PERSPECTIVES ON INSURANCE

IRVING PFEFFER, Ph.D. (CLU, CPCU)

Professor of Insurance and Finance
Virginia Polytechnic Institute and State University

DAVID R. KLOCK, Ph.D.

Assistant Professor of Insurance and Finance
Virginia Polytechnic Institute and State University

PRENTICE-HALL, INC., Englewood Cliffs, N.J.

Library of Congress Cataloging in Publication Data

Pfeffer, Irving.
    Perspectives on insurance.

    Includes bibliographical references.
    1. Insurance.   I. Klock, David R.,
joint author. II. Title.
HG8051.P53   368   73-17020
ISBN 0-13-661066-8

368
P527p

Printed in the United States of America

10 9 8 7 6 5 4 3 2 1

Prentice-Hall International, Inc., *London*
Prentice-Hall of Australia, Pty. Ltd., *Sydney*
Prentice-Hall of Canada, Ltd., *Toronto*
Prentice-Hall of India Private Limited, *New Delhi*
Prentice-Hall of Japan, Inc., *Tokyo*

To
ROBERT I. MEHR
Gentleman and Scholar

Contents

Preface

Perspectives on Insurance is a multi-disciplinary approach to the subject of risk and insurance. The insurance business is treated as a major social institution, with private and governmental sectors, that employs a set of techniques for risk management and makes important contributions to personal and business relationships by reducing uncertainty and anxiety. Insurance is studied in the light of historical, legal, psychological, economic, actuarial, managerial, and consumerist perspectives. The orientation is international rather than being limited exclusively to American practice.

The book is divided into seven parts. Part I, Historical Perspectives, provides a background of the evolution of insurance from its beginnings to the present. Part II, Legal Perspectives, discusses the nature and scope of insurance law, examines torts, agency and contracts, and explores the role and powers of the insurance commissioner. Four chapters are devoted to the analysis of the most popular forms of life, health, property and liability insurance policies. Part III, Psychological Perspectives, deals with anxiety, risk, and insurance. Gambling behavior is contrasted with insurance in the context of the literature of psychoanalytic theory. Part IV, Economic Perspectives, is an economic analysis of insurance, including its structure, competitive nature, and its role in the world economy. Part V, Actuarial Perspectives, treats the subjects of life insurance and property and liability rate-making in a non-mathematical fashion. One chapter is devoted to contemporary actuarial developments. Part VI, Managerial Perspectives, surveys the problems of insurance company management and provides techniques for measuring the performance of insurance companies. Finally, Part VII, Consumerist Perspectives, deals with social insurance, risk management, estate planning, and the consumerist movement in insurance.

Insurance is more art than science. Its foundations originate in other disciplines, such as statistics, law, economics, and psychology. Its successful practice depends upon a combination of skills, experience, and judgment brought to bear on a rapidly shifting set of contingent events. The field is very dynamic and changes of law and practice invariably outdistance published reports. Only the fundamental principles remain constant; the details are transient. Portions of this book are based on articles by the senior author which have appeared in scholarly journals and reports. The authors are grateful for permission to reprint, and for the generosity of numerous publishers who allowed us to quote from their copyright protected works.

Perspectives on Insurance is intended for use as a textbook in a college level course on risk and insurance, as well as for professional education programs and insurance training courses. It is a useful reference work for those who need to know more about this important field. Each of the parts is independent and may be read or studied in any preferred sequence. Some instructors will prefer to assign the parts in a different order than presented in the text, or in conjunction with additional materials, such as specimen policies, training manuals, or collateral reading. The authors have provided extensive footnotes as keys to the literature for those who wish to pursue particular points in greater depth. The end of the chapter questions are grouped by order of difficulty so that the first group may reasonably be assigned for answers from the text. The second group of questions provides material for short term paper or homework assignments.

Every American insurance author owes a debt to the late Solomon S. Huebner who, in 1904 at age 22, became the first professor of insurance in the University of Pennsylvania. A brilliant teacher and educational entrepreneur for more than fifty years, S.S. Huebner inspired generations of insurance scholarship. The literature is now so profuse that no author can give proper credit for the source of an idea or the inception of a custom or practice in modern insurance.

Special debts are due to John D. Long and H. Wayne Snider for critical insights, Michael Melody and Fred Bernardi for editorial finesse, Robert L. King and H.H. Mitchell for academic support, Marilyn B. Shaw for inspiration and challenge, and Phyllis Klock who not only typed but shepherded the manuscript to its final form.

The authors take full responsibility for errors and omissions, for assertions that require clarification or substantiation, and for judgments on policy matters.

Readers and users of the book are invited to offer suggestions in order that future editions of the work may be improved.

Irving Pfeffer
David R. Klock

Virginia Polytechnic Institute and State University
Blacksburg, Virginia
January, 1974

I

HISTORICAL

PERSPECTIVES

Insurance is one of the oldest commercial institutions known to man. The basic concepts and the complex superstructure can best be explained in terms of the evolution of the institution as a response to changing needs. The beginnings are in ancient Babylon, the theoretical development in Europe, the modern structure in Great Britain, and the fullest expansion in the United States.

Part I provides a short history of insurance from its origins to today and emphasizes the development of ideas that shaped the institution. The men who made the significant contributions to insurance were almost invariably better known for their non-insurance activity. Demosthenes, Barbon, Benjamin Franklin, Sir Isaac Newton, Sir William Petty, Edmund Halley, and Charles Evans Hughes would not have recognized themselves as insurance men.

The American experience has been one of adoption. Based on British practice and adapted to local needs, unique American patterns of innovation and expansion have developed.

1

The Early History
of Insurance

Insurance developed from the beginning of economic history as a technique for reducing the inevitable fear and anxiety experienced by men whose lives were filled with uncertainty. Although their technique lacked the refinements of modern insurance, risk-sharing and transfer devices are found in every ancient culture. Man recognized his need to mitigate the hazards of everyday affairs and to reduce the uncertainty of the unknown in order to maximize his security. Every culture studied by social science invented the insurance device in one form or another. Wherever anxiety exists in economic affairs, insurance emerges as a means for liberating the individual from some consequences of economic discouragement or demoralization.

THE INSURANCE IDEA

The historian seeks a broad definition of insurance that embraces many different local institutional practices. For this reason, the following generic definition is suitable:

Insurance is a device for the reduction of uncertainty of one party, called the insured, through the transfer of particular risks to another party, called the insurer, who offers a restoration, at least in part, of economic losses suffered by the insured.[1]

The principal concepts in this definition are "reduction of uncertainty," which is a lessening of the anxieties of the insured individual; "transfer of particular risks," implying that not all sources of loss may be transferred; "restoration . . . of economic losses," meaning that not all types of loss sustained by the individual can be indemnified. No insurer can hope to restore the love of a lost one or the aesthetic value of an original work of art. An insurer can only make a partial restoration of the economic loss. This is all that insurance can do today. It is all that insurance could ever do.[2]

THE BIRTH OF INSURANCE

Legend has it that Chinese merchants travelling through the treacherous waters of the Yangtze River engaged in the practice of distributing their merchandise among the various junks rather than concentrating them all in one boat. Each junk carried the merchandise of several individuals. If a boat was upset, each merchant was exposed to the loss of only a small portion of his cargo. The law of averages would presumably operate to safeguard the greater proportion of goods shipped in this manner.

The Arab version of the story relates to caravans moving across the desert and falling prey to bandits, rovers, and thieves. By distributing his wares among several caravans and among different camels in a given caravan, a merchant could be reasonably certain that in the event a disaster struck no more than a small part of his cargo would be lost. Another version referred to coastal shipping in Asia Minor in which losses due to piracy or storms were reduced in a similar manner through the distribution of cargoes.

The transfer concept of insurance is first seen, perhaps, in the doctrines relating to suretyship, in which one party guarantees the performance or contracts of another. The Old Testament is sprinkled with observations on the practice of suretyship.

My son, if thou be surety for thy friend, if thou hast stricken thy hand with a stranger, thou art ensnared with the words of thy mouth, thou art taken with the words of thy mouth.

[1] Irving Pfeffer, *Insurance and Economic Theory* (Homewood, Ill.: Richard D. Irwin, Inc., 1956), p. 53.

[2] Insurance scholars date the origins of the insurance institution differently according to the definitions which they accept. Some regard the existence of "insurance contracts" as crucial; others contend that "actuarial science" or invention of the "law of large numbers" is essential. The risk transfer idea is common to most definitions of insurance. For extended discussions of this issue, see Pfeffer, *op.cit.* pp. 12ff., and Herbert S. Denenberg, "The Legal Definition of Insurance", *The Journal of Insurance,* Vol. 30, No. 3 (Sept. 1963), pp. 319ff.

He that is surety for a stranger shall smart for it; and he that hateth suretyship is sure.

A man void of understanding striketh hands and becometh surety in the presence of his friend.

Take his garment that is surety for a stranger.

Be not one of them that strike hands, or of them that are sureties for debts.

Who is he that will strike hands with me?

Suretyship hath undone many of good estate, and shaken them as a wave of the sea; mighty men hath it driven from their homes, so that they had to wander in strange lands.[3]

In a more formal sense, the earliest contracts of insurance were legal arrangements developed centuries before the Christian Era, which embodied elements of what later became social insurance and marine insurance. The major documentation for this view is the *Code of Hammurabi* (*circa* 1750 B.C.), which provided that:

If the brigand has not been caught, the man who has been despoiled shall recount before (the) god what he has lost, and the City and Governor in whose land and district the brigandage took place shall render back to him whatsoever of his that was lost.[4]

The "insurance" provisions of the Babylonian laws merit particular attention by insurance historians. The pertinent sections are:

(23) If the highwayman has not been caught, the man that has been robbed shall state on oath what he has lost and the city or district governor in whose territory or district the robbery took place shall restore to him what he has lost.

(24) If a life (has been lost), the city or district governor shall pay one mina of silver to the deceased's relatives.

(25) If a fire has broken out in a man's house and one who has come to put it out has coveted the property of the householder and

---

[3] *Proverbs*, 6:1-2;11:15;17:18; 20:16;22:26. *Job*, 17:3. *Ecclesiastes*, 29:18.

[4] C.H.W. Johns, *Babylonia and Assyrian Laws, Contracts and Letters* (New York: Charles Scribner's Sons, 1904), p. 5. Most insurance authors date the *Code of Hammurabi* to about 2250 B.C., after C.H.W. Johns, *op.cit.* Archaeologists disagree on the precise dating, but none of the leading contemporary schools date the reign of Hammurabi earlier than 2067-2025 B.C. See G.R. Driver and John C. Miles, *The Babylonian Laws*, Vol. 1 (London: Oxford University Press, 1952), pp. xxiv-xxvi; W.F. Leemans, *Foreign Trade in the Old Babylonian Period* (Leiden, Holland: E.J. Brill, 1960) p. 3, uses the dates 1792-1750 B.C.

The *Code of Hammurabi* is engraved in a block of black diorite about 2.25 meters high, tapering from 1.90 to 1.65 meters in circumference. It was found by DeMorgan at Susa, the ancient Persepolis, in December, 1901 and January, 1902, in fragments that were rejoined. The text was published by the French Ministry of Instruction from "squeezes" by the process of photogravure, in the fourth volume of the *Mémoires de la Délégation en Perse*. The monument preserves forty-four columns with some thirty-six hundred lines.

appropriated any of it, that man shall be cast into the self-same fire.

(45) If a man has let his field to a farmer and has received his rent for the field but afterward the field has been flooded by rain, or a storm has carried off the crop, the loss shall be the farmer's.

(48) If a man has incurred a debt and a storm has flooded his field or carried away the crop, or the corn has not grown because of drought, in that year he shall not pay his creditor. Further, he shall postdate his bond and shall not pay interest for that year.

(117) If a man owes a debt, and he has given his wife, his son, or his daughter (as hostage) for the money, or has handed someone over to work it off, the hostage shall do the work of the creditor's house; but in the fourth year he shall set them free.

(125) If a man has given anything whatever on deposit, and where he has made his deposit, something of his has been lost together with something belonging to the owner of the house, either by house-breaking or a rebellion, the owner of the house who is in default shall make good all that has been given him on deposit, which he has lost, and shall return it to the owner of the goods.[5]

A primitive kind of bottomry loan, or marine insurance, can also be traced to the *Code of Hammurabi*.

INSURANCE IN THE PRE-GREEK PERIOD

As early as 5000 B.C., the alluvial plains of Babylonia in the Middle East were populated by natives under settled conditions of government and culture. The city of Babylon itself is said to have been founded about 4000 B.C., if not earlier. By 3000 B.C. there were civilizations in the valleys of the Nile, Tigris, Euphrates, and Indus Rivers. These civilizations possessed complex agricultural and manufacturing skills; engaged in extensive overland and maritime trade, with systems of writing, a knowledge of numbers and astronomy; and governed by an elaborate system of commercial law. It was inevitable that Babylonia, lying at the crossroads of world trade with access to Europe, Africa, and Asia, should have been the leading commercial nation of antiquity.[6]

The history of Western Civilization focuses on Babylon as the center of the early world economy linking China, India, and Persia with Phoenicia, Egypt, and Armenia. Located in a fertile territory bounded by the Tigris and Euphrates

[5] Johns, *op. cit.*, Ch. 11.

[6] See H.F. Lutz, "Price Fluctuations in Ancient Babylonia", *Journal of Economic and Business History,* Vol. IV (1932) and "Babylonian Partnerships", *loc. cit.,* for evidence of the economic sophistication of the merchants of the period. W.F. Leemans, *The Old-Babylonian Merchant* (Leiden, Holland: E.J. Brill, 1950) deals at length with the business and social position of the tamkaru or entrepreneurs.

Rivers and inland from the Persian Gulf, Babylon was a natural trade center for overland caravans travelling through the Middle East. Steady streams of traffic carried scarce raw materials of high unit value.

According to archaeological evidence,[7] the principal imports of Babylonia included gold, silver, copper, tin, precious and semiprecious stones, ivory, woods such as ebony, and oil, essences, wine, and slaves. Exports included agricultural produce such as barley, vegetable oils, wool, skins, and leather articles; textile fabrics and garments of all kinds; materials for making paints; and re-export of semifinished materials.

Bandits, pirates, fire, storms, and death were the constant companions of businessmen along the various trade routes. The chances of loss were very high, and the Babylonian merchants who extended credit on such vulnerable collateral as cargo in transit charged risk premiums above the interest charges on capital, which in themselves were very high. Rates in excess of 100 percent were not uncommon. The borrower customarily pledged all of his property and his family in order to secure the loan. If misfortune befell him, the borrower lost everything, and he and his family might be sold into slavery. These uncertainties were a major deterrent to commercial expansion in this early period.

Under the pressures of high risk, trade declined, and by 2250 B.C. there was little commercial activity along the trade routes of the Near East. The *Code of Hammurabi*, which formalized the concepts of *civic responsibility, bottomry,* and *respondentia,* improved trade conditions and established doctrines that were to play significant roles in the evolution of insurance.

The doctrine of *civic responsibility* provided that a city or community was responsible for payment of indemnity to victims for acts of violence or disturbances that might have been subject to control of the local authority. *Bottomry* and *respondentia* loans were maritime contracts on vessels (bottoms) or on cargoes (*res*). There were three basic elements in such agreements: (1) a loan on the vessel, cargo, or freight, (2) an interest rate on the loan, and (3) a risk premium for the chance of loss of the venture and the consequent cancellation of the debt. Under the provisions of a bottomry bond, the borrower was freed of his obligation in the event that the collateral was lost through no willful act of his own. Modern credit life and disability insurance is used in the same manner as the bottomry loan. In the event of death or total disability of the borrower the debt is cancelled. The insurance premium, which is separate from the interest on the loan, corresponds to the risk premium of ancient times.

Bottomry loans became a principal vehicle for insurance, and the technique spread through ancient civilization. This device is to be found among the Phoenicians, Rhodians, Greeks, and Romans as each, in turn, became the dominant trading or commercial nation.

---

[7]W.F. Leemans, *Foreign Trade in The Old Babylonian Period* (Leiden: E.J. Brill, 1960) pp. 120ff.

THE INSURANCE INSTITUTION IN ANCIENT GREECE

By the time the Greek era of modern history began (*circa* 750 B.C.), the two most significant insurance developments of early times had been brought to a high degree of refinement. The contract of bottomry was so well established that the great lawyer-philosopher Demosthenes prepared elaborate pleadings before the Athenian courts, some of which have been preserved in the form of a series of Orations.[8] Athenian contracts were construed very strictly, and the *Orations of Demosthenes* dealt with these matters along modern lines. Nearly every voyage in Ancient Greece was supported by a bottomry contract providing for a risk premium over and above the interest charges. Risk premium rates ranged from 10 to 25 percent for different routes, depending upon such factors as time of year, type of vessel, type of cargo, route followed, experience of the captain, etc., which is similar to the manner in which contemporary marine insurance rates are set.[9]

The concept of "general average" was also well developed in Ancient Greece. In the semantics of marine insurance "average" means "loss", and "general average" is a loss that is shared by all of the interests in the venture and not merely by the particular interest affected. Thus, if a captain is obliged to jettison some cargo in order to save a venture, he would be in a quandary about whose cargo to throw overboard, in the absence of a rule. The rule emerged from experience and was refined into one of the most fundamental legal doctrines in insurance. If the loss is deemed essential for the safety of the venture, then the captain must determine the action to be taken, and each interest bears the loss proportionate to its values at risk. Demosthenes and his colleagues in the courts of Athens were thoroughly familiar with these doctrines.

The first insurance exchange is believed to have been established in Athens in this early period. There was a news system similar to that later developed at Lloyd's of London. Bankers and merchants operated swift dispatch boats that brought intelligence reports to Athens so that shipping could be routed to safe ports and attractive markets. Bottomry bonds were arranged at the exchange, and an informal news center was developed.

The heritage of the Phoenicians, the Rhodians, and all of the maritime nations that interacted with Western Civilization was embodied in a single set of practices and customs by the Greeks when their empire and commercial development achieved a peak. Not until the resurgence of commerce in England, after the Middle Ages, was insurance again to have such a full development.

[8] Demosthenes, *The Orations of Demosthenes*, translated by Charles Rann Kennedy, London: Henry G. Bohn, 1861. See especially, "Oration Against Phormio" (circa 330 B.C.) in Vol. IV; also, "Oration Against Lacritus" (circa 341 B.C.).

[9] George M. Calhoun, "Risk in Sea Loans in Ancient Athens", *Journal of Economic and Business History*, 1930.

INSURANCE IN THE ROMAN EMPIRE

The Greek tradition in insurance was conveyed to the Romans, who adopted the practices of bottomry and its related contracts.[10] The laws of warranty and general average were further refined. The Romans even had an insurance exchange, although it is not believed to have been formalized as was the one in Athens. The major contribution of the Romans to the insurance heritage was the organized burial society, a rudimentary form of life and health insurance.

Burial societies, known as *Eranoi* and *Thiasoi*, existed in Greece for the purpose of providing prepaid burials for members, but the Romans provided more elaborate burial and benevolent services through their *collegia*. Authorized by special Senate decree, the *collegia* were the true counterparts of the fraternal insurance organizations of modern times. Members prepaid their contributions, a fund was maintained, and benefits were paid in terms of decent burial and last expenses incurred by the family of the deceased member. The *collegia* were numerous in the Roman Empire and tended to specialize on a social or occupational basis. Thus, there were *collegia* for the military in each of the provinces, *collegia* for wealthier citizens, and even the *Collegia Tenuiorum* for the lower classes. The *collegia* of the militia in Rome provided limited pensions for disability owing to wounds, and retirement benefits for enlisted men upon reaching the end of their military careers.

A further possible antecedent of modern business life insurance was the provision that indemnities might be paid to the widows of borrowers under bottomry contracts.

The annuity concept appears to have been comprehended by the Romans because they apparently solved the problem of valuation. The Falcidian Law of 40 B.C. restricted the testamentary disposition of property to not more than three-quarters of an estate being passed to persons other than the deceased's legal heirs. Because the testator might have granted some life annuities to other persons prior to his death, it was necessary to value such annuities in order to be certain that the law had not been violated. An annuity value table (Table 1.1), developed by Domitius Ulpianus (*circa* A.D. 230), was promulgated and apparently used as late as the nineteenth century by the government of Tuscany.[11] A simpler table, prepared by Aemilius Macer, a contemporary of Ulpianus, was also used in Rome.

---

[10]Buist M. Anderson, ed., *Vance on Insurance* (3rd ed.) St. Paul: West Publishing Co., 1951, p.8fn. argues that references to the work of Cicero, Livy, Suetonius, and other Latin authors have led to erroneous conclusions about the existence of insurance practices among the Romans. The standard reference work in this field is C.F. Trennery, *The Origin and Early History of Insurance*, London: P.S. King and Son Ltd., Westminster, 1926.

[11]R. Carlyle Buley, *The American Life Convention*, Vol. 1, New York: Appleton-Century-Crofts, Inc., 1953, pp. 7-8.

The *collegia* represented the distinctive contribution of the Romans to the history of insurance. By formal organization, the promise of definite benefits, and the collection of regular prepaid assessments, they are direct antecedents of the guilds of the Middle Ages and of fraternal insurance in modern times. While there is little evidence of actuarial skill, adequacy of dues collections must surely have been a criterion of membership fee setting.[12]

TABLE 1.1   Annuity Payments Table of Ulpianus

Ages	Expectation in Years	Ages	Expectation in Years
Birth to 20	30	44-45	15
20-25	28	45-46	14
25-30	25	46-47	13
30-35	22	47-48	12
35-40	20	48-49	11
40-41	19	49-50	10
41-42	18	50-55	9
42-43	17	55-60	7
43-44	16	60 and upwards	5

SOURCE: R. Carlyle Buley, *The American Life Convention*, Vol. 1, p. 8 (New York Appleton-Century-Crofts. Inc.? 1953).

INSURANCE IN THE DARK AGES

The decay and disintegration of the Roman Empire, in the fifth century A.D., brought in its wake an era of negligible international commerce and the development of small, isolated, self-sufficient, and self-contained communities. Trade route protection disappeared, and the hazards of travel and [commerce soon eliminated any substantial flow of traffic along the communication lanes of earlier times. Insurance was not snuffed out of existence, but its embers burned very low.

The *collegia* of Rome evolved into the guilds of the Middle Ages. The early Anglo-Saxon Guild was a family association loosely knit for the purpose of providing mutual aid. When a youth attained the age of fourteen years, the

[12]Terence O'Donnell, *History of Life Insurance in Its Formative Years*, Chicago: American Conservation Company, 1936, p. 55, describes the operation of the *Collegium cultorum Dianae et Antinoi* (circa 136 A.D.): "New members paid a fee of 100 sestertii, contributed an amphora of good wine and were thereafter assessed like the other members a sum of about one and one-quarter sestertii monthly . . . These assessments went into a common fund, whence 300 sestertii were paid at the death of a member, at the rate of fifty for the funeral expenses and the remainder ostensibly for the survivors of the deceased . . . Suicides forfeited all claims." O'Donnell describes the problems of attracting and keeping members in the *collegium*. Members generally refused to come to meetings or pay their dues.

Norman conquerors of England required him to find sureties to guarantee his keeping the peace. To meet this contingency, the early guilds were formed.

In time, the guilds enlarged their functions to include benefits to craftsmen, artisans, and professional persons. The full-fledged development led to religious, economic, political, and defensive organizations. About the eighth century, trade guilds in Flanders and West Germany offered mutual protection against loss arising from fire damage to livestock and against other misfortune. Early Teutonic guilds along the seacoast dealt in marine insurance contracts of Roman and Phoenician origin. But an agrarian society, based on small, isolated, autonomous communities in which the contingencies of the individual and his family were provided for, had little need for insurance. Insurance is an instrumentality of a commercial society, and until the revival of trade in Europe and Asia, there are few examples of the insurance institution in the modern sense.[13]

INSURANCE AND THE REVIVAL OF INTERNATIONAL COMMERCE

During the Middle Ages the proclivity of the men from Scandinavia to raid and pillage small towns along the north coast of Europe gave rise to the development of fortified towns. The North Sea became a Scandinavian lake as the Vikings became masters of shipbuilding and seamanship. Consequently, pillaging raids led to trade, and the products of the north: wine, fish, salt, wax, honey, furs, amber, and slaves were traded for silks, spices, wine, fruit, metalware, sulphur, porcelain, brocade, glassware, and striped fabrics. The Scandinavians' trading area spread to include most of Europe and the Near and Middle East. Ultimately, the merchants of the Hanse cities organized a league for mutual protection, and the Hanseatic League spread its influence throughout Northern Europe.

The Hanseatic League was the strongest offensive and defensive alliance of the thirteenth and fourteenth centuries. Formed to protect trade routes, to enforce strict codes of conduct, and to resist attempts to flout the authority of its regulations, this league provided a major impetus for a renaissance of commerce in Europe. At its height, the Hanseatic League included more than seventy towns, stretching from London in the west to Novgorod in the east, and from Bergen in the north to Leipsig and Cracow in the south. Until the seventeenth century, the Hanse merchants had sovereign status in a section of London called "The Steelyard."

The Crusades, with their movement of manpower across Europe, similarly created overland trade routes in the south. The returning crusaders, having tasted

---

[13] See, for example, Florence Edler DeRoover, "Early Examples of Marine Insurance", *Journal of Economic History*, 1945; W.S. Holdsworth, "The Early History of the Contract of Insurance", 17 *Columbia Law Review* (1917).

the products of Asia, created a demand for commodities that were not available in Western Europe. The Lombard merchants engaged in active trade and established a league for joint protection along the Mediterranean, where a pattern of protected towns developed. The Lombards' jurisdiction stretched from Asia Minor across the southern coast of Europe and north to London. Lombard Street, the financial center of England, originated as the counterpart of "The Steelyard"–a sovereign area in England.

Because Venice was located at the crossroads of the medieval world, it provided the locale for the rebirth of the insurance institution. A shipowner or merchant seeking insurance protection would state his needs in a contract, called a *poliza,* and would carry this policy among those known to insure marine risks. Each underwriter who accepted a portion of the risk would sign his name and indicate the portion he would bear. The amounts at risk were substantial, and most policies required many underwriters. Bottomry agreements were common in Venice, Genoa, Florence, Naples, Tarentum, and Bari before the year A.D. 1000, as evidenced by the Amalfitan Sea Codes.

Marine insurance made progress during the twelfth through fourteenth centuries, and there appears to have been a Chamber of Assurance at Bruges, about 1310, at which merchants could insure their goods upon payment of a stipulated percentage.

The antecedents of fire insurance are found in the custom, recorded as early as 1240 in the village of Verambacht, which held that a person whose house burned down was to be indemnified without delay by the whole village. By 1227, outside merchants wishing to sell their wares at local fairs could be insured against loss by fire or theft for a duty of four deniers.

By 1400, Europe's trade pattern was well-developed, considering the relatively low state of transportation technology. Small ships hugging the coastlines of Europe, caravans of small wagons travelling overland, and countless peddlers carrying their inventories on their backs supplied a network that moved goods in high demand to and from all parts of the civilized world. Because of her relative freedom from invasions, Venice became the *entrepôt* of the period, and profits ran high.

The mariner's compass, which was used by the Portuguese in venturing across the open seas to Africa and India, revolutionized the patterns of trade in the fifteenth century and transferred much of the world's economic power to Portugal. Rare goods could be imported from far distant points by ship at a cost that was only a fraction of that required by the makeshift convoys of earlier times. Almost overnight Venice lost her status and Lisbon became the most important commercial center in the world. Encouraged by the success of Portugal, other nations embarked on voyages of discovery, and Spain, Holland, France, and England came to the fore in the race for the fruits of international trade. The monopolistic protection of trade routes by the military power of the state led to the imperialistic organization of the world, which was not materially modified before the twentieth century.

While Portugal monopolized the eastern route to Africa, Persia, Indo-China, and Malaya, Spain sent its explorers west to the New World from which incredible riches were brought back to Europe. The annual shipment of precious metals from Vera Cruz and Porto Bello to Spain required twenty-seven ocean going vessels. England sent her ships to discover routes to Canada and Russia. Antwerp came to dominate the northern European routes through the Eastern trade, based on Portugal. By the middle of the sixteenth century, expansion began to take the form of wars among the great consolidated states of the west and east of Europe.

Spain conquered Portugal in 1581 and added Antwerp and the Netherlands to its domain by 1585. The defeat of the Spanish Armada in 1588 left the field to the Dutch, English, and French. Over the next two hundred years, England established her authority over all of Europe as the dominant nation in international trade during the nineteenth century.

The Hanseatic League, by ignoring the newer channels of trade, lost market after market as prices were cut below the costs of overland shipping by the direct sealanes of the Age of Discovery. Similarly, the Lombards gradually faded out of the picture as banking mechanisms were established as a universal adjunct of commerce.

Bottomry bonds were used extensively throughout the renaissance of commerce, and insurance was a basic consideration in all shipping along major routes. A cargo of armor shipped from Hamburg to London in 1560 was insured by the Hanse underwriters at a rate of 6 percent. This rate is not too far from contemporary levels.

SUMMARY

The legacy of the early history of insurance includes the practice of specialized legal documents in the form of insurance contracts serving as useful adjuncts to commerce. The *raison d'etre* of insurance as an uncertainty-reducing device was established at a very early date. The techniques of bottomry, *respondentia*, civic responsibility for indemnifying victims of specified contingent events, general average, private annuities, suretyship, and assessment life and health insurance were understood and used. A scientific foundation for the business of insurance was lacking, and it is this, more than any other criterion that distinguishes the modern institution from its historical antecedents.

REVIEW QUESTIONS

1. Why did insurance emerge at about the same time that commerce and trade began in ancient civilization? What needs did the insurance mechanism fulfill? Discuss.

2.   What proof do archaeologists or historians have that insurance contracts were used in ancient times?

3.   What contribution to the development of insurance was made by the *Code of Hammurabi*?

4.   During the Dark Ages the development of insurance as a concept and as an institution was minimal. Why? What does this tell you about the environment required for the growth and development of insurance?

5.   Discuss the nature and historical background of *bottomry* and *respondentia*.

STUDY QUESTIONS

6.   Why are bottomry bonds no longer necessary in maritime commerce?

7.   Discuss the relationship between the definition of insurance and the determination of the historical period in which the institution emerged.

8.   Initial insurance contracts were related to the extension of credit. To what extent does this relationship exist at present? Explain.

9.   Many states have enacted laws in recent years providing indemnities for the victims of crimes. How do such laws enforcing civic responsibility for the benefit of victims of socially preventable wrongs differ from the laws expounded in the *Code of Hammurabi*? Explain.

10.   The text favors the concept of insurance which stresses the transfer of risk feature rather than the grouping of risks or the formality of contracts. What are the necessary and sufficient conditions for insurance to exist?

2

The Development
of Insurance
in Western Europe

THE INSURANCE BUSINESS IN 1600

Toward the end of the Elizabethan reign, the insurance business in England was a flourishing trade with well established centers of activity, respected contracts, competitive rates, and an adequate market for most of the needs of the time. Insurance was conducted by sole proprietors on an individual basis, but it was customary for the insured to obtain joint participation of as many underwriters as were required to provide full coverage.

The beginnings of modern commercial development in England are to be found in the activities of the Hansa Merchants, who, beginning about the tenth century A.D., employed London as one of the bases in their network of international trade. These merchants were located in "The Steelyard" and conducted their activities on a virtually monopolistic basis for several hundred years. Their position was solidified because they were the principal private financiers of the Crown and consequently were granted protection as consideration for their extension of credit. The Hansa merchants observed such strict rules of conduct that they are sometimes called "monks of commerce." The entire territory north and east of Bruges was regarded as the domain of the Hanseatic League.

The Lombards and Florentines of Italy established the monopoly for trade in all of the south and west of Bruges. In the beginning of the twelfth century, the Lombards moved into England and settled in London as well—the famous Lombard Street being the center of activity. Whereas the Hansa Merchants brought trade and barter to England, it was the Lombards who brought sophisticated financial institutions, such as money and banking, international exchange, and insurance, to the English scene. Their activities came under official notice on many occasions. Marine insurance was widespread and formed the basis for most international contracts. The bottomry contract was basic, although it had come to be used more and more for emergency fund raising rather than for general financing of boats or cargo.

About 1300, the Laws of Wisby were promulgated regulating activities of members of the Hanseatic League and limiting the use of bottomry agreements in many ways. Such internal regulation was common throughout Europe, and there are numerous statutes relating to these practices. For example, an Ordinance of Barcelona in 1435 regulated bottomry. Many such ordinances, rules, and regulations are to be found in law collections prior to 1600. Probably the most authoritative such set of rules is the *Guidon de la Mer,* published in Rouen, France, approximately 1600. This insurance code spells out clearly the rules of law pertaining to insurance contracts used in international commerce at the time.[1]

The first English Statute on Insurance was enacted in 1601. It authorized the formation of a special court for the hearing of disputes relating to insurance.[2] Such a court had been established by the Grand Council of Venice in 1468. In 1574, Elizabeth authorized a bill that created a Chamber of Insurance for the sale of marine insurance. Such Chambers of Insurance were common in earlier times, one having functioned relatively well at Bruges in 1310.

By 1600, insurance was centralized in Lombard Street, as it is today in England. Most of the lines of insurance that could have been written were being written; the statutes of the land and the customs of the business made rules of operation clear; a body of law pertaining to the contracts was already being formulated by the courts.

Lacking at this time were: (1) the development of substantial financial backing for underwriters, (2) the use of uniform contracts, (3) uniform rates, (4) a body of actuarial understanding, (5) a satisfactory judicial tribunal for hearing insurance cases, and (6) a vigorous market development. All of these were in evidence by the eighteenth century.

---

[1] *The Osceola,* 1903, 189 U.S. 158, 23 S. Ct. 483, 47 L. Ed., 760 provides citations supporting the thesis that maritime law was international in character during the fifteenth and sixteenth centuries.

[2] *Statutes* 43 Elizabeth, c. 12 (1601).

THE MARINE INSURANCE INDUSTRY

The business of underwriting marine insurance is the oldest branch of the insurance industry. Continuing in a relatively unbroken line from the earliest uses of bottomry contracts or bonds and the widespread acceptance of the doctrine of general average, both the Hanseatic League and the Lombards employed the device and developed detailed sets of regulations pertaining to the practice of marine insurance. The Laws of Wisby (1300), the Ordinance of Barcelona (1435), and the *Guidon de la Mer* (1600) provided evidence of widespread development. But the industry consisted of individual underwriters each writing business for his own account. The common law had not yet developed the concept of a corporation.

The combined effect of the vastly improved systems of foreign communication and modern credit instruments, coupled with use of the master's lien for disbursement, which is now recognized by statute, virtually eliminated the bottomry bond.

Lloyd's of London emerged as the dominant organization of individual underwriters of insurance in the world. Beginning with the last quarter of the seventeenth century, the underwriters of London tended to gather in the coffee house of Edward Lloyd for the exchange of contracts and the general informal conduct of their business.[3] By 1696, there was sufficient demand for Lloyd to begin publication of *Lloyd's News,* a newspaper relating maritime news. This publication was banned for a time because it was considered controversial. It was resumed under the title *Lloyd's List* and continues to the present day.

The methods employed in the handling of insurance at Lloyd's consisted of an underwriter preparing a slip, called a bordereau, that was passed from underwriter to underwriter until sufficient names and amounts were attached to cover the full risk, at which time the insurance was bound. It was not until 1769 that Lloyd's was formally organized with a set of rules, enforceable by appropriate committees, for the conduct of its members. In 1779, the underwriters at Lloyd's adopted a uniform marine insurance contract, which is substantially the policy in use today. It was not until 1906 that the Marine Insurance Act was passed, providing statutory regulation of the marine insurance business in England. In 1909, the Marine Insurance (Gambling Policies) Act was adopted, and the modest pattern of British regulation was set as it is in substance today.

---

[3] Lloyd's coffee house was set up about 1688 in Tower Street and moved to Lombard Street about 1691. Many histories have been written of Lloyd's, including: C.E. Golding and D. King-Page, *Lloyd's,* New York: McGraw-Hill Book Co., 1952; Frederick Martin, *The History of Lloyd's and of Marine Insurance in Great Britain,* London: MacMillan and Co., 1876; Ralph Strauss, *Lloyd's, The Gentlemen at the Coffee-House,* New York: Carrick & Evans, 1938; D.E.W. Gibb, *Lloyd's of London,* London: MacMillan & Co., 1957; Charles Wright and Ernest Fayle, *A History of Lloyd's,* London: MacMillan & Co., 1928.

In 1720, Royal Charters were granted in the form of private monopolies to two corporations in consideration of a very large payment to the Crown. These first chartered companies were the London Assurance Corporation and the Royal Exchange Assurance Corporation. The monopolies that they were granted permitted them to raise public funds and to have an exclusive control of the business of corporate insurance underwriting in the marine field. These companies did not encroach upon individual underwriters at Lloyd's, whose prerogatives were unaffected. The monopoly corporate powers covered the insuring of ships and cargoes, but were later expanded to permit the writing of fire and life insurance.

In 1824, at the behest of the international banker Nathan Rothschild, the monopoly granted to the two corporations was repealed, and the Alliance British and Foreign Fire and Life Assurance Company was organized with substantial capital. This venture proved successful and initiated an era of open competition in the marine insurance business in England.

Since England was the foremost commercial nation from the seventeenth century until the twentieth, the customs and usages of the English marine insurance industry have been carried throughout the world. Lloyd's continues as one of the world's most important insurance centers, with the principal international insurance markets still converging on Lombard Street.

THE FIRE INSURANCE INDUSTRY

While numerous isolated examples may be found of fire insurance for different risks, it was not until the Great Fire of London that modern fire insurance was born. The fire, which began on September 2, 1666 and burned for five days, was the largest disaster that had occurred to private property in the history of England. Nearly one-quarter of the buildings in the City of London, where wood construction predominated, were destroyed. Nicholas Barbon, economist, dentist, and builder, who had been born Nicholas-If-Christ-Had-Not-Died-Thou-Wouldst-Be-Damned-Barebones, opened as a sole proprietorship the first specialized office for fire insurance on dwellings and business buildings. The contract he designed is much like the contract of today. He provided rather prudently that the insurer should have the right to replace or repair any loss with materials of like kind and quality. This gave his own building enterprise the opportunity of reconstructing damaged properties rather than paying cash benefits. It appears that his rates were adequate.[4]

Barbon went into business on his own in 1667 and continued as a partnership after 1680. Competition appeared in 1683 with the formation of the Friendly Society. In 1710, Charles Povey formed the Sun Fire Office which was incorporated as the Sun Insurance Office in 1726.

Since that time, the fire insurance business expanded in England, gaining

---

[4] Philip James, "Nicholas Barbon", *Review of Insurance Studies,* Vol. 1 (1954).

additional volume as industrialization gave rise to ever greater dependence on a money economy. Where the farmer of old could establish a building bee or neighborhood co-operative to rebuild a damaged home, the complexity and impersonality of cities made fire insurance imperative. Once a credit economy emerged few real estate improvement loans could be completed without the security of fire insurance policies.

THE LIFE INSURANCE INDUSTRY

As was true of fire insurance, individual instances of life insurances were not uncommon at an early date, although the writing of annuities was more common. The Laws of Wisby of the thirteenth century provided that if a merchant required a captain to insure a ship, the merchant was obliged to insure the captain's life against the hazards of the sea.

The first widespread development of the life insurance business came through the operation of tontines in France, Holland, and England. The first tontine in France occurred in 1689, and the first English tontine took place in 1692. The plan, invented by Lorenzo Tonti, was to grant annuities, for a consideration, with survivors sharing in the forfeitures of those who died prematurely, and the government obtaining the use of the funds. Despite the fact that probability and mortality theory had been developed, the initial tontines were grossly undervalued and failed to meet their objectives. A thirst for speculation through the use of tontines swept the country, and the urge to provide life insurance benefits was strong.

In 1698, the Mercers Company of London began granting annuities to beneficiaries named by member insureds. In 1699, the Society of Assurance for Widows and Orphans, a mutual assessment association, began its operations. Both companies ultimately disappeared, probably because of inadequate rates.

In 1756, the Old Equitable was founded and today is the oldest existing life insurance company in the world. It began writing business in 1762. By 1774, life insurance had progressed to the point that the English Parliament was obliged to enact a life insurance statute prescribing an insurable interest as a requisite for an enforceable insurance contract. An insurable interest in life insurance is an economic relationship between an individual and an insured such that the individual would suffer a financial loss should the insured die.

By the middle of the eighteenth century, the techniques of life insurance had become substantially scientific in nature. The major deficiency of the industry was the lack of an aggressive marketing system.

THE LEGAL DOCTRINES OF INSURANCE

The law pertaining to insurance was a part of the common law of England. It was a mixture of all the concepts that had been carried to England by the

Hanseatic League, the Lombards, and later by the evolving practices of England itself. The first comprehensive expression of the law was expounded by the great Lord Mansfield, Chief Justice between 1756 and 1788, who published many important decisions on insurance matters. In 1789, in a volume entitled *A System of the Law of Marine Insurance,* James Allan Park provided the first uniform insurance code in the English system of law. Most of the fundamental legal doctrines of insurance were expounded in cases coming before Lord Mansfield. The ideas of contract and agency, of insurable interest and insurable hazard, of tort and of indemnity were developed in the early English courts of law and equity.

THE BEGINNINGS OF ACTUARIAL SCIENCE

Credit for the invention of modern actuarial technique belongs to the French rather than to the English because it was French mathematicians, interested in maximizing gambling success, who developed the theory of probability in its classic form. Blaise Pascal, in correspondence with Fermat in the 1650s, established the basic theorems of probability by counting all of the alternatives in equiprobable situations. Others took up the work, and the doctrines were well understood before the end of the seventeenth century.[5]

Graunt published his work on the Bills of Mortality in 1661 and developed tables that could be used as the basis for calculating life expectancies and premiums. The work of DeWitt in 1671 and DeMoivre in 1718 was also noteworthy. In each case, a complete mortality table was offered based on modifications of observed mortality. Modern statistics originates with the concern for population forecasting and age distributions for use in setting conscription quotas for the militia. Sir William Petty published a demographic work based on Irish experience.

Among the most sophisticated actuaries in England was Sir Richard Price. A correspondent of Benjamin Franklin, Price published a book on Reversionary Payments in 1771 that was widely read by students of the field.

The word "actuary" was introduced in 1762 to describe the chief executive officer of the Equitable Life Assurance Society, the first and oldest insurance company in the world. In their preliminary report in 1761 the Attorney General and the Solicitor General of England wrote:

> "The success of this scheme must depend upon the truth of certain calculations taken upon tables of life and death, whereby the chance of mortality is attempted to be reduced to a certain standard; this is a mere

---

[5] Isaac Todhunter, *A History of the Theory of Probability,* London, 1865, offers one of the leading treatments of the subject.

speculation, never yet tried in practice, and consequently subject, like all other experiments, to various chances in the execution."[6]

The success of the Equitable in gaining a following during its formative years resulted in scientific approaches to life insurance. The actuary gained in stature as an applied mathematician, and during the eighteenth century actuaries became organized as a professional group.

THE HISTORIC FUNCTION OF LLOYD'S

From its inception in the seventeenth century, Lloyd's of London served as the chief insurance center of the world. This was the principal market for the establishment of contracts of insurance of every type. The pricing process was focused here. Underwriters at Lloyd's were more conversant with economic and business conditions than underwriters in any other part of the world. The communications center was in Lombard Street, and the Lutine Bell signalled every major disaster in modern commercial history. Because of their comparative freedom from government intervention, the underwriters were able to adapt their techniques and coverages to the needs of the times. Flexibility and change were and still are hallmarks of Lloyd's procedures. Even today, shipping rates quoted by the underwriters at Lloyd's are widely regarded as significant barometers of international conditions. The reputation of Lloyd's has been well earned. Its role was to make the market for the industry with particular reference to short term risks where the actuarial aspects were difficult of assessment. That it performed this role effectively provides the best explanation for its preeminence over the centuries.

LLOYD'S METHOD OF OPERATION

The basic method of doing business at Lloyd's has been unchanged since earliest times, although its facilities have improved materially. Lloyd's consists of a "room" in which underwriters have desks for the conduct of their activities. The prospective insured submits his request for coverage to his broker. The broker resubmits his proposal to an underwriter who may undertake to quote a rate then and there and sign his name to the slip, indicating the amount of risk that he is willing to bear and the rate that he is willing to offer. If this quote is acceptable, the slip is passed from underwriter to underwriter until enough names are attached to the slip to provide full coverage. At this point, the

---

[6] Maurice Edward Ogborn, *Equitable Assurances,* London: George Allen and Unwin Ltd., 1962, p. 35.

contract is bound. The term "underwriter" came from this practice of writing the name under the proposal.

When the proposal has been "underwritten," it is routed back to the insured by way of his broker, who might actually write up a policy or certificate for his client. In theory, if the rate quoted is not satisfactory, the insured could shop among the underwriters for a better quotation. In fact, however, the consultative process makes for a relatively uniform set of quotations, and it is regarded as improper to shop around for better rates. The idea that one of their number has quoted too high is repugnant to the underwriters, who function as members of a group or syndicate.

From the outset, Lloyd's underwriters accepted risks on their own responsibility without legal limitations on their personal liability. This practice follows the sole proprietorship form of organization, which prevailed prior to the first granting of corporate charters by the Crown.

CONTEMPORARY SYSTEMS AND PROCEDURES AT LLOYD'S

With the expansion in numbers of underwriters admitted at Lloyd's—there now are more than 6,000 individual members—and the increase in the volume and complexity of the business underwritten, there has been a streamlining of systems and procedures. Partly because of international restrictions on convertibility of currencies and tensions that have prevailed for many years, the financial resources of the underwriters have been considerably strengthened. While restrictive legislation, particularly in the United States, has curbed some of the market activity of the group, their preeminence remains unquestioned in the international insurance market.

Underwriters at Lloyd's are organized into more than 300 syndicates, who delegate management responsibility to the leader of each syndicate. Each manager is expert in quoting rates on particular classes of risk. Syndicate members automatically accept their proportionate shares of the business so underwritten. Thus, if one wanted to insure a church building against loss by earthquake, the broker would seek out the syndicate leader who specialized in this kind of risk and would get a quote from him. This would be the most authoritative quote and would set a pattern not only for one syndicate but for all other syndicates interested in bidding on, or underwriting, this particular type of risk. In this way shopping is minimized, quotes are rendered instantly, and coverages can be bound speedily. Because the "capacity" at Lloyd's is so large, most of the world's great risks can be covered almost immediately.

Financial guarantees behind the activity at Lloyd's have been strengthened substantially in recent years. While there have never been records of underwriters' defaults in meeting claims, the only security for insureds is the personal financial responsibility of the members. Today a complex system of reserves buttresses the individual guarantees of members. There is a premium trust fund into which all net premiums are paid and out of which all claims are settled. The underwriter has no control over this fund and merely receives net remittances with his financial statements on a monthly basis. Since an underwriter may be a member of many syndicates, each acting under the managing underwriter's discretion, a member may not know what risks he was on until he receives his bordereau statement at the end of the month. In addition to the premium trust fund, there is a member's guaranty trust fund into which he must pay a sum in excess of £10,000 to back up his underwriting commitments. The income from this fund covers the operating costs at Lloyd's.

For the American risks that are handled at Lloyd's there is yet another trust fund, maintained in New York City, amounting to more than $800,000,000. This fund was established just before the outbreak of World War II, when it appeared that Great Britain might have some difficulty in processing its American business speedily in American funds.

To provide yet further financial power, the claims function is decentralized and is not subject to the control of the underwriter on a particular risk. The chance of hedging poor underwriting judgment by resisting the payment of claims has thereby been eliminated. Finally, there is the unlimited personal financial responsibility of the member, and, since his net worth is one of the criteria for membership, this guarantee provides another enormous pool of capital. There is no joint liability at Lloyd's; in fact there is a tradition that no insured should be allowed to suffer because of the financial incapacity of a member, and this has never been a serious problem.

SPECIAL SERVICES OF LLOYD'S

The unique features of Lloyd's at present include: (1) its reinsurance capacity, (2) simplicity of its policies, (3) flexibility of rate making, (4) relative freedom from governmental regulation, (5) breadth of market for unusual risks, and (6) its formation of a world market for insurances.

Reinsurance Capacity

The reinsurance business, in which one insurance company transfers a part of the risk to another insurance company or underwriter, makes it possible for a company to distribute its risks more widely without having exposure in undue concentrations. For example, a company that writes a $100,000,000 policy might risk bankruptcy if that particular risk should occur. By means of reinsurance, an insurer may share a portion of the risk with other insurers. Just as the individual purchases insurance to reduce the chance of catastrophic loss, so too does the insurance company protect itself against the same contingency, although its ability to bear the loss is usually much greater than that of its insureds.

At Lloyd's there is an international reinsurance market where risks of all sizes may be ceded. The operations of the underwriters know no national boundaries. The underwriters can take virtually unlimited risks by tapping the entire world market for any given risk other than the unusually large exposure, where the world's private insurance capacity may not be adequate, at rates which the buyer is willing to pay. The reinsurance business is conducted in much the same manner as the ordinary insurance business, except that the ceding carrier usually handles all of the detail work of underwriting, claim settlement, and accounting by submitting a bordereau to the reinsurer either monthly or quarterly. Facultative arrangements are common where the size of any one risk is above an agreed upon level.

Simple Contracts

The policies at Lloyd's are simpler than the policies typically issued by American companies. There are fewer special exclusions, and the settlement procedures tend to be less involved. Much of the language in the policies is similar to that used in 1789, which was about the time that uniform marine policies were adopted. This simplicity of policy form has not aggravated the litigation problems, as one might expect.

Rate Flexibility

Operating without statutory regulation of rates, the underwriters at Lloyd's are able to achieve much greater rate flexibility than is characteristic in the United States. In many American states, a property-liability insurance company or organization must obtain prior approval of its rates, and this approval is contingent upon a showing of the reasonableness, adequacy, and equity of the contemplated rate. The average time for obtaining a proper rate adjustment may be very long, ranging to almost three years in some instances. The British insurance market is free of this kind of prior approval restraint and therefore can adapt quickly to changes in the market situation.

Freedom From Regulation

The U.S. Congress in World War I granted an exemption from state regulation for marine insurance, and this line of activity is competitive in the British sense. No other line of insurance has this exemption, however, and a good deal of business is transacted abroad because of rate considerations. Most states have "surplus line" laws that are intended to discourage the export of risks. The law typically states that the insurance must be placed in the domestic market unless there is no carrier admitted to do business in the market who is willing to accept the risk.[7] Only in such a case can the line be placed abroad as a surplus line. The fact that the local price is a higher one is not a permissible reason for placing the insurance in other markets.

There is relatively little formal regulation of the operating procedures at Lloyd's. The statutes proscribe contracts that are gambling contracts lacking insurable interest; there are requirements for solvency and the filing of reports with the Government, but little else. Certainly there are none of the prior approval notions that are common in the United States. This freedom from government intervention has made it possible for the underwriters and, indeed, for the companies operating in Great Britain to become major factors in the world market.

Unusual Risks

The very same attitude of underwriting, based upon intuitive judgment and experience, makes it possible for the underwriters to consider the unique risk in much the same fashion as the more familiar kind. By a process of analogy, the risk can be evaluated and rated for a proper price. If there is sufficient diversification of risks, the volume of such transactions is large enough for the average profit to be satisfactory. If the lead underwriter is too frequently unsuccessful, he will soon find himself without a syndicate to manage, and he can retreat to the comparative safety of mere syndicate membership.

Often the risk partakes of a gamble in that there is a quality of speculation surrounding the exposure. For example, some golf tournaments buy insurance policies against the hazard of a golfer hitting a hole in one. The insured amount may be $50,000. Why should anyone wish to insure this kind of event? The public relations values seem more important here than the catastrophic exposure. If the rate is high enough and capabilities of the golfers are known, the risk may be underwritten, but it resembles a gambling kind of transaction. The existence of an insurable interest keeps it out of the class of prohibited insurances.

World Market

Perhaps the most important service that Lloyd's provides in a unique way

---

[7] See, for example, State of California, *Insurance Code,* Sec. 1763, "A surplus line broker may . . . place insurance . . . with nonadmitted insurers only if such insurance cannot be procured from a majority of the insurers admitted . . .".

is an international market for both insurances of short duration and for reinsurances. Insurance carriers and brokers throughout the free world recognize that the market at Lloyd's is a central pricing institution and the meeting ground for full coverages through the various syndicates. By working through reinsurance brokers in London, it becomes possible for a company to have access not merely to markets for insurance that it wishes to cede but, also, for access to reinsurance commitments that it wishes to accept. The syndicates need all the capacity they can achieve at the most profitable levels, but there is rarely sufficient capacity in the free world to meet every situation for which insurance is sought. Hence, each company that is interested in expansion of capacity generally selects a reinsurance broker who lines up syndicates with as wide a participation as possible. Ultimately, the rate is determined by the actual experience. Lloyd's is the center of this activity, and the world insurance market is dependent upon this.

THE REGULATORY PATTERN IN GREAT BRITAIN

The British insurance tradition has always been one of self-regulation, with statutes being enacted only as indicated by special needs. There is a belief, which has long been prevalent, that the industry can be left to its own responsibility in most matters as a competitive force in the economy. Thus, rates and contracts are not regulated nearly so stringently as is the case in the United States.

The body of English statutes relating to insurance is not large. There are the Lloyd's Acts, which govern the activities of Lloyd's, the Marine Insurance Acts, and a few more statutes relating primarily to insurable interest and statutory reports.

It is of interest that there was a movement, after World War II, favoring the nationalization of the insurance industry in Great Britain, a pattern that was followed in a number of her former colonies, such as India and Pakistan. The movement was aborted largely because of the realization that some £33,000,000 in net remittances from abroad, which represented the foreign profits of the British industry, would probably stop in the face of any move to permit the state to encroach on this sphere of private enterprise. In 1972, insurance earnings contributed more than $500,000,000 in foreign exchange earnings to Great Britain.

WORLD INSURANCE TRENDS

Insurance markets throughout the free world have tended to evolve and expand in response to the demands of commerce and particularly to maritime activity. Except for life insurance, which has become a major savings outlet in advanced economies, the insurance industry has been modest in its growth and volume in most parts of the world. Great Britain has long been the principal international market, but the Scandinavian countries, Germany, Italy, Canada, Switzerland, France, and Japan have been important factors. The level of insurance activity is not nearly so high in these countries as it is in the United States or Great Britain at the present time.

In 1971, aggregate insurance premiums in the free world were in excess of $135 billion. Of this amount, the market share of U.S. companies was 54.3 percent. Other leading national groups had the following shares: Japan, 7.9 percent; West Germany, 7.5 percent; Great Britain, 5.3 percent; France, 4.1 percent; Canada, 3.2 percent; Italy, 1.8 percent; Australia, 1.5 percent; and Netherlands, 1.4 percent. No other country had as much as one percent of the market.[8]

During the twentieth century, the volume of insurance activity seems to correlate reasonably well with the level of national income. The emergence of the United States as the world's leading economic power has led to its assumption of insurance leadership. Today, one must turn to the United States and its practices and experience in order to gain a proper perspective on the world market for insurance. Whereas the United States cannot take credit for many innovations in the field, it can be credited with the greatest expansion of the insurance industry in all of its branches.

SUMMARY

The insurance industry flourished in England from the seventeenth century onward because of a combination of favorable circumstances. London was a world trade center at the junction of the two greatest commercial associations of the period, the Hanseatic League and the Lombards, and England became the dominant trading nation. A scientific basis was prepared for life insurance. Marine insurance was developed to a fine art. The Great Fire of London led to the invention of modern Fire Insurance. Lloyd's of London evolved into the greatest insurance center in the world. Freedom from government regulation of prices and coverages coupled with a powerful code of honor made Lloyd's strong and prosperous. Competition was not forthcoming from the traditional sources—France, Portugal, Italy, and Spain—because of religious and political prohibitions. On the continent of Europe there was widespread belief that fire insurance would lead inevitably to a substantial increase in arson, and that life insurance was an immoral wager upon human life. Life insurance was prohibited in France until 1820.

---

[8] Swiss Reinsurance Company, *Sigma,* March 1973. Total premium volume is heavily influenced by domestic premiums. In the international market, which is primarily reinsurance, the London market is pre-eminent.

After World War II, there was rapid growth in insurance in the developed countries and the share of the British relative to Japan and West Germany became less favorable. Between 1961 and 1971, the share of the world market held by Great Britain in gross premiums fell from 7.1 percent to 5.3 percent. Japan moved from 2.4 percent to 7.9 percent. West Germany advanced from 5.2 percent to 7.5 percent during this period. The United States, which accounted for 64.4 percent of world premiums in 1961, declined to 54.3 percent in 1971.

REVIEW QUESTIONS

1. What are the sources of financial strength which permit Lloyd's underwriters, a group of individuals, to compete with the billion-dollar insurance companies of the United States? Explain.

2. Discuss the early development of Lloyd's of London in terms of the needs that it met and the *modus operandi* of the early underwriters.

3. During the seventeenth century, the insurance mechanism developed more substantial financial backing and actuarial bases. Discuss the evolution of these most important advancements.

4. Did the granting of Royal Charters to specific insurance organizations affect the operation of Lloyd's? Why?

5. Discuss the role of Nicholas Barbon in the evolution of modern fire insurance.

STUDY QUESTIONS

6. Government annuities were significant tax revenue sources in Europe at various times. In the form of tontines, they appealed to speculative and wealthy people everywhere. What went wrong? Why did these annuities fall into disfavor? Discuss.

7. Why have Lloyd's type insurance organizations not become a significant factor in the United States insurance market? Discuss.

8. Modern fire insurance was launched as a consequence of the Great Fire of London. Does the volume of fire insurance premiums tend to spurt upward after every major property disaster? Discuss.

9. How do you account for the fact that Great Britain is losing its position of insurance leadership, in terms of market shares, to Japan and West Germany? Discuss.

10. Does the basic principle of a tontine still exist in contemporary life insurance? Discuss.

3

The Evolution

of American Insurance

THE INSURANCE ENVIRONMENT
OF THE COLONIAL PERIOD

Economic historians agree that the Colonial Period in American history was marked by the application of mercantilist doctrines to the relations between England and the Colonies. Mercantilism was a restrictive trade policy designed to enrich England by utilizing the agency of the state to strengthen the position of commercial enterprisers in trade, manufacturing, and agriculture and by attaching the overseas possessions in a subordinate capacity to the economy of the mother country. The Board of Trade, established in 1696, had as its objective the goal of making the colonies commercially profitable to England. They determined the economic development of the colonies through control of the civil service and the colonial judiciary, the power to survey colonial legislation with a view to recommending disallowance by the Privy Council, and a specific veto power over colonial encroachments on British prerogatives. Colonial shipowners and shipbuilders suffered because the Navigation Acts virtually compelled about 80 percent of the shipping between the British Isles and the Thirteen Colonies to be carried on English vessels. Many economists believe that the greatest burden for the colonies was not the taxes assessed, but the increased costs of shipment, transshipment, and middleman's profits arising from the requirement that England be used as the distribution center for goods from the colonies. Given this economic environment, it was inevitable that insurance transactions were consummated almost exclusively in the London market.

THE EARLY AMERICAN INSURANCE MARKETS

The first insurance transactions in the United States were entered into between shipowners and the English underwriters, many of whom lacked adequate financial resources to meet their commitments. In 1705, William Penn, who neglected to insure several of his ventures, explained that "Ensurers fail much."[1] John Copson is credited with forming the first domestic insurance market in 1721, when he advertised in a Philadelphia newspaper that he was starting "An Office of Publick Insurance on Vessels and Merchandizes . . . at his house . . . (and that) . . . all Assurers or Under Writers be Persons of undoubted Worth and Reputation, and of considerable Interest in this City and Province."[2] In 1725, Francis Rawle's book on *Ways and Means for the Inhabitants of Delaware to Become Rich* cited marine insurance as an outlet for "the industrious Adventurer." The London Coffee House in Philadelphia became an insurance center by 1760, with regular hours and a small staff. Next door, the New York Insurance Office was operated as a production agency for English underwriters.

The formation of a domestic market was restricted as a result of a price war launched by the English underwriters. The Americans urged prospective insureds to buy their coverage in the local market because it was their patriotic duty to keep their money in America and, furthermore, claims against the English insurers might go unsettled for months, while lengthy and time consuming correspondence and negotiations were carried by way of slow moving ocean vessels. The attraction of premium payments by paper currency, rather than in specie, was also an important consideration.

MARINE INSURANCE

Marine insurance was the first branch of the industry to gain a foothold in the American colonies. Agencies of the major underwriters of England were established in Philadelphia, New York, and Boston, and the bulk of the business was conducted through the offices of Lloyd's. Until the American Revolution in 1776, there was little economic pressure for the formation of a domestic insurance market because the premium volume was not large. English ownership

[1] Marquis James, *Biography of a Business* (New York: Bobbs Merrill, 1942) p. 19.
[2] *Ibid.*, p. 19.

of most of the vessels plying international waters in the pre-Revolutionary Period meant that most of the marine insurance business, even among the colonial ports, was in London. The route from the Caribbean Islands to the New England ports was a busy one and virtually preempted by the mother country.

FIRE INSURANCE

Fire insurance evolved at an early date because of the exposure of the small, wood-constructed towns to inadequate water supplies and a general lack of fire prevention facilities. Disastrous fires in Boston in 1630, in Philadelphia in 1730, and in North Carolina in 1740 created an awareness of the need for some kind of protection. Fire insurance in England was well developed by the turn of the eighteenth century, and the practices of the English companies were well known in the colonies.

Benjamin Franklin wrote extensively on the subject of fire protection in his *Pennsylvania Gazette* and was responsible for the formation of one of the earliest voluntary fire companies in America. By the middle of the eighteenth century, there was considerable interest in fire insurance.

The first fire insurance company was organized in Charleston, South Carolina in 1735 as a Friendly Society, operating under a royal charter. However, the company failed in the aftermath of the disastrous Charleston fire of 1741. In 1750, using his fire fighting Union Fire Company as a nucleus, Benjamin Franklin introduced fire insurance to Philadelphia. What began as a closed group was opened to the public in 1752, with the formation of the Philadelphia Contributionship for the Insurance of Houses from Loss by Fire. Three of the subscribers were later to be signers of the Declaration of Independence: Benjamin Franklin, John Morton, and Robert Morris. This company was patterned after the Amicable Contributionship of London. Both companies designated the buildings they insured with a mark designed as two clasped hands, and, because of this, both companies became known as the Hand-In-Hand.

The method of operation of the Hand-In-Hand is of interest. Perpetual policies were issued. Each member contributed a large sum of money that was invested by the Contributionship. The investment income was used to pay losses and the costs of operating the company. This company is still in business in Philadelphia and, in modified fashion, still operates this way. Each insured was given a fire mark or shield with the company emblem on it, which he attached in a prominent place to the front of his house to indicate that he was a policyholder. The Hand-In-Hand subsidized the city's volunteer fire fighting companies. These fire fighters would answer a call to fight fires in any dwelling, but they probably performed more effectively on those houses that carried the appropriate fire mark.

The fire insurance business in the colonies was able to get a healthy start because the London insurance companies were prohibited, under the terms of their charters, from writing fire insurance in America. Applications for fire insurance from Americans were universally rejected. Local market development was, therefore, inevitable. For reasons that are unclear, the local underwriters effectively resisted the granting of charters for the formation of stock insurance companies, and only a mutual could be organized.

LIFE INSURANCE

The early colonists expressed little interest in life insurance.[3] Benjamin Franklin is reported to have commented: "It is a strange anomaly that men should be careful to insure their houses, their ships, their merchandise, and yet neglect to insure their lives, surely the most important of all to their families, and more subject to loss." Probably the earliest life insurance contracts written during the Colonial Period were short term policies on the lives of ship captains and others who made ocean voyages.

In 1759, the first American life insurance company was formed by the Presbyterian Synod of Philadelphia. The Corporation for the Relief of Poor and Distressed Presbyterian Ministers and for the Poor and Distressed Widows and Children of Presbyterian Ministers, now known as the Presbyterian Ministers' Fund, insured only the clergy and did not use agents.[4] Its purpose was to provide economic assistance to the families of clergymen who were unable to provide an estate for their wives and children because of the low wages paid. Through the life insurance program, at least their dependents would be cared for. Still in operation in Philadelphia, it has broadened its insuring activities and insures other members of the church. Its success led, years later, to the formation of the Episcopal Corporation, which was organized for a similar purpose. Benjamin Franklin played a leading role in the organization of the Fund, although the Reverend Francis Alison is credited with initiating the project.

The first life insurance contracts were whole life policies, with proceeds payable on a life income basis. Premiums were payable annually in fixed installments, and benefits were payable on a fixed basis. The contract was similar in many respects to modern life insurance policies.

[3] J. Owen Stalson, *Marketing Life Insurance*, Cambridge: Harvard University Press, 1942, p. 44.

[4] Alexander Mackie, *Facile Princeps*, Philadelphia: Presbyterian Ministers' Fund, 1956. This volume provides a detailed history of the beginning of life insurance in the United States. See also, Charles K. Knight, *The History of Life Insurance in the United States to 1870*, Philadelphia: University of Pennsylvania, 1920; Terence O'Donnell, *History of Life Insurance in its Formative Years*, Chicago, 1936; A. Fingland Jack, *An Introduction to the History of Life Insurance*, New York, 1912; R. Carlyle Buley, *The American Life Convention*, New York: Appleton-Century-Crofts, 1953.

By the time of the American Revolution, insurance, in its three major branches, was well established in the colonies, although its formal organization into chartered companies had hardly begun. The "industry" was small and disorganized; legal restrictions limited its expansion in the marine insurance field; a largely agrarian society felt little need for life insurance; and the urbanization development was just beginning to create an awareness of the value of fire insurance. The technology of insurance, including its contractual and actuarial bases, had been developed. There remained only the unshackling of American entrepreneurs to permit the expansion that followed the American Revolution.

THE IMPACT OF THE AMERICAN REVOLUTION

By 1776, there were two active life insurance companies in America on a mutual basis. At least one fire insurance company was active, and numerous underwriters made a market of limited capacity for marine insurance. The break from colonial status brought with it a sharp cut in the volume of activity with the English market and forced American insurers to expand their domestic capacity.

The principal obstacle to expansion of the local industry to major proportions was its inability to underwrite large risks in the domestic market. The capital available was inadequate for underwriters in Philadelphia to hazard more than $25,000 on a single venture. The economic blockades of the 1776 War made it mandatory that the industry grow to sufficient size to provide for the insurance requirements of the American people. This became an important economic goal of the period.

THE AMERICAN INSURANCE INDUSTRY
BEFORE THE CIVIL WAR

Stock Insurance Companies.   The first American stock insurance corporation, the Insurance Company of North America, was organized in Philadelphia in 1792 and was chartered by the General Assembly of Pennsylvania in 1794. This company, which had a broad all lines charter, began by writing fire and marine insurance and continues as one of the largest companies in the world today. The Insurance Company of the State of Pennsylvania was also chartered in 1794. The corporate system launched by these two companies spread rapidly to other cities. The joint stock company, which enabled wealthy individuals to invest substantial sums of money for the purchase of common stock, made possible a much larger amount of capital and surplus than could be raised on the mutual plan. The Insurance Company of North America was founded with the largest capitalization of any firm in the United States up to its formation. With an initial capital investment of $600,000, the company was able to assume the largest marine risks of the day. Many of the most experienced insurance underwriters in Philadelphia became active promoters of the company.

Marine Insurance.   Marine insurance, because of its international ramifications, did not develop as a peculiarly American institution. Its forms, rates, and rules were standardized on an international rather than on a national basis. The history of marine insurance closely followed the cycles of international commerce. Wars have always served to increase hazards, rates, and premium volume. Such periods were not always prosperous, but they stimulated innovation and growth. The Napoleonic Wars and their aftermath and the War of 1812 swept most American shipping off the seas and brought the U.S. marine insurance industry to the brink of disaster. It was not until about 1840, when the clipper ships of the United States captured most of the English and continental trade, that the industry revived.

The clipper ship era lasted from about 1840 until 1860. The development of the English steam propelled iron ship coupled with the effects of the American Civil War caused a serious decline in American shipping.

Fire Insurance.   The history of fire insurance in the United States is the history of great fires, each one having a salutary effect on the business. There were few companies in the field by 1820, but Pennsylvania and New York passed laws prohibiting foreign companies from operating in their states. The Great Fire of New York in 1835, which destroyed 700 buildings, put an end to this discrimination—and to most companies in the fire insurance business at the time. These failures gave rise to the birth of insurance regulation, when Massachusetts in 1837 required companies to maintain a fund to guarantee fulfillment of their contracts. Gradually, all states set up reserve requirements, and a complex pattern of state regulation developed.

Casualty Insurance.   Casualty insurance began before the Civil War. About twenty companies were in the field of accident insurance. The Travelers Insurance Company, founded in 1863 for the writing of travel policies exclusively, was writing all lines by 1864.

Inland Marine Insurance.   Inland marine insurance, which extended marine contracts to cover inland waterways, and then from warehouse-to-warehouse, arose in this period as well.

Life Insurance.   Mutual of New York, founded in 1835, was the first major surviving insurance company to do a general life insurance zusiness. It still is one of the leading life insurers in the United States. Many companies were formed during the period before the Civil War, but very few managed to remain in business very long. There was a looseness of operation that required external control before the industry could move forward on a financially sound basis.

By 1860, a great number of insurance companies had been promoted and had discontinued operations for want of proper management and adequate capital. The industry was viable and aggressive. Forty-three life insurance companies were in active operation, and more than thirty fire and casualty carriers. The panic of 1857 had wiped out fifteen of the twenty-six Philadelphia stock insurance companies that had ·been "rated" in *Tucketts' Monthly Insurance Journal.*[5]

ELIZUR WRIGHT AND INSURANCE REGULATION

Massachusetts, in 1855, was the first state to organize an insurance department, followed by New York in 1859. In 1852, Massachusetts appointed a Board of Insurance Commissioners, but a separate department was launched in 1855. Shortly thereafter, such departments were formed in many other leading insurance states.

Elizur Wright, a professor of mathematics, was instrumental in launching the first insurance department, and he served for eight years as one of the two insurance commissioners. While he failed in his advocacy of federal regulation of life insurance, he did succeed in persuading the Massachusetts legislature to introduce a number of laws that helped to establish the American life insurance industry on a more sound actuarial basis.

Among the innovations introduced by Wright were:

1. the principle of state supervision of insurance from the standpoint of solvency of carriers,
2. requiring deposits as a precondition for licensing,
3. periodic reporting by carriers and the audit inspection of their accounts and records,
4. the principle of the cash surrender value and premium loan privilege in life insurance policies as a statutory requirement, and
5. the concept of the level reserve plan as a substitute for the natural reserve or increasing annual premium plan.

The role of Elizur Wright in the development of life insurance regulation was pivotal. Knowledgeable, moralistic, and mathematically versatile, he understood the needs of the business and had the power to move the legislature of Massachusetts to set the initial patterns of what later became a complex web of insurance regulation.

At an 1871 meeting in New York, the National Convention of Insurance

---

[5] *Tucketts' Monthly Insurance Journal* was the first American insurance magazine. It was published in Philadelphia in 1852 and rated companies as: "reliable," "insufficient assets", "unsafe for business", and "fraudulent". This degree of candor would be illegal in most states today.

Commissioners, whose name was changed in 1935 to the National Association of Insurance Commissioners, was formed. Its purposes were to seek cooperation in achieving a reasonable degree of uniformity in control. At the first meeting, which lasted ten days in May 1871, the commissioners adopted a uniform reporting form for annual reports. Other matters on the agenda of the meeting that year included: reciprocity between departments in accepting certificates on valuations and assets of domestic insurance companies, uniform methods of valuation, uniform insurance and taxation laws, and problems of insolvency. The American Experience Table was recommended for mortality assumptions with a 4.5 percent interest factor. Superintendent George W. Miller of New York stated that "the true object and aim of governmental supervision should be to afford the fullest possible protection to the public, with the least possible annoyance or expense to, or interference with, the companies."[6]

In 1868, the United States Supreme Court, in the leading case of *Paul v. Virginia*,[7] held that insurance is not interstate commerce. This decision proved to be a landmark from the standpoint of regulation and gave rise to affirmative regulation by the various states. The *Paul v. Virginia* decision was tested on many occasions, but it was not until the Southeastern Underwriters Association case in 1944[8] that the Supreme Court reversed itself and held insurance to be interstate commerce.

MARINE INSURANCE AFTER THE CIVIL WAR

The post-Civil War Period was a poor one for marine insurance in the United States. The Confederate Navy, assisted by English shipbuilders, had successfully played havoc with shipping off the east coast of the United States. The Confederate cruiser *Alabama* had destroyed the whaling fleet off the Azores and captured nine northern ships on its way home in the winter of 1862. By the end of 1863, forty vessels had fallen prey to this one gunboat, and marine insurance rates had doubled and tripled for shipments on American hulls. The British marine underwriters used more sophisticated rate classifications to identify profitable classes of business and were able to undercut American insurance companies by a wide margin, thereby attracting the bulk of the business. American shipowners sought foreign registry to obtain the benefits of lower rates, and the United States experienced a gradually declining share of the market.

In 1897, Benjamin Rush prepared a comprehensive analysis of marine underwriting conditions that identified problems in the American marine

---

[6] Buley, *op. cit.*, p. 84.

[7] *Paul v. Virginia*, 8 Wall. 168 (1869).

[8] *U.S. v. South-Eastern Underwriters Assn.*, 1944, 322, U.S. 533,64 S. Ct. 1162, 88 L. Ed. 1440.

insurance market after the Civil War.[9] He attributed the decline in the American share of the world market to the following conditions:

1.   The transition from wooden sailing vessels to iron steamers, which could earn more money per ton than sailing ships, largely eliminated the profits of shipowners and led to poor maintenance, ineffective management, and deliberate destruction for the purpose of collecting on insurance policies.

2.   The hazard of collision was enormously increased because of the expansion of commerce; the highways of the oceans were becoming crowded with large, fast, powerful ships running on the schedule time of a railroad, through fair or inclement weather.

3.   The substantial profits earned by some of the more careful companies led to intense competition. Rates dropped as much as 80 percent, improper claims were paid, and careless extensions of coverage were granted. These procedures resulted in substantial negligence and fraud. Price wars drove weaker companies out of the business.

While some companies were able to meet competition by more detailed reclassifications of business, more careful underwriting and claims supervision, and more profitable reinsurance arrangements, the American marine insurance business was largely in foreign hands by the beginning of the twentieth century.

FIRE INSURANCE AFTER THE CIVIL WAR

The fire insurance industry was a multimillion dollar business by 1870, with a large number of inadequately capitalized companies underwriting risks with little regard for the catastrophic hazard. Most housing was of wood frame construction with wood shingle roofs. Typically, houses were crowded together along narrow streets. Fire prevention equipment was modest in both quality and quantity; building codes were not enforced; and local insurance companies operated with little, if any, contingency reserves. Mrs. O'Leary's cow bankrupted sixty-eight fire insurance companies on October 8, 1871, as the great Chicago fire killed 250 persons and ruined 2,124 acres of the city, with losses in excess of $190,000,000. Some 202 companies shared in losses, which were insured for more than $100,000,000. In 1872, the city of Boston sustained a similarly disastrous fire, in which more than $75,000,000 of property was destroyed, some $50,000,000 of which was covered by insurance. As a result of this disaster, some twenty-five companies were forced to suspend business.

The impact of the Chicago and Boston fires on the insurance industry and on public recognition of the need for better fire prevention was a powerful one. An elaborate system of fire insurance ratings that discriminated against wooden

[9] See James, *op.cit.*, pp. 192-99.

construction, inadequate water systems, inadequate fire departments and protection, and inadequate enforcement of building codes was established. Line limits, which are maximum insurance amounts per building and per district, were set by the fire insurance companies. The public became extremely insurance conscious, and rates were at favorable levels. The end result was that hazards were reduced, rates increased, sales rose, and the insurance business became lucrative toward the end of the nineteenth century.

CASUALTY INSURANCE

Casualty insurance was the latest of the major branches of the industry to come into being. The Travelers Insurance Company of Hartford had added accident and health insurance as an adjunct to its life insurance business, and a modest amount of liability insurance was being written by the Fidelity and Casualty of New York. The first automobile insurance policy was written about 1888 as an extension of the forms used for the protection of owners of horse drawn carriages. By 1898, two hundred automobiles were manufactured in the United States, and liability insurance began its long rapid history of growth. Early resistance to such coverage on the part of insurance companies was based on the reckless driving of the first "chauffeurs." As companies and the public became aware of the increasing need for broadened coverages, new endorsements and lines of coverage were added to the point where, in the twentieth century, casualty insurance probably has more variation in forms and covers than any other branch of the business.

LIFE INSURANCE AFTER THE CIVIL WAR

The period between 1868 and 1905 in the history of American life insurance has been described as one of "revolt, recession, and resurgence," with considerable disorder in the industry. The period was characterized by major changes.

> American companies expanded into Canada and Europe; Canadian companies entered the United States; fraternal and assessment insurance arose; industrial life insurance had its beginning in this country; failures and hard times weighed heavily upon life sales throughout much of the period; competition was harsh and ruthless; the public suffered many disheartening disclosures of bad practice and bad faith in life insurance selling and management circles; there was a turning away from first principles, in a sense, when new types of sales appeals attracted support for the investment and speculative rather than for the more purely protective types of policies; and selling methods themselves were altered. It was a period of failures, of opposition to the regular companies, of

crude and venomous sales tactics, of chastisement, and of groping self-discipline; yet it was ultimately too a period of advancement and growth.[10]

A wave of mergers and bankruptcies caused much uncertainty on the part of insureds as new companies were formed and dissolved. Every life insurance company that commenced business before 1840, with one exception, failed or changed the character of its business. Of the 104 companies formed between 1868 and 1895, only 9 were still active in 1937.

TABLE 3.1   Number of U.S. Life Insurance Companies, 1759-1900

Year	Number
1759	1
1760	1
1770	2
1780	2
1790	3
1800	4
1810	2
1820	6
1830	9
1840	15
1850	48
1860	43
1870	129
1880	59
1890	60
1900	84

SOURCE: *1971 Fact Book*. New York: Institute of Life Insurance, 1971.

While regulatory officials had launched insurance departments in most states by the turn of the century, the degree of enforcement was not uniform, and in most instances the formation of an insurance department was regarded more as an avenue for better tax collection from carriers than for the maintenance of high standards of conduct.

SUMMARY

The evolution of American insurance from the Colonial Period to the end of the

[10] Stalson, *op.cit.*, p. 401.

nineteenth century is marked by the adaptation of English practices to a very different environment, both economically and politically. The early insurance offices were merely local agencies for London underwriters. Imitations of English institutions, such as the London Coffee House in Philadelphia in 1760, did a very modest business with limited capacity. The singular development and expansion of the insurance industry in the United States is attributable to the major influences of wars, catastrophic fires, urbanization, the Industrial Revolution, and the rise of Big Business.

The impact of major wars, such as the Revolution, the Napoleonic Wars, and the Civil War, with their international ramifications was to stimulate nationalistic drives for the formation of domestic insurance markets to relieve the economy of overdependence on the "capacity" of markets controlled by the "enemy."

The multinational nature of the insurance business, whereby an insurer places some of its excess risk with reinsurers abroad, who place some of their excess (a process referred to as "retrocession") with other groups of reinsurers makes it virtually impossible to identify the nationality of each insurance company that carries a portion of the risk. During World War II, American ships and cargoes were being insured by American insurance companies, which reinsured some of the risk in Swiss reinsurance companies, who retroceded some of the American business to insurance companies domiciled in Germany, Italy, and Japan. According to U.S. Army Intelligence, underwriting information about American shipping was available to the enemy by way of insurance records, and this data was used to pinpoint targets for successful submarine attacks.[11]

War also draws attention to the problems of risk and insurance and creates powerful demands for insurance coverage. While the initial impact on the insurance industry is usually one of financial stress because of adverse claims experience, the ultimate result has always been a material expansion in the size of surviving companies.

Conflagrations provided the motivation for the growth and development of municipal fire departments, water systems, building codes, and fire insurance. The rising trend of fire insurance premium volume in the United States is interrupted periodically by major losses that temporarily tax the resources of the industry and drive the weaker companies out of business. The immediate sequel to every major disaster has been an acceleration in the growth rate of the fire insurance companies, whether measured by resources or premium income.

The urbanization process is accompanied by dependence upon a money economy, which compels people to make more formal provision for premature death or sickness than is required in a rural community. Life insurance flourishes

---

[11] James Stewart Martin, *All Honorable Men,* Boston: Little, Brown and Co., 1950, p. 21, describes the World War II experience in which American ships and cargoes were being reinsured by German companies whose records were made available to their government for use by the German Navy.

in an urban society, and its growth in the United States paralleled the movement to the cities. Property insurance, likewise, expanded with the urbanization process.

The Industrial Revolution in the United States, which began after the Civil War, brought with it a radical increase in the Gross National Product and in commercial activity. As business investment rose, the need for fire insurance as a prerequisite of credit transactions was recognized, and amounts at risk in factories and commercial establishments showed parallel gains. The improvement in personal disposable income made life insurance attractive as a medium for savings as well as protection. By the end of the nineteenth century, insurance was a booming business with an army of salesmen.

The rise of Big Business had a material effect on the insurance industry because this financial institution was in command of enormous sums of money for investment in other enterprises. It was perhaps inevitable that the fiduciary nature of the insurance business would be ignored by financiers seeking maximum leverage through holding company devices in an era when government regulation was minimal. Companies were promoted in great numbers, only to disappear at the first whiff of trouble from economic recession or natural disaster.

The English experience differed from that of the United States largely because of differences in population mobility and tradition. The men in Lombard Street adhered to practices that were hundreds of years old. The gentlemen's agreement was regarded as a matter of utmost good faith, and an underwriter who dishonored his contracts was permanently banned from the financial community. In a closed English financial society there was no place for a failure to make a fresh start. The code of honor served as a regulatory apparatus. In the United States there was a breaking away from the old customs. People were proud of their ability to "bounce back." The man who failed in Boston could start again in New York, and, having failed there, could try once more in Philadelphia. The mobility of entrepreneurs created a need for new approaches to business risks. Credit references, more carefully drawn contracts, greater statutory protection for the public, and greater concern for the integrity and solvency of insurance companies were American adaptations of the insurance institution.

REVIEW QUESTIONS

1. The formation of a domestic insurance market was regarded as a major goal before the American Revolution. Why was a domestic insurance market essential for the economic liberation of the American colonies from British rule? Can one safely generalize from the American experience to that of other underdeveloped countries? Discuss.

2. "Elizur Wright was a forerunner of the contemporary consumerist movement in insurance". Explain.

3. American marine insurance markets have undergone periods of growth and decline associated with wars. Explain the nature of this cyclical pattern.

4. What has been the influence of the Industrial Revolution and of the urbanization process on the development and growth of insurance in the United States? Discuss.

5. Contrary to the English experience, the United States did not have traditions of "gentlemen's agreements" and a closed financial society. How did these differences influence the evolution of insurance regulation in the United States as compared with the English system? Explain.

STUDY QUESTIONS

6. How do you account for the tremendous impact of Benjamin Franklin on the early history of insurance in the United States? Explain.

7. How do you account for the formation of the National Association of Insurance Commissioners despite the fact that insurance was regarded as subject to state rather than federal regulation throughout the nineteenth century? Discuss.

8. What lessons were learned from the period of unregulated competition in the late nineteenth and early twentieth centuries? How might the potential adverse affects of extensive insurance market competition be avoided without also destroying the potential benefits of market competition?

9. The growth of insurance markets is often stimulated by the occurrence of natural disasters (earthquakes, floods, fires, etc.). To what extent has this correlation been true in the United States?

10. What effect, if any, did passage of the Sherman Anti-Trust Act have on the operations of insurance companies between 1890 and 1910? Explain.

4

American Insurance

in the

Twentieth Century

The history of the insurance business in the United States in the twentieth century is one of explosive growth in the face of ever-increasing regulation at all government levels and in all phases of the business. Major economic events and natural or man made disasters shaped the direction of expansion of the industry. For purposes of analysis the period may be divided into four segments:

1. the Era of Intensive Regulation, 1900-1919;
2. the Era of Economic Adjustment, 1919-1940;
3. the Era of Wartime Expansion, 1940-1948; and
4. the Contemporary Period, 1948 to the present.

THE ERA OF INTENSIVE REGULATION, 1900-1919

The first decade of the twentieth century opened with a series of major events that established landmarks and important new directions for the industry. A series of scandals, culminating in the Armstrong Investigation of the life insurance business; a series of major fire disasters; a castastrophic influenza epidemic; and the intervention of government in the insurance business all influenced this important period in American insurance history.

The Armstrong Investigation

The Armstrong Committee Investigation,[1] conducted in New York in 1905 in the course of which charges of mismanagement and malfeasance were made and widely publicized in the national press, grew out of a dispute involving control of the Equitable Life Assurance Society of the United States. This was the era of the "muckrakers" in American history, and life insurance came in for its share of adverse publicity. The findings of the Committee clearly indicated a need for reform. The resolution appointing the Committee set forth these objectives:

> To investigate and examine into the business affairs of life insurance companies doing business in the State of New York, with reference to the investments of said companies, the relation of officers thereof to such investments, the relation of such companies to subsidiary corporations, the government and control of said companies, the contractual relations of said companies to their policyholders, the cost of life insurance, the expenses of said companies, and any other phase of the life insurance business deemed by the Committee to be proper, for the purpose of drafting and reporting to the next session of the Legislature such a revision of the laws regulating and relating to life insurance in this state as said Committee may deem proper.[2]

The Report of the Committee, which included a transcript of the testimony, filled ten volumes and resulted in the enactment in New York State of the most intensive pattern of insurance regulation to be found anywhere in the world. Stimulated by the Armstrong Committee hearings, many other states and countries conducted similar investigations, and insurance regulation elsewhere was materially affected.

The recommendations of the Committee were numerous. Most were enacted into law, but a number were later relaxed because they were unnecessarily restrictive. The following list is indicative of the scope of its recommendations:

Organization of Life Insurance Companies. In order to form mutual companies, special legislative enactment was required in contrast to the requirements for stock companies. It was recommended that a law be enacted to facilitate the formation of new mutual companies by setting forth uniform standards for subscriptions and reserves.

Control of Mutuals by their Policyholders. Six recommendations for new legislation were made to curb the power that directors had to maintain

---

[1] New York Legislative Insurance Investigation Committee, *Armstrong Committee Record: Testimony, Exhibits, Report,* 10 vols. Albany, N.Y., 1906.

[2] Cited in Joseph B. Maclean, *Life Insurance,* 8th ed. (New York: McGraw-Hill Book Co., 1959), p. 591.

permanent control of the mutual companies by perpetuating themselves by automatic reelection.

1. Individual policyholders should have access to lists of policyholders so that independent candidates might run for election to the board of directors.
2. The incumbent administration of an insurance company should have the power to nominate candidates for election to the board of directors.
3. Independent nominations should be allowed.
4. Ballots listing the names of all candidates should be circulated among the policyholders.
5. All existing proxies should be cancelled.
6. Proxies should be valid for no longer than two months.

Control of Stock Companies by Policyholders. In order to permit conversion from a stock to a mutual form of company, the Committee recommended that stock companies be permitted to retire their stock and thereby to effect a change either to a "mixed" basis, with policyholders having partial control, or to a completely mutual basis.

Investments in Real Estate. Despite statutes limiting the power of a life insurance company to hold real estate as a permanent investment, many companies were heavily committed to low yielding real estate leased at substandard rents to indirectly related subsidiaries and controlled entities. The Committee recommended that schedules showing all of the relevant details pertaining to real estate held for investment be made a part of the statutory Annual Convention Blank.

Securities. Insurance companies were found to be involved, through substantial stock ownership, in the control of companies in other lines of activity; to be maintaining substantial deposits in inactive accounts in banks controlled by insurance company directors; to be participating as guarantors in syndicates for the flotation of new stock issues; and to be engaged in financial transactions on joint account with other companies. The Armstrong Committee recommended that investment in all stocks be prohibited for life insurance companies (legislation on this point was subsequently modified on a step by step liberalization basis); all stocks held in the portfolios of life insurance companies be liquidated within five years; investment syndicate participation should be prohibited; and conflicts of interest should be made illegal, as they relate to the activities of directors or officers of insurance companies.

Limitations of New Business. In order to limit the apparent increasing concentration of economic power in the giant life insurance companies, the Committee recommended that limits be set on the amount of new business a life insurance company would be permitted to write. An ultimate limit of

$150,000,000 per year was recommended. Today many companies sell in excess of $1 billion worth of new life insurance each year.

Political Contributions.   The Committee recommended that campaign donations be prohibited, or at least be given substantial publicity in the Annual Report of the companies.

Lobbying.   Lobbying activities of the three largest companies in New York had been massive and costly to policyholders in the judgment of the Committee. They suggested a prohibition on such activity.

Expenses.   The expense factors reported by witnesses were regarded as excessive. The Armstrong Committee therefore made these suggestions:

1. Limits should be set on the amount of new business a company could write in order to reduce the financial drain on surplus.
2. Commissions should be limited and standardized throughout the industry with special bonuses disallowed.
3. Vouchers should be required to justify all expenses.
4. Total expenses for new business should not be allowed to exceed total loadings on first year premiums plus a conservative estimate of the present value of mortality gains expected for the first five years of policy duration. By this means it was hoped that old policyholders would not be compelled to subsidize the acquisition costs of obtaining new policyholders.

Rebates.   Rebating, the payment of a portion of the commission by an agent to a prospective insured as an inducement to take out a policy, was illegal. Unfair discrimination was not. The Committee recommended that the person receiving the rebate be subjected to the same criminal penalties as the person granting the rebate.

Tontine Dividends.   The practice had developed of allowing dividends to policyholders to be deferred for long periods of time (five, ten, fifteen, or twenty years), with policyholders forfeiting their equity in these dividend accumulations in the event the policy was allowed to lapse, or in the event of premature death. Dividend projections that were highly speculative in nature were used in selling. To eliminate the "betting" feature, the Armstrong Committee recommended that dividends should be paid annually in cash, paid up insurance, or in reduction of premiums; the selling of deferred dividend policies should be prohibited; companies should be required to make an annual accounting of dividends for every policy in force; contingency funds should be permitted in order to minimize dividend fluctuations; and finally that companies should file a profit and loss statement with the State Superintendent of Insurance showing the amount available for distribution to policyholders, the actual dividends declared, and the method of computation used in arriving at the dividends.

Nonparticipating Policies.   Mutual companies should not be permitted to issue nonparticipating or nondividend policies because nonparticipating life insurance policyholders would find themselves either paying too much or too little, which results in inequities.

Policy Forms.   The Committee recommended that the contract be one of "entirety," not depending upon oral side agreements in order to clarify the rights of policyholders. They also urged that forms be standardized to reduce the confusion arising from catchy titles and similar sales devices.

The Committee held fifty-seven public hearings between September 6, 1905 and December 30, 1905 under the leadership of Charles Evans Hughes, who was later to become Chief Justice of the U.S. Supreme Court. Most of the Armstrong Committee recommendations were enacted into law in New York, and, later, elsewhere. As a consequence of this investigation, the life insurance industry was launched into the Era of Intensive Regulation with a widespread public awareness of the financial and managerial responsibility of life insurance companies. The purge had the effect of increasing public confidence in the institution of life insurance. When the New York Insurance Code was amended, it included the more significant recommendations of the Armstrong Committee.

The San Francisco Fire and the Merritt Committee

The San Francisco Fire of 1906, which followed in the wake of a major earthquake, resulted in the destruction of 28,000 buildings with a property loss of approximately $350 million. The total burned area was about 3,000 acres. The insurance loss was estimated at $235,000,000, most of which was placed with insurance companies admitted to do business in California; almost $270,000,000 was paid in insurance settlements. This infamous fire bankrupted a great many companies, caused a general overall increase in fire rates across the country, and forced surviving companies to cooperate more closely in rate making and other activities.

The substantial rate increases that followed the San Francisco disaster met little immediate resistance because of public appreciation of the fire hazard. Before long, questions were raised about the legality of uniform rate structures and compacts between companies that were felt to be in restraint of trade or in violation of antitrust statutes. A number of states enacted "anticompact" statutes designed to prohibit "any agreement or combination for the regulation or fixing of premiums." The practice of settling losses on an indemnity basis also came under criticism, and some states enacted so-called valued policy laws, requiring a company to pay the face of the policy in the event of total loss.

After the San Francisco fire, investigations of the fire insurance industry were conducted in some ten states, somewhat along the lines of the Armstrong inquiry. In New York the Merritt Committee was established in 1910 to investigate insurance company opposition to the numerous anticompact and valued policy bills introduced before the legislature.[3] Hearings were held between November 22, 1910 and January 6, 1911, and the Committee published its report in 1911.

The Merritt Committee Report opposed anticompact laws and arbitrary regulation of fire insurance by the states. It recommended that rating bureaus established by the companies be recognized and regulated by the states. This report was significant because it established the principle that combinations of fire insurance companies who set uniform rates were not acting contrary to the public interest. The investigation also clarified misunderstandings about profit levels. It established as fact that unrestricted price competition was a major cause of insurance company insolvency. Legislation based on the Merritt Committee Report had as important an effect on the fire insurance business as did the Armstrong Report legislation on the life insurance business. Both tended to enhance public confidence in the insurance business.

The Influenza Epidemic of 1918

The influenza epidemic of 1918 had more severe consequences for the life insurance industry than any war in history. The world-wide death impact was more than 10,000,000 lives. In the United States the number of deaths directly attributable to the epidemic was estimated at more than 450,000 or more than 3 per 1,000 of the total population. The major effect was on young lives where, because policies were relatively new, life insurance company reserves were small. The financial result was that the ratio of actual to expected mortality rose to several hundred percent for the year, and life insurance benefits vastly exceeded premiums that had been collected. New companies were so severely affected that reserve practices and patterns of reinsurance were tightened to a degree never before observed. That this catastrophe was not even more financially disastrous is attributable to the enormous spread of the business risk and to the fact that most policyholders had relatively small policies in force.

Wars in which the United States engaged generally resulted in widespread losses among young people with small policies, but war clauses effectively precluded liability. The flu epidemic resulted in an avalanche of claims that were not subject to restrictive endorsements. The mortality crises of 1918 created a greater appreciation for reinsurance and contingency reserves.

---

[3] New York State Assembly, *Report of the Joint Committee of The Senate and Assembly of the State of New York Appointed to Investigate Corrupt Practices in Connection with Legislation, and Affairs of Insurance Companies, Other Than Those Doing Life Insurance Business.* (Albany: J.B. Lyon Co., 1911).

Government Intervention as an Insurance Carrier

While various forms of state insurance existed from the turn of the century, the intervention of the U.S. Government into the insurance market through the provision of war risk insurance was a major step on the road to expanded government insurance activity.

The various war risk clauses of marine insurance policies excluded the hazards of loss by floating mines, torpedoes, and other wartime perils, with the result that very little shipping of American registry was available for the conduct of World War I. It is estimated that when the war began in 1914, American steamships registered for the foreign trade accounted for only about 2 percent of the world's shipping. On September 2, 1914 the Bureau of War Risk Insurance was established in the Treasury Department with an initial capital of five million dollars. It began issuing policies almost immediately, and the federal government embarked on a course leading to major participation in the insurance industry.

In 1917 the War Risk Insurance Act was amended to embrace insurance on personal effects of masters, officers, and crews of ships, and later to loss of life by personal injuries and compensation in case of capture. A full-fledged insurance program, allowing $10,000 of coverage on a renewable term basis, was enacted into law on October 9, 1917, and by the end of the year there were 330,941 policies in force with combined face amounts of $2,848,291,500. The government program produced long term favorable effects by creating wider recognition of the "human life value" and new awareness of the need for personal programs of life insurance.

By the end of World War I, the industry was ready to participate in the economic boom of the twenties. It had come through a period of stress, and the pattern of regulation was firmly entrenched. Next would come an era of rapid expansion in volume and in influence as the insurance industry settled into its position as a major savings and protection medium.

THE ERA OF ECONOMIC ADJUSTMENT, 1919-1940

The post-World War I period was characterized by rapid economic expansion as industry rushed to deliver goods and services to fulfill needs of the country that were unsatisfied during the war emergency. The capacity of the insurance industry had been built up to meet the needs of a war economy, and the 1920s provided an encouraging milieu for further growth.

All the major branches of insurance that are recognized today were well developed by 1920. Casualty and inland marine insurance, the newest of the categories, had both grown to substantial proportions.

Prior to 1933, all transportation insurance was known as marine insurance with no distinction made between goods carried overland or by sea. In 1933, through promulgation of the Nationwide Definition and Interpretation of the Insuring Powers of Marine and Transportation Underwriters, adopted by the National Convention of Insurance Commissioners, inland marine insurance was redefined. This branch was credited with about one-third of the marine volume; it expanded rapidly until it exceeded ocean marine premiums by a wide margin. By advancing the ocean marine approach of all risk coverage it was possible for inland marine insurance to become one of the most dynamic branches of the business in later years.

The general business expansion of the twenties inevitably resulted in a relaxation of watchfulness on the part of some life insurance companies, so the crash of 1929 and the depression of the 1930s created severe problems. To some extent the dynamics of the life insurance business require constant expansion. Cessation of growth in new writings causes a run-off of reserves with rapid shrinkage of assets. Overhead expense does not decline as rapidly as income and losses are incurred. This happened to a number of companies in the 1930s.

Perhaps the most significant events of the period under study were the Great Depression, the birth of the Social Security System, and the Report of the Temporary National Economic Committee (TNEC).

The Great Depression

The impact of the depression on life insurance companies took many forms:

1. Interest rates began a decline that was to be sustained for about fifteen years;
2. Mortality experience was aggravated;
3. Earnings on surplus declined;
4. Suicides increased to a level 30 percent above normal in the early 1930s.

Much of the excess mortality was on policies of large face amounts. As a result of loose underwriting practices, policyholders were able to abuse their disability income by malingering. This was the equivalent to unemployment insurance that is not privately insurable. The insurance company loss ratios were phenomenal.

Real estate had to be foreclosed, and investment income dropped sharply, particularly in rural areas. Many states imposed moratoria on mortgage foreclosures, which aggravated the losses of life insurance companies.

The National Bank Holiday of 1933 resulted in a moratorium being declared on the disbursement of cash and policy loan values. This was done to forestall a "run" on insurance companies. Despite the economic disaster of the Great Depression, only 20 of the 350 life insurance companies in business at that time were placed in the hands of receivers. The Reconstruction Finance Corporation made loans to some companies, which were later repaid.

The Depression also hit the fire and casualty industry because burning ratios rose to high levels as arson increased in the face of financial problems. Premiums that were related to personal disposable income declined, but expense ratios tended to decline less quickly. As a result insurance companies had unfavorable experience in this period. Desperate price cutting to achieve greater volume further reduced profits.

Marine insurance declined to a low level as commerce fell to a relative standstill.

Despite its trials the insurance industry came out of the Depression in sounder condition than ever before. The financially strong survived; the weak limited their exposures or were merged out of existence.

The Social Security System

More significant in its ultimate impact on the insurance business than any other event during the interwar period was the introduction of Social Security in the United States. Although initially designed to provide only a basic minimum of economic security for retired persons and widows through government pensions, the Social Security program quickly proliferated into a relatively comprehensive system. The rapid expansion of Social Security and of other governmental programs begun in this era is shown in Table 4.1. While there was initial resistance on the part of the life insurance industry, this dissolved in the face of the inevitable, and as with the War Risk Insurance programs Social Security made people more conscious of the value of life insurance protection.

TABLE 4.1   Old Age, Survivors, Disability and Health Insurance
($ millions)

Year	Employer and Worker Taxes in Year	Monthly and Lump Sum Payments in Year
1940	637	35
1945	1,286	274
1950	2,667	961
1955	5,713	4,968
1960	11,876	11,245
1965	17,205	18,311
1970	34,737	31,863

SOURCE: *1971 Life Insurance Fact Book.* (New York: Institute of Life Insurance, 1971).

The Temporary National Economic Committee Investigation

In 1938 President Roosevelt appointed the Temporary National Economic Committee to study and report on the question of concentration of economic power. The original purpose of the life insurance portion of their inquiry was to study the impact on the economy of investment activities of insurance companies, but the investigation soon expanded into a comprehensive study of insurance. Their principal recommendations were:

1. State insurance commissioners should be appointed on the basis of qualification, should have longer tenure of office, should have no duties other than regulation of insurance, and should have larger salaries.
2. The budget and staff of qualified personnel of state insurance departments should be increased.
3. There should be closer regulation of training and qualification of agents and methods of compensation.
4. The number of policy forms should be reduced and greater attention given to standardized forms or policy provisions.
5. Life insurance should be conducted on a competitive basis. No intercompany agreements that would prevent sound development should be permitted.
6. A fundamental change in the conduct of industrial insurance should be made.[4]

While the insurance industry emerged from the investigation with its reputation intact, the study did focus attention on some of the internal weaknesses of the life insurance business during the Great Depression.

THE ERA OF WARTIME EXPANSION, 1940-1948

The World War II and postwar periods saw a number of developments that had major significance for the insurance industry:

1. the Guertin Legislation, which updated actuarial practice in life insurance and provided new mortality tables that were almost universally adopted for reserve purposes;
2. the Southeastern Underwriters case, decided in 1944, which materially changed the technique of regulation by the states; and
3. the expansion of military service connected health and life insurance benefits through the GI insurance program.

Guertin Legislation

The Guertin Legislation[5] was a major development, more from the standpoint of public relations than in terms of substantive change in company

---

[4] Maclean, *op. cit.,* p. 604 provides an excellent summary of the TNEC Report.

[5] National Association of Insurance Commissioners, *Reports and Statements on Nonforfeiture Benefits and Related Matters* (Chicago: Actuarial Society of America and American Institute of Actuaries, 1942). Alfred N. Guertin was chairman of the Committee and is credited with the authorship of the "Standard Nonforfeiture Law".

practice. The Committee recommended a new mortality table, *CSO (1941)*; a new method of computing nonforfeiture values in life insurance policies; a new method of calculating reserves; and improved insurance terminology. The term "cash surrender value" was banished from the official vocabulary of the business, to be replaced by "nonforfeiture value."

South-Eastern Underwriters Association Decision

The S.E.U.A. decision[6] was a landmark in that it declared insurance to be interstate commerce and therefore subject to federal jurisdiction. Thus insurance was subject to such statutes as the National Labor Relations Act, the Fair Labor Standards Act, the Robinson-Patman Act, and the Sherman Anti-Trust Act. This decision was a radical one because it threatened to change the entire basis of insurance regulation from state to federal jurisdiction.

In 1945 the Congress enacted the McCarran Act, which provided that the states could continue regulation of insurance without federal intervention as long as each state law met the standards of the Sherman, Clayton, and Federal Trade Commission Acts. A moratorium on federal regulation was granted until June 30, 1948 and later extended to permit revision of state insurance laws.

The National Association of Insurance Commissioners sponsored an All Industry Committee, which recommended Model Rate Regulatory Bills that were enacted in all of the states. Additional proposals relating to unfair trade practices, unauthorized insurers service of process, and conflicts of interest were also adopted.

The result of the South-Eastern Underwriters Association decision was to discourage tendencies toward monopolistic and coercive practices in the competitive structure of the insurance industry after World War II. The states retained jurisdiction over the insurance business, but the industry was placed in the position whereby, if regulation by the states proved inadequate, federal law might still be applied.

GI Insurance

The War Risk Insurance Program, the U.S. Government Life Insurance program (USGLI), initiated in 1917 made life insurance available on application to service and auxiliary personnel in amounts up to $10,000. About $40 billion of war risk insurance was issued, and after the war insureds were given the right to convert to permanent insurance. Most of that coverage had lapsed by 1972.

---

[6] *U.S. v. South-Eastern Underwriters Assn.* (1944) 322 U.S. 533,64 S. Ct. 1162, 88 L. Ed. 1440. For a detailed review of the S.E.U.A. Decision, see Irwin M. Stelzer, "The Insurance Industry and the Antitrust Laws: A Decade of Experience," *The Insurance Law Journal* (March, 1955), pp. 137-152; H.R. Stern, "The McCarran Act 20 Years After," *The Insurance Law Journal* (October, 1966), pp. 605-614.

In 1940 the National Service Life Insurance Program (NSLI) took effect, offering five-year renewable term policies primarily on a $10,000 face amount basis. During World War II about $140 billion was issued. After the war the lapse rate was again very high.

In 1951 the Servicemen's Indemnity and Insurance Acts provided Gratuitous Indemnity of $10,000 for servicemen on active duty, and the USGLI and NSLI programs came to an end.

The veterans life insurance programs sponsored by the federal government grew from a minor war risk accommodation into one of the major sources of life insurance in the United States. At its peak in 1945, there was $98,426,000,000 in force under approximately 13,000,000 policies. By 1970 veterans life insurance in force had declined to $37.4 billions, but the federal government was in the life insurance business to stay.

CONTEMPORARY DEVELOPMENT

The Cold War, the Federal Life Insurance Company Income Tax Act of 1959, the adjustment to the S.E.U.A. impact, a high rate of innovation, rapid expansion in the face of a booming economy, consumerism, and the development and growth of cooperative insurance ventures (as between government and industry) all mark the contemporary period.

Significant trends include new coverages, the variable annuity, the homeowners policy, direct writing in the fields of fire and casualty insurance, the development of multiple lines concepts and permissive legislation, the move to an "all lines" approach with more and more carriers in the life field buying fire and casualty companies or *vice versa,* computerization of operations, and development of holding companies.

Insurance was transformed during the decades of the fifties and sixties from a conservative monoline oligopolistic industry to a more competitive structure. Hundreds of new companies entered the field; the power of the boards and bureaus, the associations and clubs was broken; mergers developed in great numbers; monoline companies, multiline companies and groups became all line. The direct writing insurance companies selling directly to the public without the use of commissioned salesmen introduced a marketing revolution, and mass merchandizing programs were launched. New products were introduced so rapidly that insurance executives had difficulty identifying the innovators. Technological changes and diffusion of product were rapid,[7] as companies strained to capture or retain their market shares.

Automation came to the insurance industry relatively early and soon

---

[7]Irving Pfeffer, "Innovations in the Fire and Casualty Business," *Best's Insurance News (Fire/Casualty Edition),* June, 1966.

displaced an army of clerical workers. The ratio of personnel per $1,000 of life insurance in force, as seen in Table 4.2, fell rapidly between 1945 and 1960. The mergers of insurance organizations after 1960 made difficult the isolation of life insurance manpower ratios. However, total employment in insurance in the United States has grown at a much slower rate than the volume of premiums, which is the measure of annual sales. The increased productivity of the insurance industry is evident in Table 4.3.

TABLE 4.2   Ratio of Life Insurance Employees to Life Insurance-in-Force, Selected Years

Year	Non-Sales Personnel (000)	Sales Personnel (000)	Total Personnel (000)	Insurance-in-Force ($ billions)	Ratio
	(1)	(2)	(3)	(4)	(1):(4)
1945	110	151	261	152	.7
1950	147	197	344	234	.6
1955	170	228	398	372	.5
1960	237	237	474	586	.4

SOURCE: *Life Insurance Fact Book.* (New York: Institute of Life Insurance, various years).

TABLE 4.3   Premiums Written and Employment in the Insurance Industry in the U.S. (1945-1970)

Year	Total Premiums (000,000)	Total Employment (000)	Premium Dollars Per Employee ($)
1945	8,389	600	13,981
1950	15,055	800	18,818
1955	23,185	900	25,761
1960	32,337	1,105	29,264
1965	44,667	1,225	36,462
1970	69,634	1,460	47,694

SOURCE: *1971 Life Insurance Fact Book.* (New York: Institute of Life Insurance, 1971) and *Best's Aggregates and Averages: Property and Liability 1971.* (Morristown, New Jersey: A.M. Best Company, 1971).

In the age of consumerism all the accumulated grievances of the private insurance system were heard as public concern stressed the rights of policyholders. Due to rising levels of education, affluence, and improved communications, the public became aware of its ability to influence the economic and political character of its environment. President John F. Kennedy proclaimed the consumer's "Magna Carta" when he asserted that the public has these rights: (1) the right to safety, (2) the right to be informed, (3) the right to choose, and (4) the right to be heard.

In addition to the consumerist movement, several events of the 1960s led to government action in the area of property and liability insurance availability. Specifically, the urban riots of 1965 to 1967 led the federal government to become involved in this field. Acting on the Kerner Commission's suggestions, President Johnson appointed the National Advisory Panel on Insurance in Riot-Affected Areas (the Hughes Commission). Its goal was to investigate property insurance availability and costs and to make recommendations for solutions to existing problems. Prior to the Hughes Commission the government had no mechanism for evaluating conflicting reports or confronting the problem of residual insurance markets. No comprehensive study of property insurance availability had ever been undertaken.

The findings of the Hughes Commission indicated that a large number of ghetto property owners could not obtain or afford adequate property insurance. The commission recommended cooperation among the insurance industry, the states, and the federal government in solving the problem. Their recommendations were summarized as follows:

1. We call upon the insurance industry to take the lead in establishing voluntary plans in all states to assure all property owners access to property insurance.

2. We look to the states to cooperate with the industry in establishing these plans; and to supplement the plans, to whatever extent may be necessary, by organizing insurance pools and taking other steps to facilitate the insuring of urban core properties.

3. We urge that the federal government enact legislation creating a National Insurance Development Corporation (NIDC) to assist in achieving the important goal of providing adequate insurance for inner cities. Through the NIDC, the state and federal governments can provide backup for the remote contingency of very large riot losses.

4. We recommend that the federal government enact tax deferral measures to increase the capacity of the insurance industry to absorb the financial costs of the program.

5. We suggest a series of other necessary steps to meet the special needs of the inner city insurance market—for example, the programs to train agents and

brokers from the core areas; to assure the absence of discrimination in insurance company employment on racial or other grounds; and to seek out better methods of preventing losses and of marketing insurance in low income areas.[8]

Some of these recommendations were implemented; others never passed the discussion stage. The *Housing and Urban Development Act of 1968* (Public Law 90-448) was inspired by the third recommendation. Title II of this act established the insurance development program and set forth guidelines for implementation of a government reinsurance program. Through the vehicle of reinsurance the federal government allows the private insurance industry to maintain its dominant position. The original arrangement was as follows: the initial reinsurance covered only the perils of riot and civil disorder and included fire and extended coverage, burglary and theft, vandalism and malicious mischief, other allied lines of fire insurance, and those portions of multiperil policies covering the above listed perils. The Housing and Urban Development program (HUD) also offered optional coverage in inland marine, glass, boiler and machinery, ocean marine, and aircraft physical damage. The law required HUD to collect in the first year of operation a fund large enough to equal the insured losses from civil disorders incurred in 1967 (approximately $75 million). Under the initial ninety day binder the companies paid 0.75 percent of the retained premiums earned in a state for 1967.

Federal reinsurance did not cover all losses in full. The affected companies were paid only 90 percent of riot and civil disorder losses (including direct expenses of investigation, appraisal, adjustment, and defense of claims). Insurers also retained losses equal to 2.5 percent of the earned premiums before payments were made by the federal government.

The HUD Act made no references to rates charged the insured, deliberately leaving rate regulation to the states. The emphasis was on federal assistance rather than federal control, since the federal legislators did not wish to usurp the powers traditionally held by the states. To further assist the states in implementing insurance availability plans (e.g., FAIR program—Fair Access to Insurance Requirements), the act provided that after October, 1968, federal reinsurance would be available only to insurance companies taking part in state programs developed to make property insurance more readily available.

Several secondary benefits were derived from the development of the federal reinsurance program. A governmental organization, the Federal Insurance Administration, was established to collect and correlate property insurance availability statistics on a national scale. In addition, the federal program indirectly forced state officials to consider some form of insurance availability program. Finally, the work in this area also encouraged the development of

---

[8] The President's National Advisory Panel on Insurance in Riot-Affected Areas, *Meeting the Insurance Crisis of Our Cities* (Washington, D.C.: U.S. Government Printing Office, 1968), p. 8.

additional reinsurance programs and cooperative ventures designed to solve additional insurance availability problems. Following the FAIR programs came federal programs to assist in the provision of both flood and crime insurance. The federal government has given official notice that it will take action to assure minimum insurance availability. During recent decades there has been a rapid expansion of the federal government into the insurance business.

SUMMARY

The contemporary history of insurance is difficult to write because there is a vast array of problems and developments that can only be examined as current issues. In perspective, the American development of insurance in all of its branches has gone far beyond the scope and magnitude of the institution in any other country. By the middle of the twentieth century the United States was the world's leading insurance power, just as it was the dominant economic power.

REVIEW QUESTIONS

1.   Discuss the scope and purpose of the Guertin Committee Report and indicate the extent to which its findings were implemented.

2.   Compare and contrast the purposes and results of the Armstrong Investigation and that conducted by the Temporary National Economic Committee.

3.   What was the significance of the *Nationwide Definition and Interpretation of the Insuring Powers of Marine and Transportation Underwriters,* adopted in 1933? Discuss.

4.   "An ironic footnote to history is suggested by the effect on accident insurance of a series of railroad disasters in the decade following 1864. On the one hand, they cost the companies large sums of benefits, but on the other gave their product an advertising value all the more welcome for the low general repute of the accident insurance business." (C.A. Kulp, *Casualty Insurance,* 2nd ed., p. 372). Can this "ironic footnote" be generalized to account for the most rapid periods of expansion of most insurance lines? Explain carefully.

5.   What were the origins of the insurance institution in the United States?

STUDY QUESTIONS

6.   Is the insurance business highly competitive in your opinion? Explain the basis for your conclusion.

7. What were the principal factors which gave rise to the original Workmen's Compensation Laws in Great Britain? Explain.

8. Outline the history of the National Association of Insurance Commissioners with particular reference to their primary objective of working toward uniformity of insurance laws.

9. Describe the principal forces underlying the rapid expansion of employee benefit programs during the decade of the forties in the United States.

10. In recent years, union negotiated health and welfare plans have been the subject of much criticism. What has been the basis for such adverse criticism?

II

LEGAL
PERSPECTIVES

Insurance is an institution that affects the lives and fortunes of everyone in society. The legal basis for insurance and its operation is to be found in every important branch of law and equity.

Part II develops the nature and scope of insurance law as a general background, and then deals with the important subjects of torts, which provide the basis for liability insurance, agency, and contracts. Insurance policies are studied in the context of contracts. Finally, the powers of the insurance regulatory authority, which set limits to insurance activity, are reviewed in terms of legislative, judicial, and executive functions.

5

The Nature
and Scope
of Insurance Law

Insurance is a social institution that directly or indirectly embraces every occupation in every part of the world. Insurance covers an unlimited variety of contingent events and involves numerous types of interpersonal relationships. Most branches of law have an insurance aspect. Insurance law may be defined as rules of conduct established and enforced by the authority, legislation, or custom of the community relating to insurance transactions. The sources of insurance law are many, but among them are constitutions, statutes, regulations, judicial decisions, and trade practices. Measured by frequency of lawsuits, the most important branches of insurance law are those usually regarded as the most fundamental to the framework of the field of law itself—contracts, agency, torts, and crimes.

CONTRACTS AND RESTITUTION

Insurance is made available to the public through the medium of contracts that detail the rights and duties of the parties to the insurance agreement. These contracts may range from implied or oral agreements, as in the binders given by fire and casualty insurance agents, to formal written contracts issued by companies. To the extent that there is a higher degree of formality in the

63

expression of an agreement, the law usually provides more certain remedies for breach of contract. The lowest degree of formality is the unwitnessed oral agreement, and the highest is a Supreme Court Decision on a contract question. The problem is one of determining the "best evidence" of the intention of the parties to the contract and the enforceability of the terms and conditions. Most insurance contracts are expressed in writing even when an oral binder initiates the transaction.

Insurance contracts are complicated because of the technical nature of the subject matter, the statutory requirement that certain language be employed, and the need to avoid terms that may be construed as ambiguous. However, the need for legal clarity may lead to a contract that is beyond the comprehension of the typical insurance consumer. Furthermore, the technical nature of many contracts often distracts from the mutual understanding of its terms by the parties to the contract. For example, a study of the readability of the "standard" automobile insurance policy found this contract more difficult to understand than Einstein's *The Meaning of Relativity*. Harding found that a college education is generally required to read and understand the automobile policy and that only 8 percent of the U.S. population had this educational background.[1] It is apparent that most insurance buyers cannot be expected to understand the technical language of this and many other policies. While sales and marketing experts stress the need for a simplified insurance contract, lawyers emphasize the problems of legal interpretation which would accompany a new and simplified contract.

Restitution or quasi-contract rights arise when there has been an unjust enrichment of someone at the expense of another. Subrogation claims are examples of this legal right. An insured person whose loss has been paid by the insurance company transfers to the insurer his rights to recover from the wrongdoer for the same claim. Without such a transfer the insured could collect twice his actual loss. Such a double recovery would violate a fundamental principle of insurance law, the principle of indemnity, which provides that the insured should recover no more than the value of that which he has lost. To permit the insured to receive compensation twice would be in effect the same as permitting him to collect from the insurer for an economic loss that has already been indemnified. This would unjustly enrich the claimant at the expense of the other insureds. When an insurance company pays the insured the loss for which it has agreed to indemnify him, it receives those rights held by the insured to proceed against the wrongdoer who caused the damages.

AGENCY

Insurance contracts may be offered by corporations, partnerships, or individuals,

---

[1] Forrest E. Harding, "The Standard Automobile Insurance Policy: A Case Study of Its Readability", *The Journal of Risk and Insurance*, XXXIV (March 1967), pp. 36-45.

but personal contact with a prospective insured is invariably made through some human agency. The public generally deals with an agent rather than directly with the insurer. Laws that refer to agency relationships are therefore fundamental elements of insurance law.

Who is an agent? When does an agency relationship arise? What are the rights and duties of agents toward their principals or toward third parties? What are the different kinds of agency arrangements found in the insurance business? What are the legal liabilities of an agent? These are some of the questions with which the law of insurance agency deals. The common law provides some essential guidelines, but in all states the legislatures have enacted detailed statutes regulating the agency relationship in insurance.

TORTS

A tort is a private wrong. It occurs whenever someone acts or fails to act in such a manner that an individual's peace of mind or rights are jeopardized. It refers to any individual's action that effectively deprives another of his right to security of person, reputation, or property. Technically, each tort is defined in terms of specific statutory or common law requirements, and these vary substantially in different jurisdictions. Negligence, assault, battery, libel, slander, trespass, fraud, and false imprisonment are examples of torts. Torts differ from crimes in that the latter are public wrongs. A crime is any act that the legislature determines to be punishable by law. The same act may include all of the elements of a particular tort and a particular crime, in which case there exists a public remedy in the form of punishment prescribed by law and a private remedy that is often in the form of monetary damages.

Torts are important in insurance because they are a major source of loss covered by liability insurance. The automobile insurance policy is essential because it provides for payment of judgments awarded by the courts in negligence cases as well as the costs of litigation or claims settlement. The comprehensive personal liability insurance policy covers losses arising from negligent conduct unrelated to the care, custody, or control of the automobile or to business pursuits. The comprehensive general liability insurance policy covers losses occurring as a direct result of negligence in many business situations.

CRIMES

Some crimes that are recognized by statute are specific to insurance, while others are relevant to insurance law because they are crimes committed to obtain funds illegally from insurance companies.

Rebating

Rebating is the crime of giving the prospective insured some part of the premium or commission as an inducement to purchase an insurance policy. This conduct by an insurance agent results in unfair discrimination among insureds and may lead to "cut throat" competition. Rebating is prohibited in most jurisdictions in the United States. A typical state insurance code provides:

> An insurer, insurance agent, broker, or solicitor, personally or by any other party, shall not offer or pay, directly or indirectly, as an inducement to insurance on any subject-matter in this State, any rebate of the whole or part of the premium payable on an insurance contract, or of the agent's or broker's commission thereon, and such rebate is an unlawful rebate.[2]

This same code makes it a misdemeanor to "knowingly accept or receive any unlawful rebate."

Twisting

Twisting is the crime of inducing an individual to terminate one life insurance policy in order to buy another to the disadvantage of the insured.

> A person shall not make any representation or comparison of insurers or policies to an insured which is misleading, for the purpose of inducing or tending to induce him to lapse, forfeit, change or surrender his insurance, whether on a temporary or permanent plan.[3]

Twisting is unlawful because the insured can easily be persuaded to surrender valuable rights under his existing contract without being aware of the nature of those rights. For example, life insurance policies commonly provide that benefits will be paid even in the event of death by suicide if the act occurs more than one or two years after the policy's inception. Replacing the existing policy with a new one after two years results in the policyholder losing the benefit of the Suicide Clause in his policy. The same is true of the Incontestable Clause, which provides that a life insurance company may not contest a policy more than one or two years after its issuance on grounds of misrepresentation in the application.

An intelligent comparison of the cost-benefit relationships in an existing policy with a new policy in a different insurance company is a complex and

---

[2] State of California, *Insurance Code*, Sec. 750. Section 751 designates as an unlawful rebate, ". . . any valuable consideration which is not clearly specified, promised or provided for in the policy, or application for the insurance." Section 752 makes it a misdemeanor to knowingly accept or receive any unlawful rebate.

[3] *Ibid.*, Section 781.

rigorous process. It is unlikely that either the agent or the policyholder can fully appreciate all the factors that should be considered in a fair comparison of different policy contracts. However, the courts allow for the possibility of lawful life insurance policy exchanges when an agent presents a detailed written disclosure of the comparative features of the contracts under consideration.[4] Proof of full disclosure is generally a good defense to the charge of twisting.

Filing of False Claims

Filing of False Claims is essentially no different from theft. In many states presenting a false claim or "any writing" in support of such a claim is a felony punishable by a heavy fine or by imprisonment in a state prison. False claims include not only the attempt to collect money from an insurance company when there is no loss, but also the padding or inflation of claims by procuring excessive and fraudulent estimates of damages.

Unlicensed Insurance Activity

Unlicensed Insurance Activity is a crime because insurance companies and their agents are required by law to be licensed. Licensing provides regulatory supervision of the insurance industry for the benefit of the public. If an unlicensed person engages in any insurance transaction that requires licensing, he may be guilty of a misdemeanor. Licensing statutes tend to be lengthy because the definition of an insurance transaction usually includes any act leading to the placement of insurance. Solicitation, advising, and selling are only part of the controlled activity.

A common form of unlicensed solicitation occurs on university campuses. Many colleges have prohibited insurance agents from entering dormitories for the purpose of selling insurance. The agent is required to limit his activities to an off campus office. However, few students initiate contacts with off campus agents. To deal with this problem some agents pay students for each prospect they are able to solicit and bring into the agent's office. The remuneration is often increased if the prospect buys a policy. This practice is referred to as "bird-dogging."

---

[4]*Regulation No. 60 of the Insurance Department of the State of New York*, effective October 1, 1971, deals with Replacement of Life Insurance Policies. This regulation sets forth elaborate precautions for the protection of the parties. The statement of purpose is: "To protect the interests of the life insurance public by establishing minimum standards of conduct to be observed in the replacement or proposed replacement of life insurance policies, by making available full and clear information on which an applicant for life insurance can make a decision in his own best interest, by reducing the opportunity for misrepresentation and incomplete comparison in replacement situations, and by precluding unfair methods of competition and unfair practices."

Defamation

Defamation by publication of material that might tend to lessen public confidence in the institution of insurance (or in any other financial institution) is prohibited by law in some jurisdictions. This provision goes beyond the ordinary limits of laws against libel and slander and creates a fine distinction between proper criticism of a financial institution and criminal libel. In the law of crimes, unlike the usual rule in the law of torts, the truth is not a perfect defense to the charge of libel or slander.

Insurance supervisory authorities must be particularly sensitive to possible lawsuits alleging defamation. Although the regulators have broad powers to control and report on activities of insurers, they are cautious about the risk of causing injury to the reputations of innocent persons or insurance companies. Government officials must treat most information of a derogatory nature as confidential until there is sufficient evidence to justify public disclosure. There is a fine distinction between protection of the public and protection of an insurer.

Arson

Arson, the felonious burning of the property of another, is not an insurance crime *per se*, but when the intent is to defraud an insurance company, the criminal definition extends to property owned or in the care, custody, or control of the insured. Arson for insurance purposes is a specific crime in most states. The act is equivalent to theft from the insurance company because the event contemplated in the insurance policy was intended to be contingent and not deliberate.

Homicide

Homicide for the purpose of defrauding insurance companies is frequently given special attention in the statutes on insurance because it violates the maxim that a criminal should not profit from his wrong. A convicted first degree murderer who is the beneficiary of the insurance policy of his victim may not collect the proceeds. Where the beneficiary of a life insurance policy murders the insured for the purpose of obtaining the proceeds of the policy or otherwise, the law presumes that there exists a constructive trust for the estate of the deceased insured. The courts regard the intent of the beneficiary as crucial and will often permit him to collect the policy proceeds in cases of unintentional homicide.

Breach of Trust

Breach of Trust by insurance agents is treated as theft in many insurance codes.

All funds received by any person acting as an insurance agent, broker, or solicitor . . . on or under any policy of insurance . . . are received and held by such person in his fiduciary capacity. Any such person who diverts or appropriates such fiduciary funds to his own use is guilty of theft and punishable for theft as provided by law.[5]

Agents receive premiums from their clients for the accounts of the insurance companies who are at risk. These premiums should not be commingled with the agent's own funds but should be maintained in a separate trust account. Whether a single trust account is used for all companies represented or a separate account established for each company is a matter of contract between agents and the insurance companies they represent. Improper use of funds held in this fiduciary capacity is a form of criminal misappropriation, or theft. Practice with respect to agents' trust accounts varies from jurisdictions that adhere strictly to the doctrine of fiduciary responsibility to those in which trust accounts are ignored.

Unfair Discrimination

Unfair Discrimination among insureds, in which different rates are charged by a single insurance company to two or more insureds with identical exposures, is illegal in many states. In some respects this is similar to illegal rebating. Antitrust laws relating to insurance pricing usually prohibit rates that are "inadequate, unreasonable, or unfairly discriminatory."

Conspiracy

Conspiracy to commit any crime is a felony in most jurisdictions. When two or more people plan and act together secretly in order to commit a crime, the law regards the activity as more serious than when a crime is committed by an individual acting alone. For this reason conspiracy to commit a misdemeanor is treated as a felony in many states. The dishonest agent who conspires with his client to defraud the insurance company by misrepresentation, by filing a false claim, or by falsifying a document is engaged in the commission of a felony—and so is his client.

These are not the only criminal acts that have relevance to insurance. Probably the most common offenses in terms of arrests and convictions are filing of false claims and unlicensed insurance activity.

CORPORATIONS

Many states provide that only a private corporation or a governmental agency may act as an insurer. In the early nineteenth century an anticharter policy was

---

[5] State of California, *Insurance Code*, Sec. 1730.

common among the states, but this policy gradually changed so that the corporation became the normal form of insurance organization. In most jurisdictions today individual underwriters or partnerships are not permitted to insure risks. Such laws explain the absence of Lloyd's of London as an admitted carrier in most American states. Lloyd's is an association of individual underwriters and not a corporation engaged in the business of insuring risks.

The organization and licensing of insurance companies differs from that of other corporations in that the insurance industry is regulated by both an insurance supervisory authority and a general corporate regulatory authority. It is important that an insurance company select a name that will not be confused with that of another insurer. Selection of a name in many states requires that certain words such as "insurance company" be used to distinguish the corporate name. With thousands of companies in operation in the United States the necessity of avoiding duplication of an existing company name is apparent. After the name has been reserved, articles must be filed with the state, after which a permit to issue securities will normally follow. Finally, if all requirements have been complied with, the insurance department of the state will issue a Certificate of Authority.

For each line of insurance that a company seeks permission to write there is usually a set of special financial requirements.[6] Most states permit multiple lines underwriting of all lines except life insurance, if capital and surplus of the insurance company is at least two million dollars. In many less populous states the financial requirements are more modest than they are in the highly industrialized jurisdictions. Insurance companies are required to file periodic financial and other reports with regulatory authorities and are subject to more rigorous audit procedures than are unregulated corporations.

The law of insurance corporations is primarily concerned with the financial security of the company and the competency and integrity of its officials. Among the primary responsibilities of insurance supervisors is securing the contractual promises given by insurers to the public. An institution that attempts to provide financial security for the public must itself be financially secure. Insurer solvency is an important goal of public policy and a principal justification for insurance company regulation. Minimum capital and surplus requirements are specified by lines of insurance; minimum reserve standards are set by law; comprehensive and complex investment regulations establish limits on the discretion of insurance company managements. The law usually authorizes the insurance commissioner to satisfy himself as to the competency of officials in a new company. If he believes that an insurance company's

[6] Allen L. Mayerson, "Regulating the Solidity of Property and Liability Insurers: Ensuring the Solvency of Property and Liability Insurance Companies", in Spencer L. Kimball and Herbert S. Denenberg, eds., *Insurance, Government and Social Policy: Studies in Insurance Regulation* (Homewood, Ill.: Richard D. Irwin, Inc., 1969), p. 146.

management is incompetent and that the policyholders' security may be jeopardized, he is empowered to suspend the company license and even in some cases to force it into conservatorship. The integrity of management, or of owners of insurance companies, is governed by laws pertaining to conflicts of interest and public disclosure. The performance record of insurance companies in the United States has been a relatively good one despite occasional instances of insolvency and malfeasance.

PROPERTY

The law of property is important for insurance because each of the categories or interests in the subject matter is treated distinctly. Property is classified as (1) buildings and structures, (2) personal property, and (3) rights of possession or use.

Buildings and structures are real property or improved real estate, and include fixtures or improvements that are permanently attached to the building. For example, pews in a church may be attached to the floor, in which case they become part of the structure; or they may be free-standing as personal property. Insurance rates are lower for buildings than for contents, a fact that may provide financial incentives to minimize the use of detached furniture and fixtures in buildings. Title to real property and rights of owners are different from those of personal property.

Personal property, for insurance purposes, falls into two groups: (1) furniture, fixtures, equipment, and other articles that are being used and are not for sale in the ordinary course of business, and (2) merchandise offered for sale by a producer, manufacturer, merchant, or storeowner. Rights of possession or use that are of concern to insurance include those described in policies covering rents or rental value, business interruption, use and occupancy, and leasehold interests.

The landlord and the tenant each has a different insurable interest in real property. Their legal rights to proceeds of insurance policies covering property risks are dependent upon the law pertaining to leasehold interests. Similarly, the rights of individuals who occupy or have custody of property depends upon their legal status.

DOMESTIC RELATIONS

The legal rights of women and children are generally different from those of men under the laws of contract, tort, and crimes. The capacity of women and children to contract depends upon the law of each jurisdiction. Some states permit women to contract freely; others grant them freedom of contract only for small sums and for family necessities; and some community property states continue to give the husband full and exclusive management control of the community property. Anyone having business transactions with a married woman must be certain that she actually has legal capacity to enter into contracts without her husband's consent. Insurance codes frequently devote sections to the insurance rights of married women.

Most laymen incorrectly believe that children do not have the capacity to contract. The rights of children with respect to contracts vary from jurisdiction to jurisdiction depending upon the kind of contract involved. Under some conditions, minors may contract for marriage, automobile insurance, life and health insurance, medical care, as well as other essential goods and services. For example, in Virginia a fifteen year old is legally permitted to contract for life insurance on his own life for his own benefit or for the benefit of immediate relatives. A fifteen year old minor may give a valid discharge for any benefit accruing or money payable under a life insurance contract. Similarly, a minor may contract for automobile insurance within statutory limits under some circumstances.

The rights of married women and minors under tort law differ from those of adult males in a number of respects with regard to liability and treatment for purposes of insurance. The presumption that women and children act as agents for the spouse or father results in imputed liability to the husband and father. The risk of liability for torts of the wife or child varies from state to state.

Criminal law often presumes that a wife operates under the influence of her husband and is therefore not responsible for certain types of crime, which she may commit. For example, a wife may use as a defense to a charge of forgery the plea that she was coerced by her husband to sign the document. Children of certain ages are presumed to have the capacity to commit crimes; their treatment by the courts varies by jurisdiction. The same crimes committed by women or children against insurance companies may have different consequences when committed by men.

Discrimination based on sexual differences is a pattern in many branches of the law; it is of considerable importance in insurance matters. Tax preferences, alimony rights, property ownership rights, and contracting powers all hinge upon this issue. A proposed constitutional amendment if ratified will substantially alter this pattern of sexual discrimination.

ADMIRALTY OR MARITIME LAW

The law of the seas is referred to as maritime or admiralty law. This branch of insurance law is unique because it originates in federal statutes and international custom rather than in local law. Once it leaves port, a vessel is treated as a special type of legal person subject to a different set of rules from nonmarine entities. A lawsuit may be filed directly against a vessel, and damages are awarded based on the duties and negligence of the vessel. Marine insurance contracts must be designed and claims paid in accordance with the customs and usages of the seas.

There are four separate sets of interests in every shipping venture, each with its own set of rights and duties:

1. the hull, the conveyance in which goods or persons are transported;
2. the carrier, who assumes liability for loss or damage to the property of the shippers;
3. the cargo, the goods being transported; and
4. the freight owner, the person entitled to money for the hire of the vessel or for the conveyance of cargo from port to port.

WILLS AND TRUSTS

A will is a privilege granted by law to specify how one's property shall be distributed after death. Historically, wills were used to dispose of real property and testaments to dispose of personal property. The expression "last will and testament" therefore encompasses all of the property that a person could dispose of at death. Because the will is a sensitive matter and testators are susceptible to special pressures by relatives and others, the statute of wills of each jurisdiction establishes requirements for what constitutes a valid will. Persons who die without leaving a valid will are said to die intestate, and the statute provides for intestate distribution of property to the heirs or the state.

A trust is an arrangement whereby one person (a grantor or settlor) transfers property (the corpus) to another person (the trustee) to hold and use for the benefit of a third person (the beneficiary). The trust may take effect immediately, in which case it is referred to as an *inter vivos* trust; or it may be a testamentary trust, taking effect at the death of the grantor.

Life insurance policies, through their beneficiary designations, permit the insured to determine the disposition of the proceeds. In this respect a life insurance policy is considered by some to be a living will. Legal distinctions between wills and contracts are important. The life insurance contract is not an "ambulatory" document taking effect only at death; it is operative immediately. The trustlike features of the contract are also important. The settlement options of life insurance policies establish the insurance company as "trustee" to manage and distribute the policy proceeds to the beneficiary. But a legal trustee has certain powers and duties that are not present in the case of life insurance. The life insurer has a contract to perform and does not act in a fiduciary capacity.

TAXATION

The tax structure of the United States has many features designed to accommodate the special characteristics of insurance. Widows and orphans who are life insurance beneficiaries have been granted special treatment in federal and state tax laws.

Exemption of the proceeds of life insurance policies from income taxation is a form of preferential treatment that applies despite the increase in value of the policy over the paid premiums. Where beneficiary designation and ownership are properly established, the proceeds of life insurance may be exempt from federal estate taxes. State inheritance tax laws frequently grant the widow a special exemption of a significant portion of life insurance proceeds.

Tax laws at all levels of government affect insurance and are adapted to the technical problems of insurance accounting. Federal corporate income tax laws have special provisions for insurance companies that recognize their problems of reserve liability determination and estimation of income. State premium taxes are designed to reach the revenues of insurance companies in an equitable manner. License and examination fees attempt to assess the business in terms of benefits conferred by the state. The field of insurance tax law is a rapidly changing complex of technical rules and interpretations, which are the province of specialists.

CONFLICT OF LAWS

Insurance companies may operate in numerous states and in many countries. Suppose a contract is initiated in state A and completed in state B; a loss arises in state C; and settlement occurs in state D. Which is the appropriate jurisdiction for resolving lawsuits arising from the contract? The insurance lawyer is often confronted with such problems.

There are rules relating to jurisdiction that apply when concerned parties have residence in different states. These rules determine when federal courts take jurisdiction, when state courts handle the matter, and which body of law is applicable to a particular dispute. The usual rule is that the forum for litigation arising out of the contract is the place where the last act necessary to make a binding contract occurred. In the example cited above, the settlement would occur in state D in accordance with the laws of state B. The possibility of having a case adjudicated in different courts in different jurisdictions could give rise to "forum shopping" in the absence of a set of rules. Insurance companies generally prefer to have their contracts completed in the state where their home offices are located.

SOURCES OF INSURANCE LAW

The original source of American insurance law is the common law of England, which became the earliest law in most of the states. That law comprises a body of precepts developed by the English courts before the beginning of the eighteenth century. American constitutions and statutes have substantially superceded these common law rules, but gaps in legislation are still commonly filled with interpretations drawn from the common law. Case law has expanded upon the bare outlines of the statutes. And when supplemented with administrative rulings on interpretations and specifications, it extends to most of the subjects of concern to lawyers and their clients.

A comprehensive search for the sources of insurance law would include the U.S. Constitution, the state constitutions, federal and state statutes, and the vast body of case law. The legal research process is simplified by the adoption in most jurisdictions of insurance codes that bring together statutory law and, with annotations, additional relevant sources of law and commentary. In many states the insurance provisions can be found in a variety of different codes: insurance, labor (workmen's compensation), corporations (securities provisions), government (public official bonds and state insurance), financial institutions (licensing regulation), penal (insurance crimes), civil (rights of minors to contract), civil procedure (jurisdiction of courts in insurance matters), and probate (testamentary disposition of insurance proceeds).

Sources of insurance law, in addition to the statutes and adjudicated cases are Opinions of the Attorney-General, of Legislative Counsel, and of the Commissioner or Superintendent of Insurance.

Each of the substantive issues that requires legal research in the field of insurance may have a different outcome because each jurisdiction in the United States operates independently. The movement toward uniform laws is slow because individual states regard their needs as unique.

THE JUDICIAL SYSTEM AND INSURANCE LITIGATION

The court systems of the United States are established on two separate bases. State courts have jurisdiction over subjects when those powers have not been delegated to or assumed by the federal government. Federal courts have jurisdiction over constitutional questions and disputes between the states.

Subject to a reservation that permits the United States to determine the extent to which international courts have jurisdiction, the highest tribunals are those associated with the United Nations. International disputes ultimately may have recourse to the International Court of Justice at The Hague. The U.S. Supreme Court is the ultimate judge of disputes within the United States.

Subordinate to the Supreme Court are the District Courts of Appeal for federal cases and the Supreme Courts of the states for constitutional cases. A wide variety of courts is established within the states to hear cases of different kinds. Beyond these local courts are administrative tribunals with a quasijudicial function. Insurance matters may be considered in any of these numerous courts, depending upon the location or status of the parties, the amount in dispute, and the grounds for appeal.

The rules of jurisdiction generally provide that where a dispute affects the rights of nations it should properly be submitted to the International Court of Justice at The Hague. This body has less activity than one might expect because each nation is free to decide whether it will be a defendant or plaintiff in an action before the court. There are no enforcement powers inherent in the court.

Federal District Courts will usually take jurisdiction in civil matters only when the amount in dispute is at least $10,000 or when a constitutional question is raised.

State courts have increasing jurisdiction according to the level of the court. A justice court may deal in very small sums or offenses, a municipal court in larger amounts, and superior courts in major issues. Appellate courts may be invoked, and, finally, the state Supreme Court has the ultimate state judicial power.

In addition to statutory jurisdiction of the court in a particular matter there must be jurisdiction over the person. By due process (usually a summons personally served within the jurisdiction) the defendant is brought before the court for an action or legal process to commence. It is necessary to serve a defendant properly or to publish an appropriate notice of service before the court can take jurisdiction.

Insurance cases are heard in all parts of the judicial system. Small claims courts of municipalities often hear cases involving unpaid premium obligations; municipal courts handle lawsuits involving insurance contracts in amounts under $5,000; state Superior Courts adjudicate suits "praying" for amounts in excess of $5,000; state Appellate Courts hear cases alleging error in judgments; state Supreme Courts take jurisdiction for lawsuits alleging violation of constitutional provisions relating to insurance at the state level; U.S. District Courts hear cases involving citizens from different states and insurance policies with large amounts in dispute; federal Appellate Courts try cases seeking writs of review; and finally the U.S. Supreme Court deals with constitutional issues. One of the most famous Supreme Court Decisions in an insurance case was *Paul v. Virginia* (1868) in which the court held that insurance was intrastate commerce and therefore not subject to federal antitrust laws. This was overruled by *U.S. v. S.E.U.A.* (1944).

SUMMARY

The task of finding and interpreting the law of insurance tends to become specialized because the field is so complex. The International Association of

Insurance Counsel comprises several thousand lawyers, barristers, and solicitors who are actively engaged in the practice of the law pertaining to all aspects of the business of insurance. Most often these lawyers work for insurance companies. Their counterpart is the American Trial Lawyers Association, an organization of attorneys who most frequently represent plaintiffs against liability insurance policyholders. The thousands of lawyers engaged in insurance law tend to specialize quite narrowly within the various subject areas of the discipline.

REVIEW QUESTIONS

1. "Insurance law may be regarded as an aspect of each of many branches of law." Identify three branches of law, other than contracts, agency, or torts; and, for each, illustrate how its precepts form a part of the body of insurance law.

2. Alfred, an eighteen year old student, bought a life insurance policy on his own life and named his mother as beneficiary. Shortly thereafter, Alfred was married and sought to change the beneficiary designation in favor of his wife. Alfred's mother attempted to block the beneficiary change on the ground that Alfred was a minor and therefore incapable of changing his contract. What are Alfred's rights in the matter? Explain.

3. Why do insurance contracts use technical jargon instead of plain English? Why don't insurance companies use illustrated booklets to make the policy self explanatory? Discuss.

4. The insured's automobile was involved in a collision and sustained damage to the front bumper and grille. There was a $50 deductible in the auto policy material damage coverage. Upon reporting the loss to his insurance company, the insured was told to obtain two estimates of the damage from auto repair shops. Instead, the insured obtained four estimates: $50, $100, $300, and $500. Realizing that the lowest estimate would not exceed the deductible, he turned in the two highest ones. Was this a criminal act? Explain.

5. What are the sources of insurance law? Discuss.

STUDY QUESTIONS

6. Laws prohibiting rebating and twisting are primarily designed to protect consumers. Do they also protect insurers? Explain.

7. What effect would passage of the Equal Rights Amendment to the U.S. Constitution have on the rights of women under insurance law? Explain.

8. Suppose that a life insurance company issues a second policy with identical terms to a policyholder three years after the first policy is issued. What benefits might there be in the earlier policy which would be of sufficient importance to the policyholder to require that he be protected against twisting? Explain.

9. The text says, "State premium taxes are designed to reach the revenues of insurance companies in an equitable manner." What is the basis of the state premium tax? Do such taxes discriminate between domestic and foreign insurance companies? Are they sufficient to cover the costs of regulation of the insurance industry? Discuss.

10. What are the purposes for which it may be necessary for the courts to define "insurance"?

6

Torts

and

Insurance

INTRODUCTION

Liability insurance is designed to indemnify the insured against the costs of certain types of legal actions arising out of conduct, which the courts regard as tortious. The liability insured against is that which arises from civil as distinct from criminal actions, and it excludes liability voluntarily incurred. The varieties of conduct that may subject the insured to damages and legal expense have multiplied substantially in recent years, but the common law doctrines that are the source of such liability have not materially changed.

DEFINITION OF A TORT

A tort is a wrongful act or omission, arising out of relationships other than contracts, that violates the legally protected right of an individual, and for which damages may be awarded as a remedy. Oliver Wendell Holmes in his classic *The Common Law* wrote:

> The business of the law of torts is to fix the dividing lines between those cases in which a man is liable for harm which he has done, and those in which he is not. But it cannot enable him to predict with certainty

79

whether a given act under given circumstances will make him liable, because an act will rarely have that effect unless followed by damage, and for the most part, if not always, the consequences of an act are not known, but only guessed at as more or less probable. All the rules that the law can lay down beforehand are rules for determining the conduct which will be followed by liability if it is followed by harm,—that is, the conduct which a man pursues at his peril.[1]

Torts may or may not be crimes depending upon whether the particular activity has been proscribed by statute, but many kinds of tortious conduct possess nearly all of the elements of related crimes. For example, consider "assault," "battery," "champerty," "conspiracy," "false imprisonment," "libel," "nuisance," "trespass," and "defamation." The absence of criminal intent, *mens rea*, is critical in most cases.

CLASSIFICATION OF TORTS

Torts are often classified as intentional or unintentional. An intentional tort is uninsurable and includes torts to the person, such as assault, battery, and false imprisonment. Also included among intentional torts are trespass to property, which includes trespass to land, trespass to chattels, and wrongful conversion. The second category, unintentional torts, is insurable and includes acts arising out of negligence and cases where the law imposes liability without regard to fault.

NEGLIGENCE

Negligence is the failure to exercise that degree of care which the law requires to protect others from an unreasonable risk of injury to person or property. There are five elements in a *prima facie* case of negligence.

1. *A Legal Duty Owed.* Since a tort is an invasion of the rights of another, a legal duty must be owed to that other. Every citizen has the right to freedom from damage to his person and property, and this right has the correlative duty imposed on all members of society to avoid interfering with the rights of any other person. The duty owed may range from merely the obligation to avoid injuring directly, to the duty to leave a person alone, to the duty to

---

[1] Oliver Wendell Holmes, *The Common Law* (Boston: Little, Brown and Co., 1923), p. 79.

exercise a high degree of care in some circumstances. The duty may be imposed by common law, by statute, or by a voluntary act.

2. *An Act or Omission.*   A tort is an act or omission that was the result of a breach of legal duty to another and that gives rise to an action for damages. In a positive sense one must act prudently. In a negative sense one must not act imprudently. One need not come to the aid of another as a rescuer, but if one does the law holds him to a standard of care appropriate under the circumstances. The act or failure to act must be distinguished from the intent.

3. *Breach of Duty.*   For a tort to occur there must have been a breach of duty by the tortfeasor. Generally, the courts recognize a reasonably prudent man standard under the particular set of circumstances as the norm against which specific conduct will be measured. A doctor will be held to the standard of care of doctors, a lawyer to the standard of lawyers, and so on. Even children will be held to a standard of care commensurate with their age and intellectual attainments.

4. *Proximate Cause.*   The breach of duty or the act must have been the actual or legal cause of the injury sustained by the plaintiff. Unless there is a casual connection between the act and the injury, a tort action will not prove successful.

5. *Damages.*   The plaintiff in a negligence action must always prove damages, and he must show that all damages claimed were sustained as a direct result of the negligent act and from no other independent cause. There is no presumption about the nature or amount of damages.

Damages have been defined as "pecuniary compensation or indemnity, which may be recovered in the courts by any person who has suffered loss, detriment, or injury, whether to his person, property, or rights, through the unlawful act or omission or negligence of another."[2] In negligence cases most courts recognize the possibility of different classes of damages. Actual damages are awarded by the court in compensation for the actual and real loss or injury sustained by the injured party. Sometimes, actual damages are referred to as compensatory or general damages. Where there is no substantial loss of injury to be compensated, but the law still recognizes a technical invasion of the rights of the plaintiff a trivial sum such as one cent or one dollar may be awarded as nominal damages. Special damages are those which are the actual, but not the necessary, result of the injury complained of. Punitive or exemplary damages are damages on an increased scale, awarded to the plaintiff over and above actual damages, where the wrong done to him was aggravated by circumstances of violence, fraud, or malice on the part of the defendant. The victim of an automobile collision caused by a wanton and reckless driver might seek actual

---

[2] Henry Campbell Black, *Black's Law Dictionary*, 4th ed. (St. Paul, Minn.: West Publishing Co., 1968), p. 466.

damages for costs incurred arising out of the accident, nominal damages for loss of reputation as a careful driver, special damages for loss of future capacity to earn a living, and exemplary damages for the reckless conduct of the defendant. In most cases where very large amounts are awarded as damages there is an element of punitive or exemplary damages involved.

At common law no recovery for negligence was permitted unless there was physical injury caused by direct contact. Today, the courts have moved away from the early doctrine and hold that mental pain and suffering are just as injurious to the victim as a bodily injury. In food cases, recovery was allowed for shock from the sight of revolting substances in food, such as dead mice, cockroaches, and the like. Other examples include the unauthorized autopsy of a close relative, mishandling of dead bodies of deceased relatives, and the burial of a wrong body in a grave. In some instances the contemplation of disfigurement, of loss of marriage opportunities, of loss of career have been held fit subjects for awards of damages.

VICARIOUS LIABILITY AND IMPUTED NEGLIGENCE

Vicarious liability arises when the law imputes to one party the negligent conduct of another. Thus, the employer is liable for the negligent acts of his employee in the course of employment; the same is true of the master-servant relationship, the principal-agent relationship and, at common law, the case of parent and child. The law imputes negligence to independent contractors where the work is inherently dangerous or where the master controls the work. There is also vicarious liability in joint enterprises, such as partnerships, where the negligence of one party is attributable to the others. The concept of vicarious liability is very important because it gives rise to the possibility of lawsuits where the defendant did not perform the negligent act.

NEGLIGENCE PER SE

Where there is a duty owed to a person by virtue of a statute specifically designed for that class of persons, such as speed laws in a school zone for the protection of children, and there is a breach of that duty, this is regarded as negligence *per se*. The burden of proof shifts from the plaintiff to the defendant to demonstrate the absence of negligence.

DEFENSES TO NEGLIGENCE

The two most important defenses to allegations of negligence are the doctrines of contributory negligence and assumption of risk.

Under the equitable doctrine that no man should come into court with unclean hands, the plaintiff could not be given a remedy for an action charging negligence unless he could show that he was not partially at fault. If the defendant could prove contributory negligence, whereby the plaintiff contributed to the injury by his own negligence, the case would be dismissed. This defense has been held to be effective except where the conduct of the defendant himself was intentional or willful, wanton, and reckless. An individual is held to a standard of due care for his own conduct.

The doctrine of assumption of risk holds that one who has knowledge or awareness of the existence of a risk and an understanding of the extent of the danger, but who exposes himself to it voluntarily, has no cause of action. A professional boxer has no cause of action for injuries sustained in the ring; a trapeze artist has none for a fall in the circus, a carpenter has none for a fall from a ladder.

In the automobile insurance field, the Automobile Guest Statute provides an important defense for negligence. Under such statutes, one who rides with the driver of an automobile as a guest for his own business or pleasure, without in any way remunerating the driver for the ride, is a guest and may not sue for negligence unless the driver's degree of care was abnormally low. Wanton and reckless, grossly negligent or intentional misconduct are the degrees of care that the guest must prove before he may successfully bring an action against the driver.

ACCIDENTS AND ACTS OF GOD

An event that could not have been foreseen even with reasonable diligence has been defined as an accident or act of God. Thus, a bolt of lightning, a sudden explosion, or an earthquake might be regarded as unavoidable acts of God. Inherent is the idea that there was no lack of due care, and these events are not treated as negligent.

LIABILITY WITHOUT FAULT

In addition to intentional torts and negligence, there is liability without fault imposed by statute or by custom in certain situations. The most familiar case is workmen's compensation where the law presumes that an employer is liable regardless of fault. It is enough to prove that an injury was sustained in the course of employment for the employee to recover damages in the form of benefits set by law. He need not show any connection between an act or omission of the employer and his injury. Strict liability is also implied in certain types of contractual situations, such as transportation or other services provided by a public utility or common carrier, and in situations where the doctrine of *res ipse loquitur*—the thing speaks for itself—prevails.

The elements of *res ipse loquitur* are:

1. the injury was unusual,
2. care of the instrumentality was in the hands of the tortfeasor,
3. the tortfeasor had superior knowledge of danger, and
4. negligence cannot be proved directly.

Res ipse loquitur shifts the burden of proof to the tortfeasor and provides a *prima facie* case of negligent causation.

The No-Fault Automobile Insurance programs that have been advanced in recent years are an extension of the doctrine of liability without fault to the automobile insurance field.[3] Absolute liability attaches to the first party in such a case. The same idea is operative in first party accident and health insurance.

LAST CLEAR CHANCE

An exception to the defense of contributory negligence is the doctrine of Last Clear Chance, which allows recovery, in spite of the plaintiff's negligence, if the defendant had a last clear chance to avoid the injury. This doctrine may ordinarily be invoked if the evidence shows that the plaintiff was in a position of danger and by his own negligence was unable to escape from such a position by the use of ordinary care, either because it became physically impossible for him to escape or because he was totally unaware of the danger; that the defendant knew that the plaintiff was in a position of danger, or should have known this with the exercise of ordinary care; and having a clear chance to avoid the accident by the exercise of ordinary care, failed to exercise such last clear chance, and the accident occurred as a proximate result of such failure. It is argued that the negligence of the defendant is the proximate cause and that of the plaintiff is a remote cause of the accident.

ATTRACTIVE NUISANCE

Where one maintains a condition upon his property that may reasonably be anticipated to present a source of danger to children, he is expected to take

---

[3] Robert E. Keeton and Jeffrey O'Connell, *Basic Protection for the Traffic Victim* (Boston: Little, Brown and Co., 1965) is the pioneering work which led to the No-Fault Automobile Insurance movement. A more recent review is Willis Rokes, *No-Fault Insurance* (Santa Monica, Cal.: Insurors Press, 1971). See also, James D. Ghiardi and John J. Kircher, "The Uniform Motor Vehicle Accident Reparations Act: An Analysis and Critique", *Insurance Counsel Journal*, Vol. XL, January, 1973, pp. 87-110.

prudent steps to protect children from the hazard. This doctrine refers only to man made hazards but, like *res ipse loquitur*, one who maintains such a nuisance is presumed negligent. Examples include excavations in the ground, piles of lumber, unenclosed swimming pools, and so forth.

COMPARATIVE NEGLIGENCE

Some jurisdictions apply the rule that contributory negligence of the plaintiff will not defeat his recovery if the negligence of the defendant was disproportionately great. If more than 50 percent of the injury was caused by negligence of the defendant, he may be given a setoff against damages rather than dismissal of the action. This is an important modification of the contributory negligence doctrine.

THE ADEQUATE AWARD CONCEPT

During the twentieth century, the doctrine of the Adequate Award has been introduced by plaintiff's attorneys as a measure of damages. It is argued that there can be no amount of money damages that can indemnify the victim for the loss of a limb, an eye, or for disfigurement. These losses are regarded as more serious than death because the victim must live with his disability. It is argued by some attorneys that the only reasonable measure of damages is mathematical. Over and above direct costs for medical care and hospitalization, a *per diem* damage amount may be calculated, and this may be multiplied by 365 and by the life expectancy of the victim to aggregate the damages for pain and suffering. In addition, to estimate the disability pension that should be commuted for the benefit of the injured victim, the work expectancy of the victim should be multiplied by the potential average income in the absence of the injury.

DEMONSTRATIVE EVIDENCE

Coupled with the doctrine of the Adequate Award is the concept of Demonstrative Evidence. It is argued that the jury and court cannot fully comprehend verbal testimony and should have the benefit of audio-visual aids—demonstrative evidence. Reconstructions of the scene of the action, maps, skeletons, and motion pictures are all examples of demonstrative evidence commonly employed in modern trials. The jury may be moved to emotional involvement in the enormity of the tort and thereby induced to grant larger amounts by way of damages. The courts have taken steps to restrict the excessive use of theatrical devices designed to play upon the emotions of jury members.

CONTINGENT FEES

The practice of payment of contingent fees is common in the personal injury field. Under this system of compensation, the attorney is paid only his out-of-pocket expenses if he loses the case and from one-third to one-half of the judgment if he wins. The contingent fee practice has been responsible for a substantial increase of tort litigation because the legal hazard is being borne largely by the attorney. The similarity to the common law crimes of champerty and maintenance, which relate to a third person having a financial interest in a lawsuit to which he is not a party, has been resolved by the substantial removal of these crimes from the statute books.

SATISFACTION OF JUDGMENTS

Most states have met the problem of the satisfaction of judgments by motorists through the enactment of financial responsibility laws. Under these statutes a motorist is required to demonstrate ability to pay judgments awarded against him up to the limits set by law. Such responsibility may be shown by a certificate of insurance, by posting a bond, or by posting a cash deposit. Usually such laws provide for proof of financial responsibility after a loss has occurred, leaving the first victim unprotected. These are sometimes called "one-bite" laws.

Compulsory automobile insurance is found in an increasing number of states. Such laws usually provide that evidence of insurance to statutory limits is a condition precedent to the issuance of a driver's license or motor vehicle registration plates. Out of state and unregistered vehicles are not ordinarily covered under such statutes.

Unsatisfied judgment laws attempt to provide for the victim of an automobile accident by creation of a fund from which unsatisfied judgments may be paid. Where a judgment is obtained against an uninsured motorist and no recovery is possible, the plaintiff, if a qualified person, may have recourse against the funds to the limits prescribed in the law.

THE LIABILITY INSURER'S PROMISES

The promises of the insurer under most liability contracts are relatively uniform. There is first the promise to defend or settle all claims alleging such negligence as is covered under the contract regardless of whether such claims are "false, fraudulent, or groundless." The insurer will provide the legal defense necessary to respond to the lawsuit. The company also promises to pay all court costs including the cost of bonds for attachment or appeal, witnesses, evidence, and related expenses. The insurer also promises to pay all judgments awarded by the court up to the limits of the policy. In essence the insurer will stand in the footsteps of the insured when the action or claim arises out of either negligence or liability without fault.

REVIEW QUESTIONS

1. When a policyholder is sued by an injured party, does the insurance company on the risk become the defendant? Explain.

2. What must be proved by a plaintiff in order to recover damages under the law of negligence? What defenses are available to the defendant?

3. What is the doctrine of last clear chance?

4. "A" double parked his car on a two-way street, blocking one lane of traffic. "B," trying to pass the parked car, hit it. "A" sues "B" for damages. Explain how the doctrine of contributory negligence and last clear chance might enter this case.

5. A child wanders onto a neighbor's unfenced lot and pets a stray dog. Unknown to the child, the dog is vicious and the child is attacked, sustaining severe injuries before some passersby come to the rescue. What is the standard of care required of the landowner in this case? Discuss.

STUDY QUESTIONS

6. A liability insurance policy promises to defend or settle all claims alleging negligence regardless of whether such claims are "false, fraudulent, or groundless." What rights does an insured have if the insurance company refuses to defend or settle a lawsuit brought against him? Discuss.

7. How much, in damages, constitutes an adequate award for a person who has been blinded as a result of negligence? How would the damages be estimated? Explain.

8. A teenager was burned when he carelessly told his brother to pour adulterated kerosene on a smoldering piece of wood. The proximate cause of the injury was found to be a combination of the negligence of the teenager-plaintiff and the abnormally low flash point of the impure kerosene. The Supreme Court of Texas awarded damages to the plaintiff despite his contributory negligence and the absence of a comparative negligence statute at the time. Explain. (*Shamrock Fuel Oil Sales Co. v. Tunks*, 416 SW2d 779 (Tex 1967).

9. The common law held the possessor of land to a different standard of care for invitees, licensees, and trespassers. This view has been held to be "contrary to our modern social mores and humanitarian values." Discuss. (*Rowland v. Christian*, 443 P2d 561 (Calif. 1968).

10. Plaintiff smoked Lucky Strike cigarettes, developed lung cancer, and died. The Court of Appeals affirmed a jury verdict for the defendant noting that "good tobacco is not unreasonably dangerous merely because the effects of smoking may be harmful." Discuss. (*Green vs. American Tobacco Co.*, 409 F2d 1166 (5 Cir 1969).

7

The Insurance Agent
and His Principal

THE NATURE OF THE AGENCY RELATIONSHIP

An agency relationship is one in which one party, the principal, delegates the authority and power to another party, the agent, to enter into agreements with third parties on behalf of the principal. Standing in the shoes of his principal, an agent has the same power to enter into transactions on his behalf as the principal does with third parties. The relationship is fiduciary in that the agent has a duty to act primarily for the benefit of his principal and to deal in good faith with him. It is a controlled relationship in that there is always an inference that the principal can limit the scope of authority of his agent. Any individual or firm can act as agent provided that the principal has legal capacity to contract. Thus, an infant going to the store to buy something for his mother is an agent. Capacity of the infant is not in question. In this case, only the mother needs legal capacity for contractual purposes.

The principles of agency, derived from the common law, are as applicable to insurance as they are elsewhere. What is unique in the insurance agency relationship is the specific set of customs and usages of the business.

CLASSIFICATION OF INSURANCE AGENCIES

There is wide variation of practice in different fields of insurance and in different jurisdictions about the designation of the persons who act as agents. The differences relate primarily to the scope of power of the agent and the party who is the principal.

Managing General Agent

A managing general agent is appointed usually exclusively by an insurance company with full authority to perform virtually all acts on behalf of the company. This includes underwriting, policy issue, and claims adjustment as well as sales. Power to run the company in the designated territory goes with a managing general agency. Thus, a foreign insurance company may have a managing general agency for its U.S. operations. A New York based insurance company may appoint a managing general agency for its California operations. The managing general agent has delegated to him the maximum authority the insurance laws permit.

The scope of authority of a managing general agent is so broad that most jurisdictions require approval by the regulatory authority of management and exclusive agency contracts. Such contracts are likely to be disapproved when they subject the insurer to excessive charges for expenses or commissions, when they do not contain fair and adequate standards of performance, when they extend for an unreasonable length of time, or when they contain other inequitable provisions that may jeopardize the security of policyholders.

General Agent

A general agent usually has fewer powers than a managing general agent, but his authority may extend beyond sales to underwriting and claims adjustment. In life insurance the designation is usually limited to authority over the sales activities of one or more agents.

Agent

An agent is appointed by an insurance company to sell its policies and perform some limited underwriting and claims reporting functions. In the property and liability insurance fields, such an agent usually has some binding authority. Often, he may have a limited claim draft authority that permits him to settle small claims at his own discretion. In life insurance the powers of agents are much more limited.

Generally, any individual, partnership, or corporation may be licensed to act as an agent for an insurance company. Such an agent may solicit, negotiate, or effect contracts of insurance or annuities on behalf of the insurer and, if authorized to do so, collect premiums on such contracts.

The authority of a life insurance agent is different from that of a property and liability agent in that the latter generally is empowered to make binding contracts for his principal. A life insurance agent is never authorized to make contracts for his insurance company principal but only to take applications for life or health insurance or annuities.

Subagent

A subagent is appointed by another agent to perform functions by redelegation of authority from the principal company. A subagent usually is restricted to the function of locating prospects for insurance. Solicitation and sale are performed by the agent.

Special Agent

A special agent may be appointed by the insurance company to perform special supervisory functions in the field. He may have the power to appoint and terminate agencies and to act as an intermediary between agents and brokers and the company. Frequently, the term special agent is reserved for any regular salaried officer or employee of a licensed insurance company who devotes all of his services to the supervision of the production activities of his company and who does not solicit, negotiate, or effect contracts of insurance except for, or in conjunction with, licensed resident agents or company representatives.

Insurance Broker

An insurance broker acts as an agent of the insured rather than as agent for the insurance company. In his legal capacity as a broker he is independent of any insurance company, and he lacks binding power. However, he may deal with any insurance company that is willing to contract with him on behalf of his clients. In many states an individual may be licensed as a broker and as an agent, in which case the insurance salesman may have binding authority with some companies but not with others.

CREATION OF THE AGENCY RELATIONSHIP

Insurance agencies may be created by mutual consent, ratification, or by estoppel.

Most insurance agencies are created as a result of mutual consent. The principal and the agent enter into a formal contract that defines the scope of authority and the powers of the agent and provides a basis for compensation. Termination by either party may be effected in accordance with provisions spelled out in the agency agreement.

Agency by ratification occurs when an agent enters into an agreement with a third party beyond the scope of his authority, and where the insurance company ratifies the action after the fact. The requirements for such an agency include the need to recognize a purported agency, the right principal must ratify the act with full knowledge of the facts surrounding the transaction, and the ratification must be complete with respect to all aspects of the particular transaction. While silence will not effect a ratification, no formality is required to accomplish the result.

Agency by estoppel occurs when the agent has acted beyond the scope of his authority, where the principal knows that this has occurred, and where the conduct of the principal is such as to lead third parties to believe that the act was done with consent of the principal. The principal will be liable to third parties if, by his conduct, he has led them to deal with his agent to their detriment. Whereas agency by ratification provides a remedy or defense to an agent toward his principal, agency by estoppel provides a defense or remedy to a third party with respect to the principal.

OPERATION OF THE AGENCY RELATIONSHIP

Once created, the agency relationship confers upon the agent the power to act for his principal within the scope of his ostensible authority. The powers of an agent go beyond the express authority given him by contract and extend to both implied or incidental authority and apparent authority. The company will be bound by acts beyond the scope of the actual authority of the agent unless it conveys to third parties the limitations on the authority of its agent. While implied authority is essential to the performance of the agency contract because not every act may be enumerated in the express contract, apparent authority leads to agency by estoppel because the third party may not know the limits of authority of the agent with whom he deals.

The customs and usages of the insurance business vary from life insurance to property and liability insurance, and in the absence of specific agreement such customs determine the powers of the agent. For example, a life insurance agent never has the power to bind his insurance company, whereas a fire insurance agent can hardly function without such power.

It should be observed that the law creates no presumption of agency. The burden lies on third parties to know with whom they are dealing. The principal has the right to limit the authority of his agent, but unless these limitations are communicated they will not affect the rights of innocent third parties.

LEGAL DOCTRINES OF AGENCY

There are important legal doctrines relating to the agency relationship that serve to clarify the rights and duties of the parties. We may state some of these briefly:

1. The acts of an agent are the acts of his principal. All acts of an agent within the scope of his authority are held to be acts of his principal.

2. The contract is the contract of the principal. When an agent enters into a contract on behalf of the principal, the latter is entitled to all of the benefits and charged with all of the obligations under the contract.

3. Knowledge of the agent is presumed to be known to the principal. The agent has a duty to communicate to his principal all material information gathered in the course of his employment as agent. Third parties who provide information to agents are entitled to believe that such information was transmitted to the principal.

4. There is no presumption that one person has authority to bind another by word or act. Such authority must be proved to have been actually or apparently given.

5. The principal is estopped to deny that his agent possesses the authority with which he has apparently clothed him.

6. Limitations upon the powers apparently possessed by an insurance agent cannot affect the insured unless communicated. Limitations of agency powers may be communicated in the application, in the policy, by oral communication, or by a writing not immediately connected with the contract. Improper limitations will not be enforced by the courts. Such limitations, occasionally found in policies include: agent of the insurer shall be deemed the agent of the insured; no agent is authorized to alter or waive any condition of the policy; the insurer shall not be charged with knowledge acquired by his agent in the course of his employment.

7. Any fraud or wrong perpetrated by the agent in the course of his employment binds the principal even though not authorized. However, an illegal act of an agent cannot bind his principal to that act.

8. An agent can only act for one party to the contract, but the person for whom he acts can only be determined by the facts of each case. Where a person is both an agent and broker, the specific nature of his role is determined in a given controversy.

TORT LIABILITY OF AGENTS AND BROKERS

An insurance broker, who has his policyholder as a principal, has an important responsibility to provide the proper insurance in adequate amounts for his client. In general, he may be liable for any damages that result from his failure to exercise due care in the handling of an account. Failure to follow specific directions given by the insured, neglecting to obtain insurance promptly, failure to notify the principal of inability to place insurance, careless placement of insurances that are void or defective may all impose liability on the broker.

The agent who informs his customer that the risk is covered is responsible for taking the necessary steps to provide for such prompt coverage in order to avoid liability for negligence. The agent is held to a standard of good faith and reasonable diligence to obtain insurance on the best possible terms. The courts have awarded damages to policyholders in some cases where the agent could have obtained the coverage on more favorable financial terms.

To cover the hazards of negligence in their agency role, agents and brokers often obtain errors and omissions coverage, which is a form of malpractice insurance covering the producer's liability to his customers or the companies he represents.

The producer also has a fiduciary duty in handling funds belonging to the company or companies that he represents, in order to conform with the law, to so maintain his fiduciary accounts that he could at any time discharge his obligations to his principal and terminate his relationship on short notice.

TERMINATION OF THE AGENCY RELATIONSHIP

The agency relationship may be terminated by action of the parties, by operation of the contract, or by operation of law.

An agency may be terminated if the principal discharges the agent or if the agent renounces the relationship. By the same token, inactivity or abandonment by the agent will effectively terminate the agency.

Most agency contracts provide for termination after a period of time, and in the absence of renewal termination is automatic. Also, cancellation provisions are common whereby either party may terminate the contract under certain circumstances.

Death, bankruptcy, and loss of license would all act to terminate agencies by operation of law. Death of the agent terminates the agency because the relationship is a personal one, although a corporate agency will survive the death of any individual subagent. Unless the agency is coupled with an interest, an agent loses his powers upon death of the principal. Bankruptcy stops the agency because the credit of the principal may no longer be pledged except by a receiver or other authorized official. Loss of license ends the agency because it would be a crime for the individual to act in a prohibited capacity.

Failure to terminate an agency relationship effectively when the agent is inactive or may have abandoned the agency is hazardous to insurance companies. The agent retains important evidence of his apparent authority in the nature of cards, application and policy forms, manuals and insignia, and may abuse his position. If he is unscrupulous, he may bind the company to undesirable risks, collect premiums for his own account, or take money under false pretenses. Sound business practice requires a prudent approach toward agency terminations.

MARKETING METHODS AND AGENTS

An insurer may distribute his product through any or all of four distinct systems: (1) independent agents, (2) captive agents, (3) employees, vending machines, mail, and other direct methods, and (4) brokers.

The independent agent usually establishes an agency relationship with numerous insurers and owns all policy records relating to his clients. He retains the rights to collect premiums from his clients and renew their policies with alternative insurers. Many independent agents have transferred the billing, financing, and collecting functions to insurers to reduce paperwork and costs. This transfer of part of the work load usually results in reduced renewal commissions, but it frees the agent's time for soliciting and servicing clients. The independent agent receives a commission from the insurer on all policies in force, and he pays his own operating expenses.

The captive agent has an exclusive contract with (and represents) only one insurer or group of insurers. Insurers represented by captive agents generally retain control over all policy records and billing. The client belongs to the insurer rather than the agent. The captive or exclusive agency system predominates in the life insurance field, but some large property and liability insurers have experienced rapid growth using a captive agency system.

Many insurers have adopted a "direct selling" distribution system whereby the insurer has direct contact with the insured through salaried employees, mail solicitation, or vending machines. While all types of insurers are represented among the direct writing companies, most have been mutual insurance companies. The direct selling system is used in all lines of insurance but has been most successful in personal lines property and liability insurance (e.g., family, auto and homeowners policies), accidental death and disability, and group insurance.

Brokers do not have agency relationships with insurers. They deal with many insurers on behalf of their clients. While a broker may not have contractual ties with insurers, he frequently develops working relationships with a few insurers who regularly accept his brokerage business. Some insurers accept applications for insurance directly from brokers while others require the broker to place his business through an agent of the company. In such cases, the broker and the agent usually split the commission. Because brokers generally receive lower commissions than agents, they tend to specialize in high premium volume business, especially commercial accounts.

LICENSING REQUIREMENTS

In order to solicit and sell insurance, an individual or firm must be licensed by the state. Licensing requirements vary significantly among states, but the trend is toward more demanding requirements. In order to become an agent, an applicant must pass a written examination and be sponsored by an insurance company. In addition, many states require specific educational prerequisites. Both the tests and the educational prerequisites are becoming more rigorous as the states attempt to raise the "professional" image of insurance agents.

In addition to restricting the entry of sales personnel, most states exercise control over the practices of agents. The most common restrictions are concerned with rebating, twisting, and commission levels.

Several states have limited the amount of commission an agent can be paid. For example, New York restricts first year commissions on a life insurance contract to a maximum established by formula written into the law. If an insurance company wishes to operate in New York, it must limit commissions to this level in every jurisdiction in which it does business.

PROFESSIONALISM

To advance their status as "professionals" thousands of insurance agents have pursued the designations of Chartered Life Underwriter (CLU) or Chartered Property and Casualty Underwriter (CPCU). Professional status requires competency as demonstrated in rigorous examinations administered by professional associations. The lawyer must pass a bar examination, and the accountant takes a CPA examination. In similar fashion, the CLU or CPCU designation is obtained only after completing a series of examinations. For example, to become a CLU an individual must pass tests in the following subjects: life and health insurance, life insurance law and company operations, group insurance and social insurance, pension planning, income taxation, investments and family financial management, accounting and finance, economics, business insurance, and estate planning and taxation. The examinations for the CLU and CPCU are far more comprehensive than state licensing tests. Accordingly, several states exempt individuals with the CLU or CPCU designation from the state licensing test requirement.

SUMMARY

The role of the individual who purports to act as agent or broker is very important. The rights and duties of all parties in the agency relationship are affected by the facts of each case. In general, the loyalty of the agent is to his principal to whom he owes the duties of proper conduct, reasonable care, fair dealing, and acting within the scope of his authority. Conflicts of interest arise where the identification of the roles of the three parties to a transaction are unclear.

REVIEW QUESTIONS

1.   Outline the duties of an agent to his principal and to his client.

2.   How is an agency relationship created by "estoppel"? Explain.

3.   When an agent advertises his expertise as a Chartered Life Underwriter (CLU), is he held to a higher standard of care than a non-CLU in his dealings with the public from the standpoint of tort liability? Explain.

4.   Charles died of tuberculosis three months after his life insurance policy was issued. The insurance company denied the claim on the ground of material misrepresentation. Charles had answered "no" to the question "Have you ever had or been told that you had tuberculosis?" The insurance company proved that Charles had been treated for tuberculosis for several years prior to applying for the insurance. Charles' widow argued that the agent never asked the question of Charles but instead merely filled in the application and Charles had signed it without reading it. What are the liabilities of the agent? Discuss.

5.   Brown recently purchased a fire insurance policy from Jones, who is a broker. Brown explains that he intends storing a large emergency supply of gasoline in his basement in the near future, and Jones tells him that this is nothing to worry about. Shortly after, Brown lit a match on the stairway leading to the basement. The house exploded and burned to the ground. The insurance company refused to pay Brown's claim on the grounds that Jones had neglected to inform them of the increased hazard arising from the storage of gasoline in Brown's basement.

   a.   What redress does Brown have against the insurer? Explain.

   b.   What redress does Brown have against Jones? Explain.

   c.   If Jones had been an agent instead of a broker, would this have altered the insurance company's position? Explain.

STUDY QUESTIONS

6.   What are the requirements for licensing of agents in your state? Are the standards for licensing sufficiently high as to protect the public against the hazards of incompetence and moral turpitude? Discuss.

7.   How can an insurance company give notice of an agency termination to third parties when it may not know the identity of those third parties? How can the public know when an agency has been terminated? Explain.

8.   An independent insurance agent is said to own his "expirations." This is the principal property asset which is transferred when an agency is sold. What are "expirations?" Why does the agent own them? Explain.

9.   The president of a life insurance company is an agent of the company as a matter of law. Officers of life insurance companies are generally prohibited from receiving commissions on business placed with the company. When the president buys a life insurance policy on his own life from the insurance company which employs him, who receives the commission? Explain.

10. From a professional standpoint, is it ethical for an agent to compromise the policy which he believes right for the client with what he believes the client is more likely to be willing to buy?

8

Insurance
Contracts

INTRODUCTION

Insurance contracts are agreements between insurance companies and insureds for the purpose of transferring from the insured to the insurer part of the risk of loss arising out of contingent events. Because the insurance contract is between parties affecting their respective interests in property, it is a personal contract. While it is a contract of indemnity, the measure of indemnity, insurable interest, may not be precise. The subject of insurance contracts may be divided into considerations of functions, nature, elements, and legal requirements.

FUNCTIONS OF AN INSURANCE CONTRACT

The principal functions of an insurance contract are: (1) to define the risk that is to be transferred, (2) to state the conditions under which the contract applies, and (3) to explain the procedure for settling losses.

Insurance contracts are usually contracts of adhesion; that is, the contract is drafted only by the insurer, and the applicant must take the contract as written or reject the offer. However, in the event that the terms of the contract are ambiguous, the benefit of any doubt is against the insurance carrier.

Therefore, the definition of the risk to be transferred requires care and must be clear and easy to interpret. The risk must be specified by time, place, persons affected, amount, and nature. For underwriting purposes, the risk exposure must be mutually agreeable. Almost without exception, the courts hold that in the event of ambiguity the contract will be construed strictly against the insurer and in favor of the insured and beneficiary.

Conditions of the contract must be carefully stated so that both parties to the contract know precisely what they may expect by way of rights and correlative duties. Conditions may be precedent, such as payment of the premium; concurrent, such as performance of certain acts; or subsequent, such as presentation of proper proofs of loss. The effect of a breach of condition is to prevent recovery of damages against the party who has made a promise subject to the condition.

Sometimes the intent or scope of the condition must be determined on the basis of laws pertaining to construction of the particular provision. For example, the "co-operation clause" in an automobile insurance contract provides that: "The insured shall co-operate with the company and, . . . assist in . . . enforcing any right of . . . indemnity against any person . . .". This condition, as interpreted by the courts, prohibits the insured from admitting or assuming liability. The clause is a material condition, and its breach can result in loss of the right to indemnity under the contract.[1]

Procedures for settling losses are precisely explained in the contract. Reference to these procedures by all parties leads to expeditious and equitable loss adjustment. When clearly established procedures are followed, there is less possibility of dispute or litigation.

Indemnity

The principle of indemnity in insurance contracts asserts that the contract is one for restoring the insured to the same economic condition he was in prior to the happening of the insured event, but not to permit him to profit from the contingency. It is this concept that legally differentiates insurance from gambling. In the one case, the insured is protected against possible loss; in the other, he deliberately risks loss for the possibility of potential gains.

While most insurance policies are contracts of indemnity, there are exceptions. Since there is no accepted means of measuring any loss, the Valued Policy is for a fixed amount regardless of the actual potential economic loss. Valued Policies are typical in life and health insurance. The value of a lost or damaged life is at best subjective. Valued Policies are also used in marine insurance. Historically, it was difficult to fix precise marine values because the

---

[1] William E. Moorly, "Admission of Liability of an Assured", *Insurance Law Journal* (October, 1958), pp. 645-50.

date of loss might not be known. This date would be important because the cargo's utility increases as it approaches closer to port. Replacement cost policies in fire insurance modify the indemnity principle as well, because such policies allow the insured full restoration of economic loss without regard to depreciation of property.

Subrogation

Subrogation is the transfer by an insured to an insurer of any rights to proceed against a third party who has negligently caused the occurrence of an insured loss. For example, an automobile insurer that has paid a collision insurance claim obtains the right to collect reimbursement from any negligent third party who caused the accident.

The doctrine of subrogation is a corollary of the indemnity principle. The insured who has been indemnified by the insurance company may neglect to prosecute the tortfeasor where liability exists, or he might prosecute in order to seek double recovery. Double recovery would violate the indemnity principle. By subrogation, the dilemma is resolved by assigning to the insurance company the right to prosecute the action against the wrongdoer and thereby recoup a portion or all of the damages paid to the insured. Such salvage by insurance companies helps to maintain lower rate levels for insureds.

NATURE OF THE INSURANCE CONTRACT

The insurance contract has been described as entire, personal, unilateral, and aleatory. Entirety means that all of the terms and conditions are to be found within the document. This is essential because its absence would require the parties to look to other evidence of the terms of the contract. If such evidence were oral it might be difficult to prove. Under the parol evidence rule, oral agreements may not be introduced as an element of proof of the intention of the parties in a written contract. The personal feature means that the contract follows the person who is the insured rather than the property. A fire insurance contract does not insure a house against loss by fire, but insures the interest of the named insured in the house against loss by fire to the extent of the insurable interest of the insured. Unilateral contracts are those in which further performance is required of only one party. For example, in fire insurance after the premium has been paid the only party with obligations to perform is the insurance company. An aleatory contract is one with performance conditioned upon an event that may or may not happen. Thus there may not be an exchange of equal dollar values between the insurance company and the insured.

ELEMENTS OF AN INSURANCE CONTRACT

There are four basic elements to every insurance contract: (1) an application, (2) a binder, (3) the policy form, and (4) endorsements.

Application

An application is required for every contract of insurance. In the application, which is an offer to enter into a contract, the prospective insured sets forth the facts and figures required by the insurance carrier's underwriting department. The application may be brief and oral, or of any length and in written form. In life insurance, the application itself becomes a part of the contract.

Binders

A binder is a memorandum specifying some of the details of the property or liability policy to be issued by the company. It is a memorandum of insurance issued pending delivery of the formal policy. The binder may be oral or written, and may be given either by an agent or a company. A broker, not being an agent of an insurance company, cannot issue binders. The binder is usually a temporary document and ordinarily would remain in force no more than ten days. For example, in automobile insurance a car buyer wants immediate coverage. By binding the insurance company to the risk, the agent need not wait for the insurance to become effective.

Binders are not used in life insurance. Given the long term nature of the contract and the insurer's inability to cancel a life insurance policy, the life insurer requires an opportunity to examine the application (and possibly the applicant) before being bound to a lifetime contract. However, in place of binders the life insurance agent can provide the applicant with a receipt (assuming the first premium installment is paid) that will provide varying insurance benefits depending on the nature of the receipt. There are basically three types of life insurance receipts:

1. Coverage is provided immediately after the application is accepted by the company. If no receipt were issued (that is, the first premium was not sent with the application), the application would only be a request for an offer, and acceptance would not occur until after the applicant received notification of an offer and paid the first premium. This first form of receipt only provides the benefit of making the application an offer and the approval by the company the acceptance, which creates a contract.

2.   Coverage is provided at the time the receipt is issued conditional upon the applicant being qualified. That is, should the applicant die before a contract is issued, payment will be made only if the applicant would have passed all normal underwriting standards. If it can be demonstrated by the insurer that the applicant had a condition that normally would have led to his rejection, payment by the insurer could be avoided.

3.   Coverage is provided at the time the receipt is issued, and payment will be made at time of death regardless of the applicant's condition. This is not a permanent contract but a temporary one subject to cancellation should the company reject the application for insurance. The type of receipt issued with the payment of the first premium will thus have a distinct effect on the nature of the insurer's obligation. The second type, or conditional receipt, is most frequently used by insurers. However, there is a trend toward the use of the third or "binding" receipt.

Policy Forms

The policy form is the formal written contract of insurance that sets forth all of the terms of the agreement. The policy is usually set up in two parts. The first page is the declarations page and identifies the risk by specifying the name of the insured, the address, location of the risk, period covered by the policy, description of the subject being insured, the amount of insurance, the amount of the premium, and any warranties or representations made by the insured. The second part is the contract itself and contains the insuring agreements, exclusions, and conditions. The insuring agreements stipulate the rights of the insured and the duties of the insurer. The company promises "To pay . . . ," "To defend . . . ," "To settle . . . ," and so on. The exclusions may list perils that the company is not willing under any circumstances to cover, such as "invasion," "civil war," "revolution," or perils that the insured can have covered under other insurance policies. The conditions define the rights and duties of the parties aside from the insuring agreements. It is here that the insured may find his duties under the contract.

Standardization of policy forms is an ongoing process, and most insurance contracts have uniform language for the greater part of their terms. Such standardization makes possible economies of operation, statistical uniformity, and better communication between the insured, his agent, and the insurance company. Where language has been standardized, determination of the meaning of the words and phrases by the courts reduces the chance of misunderstanding.

In one case the court discussed the proliferation of forms at the time in the following terms:

Forms of applications and policies . . . of a most complicated and elaborate structure, were prepared, and filled with covenants, exceptions, stipulations, provisos, rules, regulations, and conditions, rendering the policy void in a great number of contingencies. These provisions were of such bulk and character that they would not be understood by men in general, even if subjected to a careful and laborious study; by men in general, they were sure not to be studied at all. The study of them was rendered particularly unattractive by a profuse intermixture of discourses on subjects in which a premium payer would have no interest. This compound, if read by him, would, unless he were an extraordinary man, be an inexplicable riddle, a mere flood of darkness and confusion. Some of the most material stipulations were concealed in a mass of rubbish, on the back side of the policy and the following page, where few would expect to find anything more than a dull appendix, and where scarcely anyone would think of looking for information so important as that the company claimed a special exemption from the operation of the general law of the land relating to the business in which the company professed to be engaged. As if it were feared that, notwithstanding these discouraging circumstances, some extremely eccentric person might attempt to examine and understand the meaning of the involved and intricate net in which he was to be entangled, it was printed in such small type, and in lines so long and so crowded, that the perusal of it was made physically difficult, painful, and injurious.[2]

Endorsements

An endorsement is a form that is used to modify the policy contract. Endorsements may extend or restrict coverage, permit transfers of interest in property, transfer coverage, transfer coverage from one place to another, increase or decrease limits of coverage, provide for assignment of policies or changes in beneficiary designations, provide for changes in settlement options elected, or in any other legal manner permit amendments to the contract.

CLASSES OF POLICY CONTRACTS

The forms of insurance policy contract are so numerous that the semantics of the field can become confusing without some clarification. The All Risk policy is an inland marine insurance policy covering property against all risk of loss except that which is specifically excluded. A Comprehensive policy covers all risk of loss in the liability field with the sole exception of specified excluded perils. The Named Perils policy covers only perils named specifically in the policy, excluding all others. The Schedule policy covers a number of specific locations or pieces of personal property. The Blanket policy in fire insurance covers all property regardless of location under a single limit of protection in a single form. The Floater policy covers movable property in all locations. The

---

[2] *DeLancy v. Rockingham Farmers Mutual Fire Insurance Co.*, 52 N.H. 581, 587.

Standard Form is a uniform policy in use by many insurance companies. A Manuscript policy is a contract specifically designed for a given risk and is in manuscript form.

LEGAL REQUIREMENTS FOR FORMATION
OF INSURANCE CONTRACTS

The formation of an enforceable insurance contract requires the mutual assent of at least two parties, and this mutual assent must be manifested by an offer and an acceptance that is unequivocal, and made while the offer is still open. The contract must be supported by consideration for the promises bargained for. In addition, there must be mutuality of obligation, certainty of terms, legal purpose, capacity, and form. Specific insurance requirements also include that an insurable interest exists and that a loss be sustained before the insurer is obliged to perform under the contract.

The Offer

The offer to buy insurance is usually made by means of the application and consists of material representations or warranties made by the prospective insured as an inducement to the insurer to issue the contract. In life insurance the first installment may be required to accompany the application if it is to be construed as an offer. Legally, the offer is intended to provide the basis for mutual assent, and if the application includes misrepresentations of material facts or fails to disclose material facts by concealment, there can be no requisite mutual assent.

The Consideration

A contract is an agreement supported by a consideration for the promises of the insurer. In insurance this consideration is both the premium paid by the insured and more significantly the set of representations made by the applicant for insurance. Most insurance contracts give equal status to representations, warranties, and the payment of premiums. A common provision states: ". . . in consideration of the payment of the premium and in reliance upon the statements in the declarations. . . ." Another reads: "In consideration of the Application for this policy and the payment of the premium. . . ."

Mutuality of Obligation

Being a form of bargain, a contract requires that both parties be obligated to perform or refrain from performing some act or acts. In the insurance contract the insurer promises to assume certain risks, while the insured promises to pay the premium. Unless both parties have obligations, there can be no contract. An insurance contract can be repudiated by the insurance company for failure to perform by the insured. Both parties are bound or neither is bound.

Certainty of Terms

A contract is not enforceable unless the intent of the parties is clearly expressed. There must be no mistake about the subject of insurance, the period of coverage, the premiums, the location of the risk or other important details of the coverage. In the course of processing thousands of contracts it is inevitable that unintentional errors will occur. On occasion the $5,000 policy may be printed as a $5,000,000 policy. To correct such errors the insurer may proceed to a court of equity to reform the contract. However, reformation is only applicable to mutual errors by both the insurer and the insured. Only when there is fraud or excessive negligence will unilateral errors be corrected by reformation.

Legal Purpose

A contract of insurance that covers a risk promoting a business or venture prohibited by law is void. Similarly, a contract that insures goods illegally possessed or that is merely a gambling contract will not be enforced by the courts.

Legal Capacity

The parties to an insurance contract must have legal capacity. This requirement excludes persons who have been deemed incapable of contracting, such as those who have been judicially declared insane, and persons who are legally incompetent, such as infants, drunken persons, and those of unsound mind but not adjudged insane. Married women in some states are by law incompetent to enter into some types of insurance contracts. Many states regard life, health, and auto insurance as "necessaries" and permit persons otherwise lacking legal capacity to enter into them under certain conditions. A minor child above a certain age may be permitted to purchase insurance. The rules vary from state to state on this as on other contract questions. Enabling statutes permit a minor to buy life insurance on his own life, and sometimes on the life of one in whom the minor has an insurable interest. Emancipation statutes free the minor from his legal incapacity either generally, or with regard to listed business or personal transactions or situations. Many states permit the minor to insure his life at age fourteen and one-half.

Legal Form

Insurance contracts may be oral, informal memoranda, or formal policy contracts. The laws of most states require that certain statutory language be used as a condition of enforceability of some contracts. In such jurisdictions the contract must have the form required by law. Thus, the California Insurance Code requires that all fire insurance policies have the same policy language, size of type, and punctuation.

> All fire policies on subject matter in California shall be on the standard form, and, except as provided by this article shall not contain additions thereto.
> The policy shall be plainly printed. The type shall not be smaller than eight point and in a style not less legible than Century and subheads shall be in type larger than eight point and in a style not less legible than Century.
> It is a misdemeanor for any insurer or any agent to countersign or issue a fire policy covering in whole or in part property in California and varying from the California standard form of policy otherwise than as provided by this article. Any policy so issued shall, notwithstanding, be binding upon the issuing insurer.[3]

Life and health insurance policies must contain certain clauses required by law. Unless the contract conforms with the statutory provisions it is void or voidable.

Requirements relative to the covenants in an insurance contract may be classified as: required provisions, allowable provisions, and restricted provisions. For example, most states require that life insurance contracts contain specified provisions with regard to: a grace period in which late premiums can be paid and cancellation avoided, incontestability of incorrect statements in the application in the first two years after the policy is issued, adjustment of benefits in the event of misstatement of age or sex, available options, default in payment of premium, policy loans, reinstatement, and so on. Most states specifically prohibit the use of the following provisions: back dating the policy, assessable clauses, or requiring that the laws of a state other than where the policy was issued will apply to the contract. In addition, there are many provisions that may be used at the discretion of the insurer, such as clauses on the assignment and ownership of policies and policy exclusions.

Insurable Interest

An insurable interest has been defined as such a relation between the individual and the subject of insurance as would cause him to suffer financial or

---

[3] State of California, *Insurance Code*, Sec. 2070.

economic loss in the event the contingency insured against occurred. The New York Insurance Code defines insurable interest as follows:

> The term insurable interest shall mean (a) in the case of persons related closely by blood or by law a substantial interest engendered by love and affection, and (b) in the case of other persons a lawful and substantial economic interest in having the life, health or bodily safety of the person insured continue.

One has an insurable interest in property to the extent of his monetary interest in it. A mortgagee has an insurable interest in the property insured only to the extent of the balance due on the contract. One who sells property loses his insurable interest in it.

The issues of when an insurable interest must exist, when it is created or terminated, and how it may be measured can only be resolved by study of the local statutes. Normally, in life insurance, the insurable interest need exist only at the time of application, whereas in property and liability insurance the insurable interest need exist only at the time of loss. However, several states (e.g., California) have stated that insurable interest in property and liability insurance must exist at the time of issuing the policy, throughout the life of the policy, and at the time of any loss. Thus, as with many other features of insurance law, specific statutes must be consulted before relying upon generalizations.

Insurable interest is one of several factors that restrict the extent to which recovery can be had under an insurance contract. Payment beyond an individual's insurable interest would violate the concept of indemnification, might create a moral hazard,[4] and might transform the insurance policy into a gambling contract.

Occurrence of Loss

In order to collect the indemnity from the insurance company, the insured must sustain an economic loss. This is because the obligation of the insurer is a contingent one. It arises from the aleatory nature of the contract.

If an insurer is uncertain as to which of several parties should receive the proceeds of an insurance contract, it may use the remedy of interpleader. Interpleader allows the insurer to deposit the proceeds with the court, which will determine an appropriate pattern of distribution. For example, assume a life

---

[4] In *Liberty National Life Insurance Company v. Weldon* (267 Ala. 171, 100 So.2d 696, 1957), the court held that a life insurance company is liable in tort for failure to determine the insurable interest of the beneficiary. A $75,000 award was granted for wrongful death. An aunt purchased policies on the life of her niece, naming herself as beneficiary. The aunt lacked insurable interest, neither living with nor supporting the niece. The aunt later murdered the niece by feeding her arsenic, and the aunt was subsequently executed. Action was brought by the father of the niece alleging negligence.

insurance policyowner named as beneficiary "my wife, Mary". Shortly after making this beneficiary designation, he divorced his first wife (Mary) and remarried another woman named Mary. Assume further that the divorce decree made no reference to the insurance policy and both Marys have made claim for the proceeds based on the oral communication that they were named as beneficiaries. If the insurer pays the proceeds to either Mary, it may be subject to a successful suit by the other Mary. To avoid the possibility of paying the proceeds twice, the insurer may be allowed to use the remedy of interpleader and thus allow a court of equity to resolve any possible conflict.

OPERATION OF INSURANCE CONTRACTS

A valid insurance contract is one which complies with all of the legal requirements. Once formed it becomes operative, and legal questions may arise with respect to the rights and duties of the parties under the terms of the agreement. General rules of construction of contracts are applicable in addition to the laws specific to insurance.

General Rules Underlying Interpretation of Insurance Contracts

In general, the courts have taken the position that a life insurance contract is a valued policy and not a true indemnity policy. This means that the insurable interest of a person in life insurance on his own life may be any amount agreed upon between the policyholder and the insurance company.

In case of ambiguity about the meaning of provisions in the contract, the benefit of the doubt will favor the policyholder because the contract is usually one of adhesion. The policy is issued by the insurance company, and the customer is not free to change the wording of the contract. A general legal principle is that he who drafts a document is presumed to have intended exactly what he drafted and would have elaborated upon it if he intended more.[5]

If there is no ambiguity about its meaning, the court may not liberalize but must construe the contract strictly in accordance with its terms.

Endorsements in an insurance policy control the provisions of the policy. Endorsements are amendments to the contract.

Construction of a contract is governed by the law and usages of the place where the last essential act occurred in the making of the contract. However,

---

[5] In *Lisi v. Alitalia-Linee Aeree Italiane*, 253 F. Supp. 237 (SDNY 1966), the court refused to enforce what it referred to as a condition "camouflaged in Lilliputian print in a thicket of 'Conditions of Contract' crowded on page 4," as being "both unnoticeable and unreadable."

assignments are governed by the law of the place where the assignments were executed.

In a life insurance application, all statements are deemed to be mere representations and not warranties. Misstatements of age are corrected by adjustment of benefit amounts.

Legal Assumptions Related to Insurance

There are numerous situations where the law makes assumptions with regard to an unknown event. The purpose of these presumptions is to allow an action to be taken that might otherwise be delayed indefinitely, or an action to be taken that is in the public interest. Without certain legal presumptions there might be no basis on which to proceed, and inaction (or the "wrong action") might be detrimental to society or individuals. Three areas where legal assumptions affect insurance are: (1) common disaster, (2) prolonged absence or disappearance, and (3) suicide.

Common Disaster

From an insurance viewpoint, a common disaster occurs when both the insured and the primary beneficiary (e.g., husband and wife) die in the same accident, and there is no evidence to indicate which party died first. The question is who gets the proceeds of the insurance—the estate of the beneficiary or the estate of the insured? To solve this problem most states have adopted the Uniform Simultaneous Death Act. This statute provides that in circumstances where the order of survival cannot be proven, the insured is presumed to have survived the beneficiary. However if it can be proven that the beneficiary survived the insured, this does not solve the potential estate distribution problems associated with simultaneous death. In that case the proceeds must be paid to the estate of the beneficiary, which might violate the goals of the policyowner. Thus, rather than relying on the applicability of the Uniform Simultaneous Death Act, it is more efficient for the policyowner to adopt a survivorship clause which provides that the primary beneficiary must survive the insured by a stated period of time. Should the beneficiary die prior to the survivorship period, the insurer would distribute the proceeds to any secondary beneficiaries or to the estate of the insured.

Disappearance

Should the insured disappear for a lengthy period of time, there will be doubt as to whether he is alive or dead. The uncertainty as to the insured's condition may be legally removed after seven years. Should the insured disappear for seven years, he is presumed to have died some time during the seven years. Generally no specific time of death is assumed. Only if it can be demonstrated that the insured incurred a specific peril or danger at a known date will a time of death be set prior to seven years.

Suicide

During a specified period (usually the first one or two years of the policy), death by suicide is excluded by life insurance contracts. However, in all cases where there is any doubt as to the proximate cause of death, the law assumes that the insured did not commit suicide. This presumption against suicide is based on man's instinct for survival, and his inherent love of life. The burden of proof is on the insurer to prove beyond a doubt that the insured committed suicide.

Representations, Concealment, and Warranties

A representation is an oral or written statement either of such facts or circumstances relative to the proposed insurance as is necessary to enable the underwriters to form a proper estimate of the risk. Any allegation of facts by the applicant to the insurer, or vice versa, preliminary to making the contract, and directly bearing upon it, having a plain and evident tendency to induce the making of the policy is a representation. Concealment is the counterpart of misrepresentation. It is a withholding of something that one knows and that one, in duty, is bound to reveal. The terms misrepresentation and concealment have a known and definite meaning in insurance. Both have a tendency to mislead and to be material. Both are inducements to enter into a contract without mutuality of consent. Material misrepresentation or concealment will, therefore, make the contract voidable unless the injured party waives his rights.

A warranty is a statement of fact either explicit or implied that becomes a condition of the contract. Breach of warranty will make the contract voidable. A warranty is a statement by the insured upon which the validity of the contract depends. There is an absolute quality about the warranty in insurance that is much more harsh than that of a representation where the issue of materiality may be raised. If under a marine insurance contract written in the nineteenth century the shipowner informed the underwriter that the ship captain was forty-five years old, and in fact he was forty-two years old, the contract would be subject to voidance regardless of the immateriality of the error. While the use of warranties appeared excessive, they were particularly necessary during the formative years of marine insurance. Ships requiring insurance protection had no quick lines of communication. Thus the London underwriter had to have complete faith in all statements made by the shipowner. Recognizing the importance of his dependence, the doctrine of warranty was applied. As lines of communication improved, insurers were better able to verify facts relevant to the exposure. Furthermore, in other lines of insurance (e.g., fire, life, liability, etc.) the exposure was within the immediate vicinity of the underwriter and subject to examination. Thus the need for warranties declined. It was the harshness of the doctrine that has caused many legislatures to declare that warranties do not exist in most types of insurance.

Incontestability

The incontestable clause in life insurance, in accident insurance, and sickness insurance contracts provides that the insurer may not contest the policy on grounds of misrepresentation after the lapse of a definite period, such as one or two years. This statutory limitation is designed to protect the insured and the beneficiary from allegations about possible misrepresentations long after the policy is issued. It is in the public interest that the beneficiary should not suffer for the transgressions of the insured.

The grounds for an insurer overcoming the incontestable clause generally involve misrepresentations that are not merely material and fraudulent but that grossly contravene public policy. Examples include: instances where another person was substituted for the medical exam for life insurance; where the purchaser of the policy had no insurable interest in the life of the policyholder; where the beneficiary murdered the insured; where there was a failure to pay premiums; or where there was capital punishment of the policyholder.

Waiver and Estoppel

A waiver is a surrender of a known right under a contract. Where one of the parties has failed to comply with some condition of the policy and the other party permits such breach, he is said to have waived his right. It is an affirmative act. An estoppel occurs when a party is estopped from asserting a right because his past pattern of conduct indicates that he has implicitly waived his right. For example, suppose that an insurance premium is payable monthly and is due on the first day. It arrives on the tenth day and is accepted by the company without protest. This occurs month after month. After a number of months the insurer will lose its right to protest the late payments by virtue of the doctrine of estoppel.

DISCHARGE OF INSURANCE CONTRACTS

Insurance contracts may be discharged by the lapse of time, the settlement of claims, failure to pay premiums, failure to renew, or cancellation. Each type of contract has its own bases for termination.

SUMMARY

The law pertaining to insurance contracts is not fundamentally different from the general law of contracts except to the extent that specialized customs and usages of the business, the requirements of underwriters, and the public policy implications of protecting the public against improper practices by insurers tend to narrow the interpretation of the general law. The court has the duty to interpret the contract that is presented for construction rather than to remake bad contracts entered into by the parties. Where the language is unambiguous and the various provisions of the statute are complied with, the court will enforce the contract on its express terms giving an ordinary meaning to the words used.

Insurance contracts, having come under statutory regulation, must possess certain elements over and beyond the general requirements of offer, acceptance, consideration, mutuality of obligation, certainty of terms, legal purpose, and legal capacity. They also require legal form, insurable interest, and the occurrence of a loss before indemnity may be paid.

REVIEW QUESTIONS

1. What are the essential elements of an insurance contract? Must all the elements be in writing?

2. "The contract of life insurance is not a contract of indemnity." Discuss.

3. David named as beneficiary of his life insurance policy "my wife and children." What are some of the legal problems which may arise from such a designation? Discuss.

4. What are the advantages and disadvantages both to consumers and insurers of standardized or uniform insurance contracts? Discuss.

5. What is the relationship between insurable interest and indemnity? Why does the public benefit from the requirement of insurable interest?

STUDY QUESTIONS

6. At midnight on Saturday, Fred bought a car from a friend while at a party. He immediately called his agent at home and ordered automobile insurance with a $50 deductible on collision coverage. The agent said, "You're covered." The agent had authority from both the X and the Y insurance companies to give oral binders on collision coverage for drivers with "clean" records. After the party, Fred was involved in an accident in which the newly purchased car was badly damaged. When he called the agent to report the loss, Fred was told that the agent had no authority to issue oral binders without checking the traffic violation record of the prospective insured, and therefore Fred was not covered. Advise Fred.

7. George bought an automobile insurance policy from the Z insurance company. The policy provided coverage for the family without exclusions for drivers under the age of 25. After the policy had been in force for several months, a company representative asked to see the policy. Unknown to George, the agent attached a rider to the policy excluding drivers under age 25 from coverage. George learned about this after filing a claim for an accident involving his 23 year old son who lived at home. What defense does George have against the company's refusal to pay the loss? Discuss.

8. In 1865, the federal government offered a reward of $25,000 for information leading to the arrest of John H. Surratt, one of Booth's accomplices in the assassination of President Lincoln. The offer was revoked on November 24th, 1865, and the notice of the revocation was published. In April, 1866, Surratt was found serving in the military service of the Papal Government, and he was subsequently arrested. The government refused to pay the reward. Discuss. (*Shuey v. United States*, 92 U.S. 73, 23 L. Ed. 697).

9. The courts have frequently held that an insurance contract is one of utmost good faith, *uberrimae fidei*. Does this doctrine conflict with the intent of the Incontestable Clause in a life insurance policy which shields the insured against the consequences of his misrepresentation or concealment of material information in the application for insurance? Explain.

10. Plaintiff, beneficiary of life insurance policies on the life of her son who died in the Vietnam conflict, sought recovery of double indemnity benefits under the policies. The policies had a war exclusion clause in them. Plaintiff argued that the war exclusion was void because Congress had failed to declare war in the Vietnam conflict. Discuss. (*Hammond v. National Life and Accident Insurance Company*, 243 So2d 902 (La Ct App 1971).

9

Life and Health
Insurance Contracts: I

INTRODUCTION

Most individual family units rely on a flow of income generated from gainful employment. Should the death or disability of the family head lead to a discontinuance of this income flow, financial disaster for the family is a distinct possibility. In similar fashion illness to any member of the family could create a large and persistent drain on the family's financial resources. To offset these perils of death, disability, and disease the family usually tries to make arrangements either to prevent a loss of income or provide a supplementary income flow should a loss occur. Life and health insurance are two efficient techniques for dealing with the risks of income loss due to premature death, disability, accident, or sickness.

Insurance is an effective preloss arrangement for the perils of death, disability, or disease because (1) the insurance contract provides certainty of benefit flows in the event of a loss, and (2) the specific event that creates the need for a new source of income triggers the flow of cash benefits from the insurer. Unlike advances from relatives, friends, or charity, insurance benefits are contractual and not dependent upon the discretion or whims of others. Furthermore, the benefit flows from insurance are independent of the passage of time. If an individual attempted to accumulate an emergency fund to meet the risk of premature death or catastrophic illness, the plan would probably be frustrated by the occurrence of a loss prior to the accumulation of a sufficient fund. With life insurance, a postdeath estate is created immediately at the inception of the contract. For example, should the insured individual die right after the contract is issued, life insurance proceeds will be available to the beneficiary within a matter of days.

As demonstrated by Table 9.1, U.S. consumers have recognized the benefits of life insurance. Total life insurance in force grew steadily from $106 billion in 1930 to $1.6 trillion in 1972, and the average size of a policy in force increased from $2,460 in 1930 to $6,450 in 1971. The number of policies per family grew as the average amount of life insurance per family went from $2,800 in 1930 to $22,700 in 1972. The average size new "ordinary" policy in 1972 was $12,540.

TABLE 9.1   The Growth of Life Insurance in United States

Year	Life Insurance in Force ($000,000)	Average Size Life Insurance Policy	Life Insurance Per Family
1930	$ 106,413 ($\times 10^{0}$)	$2,460	$ 2,800
1940	115,530	2,130	2,700
1950	234,168	2,320	4,600
1960	586,448	3,590	10,200
1970	1,402,758	6,100	20,900

SOURCE: *1972 Life Insurance Fact Book.* New York: Institute of Life Insurance, pp. 24, 25, 27.

There are four principal groups of life and health insurance products: (1) life insurance, (2) annuities, (3) health insurance, and (4) disability income insurance. Each of these types of insurance may be sold on either an individual or a group basis.

Group life insurance is usually sold by payroll deduction, or is paid for by the employer as a fringe benefit. Most group life insurance plans are based on yearly renewable term insurance. Annuities on a group basis may be provided either by insurers or under noninsured arrangements referred to as trusteed plans.[1] Group health insurance plans may cover only a few hazards, such as

---

[1] The private pensions movement is divided among insured and trusteed plans and provides annuities on a group basis. See Joseph J. Melone and Everett T. Allen, Jr., *Pension Planning: Pensions, Profit Sharing, and Other Deferred Compensation Plans* (rev. ed.) (Homewood, Ill.: Richard D. Irwin, Inc., 1972); William F. Marples, *Actuarial Aspects of Pension Security* (Homewood, Ill.: Richard D. Irwin, Inc., 1965); Dan M. McGill, *Guaranty Fund for Private Pension Obligations* (Homewood, Ill.: Richard D. Irwin, Inc., 1970).

accidental death or dismemberment, or a broad spectrum, such as major medical insurance, which indemnifies for losses of all kinds arising out of accident or sickness. Group disability income insurance is generally provided in conjunction with employment.

LIFE INSURANCE PRODUCTS

Life and health insurance are recognized as efficient ways of managing important risks. The optimum use of these forms of insurance depends upon proper selection of policies and of the various options available with each policy. No valid generalizations can be made with regard to the "best" life or health insurance policy. The "best" policy will vary depending upon the individual's exposure to risk, the size of his present estate, his income tax bracket, his family situation, and his ability to pay premiums, among other factors.

There are three basic types of life insurance: term, whole life, and endowment. Other policies are based on a combination of these three. Term provides protection, with no savings feature; whole life and endowment insurance provide protection and savings. Thus, while term insurance is only used for creating an after-death estate for a beneficiary, whole life and endowment insurance help accumulate a living estate for the insured himself.

Table 9.2 summarizes the extent to which each of the major plans of life insurance have been sold. The table is for ordinary life insurance and thus excludes group, which is predominantly term insurance.

TABLE 9.2   Life Insurance in Force by Type of Contract (1970)

	Amount ($ millions)	Percent of Amount
Whole Life		
Straight Life	$327,500	44.8%
Limited Pay	83,000	11.4
Paid Up	31,000	4.2
Endowment	38,000	5.2
Term	179,000	24.5
Other	72,600	9.9
Total	$731,100	100.0%

SOURCE: *1972 Life Insurance Fact Book, New York:* Institute of Life Insurance, p. 28.

Term Insurance

A term insurance policy is a life insurance contract that provides for payment of benefits to the beneficiary if the insured dies within a specified period, usually one or more years. If the insured survives this period the contract expires, and there are no further benefit rights. This contract is often referred to as straight term insurance. Because there are no accumulated cash values, straight term insurance provides protection only against the peril of premature death. Straight term life insurance is like a fire insurance policy in that it provides protection against a named peril for a specified time. Furthermore, it provides this protection at a relatively low cost. No other life insurance policy sold on an individual basis provides protection for a limited period of time at a lower premium.

The main limitation of straight term insurance is its temporary nature. If the need for life insurance protection extends beyond the policy period, or perhaps for the insured's entire lifetime, straight term insurance is probably not the most appropriate plan of insurance. If the insured survives the period of the straight term policy, he may no longer be insurable. In such a case, he will be unable to buy additional protection even if he needs it.

Renewable Term.   Renewable term insurance guarantees the insured the right to renew the policy before the expiration date without evidence of insurability. The additional period for which the policy can be renewed is usually equal to the period of the original policy. The insured's option to renew, while raising the cost of the policy slightly, is an important feature that can expand the potential uses of term insurance. Specifically, the guarantee of renewal at the complete discretion of the policyowner provides a mechanism for extending the period of coverage. Should the need for protection extend beyond the original policy period, this option would prove valuable. The premium for a renewable term policy remains the same throughout each policy period, but increases to a new level with each renewal. The new premium is based on the insured's attained age at the time of renewal. While most life insurance companies offer yearly renewable term insurance, they prefer to sell five, ten, fifteen, or twenty year renewable term. Yearly renewable term insurance must be sold with very large face amounts to cover the overhead expense, or "loading" factor.

While the renewable term policy provides an opportunity to extend the period of coverage, there are important limitations on its use. Life insurance companies restrict the number of times the renewal option may be exercised and the age beyond which renewals are not permitted. These restrictions are used by the insurer to avoid adverse selection—as premiums rise with age, those in poor health are more likely to renew their policies than healthy insureds. Also, the premium for renewable term insurance increases at the time of exercise of each option and becomes relatively high. If protection is needed for a long period or for the whole of life, renewable term is inefficient and costly. In this case convertible term insurance or whole life insurance is more appropriate.

Convertible Term.   Convertible term insurance gives the insured the right to convert a term insurance contract into a form of permanent life insurance.

The conversion is at the option of the insured and requires no evidence of insurability, such as a medical examination. When the policyowner has exercised the option to convert, the premiums increase to the level required for the new policy (generally a whole life policy) at the insured's attained age. The policyowner may convert the policy at any time up to the expiration of the conversion privilege.

The conversion option eliminates one of the limitations of term insurance. While a consumer may be convinced that he will need life insurance protection for only a short period, his circumstances may change. Differences in the economic or familial condition of the insured may give rise to a need for permanent whole life insurance protection. If the consumer becomes uninsurable (e.g., as a result of a heart condition or occupational hazard) during a period of changing insurance needs, the expiration of his term insurance would leave his family unprotected. However, with convertible term insurance the new situation could be met by converting the term policy to a form of permanent protection. Today, most term insurance policies are sold with both renewable and convertible features.

Decreasing Term. Decreasing term insurance is term insurance in which the face amount of the policy decreases over the policy period. The premiums are usually paid on a level basis, and the policy is paid up before the end of its term so that the consumer has little incentive to lapse the policy when the amount of coverage has dropped to a relatively small amount. Decreasing term insurance is an efficient way of providing protection for a need, which also declines over a specific period. Mortgage protection, in which life insurance proceeds are used to pay off a declining mortgage balance, is the most common use of decreasing term insurance.

The Uses of Term Insurance. Critics of term insurance assert that "you must die to win". This contention is based on the absence of survival benefits or cash values in term insurance policies. This argument ignores the fact that reduction of the insured person's· anxiety is the primary reason for buying insurance.

Few consumers have enough money to pay for all of the life insurance benefits they want. Most buyers must make a trade off among their various needs. The two perils covered by life insurance policies are premature death and outliving one's earning capacity. While term insurance protects against the peril of premature death, it offers no cash values that might be needed during the period of retirement. However, if the need for protection against the financial consequences of premature death outweighs the need to accumulate a savings fund, term insurance may provide the answer.

Term insurance is generally recommended when the consumer has the greatest need for temporary protection. For example, there is a great need for protection when a married couple has small children and the death of either spouse might cause serious financial problems. This period is also usually a time of low family income. Recognizing that both family discretionary income and the need for a savings fund may increase over time, the convertible option is usually recommended in term insurance.

Borrowers often use term insurance as a means of providing funds with which to repay debts in the event of death. Banks and other lending institutions almost invariably require credit life insurance in term form as additional security for loans.

Whole Life Insurance

Originally all life insurance was term insurance. However, many consumers as they grew older found it difficult to pay the increasing term insurance premiums. A need developed to provide for level annual premiums during the lifetime of the insured. To meet this demand, the actuaries developed whole life insurance.

A whole life insurance policy is a contract that provides for periodic payment of premiums as long as the insured lives. The policy remains in force so long as premiums are paid. Should the policyholder decide to discontinue his policy, he may surrender it for the nonforfeiture, or cash surrender, value. Cash values grow at an increasing rate throughout the life of the policy as the policy reserves build up. Eventually, usually after about twenty years, the cash values of the policy exceed the total amount paid in as premiums by the policyowner.

As shown in Table 9.3, rates for whole life insurance are higher than for term insurance because the insurer must eventually pay either the beneficiary (death proceeds) or the policyholder (cash values) as contrasted with term insurance in which there is only the possibility that the beneficiary might have to be paid.

TABLE 9.3   Typical Premiums for Life Insurance Contracts
(cost per year per $10,000 insurance, age 21)

Contract	Participating	Non-Participating
Term		
Five Year Convertible Renewable Term	$ 47.40	$ 40.50
Twenty Year Decreasing Term	28.50	26.80
Whole Life		
Continuous Pay	156.30	117.80
Life Paid Up at 65	168.60	132.80
Twenty Pay Life	267.10	201.90
Endowment		
Twenty Year Endowment	474.70	432.90
Endowment at age 65	190.60	154.90

Types of Whole Life Insurance. The straight life insurance policy requires premium payments until death or age ninety-nine, which is the last year of the mortality table.

A limited-pay whole life policy provides for premium payments for a specified number of years, after which the policy is "paid-up." A paid-up life insurance policy no longer requires the payment of premiums in order to keep the face value of the contract in force. After the policy is paid for, it remains in force (without additional payments) until the time of death of the insured or the surrender of the policy in exchange for the nonforfeiture values. Limited-pay life insurance policies are commonly paid in twenty years, thirty years, or at age sixty-five. The level premium for a limited-pay policy is higher than that for a straight life policy issued at the same age. However, the cash values in the limited-pay policy accrue more rapidly than in a straight whole life policy. Thus, the limited-pay policy places a greater emphasis on savings and estate accumulation.

Uses of Whole Life Insurance. Whole life insurance is used to protect against a long range or permanent exposure to the financial consequences of premature death. It is also used to accumulate a savings fund. Life insurance death benefits may provide a flow of income to dependents, be used to pay estate taxes, provide an estate administrator with sufficient cash to carry out the estate plans, and so forth. Alternatively, the cash values may be used for a variety of needs, including payment of children's education, retirement income, funds for immediate business, or personal use.

Whether or not whole life insurance is an appropriate purchase depends upon the needs of the consumer. If life insurance protection is required for the duration of the consumer's life, whole life insurance is the least expensive form of individual life insurance policy. The use of term insurance to cover a permanent need for protection will ultimately require a greater financial outlay by the policyholder than a continuous pay whole life policy. This results from more conservative actuarial assumptions used in the calculation of term insurance rates. Whole life insurance is the most popular form of individual insurance because it provides permanent protection with savings and requires a fixed level annual premium for life. The cost of this insurance is low but varies considerably among companies.[2]

Endowment Plans. An endowment policy is a life insurance contract that promises to pay the face of the policy if the insured is alive at the end of a specified period or at any time during the policy term in the event that the insured dies. A "pure endowment" would be a contract that paid benefits only in the event of survivorship. From the standpoint of its structure, an endowment

---

[2] Joseph M. Belth, "The Relationship Between Benefits and Premiums in Life Insurance," *The Journal of Risk and Insurance*, XXXVI (March, 1969), p. 19.

insurance policy is a combination of term insurance and a pure endowment. A whole life policy is an endowment at age 100. Most endowments are written for varying periods between ten and thirty years. The premium for an endowment policy is higher than that for a whole life policy issued at the same age because the insurer must develop reserves equal to the face of the policy within the contract period, which is shorter than that for whole life.

The endowment policy is sometimes regarded as having two different parts: decreasing term or protection and increasing investment or savings as seen in Figure 9.1. This concept is a close approach to the actual benefit flows. With an endowment policy the insured may surrender the policy at any time and collect the nonforfeiture values. As the reserves increase so do the cash values, which represent the investment element of the endowment policy. Concurrently, the insurance protection declines to zero at maturity of the policy.

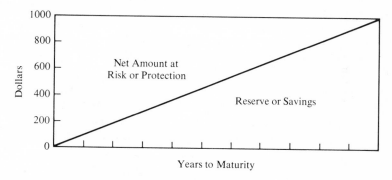

FIGURE 9.1   The Endowment Policy as Protection and Savings

The advantages of an endowment are directly related to the advantages of insurance as a savings medium. These advantages include: a strong incentive to save because of the way in which premiums are collected, a hedge against premature death during the savings period, a means of delaying or possibly avoiding federal income taxes on interest earned, and safety of principal superior to most other investments available to the individual. Some insurance analysts refer to the endowment as an "insured savings program." This is too strong a description. The guarantee of the savings program is contingent upon continued payment of premiums, just as the growth of a savings account is dependent upon periodic deposits.

If protection is the main concern of the policyowner, the endowment is the most expensive way to buy it.[3] The endowment policy is an excellent means for accumulating a fund of savings for some specific object, such as a college education or for retirement.

---

[3]Industrial life insurance sold on a weekly or monthly debit basis is most commonly on the endowment form and, per $1,000 of coverage, is the most expensive form of life insurance. It is sold primarily to low-income groups, to provide for burial expenses.

Special Life Policies

Family Income Policies.   Family income plans vary greatly but have one feature in common: they combine a certain amount of permanent (whole life) insurance with additional term insurance, the latter decreasing gradually to parallel decreasing family needs as children grow toward employment age. At the end of the family income period, the premium drops to the level necessary to cover the cost of the permanent portion of the policy.

Juvenile Insurance.   Juvenile policies covering the life of a child are common. However, these policies usually have a small face amount. While many juvenile policies are low cost continuous pay whole life insurance, many are limited-pay policies designed to provide paid-up protection when the child reaches his majority. This kind of policy is frequently bought by grandparents as gifts for their grandchildren. One popular policy is the Jumping Juvenile, a policy which automatically jumps to five times its face value when the child reaches age twenty-one. This policy provides the child with a guarantee of insurance availability regardless of his later health.

Juvenile insurance should not be purchased unless the child's parents are themselves adequately provided for. The child is dependent on the income flow provided by the parents and is best protected when those income flows are assured. The existence of a juvenile policy will do the child little good if his father dies and premiums cannot be continued.

LIFE INSURANCE RIDERS

Insurers have developed numerous "riders", which may be attached to a policy, in order to give standardized life insurance contracts some flexibility in meeting the needs of insurance consumers. The advantages of these riders are dependent upon the needs of the individual consumer. The consumer should consider the value of the riders and decide whether they are worth the cost. Table 9.4 provides data on the relative cost of the principal options. To neglect a basic

TABLE 9.4   Typical Costs of Life Insurance Riders
(per $1,000 of insurance, age 21)

Option	Amount
Guaranteed Insurability	$1.19
Disability Income	.24
Double Indemnity	.82

insurance need in order to obtain a "bargain" rider would be an inefficient use of limited funds. Two commonly used policy riders are the guaranteed insurability rider and disability waiver-of-premium rider.

The Guaranteed Insurability Rider

The guaranteed insurability rider provides that the insured may purchase, at stipulated intervals (e.g., every three years) an additional amount of insurance under his existing policy without proof of insurability. This option is available for any permanent life insurance contract and may be exercised at the election of the insured. Generally, the number of times that the option can be exercised is restricted, and it is not available after the insured reaches some limiting age, such as forty-five. For example, an insured, age twenty-five, might be guaranteed the right to purchase $5,000 of additional insurance every three years for a period of fifteen years. Thus, the insured is given five options to purchase additional policies of $5,000, or a total addition of $25,000. The cost of this rider is determined both by additional premiums waived by the insurer on those policyholders who might become high risks, and the higher losses incurred on policies selected under the option because of adverse selection against the insurance company.

The guaranteed insurability rider is particularly useful for the individual whose present need for permanent life insurance protection is minimal. While existing needs may be small, changing economic and personal conditions might dictate the purchase of additional life insurance later. The guaranteed insurability rider offers a hedge because it guarantees that the additional insurance may be purchased at a later date or dates without evidence of insurability. Thus, to cover potential future needs the insured is not forced to purchase more insurance than his present circumstances dictate. For example, a young unmarried high school or college graduate might presently require only enough life insurance to cover expenses associated with burial expense and debts. This graduate might anticipate marriage and growing family responsibilities in the next few years. His requirements for life insurance are two: immediate protection and the possibility of buying increased future protection. A small whole life policy with the guaranteed insurability rider may be a good way to fulfill both requirements. Many life insurance companies offer the guaranteed insurability benefit as a separate insurance policy rather than as a rider.

Disability Waiver-of-Premium Rider

The disability waiver-of-premium rider guarantees the policyholder's premiums will be waived should he become totally disabled. The insurer continues the policy in force until the insured recovers. Dividends are continued, and cash values increase without deduction. There is usually a six month waiting period, but premiums paid during this period are refunded if the disability exceeds the six month waiting period.

LIFE INSURANCE POLICY OPTIONS

The owner of a life insurance policy has the right to select from several sets of benefit distribution options. The most important options are nonforfeiture and settlement options. In addition, the holder of a participating policy has the right to select a dividend option. The policyholder should decide carefully among these options because proper selection can improve the flow of benefits, and improper selection may result in a misdirection of resources. However, because individual needs and goals vary there is no one set of best options.

Nonforfeiture Options

After an initial period of one or two years, all types of permanent life insurance (whole life, limited-pay life, and endowment) contain cash values that are available to a policyholder who has terminated his contract. The methods used in calculating these nonforfeiture values are prescribed by law. Prior to the adoption of nonforfeiture laws, many whole life policies contained no surrender values. It was not uncommon for destitute policyholders to auction the rights in their contracts. The highest bidder would continue premium payments and hope for the insured's early death. In some cases, the early death of an insured occurred under mysterious circumstances.

TABLE 9.5 Typical Nonforfeiture Values
(per $10,000 of whole life insurance issued at age 21)

Policy Years Elapsed	Cash or Loan Values	Paid-Up Insurance	Extended Insurance Years - Days
1	$ 000	$ 000	0/0
2	60	230	3/111
3	140	690	10/265
4	320	1,130	16/348
5	460	1,590	21/144
6	550	1,850	23/048
7	660	2,170	24/308
8	760	2,430	25/331
9	870	2,720	26/312
10	980	2,980	27/198
20	2,240	5,300	28/235
Age 62	5,500	8,270	20/340
Age 65	5,970	8,530	19/201

Nonforfeiture options, or the method by which cash values are distributed upon termination of the policy before maturity, include: cash, extended term, and paid-up insurance. Table 9.5 presents the alternative nonforfeiture benefits available from one insurer.

Cash Option.   The cash option allows the insured to receive the cash values in a lump sum. Use of the cash nonforfeiture option is not the only method that allows removal of cash funds. By use of a policy loan the insured may obtain a cash distribution without terminating the policy. If the insured needs only temporary use of the cash values, a policy loan is a better solution than lapsing the policy. However, if there is no longer a need for insurance, use of the cash nonforfeiture option is appropriate.

Extended Term Option.   The extended term option allows the insured under a permanent or endowment policy to temporarily maintain insurance protection equal to the face value of the initial policy without further payment of premiums. The cash values in the policy are used to meet the costs of term insurance coverage. The length of the term option depends on the insured's age, existing rates, and the size of the policy. For example, if an insured, age thirty-five, terminated a policy with $1,850 in cash values (for a $5,000 policy that had been in force twenty years), the extended term option might provide the equivalent of a $5,000 term policy for approximately seventeen years.

Paid-Up Insurance Option.   The paid-up insurance option provides the insured with a whole life policy with a face value less than that of the initial policy. For example, a thirty-five year old insured with $1,850 in accumulated cash values might obtain a paid-up whole life policy with a face amount of $2,800. Because the insured pays no fresh acquisition expenses, such as the costs of selling and underwriting, he obtains a larger policy than if the cash option were taken and another paid-up policy purchased with the funds.

Settlement Options

The purpose of settlement options is to provide the policyholder with alternative methods for managing the life insurance proceeds. Failure to select a settlement option that is compatible with the insured's estate goals and the capabilities of the beneficiaries may defeat the purpose of the life insurance.

Settlement options include: lump sum, interest only, fixed amount income, fixed period income, and life income. All but one of the options, the lump sum payment, stipulate that the insurer will fully manage and distribute the funds. Because it is an expense assumed in the premium calculations, management of the proceeds is not a direct cost to the beneficiary. However, the settlement options are relatively rigid in that the insurer cannot be given discretion in distributing the proceeds. They must be distributed precisely according to the terms of the option selected. This is unlike a trust, whereby the trustee may distribute the funds as in the best interests of the trust beneficiary. However, a fee must be paid to obtain trustee management. The "free" management provided by the insurer is an important benefit in a life insurance policy.

Lump Sum Option. Under the lump sum option the insurer pays the face value of the policy (less any policy loans outstanding) to the named beneficiary, and all contractual obligations are terminated. Once the proceeds are distributed under this plan, the beneficiary cannot avail himself of the options that provide management of the policy proceeds. The lump sum option is usually selected when the proceeds must be used immediately after death to pay estate taxes, administrative expenses, or to fulfill an immediate obligation (e.g., a business purchase agreement funded with life insurance). The cash option may also be used if the other options fail to meet the desired objectives of the policyholder or the beneficiary. For example, the cash may be invested in a portfolio of common stocks to offset the peril of inflation.

Interest Only. The interest only option allows for the proceeds to remain with the insurer and for the beneficiary to receive only interest payments for a predetermined period of time. In addition, the beneficiary might be given the right to make periodic withdrawals of the principal. After the predetermined period, the insurer will distribute the principal under one of the other options.

Fixed Amount Option. Under the fixed amount option, as shown in Table 9.6, the insurer distributes the proceeds in predetermined monthly sums until both the proceeds and any interest earned are distributed.

TABLE 9.6   Fixed Amount Option: Typical Proceeds Required to Provide a Desired Monthly Income

	Monthly Income			
Years of Income	*$50*	*$100*	*$150*	*$200*
	Proceeds Required			
5	2,792	5,584	8,376	11,167
10	5,203	10,406	15,609	20,812
15	7,279	14,553	21,835	29,113
20	9,075	18,149	27,224	36,298
25	10,616	21,232	31,848	42,463

Rights of withdrawal may be given with this option, but any withdrawal will reduce the length of time for which the fixed amount will be paid.

Fixed Period Option. The fixed period option stipulates that the insurer will pay all proceeds and interest over a specified period of time (See Table 9.7).

TABLE 9.7   Fixed Period Option: Typical Monthly Installments
(3 percent interest assumption)

Length of Fixed Period	$10,000 Proceeds	$20,000 Proceeds	$50,000 Proceeds
5 years	$179.10	$358.20	$895.50
10	96.10	192.20	480.50
20	68.70	137.40	343.50
30	41.80	83.60	209.00

If the beneficiary does not survive the fixed period, all remaining payments are made to a secondary beneficiary or the commuted value of the payments is paid to the estate of the beneficiary. The fixed period option does not allow for the right of partial withdrawal. If withdrawal were allowed, the insurer would incur the cost of recalculating the amount to be paid in the fixed period. However, the beneficiary may be given the right of full withdrawal.

Life Income Option. Use of the life income option furnishes the beneficiary with a fixed income for as long as she lives (see Table 9.8). This is also referred to as the annuity option. Frequently, the insurer will guarantee a specific number of payments (until the face of the policy is returned), and should the beneficiary die prior to receiving the guaranteed amount, payments will continue to a secondary beneficiary.

TABLE 9.8   Life Income Option: Typical Monthly Installments
(3 percent interest assumption)

Age of Beneficiary	$10,000 Proceeds	$20,000 Proceeds	$50,000 Proceeds
30	$32.30	$ 64.60	$161.50
40	35.70	71.40	178.50
50	45.20	90.40	226.00
60	57.20	114.40	286.00
65	66.80	133.60	334.00

Dividend Options

Life insurance issued by a mutual insurance company will usually be participating; that is, policyholder dividends are earned or paid at the end of each year. Table 9.9 indicates the dividends that were paid by a typical mutual insurance company in 1972. For competitive reasons, some stock insurers have also issued participating policies which provide for dividends. It is a misconception to think of dividends as the payment of profits that otherwise would go to stockholders. In practice, dividends represent the return of an overcharge. The premium calculated for a participating policy is based on conservative estimates of mortality, interest, and expenses. Dividends are paid out of gains resulting from variations of actual as compared to expected experience. Nonparticipating insurance policies will generally have lower gross premiums than similar participating policies written by the same company. Premiums for nonparticipating policies are calculated on less conservative cost assumptions.

TABLE 9.9   Typical Dividend Record

(per $10,000 participating whole life insurance, issued age 21)

Policy Year Elapsed	Annual Dividend	Accumulated at Interest (5%)	Total Paid-Up Additions
1	$00.00	$ 00.00	$ 00.00
2	19.20	20.00	69.00
3	24.40	45.00	155.00
4	29.70	78.00	259.00
5	34.90	118.00	279.00
10	61.60	437.00	1,217.00
20	87.20	1,680.00	3,475.00
Age 62	–	7,779.00	9,265.00
Age 65	–	9,485.00	10,377.00

Dividend options include: cash, accumulation at interest, paid-up additions, additional term, and accelerated payment of the policy.

Cash.   Under the cash option, dividends are paid directly to the policyholder or used to reduce the premium payable in the next year. If the policy is paid-up, direct payment is the only available cash option. However, if premiums are due for the following year, the bill may indicate the gross premium, dividends payable, and the resulting net premium payable.

Accumulation at Interest.   The policyholder may leave dividends with the insurer to accumulate at a guaranteed interest rate (see Table 9.9). By allowing dividends to accumulate, the policyholder emphasizes life insurance as a savings vehicle. Dividends on a $10,000 continuous pay policy issued at age twenty-one may amount to as much as $9,485 at age sixty-five in the case of a typical mutual life insurance company. Cash values at age sixty-five for the same policy would be approximately $5,970. As a matter of law, insurance companies are not permitted to guarantee or predict what future dividends will be. Such forecasts are usually misleading.

Paid-Up Additions. While dividends may provide additional savings, they can alternatively provide additional protection (either term or whole life). The paid-up additions option uses dividends to purchase paid-up participating insurance. Because the purchase is based on the net single premium rate, as opposed to the larger gross single premium normally charged consumers, this is the least expensive way of purchasing paid-up insurance. No commission or other expense loading is included in the premium for the paid-up additions. While the dividends purchase relatively small paid-up amounts, the accumulation of these sums can lead to a substantial increase in protection (see Table 9.9). For example, with an illustrative $10,000 policy, at age sixty-five, the paid-up additions would provide more than $10,000 of additional insurance protection. Furthermore, the paid-up policies accrue nonforfeiture values and may be surrendered for cash.

Additional Term Option. The one-year term option uses the dividends to purchase additional term insurance protection. However, the option usually does not allow the additional term insurance to exceed the existing face value of the initial policy. Dividends in excess of those required to purchase this limited amount of term insurance are distributed under one of the other dividend options.

Accelerated Payment of Policy. The accelerative option is used to prepay the initial contract in a shorter period of time. Dividends are credited directly to cash values, thus reducing the amount at risk for the insurer (face of policy less the nonforfeiture values). If this option is used, the payment at death remains the face value. If dividends are left to accumulate at interest, death payments would equal the face value of the policy plus all accumulated dividends.

STATUTORY PROVISIONS IN LIFE INSURANCE CONTRACTS

Most states have enacted legislation designed to standardize the terms and conditions of life insurance policies. While the law varies from state to state, most have adopted the approach of New York which defines three classes of provision as mandatory, prohibited or permissible. These provisions are important because they determine the rights and obligations of the parties to the contract.

Mandatory Provisions

Required standard provisions often required include: (1) how premiums are payable; (2) grace period; (3) entire contract; statements deemed representations; (4) incontestability; (5) misstatement of age; (6) participation in surplus;

(7) policy loans; (8) nonforfeiture benefits and cash surrender values; (9) tables of values and options; (10) reinstatement; (11) settlement; (12) table of installments; (13) title.

Generally, premiums are payable in advance. A grace period of one month is provided for late payment of premiums after the first year. The policy and the application for insurance attached to it constitute the entire contract between the parties and all statements by the insured in the absence of fraud are deemed representations and not warranties. After a policy has been in force on the life of an insured for two years the insurance company may not contest it except for nonpayment of premiums. This is the incontestable clause, one of the most important features of a life insurance agreement. The misstatement of age provision states that if the age of the insured has been misstated, the amount payable under the policy will be that which the premium would have purchased at the correct age at the time the policy was issued. Misstatement of age will not void the policy but will merely reform it.

Policyholders who have participating policies are entitled to participate in the surplus of the company to the extent that they have a right to annual credits or distributions of dividends declared by the company. This provision is designed to avoid the tontine feature whereby only long-term survivors might share in the profits of the company. The policy loan provision offers the insured the right, after the policy has been in force for at least three years, to borrow against the cash values in the policy. Nonforfeiture benefits are options available to the policyholder in case he fails to pay the premium in a life insurance policy. These include cash surrender values, extended term insurance, and paid-up life insurance. Each life insurance policy is required to include a table of values and options available under the policy each year upon default in premium payments, during the first twenty years of the policy or during the premium-paying period if less than twenty years.

The reinstatement clause provides that in the event of default in premium payments the policy may be reinstated at any time within three years from such default upon evidence of insurability satisfactory to the company and payment of arrears of premiums and the payment or reinstatement of any other indebtedness to the company on the policy with interest. It is much less costly to the insured to reinstate a lapsed policy than it is to purchase a new one. The settlement provision requires payment of claims to be made upon receipt of due proof of death. If settlement options are available, the policy must provide a table of installments showing the amounts which are guaranteed. Finally, a policy must have a title on the face and back which describes its nature and form briefly and accurately.

Prohibited Provisions

In most states a policy of life insurance may not include certain restrictive provisions. If they are found in the policy the courts will ignore them. A policy may not (1) limit the time within which a lawsuit may be commenced to less than one year after the cause of action occurs; (2) backdate a policy more than six months before the original application was made in order to lower the premium to age last birthday; (3) provide for any mode of settlement at maturity of less value than the amount insured by the policy; (4) provide for forfeiture of the policy for failure to repay any loan on the policy, or to pay interest on such a loan, while the total indebtedness on the policy, including the interest, is less than the loan value; (5) provide that the agent soliciting the insurance is the agent of the insured under the policy, or making the acts or representations of the agent binding upon the insured person.

Permissible Provisions

Mandatory provisions set minimum standards for policy provisions and may be exceeded by the insurance company. Most companies offer more liberal terms than the statutory minimums. Prohibited provisions are intended to protect the insured against unreasonable restrictions. The permissible provisions allow some latitude to insurance companies in avoiding some types of claim not calculated in the premiums. Coverage may be excluded in the event of (1) death from military service in wartime; (2) death within five years as a result of war while traveling outside the United States, its possessions, or Canada; (3) suicide within two years from the policy's date of issue; (4) death resulting from certain types of aviation accident; (5) death resulting from certain hazardous occupations, if it occurs within two years from the date of issue; (6) death if it occurs as a result of a specifically excluded "ridered" cause.

REVIEW QUESTIONS

1. Why is reinstatement of a lapsed policy more advantageous to the insured than the purchase of a new contract? Explain.

2. Joe is a junior at the university, single, healthy, and age 20. He is working his way through school doing part-time jobs on campus. He has no savings. A friend recommended to him that he should start his life insurance program right away because insurance companies charge less at younger ages. He is considering a five year term policy, a whole life insurance contract, and a twenty year endowment. All of these plans are available for the $20 per month Joe feels he can set aside. (a) Which of these plans will provide the greatest amount of protection? Which will provide the least? (b) What are the factors that Joe should consider in making his purchase decision? Explain.

3. Describe the benefits available with whole life insurance which are not available with term insurance.

4. Under what set of circumstances is term insurance best advised?

5. Under what circumstances would you recommend the purchase of an endowment?

STUDY QUESTIONS

6. It has been suggested that life insurers do not compete favorably with financial institutions which offer equity products. Discuss.

7. Describe the facts that must be proven by a life insurance company seeking to rescind a life insurance policy on the grounds of fraud.

8. Four years ago, "A" took out a $10,000 life insurance contract and designated his wife, "B," as revocable beneficiary. With "B's" consent, "A" recently assigned the contract to "C" as security for a $5,000 character loan, an absolute assignment form being used and recorded with the insurance company. A few days ago, "A" was killed in an automobile accident. What will be the disposition of the insurance proceeds? Explain. Would your answer be the same if "C" were not a creditor? Discuss.

9. The American Association of Suicidology estimates that as many as 8,000 of the nation's reported 55,000 annual auto accident deaths might properly be added to the 22,000 annual recorded suicides. One study estimated that about 15 percent of drivers in fatal automobile accidents were "conscious, goal-directed suicides." How does an insurance company determine the cause of death? How is suicide detected for purposes of the suicide clause? Explain.

10. The inflation problem is an important concern for life insurance buyers because their long-term contracts promise to pay in fixed dollars which do not increase in amount as the cost of living rises. How can life insurance policies be made inflation proof? Discuss.

10

Life and Health
Insurance Contracts: II

ANNUITIES

While life insurance is protection against the peril of premature death, an annuity is protection against the peril of living too long. An annuity protects against out-living either capital or the capacity to work. An annuity is based on the same pooling concept used in life insurance. Those annuitants who die early make a contribution toward payment of the benefits received by the annuitants who survive longer than the average. The annuity benefit is composed of three parts: return of principal, interest, and an insurance benefit. While other financial instruments, such as savings accounts, mutual funds, and trusts, provide a means of liquidating principal and interest, only an annuity furnishes the insurance benefit that results from the pooling of risks. An annuity is the only financial instrument that can guarantee a flow of benefits for exactly the same period of time as an individual lives. There are basically two types of annuities: fixed dollar and variable.

Fixed Dollar Annuities

A regular annuity guarantees the annuitant a fixed monthly income for as long as he lives. While the annuity is usually based on the continuation of one life, it is possible to arrange the benefit flow to be contingent upon the survival of several individuals. A joint and last survivor annuity provides coverage based on two or more annuitants. Payment is continued so long as any one of the annuitants is alive. This type of annuity is typically used for a husband and wife. To match benefit flows more efficiently with the needs of the annuitants, a larger amount is frequently paid while both are alive, and a reduced amount after a spouse has died. Since the cost of living is higher for two, the varying benefit flows meet the needs of the couple more appropriately.

Even if an annuity is based on several lives, there is no guarantee that total payments to all beneficiaries will reach any specified amount. For example, both the husband and the wife may die within a year of purchasing the annuity. Some annuitants seek a guarantee that the insurance company will pay back at least some minimum dollar amount. To meet this need, insurers sell a refund annuity and a period certain annuity.

Under the refund annuity, the insurer makes total payments that at least equal the premium paid. The refund to a secondary beneficiary if death of the annuitant occurs prior to receiving the full amount of the premiums may be either a lump sum or a continuation of periodic payments.

The period certain annuity is used to guarantee payments for some specified period. Following the guarantee period, benefits continue until the death of the annuitant. Although the joint and survivorship, refund and period certain annuities provide flexibility to the flow of benefits, they may also reduce the benefit amounts. The guarantees create a cost for the insurer, which is offset by reduced benefit flows. Table 10.1 indicates the benefits available under alternative annuity plans.

Variable Annuities

The fixed dollar benefit annuity provides protection against the perils of

TABLE 10.1 Typical Monthly Annuity Benefits
(per $1000 paid to insurer)

Age*	Regular Annuity	Joint and Last Survivor	Ten Years Certain
45	$6.01	$5.15	$5.82
50	6.37	5.37	6.16
55	6.86	5.63	6.65
60	7.54	6.03	7.28
65	8.49	6.62	8.01
70	9.64	7.43	8.82

*Assume husband is primary annuitant and wife is same age.

longevity, but not against inflation and a rising cost of living. To offset these two perils, insurers developed the variable annuity. Under a variable annuity, the insurer guarantees to pay a fixed number of variable annuity units per month so long as the annuitant lives. The value of the unit fluctuates as does the value of a separate portfolio of securities. Monthly benefits equal the number of units received per month multiplied by the value of each unit. The variable annuity is based on an assumption that a correlation exists between the cost of living and the value of a diversified stock portfolio. While this assumption may not be valid in the short run, the assumption has been reasonably valid over long periods.

PENSION FUNDS

While Social Security provides a source of income to the majority of the aged in the United States, the benefit philosophy of Social Security is to provide only a floor of protection; that is, a survival income. If an individual seeks to achieve a retirement income above the poverty level, he must participate in a private retirement income program. A private pension plan is one of several alternatives available for offsetting the risks associated with outliving one's capacity or opportunity to work. Other techniques include: reliance on accumulated wealth, dependency on relatives and friends, or welfare programs. However, most individuals either disdain dependency or lack the capacity to accumulate a capital fund. Thus, as shown in Table 10.2, the pension fund movement has grown rapidly as a mechanism for providing retirement security.

TABLE 10.2 Growth of Pension Program in the United States
(number of persons covered)
(000)

Year	Insured Plans	Noninsured Plans	Government Administered Plans [a]
1930	100	2,700	2,677
1935	285	2,525	2,481
1940	695	3,565	3,618
1945	1,470	5,240	6,746
1950	2,755	7,500	6,455
1955	4,105	12,290	7,713
1960	5,475	17,540	8,893
1965	7,040	21,060	10,754
1970	10,980	24,100	12,832

[a]Railroad workers, federal employees, and state and local employees.

SOURCE: *Life Insurance Fact Book 1973.* (New York: Institute of Life Insurance, 1973).

Pension Funds: The Alternative Plans

Early pension plans were seldom written contracts. They were casual promises given by the "boss" that all loyal employees would be compensated in their old age. The fulfillment of these promises was often discretionary, and funds were not earmarked for benefits. Such a program is called an informal pension plan. This is in contrast to a formal pension plan where the specific rights and requirements of all plan participants are defined in a written contract. However, a formal pension plan does not guarantee that the employer will accumulate a fund to meet all pension liabilities. Only if the pension is funded will assets be segregated. If the pension plan is not funded, payment is made out of the employer's income at the time of each employee's retirement. Unfunded plans are "owe as you go." Pension obligations accrue while the employee remains with the firm, and the obligation is paid at time of retirement if funds permit.

If the pension program is funded, the funding instrument may be either a trust or insurance. Should a trust be selected, the pension is called a self-insured plan, and if an insurer is used it is called an insured plan. If the pension program adopts both funding instruments, the plan is called a split fund.

Finally, a pension program may be classified as either non-qualified or qualified. Under a qualified program, the employer's contributions are an allowable business deduction from federal income taxes. Furthermore, the employer's contributions are not treated as taxable income to the employee in the year in which pension plan contributions are made. In order to deduct employer contributions, the program must meet specific requirements with regard to benefit structures, eligibility requirements, and funding.

Insured Pension Plans: Funding Instruments

To be flexible in meeting the funding requirements of a pension program an insurer generally offers several alternatives. Examples of insurance funding instruments include: a single premium individual annuity, a level premium individual annuity, a group deferred annuity, a group deposit ·administration annuity, or a permanent life insurance contract.

With a single premium annuity contract, the employer purchases a separate annuity contract for each employee. This approach is frequently used at the inception of a new pension program to provide benefits for employees who have retired or are approaching retirement. The single premium annuity contract is seldom used in ongoing programs.

To allow the employer to distribute the cost of funding the retirement benefits evenly over the employees' working years, an insurer can sell the employer a level annual premium annuity. So long as the level premium is paid for each employee until his retirement, the insurer guarantees a specific retirement income. As an alternative to contracting for several individual annuities, the employer might select a group deferred annuity. Under this plan the insurer provides a deferred retirement annuity for each qualified employee. Only one master contract is issued; the employee receives a certificate that indicates participation under the group contract.

Under insured annuity programs, pension liabilities are immediately offset. The employer's contributions are used to purchase annuity benefits for each employee. Assuming the insurer remains solvent, both the employer and employee are secure in their belief that specified annuity benefits will be paid. However, to obtain this security the employer reduces his flexibility with regard to the determination of his annual pension plan costs. To meet the needs of employers with varying cash flows, insurers developed the Deposit Administration Annuity. With a Deposit Administration Annuity, the employer's contributions do not immediately purchase an annuity, but rather accumulate until the employee retires. At the time of an individual employee's retirement, a portion of the accumulated funds is used to purchase a single payment immediate annuity due. Accordingly, the insurer assumes no risk and gives no guarantee until an employee's retirement. Because of the flexibility provided by the Deposit Administration Contract, this plan is the most popular arrangement presently offered by insurers. Flexibility is provided not only with regard to annual cash payments but also with regard to eventual retirement benefits (e.g., the relationship between average salary and benefits), the appropriate retirement age, and actuarial assumptions (on which to base annual payments). With regard to the latter assumptions, the employer is free to adopt the recommendation of an independent actuarial consultant. This provision allows customers to avoid using insurer actuarial assumptions which are sometimes considered too conservative.

In addition to annuity contracts, the pension obligation can be funded with the purchase of permanent life insurance; either an individual or a group contract. The cash values accompanying permanent life insurance can be used to provide the desired retirement benefits. In addition to accumulating cash values for retirement income, a permanent life insurance contract also provides protection against the premature death of an employee. Should the employee die prior to retirement, his beneficiary receives the death benefits. The size of the permanent life policy will vary according to the type of policy selected (e.g., whole life, limited pay life, endowment, or retirement income policy) and the level of retirement benefits desired.

Pension Plans: General Characteristics

In designing an insured pension plan, the employer must make decisions in the following areas of retirement plan design: employee eligibility, benefit formula, employee contributions, vesting, and costs.

(1) Eligibility.   A pension plan will seldom cover all employees. To eliminate coverage for part-time or seasonal workers and thus simplify and control administrative costs, participation in a pension program is usually restricted. Because pension benefits are usually provided as a stimulus to and reward for long service, employers generally do not cover classes of employees that have demonstrated high turnover rates. Eligibility is often contingent upon either a specified length of employment or a minimum (or maximum) age. While the Internal Revenue Service does not require that all employees be covered, qualification for tax deduction is lost if eligibility criteria are unfairly discriminatory against a class of workers.

(2) Benefit Formula.   There are two basic classes of benefit formula: (a) the defined benefit method by which benefits are fixed and employer contributions vary, and (b) the defined contribution method by which benefits vary and the employer contribution is fixed.

The defined benefit formula may be based on either a flat amount, a flat percentage, or a unit benefit. Under the flat amount formula, all participants in the pension program receive the same retirement income upon attainment of the specified normal retirement age. If the flat percentage formula is employed, benefits are related to an employee's average earnings. No reward is given for service beyond a specified maximum number of years. Finally, under a unit benefit formula the retirement income is a factor of the number of units each employee obtains multiplied by a specified value per unit. Generally a unit represents a year's service. For example, an employee might receive five dollars for each unit, and with thirty years' service his retirement income would be $150 per month.

Should a defined contribution formula be adopted, the employer (or the employer and employee) is assigned a specified rate of contribution, and actual retirement income will vary with age, income, and length of service at time of normal retirement. Employers often will insist on this arrangement because it allows them to tie their contributions to some fixed unit of production or employee effort. For example, contributions may be based on a specified number of cents per man hour worked or per item of finished product or a specified percentage of profits above a minimum level. Such a program allows the firm to budget the cost of the pension plan. While this method provides definite costs for the employer, it does create uncertainty as to eventual benefits. Generally, benefits will equal the amount that the defined contributions can obtain.

(3) Employee Contribution.   If the cost of a pension program is fully paid by the employer, it is called a non-contributory plan. However, should the employee be required to make partial payment, the program is referred to as a

contributory program. While the non-contributory plan has the advantage of automatically covering all qualified employees at no cost to the employees, it has the potential disadvantage of providing inadequate benefits. In some cases, employee contributions are a prerequisite to the initiation of any pension program, particularly if the employer does not have sufficient discretionary funds to support a viable pension program. In addition, when the employee makes a contribution to the pension plan his dollars purchase more benefits than they could in most individual private programs. It is argued by proponents of contributory plans that such programs generate better employee appreciation and understanding of the program. If the employee makes a contribution (however slight) to the cost of the program, the plan is less likely to be ignored or allowed to be mismanaged. Alternatively, employers may prefer a non-contributory plan as it may allow them complete discretion in the management of the program. However, even in non-contributory plans unions insist upon participation or review of pension management. The strongest support for a non-contributory plan relates to the tax status of payments. Employer payments to a qualified pension are deductible for income tax purposes, while contributions made by employees are made from after-tax personal income.

(4) Vesting. An employee has a right to recover his contribution to a pension plan should he leave the program prior to retirement. However, whether the employee who withdraws from employment can reach the contributions of the employer will depend on the extent of vesting. Vesting has been defined as "attainment by a participant of a benefit right, attributable to employer contributions, that is not contingent upon a participant's continuation of specified employment."

Vesting may be: immediate or deferred; conditional or unconditional; full or partial. If vesting is immediate, the employee has immediate rights in the contributions of the employer. However, if deferred vesting is used the employee does not obtain rights in employer contributions until the fulfillment of a specified condition such as age or years of service. Conditional vesting occurs when the program prescribes conditions which must be met before vesting will occur. For example, a common condition for vesting is that the employee leave his cash contribution in the program. Should he voluntarily withdraw his contribution prior to a specified date, vested benefits would be sacrificed. With regard to the amount of vesting, the right to the employer's contribution may be full or partial. Partial vesting exists when only a specified portion of the employer's contribution becomes available as a vested benefit for each employee. An example of partial vesting is graded vesting. Under this arrangement, the amount of vested benefits increases with each year of additional service, and after a specified number of years full vesting may be obtained.

(5) Costs.   In determining or estimating the potential costs of a pension fund, an actuary must make careful estimates as to mortality and morbidity or sickness rates for the group covered by the pension, interest earned, expenses incurred, average retirement ages, future salary levels, withdrawal rates, and changes in compensation levels. However, these are only the objective factors that contribute to the net cost of a pension plan. Subjective factors such as employee morale and productivity and employee turnover rates, while admittedly difficult to measure, must also be considered.

Separate Accounts

Until the 1960s trustees had greater flexibility in meeting the investment demands of pension managers than insurance companies. Trustees were not restricted, as were insurers, to investing most of the fund's assets in fixed dollar obligations. Life insurers were severely limited in the extent to which they could invest pension fund contributions in common stock. With a trust fund program contributions could be invested in any medium which met both the dictates of the trust agreement and the laws pertaining to investments for trusts. To offset this competitive advantage inherent in a trust arrangement, insurers were allowed to establish separate accounts for pension fund assets. Separate account assets are not commingled with the general assets of an insurer, and general policyholders assume none of the investment risk associated with a separate account. Accordingly, regulators allow insurers to invest separate account assets with virtually the same flexibility and discretion given trusts. While some pension programs are sufficiently large to justify the establishment of a special separate account, most separate accounts include the contributions of several pension programs.

HEALTH INSURANCE

Health insurance provides indemnification of the direct financial expenses associated with illness or accident. The indirect loss of income which may accompany a loss of health is covered by disability income insurance. Health insurance benefits include: hospitalization, surgical and medical expense, major medical and comprehensive insurance. In 1972, according to the Health Insurance Institute, Americans received $21.4 billion in private health insurance benefits of which $10.7 billion was paid by insurance companies.[1] Those

---

[1] *The Weekly Underwriter*, May 12, 1973, p. PH 4. In the 1972 *Economic Report of the President* (U.S. Gov't. Printing Office, Washington: 1972), p. 135. The Nation's medical expenditures for all types of medical care in fiscal 1971 were estimated at $75 billion. Life

persons covered by insurance company policies received $3.8 billion toward hospital bills, $1.1 billion for surgical and dental fees, and $2.0 billion in disability income insurance benefits. In addition to the $4.9 billion paid out for hospitals, surgical and dental costs under commercial policies, an additional $3.3 billion was paid out through major medical expense insurance. The fastest growing branches of the health insurance field in 1973 were major medical expense and disability income. In 1946, there were 26 million persons with loss of income protection, including 14 million through insurance companies. In 1972, there were 60 million with short term protection, through insurance companies, formal paid sick leaves and employee benefit plans, and an additional 13 million Americans had long term protection.

Hospitalization

Hospitalization coverage is designed to pay for hospital expenses. The types of expense covered, and the amounts paid, vary by type of policy. For example, the insurance may pay up to $30 per day in the hospital to cover room and board, or the coverage may be for the cost of a semiprivate room with no specific daily maximum allowance. Obviously, the premium varies with the extent and amount of coverage.

Hospital insurance is the most popular health insurance coverage in the United States. Policies are issued by insurance companies, by Blue Cross Associations, and by independent prepayment plans. The rapid inflation of hospital costs has created a serious lag between *per diem* benefit levels and actual hospital charges.

Surgical and Medical Expense Insurance

Surgical and medical expense insurance covers the costs associated with specified surgical procedures and ordinary in-hospital physicians' care. The benefits are usually scheduled at a specified maximum amount for each of many surgical procedures, and premiums vary with the extent and amount of coverage.

Surgical schedules are designed in terms of relative value units as determined by the various medical associations. The limit per procedure is

insurance companies accounted for less than 15 percent of the total health bill. Health benefit payments by all insurance companies in 1971 were $9.7 billion. The U.S. Social Security Administration, Office of Research and Statistics estimated that insurance payments for personal health care expenditures were $0.9 billion in 1950, or 8.5 percent of a $10.5 billion total, and $19.0 billion in 1972, or 26.4 percent of a $71.9 billion total. These figures include more sources than private health insurance carriers. See *Building a National Health-Care System* (New York: Committee for Economic Development: 1973), p. 13.

intended to reflect the relative cost of that procedure as compared with other surgical procedures. For example, an operation for miscarriage of a child might have a scheduled benefit of $25; removal of a malignant tumor of the skin, $50; appendectomy, $100. By setting relative value limits, insurers hope to reduce possible abuse. Unfortunately, the insured has no way of knowing in advance what procedures he may need during the policy period, and he has difficulty in deciding what schedule of benefits is most appropriate for his case.

Major Medical and Comprehensive Insurance

Major medical insurance is designed to provide coverage for the catastrophic event. Major medical is blanket coverage for all medical bills above a deductible amount, which is usually large. The deductible may be the amount of benefits generally provided under hospitalization and surgical insurance plus a small fixed dollar deductible. For example, a major medical policy might provide $10,000 of blanket coverage above: (1) what a basic health insurance policy pays, and (2) a $100 deductible. Furthermore, there usually is a coinsurance clause that restricts indemnification to a specified percentage, usually 80 percent of all covered expenses. Thus, after the basic coverage was exhausted, major medical might pay 80 percent of all expenses, up to $10,000, less $100.

Prepaid Medical Service

While a significant portion of health insurance is furnished by private health insurance companies, a growing share is provided through group prepaid service organizations (i.e., Producers' Cooperatives). Included in this latter group are: (1) the "blues", and (2) group practice prepayment programs. Blue Cross and Blue Shield are cooperative health insurance plans offered by nonprofit corporations. Blue Cross does not pay the insured but rather furnishes the services of hospital care in authorized hospitals (i.e., a cooperating hospital). Blue Cross is not a single national program. It is a system of more than seventy-five regional corporations. Coordination of the regional corporations is a task of the American Hospital Association and the Blue Cross Association. Blue Shield is a similar program of more than seventy-five regional corporations organized by medical societies for the provision of surgical services.

Of growing importance are group prepayment plans designed to provide most or all of an individual's medical needs for a specified monthly fee. The most significant group prepayment plan is the Kaiser Foundation Program, which provides coverage for more than 2,000,000 individuals. Because this program covers most medical services, including periodic visits to doctors' offices, it places an important emphasis on loss prevention activities. This is expected to lead to reduced demand for hospital services and a decline in overall health protection costs.

DISABILITY INCOME INSURANCE

The consequential loss of income resulting from illness or injury may have a catastrophic effect on an individual's financial program. To offset this risk, a person may buy a disability income insurance policy that provides monthly payments in case of interruption of income due to accident or illness. The extent of payment usually depends upon whether the insured is totally or partially disabled, and whether the disability is temporary or permanent. Furthermore, benefits do not generally begin until after a waiting period. The longer the waiting period, the lower the premium. However, as the waiting period increases, the decline in premiums becomes proportionately smaller. Most policies pay benefits for a maximum number of months or years, but lifetime benefits or benefits until age sixty-five are available.

Disability Defined

Of particular importance to the purchaser of disability income insurance is the definition of the term "disability." The definition may vary significantly by policy and by company. For example, one policy may define disability as inability to perform the duties of one's *own* occupation. Another insurer may define disability as inability to perform the duties of *any* occupation. This is generally interpreted to encompass any occupation that the insured may perform considering his training, experience, and education. Whereas the latter definition is less liberal, its use should result in lower premiums. The definition of partial disability also varies widely among insurance policies.

Work Incentives

The provision of partial disability benefits may serve as an incentive for returning to work. If partial disability benefits are provided, the insured does not need to remain totally incapacitated to continue receiving benefits. The insured may return to work in a limited capacity and continue to collect partial disability benefits. Not only does this reduce the insurer's cost, and thus the cost of the insurance, but it also provides the disabled worker with the pride of self-support.

PROBLEMS AND ISSUES IN HEALTH INSURANCE

The health insurance field is controversial because of public demand for better health care delivery systems and improved coverage by private health insurance companies. Critics contend that too small a proportion of the health bill is actually paid from insurance company benefits. In part, this is because policyholders are unwilling or unable to pay the cost of full coverage and the moral hazard of overutilization of services makes full coverage extrahazardous to insurance companies. The ways in which insurers have limited their exposure give rise to important questions of public policy.

One of the issues is whether the commercial insurer, paying cash benefits, is more effective than the nonprofit plan paying benefits in terms of units of hospital, surgical, or medical service. How important is freedom of choice in the selection of hospitals, surgeons, and physicians? How can costs be compared when the services being offered are so varied in quality and quantity?

A second issue is the extent to which the population is covered by voluntary health insurance. Commercial insurers are only able to reach a fraction of the market. Through community enrollment procedures, some of the private nonprofit plans have been able to extend that market. But until virtually the entire population is covered by some form of health insurance, the average costs and distribution of coverages will probably be higher than they need to be.

The problem of overutilization is a difficult one because the capacity of the medical care system in the United States cannot meet the needs of those for whom hospitalization or medical care might properly be recommended. Various studies have shown that overutilization varies widely among patients with no insurance, limited commercial insurance, and Blue Cross insurance.[2] Controlling overutilization by requiring financial contributions by the patient is counterproductive because it provides him with incentives to avoid obtaining proper medical care in time because of the cost factor.

Matters that are of current concern are: policy limitations, such as cancellation clauses, which give the insurer the right to cancel a policy upon the occurrence of an accident or illness; nonrenewal clauses, which permit the insurer to get off the risk at time of policy renewal; preexisting conditions clauses, which permit the insurer to deny claims for accidents or illnesses arising out of conditions that existed prior to inception of the policy; schedule benefit limits, which are grossly inadequate to cover actual outlays for health care services; and substantial delays in delivery of medical care services.

SUMMARY

Life and health insurance are generally considered as efficient means for offsetting the financial consequences of death, disease, or disability. To provide the desired security from these perils, the consumer may select from a broad

---

[2] See O. D. Dickerson, Jr., *Health Insurance*, 3rd ed. (Homewood, Ill.: Richard D. Irwin, Inc., 1968), p. 383.

spectrum[3] of life and health insurance products. Life insurance products include: term insurance, whole life insurance, endowments, and annuities or pensions. Health insurance products include: hospital and surgical covers, group prepaid medical plans, major medical policies, and disability income insurance.

Selection of the most efficient set of policies depends upon the needs and financial resources of the individual consumer. In addition to the various policies there are numerous riders and options provided by the insurer to give flexibility to the contract. Judicious selection of these options plays a key role in achieving the specific insurance goals of an individual.

REVIEW QUESTIONS

1.   Outline the principal types of annuity available at present. Explain each briefly.

2.   Differentiate between Blue Cross, commercial health insurance, and prepaid medical service.

3.   Should an employee be obliged to contribute toward his pension or retirement fund? Explain.

4.   Discuss the pros and cons of compulsory retirement at age 65 from the standpoint of pension and business economics.

5.   Distinguish between *funding* and *vesting* in pension plans.

STUDY QUESTIONS

6.   Jefferson claims that he does not need health insurance because he is covered by both workmen's compensation and unemployment insurance. Do you agree? Discuss.

7.   Describe the principal features of a group major medical insurance contract.

8.   Health Maintenance Organizations (HMOs) with prepaid comprehensive service are regarded by many critics of the American health care delivery system as the optimum solution to the medical economics problem. HMOs provide members with service on a group practice basis rather than cash indemnities. However, freedom of choice of physician or hospital is restricted. Compare and contrast the programs offered by commercial insurance companies and those of HMOs in terms of costs and benefits provided.

9.   What is the difference between a profit sharing plan and a pension plan funded with insurance? Explain, indicating the relative merits of the profit sharing agreement.

---

[3]William Rudelius and Glenn L. Wood, "Life Insurance Product Innovations," *The Journal of Risk and Insurance*, XXXVII (June, 1970), p. 169.

10. The Ajax Electronics Corporation has an executive staff of 22 senior officers, a technical staff of 250 engineers, and an unclassified staff of sales clerks, typists, warehousemen, etc., of 2,000. The officers of the corporation want to install a pension plan which will provide each of the 22 senior officers with full income for life upon retirement at age 60; the technical staff are to receive 30 percent of their final pay for life upon reaching age 65; the remaining staff are to pay for their own retirement, which is compulsory at age 70. Are there any tax problems with which this firm is likely to be beset? If no, explain. If yes, outline the statutory requirements of a qualified plan.

11

Property and Liability
Insurance Contracts: I

INTRODUCTION

In 1946, the U.S. property and liability insurance industry collected slightly over
$3 billion in premiums, held approximately $7.8 billion in total assets, and had
accumulated policyholder surplus equal to $3.8 billion. As indicated by Figure
11.1, by 1970, the same industry accounted for over $27 billion in written
premiums, $50 billion in assets, and $20 billion in policyholder surplus. The
American consumer has an increasing need for the protection offered by
property and liability insurers. The increased demand for insurance results in
large measure from three factors: (1) the number of exposures to risk has grown,
(2) the value of the individual risks has increased as a result of inflation, and (3)
the consumer is more conscious of his need for insurance protection.

PROPERTY INSURANCE

Property insurance indemnifies the insured for physical damage to, or
destruction of, personal or commercial property resulting from the occurrence
of specified perils. All risk policies cover loss caused by any perils except those
enumerated among the exclusions. Losses covered include both the cost of

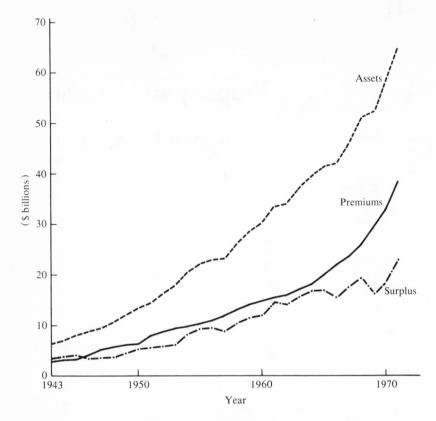

FIGURE 11.1   Growth of Property and Liability Insurance: U.S.A.

replacing or repairing the destroyed or damaged property and the indirect or consequential losses. Consequential losses may be instantaneous, such as spoiled food because the refrigeration system was damaged, or continuing, such as lost earnings because a manufacturer could not fill orders for goods. The potential for loss is a direct function of both the amount of property at risk and the usefulness or replaceability of the property.

A rising standard of living and the mechanization of industry have increased the number of personal and commercial exposures to property damage. As the number of cars, boats, and other items of personal property has increased, so has the number of real property exposures, such as homes and commercial buildings. Added to these are the increasing values of commercial and industrial equipment, fixtures, and inventory. The consequential losses that accompany the destruction of property have also increased. These are measured by lost profits or added expense. As the income generated from property increases, so does the potential for consequential losses. Furthermore, as the cost of replacing the services provided by property increases, so does the potential for consequential loss.

Inflation and increased productivity have also caused the value of potential individual losses to increase. Consumers are aware of the rising cost of two of their major purchases: the house and the automobile. Businessmen are conscious of the inflated cost of buildings, equipment, and production inputs. Furthermore, the improved productivity of commercial and personal property has resulted in higher replacement values. Figure 11.2 demonstrates the improvements in industrial productivity since 1950.

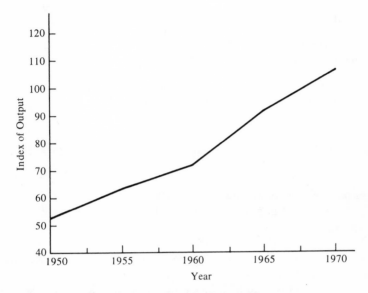

FiGURE 11.2   Industrial Productivity (1967 = 100%)

SOURCE: Statistical Abstract, U.S. 1972, p. 232.

Belted tires, seatbelts, disc brakes, and power equipment have both improved the safety of a car and increased its cost. Similarly, automatic welding machines have reduced the time to assemble a car, but they are more costly to replace than individual units of welding equipment. Furthermore, when a highly productive specialized piece of equipment is destroyed, an entire plant may be forced to close temporarily, and consequential losses may exceed the cost of replacing or repairing the damaged machine.

The growth of property insurance coverage in the United States is clearly seen in Table 11.1.

LIABILITY INSURANCE

Liability insurance indemnifies the insured for losses arising from his liability for damages to the property or person of others. The insurer agrees to pay damages

TABLE 11.1   Property Insurance Growth in the United States
($000,000)

	Stocks		Mutuals	
	1960	*1970*	*1960*	*1970*
Auto Physical Damage	$1,439	$3,275	$554	$1,548
Homeowners	617	1,960	146	604
Fire	1,387	1,835	279	363
Commercial Multi-Peril	50	1,118	4	212
Inland Marine	346	722	35	89
Extended Coverage	480	541	94	102
Ocean Marine	212	409	17	55
Allied Fire	122	227	43	78
Burglary and Theft	106	116	9	19
Boiler and Machinery	62	101	22	13
Glass	42	33	5	7

SOURCE: *Best's Aggregates and Averages: Property and Liability 1971* (Morristown, New Jersey: A.M. Best Company, 1971).

to third party claimants who have valid claims against the insured. Liability may arise from intentional interference with the rights of another, negligence, or as a matter of law.

Intentional interference includes deliberate destruction of property, trespass, vandalism, and malicious mischief. It also includes assault, battery, defamation, and false imprisonment.

Absolute liability may be imposed by law regardless of fault. Society has concluded that certain activities are so inherently dangerous that those engaging in them should be held responsible for damages resulting from accidents without requiring the victims to prove negligence. For example, absolute liability is associated with the use of dynamite or the storage of explosives.

Accompanying the growth in property ownership is an increasing liability exposure. The negligent use of property may result in a tort action against the property owner. Furthermore, just as property damage repair costs have risen, so have medical and legal costs. Not only do doctors charge higher fees for their services, but medical research and publicity have generated a demand for the benefits of an array of costly new medical care services. Table 11.2 shows the expansion of volume in the liability insurance field in the United States since 1960.

SURETY AND FIDELITY BONDS

A surety bond is a contract whereby one party, the surety or guarantor, guarantees the performance of a second party, the principal, for the benefit of a

TABLE 11.2 Liability Insurance Growth in the United States
($000,000)

	Stocks		Mutuals	
	1960	*1970*	*1960*	*1970*
Auto Bodily	$1,873	$4,093	$851	$2,116
Injury Liability	$1,873	$4,093	$851	$2,116
Workmen's				
Compensation	942	2,489	476	1,003
Auto Property				
Damage Liability	783	1,792	374	957
Miscellaneous				
Bodily Injury				
Liability	609	1,358	171	304
Miscellaneous				
Property Damage				
Liability	147	400	34	77
Fidelity and Surety	300	539	12	23

SOURCE: *Best's Aggregates and Averages: Property and Liability 1971* (Morristown, New Jersey: A.M. Best Company, 1971).

third party, the obligee. Should the principal fail to perform his agreement with the obligee, the surety will be required to pay the penalty and will be subrogated to the rights of the obligee against the defaulting principal.

A bail bond is a common type of surety contract. An accused person, the principal, obtains a bond covering the amount of bail required by the court, the penalty, from a bail bondsman, the surety. If the accused fails to appear in court at the scheduled time, the bail bondsman will forfeit the bail. Because the bail bondsman is unlikely to recover the penalty by subrogation against the "bail jumper," the accused will generally have to post collateral with the bondsman before the bond is issued. In case of default, the bondsman is indemnified by the sale of the collateral. Collateral in such cases is usually provided by the family and friends of the accused and may take many forms, such as mortgages to property, chattel mortgages, personal jewelry, and the like. The most common classes of surety bonds are judicial, license, contract, and public official bonds.

Fidelity bonds, unlike surety bonds, cover the infidelity or dishonesty of employees. They protect employers and other principals against embezzlement, forgery, and other forms of theft by employees or agents.

MARINE INSURANCE

Marine insurance contracts cover losses related to transportation. These may involve hulls, cargo, or freight. Marine contracts also cover instrumentalities of transportation such as bridges, dams, and lighthouses. Ocean marine insurance covers mainly perils of the sea. Inland marine insurance covers against losses arising from transportation other than on the ocean and on certain types of personal property wherever located. The personal property floater policy is a common example of an inland marine contract.

Marine insurance was exempted from state regulation in the United States. This permitted a greater degree of freedom for innovation in the development of multiperil policies. With the liberalization of laws relating to the branches of insurance a single company might write, property and liability insurers began to offer a wide variety of comprehensive package policies and multiperil contracts.

THE FIRE INSURANCE POLICY

Development of a Standard Contract

The provisions and wording of the fire insurance policy are prescribed by statute and are standard throughout most of the country.[1] This was not always the case. In the initial years of fire insurance there was little or no state supervision of contract provisions, and each insurer developed and implemented its own fire insurance contract. The confusion that surrounded the multitude of contracts led the states to adopt standard policies. In 1873 Massachusetts adopted the first standard fire policy, and other states gradually required one of several standard forms. Today, the 1943 New York Standard Fire Policy has become the required fire contract in all but five states. And the standard policy in these five states closely resembles the New York contract.

The growth of a standard fire insurance policy can be attributed to the following benefits of contract standardization. First, since the contract must comply with the requirements of the law, consumers have a better opportunity to determine the meaning of the policy terms. The insurer must adopt the standard contract and cannot "take away in small print what it gives in the large print." Thus, the use of a standard contract guards against the potential for insurer malpractice. Second, prolonged use of a standard contract eventually leads to the development of a detailed set of court interpretations on all wording in the contract. The body of legal precedents as to the meaning of contract language reduces the number and cost of contested claims. Third, the statutory removal of discrepancies between different fire insurance contracts expedites the settlement of losses where two or more policies cover the same property.

Despite these advantages, standardization creates potential problems. First,

---

[1] William H. Rodda, *Property and Liability Insurance* (Prentice-Hall, Inc.: Englewood Cliffs, N.J., 1966) offers detailed analyses of policy developments in fire insurance. A comparison of the California and New York versions of the Standard Fire Insurance Policy is found in Board of Fire Underwriters of the Pacific, *Comparative Digest, Index, and Timetable*, San Francisco, 1949.

product innovations are more difficult to implement. It might take several years to change a statute, and during this period of legislative consideration the consumer may not receive the benefits of product improvement. Second, contract standardization may reduce the potential for healthy competition. For example, an insurer that develops a contract innovation will not receive the exclusive benefits of its innovation because the new provision must become a part of the standard contract available to all insurers. However, while insurers are required to adopt the same basic fire insurance contract, product competition can be initiated with the use of endorsements and riders that extend or otherwise modify coverage. Furthermore, the use of standard contracts does not affect competition in the important areas of price and service.

Declarations

The declarations page in an insurance contract is designed to provide information about the risk to be insured. The declarations page of the New York Standard Fire Insurance Policy is used to identify the following:

1. the insured: his name and address
2. the property insured: its location, type of construction, and any other relevant descriptive material
3. the insurance company: its name and location
4. the insurance policy: its number
5. the premium to be paid
6. the mortgagee: its name and extent of interest in any loss payment
7. the agent who obtained the contract for the insurer
8. any endorsements or forms added to the standard policy

Insuring Agreement

Immediately following the declarations is the insuring agreement, which sets forth information on the rights and duties of the parties to the contract. The insuring agreement of the standard fire policy states:

In Consideration of the Provisions and Stipulations Herein or Added Hereto and of the Premium Above Specified (or specified in endorsement(s) made a part hereof), this Company, for the *term shown above* from *inception date shown above* at noon (Standard Time) to *expiration date shown above* at noon (Standard Time) at location of property involved, to an amount not exceeding the limit of liability above specified, does insure *the Insured named in the Declarations above* and legal representatives, to the extent of the actual cash value of the property at the time of loss, but not exceeding the amount which it would cost to repair or replace the property with material of like kind and quality within a reasonable time after such loss, without allowance for any increased cost of repair or reconstruction by reason of any ordinance or law regulating construction or repair, and without compensation for loss resulting from interruption of business or manufacture, nor in any event for more than the interest of the Insured, against all DIRECT LOSS BY FIRE, LIGHTNING AND OTHER PERILS INSURED AGAINST IN THIS POLICY INCLUDING REMOVAL FROM PREMISES ENDANGERED BY THE PERILS INSURED AGAINST IN THIS POLICY, EXCEPT AS HEREINAFTER PROVIDED, to the property described herein while located or contained as described in this policy, or pro rata for five years at each proper place to which any of the property shall necessarily be removed for preservation from the perils insured against in this policy, but not elsewhere.

Assignment of this policy shall not be valid except with the written consent of this Company.

This policy is made and accepted subject to the foregoing provisions and those hereinafter stated, which are hereby made a part of this policy, together with such other provisions, stipulations and agreements as may be added hereto, as provided in this policy.

Inception, Termination, and Renewal.   While the written contract does not go into effect until noon of a specified day, an agent can bind the contract immediately. Thus, an oral contract is usually implemented until a formal written contract is received by the insured. The termination date specifies a time after which coverage is not in effect. However, the insurer must pay for any loss which started prior to the time of termination. So long as the proximate cause of the fire originated before termination, the insurer is liable for the full loss.

Normally, the fire insurance contract runs for one, three, or five year periods. However, on occasion an insurer may issue a perpetual policy. Most standard fire contracts make no reference to the renewal of the contract.

Property and Locations Covered.   Coverage is limited to property listed in the declarations. A more detailed description of the property is usually set forth in a "form." For example, the "dwelling and contents form" is commonly used to identify the covered property. Coverage is generally restricted to property "while located or contained as described in this policy." However, coverage is extended to locations, not described, to which the property is taken for the purpose of protection from further loss by fire.

Person(s) and Interest(s) Insured.   Like all insurance policies, the fire policy is a personal contract. The policy does not insure property, but rather covers the interest that an individual has in the property.

Measurement of Indemnification.   Probably the most important part of the insuring agreement is that section which limits the amount of money to be paid in the event of an insured loss. The contract provides four factors which limit the extent of recovery: face of policy, actual cash value of loss, cost to repair or replace the damaged property, and insurable interest. The limitation imposed by the face value of the contract is given in the declarations page. Actual cash value refers to the objective material value of the property. Sentimental or subjective value is beyond the scope of analysis (except in those cases where subjective factors affect a known market value for the property). Actual cash value is usually defined as replacement cost less economic depreciation or obsolescence. The determination of replacement cost and obsolescence is not an easy task, and the results may be subject to arbitration. The standard fire policy provides procedures that will be used if the insured and insurer cannot agree as to an appropriate cash value of the loss.

The limiting factor of "cost to repair or replace" does not require the insurer to undertake the repair of the property, but rather limits payment to the costs associated with repairing or replacing the damaged property. The insured cannot be required to replace or repair the damaged item.

Finally, the insured's recovery is limited by the extent of his insurance interest in the property. For example, a partner who owns one-half of a $100,000 building is limited to a $50,000 recovery regardless of the face value of the policy. Accordingly, it is imperative that all insurable interests in the property be clearly stated in the contract.

Insured Perils. The standard fire policy covers direct loss due to fire, lightning, and removal. "Direct" loss means that a covered peril must be the proximate cause of actual damage to property. A proximate cause is one that initiates a chain of events that result in the occurrence of a contingency. Whether a fire is the proximate cause of a loss is often a question of fact to be determined by the courts.

While not precisely defined in the contract, the meaning of the three covered perils has been explored and refined by the courts. Fire has been defined as "rapid oxidation sufficient to produce either a flame or a glow." While the presence of heat or smoke may provide evidence of a fire, it does not prove that a fire existed. Ignition must be demonstrated. For example, a small scorch hole caused by a cigarette generally does not constitute a fire loss. The courts have also interpreted the standard fire policy to cover only an "unfriendly" fire. To be classified as an unfriendly fire, the fire must occur outside the container for which it was intended. For example, a fire kindled in a fireplace or furnace and remaining within these receptacles is a "friendly" fire. Once the fire jumps or spreads beyond these controlled areas, it becomes an unfriendly fire.

The New York Standard Fire Insurance Policy covers loss by lightning, which is defined as the natural discharge of electricity in the atmosphere. At one time lightning was not covered by the standard fire policy. However, lightning is a frequent cause of fire damage, and insurers found it difficult to distinguish between lightning and ensuing fire damage. Thus, the standard policy was amended to add the peril of lightning.

To stimulate loss reduction, the standard fire policy requires insureds to take all "reasonable" action to protect property threatened by fire. The contract provides coverage for any loss sustained to property in the process of removal or while exposed to the weather. While such removal losses might be interpreted as fire loss (i.e., fire was the proximate cause of the need to remove property), the inclusion of the removal peril reduces any potential confusion as to the extent of coverage.

Assignment of Policy. The fire insurance policy is a personal contract, so coverage does not automatically follow property that is sold or given as collateral. To transfer a fire policy, it must be assigned from one party to another, and to be valid this assignment must receive the approval of the insurer. The insurer desires an opportunity to evaluate the insurability of the interest of the assignee prior to granting coverage. Should the assignee be considered a higher risk than the assignor, the assignment may not be allowed. For example, an insurer does not want a suspected arsonist to have an interest in a fire insurance policy. Such a moral hazard is unacceptable. Accordingly, fire insurers consider it imperative that they retain the right to determine the parties who will have an interest in a policy. Failure to obtain insurer approval does not void the contract but rather voids the assignment. Should a loss occur, an unapproved assignment might not be honored by the insurer.

Conditions

The conditions and exclusions relevant to the policy appear in that portion of the contract called the "165 lines." Figure 11.3 provides the 165 lines of the New York Standard Fire Insurance Policy.

Concealment and Fraud. Lines 1 to 6 indicate two factors that can lead to voidance of the contract: willful misrepresentation and concealment. A misrepresentation is a statement made in either an application for insurance or a claims form that is both false and material to the insurer's evaluation of the risk. To void the contract, however, the misrepresentation must be known to the insured. Concealment includes both an intentional hiding of facts and a passive failure to provide pertinent information. However, the courts usually do not require the insured to reveal information unless asked by the insurer or agent.

Excluded Property and Perils. Lines 7 to 10 list certain property that is excluded (accounts, bills, currency, deeds, evidences of debt, securities, etc.), and lines 11 to 24 provide a list of perils not covered (war, destruction by civil authorities, neglect, theft, etc.). Property is excluded either because of the inherent problems of determining an indemnification value (e.g., manuscript) or

1 **Concealment,** This entire policy shall be void if, whether
2 **fraud.** before or after a loss, the insured has wil-
3 fully concealed or misrepresented any ma-
4 terial fact or circumstance concerning this insurance or the
5 subject thereof, or the interest of the insured therein, or in case
6 of any fraud or false swearing by the insured relating thereto.
7 **Uninsurable** This policy shall not cover accounts, bills,
8 **and** currency, deeds, evidences of debt, money or
9 **excepted property.** securities; nor, unless specifically named
10 hereon in writing, bullion or manuscripts.
11 **Perils not** This Company shall not be liable for loss by
12 **included.** fire or other perils insured against in this
13 policy caused, directly or indirectly, by: (a)
14 enemy attack by armed forces, including action taken by mili-
15 tary, naval or air forces in resisting an actual or an immediately
16 impending enemy attack; (b) invasion; (c) insurrection; (d)
17 rebellion; (e) revolution; (f) civil war; (g) usurped power; (h)
18 order of any civil authority except acts of destruction at the time
19 of and for the purpose of preventing the spread of fire, provided
20 that such fire did not originate from any of the perils excluded
21 by this policy; (i) neglect of the insured to use all reasonable
22 means to save and preserve the property at and after a loss, or
23 when the property is endangered by fire in neighboring prem-
24 ises; (j) nor shall this Company be liable for loss by theft.
25 **Other Insurance.** Other insurance may be prohibited or the
26 amount of insurance may be limited by en-
27 dorsement attached hereto.
28 **Conditions suspending or restricting insurance. Unless other-**
29 **wise provided in writing added hereto this Company shall not**
30 **be liable for loss occurring**
31 (a) while the hazard is increased by any means within the con-
32 trol or knowledge of the insured; or
33 (b) while a described building, whether intended for occupancy
34 by owner or tenant, is vacant or unoccupied beyond a period of
35 sixty consecutive days; or
36 (c) as a result of explosion or riot, unless fire ensue, and in
37 that event for loss by fire only.
38 **Other perils** Any other peril to be insured against or sub-
39 **or subjects.** ject of insurance to be covered in this policy
40 shall be by endorsement in writing hereon or
41 added hereto.
42 **Added provisions.** The extent of the application of insurance
43 under this policy and of the contribution to
44 be made by this Company in case of loss, and any other pro-
45 vision or agreement not inconsistent with the provisions of this
46 policy, may be provided for in writing added hereto, but no pro-
47 vision may be waived except such as by the terms of this policy
48 is subject to change.
49 **Waiver** No permission affecting this insurance shall
50 **provisions.** exist, or waiver of any provision be valid,
51 unless granted herein or expressed in writing
52 added hereto. No provision, stipulation or forfeiture shall be
53 held to be waived by any requirement or proceeding on the part
54 of this Company relating to appraisal or to any examination
55 provided for herein.
56 **Cancellation** This policy shall be cancelled at any time
57 **of policy.** at the request of the insured, in which case
58 this Company shall, upon demand and sur-
59 render of this policy, refund the excess of paid premium above
60 the customary short rates for the expired time. This pol-
61 icy may be cancelled at any time by this Company by giving
62 to the insured a five days' written notice of cancellation with
63 or without tender of the excess of paid premium above the pro
64 rata premium for the expired time, which excess, if not ten-
65 dered, shall be refunded on demand. Notice of cancellation shall
66 state that said excess premium (if not tendered) will be re-
67 funded on demand.
68 **Mortgagee** If loss hereunder is made payable, in whole
69 **interests and** or in part, to a designated mortgagee not
70 **obligations.** named herein as the insured, such interest in
71 this policy may be cancelled by giving to such
72 mortgagee a ten days' written notice of can-
73 cellation.
74 If the insured fails to render proof of loss such mortgagee, upon
75 notice, shall render proof of loss in the form herein specified
76 within sixty (60) days thereafter and shall be subject to the pro-
77 visions hereof relating to appraisal and time of payment and of
78 bringing suit. If this Company shall claim that no liability ex-
79 isted as to the mortgagor or owner, it shall, to the extent of pay-
80 ment of loss to the mortgagee, be subrogated to all the mort-
81 gagee's rights of recovery, but without impairing mortgagee's
82 right to sue; or it may pay off the mortgage debt and require
83 an assignment thereof and of the mortgage. Other provisions

84 relating to the interests and obligations of such mortgagee may
85 be added hereto by agreement in writing.
86 **Pro rata liability.** This Company shall not be liable for a greater
87 proportion of any loss than the amount
88 hereby insured shall bear to the whole insurance covering the
89 property against the peril involved, whether collectible or not.
90 **Requirements in** The insured shall give immediate written
91 **case loss occurs.** notice to this Company of any loss, protect
92 the property from further damage, forthwith
93 separate the damaged and undamaged personal property, put
94 it in the best possible order, furnish a complete inventory of
95 the destroyed, damaged and undamaged property, showing in
96 detail quantities, costs, actual cash value and amount of loss
97 claimed; **and within sixty days after the loss, unless such time**
98 **is extended in writing by this Company, the insured shall render**
99 **to this Company a proof of loss,** signed and sworn to by the
100 insured, stating the knowledge and belief of the insured as to
101 the following: the time and origin of the loss, the interest of the
102 insured and all others in the property, the actual cash value of
103 each item thereof and the amount of loss thereto, all encum-
104 brances thereon, all other contracts of insurance, whether valid
105 or not, covering any of said property, any changes in the title,
106 use, occupation, location, possession or exposures of said prop-
107 erty since the issuing of this policy, by whom and for what
108 purpose any building herein described and the several parts
109 thereof were occupied at the time of loss and whether or not it
110 then stood on leased ground, and shall furnish a copy of all the
111 descriptions and schedules in all policies and, if required, verified
112 plans and specifications of any building, fixtures or machinery
113 destroyed or damaged. The insured, as often as may be reason-
114 ably required, shall exhibit to any person designated by this
115 Company all that remains of any property herein described, and
116 submit to examinations under oath by any person named by this
117 Company, and subscribe the same; and, as often as may be
118 reasonably required, shall produce for examination all books of
119 account, bills, invoices and other vouchers, or certified copies
120 thereof if originals be lost, at such reasonable time and place as
121 may be designated by this Company or its representative, and
122 shall permit extracts and copies thereof to be made.
123 **Appraisal.** In case the insured and this Company shall
124 fail to agree as to the actual cash value or
125 the amount of loss, then, on the written demand of either, each
126 shall select a competent and disinterested appraiser and notify
127 the other of the appraiser selected within twenty days of such
128 demand. The appraisers shall first select a competent and dis-
129 interested umpire; and failing for fifteen days to agree upon
130 such umpire, then, on request of the insured or this Company,
131 such umpire shall be selected by a judge of a court of record in
132 the state in which the property covered is located. The ap-
133 praisers shall then appraise the loss, stating separately actual
134 cash value and loss to each item; and, failing to agree, shall
135 submit their differences, only, to the umpire. An award in writ-
136 ing, so itemized, of any two when filed with this Company shall
137 determine the amount of actual cash value and loss. Each
138 appraiser shall be paid by the party selecting him and the ex-
139 penses of appraisal and umpire shall be paid by the parties
140 equally.
141 **Company's** It shall be optional with this Company to
142 **options.** take all, or any part, of the property at the
143 agreed or appraised value, and also to re-
144 pair, rebuild or replace the property destroyed or damaged with
145 other of like kind and quality within a reasonable time, on giv-
146 ing notice of its intention so to do within thirty days after the
147 receipt of the proof of loss herein required.
148 **Abandonment.** There can be no abandonment to this Com-
149 pany of any property.
150 **When loss** The amount of loss for which this Company
151 **payable.** may be liable shall be payable sixty days
152 after proof of loss, as herein provided, is
153 received by this Company and ascertainment of the loss is made
154 either by agreement between the insured and this Company or
155 by the filing with this Company of an
156 award as herein provided.
157 **Suit.** No suit or action on this policy for the recov-
158 ery of any claim shall be sustainable in any
159 court of law or equity unless all the requirements of this policy
160 shall have been complied with, and unless commenced within
161 twelve months next after inception of the loss.
162 **Subrogation.** This Company may require from the insured
163 an assignment of all right of recovery against
164 any party for loss to the extent that payment therefor is made
165 by this Company.

IN WITNESS WHEREOF, this Company has executed and attested these presents; but this policy shall not be valid unless countersigned by
the duly authorized Agent of this Company at the agency hereinbefore mentioned.

FIGURE 11.3   The New York Standard Fire Insurance Policy

the potential for a moral hazard (e.g., money). However, several of the excluded items can be covered by an endorsement which indicates a specific value to be paid in the event of a loss. Certain perils are excluded because either: (1) the insurer does not include these factors in the calculation of rates since they may be covered by endorsements (see lines 38 to 55), (2) credible loss on which to base a charge is not available, or (3) the peril creates a catastrophic loss potential.

Suspension of Coverage.   Lines 28 to 37 give the following three conditions that suspend or reduce coverage: while the hazard is knowingly increased; while the property is unoccupied for sixty consecutive days; and following an explosion. The first two conditions only suspend coverage. Once an increase in the hazard is removed or the property reoccupied, the suspension is lifted. The rate charged the insured is based upon the status of the risk prior to issuance of the policy. Any significant increase in the hazard changes the nature of the risk. Should this occur, the insurer must have an opportunity to reevaluate the risk and decide whether to charge a higher premium or to withdraw the insurance.

Should an explosion occur, coverage is not suspended but is limited to the fire loss. However, the need to differentiate between fire and explosion damage is avoided as few fire policies are sold without an endorsement covering explosion.

Cancellation.   Lines 56 to 67 set forth the rights of each party and procedures relevant to policy cancellation. Should the insurer wish to terminate the contract, it must make a return of premium computed on a "pro rata" basis. Thus, if the insurer cancelled on March 30 a one year policy issued on January 1, it would be required to return three-fourths of the premium.

If the insured cancels the policy, the return of premium is computed on a "short rate" basis, which is an amount less than the pro rata share. Many of the expenses associated with the writing of an insurance policy are incurred prior to the inception of the policy. If a pro rata return of premium were required, the insurer would not recoup these expenses. If the insured instituted the cancellation, the insurer should not incur a financial loss. Accordingly, the short rate is used. For example, cancellation of a one year policy after four months would result in a return of only 56 percent of the total annual premium (or the insured would pay 44 percent for the four months of coverage).

Notice of cancellation by the insured may be written or oral and becomes effective at the time of its receipt by the insurer. Notice of cancellation by the insurer must be written and does not take effect until five days after the insured has been notified.

Losses.   Lines 68 to 85 deal with the rights and duties of a mortgagee in the event of a loss. Even though the mortgagee is not a direct party to the contract, it has distinct rights that are recognized in the contract. However, to protect these rights the mortgagee must fulfill certain conditions. For example, should the insured fail to file a proof of loss statement (i.e., a required inventory of losses), the mortgagee must file one if it is to retain a right of collection.

Lines 86 to 89 introduce and define the concept of pro rata liability. If there is more than one fire insurance policy covering an interest in the same property, recovery from any one insurer is limited to each insurer's proportion of the total loss. For example, assume a building has an insurable value of $300,000 and that insurers A and B have each written a $200,000 insurance policy on the property. Assume further that there is a total loss due to fire. Each insurer will pay its proportion of the loss; that is, $150,000 each. Because of the pro rata liability clause, the insured will not collect $200,000 from each, or a total of $400,000. If the insured could collect $400,000, the concept of indemnification would be violated, and a socially unacceptable moral hazard would be created.

Lines 90 to 122 outline the following steps an insured must take in the event of a loss: (1) give immediate notice, (2) protect the property from further loss, and (3) file a "proof of loss" within sixty days of the loss. The terms "immediate" and "protect" are subjective, and the insurer will pay so long as the insured is reasonable in complying with these fundamental requirements. Because they recognize the insurer's vested interest in any loss, the courts tend to use a narrow translation of the term "immediate." Immediate notice allows the insurer to (1) institute an investigation of the loss while the evidence is still available and fresh, and (2) take action to reduce further damage to the property.

Should the insured and the insurer disagree as to an appropriate loss settlement, lines 123 to 140 provide the avenues of redress. Each party selects an appraiser, and the two appraisers select a neutral umpire to review the loss. The majority decision is binding.

While the insurer usually pays the insured in cash, lines 141 to 147 specify that the insurer has the option to repair, replace, or rebuild the damaged property. In practice most insurers avoid this option because of the potential for litigation on the quality of their repair work.

Lines 148 to 149 indicate that the insured cannot abandon the damaged property to the insurer. The damaged property remains the responsibility of the insured.

As indicated in lines 150 to 156, the insurer is required to pay all losses within sixty days after both receipt of the proof of loss and agreement by the two parties on an appropriate settlement.

The subrogation rights of the insurer are given in the last few lines. The insurer, upon payment of the loss, obtains the insured's right to proceed against and collect from any third party whose alleged negligence caused the loss.

Need for Endorsements

In itself the standard fire contract is not a complete or valid insurance policy. The fire contract must be supplemented with one or more forms that describe either additional property, perils, or losses covered. The purpose of the added forms is to clarify or extend the coverage. By judiciously selecting among the over 200 forms that can be used with the standard fire policy, the insured can design a policy that is compatible to his specific needs. The insuring agreement of the standard fire policy is intentionally general in nature; the forms are designed to specifically define the property, perils, and losses particular to an individual policy. While most of the over 200 forms have been developed by the rating bureaus, the large or unusual insured (e.g., large corporate risks) may be able to negotiate with an insurer in the design of unique forms.

COMPREHENSIVE AND SCHEDULED POLICIES

In addition to the sale of individual policies designed to cover specific perils, property and liability insurers offer all risk, or comprehensive, insurance. The term "all risk", while frequently used in insurance, is a misnomer. No rational insurer is willing to cover risks to property or people regardless of potential hazard. Not only would the cost be prohibitive, but the resulting moral and morale hazards might violate the public interest. Of all the policies written by property and liability insurers, the Comprehensive Glass Insurance Policy is one of the few which most nearly approaches all risk. However, even this policy excludes the perils of destruction or damage by fire, rebellion, war, and nuclear energy.

The comprehensive policy is a contract which indemnifies the insured, under one insuring agreement, for losses caused by all risks with the exception of specifically excluded individual perils. The comprehensive policy may be contrasted with the scheduled policy, which is a contract to indemnify for loss resulting from one or more specific perils. A peril must be named in order to be covered by a scheduled policy. In a comprehensive policy, all perils are covered unless specifically excluded in the contract.

ANALYSIS OF THE HOMEOWNER'S POLICY

The Homeowner's policy as shown in Figure 11.4 is the most popular form of property insurance coverage in the United States for individuals and families. It is a multi-peril policy covering most of the risks associated with home ownership, including dwelling and contents property damage by fire and allied perils, theft, consequential losses, and some forms of personal liability. Those who rent apartments or houses, as tenants, may obtain a similar policy covering their insurable interests.

The advantages of the comprehensive homeowner's policies include: broad and necessary protection without expensive overlaps or dangerous gaps in coverage, and reduced costs of sales, underwriting and service for the one contract as compared with the separate agreements which were formerly necessary. The cost of the homeowner's policy is less than the premiums charged for separate policies for all of the covered perils. Furthermore, the package approach results in more extensive use of certain types of insurance, such as windstorm and hail, which might otherwise not be purchased. Finally, dwellings covered under such policies usually have higher insurance to value ratios, which make possible reduced costs per $100 of insurance.

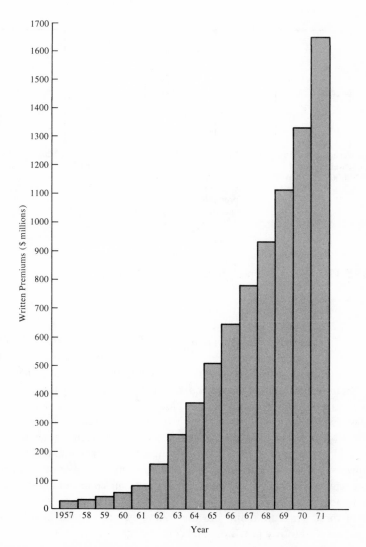

FIGURE 11.4   Growth of Homeowner's Insurance (000,000)

SOURCE: Insurance Facts 1972, p. 13

The homeowner's policy has evolved into five standard forms:[2] (1) basic, (2) broad, (3) special, (4) contents broad, and (5) comprehensive. The broad form is the most widely adopted. As shown in Figure 11.5, the Broad Form Homeowner's Policy is divided into two distinct parts: Property Insurance (Section I), and Liability Insurance (Section II).

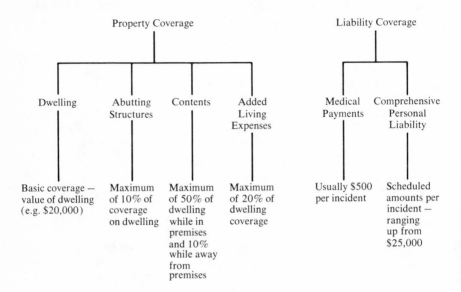

FIGURE 11.5   Homeowner's Insurance (Broad Form)

Property Coverage (Section I)

Perils Covered.   The standard fire policy and the extended coverage endorsement provide the basic contract for the coverage of property risks. The insuring agreement is the same as with the standard fire insurance policy.

Section I of the homeowner's policy lists the following "other perils insured against": windstorm or hail; explosion; riot or civil commotion; aircraft; vehicles; sudden and accidental damage from smoke; vandalism and malicious mischief; breakage of glass; theft; falling objects; weight of ice, snow, or sleet; collapse of buildings or any part thereof; sudden and accidental tearing asunder, cracking, or bulging of a steam or hot water heating system or of appliances for heating water; freezing of plumbing, heating, and air conditioning systems; and sudden and accidental injury from electric currents artificially generated. While many of these perils are defined in the policy, the precise meaning of each term depends upon statutory provisions and court interpretations.

---

[2]John Eugene Pierce, Development of Comprehensive Insurance for the Household. (Homewood, Ill.: Richard D. Irwin, Inc., 1958) provides an excellent background description of the evolution of comprehensive personal coverages.

Exclusions. Some losses caused by listed perils are not insured. The "war exclusion" of the standard fire policy is frequently used to restrict or limit the extent to which loss by a named peril is covered. Furthermore, the property section of the policy contains the same list of excluded losses as given in the standard fire policy. These exclusions include flood, earth movement, the enforcement of local or state ordinances relevant to the construction or repair of property and power or heating failure.

Property Covered. The homeowner's policy does not cover all of the property owned or controlled by the insured. While coverage on contents is comprehensive, coverage on the dwelling and appurtenant structures is scheduled. For a structural item to be covered, it must be specifically listed on the declarations page of the policy. However, all contents in the structure are covered, except for the eight types listed in Coverage C—Unscheduled Personal Property.

Description of Property and Interests Covered
Coverage A—Dwelling

This policy covers the described dwelling building, including additions in contact therewith, occupied principally as a private residence.

This coverage also includes:

1. if the property of the Insured and when not otherwise covered, building equipment, fixtures and outdoor equipment all pertaining to the service of the premises and while located thereon or temporarily elsewhere; and
2. materials and supplies located on the premises or adjacent thereto, intended for use in construction, alteration or repair of such dwelling.

Coverage B—Appurtenant Structures

This policy covers structures (other than the described dwelling building, including additions in contact therewith) appertaining to the premises and located thereon.

This coverage also includes materials and supplies located on the premises or adjacent thereto, intended for use in construction, alteration or repair of such structures.

This coverage excludes:

1. structures used in whole or in part for business purposes; or
2. structures rented or leased in whole or in part or held for such rental or lease (except structures used exclusively for private garage purposes) to other than a tenant of the described dwelling.

Coverage C—Unscheduled Personal Property

This policy covers unscheduled personal property usual or incidental to the occupancy of the premises as a dwelling and owned or used by an Insured, while on the described premises and, at the option of the Named Insured, owned by others while on the portion of the premises occupied exclusively by the Insured.

This coverage also includes such unscheduled personal property while elsewhere than on the described premises, anywhere in the world:

1. owned or used by an Insured; or
2. at the option of the Named Insured,
    a. owned by a guest while in a residence occupied by an Insured; or
    b. owned by a residence employee while actually engaged in the service of an Insured and while such property is in the physical custody of such residence employee or in a residence occupied by an Insured.

The limit of this Company's liability for the unscheduled personal property away from the premises shall be an additional amount of insurance equal to 10 percent of the amount specified for Coverage C, but in no event less than $1,000.

This coverage excludes:

1. animals, birds or fish;
2. motorized vehicles, except such vehicles pertaining to the service of the premises and not licensed for road use;
3. aircraft;
4. property of roomers and boarders not related to the Insured;
5. property carried or held as samples or for sale or for delivery after sale;
6. property rented or held for rental to others by the Insured;
7. business property while away from the described premises; or
8. property which is separately described and specifically insured in whole or in part by this or any other insurance.

Coverage D—Additional Living Expense

If a property loss covered under this policy renders the premises untenantable, this policy covers the necessary increase in living expense incurred by the Named Insured to continue as nearly as practicable the normal standard of living of the Named Insured's household for not exceeding the period of time required:

1. to repair or replace such damaged or destroyed property as soon as possible; or
2. for the Named Insured's household to become settled in permanent quarters; whichever is less.

This coverage also includes:

1. the fair rental value of any portion of the described dwelling or appurtenant structures covered under this policy, as furnished or equipped by the Named Insured, which is rented or held for rental by the Named Insured. The fair rental value shall not include charges and expenses that do not continue during the period of untenantability. Coverage shall be limited to the period of time required to restore, as soon as possible, the rented portion to the same tenantable condition;
2. the period of time, not exceeding two weeks, while access to the premises is prohibited by order of civil authority, as a direct result of damage to neighboring premises by a peril insured against.

The periods described above shall not be limited by the expiration of this policy.

This coverage excludes expense due to cancellation of any lease, or any written or oral agreement.

Conditions. The insurer places a number of restrictive conditions upon the coverage to reduce the chance of unexpected losses caused by significant increases in hazard. The standard fire insurance policy contains the following conditions which also provide a basis for suspension of coverage in the homeowner's policy: (1) while the hazard is increased by any means within the control or knowledge of the insured, or (2) while the described building whether intended for occupancy by owner or tenant, is vacant or unoccupied beyond a period of sixty consecutive days. Failure to meet the foregoing conditions may result in termination of the policy or denial of a claim.

Liability Coverage (Section II)

Perils. A typical liability insuring agreement in a homeowner's policy provides the following covers:

1. Personal Liability

This Company agrees to pay on behalf of the Insured all sums which the Insured shall become legally obligated to pay as damages because of bodily injury or property damage, to which this Insurance applies, caused by an occurrence. This Company shall have the right and duty, at its own expense, to defend any suit against the Insured seeking damages on account of such bodily injury or property damage, even if any of the allegations of the suit are groundless, false or fraudulent, but may make such investigation and settlement of any claim or suit as it deems expedient. This Company shall not be obligated to pay any claim or judgment or to defend any suit after the applicable limit of this Company's liability has been exhausted by payment of judgments or settlements.

2. Medical Payments to Others

This Company agrees to pay all reasonable medical expenses, incurred within one year from the date of the accident, to or for each person who sustains bodily injury to which this insurance applies caused by an accident, while such person is:

1. on an insured premises with the permission of any Insured; or
2. elsewhere, if such bodily injury
   a. arises out of a condition in the insured premises or the ways immediately adjoining,

    b. is caused by the activities of any Insured, or by a resident employee in the course of his employment by any Insured,

    c. is caused by an animal owned by or in the care of any Insured, or

    d. is sustained by any residence employee and arises out of and in the course of his employment by any Insured.

While the personal liability section has been referred to as comprehensive liability protection, it is more appropriately classified as specified peril coverage. The cost of liability resulting from the hazard of negligence is the one peril against which the insured is protected. This is comprehensive only to the extent that it covers all losses resulting from the alleged negligence of the insured.

Supplementary Payments. In addition to reimbursement for losses due to a long list of named perils, the insurer usually agrees to pay (in addition to any specified policy limits):

    1. all expenses incurred by this Company, all costs taxed against the Insured in any defended suit and all interest on the entire amount of any judgment therein which accrues after entry of the judgment and before this Company has paid or tendered or deposited in court that part of the judgment which does not exceed the limit of this Company's liability thereon;

    2. premiums on appeal bonds required in any such suit, premiums on bonds to release attachments for an amount not in excess of the applicable limit of liability of this policy, but without any obligation to apply for or furnish any such bonds;

    3. expenses incurred by the Insured for such immediate medical and surgical relief to others as shall be imperative at the time of the accident;

    4. all reasonable expenses, other than loss of earnings, incurred by the Insured at this Company's request.

Exclusions. The principal exclusions found in the Liability Section of the homeowner's policy include bodily injury or property damage liability arising out of: ownership, maintenance, operation, use or loading of any aircraft, motor vehicle, recreational vehicle or watercraft; rendering of or failing to render professional services; and business pursuits of any insured. These exclusions eliminate aspects of the liability risk that can be covered more efficiently under other insurance contracts. For example, the insurer selling homeowner's insurance has no desire to duplicate protection provided by an automobile insurance contract. Such duplication would tend to increase the cost of providing homeowner's protection and penalize insureds not exposed to the automobile liability risk.

Additional exclusions include: liability assumed by the insured under any contract or agreement not in writing, and injuries covered by workmen's compensation.

Persons Covered. The term "insured" generally means the named insured stated in the declarations of the policy, a spouse, relatives, and children (under age twenty-one) who are residents of the household.

REVIEW QUESTIONS

1. What is the relationship between the growth of industrial productivity and the need for property insurance?

2. What is the meaning of "fire" as it appears in the insuring clause of the fire insurance policy, and what kind of fire is covered? Explain.

3. Phil is insured under a fire insurance policy covering his personal property in his apartment. Last night there was a fire which caused a lot of damage. What are the requirements which Phil must meet in order to collect for this loss? Explain in terms of the standard fire insurance policy.

4. "The Homeowner's Policy is the final word. It puts everything the insured needs into a single policy. With a life insurance program and a Homeowner's Policy, there are no further gaps." Do you agree? Discuss.

5. What are the advantages to both the insurer and the consumer of a comprehensive policy?

STUDY QUESTIONS

6. Given the following facts, how much can the insured collect from his insurance company?

Value of property	$100,000
Face of policy	$ 30,000
Coinsurance requirement	80 percent
Loss	$ 2,400

7. Helen was a guest at a dinner party in the home of Florence. During dinner, Helen reached over a lighted candle to spear an olive. The flame set fire to Helen's sleeve, and the damage was estimated at $30. Helen carries $10,000 fire coverage on her home and $4,000 on her furniture. Florence carries $5,000 on her home and $1,000 on furniture. Under which policy is Helen's damaged sleeve covered and paid? Under which policy is it excluded? Explain.

8. Fire forced the closing of a college one week after the beginning of the fall term. Students were dismissed for the entire quarter, and tuition was refunded to all students whose accounts were paid. All of the faculty were under full salary for the quarter. What coverage would protect the college against loss of tuitions, faculty salaries, and so on? Explain. Would your answer be different if the fire had occurred one week before the beginning of the quarter? Discuss.

9.   What features of the fire insurance policy attempt to control moral hazard? Discuss.

10.   Company "X" insured the home of "A" for $10,000. Company "Y" was also on the line for $5,000. A fire caused damage which was adjusted for $2,000. Does "A" collect $1,000 from each insurance company? Explain.

12

Property and Liability
Insurance Contracts: II

THE FAMILY AUTO POLICY

The percentage of families owning one or more cars, as shown in Table 12.1, has been rising steadily in the United States. This increase in motorization is a world-wide phenomenon. The operation of an automobile exposes an individual to a number of potential sources of loss, including property damage and personal injury. In addition, there are varying degrees of exposure to tort liability. Figure 12.1 shows the growth of economic losses arising from auto accidents.[1]

The noncommercial automobile owner may purchase any one, or all, of the following coverages: liability insurance (both property and bodily injury); physical damage insurance; medical payment insurance; and uninsured motorists' insurance. While each policy can be purchased separately, they can be obtained in a package called the Family Automobile Policy. Table 12.2 outlines the coverages available and the limits of payment under each section of the Family Auto Policy. The Family Automobile Policy is available to both individuals and to sole proprietors or partnerships. It is the most popular of the many policy forms sold in the United States.

[1] Calvin H. Brainard, *Automobile Insurance.* (Homewood, Ill.: Richard D. Irwin, Inc., 1961) is a comprehensive text on this subject. See also, C.A. Kulp and John W. Hall, *Casualty Insurance,* 4th ed. (New York: The Ronald Press Company, 1968).

169

TABLE 12.1   Households Owning Cars

	CARS	
	One or more	Two or more
1960, all households	75.0%	16.4%
1970, all households	79.6	29.3
Annual income: $		
Under $3,000	42.5	4.5
$3,000–$3,999	64.1	9.7
$4,000–$4,999	75.7	17.9
$5,000–$5,999	83.2	17.8
$6,000–$7,499	88.9	25.3
$7,500–$9,999	91.6	34.7
$10,000–$14,999	95.9	48.4
$15,000–$24,999	96.6	62.2
$25,000 and over	95.3	66.6
1971, all households	80.0	29.8
Annual income: $		
Under $3,000	43.6	5.6
$3,000–$4,999	70.2	11.3
$5,000–$7,499	85.2	22.4
$7,500–$9,999	91.3	32.9
$10,000–$14,999	94.9	46.3
$15,000–$24,999	96.9	61.5
$25,000 and over	95.5	67.2

SOURCE: *Statistical Abstract of U.S.,* 1972, p. 328.

The Family Automobile Policy is designed to provide broad coverage for those perils associated with the ownership, maintenance or operation of an automobile. The policy is generally divided into four sections: (1) physical damage to the automobile of the insured, (2) liability arising out of the use of the insured's car, (3) medical payments, and (4) uninsured motorists' protection.

Physical Damage

The physical damage section of the automobile policy usually covers the insured for the following perils:

1. Comprehensive (excluding Collision): to pay for loss caused other than by collision to the owned automobile or to a non-owned automobile. For the purpose of this coverage, breakage of glass and loss caused by missiles, falling objects, fire, theft or larceny, explosion, earthquake, windstorm, hail, water, flood, malicious mischief or vandalism, riot or civil commotion, or colliding with a bird or animal, shall not be deemed to be loss caused by collision.

2. Collision: to pay for loss caused by collision to the owned automobile or to a nonowned automobile but only for the amount of each such loss in excess of the deductible amount stated in the declarations as applicable hereto. The deductible amount shall not apply to loss caused by a collision with another automobile insured by the company.

3. Fire, Lightning, and Transportation: to pay for loss to the owned automobile or a nonowned automobile caused (a) by fire or lightning, (b) by smoke or smudge due to a sudden, unusual and faulty operation of any fixed heating equipment serving the premises in which the automobile is located, or (c) by the stranding, sinking, burning, collision or derailment of any conveyance in or upon which the automobile is being transported.

4. Theft: to pay for loss to the owned automobile or to a nonowned automobile caused by theft or larceny.

5. Combined Additional Coverage: to pay for loss to the owned automobile or to a nonowned automobile caused by windstorm, hail, earth-

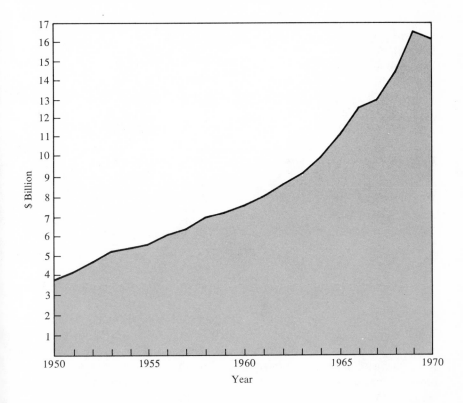

FIGURE 12.1   Economic Losses from Traffic Accidents, 1950-1970

SOURCE: *Insurance Facts 1972,* (N.Y. Insurance Information Institute, 1972), p. 48.

quake, explosion, riot or civil commotion, or the forced landing or falling of any aircraft or its parts of equipment, flood or rising waters, malicious mischief or vandalism, external discharge or leakage of water except loss resulting from rain, snow or sleet whether or not wind driven; provided, with respect to each automobile $25 shall be deducted from each loss caused by malicious mischief or vandalism.

6. *Towing and Labor Costs:* to pay for towing and labor costs necessitated by the disablement of the owned automobile or of any nonowned automobile, provided the labor is performed at the place of disablement.

TABLE 12.2 Family Auto Insurance

Coverage	Limits
A. Physical Damage	
Comprehensive	Replacement
Collision	cost less Depreciation
Fire, Lightning and Transportation	
Theft	
Combined Added Perils	
Towing	Specified (e.g., $25)
B. Liability	
Property Damage	Specified (e.g., $10,000)
Bodily Injury	Specified per person and per Accident (e.g., $50,000/$100,000)
C. Medical Pay	Cost of services up to specified amount (e.g., $5,000)
D. Uninsured Motorists	Indemnity for personal injury or costs legally due from an uninsured, financially irresponsible or unknown party

Furthermore, the following supplementary features are usually provided:

1. reimburse the insured for transportation expenses incurred during the period commencing 48 hours after a theft covered by this policy of the entire automobile has been reported to the company and the police, and terminating when the automobile is returned to use or the company pays for the loss; provided that the company shall not be obligated to pay aggregate expenses in excess of $10 per day or totaling more than $300.

2. pay general average and salvage charges for which the insured becomes legally liable, as to the automobile being transported.

Coverage is afforded to the named insured or any person (or organization) who maintains, uses, or has custody of the named automobile with the permission of the insured.

Coverage does not apply under conditions found in a typical exclusion clause, which relates:

> to any automobile while used as a public or livery conveyance; to loss due to war; to loss to a nonowned automobile arising out of its use by the insured while he is employed or otherwise engaged in the automobile business; to loss to a private passenger, farm or utility automobile or trailer owned by the named insured and not described in this policy or to any temporary substitute automobile therefor, if the insured has other valid and collectible insurance against such loss; to damage which is due and confined to wear and tear, freezing, mechanical or electrical breakdown or failure, unless such damage results from a theft covered by this policy; to tires, unless damaged by fire, malicious mischief or vandalism, or stolen or unless the loss be coincident with and from the same cause as other loss covered by this policy; to loss due to radioactive contamination; to breakage of glass if insurance with respect to such breakage is otherwise afforded.

As the cost of repairing or replacing the automobile has increased, the importance of insuring against physical damage to a car has also increased. Table 12.3 demonstrates the rise in auto repair costs.

Liability

The liability section of the family auto policy is divided into two parts: property damage and bodily injury. With respect to both, the insurer generally

TABLE 12.3   Costs of Replacing Selected Auto Parts, 1967 vs. 1972

	1967 Standard Size 4-door Chevrolet		1972 Standard Size 4-door Chevrolet	
	Parts	*Labor*	*Parts*	*Labor*
Bumper	$ 50.20	$28.80	$118.62	$ 59.40
Grill	25.75	8.40	64.91	26.10
Hood	74.00	12.60	124.53	19.80
Fender	61.95	21.60	122.07	46.80
	211.90	71.40	430.00	152.10
Total		$283.30	Total	$582.23

SOURCE: *Insurance Information Service 1972*, p. 50.

agrees to pay, on behalf of the insured, all sums which the insured shall become legally obligated to pay as damages because of:

1.   bodily injury, sickness or disease, including death resulting therefrom, hereinafter called "bodily injury," sustained by any person;

2.   injury to or destruction of property, including loss of use thereof, hereinafter called "property damage;"

arising out of the ownership, maintenance or use of the owned automobile or any nonowned automobile, and the company shall defend any suit alleging such bodily injury or property damage and seeking damages which are payable under the terms of this policy, even if any of the allegations of the suit are groundless, false or fraudulent; but the company may make such investigation and settlement of any claim or suit as it deems expedient.

In addition to the applicable limits of liability, the company also agrees to pay:

1.   all expenses incurred by the company, all costs taxed against the insured in any such suit and all interest on the entire amount of any judgment therein which accrues after entry of the judgment and before the company has paid or tendered or deposited in court the part of the judgment which does not exceed the limit of the company's liability thereon;

2.   premiums on appeal bonds required in any such suit, premiums on bonds to release attachments for an amount not in excess of the applicable limit of liability of this policy, and the cost of bail bonds required of the insured because of accident or traffic law violation arising out of the use of an automobile insured hereunder, not to exceed $100 per bail bond, but without any obligation to apply for or furnish such bonds;

3.   expenses incurred by the insured for such immediate medical and surgical relief to others as shall be imperative at the time of an accident involving an automobile insured hereunder and not due to war;

4.   all reasonable expenses, other than loss of earnings, incurred by the insured at the company's request.

However, the policy does not apply to:

1.   any automobile while used as a public or livery conveyance, but this exclusion does not apply to the named insured with respect to bodily injury or property damage which results from the named insured's occupancy of a nonowned automobile other than as the operator thereof;

2.   bodily injury or property damage caused intentionally by or at the direction of the insured;

3. bodily injury or property damage with respect to which an insured under this policy is also an insured under a nuclear energy liability policy issued by Nuclear Energy Liability Insurance Association, Mutual Atomic Energy Liability Underwriters or Nuclear Insurance Association of Canada, or would be an insured under any such policy but for its termination upon exhaustion of its limit of liability;

4. bodily injury or property damage arising out of the operation of farm machinery;

5. bodily injury to any employee of the insured arising out of and in the course of (1) domestic employment by the insured, if benefits therefor are in whole or in part either payable or required to be provided under any workmen's compensation law, or (2) other employment by the insured;

6. bodily injury to any fellow employee of the insured injured in the course of his employment if such injury arises out of the use of an automobile in the business of his employer, but this exclusion does not apply to the named insured with respect to injury sustained by any such fellow employee;

7. an owned automobile while used by any person while such person is employed or otherwise engaged in the automobile business, but this exclusion does not apply to the named insured, a resident of the same household as the named insured, a partnership in which the named insured or such resident is a partner, or any partner, agent or employee of the named insured, such resident or partnership;

8. a nonowned automobile while maintained or used by any person while such person is employed or otherwise engaged in (1) the automobile business of the insured or of any other person or organization, (2) any other business or occupation of the insured, but this exclusion does not apply to a private passenger automobile operated or occupied by the named insured or by his private chauffeur or domestic servant or a trailer used therewith or with an owned automobile;

9. injury to or destruction of (1) property owned or transported by the insured, or (2) property rented to or in charge of the insured, other than a residence or private garage;

10. the ownership, maintenance, operation, use, loading or unloading of an automobile ownership of which is acquired by the named insured during the policy period or any temporary substitute automobile therefor, if the named insured has purchased other automobile liability insurance applicable to such automobile for which a specific premium charge has been made.

Medical Payments

The insurer agrees to "pay all reasonable expenses incurred within one year from the date of accident for necessary medical, surgical, X-ray, and dental services, including prosthetic devices, and necessary ambulance, hospital, professional nursing, and funeral services" for all injuries caused by an automobile accident.

Coverage is provided for the named insured, relatives domiciled with the insured, and other persons who sustain bodily injury while occupying the insured's automobile. However, medical payments insurance does not apply to bodily injury:

1.   sustained while occupying (a) an owned automobile used as a public or livery conveyance, or (b) any vehicle while located for use as a residence or premises;

2.   sustained by the named insured or a relative while occupying or through being struck by (a) a farm type tractor or other equipment designed for use principally off public roads, while not upon public roads, or (b) a vehicle operated on rails or crawler-treads;

3.   sustained by any person other than the named insured or a relative, (a) while such person is occupying a nonowned automobile while used as a public or livery conveyance, or (b) resulting from the maintenance or use of a nonowned automobile by such person while employed or otherwise engaged in the automobile business, or (c) resulting from the maintenance or use of a nonowned automobile by such person while employed or otherwise engaged in any other business or occupation, unless the bodily injury results from the operation or occupancy of a private passenger automobile by the named insured or by his private chauffeur or domestic servant, or of a trailer used therewith or with an owned automobile;

4.   sustained by any person who is employed in the automobile business, if the accident arises out of the operation thereof and if benefits therefor are in whole or in part either payable or required to be provided under any workmen's compensation law;

5.   due to war.

Medical payments coverage is regardless of "fault". The insurer, by commencing immediate payment, hopes to reduce the ultimate costs of claims. No-Fault Plans seek to extend this principle to all persons involved in automobile accidents.

Uninsured Motorist Protection

Uninsured motorist coverage is designed to indemnify the automobile policyowner against the costs of bodily injury caused by the negligence of an uninsured, and financially irresponsible, third party motorist. A hit and run driver is a common source of claims under the uninsured motorist clause. The insurer agrees that it will:

> pay all sums which the insured or his legal representative shall be legally entitled to recover as damages from the owner or operator of an uninsured automobile because of bodily injury, sickness or disease, including death resulting therefrom, hereinafter called "bodily injury," sustained by the insured, caused by accident and arising out of the ownership, maintenance or use of such uninsured automobile; provided, for the purposes of this coverage, determination as to whether the insured or such representative is legally entitled to recover such damages, and if so the amount thereof, shall be made by agreement between the insured or such representative and the company or, if they fail to agree, by arbitration.
>
> No judgment against any person or organization alleged to be legally responsible for the bodily injury shall be conclusive, as between the insured and the company, of the issues of liability of such person or organization or of the amount of damages to which the insured is legally entitled unless such judgment is entered pursuant to an action prosecuted by the insured with the written consent of the company.

UNDERWRITING THE AUTOMOBILE RISK

In the absence of statutory prohibitions, insurance carriers attempt to select their private passenger automobile insurance risks in such a manner as to insure only those who are responsible and stable drivers. Experience indicates certain characteristics of drivers and their cars which correlate with accident frequency and severity. Underwriting guidelines provide for special review of applications from members of the most hazardous classes. Frequently, the guidelines will classify risks by (a) driver, (b) occupation, and (c) automobile.

Drivers

Most companies will not permit agents to bind them for automobile insurance for elderly drivers over 70 years of age or young drivers, where the principal operator of the vehicle is married but under age 21, or single and under age 25. Such drivers must submit additional evidence in support of their acceptability for insurance by the company. Drivers who are physically handicapped; mentally impaired; or in poor health that in any way might affect driving ability; who have a criminal record or are of poor financial or moral repute; license suspended or revoked; or requiring a Financial Responsibility filing because of accident or conviction record; unable to speak, read, and write English; excessive use of intoxicant or drugs are members of undesirable classes of risk. Most insurers are also reluctant to insure drivers with a history of claim frequency or repeated moving violations; drivers with a serious violation such as driving while intoxicated, hit and run, reckless driving or operating a car while unlicensed or under suspension. Drivers whose insurance has been cancelled, rejected or renewal refused by another company are suspect, as are drivers with less than one-year's recent driving in the United States or Canada. Each case is treated on its merits, but the insurer expects supplemental information from or about the insured before it will provide coverage.

Occupation

Certain occupations are associated with poor driving records, even when engaged in on a part-time basis. These include: tavern, bar, night club owners and employees and others engaged in the sale of alcoholic beverages; amusement and entertainment industry including entertainers, professional athletes, promoters, and musicians other than teachers and classical musicians; slot, game machine and juke box industry, employees of race tracks and gambling businesses or any suspected illegal operations; hotel, motel, restaurant and theatre employees other than administrative and clerical personnel. Other occupations which are unattractive to automobile insurance underwriters include: canvassers, solicitors, salesmen and others whose duties require extensive travel, or continued use of the insured vehicle in connection with sales, delivery, or service. Temporary residents of the country, transients, itinerants, migratory workers, and those with indefinite addresses are also difficult to insure. Finally, unemployed persons and those with no apparent means of support are believed to lack the requisite responsibility and stability to be good risks.

Automobiles

Vehicles which are over ten years old, or not in good physical mechanical condition present special problems for automobile insurers. Sports cars, high performance cars (any vehicle weighing 4,000 pounds or less with a weight to horsepower ratio of 10.5 or less), customized, altered or specially rebuilt stock automobiles, motorcycles, motor scooters, motor bikes and midget cars are treated as substandard risks for the purposes of the family auto policy.

THE SPECIAL MULTI-PERIL POLICY

Property and liability insurance for a business risk has evolved from single peril policies, such as the fire insurance policy, toward increasingly broad extensions of coverage in packages designed to cover most of the needs of the typical business risk. There are special package policies available for every conceivable type of business. The Special Multiperil Policy emerged as a common denominator of the multiplicity of forms.[2]

The Special Multiperil Policy (SMP) has four parts, two of which, liability and property, are mandatory for both building and contents. The other two, crime and boiler and machinery, are optional.

Liability Insurance

Under the liability insurance section of the Special Multiperil Policy, protection is given for all losses to the person or property of a third party that the insured becomes legally obligated to pay. Responsibility, and thus potential liability, arises out of ownership, maintenance, or use of insured property named in the contract. In addition, coverage is provided for business operations that are incidental to the insured property. The specific exclusions are for liability assumed under contract, liability arising out of ownership or operation of automobiles and snowmobiles, liability to employees injured while on the job, liability arising from "dram shop" laws (relating to the manufacture and sale of alcoholic beverages), and liability due to demolition operations. These exclusions can be covered under separate policies.

The SMP covers the cost of all legal obligations arising from either property damage or bodily injury. In addition, the SMP pays any reasonable costs for immediate medical services to an injured party. These payments are made regardless of whether the insured is liable. The insurer seeks to secure immediate medical care for accident victims. If the insured is responsible for the injury, such care can substantially reduce any eventual required settlements. The insurer also promises to pay costs associated with the legal defense of the insured. Coverage of the judicial risk can be a very important benefit. It costs very little to file a lawsuit, but the expense of defending one is a time consuming financial burden.

The SMP provides protection primarily for the acts of the named insured(s) or, if a corporation, for the officers, stockholders, or directors of the firm. The latter are covered only if acting in a capacity relating to the business. Liability protection for the other employees is provided only to the extent that they operate registered mobile equipment (e.g., off-road equipment).

---

[2] See, for example, the treatment of combination policies in John H. Magee and David L. Bickelhaupt, *General Insurance*, 8th ed. (Homewood, Ill.: Richard D. Irwin, Inc. 1970); John H. Magee and Oscar Serbein, *Property and Liability Insurance*, 4th ed. (Homewood, Ill.: Richard D. Irwin, Inc. 1967); William H. Rodda, *Property and Liability Insurance*, (Englewood Cliffs, N.J.: Prentice-Hall, Inc., 1966).

Property Insurance

The SMP covers loss from damage to buildings and contents caused by specified perils, such as fire, lightning, windstorm, hail, explosion, riot, civil commotion, falling aircraft, vehicles, and smoke. Coverage is for all direct losses and some specified consequential losses (e.g., cost of removing debris, expenses associated with reconstruction of valuable papers, and extra expenses incurred to resume normal operations). The property that is covered is identified in the contract. Any newly acquired and unlisted property is automatically covered for thirty days.

Recovery under the SMP property insurance section is restricted by clauses relating to: (1) value of loss, (2) insurable interest, (3) policy limits, (4) deductibles, and (5) coinsurance.

Value of Loss. The Special Multiperil Policy is a contract of indemnification, and the insured should not receive payment in excess of actual losses. The valuation of a loss depends on the replacement cost and depreciation. If economic depreciation were not deducted from the replacement cost, the insured's position after adjustment would be improved.

Generally, the insurer uses the services of an independent adjuster to appraise damaged property. The judgment of competent appraisers is relatively accurate for labor, material, and overhead costs in replacing or repairing property. However, depreciation is more subjective. As used by insurance adjusters, depreciation is directly related to economic obsolescence and not to age alone.

Insurable Interest. The extent of insurable interest is a limitation to total recovery under the SMP Policy. Payments in excess of one's insurable interest violate the concept of indemnity.

Policy Limits. Policy limits for property damage vary by type of property. The limits are usually given as a specified dollar amount for each building per occurrence. Other limits include: 10 percent of the limit on described buildings for coverage of newly acquired buildings; $500 for personal effects; $500 for valuable papers and records; $1,000 for trees and shrubs; and $1,000 for extra expenses.

Deductibles. The property damage section of the SMP uses "disappearing" deductibles. The insurer pays 111 percent of all losses above a deductible of $50. Thus, after losses of $500 the deductible will "disappear", and losses are paid based on 100 percent of the loss.

Coinsurance. Coinsurance is designed as an incentive for the insured to carry an appropriate amount of insurance relative to the property value. Most losses are small, and, in the absence of a coinsurance clause, the insured would be tempted to have a low insurance to value ratio. Coinsurance requires the insured to assume a portion of all losses if he does not buy at least a specified amount of insurance. The SMP generally includes an 80 percent coinsurance clause.

If an insured buys coverage equal to at least 80 percent of the property value, all losses up to the policy limit will be paid. However, if the amount of insurance is less than 80 percent of the property value, the amount of recovery will be determined as follows:

$$\frac{\text{Insurance Carried}}{\substack{\text{Insurance Required} \\ \text{(Coinsurance \% x} \\ \text{Value of the Property)}}} \quad \text{x} \quad \text{Loss} \quad = \quad \text{Recovery}$$

Thus, if the insurance policy was for $50,000, the building was worth $100,000, the coinsurance requirement was 80 percent, and the loss was $40,000, the amount of recovery would be:

$$\frac{\$50,000}{\$100,000 \text{ x } 80\%} \quad \text{x} \quad \$40,000 \quad = \quad \$25,000$$

Because he was underinsured, the operation of the coinsurance clause would require the insured to act as a "coinsurer" to the extent of the remaining $15,000.

Crime Insurance

Among the optional coverages available with the SMP is a comprehensive crime endorsement. This endorsement provides coverage for any of the following: employee dishonesty, loss inside covered buildings, loss outside covered buildings, counterfeit, and depositors' forgery. The premium will vary depending on the number of covers selected and the policy limits purchased.

Employee dishonesty can be insured against with either a commercial blanket bond or a blanket position bond. The former sets a limit per loss, while the latter sets a limit per person associated with a loss. However, both cover losses of property due to employee dishonesty. The coverage of loss inside and outside the insured's premises is designed primarily to protect against the loss of monies or securities. The coverage includes loss of money or securities due to natural causes as well as burglary or theft. Because the regular property form provides only limited insurance for money or securities, this coverage fills a potential void. While money and securities receive extensive coverage under the optional crime endorsement, other property is covered only for the perils of burglary from a safe or robbery.

Boiler and Machinery Insurance

Many businesses have large, complicated boilers and machinery that are necessary to the functioning of the entire firm. To protect these key pieces of equipment, a firm may select the optional boiler and machinery coverage under the SMP Policy. This provides protection against both direct loss of property and the liability that may arise as a result of accidents. While these two covers are important, the primary benefits of boiler and machinery insurance are the loss control and prevention services provided by the insurer. Because damage to important pieces of equipment may shut down the entire plant, it is imperative to prevent losses. Most buyers of boiler and machinery insurance are concerned more with the inspection services provided than with any other facet of the product. It is not uncommon for over one-third of the premium payment to be used for the cost of inspection services.

WORKMEN'S COMPENSATION INSURANCE

Workmen's compensation insurance[3] provides coverage for liability imposed on an employer by a workmen's compensation law. The policy is designed to cover not only the exposures that the law of the particular state specifies in terms of covered persons, covered perils, and benefit amounts but also nonstatutory employer liability. Workmen's compensation is mandatory coverage in most states, but coverage requirements are constantly reviewed and changed with each session of the state legislatures. An analysis of the policy must consider: (1) coverage, (2) benefits, and (3) costs.

Coverage

Most persons in employee status are covered under workmen's compensation laws. Certain categories of worker, however, are frequently excluded from coverage for various reasons. These include migrant farm workers and domestic servants.

The law usually covers accidents or illness arising out of, and in the course of employment. However, the definition of covered accident or illness has been liberally construed, and many industrial diseases and accidents only indirectly related to employment provide eligibility for benefits to their victims.

---

[3] See Herman Miles Somers and Anne Ramsay Somers, *Workmen's Compensation* (New York: John H. Wiley and Sons, Inc., 1954). A more current treatment is found in C.A. Kulp and John W. Hall, *op. cit.*

Benefits

After an initial waiting period, injured employees may receive specified cash indemnities based upon the severity of loss, their previous average earnings, and reimbursement for all medical and hospital costs. In the event of death arising from a compensable injury, survivor benefits may be payable to the dependents of the covered employee.

In most states, an injured employee may have a cause of action beyond the workmen's compensation statute. In such a case, the accident victim may sue the employer for more than that which is granted under workmen's compensation laws. Employers' liability coverage provides for defense and related costs as well as payment of any judgment awarded within policy limits.

Costs

Most workmen's compensation rates are set by private or state bureaus. The National Council on Compensation Insurance provides rates for insurers in over half the states. Thus, there is little opportunity for direct price competition in workmen's compensation insurance. The rate charged is based on payroll, and exposure units are expressed in terms of $100 of payroll. Rates are based on experience. Modified rating based on favorable experience of the policyholder is used extensively in workmen's compensation and is the basis for limited price competition.

MISCELLANEOUS PROPERTY AND LIABILITY INSURANCE

There is an enormous variety of property and liability insurance coverages available for virtually every imaginable contingency.[4] Camera floater policies, stamp collectors' floater policies, earthquake insurance, insurance agents' errors and omissions policies, surgeons' malpractice insurance, and title insurance merely suggest some of the possibilities. The manuals of insurance companies provide coverages and rates for most of the hazards of concern to the individual. Each form is unique and must be examined carefully in order to assure that it provides the required coverage.

---

[4]William H. Rodda, *Marine Insurance: Ocean and Inland*, 3rd ed. (Englewood Cliffs, N.J.: Prentice-Hall, Inc., 1970) provides an excellent overview of the possible coverages. *Fire, Casualty, and Surety Bulletins*, 3 volumes, (Cincinnati: National Underwriter Company) is a loose-leaf service which provides the most comprehensive review of each of the exposures and coverages.

SUMMARY

Individuals and businesses are exposed to a range of property and liability perils, the occurrence of which could result in financial disaster. To offset these exposures, and to provide financial security, property and liability insurers furnish coverage for both individual perils and for groups of perils.

Families and businesses have discovered that comprehensive packages are useful ways of obtaining necessary insurance protection. For individuals, the most commonly used insurance packages are the Homeowner's Policy and the Family Automobile Policy. Businessmen favor the Special Multiperil Policy to meet their property and liability insurance needs.

Each family unit and business must examine its own exposures and select the grouping of policies that best meets its needs. In reviewing alternative property and liability insurance contracts, the consumer should be concerned particularly with the perils covered or excluded, the dollar limits of coverage, the specific items or individuals covered or excluded, the nature and extent of restrictions on coverage and supplementary services provided by the insurer.

REVIEW QUESTIONS

1. Why does the standard workmen's compensation policy include employer's liability as well as workmen's compensation insurance? Explain.

2. The word "integration" refers to a process of unifying things to form an increasingly complete and perfect whole. In insurance, integration connotes the joining together of coverages to form policies which approach the ideal of completeness relative to the insurance needs of a particular type of risk. Explain the ways in which the principle of integration is operative in the case of the Special Multiperil Policy.

3. After stealing your car, a thief was involved in a collision which caused him some bodily injury and resulted both in property damage to a store and material damage to your car. What is your legal liability in such a case? Are you covered for these losses under the terms of the family auto policy? Will the damage to your car be paid? If so, will payment be made under the collision coverage or under the theft provisions? Explain.

4. Prepare a chart showing the principal perils to which a small business is exposed and the specific insurance policies which might be obtained to cover each of these perils. Does the Special Multiperil Policy cover all of the perils you have identified? If not, explain.

5. Discuss the principal advantages and disadvantages of workmen's compensation insurance from the standpoints of (a) the employer, and (b) the employee.

STUDY QUESTIONS

    6. Washington, a second year law student, worked part-time in the university cafeteria. While preparing a toasted sandwich, he was electrocuted by a faulty electric connection. As a result, he became permanently and totally disabled. In a letter to the insurance company, his lawyer described him as a "vegetable." What is the maximum amount the insurance company would have to pay if there were a valid workmen's compensation policy covering the employer? Explain. What would your answer be if the university claimed "governmental immunity"? Discuss.

    7. From an underwriting standpoint, why do auto insurance companies discriminate against youthful drivers? Is this justified? Discuss.

    8. Ten days after his car had been given a check-up by his auto dealer, Tom was involved in a serious accident resulting from his faulty brakes. The driver of the other car was taken to the hospital. The front seat passenger in the other car took Tom's license number and recorded the name of Tom's insurance company. Being emotionally upset, Tom said, "The whole thing was my fault. If I had been more careful, this accident would never have happened. At least you can be sure that my insurance company will pay whatever it costs to take care of things." Tom did not know that upon arrival at the hospital, his victim was found to be hallucinating from drugs but was otherwise unhurt. Did Tom breach the family auto policy by admitting liability? Will his statement be used against him in court? What should Tom have done under the circumstances? Explain.

    9. White contends that he has no need for parcel post insurance from his insurance company because the Post Office provides very low cost protection. Why do people buy parcel post insurance privately? Explain.

    10. A bail bondsman offers surety guarantees to the court on behalf of persons accused of crime. How can the bail bondsman underwrite this risk when his customers are usually from the lowest class of society? Discuss.

13

The Insurance Commissioner

and

Public Policy

INSURANCE AS A PUBLIC SERVICE

The public and the members of the insurance industry in the United States have long regarded the business as one affected with a public interest. It has even been suggested that the insurance industry is a public utility, in that the chartering provisions of companies are restrictive, rates are subject to regulation, licensing of agents is designed for the protection of the public, triennial audits are intended to secure performance of obligations, freedom of selection of insureds is somewhat limited, the right to cancel policies is restricted, and a public body has been appointed with the powers of a public utility commission to license corporations seeking to engage in the business and to regulate their practices in specific ways to protect the public. If the full public utility designation has not yet been earned, it is a pronounced trend.[1]

---

[1] See especially, Spencer L. Kimball, *Insurance and Public Policy* (Madison, Wisconsin: University of Wisconsin Press, 1960), pp. 304ff. Also, Herman H. Fracksel, *Public Utility Regulation* (Homewood, Ill.: Richard D. Irwin, Inc., 1947); Eli W. Clemens, *Economics and Public Utilities* (New York: Appleton-Century-Crofts, Inc., 1950).

186

DEVELOPMENT OF THE OFFICE
OF INSURANCE COMMISSIONER

Prior to 1818, insurance companies were virtually free of state regulation in the United States. They were incorporated, paid local taxes, were subject to the laws pertaining to corporations, but were not required to prepare any special reports nor have their practices regulated in any specific manner. In 1818, the Commonwealth of Massachusetts enacted the first regulatory statute requiring all domestic insurance companies to file annual reports of their financial condition with the state comptroller. The purpose of this enactment was to provide a basis for the levying of taxes.

In 1851, the State of New Hampshire set up a three man insurance commission to examine the affairs of insurance companies doing business in that state. In 1869, New Hampshire appointed a single commissioner to have full responsibility for the supervision of insurance companies and their activities. This was the first instance of the appointment of a single officer to supervise the activities of insurance companies. Prior to this time, there were Boards of Commissioners in various states, and in New York State an insurance department was formed in 1860 as a regulatory body.

During this early period, the commissioners did little more than review annual reports of insurance companies and process applications for licenses. By 1890, seventeen states had insurance commissioners. By the turn of the century, the principle was well established that there should be a government official with primary responsibility for insurance regulation.

EARLY DUTIES OF THE COMMISSIONER
OF INSURANCE

The early duties of the insurance department[2] were largely confined to four activities: (1) prescribe the form of annual statements to be used by insurance companies, (2) act as custodians for securities required to be deposited by life insurance companies, (3) examine insurance company records at the home offices whenever deemed necessary, and (4) publish an annual report of the department.

The concept of standardized annual reports of insurance companies, so that intercompany comparisons and uniform industry statistics could be

---

[2] The classic work on the office of the insurance commissioner is Edwin W. Patterson, *The Insurance Commissioner in the United States* (Cambridge: Harvard University Press, 1927).

developed, was among the early goals of the commissioners. Today, this remains a major area of interest for the regulatory authority.

Early statutes required deposits to be made with the insurance departments as security for policyholder reserve obligations. In recent years, this function has been conducted by the state fiscal officers as agents for the departments of insurance.

Insurance company examinations were perfunctory at first, the primary objective being to assure a fair statement of the tax base, but such examinations became increasingly intensive, to the point where the convention examination, a comprehensive investigation of the financial status and statutory compliance of an insurance company, is one of the most vital functions of the department of insurance.

The annual reports of the insurance departments vary in form from valuable and elaborate statistical documents, such as those published by ʹCalifornia and New York, to the very brief reports of some of the less populous states, which contain little more than the names and addresses of domestic insurers. One of the principal weaknesses of all such reports is the time lag between the close of the fiscal year reported on and the appearance of the annual report. Lags of two and three years are not uncommon. The timeliness of the data is largely vitiated by publication delays.

The staff reports of the National Association of Insurance Commissioners have played an important role in increasing the power of the office of commissioner by supplying understaffed states with information and assistance in regulating the insurance business. Major research studies on automobile insurance, premium taxation, the measurement of profitability, and the treatment of investment income in property and liability insurance, credit life and disability insurance as well as regulation of mass marketing of property and liability insurance were published in the early 1970s. Studies of techniques for monitoring the effectiveness of competition as a regulator of rates in property and liability insurance, variable life insurance and mass merchandizing of health insurance through both the media of the radio and television as well as through the mails contributed to better insurance regulation. These analyses were of importance for their influence on model legislation and regulations.[3]

SOURCES OF POWER
IN THE COMMISSIONER'S OFFICE

In analyzing the power of the office of the insurance commissioner, it should be recognized that any senior regulatory official may be cast by the administrative process in the role of czar. The insurance commissioner is in the unusual position

---

[3]John S. Hanson, "The National Association of Insurance Commissioners: Its Nature and Scope," *CPCU Annals*, Vol. 26, No. 1, March 1973, pp. 10-15.

of commanding, within wide limits, the legislative, judicial, and executive branches of the insurance regulatory apparatus.[4]

The commissioner usually is selected from the ranks of insurance industry executives and is presumed to be an expert in insurance technology. There is a natural tendency for the governor and the legislature to look to the commissioner and his department for advice and programs of reform. Because of the presumption that the department will be more conversant with the details of regulatory problems, there may be a gradual shift of decision making from the legislative committees to the department of insurance. Insurance bills, which are enacted by state legislatures and signed by governors, are often initiated by the staffs of insurance departments. Gradually, legislative initiative and power has shifted toward the office of the commissioner.

State statutes provide that violations of the insurance code shall be heard by the department in the first instance, and entry to the civil or criminal courts for many matters must first proceed by way of a departmental hearing. The powers of subpoena, license suspension, privileged communication, and ready access to injunction powers provide the insurance regulator with substantial judicial powers.

The executive authority of the regulator is the clearest source of power because the insurance commissioner is in command of the machinery of enforcement. Clearly, careful use of the sources of power can make the commissioner one of the most important men in the insurance industry. Carelessness or abuse can lead to disastrous personal consequences both for the incumbent of the office and for those who are subject to regulation.

ADMINISTRATIVE REGULATORY POWERS
OF THE COMMISSIONER

The modern insurance code is so extensive and complex that one must generalize that virtually every topic which might be covered by legislation is touched upon somewhere in the code and its interpretative regulations. Under the administrative function of the insurance department, the principal aspects of the business subject to regulation are: (1) financial, (2) product, (3) business methods, and (4) liquidation of companies.

In the financial area, the law charges the commissioner with responsibility for regulating insurance rates adopted by insurance companies. In life insurance, such rates are regulated indirectly by establishing minimum standards for reserves that insurance companies must meet. The deficiency reserve, a formula

---

[4] See Spencer L. Kimball, "The Purpose of Insurance Regulation: A Preliminary Inquiry in the Theory of Insurance Law," *Minnesota Law Review* (March, 1961). Also, Charles C. Center and Richard M. Heins (eds.) *Insurance and Government* (New York: McGraw-Hill Book Company, 1962).

that penalizes a company for charging a premium less than cost, helps establish a floor for rates. Competition sets the ceiling. In other lines of insurance, the requirement that rates be adequate, reasonable, and not unfairly discriminatory leaves the power in the hands of the commissioner to determine what these words mean in any given situation. The statutes define these terms only in a general way.

Rate regulation varies among the states: the most permissive, where rates need only meet the criteria of adequacy, reasonableness, and fairness and be subject to review at any time after their implementation; to filing states where rates must be filed subject to disapproval within a fixed period of time, such as thirty days; to prior approval states where no rate can be used without first being justified by the user and approved by the insurance commissioner. The possibilities for political determination of rate changes where they rest exclusively in the control of a political official serving frequently "at the pleasure of the governor" are ever present.

Company expenses are closely regulated on a direct basis in some states, such as New York, and indirectly in most other states. Perhaps the principal restraint on company expense other than sound business judgment is the statutory accounting procedure imposed on property and liability insurance companies. Such companies must use an accrual method for their income and a cash method for expenses, so that the latter constitute a drain on surplus. A company that writes an increasing volume of business will be obliged to minimize its expense factor in order to avoid undue surplus strain.

Both the types and amounts of insurance company reserves are prescribed by state law. Criteria for each class of reserve, whether it be for unearned premiums, losses incurred, reserves for life, or other contingencies are set with a view to assurance of adequacy in order to secure the interest of the actual or potential claimants. The goal is a conservative statement of potential liabilities.

The valuation of assets on the balance sheet of an insurance company is governed by a complex set of formulae designed to prevent overstatement of values. Each class of security has an assigned basis for valuation or a specific value assigned by the National Association of Insurance Commissioners. Real estate must be shown at cost or amortized value. Stocks must be carried at prices stipulated in the *Book of Valuations* of the NAIC. The power to determine the admissibility of assets for balance sheet purposes has great significance, particularly in the case of small companies. Thus, a home office building, which may be the largest single asset of an insurance company, may be disallowed as an admitted asset by the insurance department, thereby rendering the company technically insolvent. How assets shall be valued and their admissibility is largely within the discretion of the commissioner.

Investments are closely regulated in terms of eligibility for the portfolio and divided into classes based upon presumptive safety and liquidity. Thus there are "excess funds" investments that are subject to more liberally defined criteria than conservative permissible investments, which are offsets to statutory reserves. In addition, a company may make certain investments, such as excessive amounts in equipment, particular securities, or real estate that may be treated as "nonadmitted" assets.

Although the insurance codes spell out minimum standards, financial requirements for organization and licensing of companies are largely determined by the insurance commissioner. Usually, the code asserts that all of the licenses are privileges that may be granted within the discretion of the commissioner if, in his judgment, it would be in the public interest to grant such a license. This can lead to widely different standards of practice with respect to gaining admission to do business in the various states.

Supervision of deposit of securities usually with the state treasurer is within the domain of the commissioner. This can be an important source of power, particularly as it relates to the operations of small companies. In several states the security deposits of insurance companies aggregate over one billion dollars.

In the area of product regulation, the commissioner is authorized to regulate policy forms in use by insurance companies. At the one extreme of regulation the policy analysis division of the insurance department may review every policy form in use in the state, and at the other extreme, such forms are merely filed with the department. Much of the language of the policy forms is set by statute or by administrative decree.

Business methods supervised by the commissioner in his administrative capacity include the licensing of agents and brokers, and the enforcement of laws relating to misrepresentation, twisting, rebating, and unfair discrimination. It also embraces Unauthorized Insurers Service of Process Act enforcement. The insurance codes dictate that a license may be granted if in the judgment of the commissioner an applicant is a person of good moral character.

Insurance companies are not subject to the National Bankruptcy Act. Their dissolution is within the jurisdiction of the insurance commissioner. He has the power to determine the time and manner of their birth, operation, and death. Insurance companies rarely become bankrupt; instead they are taken into conservatorship or receivership and are liquidated either by runoff of claims or by portfolio reinsurance. There are stages or degrees of control possible when a company is in distress. The commissioner may temporarily suspend the license; he may permanently suspend it; he may place the company into a conservatorship (where he is the conservator); or he may liquidate the company in the best interests, primarily, of the policyholders or claimants.

LEGISLATIVE POWERS

The legislative functions of the commissioner appear indirectly at the level of statute drafting, but more directly in the regulations promulgated by the department under the provisions of various statutory codes. The principal powers include: to disseminate information, to prescribe forms of report and modes of accounting, to determine the sufficiency and validity of securities, and to establish licensing regulations.

While hearings are usually provided for in various statutory codes, the transcript of the hearings is merely advisory, and the commissioner is free to adopt such regulations as conform with the intent of the statute. In practice, it is the commissioner's application of specific regulations and his determination of which statutes will be vigorously enforced that prescribe the permissible day to day activity of companies and their agents.

JUDICIAL POWERS

The judicial powers of the commissioner of insurance are very extensive. He has privileged communications because all his records are treated as confidential and not subject to court action. He cannot be subpoenaed with his records, nor can he be compelled to testify on actions taken in the course of executing the duties of his office. He may hold official hearings and issue orders, rulings, and decisions in his judicial capacity, the violation of which is punishable as contempt of court. He has the power to subpoena witnesses and require them to testify under oath. He may issue subpoenas for witnesses with their records and files. He certifies facts of violations for prosecution by the district attorney. Under appropriate circumstances, he has the power to cancel contracts, to enjoin conduct, to seek injunctions, and to take depositions.

APPOINTMENT AND TENURE

There is a strong trend toward the upgrading of the office of the insurance commissioner and reducing the potential for political pressure on the office. This has been done by having his appointment independent of the term of office or the pleasure of the governor, and by giving him a measure of tenure. Coupled with rising compensation levels, these actions may make for more competent regulation while enlarging the powers of the office.

THE NATIONAL ASSOCIATION
OF INSURANCE COMMISSIONERS (NAIC)

The National Convention of Insurance Commissioners, later the National Association of Insurance Commissioners, was founded in 1871 to obtain uniform standards among the states in matters of regulation. The NAIC is not a statutory body. It is an association of insurance commissioners who meet regularly for the purpose of discussing mutual problems and preparing model legislation for recommendation to their respective legislatures. Figure 13.1 outlines the committee structure and duties of the NAIC.

By reciprocity, the commissioners have developed systems for cooperative company audits, simultaneous investigations of interstate problems, and information exchanges that increase efficiency in the regulatory process. By virtue of its high *esprit de corps,* the NAIC has overcome much of the burden of conflicting regulation in the different jurisdictions of the United States.

In addition to the group activities of the commissioners, the NAIC has established a permanent professional staff that is charged with research and legislative representation activities. Members of this staff often testify before state legislatures and Congress. Furthermore, they have produced extensive studies on various problems that are important in contemporary regulation. While the NAIC staff is relatively small in number, their influence on the actions of the NAIC, and the individual commissioners, is significant. The relatively small permanent staff of the NAIC is likely to expand both in size and in influence.

TRENDS IN THE POWER STRUCTURE
OF THE INSURANCE DEPARTMENT

The National Association of Insurance Commissioners has fought to preserve state regulation in the face of congressional inquiries and pressures from federal regulatory authorities. The larger states, such as California and New York, are leaders in the fight to preserve state regulation of insurance. Gradually, there has been a raising of standards in the office of the department with larger budgets, better staffs, and career oriented department personnel. Concurrently, there has been an enlargement of the powers of the commissioner of insurance. Finally, there has been increasing cooperation with the insurance industry. Many commissioners and industry leaders frequently speak with the same voice.

THE ISSUE OF FEDERAL VS. STATE REGULATION

The issue of federal vs. state regulation of the insurance business is fundamental in the United States because there is a very real conflict of laws. The public policy of the United States prior to World War II held that insurance was essentially intrastate business and therefore subject exclusively to state regulation. This meant that there were no federal statutes affecting the business, and the entire body of antitrust law was inapplicable. As a result of a major scandal in the State of Missouri in the early 1940s the issue was brought to the Supreme

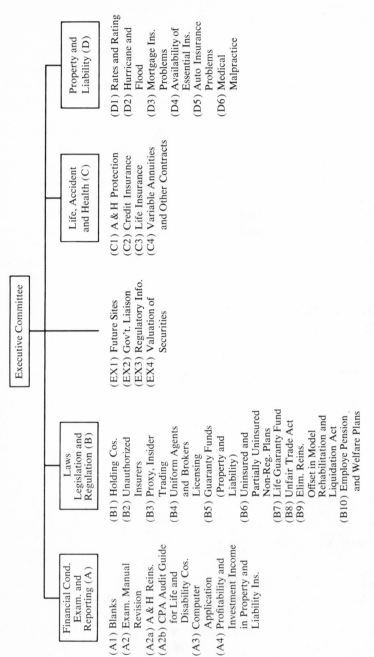

FIGURE 13.1 Organization Chart of The National Association of Insurance Commissioners

Court in a landmark case, *United States v. Southeastern Underwriters Association,* and it was resolved that insurance is interstate commerce and subject to federal regulation under the Constitution.

The Congress debated the question and enacted the McCarran-Ferguson Act in 1945, which provided that to the extent that the standards of state regulation were equivalent to those at the federal level, it was the intent of the Congress that the states should continue to regulate the insurance business. A moratorium on enforcement of federal regulation was granted until 1948, by which time the states had introduced legislation that eliminated some of the practices proscribed by federal antitrust legislation. The industry entered a highly competitive phase, and subsequently each time a federal agency interposed a fresh subject matter in need of additional regulation, the states rapidly proceeded to fill the void.

The relative merits of federal vs. state regulation of the business are controversial, but the test of the borderline between federal statutes and interpretations and the adequacy of state regulation is constantly before the NAIC and the courts.[5] Federal jurisdiction is operative only where the states fail to regulate or where the Constitution enjoins the states from acting.

The principal federal statutes affecting insurance as interstate commerce include the Sherman Act, the Clayton Act, the Robinson-Patman Act, the Federal Trade Commission Act, and various laws administered by the Securities and Exchange Commission.

The Sherman Act enjoins monopolistic activity arising out of the collusive acts of competitors in business and commerce. Agreements to fix prices, control agency representation, establish uniform commission scales, predetermine practices in common matters of marketing, underwriting, claims settlement, and so forth would tend to be in violation of the Sherman Act. State antitrust laws have attempted to preempt this field with considerable success.

The Clayton Act is concerned with activities that may result in lessened competition or increasing concentration of industry.

The Robinson-Patman Act prohibits unlawful price discrimination between different buyers of the same commodity or service.

The Federal Trade Commission Act deals with unfair trade practices, such as false and misleading advertising.

The Securities and Exchange Commission (SEC) administers laws regulating the sale of securities in interstate commerce. The variable annuity has been deemed to be a security and is regulated by the S.E.C. Questions have arisen in the matter of insurance securities regulation by the Securities and Exchange Commission, particularly with respect to the sale of variable annuities. In

[5]See, for example, *F.T.C. v. Travelers Health Association,* 362 U.S. 293,80 S. Ct. 717 (1960). Also, *State Board of Insurance v. Todd Shipyards,* 370 U.S. 451,82 S. Ct. 1380 (1962); *S.E.C. v. United Benefit Life Insurance Company,* 387 U.S. 202,87 S. Ct. 1557 (1967).

addition the Commission has dealt with the issue of proxy solicitation and the submission of annual reports to stockholders.

The Federal Trade Commission has been involved in the regulation of advertising practices, particularly of mail-order accident and health insurance. The NAIC has been concerned with the mail-order business because this clearly falls within the province of the Federal Trade Commission or the Post Office.

The sale of insurance on military bases has concerned the Department of Defense as well as commissioners of insurance.

The National Association of Insurance Commissioners is firmly committed to state regulation of insurance on political grounds. They contend that state regulation is desirable because it exists in the form of a long-established and known system with an aggregate staff of over 4,500 and combined budgets of more that $50 million in all the states.[6] They argue that the diversity and pluralism of the system makes for greater vitality and experimentation and brings regulation closer to the people. The threat of federal intervention keeps the state departments alert. Advocates of states' rights believe that undue concentration of power in Washington is unwise from any point of view.

Those who argue for a greater federal role note the high cost of doing business in 50 jurisdictions each with a different set of rules governing a product which is sold nationally. The quality of personnel in the various states is uneven and the degree of enforcement is a variable depending upon the jurisdiction.[7] Many states are too small for effectively securing the rights or requirements of policyholders against insurer insolvency or catastrophic hazards. The advocates of a national role argue that market segmentation by political subdivisions is uneconomic and results in undue concentration of regulatory power in the hands of state insurance commissioners.

Ulysses S. Grant observed that, "The best way to get rid of a bad law is to enforce it rigidly." If the commissioners use their powers to the full, they will surely lose them. The state insurance commissioners will probably retain their powers so long as they exercise restraint.

SUMMARY

The office of the insurance commissioner emerged more than one hundred years ago as the regulator of a major industry with a strong consumer interest. Beginning with simple reporting requirements, the powers of the office were

---

[6] John S. Hanson, *op. cit.*, p. 14.

[7] The U.S. Senate Committee on the Judiciary's Subcommittee on Antitrust and Monopoly has frequently been critical of the quality of state regulation but has not proposed that the federal government repeal the McCarran Act. See, for example, *The Insurance Industry: Aviation, Ocean Marine and State Regulation*, Report of the Subcommittee on Antitrust and Monopoly, 86th Congress (1960).

steadily enlarged as new problems were identified and the scope of regulation was expanded. The expertise of the insurance department staffs, the continuity in office of the civil servants through different political regimes, and the administrative capability of the departments led to an accumulation of power in the office of the commissioner. The insurance commissioner acquired the status of executive, legislator, and judge in insurance affairs. This power was reinforced by the successful maintenance of state regulation through the work of the National Association of Insurance Commissioners and the insurance industry. The *Proceedings of the N.A.I.C.* bear witness to the speed with which the commissioners are able to develop Model Bills to provide for continuing state regulation of subjects which are of federal interest.

REVIEW QUESTIONS

1. Why is insurance considered a "business affected with the public interest" and therefore subject to intensive regulation? Discuss.

2. Perhaps the most heated jurisdictional controversy of the mid-century in the insurance business was the issue of federal versus state regulation. Discuss the current status of the controversy and indicate some of the principal developments leading to the present situation.

3. "The insurance commissioner is at once the prosecutor, judge, jury, and counsel for the defense; he is executive, legislative, and judicial in his roles; he is a benign commissar." Discuss.

4. "It is a widely held belief that, because of certain unique characteristics of the insurance industry, rate competition of the kind envisaged in the Sherman Act is undesirable and can only lead to chaos." How are insurance rates regulated at present in the U.S.? Discuss.

5. What are the principal activities subject to insurance regulation? Explain four of these briefly.

STUDY QUESTIONS

6. "A" has been informed by a friend that the "X" Casualty Insurance Company with which he has his automobile insurance policy is in serious straits as a result of financial reverses. He is concerned that he will lose both his premiums and his insurance. What is the procedure by which an insurance company may cease operations without loss necessarily occurring to the insureds?

7. If no-fault insurance is implemented at the federal level, what would be the role of the states in auto insurance regulation? Discuss.

8. Is variable life insurance a security and hence subject to the federal securities laws, or is it strictly life insurance and thereby outside of SEC jurisdiction? What effect would this decision have upon state insurance regulators? Explain.

9.   If you were asked to establish an insurance regulatory system, what would be the most important goals of your system? How might these goals be achieved? Would your goals vary from those of current insurance regulation? Explain.

10.   What is the likelihood that the power of the state insurance commissioners will increase during the next decade? What are some of the factors which are likely to alter the trend? Discuss.

III

PSYCHOLOGICAL
PERSPECTIVES

Insurance exists because human beings are concerned about financial security and the consequences of adverse economic conditions. People are both attracted to and repelled by risk. They engage in betting or gambling behavior, and they buy insurance.

An understanding of behavior in the insurance market depends on a number of important ideas that help explain why the individual consumer buys insurance and why insurance companies believe they can supply the product on a profitable basis.

14

Anxiety,
Risk,
and Insurance

INTRODUCTION

Insurance is a technique, a concept, and an economic institution. It functions in a variety of ways with numerous forms and with much complexity. It may involve the transfer of specific risks or the pooling of experience; it may be highly scientific or be merely a collection of rules of thumb. Its object is to relieve the burden of uncertainty or anxiety of the insured. Insurance is an anxiety reducing device. To understand the nature and purpose of insurance one must be able to comprehend the nature of anxiety and the ways in which man deals with this state of mind.

PSYCHOLOGICAL UNCERTAINTY AND ANXIETY

Fear

The psychologist recognizes fear as a universal fact of life. People fear the nearness of danger, evil, or pain. Fear is a specific response to an unpleasant shock. Fear has a unique focus. It is undesirable. Fear tends to be irrational and shifting in quality. The objects most feared are those to which there has been the least exposure or which have not been the subject of personal experience. In studies of fears among children it has been observed that fears were rarely directly related to the experienced misfortunes of children. The most frequent sources of fear were unknowns, such as animals or ghosts. Fear can be isolated as a single experience relating to some specific event or object. In this sense it belongs in the same category as an expectation, a hope, an impression, a dream, a phantasy, or a desire. Fear is a subjective emotional state manifested by psychological and physiological signs and symptoms.

Anxiety

Anxiety is defined as a collection of fears and may be expressed as painful uneasiness of mind, generalized pessimism, or various risk aversion attitudes. Anxiety is regarded by many as the central problem of mental health. Psychologists consider that an individual's capacity to tolerate and manage anxiety is a sensitive measure of the healthy integration of his personality. In contrast, in states of intense anxiety, the individual's fears characteristically become less specifically identifiable and he tends to become severely troubled and dysfunctional. As Rollo May expresses it: "The capacity to bear anxiety is important for the individual's self-realization and for his conquest of his environment."[1]

Anxiety is not an absolute condition in terms of degree. It has a range extending from extreme neurotic anxiety, in which the reaction to danger is disproportionate to the objective threat and involves abnormal responses such as repression and intrapsychic conflict or development of neurotic symptoms, to a range of normal anxiety, which is a reaction proportionate to the objective threat. Normal anxiety can be dealt with constructively at the level of conscious awareness or can be relieved by various objective techniques of risk management.

Degree of Belief

The measure of anxiety or fears is the strength of conviction with which they are held. This may be the degree of belief viewed as a psychological as opposed to a statistical term. The concept of a degree of belief does not relate directly to the statistical idea of subjective probability because this latter term implies more precision than can be found in the psyche of the individual in a

[1] Rollo May, *The Meaning of Anxiety* (New York: The Ronald Press, 1950), p. 56. The classic works in this field are: Soren Kierkegaard, *The Concept of Dread*, translated by Walter Lowrie (Princeton, N.J.: Princeton University Press, 1944), originally published in Danish in 1844, and Sigmund Freud, *The Problem of Anxiety*, translated by H.A. Bunker (American Edition), (New York: W.W. Norton and Co., Inc.).

state of normal or neurotic anxiety. Degree of belief is not a cardinal measure and probably is not invariably consistent.[2]

Doubt

The degree of belief of the individual is clouded by doubt, and these notions are roughly analogous to the statistical idea of a dispersion or variance. It is a range within which the individual constantly vacillates in his wavering strength of conviction about the many events that induce fear and anxiety. The psychologist uses the term threshold limits to measure this attribute of degrees of belief.

The source of doubt is probably ignorance of outcomes and concern about the inability to forecast such outcomes. As predictions increase in reliability, presumably the uncertainty or doubt of the individual is diminished and the degree of belief tends to waver less widely.

Insurance and Anxiety Reduction

The role of insurance becomes clear within this subjective frame of reference. Insurance is one of the devices for the reduction of psychological uncertainty. In this respect it is similar in its effect to psychiatry, voodooism, education, faith, and other anxiety reducing mechanisms. Insurance enhances peace of mind, financial security, and is a partial relief from anxiety. The insurance salesman has almost always taken advantage of this element even when he has not understood its basis. The buyer's readiness to buy has been recognized as a function of his information and emotional set. The salesman strives to paint pictures of freedom from anxiety rather than to rationalize benefits in factual cost benefit terms.

This approach helps explain why the individual behaves as he does in his insurance conduct. He is operating at the subjective level and is driven by a need to reduce his anxiety, not only because such anxiety is inhibiting but also because it is in the nature of the healthy organism to seek relief from insecurity by whatever devices it can. The normal reaction is to resolve anxiety. In the abnormal case, the anxiety will be fed by neurosis or withdrawal efforts.

What we learn from anxiety theory is that anxiety is an inhibitor, and the healthy or normal response is to deal with it constructively. This is done through mechanisms such as insurance that, instead of repressing the fears, threats, or conflicts, transfers the source of insecurity and permits the individual to make a

---

[2] Armen A. Alchian, "The Meaning of Utility Measurement," *American Economic Review*, XLIII (March, 1953) provided an early treatment of the relationships between cardinal and ordinal measurement of utility in economics. Ordinality and inconsistency of degrees of belief frustrates mathematical treatment of the subject.

better adjustment to his environment. This explanation does not account for the phenomena of gambling or betting, which is also indulged in by insurance minded individuals.

RISK PRONE BEHAVIOR

The relationship of gambling to insurance is important, and the courts have long recognized both types of transaction as aleatory or contingent in nature. If the gambler is an individual whose conduct is at the opposite extreme from that of the insurance minded person, insights into the demand for insurance can be gained from an analysis of gambling conduct. But first the chronic gambler should be differentiated from the casual bettor who is often referred to as indulging in gambling behavior.

The Compulsive Gambler

The most widely held theory of gambling is based on studies of the behavior patterns of chronic gamblers and the nature of their drives. According to Edmund Bergler,[3] the characteristics of the gambler are these:

1. Gambling is a typical, chronic, and repetitive experience in his life.
2. Gambling absorbs all his other interests like a sponge.
3. The gambler is pathologically optimistic about winning and never "learns his lesson" when he loses.
4. The gambler cannot stop when he is winning.
5. No matter how great his initial caution, the true gambler eventually risks more than he can afford.
6. The gambler seeks and enjoys an enigmatic thrill that cannot be logically explained, since it is compounded of as much pain as pleasure

Bergler points out that gambling is not a profession, it is a dangerous neurosis. The gambler does not gamble because he consciously decides to gamble; he is overcome by unconscious forces. He is objectively a sick person who is subjectively unaware of his sickness.

The gambler is a psychic masochist. He is an individual who for unconscious reasons counteracts his own success. He cannot stop with his winnings but must play the game to the very end. The mechanism is described as follows:[4]

[3]Edmund Bergler, *The Psychology of Gambling.* (New York: Hill and Wang, 1957), p. 7.

[4]*Ibid.*, p. 32.

1. Losing is the penalty paid for trying to recreate omnipotence through aggression against parents and educators.
2. Losing satisfies the psychic masochistic urge, the end product of the infantile conflict.
3. Losing provides an alibi for the inner conscience. "I am not masochistic. The world is unjust, and I am an innocent victim."
4. The anticipation of losing provides a thrill, secondarily desired for its pain-pleasure tension *per se.*

Within the gambler's personality there is a conflict between the conscious wish to win and the unconscious wish to lose—and the will to lose must ultimately prevail in order to relieve the gambler of his guilt feelings.

Robert Lindner[5] developed an elaborate Freudian thesis that the gambler unconsciously wishes to lose. In essence, he argued that the gambler wishes to lose because in his unconscious vocabulary, winning means proof positive that his omnipotence was effective in the matter of his responsibility for the Oedipal father's death. The other form of the gambler's dilemma is a bet: the gambler forfeits the omnipotence on which he had based his life and exposes himself to the terrible penalty to be extracted for his incestuous desires. Hence, losing relieves the gambler from guilt. The gambler must win and lose at the same time for his sanity's sake, and this can never be done.

Bergler[6] accounts for the popularity of gambling today in these terms:

> Society ridicules the man who makes an out-and-out claim to omnipotence, and brands him a psychotic. The gambler, however, entertains the same unreal fantasy under conditions that can be misunderstood by the outsider as having a "rational" aim—that of winning money. This pseudorational social approval perpetuates gambling.

Gambling vs. Insurance

The psychiatrists' view of gambling is that it is a form of withdrawal from reality and a response to an underlying anxiety. Insurance is a healthy, normal reaction to anxiety, and gambling is the negative response. Psychodynamic theory holds that as the individual finds his independence he feels a sense of isolation and guilt because he is breaking the infantile parental ties. To overcome this sense of guilt he is led into gambling behavior where his omnipotence feelings can be dashed to the ground in failure. This theory suggests that gambling odds are not too important for the analysis of gambling behavior because they are merely a test of the degree of faith in luck that the individual

[5] Robert M. Lindner, "The Psychodynamics of Gambling," *The Annals of the American Academy of Political and Social Science* (May, 1950).

[6] Bergler, *op. cit.,* p. 240.

has. That he should believe in his luck in the face of known probabilities is a form of nonrational behavior, which is accounted for by other than economic considerations. Economic man might engage in betting activity for the thrill and excitement, but he would never gamble since he must inevitably lose.[7]

By contrast, the man who buys insurance is seeking a normal and healthy outlet for the relief of his anxiety. He wishes to avoid unnecessary risk.

The Accident Prone Personality

The incidence of accidents does not appear to be random. Some individuals have a higher frequency of accidents than others. Those who have a disproportionate number of accidents are described as accident prone, and this group of persons has been the subject of considerable research. Accident prone individuals tend to be antisocial in their behavior, nonconformist, and relatively materialistic. One study[8] characterizes them in terms of seven traits:

1. Difficulty in concentrating; easily distracted
2. Lack of personal restraint
3. Independent, even negative attitude toward others, resulting in uncooperativeness
4. Little sensitivity to views and opinions of others; therefore, few guilt feelings
5. Relative insensitivity to pain
6. Strong need to feel and act superior
7. Need to attract attention to themselves

Increasingly, insurance companies are seeking ways of identifying the accident prone individual in order that they may charge rates that are adequate for the special risks involved.

Measurement of Risk Taking Attitudes

Numerous experiments have been undertaken by psychologists and others in attempts to validate a profile of the risk taker.[9] In the early scientific tests, groups of individuals were placed in situations that required them to make

---

[7] Paul A. Samuelson, *Economics,* 9th ed. (New York: McGraw-Hill Book Company, 1973), pp. 424-26, argues on the basis of the law of diminishing marginal utility that gambling is economically bad and insurance advantageous. This is a standard economic argument.

[8] T.N. Jenkins, "The Accident-Prone Personality." *National Insurance Buyer* (March, 1957), pp. 6ff., cited in Herbert S. Denenberg, Robert D. Eilers, G. Wright Hoffman, Chester A. Kline, Joseph J. Melone and H. Wayne Snider, *Risk and Insurance.* (Englewood Cliffs, N.J.: Prentice-Hall, Inc., 1964), p. 61.

[9] Mark R. Greene, *Risk Aversion, Insurance and the Future.* (Bloomington, Indiana: Indiana University Press, 1971) provides a valuable bibliographic reference source for studies of risk-taking and risk-aversion.

choices in the face of uncertainty, and patterns of "utility preferences" were observed. Such experiments usually failed to provide a sufficiently realistic environment, and the inferences drawn from them are of little pragmatic value. Some insurance companies have introduced "good student" discounts in automobile insurance, based upon a high correlation between higher than average academic standing in high school and low frequency of automobile traffic violations and accidents. These studies have been too limited in scope to warrant generalizations about their results.

In one of the earliest treatises of interest to insurance scholars, Daniel Bernoulli posed the famous Petersburg Paradox. Suppose A offers to bet on a coin toss with B under the following terms: if a head comes up, A will pay one dollar; if not, then on the second toss two dollars; if not, then on the third toss four dollars, and so on indefinitely. The value of the offer, A's mathematical expectation, is infinitely large. A should be willing to pay B a very large sum for the opportunity. In fact, A does not do this because his moral expectation, or marginal utility of money, is not constant. The compulsive gambler, however, is relatively unconcerned with rational considerations.

BEHAVIORAL PERSPECTIVES

The successful insurance agent is aware that psychological factors can significantly influence human behavior with regard to the insurance purchase decision. By recognizing behavioral influences, an agent can vary his approach to clients to stimulate and meet individual needs.

Culture and Society

Culture is a pattern of traditional ideas and values that continually evolve and accumulate as basic values and beliefs. Cultures are constructed from subcultures that continually shift within the central entity. In contrast to a culture, a society is a more organized group of individuals. While members of a culture are bound by a set of values, members of a society are tied by functional needs, trade, or business. However, because a society usually is required to have internal consistency or a lack of inherent conflict, societies and cultures are often intermingled and are difficult to distinguish.

Within the American culture or society the following basic values influence the insurance purchase decision: dignity of the individual, personal freedom, self-reliance, and concern for material success. The primary function of insurance is to reduce uncertainty and thus allow an individual to pursue his other activities with less anxiety. This adds to personal freedom and dignity. Furthermore, the indemnification provided by insurance allows an individual to be more self-reliant in the face of uncontrollable risks. In addition, insurance protects the economic value accumulated in material possessions and in certain instances (e.g., life insurance) may be a financial asset. While many individuals recognize social goals and adhere to a pattern of behavior that is consistent with their attainment, others require a stimulus. Agents have often been successful in persuading a client to purchase insurance by stressing a social role for insurance. For example, society expects a man to provide a flow of income for his family. Failure to have a supplementary income in the event of his death or disability would be in conflict with this expected social role. The purchase of insurance guarantees a husband that he will fulfill the imputed responsibility to his family.

The emphasis on expected role within a culture is frequently employed when an individual is about to enter a different subculture. For example, students who will soon graduate and enter the work force are often told that life insurance must be a part of their new way of life. Like the new car, the expanded wardrobe, or other material signs of achievement, the life insurance policy is bought to demonstrate membership in the new group.

Emotions and Motivations

While most people believe that they act in a rational manner, emotions are a primary determinant of behavior. This is especially true of the insurance purchase decision. Emotions are learned reactions to a set of experiences or perceptions that have either been very favorable or very distressing. Contact with events or thoughts that recall these experiences can stimulate a desire to remove or satisfy the resulting emotions. For example, individuals who have experienced dire poverty attempt to avoid recurrence of this status for themselves or their families. One response may be the purchase of life insurance to protect existing and future income flows.

Emotions can be learned from the experiences of others. Because emotions can thus be generalized from one set of circumstances to another, many agents are successful in communicating to a client the emotional consequences of failing to obtain insurance protection. By supplementing or controlling a client's feelings, the agent motivates the individual to buy insurance. The purchase of insurance provides the individual with an overt and constructive outlet for his emotions.

Personality

Personality is a set of forces (wants, drives, abilities, etc.) within an individual that determine his reaction to a changing set of environmental stimuli. As our personality emerges, so does our set of values and attitudes. Personality traits, which evolve from a learning process, can play a significant role in the purchase decisions of a consumer. Of particular interest to the insurance purchase decision is an individual's risk preferences, or his subjective utility values assigned to either risk avoidance or risk assumption. When exposed to a similar set of perils, two individuals may react quite differently. One may have a low tolerance for risk and seek full insurance coverage at any reasonable cost; the other may be willing to assume the risk.

OBJECTIVE PROBABILITIES AND RISK

Peril

The objective aspect of fear and anxiety is analogous to the subjective. The individual is objectively exposed to a variety of events, incidents, or occurrences that may be labelled perils. Hazard may create or increase the chance of loss arising from a given peril, but peril is the event itself. Fire, accident, and automobile collision are examples of perils.

Hazards may be classified as either physical, morale, moral, or legal. Physical hazards are objective factors that tend to increase the chance of loss. Examples include oily rags in a cellar, dynamite stored near a furnace, or faulty brakes on a car. Morale and moral hazards are subjective factors that increase the chance of loss. The morale hazard results from carelessness and indifference, whereas the moral hazard results from intentional dishonesty or fraud with intent to benefit from insurance proceeds.[10] Legal hazard arises from the uncertainties of the legal process.

Risk

The term risk is often used in an objective sense to represent a combination of perils. Insurance companies speak of being "on the risk" or having an "amount at risk." The risk is perceived to be the combination of perils and their probable economic consequences. Dictionaries define risk as exposure to loss or injury. Risk is sometimes defined as the chance of loss or the degree of probability of a loss. The risk in a fair coin toss is 50 percent and the risk of an event that is certain to happen is 100 percent. Risk can also be defined as the probability of any outcome different from that which was expected—as a measure of surprise. Many scholars define risk as uncertainty concerning loss. They would gauge the degree of risk by the probable variation of actual as compared with expected experience.[11] For our purposes, the term risk usually refers to perils to which the individual is objectively exposed at any time.

[10] Irving Pfeffer, *Insurance and Economic Theory* (Homewood, Ill.: Richard D. Irwin, Inc., 1956) discusses moral and morale hazard in terms of the requirements of insurability.

[11] Curtis M. Elliott and Emmett J. Vaugh, *Fundamentals of Risk and Insurance* (New York: John Wiley and Sons, Inc., 1972), pp. 4ff. treat current choices of definition of risk in a systematic manner.

Probability and Variance

Risk is measured by probability, which is a statistical or mathematical idea. Because it is both widely used and because it serves better than some alternative approaches that are available, the statistical relative frequency concept is the meaning of probability most appropriate in insurance. Probability, or chance of loss, is characterized by dispersion or deviations from expected results and by higher order probabilities. These are described statistically by the use of measurements of variance. Dispersion is the probability that a given observed probability is correct. Dispersion will tend to vary according to the size of the sample being studied and some of its other characteristics.

Insurance and Risk Management

The means of altering either dispersion or probability of loss is by physical or other objective action. Prevention, protection, combinational devices, hedging, and transfers are the analogs of insurance, psychiatry, voodooism, and faith. The one set operates at the objective level and the other at the subjective. Insurance, as a transfer mechanism, has a real world legal basis in addition to operating on the psyche of the individual.

The paradigm of fears and perils, Figure 14.1, illustrates the parallelism between the subjective and objective aspects of the phenomena we have been describing. The categories are not mutually exclusive because there are interactions and overlaps, but the notion that there is a set of events in the real world that must be dealt with in external terms and another set in the mental or emotional world that must be dealt with psychologically is clear.

HUMAN KNOWLEDGE AND INSURER BEHAVIOR

The varieties of human knowledge which affect the operations of insurers and the consumer's insurance purchase decision may be classified as scientific, aesthetic, or transcendental.

Scientific

Scientific knowledge is that which is derived from observation, study, and experimentation. The realm of controlled experiment is relatively small in our total experience, and in the field of behavioral science the range is even smaller than it appears to be in the physical sciences. The limits of scientific knowledge in the field of insurance are quite narrow because the variables are so numerous and the parameters constantly changing. The testing of hypotheses appears to be too abstract a preoccupation to interest most business practitioners.

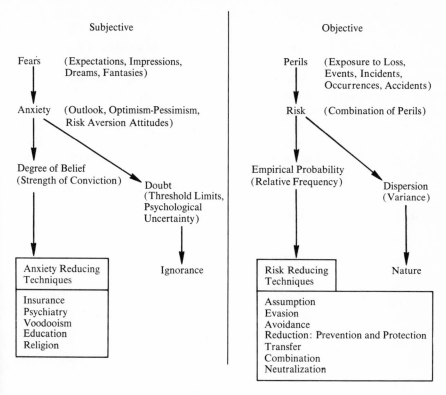

FIGURE 14.1   Paradigm of Fears and Perils

Aesthetic

Aesthetics, which may be defined as the study of the fine arts, deals with taste and intuition. The content is usually perceived as more visceral than cognitive.[12] The rules of aesthetics are not the same as the rules of science.

Transcendental

Transcendental knowledge is not derived from experience but is based on the *a priori* elements of experience, which are held by one school of philosophy to be necessary conditions of human knowledge. The transcendentalist argues from the supernatural, the abstract, and the metaphysical. He depends on faith

---

[12] Aesthetic judgments are not irrational. They are based upon a different set of premises than scientific judgments. Ultimately, if the weights for intuitive hunches could be known, aesthetics could have a scientific basis. Insurance underwriters and claimsmen frequently base their decisions upon such hidden variables as their personal tastes in physical appearance, personal behavior, and socio-economic impressions.

or belief, intuition, or spirituality rather than on testing hypotheses or mere consensus.

Among these forms of human knowledge (scientific, aesthetic, and transcendental) there is no primacy in fact. Most of us employ each of the three sources, and our everyday judgments are based as much upon the nonscientific as the scientific components of thought. It is this eclectic approach to knowledge that conditions our responses to risk and anxiety and sets limits on the knowledge that we can usefully employ. The weight of evidence in support of our belief is usually expressed in terms of a probability notion. Thus, there are many different ideas of the nature and meaning of probability, but the central ideas are crucial for insurance.[13]

RISK MANAGEMENT TECHNIQUES

There are in general seven possible responses to risk and anxiety situations:

1. Assumption
2. Evasion
3. Avoidance
4. Reduction: Prevention and Protection
5. Transfer
6. Combination
7. Neutralization

Usually these techniques are employed in combination, but they may be employed individually as well.

Assumption

Most widely used, assumption is merely the absorption of the risk of loss without transfer to another. This may take the form of mindless disregard of the perils or blind assumption; it may be more rational and entail contingency reserves, particularly where there is adequate time for the build-up of such funds. In the highest form, it may involve self-insurance, real or imagined.

A real self-insurance scheme is one in which the insured replicates the technique of the insurance carrier but without actual risk transfer. The law of large numbers is used, records are maintained, and there may even be the actual segregation of a premium fund beyond the mere accounting entry. When a loss occurs, it can be absorbed from the funds set aside in the self-insurance fund.

[13]Irving Pfeffer, *op. cit.*, pp. 153-85 discusses "The Foundations of Probability."

Evasion

Evasion, which is not usually regarded as a risk management technique, encompasses the possibilities of default in meeting obligations, which is a method of avoiding responsibility for loss reduction where it is successful. Negotiated settlement of losses at a fraction of their worth is another aspect of this. Ultimately, bankruptcy is the best known application of the evasion approach. Other aspects of this same phenomenon include neurotic behavior and compulsive gambling.

Avoidance

Avoidance occurs when the individual or business removes itself from exposure to a risk. A business can avoid a product's liability exposure by discontinuing the product. An individual can avoid the liability exposure resulting from owning a car by selling the car. While avoidance is not always a viable alternative, there are numerous situations where an individual has a choice between exposure to risk or avoidance of it.

Reduction: Prevention and Protection

Prevention is defined as measures taken before the misfortune occurs. This would include fireproofing, burglar alarms, safety tires, and so on. Protection is the collection of acts taken to reduce loss after the event occurs. Fire hoses and hydrants, covers, guards, and the like would be examples. Limitations of liability in many forms are part of the reduction technique. Such limitations include corporate limited liability of shareowners, hold harmless agreements, sidetrack agreements, and stop loss orders on the stock exchange. Each of these is designed to reduce the exposure to loss by the recipient of the benefit.

Transfer

Transfer of risk results in reduction of anxiety. Insurance is a fine example. The insurer agrees to stand in the place of the insured in the event that loss occurs. He offers to defend, pay, repair, rebuild, or replace on behalf of the insured. By the same token, hold harmless clauses achieve the same effect of transferring the liability risk to another. Guarantee or suretyship also has the same result. The obligee is protected against the financial consequences of default by the principal.

Combination

Any grouping of risks that can permit averaging to occur is a technique of combination that may be valuable. Insurance, cosuretyship, and corporate limited liability are illustrations of combination at work.

Neutralization

Neutralization is hedging. The nature of the hedging operation is to reduce risk by offsetting transactions. For example, a buyer who anticipates a future price rise may purchase a contract for future delivery today from a seller who does not anticipate a future price rise. Speculators make a market in future contracts for those who have differing expectations of change. Neutralization thereby reduces the risk of undesirable price rises from the buyer's point of view and equally undesirable price declines for the seller.

Each of us employs one or more of these techniques in our efforts to reduce the chance of loss and of risk. Our motivation is in large part a desire to reduce anxiety, and this is achieved by the realization that measures have been taken to deal with risk. It is the unknown that causes us the greatest apprehension. Objectively coping with the reality of accidents reduces our fear and thereby our anxiety.

A DEFINITION OF INSURANCE

Insurance may be defined in the context of psychology as a device for the reduction of the anxiety of the insured by transfer of part of the risk to which he is, or believes he is, exposed to another, the insurer, who promises to indemnify him for the financial losses that arise from the perils insured against.[14]

INSURANCE AND THE PUBLIC INTEREST

Because of the pervasive nature of risk and anxiety and the complexity of insurance, public policy holds insurers responsible for a reasonable standard of conduct in their relations with the insured. Insurance is indispensable to the conduct of commerce and the provision of personal economic security. It is a

---

[14] *Ibid.*, p. 53 offers a more rigorous definition of insurance.

desirable service and therefore in need of public regulation of its security, reasonableness, and fairness. Insurance is almost a public utility. That its franchise is nonexclusive removes it from the utility class, but regulatory attitudes treat it as a quasi-public utility. Therefore, it is in the public interest that companies be responsible and have a positive economic effect on society. It is the dependency of the public on insurance companies that requires the consumer be protected from the consequences of ignorance in insurance matters.

SUMMARY

Fear and anxiety about the financial consequences of adverse surprise inhibit individuals in their decision-making activity. Subjectively, there are psychological factors that can explain the nature of this anxiety. Insurance is one of the means of dealing with it. Abnormal anxiety found in risk prone or gambling behavior does not evoke an insurance response.

Objectively, the idea of probability provides a basis for making predictions about possible events, which is essential for sound insurance operations. It is the basis for the laws of large numbers.

Risk management techniques attempt to alter the objective exposure to risk by changing the hazards and thereby reducing potential loss.

REVIEW QUESTIONS

1. The text describes seven approaches to management of risk. Describe two examples of each of these approaches, indicating the circumstances under which they might be used.

2. Williams decides that he is not going to buy insurance against the risk of theft of his personal effects but will assume the risk himself. Is this self-insurance? Explain.

3. Define:
   a. risk   b. hazard
   c. peril   d. anxiety
   e. uncertainty.

4. Anxiety reduction is an important motive for buying insurance, but there are other important motives as well. What are some of these? Discuss.

5. "Risk and uncertainty are terms employed to distinguish external or objective phenomena from the states of mind which are their subjective counterparts." Discuss.

STUDY QUESTIONS

6. Three months hence, the treasurer of the International Widget Corporation must pay in Swiss francs for a shipment of watch movements. He is concerned that the value of the dollar may decline by as much as 10 percent during this time. The forward exchange rate for 90 day money shows Swiss francs selling at no premium. How might the treasurer neutralize his risk? Explain. What is the role of a speculator in this field? Discuss.

7. Discuss the nature and significance of each of the following types of hazard: moral, physical, morale, and legal. How does the presence of each type of hazard affect the predictability of future loss experience from the standpoint of an insurance company? Explain.

8. "The insurance institution, while concerned with the reduction of loss, is primarily concerned with the reduction or minimization of loss variation." Discuss.

9. The varieties of human knowledge are said to be scientific, aesthetic, and transcendental. Describe an example in which each of these three sources of knowledge might be used by a prospect for insurance in making a buying decision.

10. If gambling is "sick" behavior, how do you account for the fact that lotteries are popular government institutions in many states and foreign countries? Explain.

IV

ECONOMIC
PERSPECTIVES

The structure and competitive nature of the insurance industry in both its micro and macroeconomic aspects are important elements to understand what the insurer can and might be expected to do. The insurance industry is composed of governmental and private sectors, companies owned by stockholders and by policyholders, individuals underwriting each for his own account, and of multibillion dollar corporations. The diversity of form, product, marketing strategy, and goals presents special problems in the study of insurance economics.

Economic development throughout the world has expanded the role of insurance in all of the developed countries and made critical the problems of international trade in insurance for underdeveloped nations.

15

Structure

and Competition in

the Insurance Industry

Some insurance codes define insurance as a contract whereby one undertakes to indemnify another against loss, damage, or liability arising from a contingent or unknown event. The insurer is the party who undertakes to indemnify another by insurance, and the insured is the person indemnified. This may serve as an operational definition for exploring the structure of the insurance industry in economic terms. Thousands of insurers provide a remarkable array of different insurance practices and services. Insurance organizations take many different legal forms, adopt different marketing approaches, operate in different parts of the country (many in only a single county), and have different patterns of ownership and control. Insurers may be in either the private or government sector.

PRIVATE VS. SOCIAL INSURANCE

The United States, unlike many other countries, maintains a well defined separation between private and public sectors of the insurance business. In some countries the insurance industry has been completely or partially nationalized; other countries have equity ownership in what appear to be privately operated insurance companies. Still other countries, such as the U.S.S.R. and the People's

Republic of China, have stock insurance companies whose principal or entire activity is outside their national boundaries.

The distinction between private and public sectors in the United States is given a legal foundation by discriminatory insurance statutes, which provide that a "certificate of authority" shall not issue to any insurer owned, operated, or controlled directly or indirectly by any other state, province, district, territory nation, or any governmental subdivision or agency thereof.

Perhaps the clearest distinction between social and private insurance identifies social insurance with compulsory plans and private insurance with voluntary plans. Most forms of social insurance are designed for the benefit of persons with low and uncertain incomes who have a presumptive need for basic economic security. Statutes provide the contract, the taxing power of the state the ultimate guarantee, public policy the flexibility, and cost estimates the actuarial basis for benefits in social insurance.

Philosophically, the position implicit in the American insurance industry is that government should be responsible only for coverage of those hazards that cannot be adequately insured by private industry because of their catastrophic potential. These include unemployment, war insurrection, rebellion, invasion, flood, property expropriation by foreign governments, and collapse of the

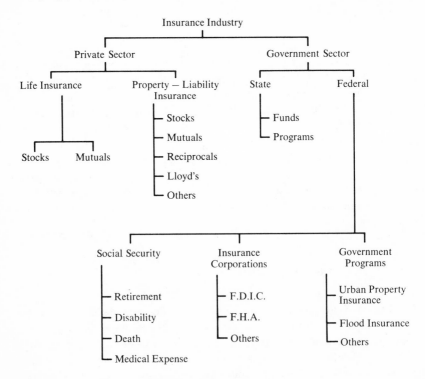

FIGURE 15.1   Structure of the U.S. Insurance Industry

banking system, among others. Where private industry is willing and able to provide insurance services on an acceptable basis, the government tends to play a relatively inactive role. Despite their proliferation, in the aggregate government programs collect less revenues than private insurance in the United States. It is significant that government insurance programs have entered fields once considered the exclusive province of the private insurance industry.

SUBINDUSTRIES WITHIN THE PRIVATE SECTOR

The private sector of the American insurance industry offers individual insurance contracts embracing every type of insurable hazard. For historical reasons two subindustries are given separate treatment: life and health insurance and property and casualty insurance. This separation is not made so clearly in other countries. Table 15.1 lists the products commonly sold by each of the two major subindustries. In addition to the division between types of insurance, there is an important distinction between stock and mutual insurers. Stock insurers are owned and controlled by common stockholders, whereas mutual insurers have no common stockholders and are owned and controlled by their policyholders.

TABLE 15.1   Insurance Products

*Property and Liability**	*Life and Health*
Automobile Liability	Whole Life Insurance
Automobile Physical Damage	Term Life Insurance
Fire Insurance and Allied Lines	Endowment
Liability (other than Auto)	Annuities
Workmen's Compensation	Disability Income Insurance
Homeowners Multiple Peril	Hospitalization
Commercial Multiple Peril	Surgical Expense
Inland Marine	Major Medical
Surety and Fidelity	Dental Expense
Ocean Marine	
Burglary and Theft	
Crop-Hail	
Boiler and Machinery	
Glass	

*Listed by order of 1971 total premiums.

SOURCE: *Insurance Facts 1972.* (New York: Insurance Information Institute, 1972).

Life insurance companies are permitted to write all types of life insurance and annuity contracts. In addition, they are authorized to write health insurance in all its forms, as are liability insurance companies and specialty health insurance carriers. As seen in Table 15.2, life insurance is a substantial growth industry, approximately doubling its aggregate assets, premiums, benefits, and insurance-in-force every decade since 1900.

TABLE 15.2   Life Insurance Industry Size and Growth
           ($ millions omitted)

	1940	1950	1960	1970
Premiums	3,887	8,189	17,365	36,767
Benefits	2,664	3,730	8,118	16,449
Assets	30,802	64,020	119,576	207,254
Insurance-in-Force	115,530	234,168	586,448	1,402,758

SOURCE: *1972 Life Insurance Fact Book.* (New York: Institute of Life Insurance, 1972).

There are more than 1800 companies in the life insurance business. More than 1650 are owned by stockholders with the remainder mutual companies. Stock companies account for less than 35 percent of the total assets of all U.S. life insurance companies; mutual life insurance companies control the balance. Of the insurance-in-force, stock companies have 48 percent; the mutuals control 52 percent. Since World War II, stock life insurance companies as a group have had higher average growth rates than the mutuals, but the market share of stock life insurers is still relatively small.

The general insurance or property and liability branch of the industry is smaller in asset size than the life branch, although the variety of product lines and the number of companies is much larger. There is greater diversity among companies within the property and liability subindustry. As shown in Table 15.3, the stock companies have the largest share of the property and liability insurance market, followed by mutuals. Over the years the trend has been toward an increasing share of the property and liability insurance market being held by stock companies. This is in part a function of the stock companies' inherent ability to attract external capital funds, as contrasted with the limited internal capital resources of mutuals and other categories of companies. In recent years relatively few property and liability insurance company charters have been granted to firms other than stock companies.

THE STRUCTURE OF THE INSURANCE INDUSTRY

Structure refers to the pattern of sellers and buyers who constitute a specific market. It identifies the organizational characteristics of a market and is determined by the relationships between market participants who influence the extent and nature of competition. The primary determinants of insurance

TABLE 15.3   Property and Liability Insurance Size and Growth
($000,000)

	1946	1950	1960	1970
Stock				
Assets	4,229	10,602	22,776	42,467
Premiums	1,729	5,137	10,527	22,429
Policyholders Surplus	2,208	4,216	9,494	14,014
Mutual				
Assets	821	2,551	6,580	14,139
Premiums	443	1,506	3,899	8,979
Policyholders Surplus	377	989	2,163	4,045
Reciprocal				
Assets	81	286	727	1,830
Premiums	50	199	522	1,432
Policyholders Surplus	41	114	262	442
Lloyd's				
Assets	12	34	47	55
Premiums	5	23	22	24
Policyholders Surplus	4	9	9	17
Total				
Assets	5,143	13,473	30,130	58,491
Premiums	2,227	6,865	14,970	32,864
Policyholders Surplus	2,630	5,328	11,928	18,518

SOURCE: *Best's Aggregates and Averages: Property and Liability 1971.* (Morristown, New Jersey: A.M. Best Company, 1971).

industry market structure are seller concentration and conditions of entry and exit. Structure is important because the existence of certain conditions may determine specific market performance by the industry. High barriers to entry in an industry and a high degree of concentration in sales usually lead to excessive profits. However, this does not mean that high barriers and concentration will always lead to bad performance or that low concentration and no barriers to entry will necessarily guarantee nonexcessive profits. High concentration and barriers to entry suggest that undesirable market performance may exist or may be forthcoming.

Seller Concentration

Economic studies of markets often utilize the concept of concentration to describe the structure of an industry. Concentration ratios are widely used. They measure in percentages such variables as assets, sales, or number of employees controlled by a select number of industry members. Concentration may be defined as "a process of growth of the relative share of output by big enterprises in the aggregate output of an economy or industry . . . The result of the process of economic concentration is clearly that fewer and larger units control production."[1] The Department of Transportation report on structural trends in automobile insurance summarizes the importance of reviewing concentration:

> Concentration measures, along with the number and relative size distribution of sellers, are used as an indicator of independent behavior in making various market decisions, particularly pricing decisions. Thus, the greater the degree of concentration the greater the likelihood of either covert or overt interdependent price making decisions.[2]

Until recently most observers contended that the insurance industry was relatively low in its degree of concentration of power.[3] A study by the American Insurance Association found that levels of concentration in the insurance industry are below those of most other large American industries. A report by the New York Insurance Department indicated that the property and liability insurance industry is one of the least concentrated industries in the United States. Table 15.4 provides a comparison of insurance product concentration ratios with other products.

During the late 1930s and 1940s there were several Congressional investigations into the degree of concentration in the life insurance business. Allegations of dangerous degrees of concentration were not substantiated. If anything, these Congressional inquiries suggested that the life insurance industry was undergoing deconcentration. In particular, stock life insurers demonstrated significant growth since World War II. In 1942, 61 mutual life insurers had issued about 75 percent of the policies in force and controlled approximately 80 percent of life insurance assets. By 1969, the number of mutual life insurers had increased to 155, while their control of total life insurance industry assets fell to 68 percent. During the same period the number of stock life insurers increased by 1,292 to a total of 1,633 companies, and their share of issued policies increased from 25 percent to 50 percent.

---

[1] Bastiaan Fortman, *Theory of Competition Policy* (Amsterdam: North-Holland Publishing Company, 1966), p. 106.

[2] *Structural Trends and Conditions in the Automobile Insurance Industry,* Report of the Division of Industry Analysis, Bureau of Economics of the Federal Trade Commission to the Department of Transportation, April 1970, p. 34.

[3] See *Prices and Profits in the Property and Liability Insurance Industry.* Arthur D. Little, Inc. (November, 1967); Roy Hensley, *Competition, Regulation and the Public Interest in Non-Life Insurance* (Berkeley, Cal.: University of California Press, 1962); New York Insurance Department, *The Public Interest Now in Property and Liability Regulation* (New York: Insurance Department of the State of New York, 1969); *The Stanford Report,* (Stanford, Cal.: Stanford Research Institute, 1967), Vol. 1.

TABLE 15.4 Comparative Concentration Ratios

Product	Concentration Ratios		
	% Top 4	*% Top 8*	*% Top 20*
Auto Physical Damage Insurance[a]	27.19%	38.29%	54.98%
Auto Property Damage Liability Insurance[a]	28.10	40.01	58.34
Auto Bodily Injury Liability Insurance[a]	28.94	40.66	59.57
Homeowners Insurance[a]	21.48	34.44	55.49
Fire Insurance[a]	20.96	35.02	60.27
Commercial Multiperil[a]	27.99	46.23	74.21
Ordinary Life Insurance[b]	29.05	38.23	55.38
Group Life Insurance[b]	32.13	52.40	72.17
Steel[c]	57.80	76.00	—
Computer Machinery[c]	68.00	76.00	—
Aircraft[c]	67.00	88.00	—

SOURCES: [a]Denenberg *et. al.* "Competition and Concentration: The Reality and Mythology of Economic Concentration in the Insurance Business." *CPCU Annals* (September, 1970), p. 267.
[b]Denenberg *et. al.* "Concentration in the U.S. Life Insurance Industry." *The Journal of Risk and Insurance* XXXIX (June, 1972), p. 184.
[c]*Studies by the Staff of the Cabinet Committee on Price Stability.* Washington, D.C.: U.S. Government Printing Office. January, 1969, p. 93.

Recent studies have questioned the validity of the foregoing findings.[4] The primary criticism focuses on the lack of sufficient subdivision of the market. The earlier studies examined data for the national market in broad categories of insurance. Critics argue for the need to refine the market definitions and present concentration data calculated by state and by specific line of insurance (see Table 15.5). For example, the analysis of automobile insurance written premiums by state reveals a wide variation in concentration ratios. The Department of Transportation report on automobile insurance stated:

There is considerable dispersion of four, eight, and twenty company concentration ratios by state. Four company concentration in the bodily

[4]See Herbert S. Denenberg *et. al.,* "Competition and Concentration: The Reality and Mythology of Economic Concentration in the Insurance Business-Part 1," *CPCU Annals* (September, 1970); *Structural Trends and Conditions in the Automobile Insurance Industry,* op. cit.; J. David Cummins, Herbert S. Denenberg and William C. Scheel, "Concentration in the U.S. Life Insurance Industry," *The Journal of Risk and Insurance,* XXXIX (June, 1972); Gerald Hartman, "Insurance Experience and Rating Laws," *The Journal of Risk and Insurance,* XXXVII (June, 1970), p. 203.

TABLE 15.5   Cumulative Market Shares: Ordinary Life Insurance

State	Insurance Written				
	% Top 4	% Top 8	% Top 20	Herf. Index	Rank [a]
Alabama	30.90	42.26	61.53	0.0448	11
Alaska	49.28	66.17	84.49	0.0858	3
Arizona	21.93	34.51	58.00	0.0225	39
Arkansas	17.48	30.59	55.57	0.0185	46
California	24.93	35.47	54.83	0.0236	37
Colorado	23.42	33.86	53.58	0.0218	41
Connecticut	44.35	56.35	75.13	0.0620	8
Delaware	32.40	45.94	69.63	0.0442	12
District of Columbia	36.17	47.24	65.41	0.0567	9
Florida	22.78	34.29	52.56	0.0213	42
Georgia	17.76	28.34	48.89	0.0155	49
Hawaii	26.27	41.50	67.65	0.0301	25
Idaho	26.51	40.22	62.52	0.0279	30
Illinois	30.89	42.20	62.19	0.0357	16
Indiana	27.06	41.25	63.76	0.0332	19
Iowa	23.22	36.61	58.20	0.0237	36
Kansas	21.57	32.12	53.09	0.0206	44
Kentucky	29.30	43.41	64.70	0.0322	22
Louisiana	22.80	32.69	52.03	0.0202	45
Maine	52.21	63.16	80.78	0.0886	1
Maryland	26.56	39.77	61.06	0.0298	27
Massachusetts	47.30	59.34	77.51	0.0723	6
Michigan	29.68	41.26	60.42	0.0316	23
Minnesota	20.95	32.53	56.44	0.0225	38
Mississippi	21.11	32.90	56.78	0.0218	40
Missouri	23.70	36.14	56.12	0.0243	34
Montana	32.69	43.89	61.47	0.0395	14
Nebraska	19.62	33.17	60.09	0.0213	43
Nevada	29.57	41.16	61.96	0.0331	20

injury line ranged from a low of 24.2 percent in Texas to a high of 54.8 percent in Nevada. Concentration ratios are of a similar magnitude for physical damage and property damage liability coverages, although property damage coverage is somewhat less concentrated on the average than the liability automobile lines.[5]

While the data indicate that concentration is relatively low in the insurance industry, contemporary studies have revealed that when the market is more precisely defined market shares are not as small as might appear from aggregate statistics.

[5] *Structural Trends and Conditions in the Automobile Insurance Industry*, op. cit., p. 25.

TABLE 15.5   *Continued*

State	Insurance Written				
	% Top 4	% Top 8	% Top 20	Herf. Index	Rank[a]
New Jersey	47.18	56.26	71.87	0.0775	5
New Mexico	29.28	38.67	57.94	0.0281	29
New York	44.81	56.89	75.77	0.0637	7
North Carolina	24.49	39.42	63.98	0.0282	28
North Dakota	21.73	35.28	62.76	0.0240	35
Ohio	32.13	45.55	65.49	0.0395	13
Oklahoma	16.19	27.01	49.96	0.0150	50
Oregon	24.34	38.36	60.34	0.0251	33
Pennsylvania	38.41	47.73	63.26	0.0542	10
Rhode Island	50.88	59.80	77.42	0.0873	2
South Carolina	27.41	40.22	62.93	0.0337	18
South Dakota	28.06	39.89	64.50	0.0301	26
Tennessee	18.18	28.42	50.93	0.0166	48
Texas	18.29	29.63	49.99	0.0168	47
Utah	32.69	43.95	64.42	0.0368	15
Vermont	49.21	63.77	86.32	0.0777	4
Virginia	25.41	38.79	57.81	0.0253	32
Washington	26.96	35.49	53.95	0.0265	31
West Virginia	29.07	42.13	64.38	0.0327	21
Wisconsin	31.21	43.89	63.83	0.0352	17
Wyoming	28.48	40.62	61.99	0.0310	24
Mean	29.54	41.60	62.52	0.0366	
Standard Deviation	9.56	9.69	8.78	0.0202	
Coef. of Variation	0.32	0.23	0.14	0.5507	

[a]Rankings are from largest to smallest according to the Herfindahl Index.

SOURCE: Denenberg *et. al.* "Concentration in the U.S. Life Insurance Industry." *The Journal of Risk and Insurance.* XXXIX (June, 1972), pp. 186-7.

Conditions of Entry

Entry into specific markets of the insurance industry is relatively easy.[6] The main hurdles are the initial capital and surplus required by the law and the implementation of an effective marketing system.

State statutes vary with respect to their requirements for new insurance companies (as illustrated in Table 15.6). Furthermore, there are different requirements in each state for different types of insurance companies. For

[6] Any study of concentration should deal with conditions of entry because low barriers can offset the potential monopoly effects of high concentration.

TABLE 15.6   Minimum Capital and Surplus Requirements of Each State for Domestic Life Insurance Companies, 1970

State	Requirement		Statute
	$ Capital	$ Surplus	
Alabama	200,000	300,000	Ala. Stat. Title 28 S1 (1967)
Alaska	200,000	100,000	Alaska Stat. 21.09.070 (1966)
Arizona	20,000	50,000	Ariz. Rev. Stat. 20-210 & 20-211 (1966)
Arkansas	100,000	100,000	Ark. Stat. SS66-2207, 66-2208 (1967)
California	450,000	550,000	Calif. Ins. Code 700.05 & 10510 (1965)
Colorado	200,000	100,000	Colo. Rev. Stat. S72-1-36 (1963)
Connecticut	Created by Legislature		
Delaware	300,000	150,000	18 Del. Code S511 (1968)
D.C.	200,000	100,000	D.C. Code SS35-508, 35-601 (1964)
Florida	500,000	750,000	Fla. Stat. SS624.0206, 624.0207 (1968)
Georgia	200,000	200,000	Ga. Code SS56-306,-307 (1963)
Hawaii	200,000	100,000	Hawaii Ins. Law 431-88, -89 (1963)
Idaho	400,000	400,000	Idaho Ins. Code S41-313 (1969)
Illinois	400,000	200,000	Ill. Stat. S73:625 (1965)
Indiana	400,000	600,000	Ind. Stat. Ann. S39-3614 (1967)
Iowa	350,000	400,000	Ia. Code S508.5 (1965)
Kansas	200,000	100,000	Kan. Gen. Stat. S40-401 (1965)
Kentucky	500,000	750,000	Ky. Rev. Stat. S304.072 (1966)
Louisiana	100,000	200,000	La. Ins. Code S22:71 (1966)
Maine	500,000	1,000,000	Maine Ins. Code 24-A S410 (1970)
Maryland	500,000	750,000	Md. Stat. Code Art. 48A S48,49 (1965)
Massachusetts	400,000	800,000	Mass. Gen. Laws c. 175 S48, 51 (1968)
Michigan	1,000,000	500,000	Mich. Stat. Code 500.410 (1965)
Minnesota	200,000		Minn. Stat. S60.29 (1963)
Mississippi	200,000	300,000	Miss. Code S5660 (1962)
Missouri	200,000	200,000	Mo. Stat. Ann. S376.280 (1964)
Montana	100,000	100,000	Mont. Rev. Code SS40-2808 (1965)

example, to organize a new stock life insurance company in New York the organization must provide a minimum of $1 million in capital and $2 million in paid-in surplus. In Illinois the same company can be formed with $400,000 in capital and $200,000 in paid-in surplus.

A new insurer must be able to acquire or develop an effective distribution system. Most new companies rely on the existing independent agency and broker system and do not invest in distribution systems based on salaried salesmen. However, most agents and brokers already have outlets for their sales efforts. To provide special incentives, the new insurers will usually be required either to pay higher than average commissions or to implement a bonus program.

While state supervisory authorities examine the character and past record of the founders of a new insurance company, this has not been a significant barrier to entry into the industry.

TABLE 15.6 *Continued*

State	Requirement		Statute
	$ Capital	*$ Surplus*	
Nebraska	500,000	500,000	Neb. Stat. 44-214 (1967)
Nevada	200,000	100,000	Nev. Rev. Stat. S682.160 (1963)
New Hampshire	600,000		N.H. Stat. S411:1 (1969)
New Jersey	800,000	1,700,000	N.J. Stat. S17:17-6 (1968)
New Mexico	100,000	200,000	N.M. Stat. Ann. S58-18-24 (1965)
New York	1,000,000	2,000,000	N.Y. Ins. Law S191 (1967)
North Carolina	300,000	300,000	N.C. Ins. Laws S58-777 (1963)
North Dakota	150,000	75,000	N.D. Rev. Code S26.08-04 (1963)
Ohio	400,000	600,000	Ohio Rev. Code 3907.05 (1965)
Oklahoma	250,000	125,000	Okla. Ins. Code 36 S610, 611 (1967)
Oregon	500,000		Ore. Rev. Stat. S731:554 (1967)
Pennsylvania	300,000	150,000	40 Penn. Stat. Ann. S383 (1967)
Rhode Island	Created by Legislature		R.I. Gen. Laws S7-1-5 (1956)
South Carolina	100,000	100,000	S.C. Code S37-181 (1963)
South Dakota	200,000	200,000	S.D. Code S31.1510 (1959)
Tennessee	150,000	150,000	Tenn. Code Ann. SS56-303, 305 (1961)
Texas	100,000	100,000	Texas Insurance Code Art. 3.02 (1963)
Utah	200,000	500,000	Utah Ins. Laws S31-11-1 (1967)
Vermont	250,000	150,000	8 Vt. Stat. Ann. S3304 (1968)
Virginia	500,000	300,000	Va. Ins. Laws S38.1-88 (1966)
Washington	400,000	400,000	Wash. Rev. Code S48.05.340 (1967)
West Virginia	750,000	375,000	West. Va. Code 33-3-5 (1968)
Wisconsin	400,000	100,000	Wisc. Ins. Code 201.04 (1966)
Wyoming	200,000	100,000	Wyo. Ins. Laws 26.1-57 (1965)

SOURCE: E.J. Leverett. "Paid-in Surplus and Capital Requirements of a New Life Insurance Company." *Journal of Risk and Insurance*, XXXVIII (March, 1971), p. 16.

Unlike many foreign governments, most U.S. regulators do not implement a "needs" test. A needs test allows entry only if the market demand is sufficient to justify the additional capacity of a new insurer. United States regulators believe that government should not attempt to restrict the opportunity for sound insurance companies to enter the field and compete. Spencer Kimball in a discussion of the goals of regulation states:

Another important economic objective is freedom of entrepreneurs to form new units and enter the market. We might also call this goal one of freedom of access to the market. In some European countries, this objective of insurance regulation is rejected—it simply does not exist. Some European countries thus have a "needs" test for the admission of new enterprises to the market, a kind of "certificate of convenience and necessity" applied to the insurance field. We have resisted this in this country and have regarded as an important value accessibility of the insurance market to new enterprises.[7]

Technical capabilities are not a significant barrier to entry because a new insurer may join a rating bureau or trade association and, as a benefit of membership, receive product advice and proposed rates as promulgated for all members. Furthermore, a new firm is not required to institute its own claims department. Independent claims adjusters are geographically dispersed across the country, and they are readily available. In addition, time sharing computers are used as an economic alternative to computer ownership. Software packages are available for most common applications of data processing in insurance.

Assuming that a new entrant to the insurance business can transfer start up costs (such as high commissions and higher cost of using outside technical services) to the consumer, entry is not difficult. However, there are two important factors that may impede entry. First, a new insurer will require reinsurance. Until it is able to attract sufficient exposures to meet the requirements of the "law of large numbers," a new insurer must reinsure most of its business. The degree of risk (or potential variation of actual results from the predicted results) would be too great for a new company to assume all new business. If reinsurance is unavailable or excessive in cost, entry may be prevented. Second, while entry into a local city wide or state wide insurance market may be open, entry into a national market may be restricted by competition with the many established national firms. A national insurance firm will probably not resist entry by a new company into a specified local market, but resistance will be forthcoming if the same new company attempts to expand into many markets. Furthermore, the large national insurers have the potential weapon of product differentiation. Given the intangible nature of the product, the long established national insurers have been able to establish customer preferences for their products.

Exit

Exit from the insurance industry may occur by several means:[8] (1) failure and resulting liquidation; (2) diversification or the use of insurer resources to develop, market, and service noninsurance products; and (3) transfer of capital (and thus insurance capacity) from an insurer to a parent holding company. Although only a few insurance companies fail each year, exit of insurance

[7]Spencer L. Kimball, "The Regulation of Insurance," in Spencer L. Kimball and Herbert S. Denenberg (eds.), *Insurance, Government and Social Policy* (Homewood, Ill.: Richard D. Irwin, Inc. 1969), p. 8.

[8]For an analysis of the attrition among firms in the property and liability insurance industry, see Robert E. Nelson, "Property-Liability Company Exits," *The Journal of Risk and Insurance*, XXXVIII (September, 1971), pp. 357-66. See also, Irving Pfeffer and Seev Neumann, "The Survival Probability of a New Life Insurance Company," *The Journal of Risk and Insurance*, XXXIV (March, 1967).

capacity via diversification or holding company formations has played an increasing role. The latter two forms of exit are more frequently voluntary and thus more relevant for their impact on competition.

Life insurers have been most active in the area of noninsurance product diversification, particularly in the development and sale of equity products (e.g., mutual funds). The results of a 1972 diversification study[9] reveal the extent of this form of exit. Of the nearly 200 largest (in terms of assets) life insurers responding to the survey, 48 percent indicated that they were also marketing mutual funds. In addition, 29 percent were involved in the real estate business, 13 percent in consumer financing, and 28 percent in other financial services. The trend toward an increasing provision of noninsurance services was apparent. When compared with the results of a similar study made in 1970, all noninsurance services showed an increase from 1 to 10 percent.

The transfer of capital from an insurer to a holding company can be accomplished by several means: (1) the insurer declares a substantial cash dividend; (2) the insurer declares a securities dividend to be paid to the parent company; (3) the insurer transfers both cash and securities to its parent; and (4) the insurer buys its stock for cancellation as treasury stock from the holding company. Each of these techniques was employed by holding companies during the decade of the 1960s.

The transfer of funds from insurers to parent holding companies is generally attributed to the relatively low earnings available in the insurance business relative to the inherent risk and the excess of surplus in many insurers that was not being used efficiently; that is, the insurance subsidiary was operating with a surplus to premium ratio higher than is generally required or considered necessary by prudent management.

COMPETITION IN THE INSURANCE INDUSTRY

The sellers in the insurance markets are of sufficient size and number that no one insurer, or small group of insurers, can dictate what prices and product variations will prevail. Entry into these markets is not artificially restricted. These facts establish that competition is possible, but whether insurers actually engage in competitive activities is a separate issue.

Competition Defined

An appropriate description of the concept of competition views it as a contest in which independent sellers offer their services or products at prices of their own choosing to independent buyers who elect to buy according to their own best interests.

[9] "Diversification Survey," *Best's Review (Life/Health Insurance Edition)*, LXXII (January, 1972), pp. 16-18.

Competition can take many forms: reduction in price, improvement in the quality of the product, provision of complementary services, advertising of favorable credit terms, exaggeration of the qualities of the product, real and unreal product differentiation, disparagement of the quality of a competitor's products, and obstruction of competitors' operations. These are only some of the many bases of competition available to an insurer. The possibilities can be classified as positive competition, whereby the seller improves the attractiveness of his own products; and defensive competition, in which the seller adopts a strategy that detracts from his competitor's products or restricts the competitor's ability to operate profitably. Positive competition may be perceived as price competition or nonprice competition.

Price Competition

The insurance industry engages in considerable price competition. There are no obvious price leaders, as appear in other industries. It is an industry with patterns of product variation and concomitant price variation. But just as the product tends toward clusters with several hundred companies having the same product, so also do prices tend to be grouped. While many companies offer insurance at similar prices, others are successful in selling their products both below and above the average price. Consider the price of an annuity at age 65: the price range for a life annuity of $100 a month at age 65 may vary from a low of $12,000 to a high of $30,000. However, as many as 150 companies are clustered around $15,000, with other clusters depending on the particular way in which the product is formed and priced.

The intensity of price competition varies by type of carrier, type of insurance, and type of customer. Insurers who must generate a large volume of business to match the overhead of a salaried sales force have instituted extensive price competition. Some companies have been very successful in obtaining a low price image for equal products. Direct selling companies strive for a low margin of profit on a high volume.

The consumers of several types of insurance have for various reasons demonstrated a willingness to shop for insurance based on price. For example, businessmen under pressure to cut costs have found that insurance outlays could be reduced without material reduction in coverage. Government institutions, under pressure from rising costs and declining tax bases, have also had success in reducing insurance costs by shopping for insurance. Rather than merely renewing their insurance programs, such businesses and institutions seek lower costs by means of a bidding process and risk management. Insurers wishing to retain their large premium customers must match or undercut competitors' prices.

While price competition is important in the insurance industry, constraints based on custom, tradition, or state intervention limit its extent. First, all states directly or indirectly regulate the prices that may be charged by insurers. The rates of property and liability insurers either require the approval of the states before changes can be implemented or are subject to disapproval by the regulator after implementation. Life insurance rates are indirectly controlled by the laws governing minimum statutory policy reserves.

Second, because of the actuarial need to obtain a large number of exposures on which to base prices, property and liability insurers have been allowed to set prices in concert; that is, to form joint pricing mechanisms called bureaus. The purpose of the bureaus is to collect loss data from their members, to assimilate and analyze the joint data, and to provide a set of suggested rates. While most states allow members of a bureau to deviate from bureau rates, the legal process required for a deviation can be expensive and time consuming. This is especially true if the bureau is allowed to act as an aggrieved party and thus institute a hearing on any rates filed independently of the bureau. The bureau request must be based on a claim that the independent rate is either inadequate or the result of insufficient statistical data. Some critics contend that the motives of bureaus in opposing independent rate filings are not public protection but rather protection of bureau members from price competition. The problems inherent in bureau rating have been reduced or eliminated in those states that have either changed the status of the bureau from rate promulgator to rate advisor or removed the regulator from the role of approving rates prior to their implementation. In either case, the power of the bureau as a controller of rates is significantly reduced.

Third, insurers have traditionally used selection of risks as the primary method of obtaining profitable business. Risks were not priced but were selected within the limits of a narrow range of prices for each particular company. This practice tended to reduce price competition because companies sought only those risks that most appropriately matched their prices. For example, automobile insurance companies either classified certain drivers with bad driving records or young drivers as substandard risks. These insurers believed that such risks would incur more frequent and more severe losses. Many automobile insurers did not attempt to price the insurance to meet the potential losses of the substandard group, but rather refused to insure the risk. To obtain insurance, the substandard insured had to seek insurers that specialized in high risk automobile insurance. Too often, the high risk insurers provided an inferior product at a price far in excess of potential losses. This is changing as major insurers attempt to broaden their markets.

The rates charged by standard insurers when they enter previously neglected markets are frequently below the rates charged by the high risk insurers. For example, in the central city section of Chicago a group of high risk insurers was charging between $489 and $648 for a package automobile insurance policy on a specific exposure. The same exposure was charged between $315 and $489 by a group of standard insurers who entered into active participation in this market.[10]

Nonprice Competition

Nonprice competition is important in the insurance industry. While some economists claim that nonprice competition is less viable as a market force than price competition, the quality of nonprice competition in terms of net benefits to the consumer can equal or approach that achieved with price competition. Applied to the insurance industry, nonprice competition can benefit the consumer by the provision of better and more economically attractive policies and concomitant services. Nonprice competitive innovations may be classified as product, service, or distribution innovations.

Product. In most states the fire insurance contract is required to be standardized by statute, so that competition is only available to insurers by means of deviation from or addition to the standard forms. The accelerating use of such deviations and additions culminated in the 1950s with the introduction of the Homeowner's Policy. The industry response to this innovation was both quick and extensive, so that within a few years the Homeowner's Policy was the standard coverage for individual owner occupied dwellings. This type of product competition, while varying in its extent, can be found in all other sectors of the insurance industry. Other product innovations include the Family Automobile Policy, the Variable Annuity, Split Life Insurance, Cost of Living riders, and Graded Premium Life Insurance.

While insurers have provided many beneficial product innovations, some have argued that this has been carried to excess. The consumer receives no benefit from unreal product differentiation. Product variation is common in the life insurance industry, although there are basically only five products sold by a life insurance agent: term, whole life, limited pay life, endowment insurance, and variable life insurance. But the titles and descriptions of policies sold by life insurers could easily lead a consumer to conclude that each company sells a much larger set of unique policies. There is the Executive Policy, the Presidential Plan, the College Special Plan, and numerous other specialized packages. The foregoing are often presented as unique contracts, when in fact they are policies constructed from one or more of the five basic life policies. The development of the variable life policy indicates the competitive advantage to be gained from genuine product differentiation.

[10]Data furnished by the Illinois Department of Insurance. For a further discussion of the reasons for price variation in automobile insurance, see David R. Klock, "The Development and Pretest of a Methodology to Investigate the Competitive Status of Markets for Property-Liability Insurance: Summary of Report to State of Illinois Department of Insurance," *Proceedings of the National Association of Insurance Commissioners,* II (1971).

Service. Service to the customer has proven to be an important competitive tool for insurers. Given the complex and subjective nature of the insurance product, the service provided by the company may be as important to the consumer as the actual policy commitments. Service competition in the insurance industry has taken many forms. Loss prevention engineering and advice is important in property insurance, general liability insurance, and workmen's compensation. In lines such as boiler and machinery insurance expert inspection service is considered more important than indemnification. The insurer who provides the best inspection service has a distinct competitive advantage. In workmen's compensation some insurers operate rehabilitation centers for injured employees.

In automobile insurance some companies have provided a stimulus for buying safer cars by offering a substantial discount on collision insurance for cars that can withstand collisions at varying speeds. Loss adjustment through independent adjusting organizations or through full-time salaried personnel is a part of the competitive framework. Promptness, fairness, and accessibility of loss service are important service based forms of competition. The large automobile insurer that is able to provide claims service within a few miles of potential clients has a distinct advantage over the company that can only provide an adjuster in the area once a week.

Installment payment plans have proliferated. The first competitive innovation in this area was the level premium concept for life insurance. However, this is based on an annual premium payment, and the contemporary consumer is usually not prepared to make large annual payments. Credit and monthly payments have become a financial reality, and a series of competitive techniques aimed at easing the payment of premiums has evolved. Some companies send monthly bills, while others have arrangements with the customer's bank so that the bank pays the bill monthly. Those insurers that write all lines of insurance needed by the typical family stress the advantage of one monthly payment for all insurance.

While most insurance needs can be met within the framework of existing contracts, some insurers have achieved competitive leadership by a willingness to write unusual risks with specialized contracts.

Distribution. Distribution efficiency and product promotion have advanced the competitive position of numerous insurers. A review of marketing activities in the insurance industry during the past few decades reveals a revolution in the making. Companies with the most rapid growth or expansion of market share have been those willing to exploit weaknesses in the "traditional" marketing structure. The history of contemporary insurance marketing shows a series of innovations with rapid diffusion throughout the industry. When one company introduced the branch office system as a means of bringing the home office closer to the public and the agent, other companies began their own conversion from the general agency system and from direct reporting to the home office. When direct writing mutuals made inroads on the workmen's compensation accounts of agency stock companies, the advantage was soon reduced through the use of retrospective rating. When independent agents of the "American" agency system failed to contact small individual customers in the insurance market, some companies used improved mass merchandizing techniques to capture that market. When it became evident that the prevailing distribution system was too expensive a method of operation—costs of distribution per policy did not decline as value increased—companies began to contract with agents under exclusive arrangements.

When some companies created both personal lines and commercial risk departments in order to cultivate each market separately, others began changing their internal structures. When one company began utilizing a portion of its agents' time in captive department stores, other insurers experimented with similar arrangements in community shopping centers. When multiple line and all line underwriting became an accepted practice, mergers among companies began to appear as parent organizations attempted to expand sales organizations and add ready-made new lines. When the concept of advertising turned from the institutional corporate image to product selling, many companies began to present information on specific contracts, services, and prices. When the economies of selling to large numbers at one time became evident, insurers emphasized group insurance. And when the concept of one stop financial service evolved, insurers expanded into mutual funds and other complementary financial services, while other institutions (banks and stockbrokers) expanded into insurance sales.

Nonprice competition is vital to the insurance industry and stimulates the provision of better and more economically attractive policies. Unless an insurer is willing to provide product innovation, to modernize procedures, and to be flexible in anticipating and meeting the changing needs of the insurance consumer, it may lose its competitive position in the insurance industry.

Defensive Competition

Defensive competition may be defined as actions intended to either restrict the ability of a competitor to penetrate a specific market or demean a competitor. The former may be carried out by trade associations, using legislative pressures; the latter is sometimes indulged in by agents.

The insurance industry has formed literally hundreds of trade associations designed to serve the interests of specific groups of insurers or agents. Among the primary tasks of an insurance trade association is to argue against (for) any legislation that might be detrimental (beneficial) to an association member or might improve (hurt) the position of a member's competitors. Virtually all of the activities of an insurance company and of its agents come under supervision by a regulatory body. Therefore, lobbying activities are extremely important to the industry.

By way of illustration, group life insurance has become an important part of most individuals' insurance portfolios. Group insurance is usually provided as an employee benefit, and the cost to the employee may range from 0 to 100 percent of the premiums. Even if the employee pays all the costs, the premium will usually be lower than the same insurance purchased on an individual basis. Thus, group life insurance is an attractive alternative to individual coverage. The maximum amount of group term life that any one individual can receive is restricted by most states (e.g., $40,000 in many states). Attempts to increase this maximum are opposed by life insurance agent associations and by some insurers who do not sell group life. Lobbyists for these associations argue that an extension of group life insurance will reduce or eliminate the valuable insurance programming services provided by the agent.

Another example of defensive competition is the resistance to open rating laws that would both increase the potential for price competition and reduce the influence of rating bureaus. Competitive rating laws usually change the status of bureaus from that of rate promulgators to rate advisers and impair the power of the bureaus to oppose independent and deviated rates. Insurers who either file their rates with the state independently of the bureau or file deviations from bureau rates have supported competitive rating laws. Alternatively, bureau members who prefer to avoid competition have tended to oppose competitive rating laws.

Actions intended to discredit the worthiness of a competitor's product are frequently self-defeating, but they are indulged in by some insurance agents. The two most common tactics are misrepresentation and twisting. While both actions are illegal and constitute bases for license revocation, they are still practiced by some insurance salesmen. Misrepresentation consists of misleading statements concerning the financial condition or reputation of a competitor (either company or agent) or the presentation of incomplete information that mistakenly leads the prospective client to conclude that a competitor's product is inferior. Twisting is misrepresentation that leads a consumer to drop a competitor's life insurance product in order to release funds to purchase the policy of a different company.

SUMMARY

The insurance industry in the United States is a very large complex of thousands of suppliers of countless products and services, organized under private and governmental auspices, characterized by vigorous price and nonprice competition. The structural characteristics are gradually shifting, and the nature and forms of competition are becoming increasingly significant.

REVIEW QUESTIONS

1.   What are the basic differences in goals between private and social insurance systems? How do the differences of goals affect the differences in practices? Discuss.

2.   Describe the forces which affect the nature of competition in the insurance industry.

3.   What are the potential social advantages and disadvantages of "defensive" competition in the insurance industry?

4.   Has the concentration of power in the insurance industry tended to increase or decrease in the past few decades?

5.   Discuss the role of the federal government as an insurance carrier in the United States, showing the lines of coverage with the highest growth rates.

STUDY QUESTIONS

6.   Is the life insurance industry an example of oligopoly in the United States? Discuss.

7.   In affecting the market share of an insurance company, is nonprice competition more significant than price competition? Explain.

8.   The total assets of the life insurance industry are substantially more than those of the property and liability industry. Why?

9.   How do you account for the growth of insurance-based holding companies? What are the advantages to the consumer of such developments? Discuss.

10.   Determine the regulatory requirements for entry into your state for each of the following types of insurer: (a) a life and health insurer, and (b) a multiple line property and liability insurer.

16

Insurance
Microeconomics

INTRODUCTION

Microeconomics relates to the theory of the firm and the industry. Included in a discussion of insurance microeconomics are factors affecting the (1) supply of insurance, (2) demand for insurance, and (3) price of insurance. In addition, microeconomics is concerned with an explanation of those forces that influence both the balance between supply and demand and the free movement of prices.

INSURANCE AND STATIC ECONOMICS

The literature of economics has very little discussion of insurance, despite the fact that insurance is one of the largest financial institutions in the United States. A multi-billion dollar institution, employing over a million persons, insurance is pervasive in every business relationship. Every business enterprise has a major concern with risk and insurance.

Economists have neglected insurance because economic theory generally assumes perfect knowledge and static analysis in its models.[1] Economists usually assume demand and supply functions that are instantaneous with perfect flexibility of adjustment. But insurance exists because knowledge is imperfect and adjustments to change are somewhat uncertain.

A theory of economics that is static in nature requires no discussion of insurance or any other phenomenon that has a time dimension. The economist deals with uncertainty by discounting for it. He then can use a discount function as a substitute for the uncertainty situation. In effect, he ignores the uncertainties related to insurance by assuming that he can determine the discounted value of cash flows required for insurance premiums. The premium is treated as a substitute for risk, and if discounted in this fashion the net result is a simple movement of the appropriate curve. The economist contends that there is no more reason to focus on the foregoing movement of the curve than on other shifts (e.g., movements caused by advertising, education, etc.). Thus, insurance is treated as an institutional topic. However, if the static assumptions are removed the need to consider the role of insurance becomes apparent.

ECONOMIC ROLE OF INSURANCE

The function of insurance is the reduction of anxiety or psychological uncertainty. To the extent that insurance performs this function, it has an economic role. Uncertainty acts as an inhibitor in economic affairs. Uncertainty causes individuals to be less willing to venture forth. By reducing or removing one set of uncertainties, insurance stimulates the willingness of individuals to assume those business and financial risks that might benefit the economy.

In 1601, the preamble of one of the first insurance statutes recognized this benefit:[2]

> Whereas it ever hathe bene the policie of this realme by all good meanes to comforte and encourage the merchante, therebie to advance and increase the general wealthe of the realme, her majesties customes and strengthe of shippinge, which consideracion is nowe the more requisite because trade and traffique is not at this presente soe open as at other tymes it hathe bene; And whereas it has bene tyme out of mynde an usage amongste merchantes, both of this realme and of forraine nacyons, when they make any great adventure (speciallie to remote partes) to give some

---

[1] "The classical theory is a theory of a man choosing among fixed and known alternatives, to each of which is attached known consequences. But when perception and cognition intervene between the decision-maker and his objective environment this model no longer proves adequate." Herbert A. Simon, "Theories of Decision Making in Economics and Behavioral Science", *Surveys of Economic Theory*, III (New York: MacMillan and Company, 1967), p. 19.

[2] 43 *Elizabeth* C.12,1601. Cited in William D. Winter, *Marine Insurance*, 3rd ed. (New York: McGraw-Hill Book Company, 1952), p. 12.

consideracion of money to other persons (which commonlie are in noe small number) to have from them assurance made of their goodes, merchandizes, ships and things adventured, or some parte thereof at suche rates and in such sorte as the parties assurere and the parties assured can agree, which course of dealinge is commonlie termed a policie of assurance; by means of whiche policie of assurance it comethe to passe that upon the losse or perishinge of any shippe there followethe not the undoing of any man, but the loss lightethe rather easilie upon many than heavilie upon fewe, and rather upon them that adventure not than those that doe adventure, whereby all merchante, speciallie the younger sorte, are allured to venture more willinglie and more freely.

In the absence of insurance coverage, a rational businessman would justifiably be concerned about the risks confronting him. To the extent that insurance is able to reduce some of the anxieties to which a businessman is exposed, he is better able to handle the dynamic risks of the business in which he is involved. For example, a shirt manufacturer has enough difficulty trying to guess the right style of shirts to produce without having to worry whether his factory or inventory is going to be destroyed by fire. This reemphasizes the important economic function that insurance plays: it removes some of the economic inhibition that is created by our uncertainties. If one could be certain of financial security in his old age, it would not be so necessary to save during one's working years. This would permit a higher level of current consumption, active investment, and a higher standard of living. Thus, insurance removes some of the constraints on spending and allows individuals to proceed with their ventures and their life styles in greater confidence. This essential function of confidence creation is at the core of most insurance purchasing. It is the anxiety relieving aspect that is crucial for insurance.

INSURANCE AS AN INCOME PRODUCING SERVICE

The economic distinction between income producing and output producing categories of goods or services helps to explain the role of insurance in economic theory. Classical economics was concerned primarily with output producing goods rather than income producing goods. The classical economist was concerned with land, labor, and capital. His illustrations were agricultural or manufacturing firms. The service industries, which are income producing but not necessarily output producing, are relatively modern.

Advertising, for example, is an income producing industry. The firm that makes an investment in advertising does not change its output capacity. However, advertising may increase income by causing a move to a higher point on the demand curve. The same is true of insurance. It is an income producing factor rather than an output producing one.

At one time it was argued that insurance was significantly different from other goods and services because insurance was not desired for the same reasons. "Insurance is not a material good . . . its value to the buyer is clearly different in kind from the satisfaction of consumer desires for medical treatment or transportation. Indeed unlike goods and services, transactions involving insurance are an exchange of money for money, not money for something which directly meets needs."[3] This is a very restrictive view. The demand for insurance is derived from the needs that it fulfills, just as the demand for production factors is determined by a contribution to final output.

SUPPLY OF INSURANCE

Price theory indicates that there are two primary factors in the determination of output: (1) the technological relationship between the factors of production, or the fixed and variable costs of production, and (2) the motivation of the firms that produce and distribute the product. While these two forces are operative in the insurance industry, the factors of production and the production process are unique. Furthermore, there are two constraints that tend to limit the extent to which insurance can be supplied: prudent underwriting practices, and regulatory requirements.

Underwriting Constraints

Unlike most other industries, insurance companies do not sell their products to every prospective buyer. The insurer must select the risks he will accept because the insurance buyer may be the source of loss due to moral hazard. One of the ways an insurer can control its costs is to choose carefully those whose interests it insures. This concept of discrimination is better understood if the insurer is viewed not as a seller of insurance but as a purchaser of risk. The insurer seeks to purchase only those classes of risk for which it must pay in claims less than it will receive in premiums.

Regulatory Constraints

The constraint on supply imposed by regulation affects two areas: premiums written per dollar of policyholders' surplus, and rate flexibility. While these constraints apply to most areas of insurance, the primary restrictions are placed on property and liability insurers. In the property and liability insurance industry it is considered prudent financial practice not to allow premiums to

---

[3]Kenneth J. Arrow, *Aspects of the Theory of Risk Bearing*, Helsinki: Yrgo Jahnssoniøn Saatio, 1965, p. 45.

exceed surplus by some predetermined multiple. The use of this surplus to premium ratio, as an indication of financial propriety, has no specific basis in theory. However, empirical evidence has led industry practitioners and regulators to establish maximum allowable surplus to premium ratios. For example, the Illinois Department of Insurance has ruled that the surplus ratio of a property and liability insurer should not exceed four to one, and the New York Department of Insurance considers a surplus ratio higher than two to one to be beyond a reasonable limit.

The prices charged by a property and liability insurer come under the direct supervision of state insurance departments. The extent of supervision varies from *ex post* observation to *ex ante* control. The majority of states exercise a right of prior approval over the rates that a property and liability insurer desires to use. It has been contended that the approval process restricts the supply of insurance by both imposing price rigidity and increasing the cost of operation. It is further argued that the removal of *ex ante* price controls would provide insurers with greater pricing flexibility and an ability to change prices more quickly in response to changes in the costs of providing the insurance product. Freedom to set rates competitively might provide an incentive to enter or expand sales activities in previously neglected markets. Believing that these arguments are valid and desiring to increase the supply of insurance, several states have switched from prior approval to open rating laws.

Fixed and Variable Costs

The supply curve that is operational for various insurance products is a function of fixed and variable costs. Fixed costs cover permanent overhead. Overhead includes office equipment, computer facilities, and executive and other full-time salaried personnel. Variable costs include opportunity costs of funds maintained against legal reserves, sales commissions, underwriting expenses, and claims payments.

To protect the rights of policyholders and clients, regulators require that insurance companies maintain minimum liabilities called legal reserves. In addition to requiring a minimum legal reserve, insurance statutes generally restrict insurers with respect to investments of the assets that match reserve liabilities. The allowable investment outlets usually are high safety, low return securities, such as federal and state obligations, high-grade bonds and mortgages, and "blue chip" stocks. If it were not for these restrictions, insurers could invest funds more freely in an attempt to optimize investment returns. Thus there is an opportunity cost associated with the reserves. This opportunity cost is a variable cost because the size of the reserves will vary with the risks insured.

The cost of providing the sales function varies by type of distribution system, company, and product. While the distribution cost may be fixed in the short run if a salaried sales force is used, most insurance salesmen are compensated on a basis of commissions. In life insurance the usual commission is a high percentage of the first year premium, a lesser percentage for the second year, and then a reduced percentage of the annual premium either for a specified period or for the life of the policy. In property and liability insurance, the commission is usually a flat percentage of each year's premium.

The purpose of underwriting is to achieve a profitable distribution of exposures. This requires both screening of applications and the assignment of appropriate rates. Underwriting costs include the expense of processing applications, examination of exposures, whether it be a medical examination or inspection of property, and analysis of credit reports.

Claims costs include not only the payment of losses but also the costs associated with investigation and legal defense. The costs associated with life insurance claims are primarily administrative because there is a definite loss, the cause of which is usually irrelevant (except in cases of suicide in the first two years of the policy). Property and liability insurance is generally a contract of indemnity, and the value of the loss must be determined *ex post.* Furthermore, in property and liability insurance the cause of the loss will affect not only the decision to pay but also the potential for subrogation. Thus, claims administration costs are more significant in the field of property and liability insurance.

Short Term vs. Long Term Supply

In economics the short term is too brief to allow for change in the productive capacity of an industry, while the long term is a time span sufficient to permit changes in the quantity of employed resources. In addition, the long run is a period of time sufficient to allow for industry entry and exit. Given the restrictions on the premium to surplus ratio, capacity in the insurance industry is not a function of plant and equipment but is a direct function of capital and surplus funds. Additions to surplus result from underwriting gains, investment returns, increases in the market value of investment portfolios and external inflows of capital. Reductions in surplus result from underwriting losses, decreases in the market value of investments, payments of dividends, and exit of insurers from the industry.

The primary determinant of the direction of capital flows in any industry is the profitability of the firms in relation to all the risks inherent in that industry.[4] These same factors are operative in the insurance industry While life insurance companies have generally achieved an enviable record of earnings, property and liability insurers have claimed frequent periods in which their returns have not equalled those achieved in less risky industries. It has been argued that an inability to earn an adequate rate of return has periodically created a "capacity crunch," or periods in which surplus could not keep pace with an increasing demand for property and liability insurance products. The

---

[4]If an enterprise is to obtain capital, it must reward prospective investors with a return sufficient to offset any risks that are incurred.

statistics on industry surplus appear to support this claim. During the 1968-1969 capacity crunch, surplus in all property and liability insurers declined from approximately $19 billion to $16 billion.[5] The decline in surplus was a result of: (1) underwriting losses, (2) a stock market decline, (3) upstream dividends paid to holding companies that sought more profitable investment outlets, and (4) the drain on surplus concomitant with increased premium writings.

Economies of Scale

As the size or scale of a business becomes larger, the per unit cost of output may be reduced. If this reduction occurs, the firm has incurred economies of scale. Economies of scale in the insurance industry are technical, financial, and distributive.[6]

Electronic data processing equipment, and the accompanying software have had an extensive impact on the operations of insurance companies. However, if an insurer is to use the computer efficiently, a large scale of operation is required. Few items of equipment are more costly than an idle, high-powered computer. While time sharing may be available to the smaller insurer, the average cost will be higher than an efficiently used in plant unit if the necessary software is not available from the time share facility.

Financial economies result from the ability of larger firms to attract external funds at a cost below that incurred by small or intermediate sized firms. The large insurers, particularly the stock companies, often have the following financial advantages: listing on a major stock exchange, access to investment bankers for raising additional capital, and the availability of lines of credit from large commercial banks with interest at the prime rate.

Distribution economies are achieved through marketing by means of direct sales offices and by mass merchandising. Both techniques require substantial volumes of sales to offset the high initial fixed costs. However, once volume exceeds the break even point, average cost per unit may decline significantly. The large insurer also achieves a distribution economy by being able to offer a wider range of products. Furthermore, it is obvious that the larger insurer is better able to afford the costs associated with genuine product development. This potential advantage is short-lived because other insurers can quickly provide identical products with impunity. The innovating insurer must file new products for approval by regulatory officials. The resulting lag between development and implementation increases the time available for a competitor to reach the market

---

[5]*Insurance Facts* (New York: Insurance Information Institute, 1970), p. 27.

[6] "The theory of economies of scale is the theory of the relationship between the scale of use of a properly chosen combination of all productive services and the rate of output of the enterprise." George J. Stigler, "The Economies of Scale," *Journal of Law and Economics*, 1 (October, 1958). For an empirical review of economies of scale as they apply to insurance, see: J.D. Hammond, E.R. Melander and N. Shilling, "Economies of Scale in the Property and Liability Insurance Industry," *The Journal of Risk and Insurance*, XXXVIII (June, 1970), pp. 181-91.

with a reasonable facsimile of the innovation. There are no patents available to protect inventors of new policy forms.

If an insurer obtains the benefits of economies of scale, it will have a downsloping long run average cost curve. Firms unable to achieve economies would be at a competitive disadvantage because they will be unable to achieve the larger firm's lower costs. However, many of the potential advantages of large scale insurance company operation can be: (1) obtained by membership in a bureau (e.g., statistical analysis), (2) received as a part of a holding company or conglomerate (e.g., financial economies), (3) purchased from a service organization (e.g., time sharing computers), or (4) short-lived (e.g., product development). Furthermore, those insurers with higher average costs may be able to differentiate their product to the public and thus be successful in charging higher prices. The existence of economies of scale in the insurance business has not led to an industry comprised only of large scale producers.

DEMAND FOR INSURANCE

Insurance supply is a technical phenomenon. However, the concept of insurance demand is relatively subjective. There is no easy way to quantify the factors that cause people to act in a given way with respect to anxieties or uncertainties. It is almost as difficult to measure the demand for this product as it would be to measure demand for advertising, education, or other income producing services. This would be a virtually impossible task for the individual insurance firm. The factors that help explain the demand for the product include political, economic, and personal variables.

Political Factors

Under capitalism, the self-sufficiency of the family or the firm as economic units is fundamental. It is a basic assumption of economics that the family or the firm, as independent units, must survive. Everything else is subordinate to this premise. If entrepreneurs were unconcerned about survival of their firms, business behavior would be much more unpredictable than it is. There would be no need for caution. The same concept applies to the family unit. If it were not very important whether or not the family unit survived, contingency plans would play a smaller role in society. The extent to which the state provides for economic security is an important determinant of the demand for insurance.

Economic Factors

Among the economic services of insurance are: (1) capitalization of potential income requirements, (2) provision of an outlet for savings and investment, (3) security and collateral for credit, (4) reduction of margins for safety in business projections, and (5) reduction of burdens on society resulting from inability of victims to cope with the financial consequences of insurable contingencies.[7]

It is frequently asserted that a person in the United States with a college 'education will probably earn half a million dollars in his lifetime, while the high school graduate will on the average earn less than a quarter of a million dollars. However, since few people personally identify with such large numbers, the figures appear meaningless. It is difficult to perceive lifetime earnings of $500,000, when the monthly bills are unpaid. To help the consumer provide for his life insurance needs, the insurance industry developed a procedure called income programming. The programming technique, instead of capitalizing earnings, estimates and capitalizes income needs. The capitalization of income requirements provides a powerful incentive to the individual consumer and to the corporation with key employees seeking to insure against the loss of income in the event of premature death.

For those individuals who seek management of their portfolios, diversification, and freedom from investment risk, life insurance serves as an outlet for savings and investment. The entire resources of the life insurance company provide a guarantee of safety of principal for the insured's investment. However, in exchange for the security of a guaranteed fixed return, the consumer receives a relatively low fixed dollar return and must assume the risks associated with inflation and a rising cost of living.

Financial institutions are unlikely to lend money on the basis of security that could too easily be destroyed. To secure payment of an obligation by a borrower, the financial institution may require an insurance policy with benefit rights assigned to the creditor. Even if policy assignment is not required, information on existing insurance policies is considered an indicator of an individual's financial responsibility, and may be a factor in deciding whether to make a loan.

Insurance reduces contingency margins on business projections. The presence of appropriate insurance coverages assists in business and personal planning. Specifically, the use of insurance replaces a large possible future cost with a small certain annual cost.

Finally, insurance reduces the economic burden on society caused by failure to provide for the contingencies of premature death or other perils. Individuals who seek to avoid the risk of bankruptcy or destitution take precautions to protect themselves against the consequences of perils that might cause financial ruin. The determination to be financially independent is a motivation to purchase insurance.

---

[7]See S. S. Huebner, *The Economics of Life Insurance,* 3rd ed. (New York: Appleton-Century-Crofts, Inc., 1959), and S. S. Huebner and Kenneth Black, Jr., *Life Insurance,* 7th ed. (New York: Appleton-Century-Crofts, Inc., 1969) for extended treatments of economic factors in the demand for life insurance.

Personal Factors

Personal factors that account for insurance demand include: (1) the desire to fulfill family responsibilities, (2) the urge to optimize income, assets, and net worth, (3) status, (4) tax reduction, and (5) indemnification for losses.

The average person is vulnerable to the argument that he has not been able to save enough. The savings of the average person are slight and arise primarily because of involuntary savings. Specifically, the most common source of equity is in a home, where there is no choice about meeting the mortgage payments and reducing the principal. In the same fashion, life insurance premiums may be treated as a debt, rather than a medium for savings. The savings are a derivative benefit.

Insurance-ownership is a status symbol because it is both a mark of responsibility to one's family and a sign of wealth. For individuals with moderate income, insurance is a relatively inexpensive source of prestige. For the rich, insurance may be a status symbol as well. Many one-million-dollar life insurance policies are sold each year. The effects of status must be considered as a realistic influence on insurance demand.

When an individual buys a large life insurance policy, he frequently is concerned about a tax problem for which life insurance is helpful. The proceeds of a life insurance policy can be made exempt from probate and estate taxes. The income generated through a life insurance policy may be free of income taxes. Premiums, if properly spread, are free of gift tax. Insurance is one of the best available investments with special tax advantages.

Finally, both individuals and firms attempt to make pre-loss arrangements for post-loss needs. Insurance is sought when cost-benefit analysis indicates that insurance would be the most effective pre-loss arrangement for indemnification of losses.

THE PRICE OF INSURANCE

Under conditions of imperfect competition, the pricing procedure suggested by economic theory consists of finding maximum profit at the point where marginal revenue equals marginal costs. However, few firms are able to determine their marginal revenue or marginal cost curves. To provide a profit, they rely on marking up the average cost per unit by some given percentage. While prices may be allowed to decline below average cost, prices will not be set below unit variable cost. Insurers tend to follow the same pricing practices. However, insurance pricing must contend with the following problems:

1.   Average costs in insurance are predominantly variable in nature and to a large extent beyond the control of the insurer.

2.   Accurate projections of average costs, particularly claims items, require sufficient numbers of exposures to allow the "law of large numbers" to operate. Small firms are thus forced to pool their exposures and price in concert.

3.   Prices may violate the economic rule and be set below unit variable cost, if losses and claims expenses are far in excess of those projected by the actuaries, or in excess of those expected by the regulator.

4.   For many insurers, within the constraints of capacity, unit cost does not change significantly with volume of sales.

5.   The insurer markup is not solely for profit but also includes an input for contingencies that are somewhat unpredictable, such as losses incurred but not yet reported.

The influence of price on the demand for insurance varies depending on the specific product and market. For example, in life insurance price is not a dominant variable, and the life insurance demand curve is relatively inelastic (i.e., has a steep slope). The inelasticity of life insurance results from the fact that the true price of life insurance is not generally known. An examination of the premiums charged does not reveal the actual long run cost. In addition to premiums, the astute consumer must know the timing of cash value and dividend flows in order to determine variations in opportunity costs. However, since few consumers are sufficiently sophisticated to undertake price comparisons in life insurance, such shopping for price is rarely done. The life insurance industry makes little effort to sell on a price basis. Most competition in life insurance depends on nonprice product and service differentials.

By contrast with life insurance, price is an important consideration in the purchase of personal line property and liability covers, such as automobile and homeowner's insurance. This price sensitivity in nonlife personal lines of insurance is supported by the success of companies that engage in vigorous price competition. Where price is a significant variable, the supply curve will be relatively elastic. A drop in price will result in an appreciable increase of sales.

The foregoing discussion of price relates to the elasticity or inelasticity of the demand curve faced by individual suppliers of a specific product. A different question is: does price play a significant role in creating demand for an entire market or product? In most cases, the answer is negative. Underlying anxieties and uncertainties create the product demand. Price may only play a role in determining where, when, and how the need is filled. However, sometimes the illusion of extremely low prices can stimulate total demand. A prime example is flight insurance, sold at counters and machines in airports across the nation. For as little as fifty cents, or one dollar, a customer can purchase several thousand dollars of accidental death insurance for the time he is on a specified flight. While many purchasers of this product have a genuine need for coverage, others are attracted by an apparent bargain.

FORECASTING

Forecasting consists of identification and analysis of important indicators of future behavior. There are many relatively stable relationships that are helpful in forecasting the demand for insurance:

1.   The correlation between insurance premiums and disposable personal income has been very high for several decades in the United States.

2.   The ratio of life insurance premiums to average ages is a stable relationship because the bulk of premiums are paid in the middle years of the purchaser's life.

3.   The relationship between life insurance premiums and level of education shows a positive correlation. The higher the average level of education the higher the premium volume.

4.   Premiums correlate with family unit size. The larger the family unit size, the higher the premium volume.

5.   *Per capita* income and life insurance outlays show a positive relationship.

6.   Fire insurance premiums and business cycles move together. In periods of high Gross National Product, property values increase, and fire insurance premiums rise. The same relationship holds in economic troughs.

7.   Workmen's compensation premiums correlate with payrolls because premiums are based on payroll statistics.

8.   Automobile insurance is a function of automobile registrations.

9.   Life insurance-in-force correlates with total population.

By means of correlated economic aggregates, insurance companies are able to make relatively precise forecasts of the future size of the insurance market. The basic problem is to obtain current and accurate economic statistics.

IMBALANCES IN SUPPLY AND DEMAND

Theoretically, imbalances between supply and demand should not persist because price will be adjusted to clear the market. However, there have been certain insurance markets where demand has exceeded supply. For example, in certain urban core areas property insurance was not sufficiently available to meet demand. The imbalance was a result of two factors: (1) prices could not move freely to clear the market, and (2) demand was relatively inelastic, and a minimum required demand was set by society. The following example may help to explain. Figure 16.1 presents hypothetical supply and demand curves for a property insurance product. P_1 is a limit price that outside forces (e.g., a department of insurance operating under a prior approval rating law) would allow, and Q_1 is the quantity that insurers would supply at the price of P_1. However, at the price of P_1 consumers desire a quantity of Q_2. Furthermore, society may have dictated that a level of Q_2 is socially desirable or necessary. Thus, a solution that leads to a supply of insurance at Q_1 is economically and socially unacceptable. Since the quantity of insurance necessary to society (demanded) is held relatively constant, a viable solution will come by either moving up the supply curve or by shifting the supply curve to the right, that is, either increase the consumer's ability or willingness to pay or decrease the costs of providing the product. The following have been suggested as means by which the government could solve the imbalance:[8] (1) pay a direct subsidy to the insurance consumer. Such a program would allow the market mechanism to operate with a minimum of government intervention; (2) provide low cost reinsurance to the insurer. This would lower the costs and risks to the insurers and thus shift the supply curve to the right; (3) contract with insurers to provide the desired product on a cost-plus basis. Such a program would be similar to government procedures with defense contractors. Where action has been taken, option (2) has usually been used as in the Fair Access to Insurance Requirements (FAIR) Program. If such a program leads to a shift from the supply curve S_1 to supply curve S_2 the market will clear at both an economic and socially acceptable solution.

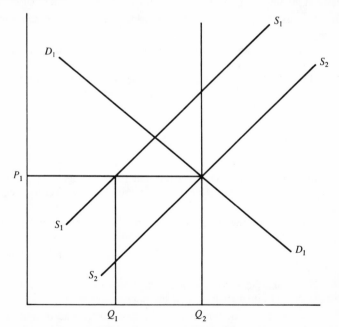

FIGURE 16.1 Model of Demand and Supply for Insurance.

[8] J.J. Launie, "The Supply Function of Urban Property Insurance," *The Journal of Risk and Insurance*, XXXVI (June, 1969), pp. 269-83.

SUMMARY

The supply of insurance is limited by the ability of insurance companies to absorb risks because of their lack of a dependable theory of retention limits, statutory rate making, minimum capital and surplus requirements, and above all, the fact that the most important variable cost—losses—is not known at the time prices must be set.

The demand for insurance is based upon a large variety of factors, all of which influence the individual in his search for security.

The role of price as a competitive factor in insurance is less significant than product and service variations. The consumer has great difficulty in pricing insurance services accurately because it is difficult to specify the unit of insurance that constitutes the product.

REVIEW QUESTIONS

1.   Are economies of scale operative in the life insurance business? Discuss.

2.   What is the correlation between life insurance in force and disposable personal income in the United States during the last decade? Discuss.

3.   Discuss the principal factors which account for the individual *demand* for life insurance.

4.   Insurance is an income producing factor as opposed to an output producing factor. Explain.

5.   How might a variation in the political system (e.g., capitalist, socialist, communist) affect the demand for insurance?

STUDY QUESTIONS

6.   Insurance pricing has been referred to as average cost pricing. Does this approach to pricing differ from that used by manufacturing concerns? Explain.

7.   How might the long term supply of an insurance product be increased? Discuss.

8.   How might you forecast the demand for variable life insurance? Discuss.

9.   Using marginal utility analysis, how can one demonstrate the proposition that insurance is good and gambling is bad? Explain.

10.   If insurance is an income producing rather than an output producing factor of production, how can its economic contribution be measured?

17

Insurance

Macroeconomics

INTRODUCTION

Insurance macroeconomics relates to those aspects of insurance that are extraindustry in nature having their primary effect on the economy as a whole. Insurance macroeconomics includes the relationship of the insurance industry to: (1) total output of the economy as measured by Gross National Product (GNP), (2) employment of capital resources as between savings and investment, (3) employment of human resources, (4) income distribution, and (5) business fluctuations and imbalances resulting from inflation, population changes, and fiscal and monetary policy.

THE GROSS NATIONAL PRODUCT AND INSURANCE

The Gross National Product measures the level of economic activity as an aggregate. While the national accounts, summed in GNP, provide an estimate of the output of the economy for a static period of time, they do not indicate why there was a specific output and what determined any change in the economy during a specific period. The role of the insurance industry in GNP results from its expenditures for wages and salaries to employees, interest and dividend payments to policyholders and stockholders, rental payments, and taxes paid. The investments of insurance companies affect GNP to the extent that pools of capital are made available for use by government and industry, who, in turn, are assisted in generating additional streams of income.

LIFE INSURANCE AS A SAVINGS MEDIUM

When premiums are prepaid, the operation of an insurance company generates substantial pools of funds. For example, life insurance contracts are generally for a long period. Premiums will be greater than required in the early years to build a fund for death payments in later years. Savings in life insurance may be measured by the increase in policy reserves, plus accumulated dividends, less policy loans and premium notes. While growing at a rate less than that of competing savings outlets (see Table 17.1), these savings are substantial and are a major component of national income.

Life Insurers
as Financial Wealth Intermediaries

Institutions that specialize in the ownership and administration of financial assets may be called financial wealth intermediaries as opposed to real wealth intermediaries. The latter institution invests in tangible assets. Life insurers are in the former category because they make it feasible for many small wealth owners to obtain indirect ownership in primary securities. The ownership is indirect because the policyholder never holds title to the primary securities, but holds a fixed claim (increasing as a life insurance policy approaches maturity) against the pool of financial assets. However, the policyholder does not .assume the investment risk associated with the pool of securities. Furthermore, the claim in the savings pool is contingent upon forfeiture of the policy. If a death claim is paid, rights to the savings pool are terminated.

The Merits of Life Insurance
as a Savings Medium

Life insurance as a savings outlet is examined in the light of criteria used to judge any investment vehicle: liquidity, freedom from management, safety of principal, return, and favorable tax treatment.

Liquidity refers to the ease or speed with which the savings instrument may be converted to cash with little or no loss of value. While life insurance cash

TABLE 17.1 Annual Change in Financial Assets of Households

Year	Savings Associations	Mutual Savings Banks	Commercial Banks	Credit Unions	Life Insurance Reserves	Pension Fund Reserves	Credit and Equity Instruments	Total
				($ billions)				
1960	$7.6	$1.4	$2.8	$0.6	$3.2	$8.4	$4.5	$28.5
1965	8.5	3.6	13.3	1.0	4.8	12.3	2.5	46.0
1970	11.0	4.4	15.8	1.1	4.9	18.6	10.5	66.3
				(Percentage Distribution)				
1960	26.7%	4.9%	9.8%	2.1%	11.2%	29.5%	15.8%	100.0%
1965	18.5	7.8	28.9	2.2	10.4	26.7	5.4	100.0
1970	16.6	6.6	23.8	1.7	7.4	28.1	15.8	100.0

SOURCE: *Savings and Loan Fact Book '72* (Washington, D.C.: United States Savings and Loan League, 1972).

values are not a close money substitute, they are relatively liquid. Usually, the cash values in a policy can be obtained within a few days. This time can be reduced to a matter of hours if the policyholder takes the contract to a company office. While the insurer can legally defer payment for six months, this privilege is seldom enforced.

Managerial or investment skills are not required of the policyholder in life insurance. The insurer assumes all managerial functions, including the tasks associated with reinvestment of income and capital gains.

While the insurer guarantees the safety of principal and a modest return on investment, the fulfillment of this promise is contingent upon the insurer's financial survival. Historically, few financial institutions can match the reputation of insurers for safety of principal. This strength is based primarily on an insurer's constant cash inflows from new and existing policies and conservative fixed income investments. Even during the depression of the 1930s the life insurance industry was able to maintain a stable flow of total income. While life insurance policyholders do not have the guarantee of the Federal Deposit Insurance Corporation, the stability of the life insurance industry warrants a high mark for safety of principal.

Savings by means of a life insurance policy may also provide favorable tax treatment. Funds that build up in policy reserves are not taxed until they are distributed to the policyholder. Thus, tax liability can be deferred to a later year when the tax rate may be lower.

The foregoing advantages have led to life insurance being a significant force among savings institutions. However, the fixed and relatively low returns concomitant with savings in a life insurance policy have led to a leveling off in the growth of life insurance savings. While the measurement of the return achieved on the savings element of a life insurance policy is uncertain, a well known method for measuring this return was suggested by M. Albert Linton. Using his technique (and 1963 dividend scales), Linton found the yield on the savings element of a $10,000 whole life policy, issued at age 35 and surrendered at age 55, to be 4.78 percent. However, Belth, in a study of over eighty life insurers, found a set of returns varying from 1 percent to just over 5 percent.[1]

The application of the Linton method is complex, but even though the typical consumer is unable to calculate the exact return on the life insurance savings element, he has apparently concluded that the fixed return available from life insurance is lower than that available in alternative investments. The alternatives may not provide the same safety of principal, but concern over both

---

[1] Joseph Belth, "The Cost of Life Insurance to the Policyholder—A Single Year Attained Age System", *Journal of Insurance*, XXVIII (December, 1961) pp. 23-31. See also Haim Levy and Jehuda Kahane, "Profitability of Saving Through Insurance Companies", *Journal of Risk and Insurance*, XXXVII (June, 1970) pp. 233-40; J. Robert Ferrari, "Implications of Viewing Interest Foregone as an Opportunity Cost of Life Insurance", *The Journal of Risk and Insurance*, XXXVI (June, 1969), pp. 253-65.

the rising cost of living and the declining value of the dollar has caused many consumers to seek higher returns elsewhere.

Unique Features of Life Insurance as a Savings Medium

While life insurance as a savings medium may be compared with other savings vehicles, there are two basic differences that reduce the validity of any comparison. First, life insurance can be considered as forced savings; that is, the premium payments are similar to current debts. Furthermore, the payment of the bill may be done before the insurance consumer receives his discretionary income; the premium may be paid as a payroll deduction for life insurance. Second, the motivation underlying the decision to save differs. Life insurance savings are generally a derivative of the desire for long term protection against uncertainty of death, rather than a desire to gradually accumulate an estate.

Stability of Life Insurance as a Savings Medium

Cash inflows into life insurance tend to be stable because of the motivations of life insurance savers. As shown in Figure 17.1 policy reserves have grown rapidly from $1.2 billion in 1896 to over $167 billion by 1970. However, due to economic conditions the growth of these reserves was irregular but consistently positive. For example, while life insurance reserves grew by about 150 percent during the 1920s ($6.2 billion to $15.3 billion), the depression of the 1930s reduced the growth rate to 79 percent between 1929 and 1939. Another example occurred in the late 1960s, when high interest rates increased the attractiveness of policy loans (at interest rates between 4 and 6 percent) and slowed the net growth of life insurance savings.

INVESTMENT

A savings pool, to the extent that it is not used for consumption or real investment purposes, is a depressant in terms of national income. Keynesian economics defines an equilibrium relationship as an equality between savings and investments. It is only when the vast sums are deployed in terms of real investment that institutional savings become a positive force in the economy. Investment is the movement of resources into capital formation and consumption. The investments of insurance companies must therefore be analyzed in terms of real vs. financial investment. The one enlarges the economy; the other is largely an exchange of titles to existing property.

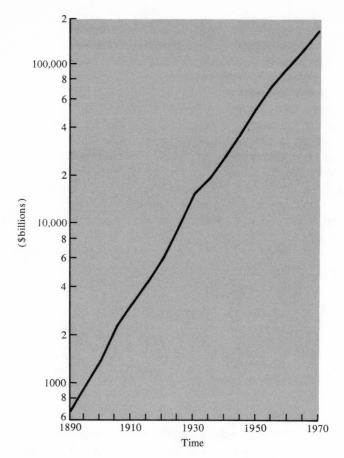

FIGURE 17.1   Life Insurance Policy Reserves

> *SOURCE:*   Institute of Life Insurance, *1972 Life Insurance Fact Book.* (New York: Institute of Life Insurance, 1972).

Equity Capital

Generally, financial investments are reflected in stocks rather than bonds. But insurance companies, especially in the life insurance industry, traditionally avoid extensive (in terms of percentage of investment funds) stock investments.

Life Insurers and Equity Capital.   Three constraints reduce a life insurer's desire and ability to invest in equity capital: (1) conservative business practices resulting from pressure to guarantee principal rather than to optimize return, (2) regulatory restrictions as to where insurers can invest, and (3) valuation procedures as required by statute or regulatory promulgation. Insurers generally make fixed commitments to policyholders. To assure that a company will be able to meet the foregoing commitments, the investment departments of life insurance companies tend to be conservative. While the states restrict life insurers primarily to fixed income ventures, the statutes of the various states usually allow a small percentage of unrestricted investment. However, even the unrestricted funds are not entirely invested in equity. They are also partly invested in fixed income securities. The aversion to common stocks results from the greater potential for fluctuation in market value. Common stocks must be recorded at market price, or at approved values as set by the National Association of Insurance Commissioners. A significant fall in market values may be reflected in the next annual statement and thus could endanger an insurer's surplus. However, most fixed income investments not in default are recorded at their amortized value.

There are exceptions to the bias against common stock investments for life insurance companies. Life insurers may establish segregated funds for specific groups that are willing to assume the investment risk (e.g., pension funds or variable annuities). The insurer is given greater latitude with respect to the investment of segregated funds. Since neither the insurer nor the general policyholders are affected by fluctuations in the market value of segregated funds, heavy equity investment would not violate any principle of sound fiduciary management.

While common stock may not account for a large percentage of life insurance company assets (see Figure 17.2) the total amount is significant. In 1971, 9.3 percent of the assets of U.S. life insurance companies were invested in common and preferred stocks. However, the 9.3 percent represented over $20 billion. Furthermore, the share of assets invested in stocks has increased steadily since 1968, when stocks accounted for only 4 percent of life insurer assets. This growth may be attributed to the growth of insured pension plans and other separate accounts. In 1971, common stock investments for separate accounts equaled over 31 percent of the common stock holdings of U.S. life insurers.

Property and Liability Insurers and Equity Capital. Property and liability insurers are allowed to invest more extensively in common stocks. Approximately one-third of the assets of the property and liability insurance industry are represented by stocks. In addition to the more permissive regulatory climate, three factors account for the more extensive use of equity by property and liability insurers: (1) the obligations of property and liability insurers are typically short term in nature, (2) property and liability insurers are not a savings medium and thus are not concerned with guaranteed long term yields on a savings element, and (3) investment income has played an increasing role in the

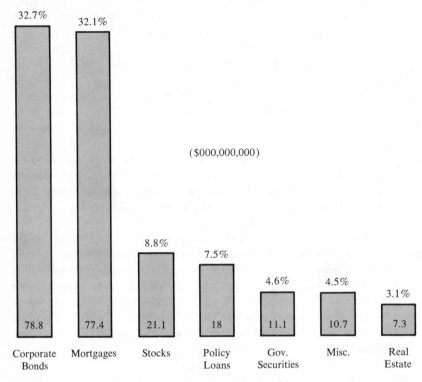

FIGURE 17.2   Asset Distribution of U.S. Life Insurance Companies: 1973

SOURCE: Institute of Life Insurance.

net income of property and liability insurers. When underwriting profits diminish, investments become a key source of income and additions to surplus.

Impact of Stock Markets.   Stock markets have little impact on life insurance companies because of their small equity holdings (mostly preferreds) and because of their traditional antipathy toward speculation or the maintenance of trading accounts. However, many multiple line companies have heavy equity commitments, both directly through their portfolios and indirectly through public ownership of their securities. Thus, they operate virtually as closed end investment trusts with billions of dollars of asset values committed. But generally, stock market fluctuations affect only a small fraction of the industry, and conversely the industry plays a small role in the determination of stock prices.

Debt Instruments

Bond issues in the primary markets, real estate mortgage commitments, direct placements, as well as other debt obligations, provide important avenues for insurance company investment. The role of the insurance industry in net real capital formation is significant. The industry is one of the principal institutions in the capital markets. In 1970, life insurers accounted for approximately 9 percent of the financial capital provided the economy from all sources.

Life Insurers and Debt Markets. Life insurance companies have invested the majority of their $200 billion of assets in fixed income securities, which offer a high degree of safety of principal. By 1971, U.S. life insurers had invested 35.7 percent of their assets in corporate bonds, 34 percent in mortgages, 4.9 percent in government securities, and 7.7 percent in policy loans. Of the foregoing, government securities have been declining, and corporate bonds have increased. While government securities offer greater safety, the returns available have generally been below those obtainable from high grade corporate bonds. Life insurers have also been attracted to the mortgage market because of the relative safety and yields higher than attainable from government securities. While the insurer incurs a risk of default with corporate bonds and mortgages, the slight risk has apparently been more than justified by the higher returns. The mortgages held by life insurers include (in order of importance) one- to four-family residences, apartments and commercial property, and farm property.

Property and Liability Insurers and Debt Markets. Property and liability insurers invest only a small percentage of their assets in mortgages, but they do invest a significant portion of their assets in corporate bonds; more so than life insurers. Furthermore, there is a substantial difference in the investment practices of stock as contrasted with mutual property and liability insurers. Mutuals tend to invest more in corporate bonds, with over two-thirds of their assets in corporate bonds, as compared to less than one-half for stock property and liability insurers.

Private Placement Loans. A significant economic contribution of insurers arises from their extensive participation in the private placement market. Estimates of this participation range upward to three-fourths of all privately placed bonds. Through the use of private placements, insurers can: (1) directly negotiate with the borrower on both indenture covenants (e.g., limitations of the borrower's right to refund early) and the interest rate, (2) place a large block of funds with one borrower at a predetermined and convenient time, and (3) enter into a more risky investment, but still retain some indirect control over the venture by use of special protective covenants. The major risk inherent in investment by means of direct placements is the reduced marketability of the securities.

Policy Loans

Life insurance policies (except term insurance, which has no cash values) include a provision that allows the insured to borrow from the insurer an amount up to the existing nonforfeiture value of the policy. The insurer cannot refuse the loan but does have the right to charge an interest rate fixed in the policy (e.g., 5 or 6 percent).

Policy loans are a unique form of investment. While the life insurer has little control over their issuance, they are fully secured; that is, failure to repay a loan will result in either the reduction of cash values at forfeiture or the proceeds at maturity of the policy.

During periods of tight money and high general interest rates, the availability of policy loans can reduce the potential earnings of the life insurer; that is, there will be selection against the company. The policyowner is able to obtain a risk free arbitrage profit by borrowing at the low interest rate of the policy loan and investing for a higher return in equally safe and liquid instruments such as savings accounts, commercial paper, or short term government securities. Furthermore, if a policyholder is in need of money, and interest rates are high, the policy loan becomes an attractive and available alternative.

It is during periods of high general interest rates that an insurer would like to place its assets in long term, high yielding securities. Not only will the insurer obtain the benefit of higher fixed returns, but there is a greater potential for capital appreciation (i.e., assuming interest rates will eventually return to some lower "normal" levels). If the assets are placed in policy loans, the opportunity for increased returns cannot be realized. There have been significant increases in policy loans during both periods of depression (1930s) and periods of relatively high general interest rates (1915-1920, 1965-1970, 1973).

Insurer Efficiency
in Allocating Capital

Economic Criteria.   United States insurers are relatively efficient allocators of scarce capital in their investment practices. Not only are insurers active in all sectors (product and geographical) of the financial market, but they are also responsive to economic forces. The U.S. economic system is based on fluctuating prices as a market clearing mechanism; that is, if the economy demands more of a particular product or service, the price of this product or service will rise until demand equals supply. Correspondingly, if a sector of the economy demands additional scarce financial capital, there will be upward pressure on the interest rates of this sector's financial instruments. Interest rates will rise until demand is met and the market is cleared. Investors who satisfy this new demand for funds will be rewarded with higher returns. Thus, if it can be assumed that insurers act to optimize their investment income, insurers are efficient allocators of capital. Within the constraints of conservative and prudent financial management, insurers do attempt to optimize investment income. The need to achieve optimum investment yields is based on a desire to maintain competitive prices (including policyholder dividends), increase the surplus base for premium growth, and to increase the flow of benefits to stockholders in the case of stock insurers. Thus, insurers have an incentive to direct funds where market priorities and returns are the highest.

Social Criteria.   In general, the investment practices of insurers have been responsive to social needs. First, insurers have been significant purchasers of residential and commercial mortgages. Even during periods of higher return on alternative investments, insurers have continued to be large suppliers of funds to the mortgage markets. While the heavy purchase of mortgages is partially dictated by regulatory restrictions, insurers have found mortgages to be an investment vehicle that complements their needs. A mortgage is long term, it is secured, and it offers a good return relative to its inherent risk. Second, insurers have recognized a need to assist small businesses by the direct negotiation and placement of debt and by participation in small loan programs. Third, insurers have demonstrated a willingness to innovate and respond to contemporary social issues. For example, a group of life insurers committed $2 billion for residential and small business loans in the core areas of major cities during a period of tight credit.[2] In a similar fashion, insurers contributed to the financing of large scale housing projects following World War II. Both of these projects were designed to reduce shortages of low cost housing in metropolitan areas.

EMPLOYMENT AND THE INSURANCE BUSINESS

Employment in the insurance industry is relatively stable. About 1.5 million persons are engaged in the industry from home office to the part-timer in the field. While employment in the industry has continued to rise, the number of employees relative to sales has declined. Increase of efficiency of existing employees, electronic data processing, and other automated procedures have reduced the need for additional clerical employees. Clerical work (as compared to professional, technical, or sales work) comprises nearly one-half of the jobs in the industry. This percentage should decline as the industry continues to use the computer and as mass marketing approaches reduce the need for relatively unskilled sales personnel. This trend could be detrimental to the already poor

[2] Charles Moeller, Jr., "Economic Implications of the Life Insurance Industry's Investment Program in the Central Cities", *The Journal of Risk and Insurance*, XXXVI (March, 1969), pp. 93-101.

employment levels of the uneducated or untrained because insurers have been a consistent employer of relatively unskilled clerical workers.

The insurance industry through the institution of insured private pensions sets up barriers to labor mobility. The fear of loss of pension rights because of lack of transferability tends to freeze older workers into jobs.

INCOME REDISTRIBUTION

Perhaps the most significant macroeconomic impact of the insurance mechanism is on income redistribution. Life insurance essentially serves to transfer funds from currently employed persons via premium payments to unemployed persons, beneficiaries, and thereby helps alleviate the problem of economic distress. This is also true of older persons who obtain the living benefits, or cash surrender values, of a life insurance policy. Insurance proceeds are an important element in the economic well-being of dependents. Government insurance programs strive more comprehensively and directly to achieve the same goal.

Private or social insurance programs provide an attractive alternative to a public welfare system. Specifically, insurance programs provide *ex ante* certainty that if a specific contingency occurs, funds will be provided. A state welfare system does not remove uncertainty, but at times compounds it. For example, unemployed individuals who are able to collect disability income insurance benefits are reasonably certain that they will receive a specified stipend for a given period of time. No controls are exerted over how the money is spent, and the recipient is not required to undergo humiliating checks on his or her domestic life. Likewise, the elderly person who has qualified for Social Security need only fill out a few forms, and the retirement benefits can commence. Again, the benefit recipient is certain of specified benefits before retirement and of their continuation once retired. The recipient does not have to be exposed to any anxiety producing restrictions on how the money can be spent.

However, if disabled workers or elderly retirees are unable to collect private or social insurance benefits and have no alternative source of income, they must rely on the uncertain assistance of the public welfare system. If they move from one state to another, their benefits may be reduced or discontinued. Furthermore, they may be restricted as to how the money can be spent, and in some areas they must undergo unwanted investigations of their personal affairs.

INFLATION AND BUSINESS CYCLES

Inflation

Inflation, or a rapidly rising price level for consumer and industrial goods, has an adverse effect on the insurance purchaser. Inflation depresses the real economic value of the dollar and thereby reduces the purchasing power of life insurance proceeds and cash values. Particularly hard hit are individuals, such as annuitants, living on fixed incomes. Indeed, the long term post-World War II price level increases significantly reduced the demand for ordinary fixed annuities. Instead, a variety of financial products, such as the variable annuity, mutual funds, and equity funding, entered the economy to fill the gap created by the failure of fixed dollar plans to meet the need. The development of the variable life policy is also a response to the threat of inflation.

Inflation also directly affects the financial performance of insurance companies. Even though premium levels have increased, increasing expenses and increasing claims costs have reduced the potential underwriting gains of the insurance industry on previously written business.

Conversely, the industry has had a slight impact on inflation by directing dollars from consumption into savings and investment.

Business Cycles

Business cycle impacts have not been pronounced. There has been a tendency for the insurance industry to have a contracyclical impact. Employment falls off less rapidly in periods of recession than it does in most other industries. Policyowner loans provide consumption expenditure moneys in recession periods, despite the fact that such loans correlate only partially with changes in national income. Furthermore, the pressure of cash flows into insurance companies compels them to maintain investment programs that direct savings into investment in all stages of the business cycle.

POPULATION CHANGES

Population changes materially affect the nsurance industry because of the economic consequences of changing rates of birth, death, marriage, and family formation. The shifting age distribution affects the kinds and amounts of insurance the public will buy.

Furthermore, a trend toward urbanization and congestion in a few geographical areas led to a deterioration of the environment in which insurers operate. Specifically, the urban core areas became undesirable exposures as crime rates increased and property owners were unable or unwilling to maintain their property in face of rising tax rates. As cities deteriorate, insurers find it more difficult to supply urban property insurance at reasonable rates. In addition, the congestion of property values in a few geographical areas increases the potential for catastrophic losses. Prudent insurers must limit the number of exposures in any one congested area.

Population changes have also affected the investment patterns of insurers. The movement of workers away from the farm reduced the need for farm mortgages, while the move to the suburbs increased the need for housing developments and shopping centers. Insurers participated in this growth both as direct investors and as providers of mortgage funds.

FISCAL POLICY

Fiscal policy consists of government activities to direct aggregate demand, aggregate supply, or prices, in order to achieve the predetermined social goals of full employment, price stability, and economic growth. Fiscal policy includes: (1) the timing and amount of government spending, (2) the timing and amount of taxation, (3) the extent to which the government exercises direct control over the business system or any one component, and (4) moral suasion.

Government Spending

If government spending results in an increase in aggregate demand, more industrial concerns will find it profitable either to come into existence or expand present production facilities. If industry is successful in filling the rising demand, consumers will acquire additional goods. The net result will be an increase in property held by consumers and industry and a rising level of personal and industrial income. The increases in property assets and income require additional insurance protection. For example, as shown in Table 17.2 there is a rising ratio between disposable personal income and life insurance purchases. Furthermore, growth in government spending and thus the industrial base provide the insurer with additional investment outlets for rising cash flows. Alternatively, if a decline in government spending causes a decline in aggregate demand, insurable property, investment opportunities, and income will decline.

By providing the government with a source of funds, insurers contribute to the government's ability to manipulate aggregate demand. While insurers have reduced their use of government securities, they still are an important purchaser. However, the savings automatically available to the life insurance policyholder tend to destabiliz the effect of a government policy to tighten the economy because policy loan availability is unregulated by the federal government. This financial disintermediation may increase the time necessary to implement restrictive fiscal policy, but the results have only gradual and modest effects on the economy.

Taxation

Specific tax laws can indirectly influence the demand for insurance. For example, changes in the tax laws that allow accelerated depreciation or investment credits can cause an increase in capital investment which in turn will require additional insurance coverage. More directly, the laws governing the

TABLE 17.2 Ratio of Disposable Personal Income to Total Life Insurance Purchases: U.S.A.

Year	(1) Disposable Personal Income ($ Billions)	(2) Total Life Insurance Purchases ($ Billions)	(3) Ratio of (2) to (1)
1946	158.9	21.702	13.7%
1947	169.5	22.425	13.2
1948	188.4	22.449	12.0
1949	186.4	22.550	12.1
1950	206.9	28.796	14.0
1951	226.1	27.467	12.1
1952	237.4	31.539	13.3
1953	250.2	36.238	14.5
1954	254.4	38.746	15.2
1955	274.4	46.527	17.0
1956	292.9	55.313	18.8
1957	308.8	66.726	21.6
1958	317.9	66.831	21.0
1959	337.3	70.854	21.0
1960	349.9	74.408	21.3
1961	364.7	79.035	21.7
1962	384.6	79.577	20.7
1963	402.5	89.573	22.3
1964	438.1	105.008	24.0
1965	473.2	114.366	24.2
1966	511.9	121.990	23.83
1967	546.3	132.568	24.27
1968	591.0	146.075	24.72
1969	634.4	159.283	25.11
1970	689.5	176.574	25.61
1971	744.4	189.175	25.41
1972	795.1	212.274	26.70

SOURCE: Institute of Life Insurance, *Life Insurance Factbook,* New York.

taxation of insurance benefits and reserves can stimulate demand for insurance. For example, under present tax laws, funds that accumulate in life insurance reserves are not taxed until distributed. Thus, income taxes can be delayed and possibly avoided if the insured dies prior to taking cash values on a nonforfeiture option. Furthermore, through the use of an appropriate life insurance settlement option, a widow can avoid taxes on a portion of her income. The tax laws place insurance in an advantageous position with regard to the solution of certain estate planning problems.

Direct Controls

Whereas in some countries the insurance industry is under the direct supervision of government, the U.S. government normally allows the insurance industry to operate free of federal supervision. However, there are three qualifications. First, the federal government does not regulate the insurance industry because it has granted jurisdiction to the states. The states have tended to restrict insurers to those investments (government securities, mortgages, and corporate bonds) that are most susceptible to fiscal and monetary policy control by limiting the investment outlets available to insurers. Second, where the federal government has determined that the aggregate supply of a necessary insurance product has been insufficient (thus a detriment to economic growth), the government has either instituted programs to assist private insurers or has established a public insurance mechanism. Third, the price freeze of 1971 and the price controls following the freeze affected the insurance industry's ability to implement price changes.

Moral Suasion

Fiscal policy may be implemented without specific action by the government. In some cases, the threat of potential government intervention may be sufficient to bring about the desired economic change. Knowing that the federal government can and has entered into the insurance business has an influence on the decisions of insurance executives. Furthermore the government has used moral suasion to obtain assistance from the insurance industry. The requested assistance has included redirection of investment into specific depressed sections of the economy.

MONETARY POLICY

The monetary policy of government, to the extent that it is expansionary by manipulation of interest rates and the supply and demand of funds, is an important influence in the operation of an insurance company.

Tools of Monetary Policy

General monetary policy is implemented in the following areas: (1) the rate of interest (discount rate) charged banks that borrow from the Federal Reserve System, (2) the reserve requirements of banks, and (3) the purchase and sale of government securities by the Federal Reserve System. In addition, the Federal Reserve System has available several selective credit controls. Selective controls include the purchase and sale of securities in specific sectors of the money markets and the placing of restrictions on limited categories of financial institutions.

The Influence of Monetary Policy

Since they are substantial holders of government debt obligations, fluctuations in government bond prices as a result of monetary policy have significant influence on insurers. Alternatively, the willingness or unwillingness of insurance carriers to buy particular issues can sometimes influence the structure of the national debt and indirectly influence the effectiveness of specific tools of monetary policy.

Many economists agree that the demand for money is of three types: transaction demand, speculative demand, and precautionary demand. The existence of insurance reduces the precautionary demand; that is, individuals with insurance do not require a precautionary reserve for protection against the insured peril. If, as a result of restrictive monetary policies, the demand for money becomes greater than supply, people may hold less insurance. In a period of tight money the purchase of necessary goods (transaction demand) may use most of the existing supply of money. However, if the money supply exceeds that required for the transaction demand, individuals will fulfill a desire for security and purchase insurance. Furthermore, individuals may also invest (speculative demand) in life insurance cash values.

There is extensive debate as to the influence of general credit controls on the investment activities of insurers. However, there is little debate as to the existence of this influence. Insurers participate in numerous investment markets that are strongly influenced by activities of the Federal Reserve System. For example, if monetary policy is expansionary and thus provides the banking system with additional loanable funds, the effective demand for commercial loans is increased. If the banks are able to reduce interest rates because of additional funds, insurers are forced to follow to remain competitive.

Alternatively, if monetary policy becomes restrictive and leads to a tighter money supply and rising interest rates, there will be a tendency for firms to seek long term loans. Borrowers will attempt to avoid higher short term rates and the potential for higher long term rates in the immediate future. As insurers recognize the trend toward higher yields, they may maintain a more liquid position to take advantage of expected increases. This withdrawal of funds contributes to the upward movement of rates. Furthermore, when insurers enter the investment markets, it is in those areas where rates have been less rigid. Insurers tend to stress direct placement of commercial bonds in preference to government securities or mortgages.

The Gurley-Shaw Thesis

The debate on the influence of monetary policy on insurers (and other non-financial intermediaries) centers around the validity of the Gurley-Shaw

Thesis.[3] The thesis asserts that nonmonetary intermediaries issue "indirect securities" (e.g., a cash value life insurance policy) that are liquid assets that may be close money substitutes, and while monetary authorities can control the extent to which commercial banks create money, the Federal Reserve System cannot control the extent to which the nonmonetary intermediaries supply close money substitutes. Gurley and Shaw conclude that if the government is to control aggregate liquidity and thus inflation, direct controls over the nonfinancial intermediaries may be required.

The foregoing theory is subject to two criticisms. First, it may be argued that most life insurance purchasers do not consider their policy reserves or cash values a liquid money source. Second, while insurers are not subject to direct controls by monetary authorities, the indirect controls exerted by the Federal Reserve System are effective in influencing the investment decisions of insurers.

INTERNATIONAL TRADE

In dollar terms, insurance is a relatively minor factor in the economics of international trade. However, such trade would probably not exist in the absence of an insurance market. Treated as an "invisible" item in the Balance of Payments, the net flow is very modest for the United States. Only a few nations, such as Great Britain, Switzerland, and the Scandinavian countries, have large favorable balances of payments.

SUMMARY

Insurance macroeconomics is concerned with the impact of the insurance industry on the economy and the impact of the economy on the insurance industry. The macroeconomic role of insurance is important in Gross National Product formation as a savings medium and as an investment outlet. The employment of more than one million persons directly in the industry adds to the quantity of wages and salaries in the national income. The redistributive effects of insurance, shifting income from persons in productive years to others in periods of dependency, is relevant for the stimulation of consumption expenditures. Inflation is a serious threat to insurance companies. The implications of fiscal and monetary policy are important more from an asset management viewpoint than from the perspective of restraints on insurance company operations.

[3] John G. Gurley and Edward S. Shaw, "Financial Intermediaries and the Savings-Investment Process", *Journal of Finance*, XI (May, 1956), pp. 257-66.

REVIEW QUESTIONS

1. As the investment manager of a life insurance company you have been asked to grant a direct placement loan to a large business concern. What are the advantages and disadvantages to this arrangement as opposed to the purchase of issued stocks or bonds?

2. Has the life insurance institution been able to maintain its relative position among financial institutions in the United States as an outlet for savings in recent years?

3. Discuss the merits of insurance as a mechanism for income redistribution.

4. In periods of prosperity, policy loans increase. Explain why.

5. Property and liability insurers are allowed by statute to invest more heavily in common stocks than are life insurers. Why?

STUDY QUESTIONS

6. Should social criteria play a role in the investment decisions of an insurance company? Discuss.

7. Many countries have experienced extremely high rates of inflation since World War II. What do you suppose has been the effect of such hyperinflation on life insurance sales? Life insurance company profitability? Explain.

8. "The financial disintermediation may increase the time necessary to implement restrictive fiscal policy, but the results have only gradual and modest effects on the economy." Explain.

9. What proportion of the national debt is held by the insurance industry in the form of government bonds? Is this rising over time? Discuss.

10. "The insurance industry is an important source of tax revenues, but it is also an enormous engine for deferment of tax payments." What tax revenues are referred to in the quotation? What tax deferments? Explain.

18

Insurance
in the
World Economy

By virtue of its long history, tradition and inextricable involvement in world trade, insurance is an international business. As it was in Elizabethan times so it is today: ships do not sail and capital is not deployed abroad without adequate insurance protection. Every nation is concerned with insurance and its monetary impact. The United Nations and regional organizations such as the European Economic Community are vitally concerned with money flows arising out of insurance transactions. Insurance is a small but important factor in the international balance of payments.

INSURANCE OF FOREIGN TRADE

Most foreign trade is conducted by means of common carriers. Shipping companies and airlines have virtually absolute liability and must provide by means of insurance for the financial consequences of disaster. Marine insurance is incorporated in the Bill of Lading used in international trade. Cargoes move from inland locations, which causes inland marine insurance to be important. The security of the warehouse or factory is no less critical to the fulfillment of a merchant's contracts than prompt shipment of goods, and property insurances of all kinds are required. Bonding and crime coverages, workmen's compensation, liability insurances, and personal coverages are also important for world trade. In the course of international business there is no way of avoiding some involvement with virtually all lines of insurance. The shipper prefers to have his own insurer handle all aspects of his risk management activity without having to depend on foreign companies whose service and financial responsibility may be uncertain.

The shipper expects his insurance company to provide coverage for him at home and abroad under familiar contract terms and at fixed or at least determinable rates. The intricacies of foreign markets call for expertise on the part of insurers. The insurance company seeking to obtain business from shippers must be prepared for the problems of operating in foreign markets. This brings the insurer into the web of foreign exchange, foreign languages, foreign laws, and foreign customs. The risks of expropriation, of discrimination, of partial or total nationalization, and of currency control or blockage are problems incurred by the domestic insurance company that enters foreign markets.

The overseas insurance buyer would also prefer that the documentation be in his language, currency, and legal framework. The foreign insurance carrier must therefore find ways to enter other jurisdictions to do business. Once established in a country, it is natural that the insurer will seek to expand its business by seeking domestic risks as well. So it is that in the United States foreign companies account for a substantial volume of business. Canadian life insurance companies rank high in the American market. British, Swiss, and German insurers and reinsurers rank high as well.

COMPETITION IN THE INTERNATIONAL MARKET

There is extensive competition in the world market. There are more than 13,500 insurance companies striving for reasonable shares of the available business. Despite movements toward partial oligopoly by line and class of business and by country, there is vigorous competition on price, product, and service. There is a worldwide tendency for prices and terms to converge, and major discrepancies are usually removed rather quickly. Most companies are submarginal by volume and are unable to compete effectively either because of excessive overhead costs or inadequate underwriting skills. Standards of performance are established informally by the major reinsurance companies who operate throughout the world. These companies have computerized their results by class in such a manner that they can readily make corrective suggestions to primary insurance carriers whose standards deviate beyond acceptable limits.

Those insurers who enter the world market and actively compete in foreign territory must conduct themselves with greater than normal caution. The parameters of operating abroad are somewhat different, and the likelihood of failure is high, especially in the first few years of market participation. Considerations for survival should include adequate capitalization prior to entry and a cautious attitude toward retention limits after entry. Working with and through nationals of the country involved is essential.

CAPACITY PROBLEMS

The insurance capacity problem is international in scope. There has been a major escalation in values relating to property and liability risks of various kinds. Jumbo jets with payloads in the tens of millions, massive supertankers for oil transport carrying literally millions of gallons of oil, skyscrapers, major bridges and dams, and major transmission systems for nuclear power are only a few cases that require limits of insurance beyond the capacity of the entire domestic market. Therefore, international insurance or reinsurance is mandatory for local insureds, and domestic carriers are compelled to enter the international market to seek reinsurance coverage. Some reciprocity is expected, so it is difficult to avoid competition in the broader arena. As the capacity problem is exacerbated by inflation and economic development, the demand for international insurance grows, and competition for the better risks is expanded

In developing countries the insurance industry is confronted with a dual form of the capacity problem. If the industry is relatively disorganized and competitive, it must deal with the hazard of cumulation of liability. A reinsurer may discover that instead of obtaining a normal share of a risk it has received several shares beyond its desired limits of retention. In a small market, capacity problems force movement of business indiscriminately through reinsurance channels. Furthermore, the industry is dependent upon foreign reinsurance markets to meet its risk obligations. It is awkward to seek help from competitors who may learn underwriting policy details, but it is even worse to have one's agents and brokers seek out competing insurance companies in order to complete insurance lines. This conflict provides an incentive to avoid larger risks and to seek reinsurance abroad wherever possible. The insurance carrier is in the position of a broker *vis-à-vis* his large reinsurance partner. A pattern of modest retentions and high reinsurance commission income tends to develop.

Ultimately, the alternatives are government intervention in the form of mandatory domestic retention programs or reinsurance programs with the government acting as carrier of last resort. There is in fact an international network whereby all companies are subjected to a degree of common control by the reinsurers. The major reinsurers provide the capacity that makes survival possible for a small carrier in an underdeveloped country.

NATIONALIST INFLUENCES

The process of nationalist restriction of insurance activity began about the time of the First World War in Europe. International trade in direct insurance declined relative to the expansion of commerce.

> Direct insurance in most of the European countries managed to establish near self-sufficiency without actual legal discrimination against foreign companies. In countries such as Denmark, Finland, Italy, Sweden,

Switzerland, etc., where foreign companies are free to operate on legally equal terms with the local companies, the formerly considerable business of the foreign companies has withered to little significance since 1914. In Switzerland it has declined from 35 percent to 1 percent. In Finland from 13 percent to 4 percent; in Norway from 20 percent to 4 percent, etc.[1]

The pace of the movement toward autarky quickened after the Second World War. Cross currents are to be found in trade liberalization efforts by the European Common Market countries.

There were two noteworthy trends that developed after World War II: (1) the growth of state insurance in all possible legal forms in various countries, from government owned stock companies and mixed enterprises to state corporations and public utilities, and from competitive offices to outright monopolies, and (2) a gradual narrowing of the geographical sphere of international insurance transactions with a reduction of the relative shares of foreign companies in the total available business of countries in which operations are still permissible.

DEVELOPMENT OF MAJOR INSURANCE COUNTRIES, 1960-1970

Economic Development

During the 1960s, insurance passed through a phase of rapid growth similar to that of the overall world economy. The insurance markets of industrialized West European countries and Japan benefited most from the favorable trend.[2] World premium volume (excluding the Communist bloc) increased during the period 1960-1970 from approximately $48 billion to about $115 billion. Thus, it more than doubled during this ten-year period, with an average annual growth rate of 9 percent. During the same period the population of the free world increased from 2 billion to 2.5 billion, and world income grew from roughly $900 billion to $2 trillion. This corresponds to average annual growth rates of 2.2 percent and 8 percent respectively.

World Insurance Transactions

Private insurers transact business under widely differing economic and political circumstances with the result that the statistics of private insurance in different countries are not strictly comparable. Nevertheless, a survey of the

---

[1] S. J. Lengyel, *International Insurance Transactions: Insurance in the Balance of Payments* (London: Wadley and Ginn, 1953), p. 7.

[2] Swiss Reinsurance Company, *Sigma* (April, 1972). This material is based largely on data from *Sigma* and is used with permission of the Swiss Reinsurance Company.

major insurance countries of the world including all countries with a premium volume exceeding $100 million in 1970 gives a realistic picture of the economic importance of insurance in these countries (see Table 18.1).

The United States heads the list by a significant margin with a share of nearly 60 percent of the world premium volume. While the United States contains only 8 percent of the free world population, its share of world income represents more than 40 percent. In 1970, Western Europe accounted for 15 percent of the world population, 23 percent ($27 billion) of the world premium volume, and about 30 percent of the world income. The Japanese insurance industry has achieved an astonishingly dynamic growth. It moved from sixth position in 1960 to second position in 1970. On the other hand, Great Britain slipped from second to fourth position and Canada from fourth to sixth.

In a comparison of the relative shares of individual countries in total premiums, national income, and population, three main groups emerge:

1.   Countries whose share in the overall total of premiums is higher than their share of world income and population. These include the more developed insurance countries: United States, Canada, Australia, the Netherlands, Switzerland, and New Zealand.

2.   Countries whose relative share in world premium volume is lower than their share of world income—their relative share in premiums being at least one-half as high as their relative share in the world economy. With regard to insurance, these are the developed countries. They include Japan, Germany, Great Britain, France, Sweden, Belgium, South Africa, Denmark, Austria, Norway, Finland, Ireland, and Israel.

3.   Countries whose percentage share in the world premium volume is less than 50 percent of their relative share in world income. From the standpoint of insurance, these are the less developed countries that generally show a low per capita income: Italy, Spain, India, Argentina, Brazil, Mexico, Venezuela, the Philippines, and Pakistan. Italy figures in this group in spite of its relatively high level of economic development because until 1971 it had no compulsory automobile third party liability insurance, and additionally it had a relatively low density of life insurance.

Relative Development
of Insurance Markets

Ratio of Premium Volume to National Income.   With the exception of Canada and Norway, premium income has increased more rapidly than national income in all countries surveyed over the decade of the sixties (see Figure 18.1). As might be expected, the highest ratios are shown by countries with the highest standards of living. The United States has the highest ratio at 8.5 percent (1960: 7.6 percent), followed by Australia with 6.7 percent (5.7 percent), Canada 6.3

Position		Country		Premiums in millions of national currency			US$	Share in world total in %		
1960	1970			Non-Life	Life	Total	Total	Premiums	National Income	Population
1	1	USA	$	42 510	25 400	67 910	67 910	59.05	40.82	8.15
6	2	Japan	Yen	1 007 990	1 800 000	2 807 990	7 852	6.83	8.10	4.11
3	3	W. Germany	DM	16 971	10 781	27 752	7 603	6.61	7.35	2.45
2	4	Great Britain	£	721*	1 429*	2 150*	5 139	4.47	4.74	2.21
5	5	France	F	19 500*	5 400*	24 900*	4 511	3.92	5.85	2.01
4	6	Canada	$	2 228	1 765	3 993	3 953	3.44	3.24	0.85
8	7	Italy	Lit.	895 249	269 626	1 164 875	1 870	1.63	3.70	2.13
7	8	Australia	A$	895	700	1 595	1 773	1.54	1.35	0.50
9	9	Netherlands	hfl	3 160*	2 464	5 624*	1 562	1.36	1.31	0.52
10	10	Sweden	sKr.	2 887	2 425	5 312	1 027	0.89	1.37	0.32
11	11	Switzerland	sFr.	2 250*	2 100*	4 350*	1 008	0.88	0.88	0.25
12	12	Belgium	bFr.	31 193	12 425	43 618	878	0.76	1.05	0.38
13	13	South Africa	R.	207*	405*	612*	851	0.74	0.74	0.80
16	14	Spain	Ptas	47 469	4 331	51 799	743	0.65	1.40	1.32
14	15	India	Rp.	1 350*	2 869	4 219*	557	0.48	2.17	21.84
15	16	Denmark	dKr.	2 700*	1 450*	4 150*	554	0.48	0.60	0.20
20	17	Austria	Sch	9 192	2 018	11 210	433	0.38	0.55	0.29
19	18	Argentina	N.Pes.	1 444	173	1 617	404	0.35	1.03	0.97
17	19	Norway	nKr.	1 651	880	2 531	354	0.31	0.43	0.15
21	20	Brazil	Cruz.	1 376	298	1 675	338	0.29	1.40	3.78
22	21	Finland	Mk.	718	603	1 321	316	0.27	0.41	0.19
23	22	Mexico	Pes.	2 273	1 405	3 678	294	0.26	1.42	2.01
18	23	New Zealand	NZ.$	118	133	251	279	0.24	0.23	0.11
26	24	Philippines	Pes.	425*	275*	700*	178	0.15	0.41	1.53
25	25	Ireland	ir.£	29	43	72	172	0.15	0.16	0.12
24	26	Venezuela	Bs.	500*	200*	700*	156	0.14	0.48	0.41
27	27	Portugal	Esc.	3 649	665	4 314	150	0.13	0.28	0.38
28	28	Israel	I£	390	124	514	147	0.13	0.22	0.11
29	29	Pakistan	Rp.	320*	330*	650*	135	0.12	0.75	4.53

*) estimated

TABLE 18.1   Important Insurance Countries—1970

SOURCE: Swiss Reinsurance Company.

277

percent (6.7 percent), New Zealand 6.2 percent (5.3 percent), and the Netherlands 6.1 percent (5.0 percent). The number of countries with ratios of premiums to national income of 5 percent or more increased from 7 to 11 during the ten-year period. Even in less developed insurance countries, the growth of insurance was higher than overall economic growth. In 1960 nine countries showed a ratio of less than 2 percent, only five did so in 1970. The arithmetic mean of the twenty-nine ratios of premiums to national income increased in the decade from 3.3 percent to 4.1 percent.

Premiums Per Capita.   Per capita premiums (see Table 18.2) indicate the distribution of insurance in individual countries. The United States, with $331 premiums per capita in 1970 (+89 percent compared with 1960), ranked as the most developed insurance market. The per capita premiums were about one-half as high in the following countries: Canada $185 (+80 percent), Switzerland $161 (+137 percent), and Australia $141 (+108 percent). These were followed by Sweden with $128 (+118 percent), Germany with $124 (+204 percent), the Netherlands with $120 (+194 percent), and Denmark with $113 (+163 percent). Eight countries exceeded the $100 premium per capita mark in 1970 as compared with only two (United States and Canada) in 1960. In some countries (Brazil, Mexico, India, the Philippines, and Pakistan) the 1970 average per capita premium was less than $6 (on average $3.2); nevertheless, this doubled between 1960 and 1970. Per capita insurance premiums showed the highest growth during the ten-year period in Japan (+589 percent), Spain (+330 percent), Pakistan (+300 percent), and Italy (+259 percent). The increase was higher than 200 percent in Germany, Finland, and Austria. The average growth of per capita premiums in all countries amounted to 162 percent.

Life vs. Nonlife Insurance.   A shift in favor of nonlife as compared with life insurance business is evident from 1960-1970 (see Figure 18.2). The share of nonlife business in total insurance portfolios increased in seventeen of the twenty-nine countries covered. These seventeen countries included both indus-trialized and developing countries. The shift in favor of nonlife business was most pronounced in the Philippines, Holland, and Venezuela. The arithmetic mean of the share of nonlife business for the twenty-nine countries increased from 59.8 percent to 61.4 percent. In eight countries nonlife business constituted between 75 and over 90 percent of the total business: these were Spain, Argentina, Portugal, Brazil, Austria, France, Italy, and Israel. Life insurance does not attain such a high share of the total business in any of the other countries covered. The highest levels (between 64 percent and 68 percent) are found in India, Great Britain, South Africa, and Japan. Otherwise, only Ireland, New Zealand, and Pakistan show shares of more than 50 percent. Therefore, in 1970 life insurance accounted for more than half of the total business in seven countries, while in 1970 this was true of nine countries.

= 1970
= 1960

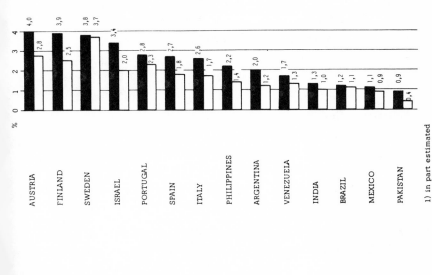

%

AUSTRIA 4,0 / 2,8
FINLAND 3,9 / 2,5
SWEDEN 3,8 / 3,7
ISRAEL 3,4 / 2,0
PORTUGAL 2,8 / 2,3
SPAIN 2,7 / 1,8
ITALY 2,6 / 1,7
PHILIPPINES 2,2 / 1,4
ARGENTINA 2,0 / 1,2
VENEZUELA 1,7 / 1,3
INDIA 1,3 / 1,0
BRAZIL 1,2 / 1,1
MEXICO 1,1 / 0,9
PAKISTAN 0,9 / 0,4

1) in part estimated

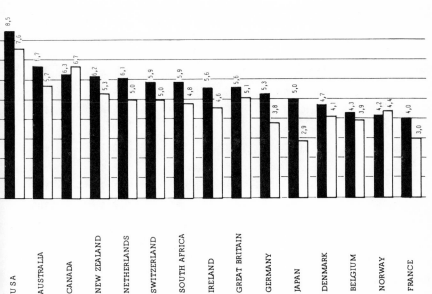

USA 8,5 / 7,0
AUSTRALIA 6,7 / 5,7
CANADA 6,3 / 6,7
NEW ZEALAND 6,2 / 5,3
NETHERLANDS 6,1 / 5,0
SWITZERLAND 5,9 / 5,0
SOUTH AFRICA 5,9 / 4,8
IRELAND 5,6 / 4,6
GREAT BRITAIN 5,6 / 5,1
GERMANY 5,3 / 3,8
JAPAN 5,0 / 2,9
DENMARK 4,7 / 4,1
BELGIUM 4,3 / 3,9
NORWAY 4,2 / 4,4
FRANCE 4,0 / 3,0

FIGURE 18.1 Premiums in Percent of National Income

SOURCE: Swiss Reinsurance Company.

279

Position			1970	1960	Increase in %
1960	1970				
1	1	USA	330.6	175.0	89
2	2	Canada	184.6	102.6	80
4	3	Switzerland	160.5*	67.8	137
3	4	Australia	141.3	68.1	108
6	5	Sweden	127.6	58.5	118
11	6	W. Germany	123.3	40.5	204
10	7	Netherlands	120.0*	40.8	194
8	8	Denmark	112.6*	42.9	164
5	9	New Zealand	98.9	63.7	55
7	10	Great Britain	92.2*	57.3	61
9	11	Norway	91.2	42.3	116
12	12	Belgium	90.7	38.9	133
13	13	France	88.9*	31.3	184
19	14	Japan	75.8	11.0	589
15	15	Finland	67.2	22.1	204
14	16	Ireland	58.5	24.3	141
16	17	Austria	58.4	19.3	203
18	18	Israel	50.9	17.9	184
17	19	South Africa	42.3*	18.0	135
21	20	Italy	34.8	9.7	259
24	21	Spain	22.3	5.2	330
22	22	Argentina	16.6	6.9	141
23	23	Portugal	15.6	5.8	169
20	24	Venezuela	15.0*	10.4	44
25	25	Mexico	5.8	2.7	115
26	26	Philippines	4.6*	2.4	92
27	27	Brazil	3.5	1.7	106
29	28	Pakistan	1.2*	0.3	300
28	29	India	1.0*	0.7	43

*) estimated

TABLE 18.2   Insurance Premiums Per Capita ($ U.S.)

SOURCE: Swiss Reinsurance Company.

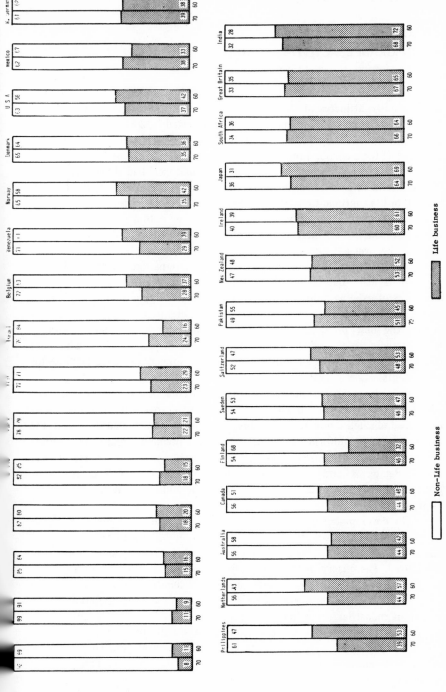

FIGURE 18.2 National Insurance Markets: 1960 and 1970 (Share of Life and Nonlife Business in Percent of Total Business)

SOURCE: Swiss Reinsurance Company.

REASONS FOR
U.S. INSURANCE ACTIVITY ABROAD

There are hundreds of U.S. based multinational industrial corporations, and sales of the foreign affiliates of these giants have grown by billions of dollars since 1960. Multinational U.S. corporations had invested $32 billion in plant and equipment by 1960. By 1970 their investment had swelled to over $78 billion. The need of these corporations for international insurance covers is both obvious and extensive. With regard to these needs, risk managers had three alternatives: (1) use the facilities of local insurance markets, (2) take business to the London market, or (3) continue to have their needs satisfied by U.S. insurers.

U.S. insurers have attempted to make the last option more attractive for various reasons. First, there is the obvious purpose of generating business by insuring the overseas operations of existing customers. To do otherwise would concede these risks to local insurers or other international insurers. Second, there is a fear that abandonment of overseas business would make U.S. exposures of existing multinational clients vulnerable to competition by foreign insurers. Third, there is a desire to explore the potential profitability of introducing new products and U.S. selling techniques to overseas markets. Fourth, there is a need to meet the demands of U.S. brokers who have established overseas branches and have requested foreign insurance facilities for their clients.

Risk managers working for U.S. based international companies have not only been receptive to proposals of U.S. insurers to provide international covers but have indicated a preference for this procedure. Among the advantages to the risk manager are uniform terms and conditions, premium credits for multiple location exposures, minimum currency and language problems, convenience in negotiating terms, and optimal corporate and national balance of payments position. Clearly, corporate officials desire both multinational and centralized insurance programs.

The development of multinational operations results in increasing central-ization of product, market, and fiscal planning. It follows that the corporate insurance programs for such firms must become both multinational and centralized. There is a growing demand for international insurance coverage. The advantages of global covers include simplicity, standardization, efficiency of covers, possible premium economy, and protection against inflation. While American industrial firms have not ignored the benefits of using either local markets or the extensive London market, the proximity of the U.S. market has provided U.S. insurers with distinct competitive advantages. The increasing thrust of American insurers abroad is an attempt to capitalize on these potential advantages.

Even if a risk manager for a U.S. based international firm preferred to place his insurance in overseas markets, sufficient capacity might not be available. As industrial plants have increased in size and complexity, the potential for costly catastrophe has become a concern of all insurers. There is increasing pressure to spread exposures over a broad international base. This problem has two effects on the ability and desire of U.S. insurers to penetrate international insurance markets. First, the insurance capacity of large U.S. insurers is considered a necessity to meet the accelerating demands for insurance in foreign markets. Second, to reduce the catastrophe potential and the accompanying degree of risk, U.S. insurers seek to obtain geographic dispersion of their exposures. Pressures on insurance capacity increase with industrialization of underdeveloped countries and advances in technology. Capacity problems not only require more international cooperation among insurance markets, but also new and imaginative uses of existing underwriting capacity.

U.S. INTERNATIONAL REINSURANCE ACTIVITY

United States insurers have accepted a growing volume of reinsurance business. In fact, premiums ceded to U.S. insurers have grown at a faster pace than those ceded overseas. In 1955, reinsurance premiums accepted from abroad by U.S. insurers were only $33 million, but by 1971 this had increased to 309.1 million (9.3 times that accepted in 1955). However, the $470.9 million paid in 1971 to foreign reinsurers was only a little more than twice the $209.1 million ceded in 1955.[3]

Complementing the need for increased U.S. participation in reinsurance markets is a need for U.S. reinsurers to obtain a wider geographic spread of their exposures. A large reinsurance company must develop business on a worldwide scale because only by means of this geographical spread—in addition to a spread in time—can the balance of risk be obtained which is the *raison d'être* of a reinsurer.

EMPLOYEE BENEFITS

Concomitant with the demand for international commercial covers is a growing awareness of and need for employee benefits and individual personal line covers. As U.S. firms expand their overseas plant and equipment, they also expand the number of overseas employees, both American and local. American management teams take with them their foreign management staffs, and colleagues request

---

[3] "U.S. International Reinsurance Transactions, 1962-1969," *International Insurance Monitor*, XXXV (January, 1971), p. 30. Later data from U.S. Dept. of Commerce.

the same level of employee benefits. To fulfill these needs many U.S. corporations turn to their U.S. insurers. After establishing overseas service facilities to handle the employee benefit needs of American firms, U.S. insurers frequently seek out domestic clients for employee benefit covers.

Industrial growth in numerous foreign markets leads to increasing demand for personal insurance programs. Of importance to U.S. insurers are increases in standards of living, personal incomes, and purchases of homes and automobiles. These contribute to growth in the insurance needs of the man in the street. Because markets, such as the European Economic Community, have the potential to equal or surpass the United States in importance, American insurers cannot afford to neglect the foreign man in the street.

Two additional factors contribute to United States expansion in foreign markets for employee benefits and personal lines: (1) the relative inexperience of many local insurers in marketing and servicing these programs, and (2) the insufficient capacity of local markets. Only recently have foreign insurers begun to operate in the group field on a major scale. The large asset base of U.S. insurance companies makes it possible for foreign partners to retain larger risks than they could on their own or in cooperation with other overseas partners.

U.S. INSURERS AS INTERNATIONAL FINANCIAL INTERMEDIARIES

While the primary function of an insurer is to provide indemnification, the supplementary function of financial intermediary has also been an important factor in the expansion of U.S. insurers abroad. Life insurers have demonstrated an ability to make substantial contributions to the accumulation and distribution of capital. Thus, the American life insurance industry has found a hospitable climate particularly in developing countries. The U.S. life insurance industry is an economic catalyst creating substantial investments of new capital for the development of industry, advanced agriculture, and consumer services abroad. Because of the need for domestic capital, many nations require investment of funds resulting from local operations in local assets as a prerequisite to selling insurance in their markets.

> In a few developing countries, there is a tendency for companies to invest funds in excess of these minimum government requirements. . . . The developing nature of these economies and the inadequacy of local capital markets often mean that there is generally a high demand for external finance. Insurance companies frequently decide to satisfy these local demands in order to stimulate demand for their insurance products.[4]

[4]Gerald M. Dickinson, "Classification of Foreign Capital Flows of Insurance Companies," *The Journal of Risk and Insurance,* XXXVIII (March, 1971), pp. 93-98.

Complementing the demand for effective financial intermediation is the desire of American insurers to find profitable and possibly less restrictive investment outlets. United States companies can be lured by the stimulus of higher returns on funds held abroad. In addition to the potential for high returns, U.S. insurers invest abroad to obtain geographical dispersion of investments and concomitant profit stability.

ENTRY INTO FOREIGN MARKETS

There have been four basic methods of entry into foreign markets:

1. setting up a branch office or authorized representative,
2. starting a new subsidiary or affiliated insurer,
3. purchasing an interest in an existing local insurer, and
4. establishing a cooperative agreement with one or more local insurers.

Direct entry via a branch office or subsidiary assures complete control over the quality, quantity, and cost of underwriting and services, but the direct entrant may have insufficient market information and may have to make a substantial investment to obtain the facts he needs. Indirect methods by means of association with existing local insurers offer less control over operations, but offer familiarity with and feasible solutions to local problems.

Direct entry was used by the earliest U.S. entrants to international markets. However, direct writing of overseas exposures through agents or branch offices did not increase rapidly until the 1950s and 1960s. While precise statistics on the extent of this development are not available, it has been estimated that during the early 1970s annual direct overseas premiums (excluding reinsurance) for nonlife exposures were approximately $500 million.[5]

While direct entry has traditionally played an important role, indirect entry has been used most in recent years. Two factors account for the growth of indirect penetration: (1) an increased awareness of the need for local expertise and admitted covers, and (2) the growth and development of local insurers. Indirect entry via a cooperative agreement with a local insurer provides the U.S. partner with the valuable national identity associated with a long established admitted insurer. With expanding nationalism admitted status will play an increasing role. However, partnership with a foreign insurer is not justified solely on the basis of possible need for local insurance forms. The success of a cooperative contract is dependent upon joint contribution to the profits of each

[5] F. Arthur Mayes, "U.S. Insurance Companies and the International Market," *International Insurance Monitor*, XXXV (January, 1971), p. 4.

participant. The U.S. insurer provides capacity and technical capabilities, and the foreign partner provides recognition of and solutions for local problems.

Some U.S. insurers have entered into cooperative agreements with a few multinational foreign insurers; others have preferred formal relationships with insurers in each country or area of the world. While the former method reduces potential problems of negotiation and communication, there is no guarantee that the foreign multinational insurer will not incur the same problems that a U.S. insurer would incur upon direct entry; that is, the multinational insurer is foreign to many of the markets it might service for a U.S. insurer.

The types of indirect entry vary. The following indicate some of the more common arrangements for employee benefits:

1. A typical arrangement consists of a network of companies in the various nations where the originating insurer has or expects to have a need for local cover. The originating carrier, i.e., the insurer of the employee benefit plan covering the parent corporation in its country of domicile, when presented with a request to expand the cover to employees of a branch, subsidiary or affiliated company in a foreign land, will inform a national company, i.e., its associated member in the particular country, of the coverage required. The national company will then develop a proposal and submit a quotation. If satisfactory, this will be accepted and the national company will write the policy under its own masthead. Typically the national company will reinsure a quota share of the case to the originating insurer, although this is not universally done and in fact may be impossible in some countries because of the existence of a national monopoly on reinsurance or other applicable restrictions.[6]

2. We develop together limits on experience and profit charges to be made by each foreign insurer, that are reasonable and in line with the expectations of the American buyer. . . . We exchange with each partner knowledge of American and foreign employee benefit practices and related techniques, first in a two week gathering of technical people and thereafter on a continuous basis. . . . We sign a reinsurance cooperative agreement with each company and set up the mechanism for a worldwide experience rating system which ties us all together.[7]

There are at least three potential benefits of these agreements.

First, there is more efficient and potentially less costly service to clients. Once an agreement is reached, U.S. insurers can immediately extend foreign services to their international corporate clients. The team of partners works

[6]John H. Miller, "International Cooperation in Life Insurance," Pacific Insurance Conference, 5th Biennial Meeting, Hawaii, Sept. 19-24, 1971, p. 1.

[7]John Hill, "The Burgeoning World Insurance Market," *Insurance* (April 15, 1967), p. 106.

together to provide the corporate client with a consistent worldwide package of covers, which approximate or equal U.S. style programs. Because of the worldwide service, risk managers and insurance brokers are not deterred from attempting to plan international insurance programs. U.S. insurers with cooperative contracts are able to provide risk managers and brokers with all pertinent information on foreign insurance conditions. Furthermore, these arrangements can save the client money. If the U.S. partner is ceded a portion of the covers and combines these with U.S. exposures, the client can be rated with a lower risk factor applicable to a larger number of exposures and participate in any dividends resulting from overall experience.

Second, cooperative agreements usually expand the potential underwriting capacity of the partners by mutual provision of reinsurance facilities. With partners located in many parts of the world, the level of capacity within the joint venture should become more stable.

Third, joint ventures should expand the knowledge and capabilities of the partners via exchanges of information and personnel. A mutual exchange of ideas and experiences could contribute to more effective operations for all partners and to a reduction of unnecessary and inefficient differences in insurance policies and practices between the domicile countries of the partners. Thus, complementing the entry of U.S. insurers into foreign markets has been the exportation of U.S. policies, practices, and technical capabilities. For example, foreign underwriters placed little emphasis on inspection as a potential loss prevention tool but rather used inspection solely as a means of ascertaining the nature of the risk. However, U.S. insurers emphasize loss prevention (particularly with large corporate exposures), and this philosophy is now receiving more attention by foreign underwriters.

In addition to providing foreign partners with technical assistance, U.S. insurers have also entered some international markets not as indemnifiers but as sellers of technical services. The sale of these services is particularly important in countries where entry is severely restricted or where the state maintains an insurance monopoly. The services available for sale include computer software, investment analysis, underwriting procedures, loss control and prevention services, actuarial consultation, and personnel training.

BARRIERS TO ENTRY ABROAD

Problems incurred by U.S. insurers attempting to enter foreign markets include staffing difficulties, an information gap, varying regulatory systems, local economic problems, increased competition from local insurers, and growing use of captive insurers.

Although there is a set of problems that U.S. based international insurers have experienced in varying degrees, there are no problems common to all companies or common to entry into any country. Each company and country presents a different set of relevant problems depending on economic conditions, regulatory philosophy and practices, language, market conditions, and labor conditions. Entry into world markets requires an understanding of a complex of situations, which represent a microcosm of the world's varying cultures. Societies are not static, and insurers are always dealing with different and dynamic environments.

Staffing Problems

Staffing problems include: a shortage of executives trained in a specific insurance organization with experience in a specific overseas market, and the hiring, training, and motivating of foreign employees. To familiarize trained executives with a new market, many companies use a technique common to international insurers: they exchange executives with a European partner in order to provide them with immediate experience in a specific market. Through his temporary assignment to a foreign partner, an executive acquires expertise in a specific market. Another approach is the use of consultants and experienced international brokers. For example, major U.S. insurance brokers have established consulting branches abroad. These pools of talent are used by both insurance buyers and companies.

Insurers have had difficulty in hiring and motivating local agents. Typically, European agents are "captive" and unable to contract with more than one insurer. Insurers have also had difficulty in getting local agents to adopt U.S. sales techniques. Some insurers have found it difficult to motivate their agents located abroad because these agents were not reared in a sales oriented culture.

Information Gap

The primary informational inputs to a successful foreign insurance operation are the product requirements of local insurance markets and local economic conditions. Obtaining this information has been a difficult and slow task, and the problem is compounded by the diversity of foreign markets. Few countries offer identical conditions. Even the highly developed and geographically linked countries of Western Europe are dissimilar in terms of insurance; as a group they differ enormously in benefit practices from countries elsewhere in the world, especially from the developing countries of Latin America and Asia. Insurers must be able to separate long accepted myths from market realities. For example, it has been suggested that employee benefits are more frequently used abroad than in the U.S. and that foreign style benefits are more extensive.[8] However, this contention is difficult to prove.

---

[8] Mark R. Greene, "International Levels of Employee Benefits–An Exploratory Study," *The Journal of Risk and Insurance,* XXV (March, 1968), pp. 1-15.

Regulatory Variations

While the type and extent of regulation vary from country to country, most U.S. insurers have demonstrated an ability to adapt to the appropriate rules of participation. Given the U.S. system of state regulation of insurance, U.S. insurers have learned to operate under a regulatory environment that lacks uniformity. However, regulation does create a problem if it is a significant barrier to entry or successful participation in a foreign market. Such restrictive regulation can originate in either the country of entry or in the United States.

Restricted entry may result from the application of (1) nationalistic measures designed to reduce or eliminate foreign competition, or (2) the Swedish type of "needs" test that attempts to keep the number of market participants within the requirements of the specific market and within the effective control of the regulator. Nationalistic policies are frequently found in Latin America (e.g., Argentina, Chile, Mexico, and Brazil), the Arab Middle East (e.g., Iraq, the U.A.R., and Algeria), and the Orient (e.g., Burma, Sri Lanka, and Japan). While most of these countries have not totally barred foreign penetration, they have taken action to limit direct foreign insurance participation. For example, in Brazil all property and liability insurance must be reinsured with the government, and in Mexico and Peru only those companies controlled (50 percent or more ownership) by nationals are permitted to do business.

The needs test is primarily applied in European countries and allows entry only to unsaturated markets or to those companies believed to have genuine and valuable product innovations.

Entry restrictions have influenced the decision of U.S. insurers as to the most appropriate method of participation in foreign markets. First, insurers have recognized that partnership and cooperation are more viable than conquest. Second, in some markets insurers have conceded the indemnification process to national companies and have been content to profit from the provision of technical services.

In addition to regulations restricting entry, there is a concern for potential regulation restricting exit from the United States. There is pressure on Congress to restrict the export of capital. Labor groups are concerned about the exportation of jobs. International firms are aware that their activities are not without opposition.

Unstable Economies

Unstable social and economic conditions can create an atmosphere detrimental to an international insurer. Varying rates of inflation and currency valuation can easily reduce or eliminate underwriting gains. Basic changes in the economic goals of a foreign government can affect the ability of an international insurer to prosper within that country. For example, countries within the European Economic Community may adjust their social and economic goals and policies to be compatible with any agreed upon Community goals. The international insurer must be able to discern such changes and respond to the new environment.

Local Competition

United States based international insurers face the problem of more vigorous competition from both local insurers and captive insurers. Foreign insurers are adopting American selling methods and products and are demonstrating an ability to implement technical processes previously used primarily by U.S. insurers (e.g., loss prevention and control techniques). In many foreign markets the services and products offered by U.S. insurers may no longer be unique. While this does not remove competitive advantages (e.g., proximity) enjoyed with U.S. industrial firms, it does increase the problems associated with attracting and holding local clientele.

Captive Insurers

In response to increasing cost and decreasing availability of some commercial insurance covers, many international industrial firms have established or acquired captive insurance companies—a financial tool used by large firms. The expansion of captives into international markets is a recent trend. These small insurance companies do not restrict their writing to the exposures of the parent company but seek clients throughout the world.

AREAS OF ENTRY

The *International Insurance Monitor* reported that,[9]

> . . . the premium volume of all private insurance companies operating in the free world, reached in 1969 an amount estimated at $100 billion, as against $44 billion in 1959. This corresponds to an average annual growth of 8.5 percent, which is considerably above the average increase . . . in national income. North America's share in the 1969 total world premium volume was 62 percent, followed by Western Europe with about 26 percent. The business share of the E.E.C. nations was 14 percent, and this relatively high portion has shown a growing trend during the last years as the relative share of North America has been diminishing at the same time.

[9]Charles Zwonicek, "Insurance Development in the E.E.C. Countries," *International Insurance Monitor*, XXXV (January, 1971), p. 12.

Thus it is not surprising that the developed countries of western Europe have offered the most attractive foreign market to U.S. based insurers. The ratio of insurance-in-force to national income is a key indicator of insurance development. A little more than 4 percent of national income is spent for insurance in the Common Market, while in the United States 8 percent of national income is spent for insurance protection. Europe still offers a large market for U.S. insurance products.

While the majority of U.S. based international insurers have concentrated their efforts on European markets, U.S. insurers have also explored and entered markets in the Far East, South America, and Africa. Because of their potential for industrial growth and increasing personal income (with resultant growth in insurance needs), the developing countries have been of exploratory interest to U.S. insurers. Other potential markets include the Communist countries of Eastern Europe. The United States and the Soviet Union shared exposures in the London reinsurance market throughout the Cold War Era.[10]

Europe

Two factors make Europe the most attractive foreign market to U.S. insurers: (1) the European Economic Community (E.E.C.) has been a large and growing market, and (2) American insurers could enter this market with little or no restriction. The population of the E.E.C. by the early 1970s was more than 185 million; with the entry of Great Britain this number exceeded the population of the United States.

The per capita income of the E.E.C. nations is approximately one-half that in the United States, but the economic gap between the two areas is gradually becoming smaller. However, the difference between the United States and E.E.C. nations is greater for private insurance spending than for income. In the United States during 1969 per capita spending on private insurance contracts was approximately $304, as compared to only $77 in E.E.C. countries.[11] This difference results from greater use of government insurance and more untapped insurance markets in E.E.C. nations. Many U.S. insurers believe that the second factor is a more appropriate explanation, and they are therefore interested in penetrating the untapped and potentially profitable markets of Europe. Also, U.S. insurers are anxious to enter European markets before they are closed to non-E.E.C. nations. Officials of the E.E.C. have frequently warned of future restrictions on entry. Of all the European nations, Great Britain has been the

[10]The Black Sea and Baltic Insurance Company is a U.S.S.R. owned multiple lines insurer and reinsurer based in London and doing a world-wide business. Insurers from many Iron Curtain countries reinsure portions of U.S. risks and *vice versa*.

[11]Charles Zwonicek, *op. cit.,* p. 15.

most popular with U.S. insurers. This is partly the result of historic ties between American and English insurers. Also responsible is the relative ease of entering the English insurance market.

The Orient

The Orient offers markets equal in size to Europe. However, two factors have diminished the desire or ability of U.S. insurers to enter these markets. First, economic expansion in these nations (excluding Japan) has been retarded compared to Europe, and second, the Japanese market has been severely restricted by government policy.

Japan is recognized as one of the largest insurance markets in the world it ranks second only to the United States in terms of life insurance-in-force. The majority of life policies sold in Japan have a high savings element (e.g., endowments). Given the U.S. trend away from life insurance as a savings device, this trait of the Japanese life insurance market makes Japan even more attractive to U.S. insurers. Until recently the Japanese government had not permitted foreign companies to participate directly in their insurance markets. In fact, even the number of Japanese participants declined. In 1920 there were forty-two Japanese life insurance companies, but by 1971 this had declined to sixteen mutual and four stock life insurers.

There has been some relaxation of the rigid restraints on foreign investment in Japan. The government recognized the necessity of international-ization and liberalization of systems and customs, but the process has been slow. Two factors may hasten liberalization: the pressure placed on Japan by U.S. economic policy and the potential inability of the Japanese insurance industry to meet increasing demands for insurance. In several lines of insurance Japanese industrial firms require more than the entire capacity of their insurance industry. The Japanese need for increased capacity is opening the door to U.S. insurers.

SUMMARY

Insurance is playing an increasingly important role in the world economy. A natural complement of world trade expansion, insurance is subject to intense international competition. The existence of a capacity problem compels most countries, even the most nationalistic, to consider permitting foreign companies to do business relatively freely. The major insurance countries have expanded materially since 1960, and the United States continues to play a major role, although a declining one in relative terms. American firms must do business abroad to meet the needs of their multinational clients. Entry into foreign markets is complex, requiring considerable ingenuity. Barriers to entry abroad are substantial, but American and other insurers have found ways of penetrating the important economic blocs in efforts to obtain suitable market shares.

REVIEW QUESTIONS

1. Discuss the manner in which international reinsurance serves to increase capacity for large risks.

2. What are the principal approaches used by U.S. insurers in entering foreign markets?

3. To what extent is insurance a prerequisite to international trade?

4. What are the principal barriers to a major foreign expansion of the American insurance industry? Discuss.

5. What criteria or yardsticks are most appropriate for a comparative study of insurance development in different countries?

STUDY QUESTIONS

6. Why is self-insurance not more widely used for transactions in international trade? Explain.

7. How do you account for the dramatic growth of the Japanese insurance industry in the international market? Discuss.

8. Underdeveloped countries are concerned about the balance of payments aspects of their insurance markets. Their reaction has been discrimination against foreign companies, or outright nationalization. What are the advantages and disadvantages of such protectionism for an underdeveloped country? Discuss.

9. As contrasted with fire or casualty insurance, relatively little life insurance is sold across international borders. Why? Discuss.

10. The main goals of the European Common Market with regard to insurance are freedom of establishment and freedom of services. How will these goals affect the operation of European insurers? How will they affect the existing and potential European operations of U.S. insurers?

V

ACTUARIAL
PERSPECTIVES

The actuary is the principal technician in the insurance field. As analyst, mathematician, statistician, data processor, economist, businessman, he establishes prices, reserves, retentions, and underwriting guidelines. Part V explains the development of actuarial science: how life and nonlife insurance premiums are determined, how insurance reserves are set, and the practical and theoretical problems confronting the actuary today.

19

The Rise

of

Actuarial Science

INTRODUCTION

Actuarial science deals with monetary questions involving the mathematical doctrine of probabilities and the principles of compound interest. For more than two hundred years, the actuary has served as the engineer of insurance companies and as the technician responsible for performing a wide range of mathematical and clerical functions.

THE ELEMENTS OF ACTUARIAL SCIENCE

In the twentieth century the actuary is more concerned with the business and regulatory aspects of insurance than he is with the theoretical portion of his discipline. The elements of his science are tables of contingencies, annuity, and compound tables and a great variety of ratios relating to risks. Probabilistic mathematics, other than for relatively fundamental theorems, is not extensively employed. The pure mathematics adopted by the actuary is concerned with the smoothing of mortality and annuity curves, interpolation and summation formulae, and specific parts of the theory of probability and statistics.[1]

[1] Manuel Gelles, "Developments in Actuarial Work," *The Journal of the American Society of Chartered Life Underwriters* (December, 1951), p. 15.

Clearly defined contingencies, such as mortality, accident and sickness, and tables of relative frequency of occurrence of different kinds of loss are tools that are central to the science. Sampling theory, applied statistics, and interest tables are also important for purposes of discount and capitalization on various bases.

The life actuary uses a priori probability in calculating life contingencies and relative frequency probability in group insurance rate making. Subjective probability enters in judgment or schedule rating in marine and property insurance. Commutation columns, mathematical expansions, and summations are basic. The property and liability actuary is concerned more with relative frequency concepts, such as pure premiums and loss ratios, than with a priori concepts.

Basically, there are just a few significant actuarial ideas that form the foundation for all of modern scientific insurance work. These ideas can be identified with specific individuals of the seventeenth and eighteenth centuries. The tools are limited in number, the mathematical statistics are highly specialized, and the element of business discretion and judgment is greater than the layman may imagine.

A SHORT HISTORY
OF ACTUARIAL SCIENCE

The history of modern actuarial science can be traced back to the seventeenth century. Some types of life insurance were known before this time, but the basis of these contracts seems to have been rather arbitrary. In the seventeenth century life insurance tended to be regarded as a wager or a game of chance. Initial life insurance contracts were short term in nature, rarely for more than a year. The problem of long term liabilities and the establishment of appropriate reserves required more than the intuitive judgment of skillful underwriters. There was a need for a theory of probability, mortality statistics, and mathematical tools to fashion a new science.

Theory of Probability:
Pascal and Fermat

One of the most important ideas in modern actuarial science is the theory of probabilities.[2] The basis for statistical analysis of insurance agreements was provided by Blaise Pascal in 1654. In that year, the Duke of Burgundy decided to mathematically determine what the chances were of a number occurring in a

---

[2] Irving Pfeffer, *Insurance and Economic Theory* (Homewood, Ill.: Richard D. Irwin, Inc., 1956), pp. 57-60 discusses the evolving role of the actuary.

game of chance. The Duke's concern in presenting this problem to Pascal was simply to obtain a gamester's advantage. His desire to win gave impetus to the discovery of the theory of probabilities, which was destined to make modern life insurance possible. Pascal was aided in finding a solution to the Duke's problem by Pierre de Fermat. Their approach was simply to count all possibilities that existed with respect to dice and to develop tables showing what the probabilities were for the different combinations of dice. While there was no attempt on their part to create a mathematical theory of probability, they did develop a simple table from which to read the relevant probabilities.

Pascal presented the theory of probability in outline form, and it was left to other mathematicians to continue where he left off. In this manner the doctrine of chances was advanced during the following years.

Huygens' Treatise on Probability

In 1657, Christian Huygens, a noted French scholar, found that the chances of an event occurring could be indicated by a fraction. Huygens wrote the first treatise on probability. For more than fifty years this treatise, printed as a collection of mathematical exercises, provided the best account of the subject of probability. It was during this period that the foundation of actuarial science was established.

Invention of Statistics

Statistics was probably invented by John Graunt in a book called *Natural and Political Observations Made Upon the Bills of Mortality,* which was printed in 1662.[3] It was the first attempt to interpret mass biological phenomena and social behavior from numerical data—in this case, fairly crude figures of births and deaths in London from 1604 to 1661. Graunt obtained the information for his study from the Bills of Mortality, which were weekly and yearly returns of the numbers of burials and christenings in the several London .parishes. The practice of recording such figures seems to have arisen in times of plague—when the causes of death were followed with special interest—and probably dated back to the beginning of the sixteenth century.

At the time Graunt was gathering information for his studies, about 130 parishes were included in the scope of the Bills. The cause of death was established by the "two honest and discreet matrons" appointed in every parish, whose sworn duty it was, upon being informed of a death by the sexton, to "search the body," and to report to the parish clerk the cause of the death.

---

[3] John Graunt, *Natural and Political Observations Mentioned in a Following Index, and Made Upon the Bills of Mortality* (1662). Reprinted in James R. Newman, *The World of Mathematics,* Vol. III (New York: Simon and Schuster, 1956), pp. 1421-33.

Graunt believed that this information would be valuable for military purposes and as general information about the population. He did not use frequency distributions as such. He tabulated his observations and published them. For example, one of the pages of his report is headed "The diseases and casualties this year being 1632". He then catalogued the number by cause of death:

Abortive and Still-Born	445
Affrighted	1
Bit with a Mad Dog	1
Bleeding	3
Bloody Flux	348
Burnt and Scalded	5
Colds and Coughs	55
Dead in the Street and Starved	6
Consumption	1797
Executed and Pressed to Death	18
Gangrene	5
Grief	11
Killed by Several Accidents	46
Lethargy	2
Made Away Themselves	15
Murdered	7
Over Laid	7
Piles	1
Rising of the Lights	98
Suddenly	62
Teeth	470
Vomiting	1

From this data he was able to develop mortality estimates. This statistical work was followed by the work of Sir William Petty and others, which provided the early basis of modern statistics.

Graunt expressed doubts as to the accuracy of the reports given by the "perhaps ignorant and careless Searchers," especially in cases of death from obscure or disreputable diseases. He began his book with an account of the Bills of Mortality, their history and their gradual increase in scope as more parishes were included and more information became available. The book concludes with a number of analytical tables that summarize all the Bills analyzed by Graunt. Graunt's study of the Bills of Mortality marked a period of special interest in mortality tables, the basis of all scientific life insurance.

The value of Graunt's *Observations* was immediately recognized and encouraged others on all parts of the continent, particularly in France and England.

Development of Mortality Tables

A mortality table is a statement of the numbers of persons living and dying in each year of age from birth until death (see Appendix A). The radix, or beginning age, is usually zero, and the terminal age represents that at which the last person in the sampled population is presumed to die. Such tables may be developed for any kind of population, and in fact they have been created for telephone poles, railroad ties, automobiles, animals, and so forth. Depreciation tables are forms of mortality tables.

In 1662, Graunt's table, being based on London experience, was given wide currency.

In 1693, Edmund Halley published his *Estimate of the Degrees of the Mortality of Mankind,* establishing a set of rates to be used in the computation of annuity values.[4]

From these beginnings the mortality table took form and, modified by experience, it has come to its current development.

Morbidity Tables

The Bills of Mortality were the source of early morbidity data, although such tables have limited value because of the rapid change in the nature and costs of the sickness contingency. Accident and sickness tables have been developed, but their credibility is limited.

Probability and Annuities

Mortality tables did not come into use in the modern era until the seventeenth century when they were used as a basis for calculating annuities. At that time, it was the practice of some states to raise money for waging war by soliciting funds from individuals with the promise to pay them certain amounts for the remainder of their lives. In 1671, John de Witt, Grand Pensionary of Holland, wrote a paper for the States General showing how to apply the theory of probability to the value of a life annuity. It was the practice of the Dutch government at the time to issue annuities requiring fourteen years' purchase. De Witt's report attempted to show that a life annuity at fourteen years' purchase yielded a better return to the purchaser than a redeemable annuity at twenty-five years' purchase. Only a few copies of this report were printed and,

[4]Edmund Halley, *An Estimate of the Degrees of the Mortality of Mankind, Drawn from Curious Tables of the Births and Funerals at the City of Breslau: With an Attempt to Ascertain the Price of Annuities Upon Lives* (1693). Reprinted in James R. Newman, *op. cit.,* pp. 1437-51.

because De Witt was forceably driven from power in 1672 (a year after the report was written), all traces of the report were lost, although the fact that it had been written was known. A copy of the report was finally recovered in the Netherlands archives about the middle of the nineteenth century.

Edmund Halley
and the Breslau Data

Thirty years after Graunt's *Observations* appeared, a valuable mortality table (Table 19.1) was published by Edmund Halley in the *Philosophical Transactions* with applications to the calculation of life annuities. This work was entitled *Estimate of the Degrees of Mortality of Mankind Drawn from Curious Tables of the Births and Funerals at the City of Breslau: With an Attempt to Ascertain the Price of Annuities Upon Lives.* Printed in 1693, it is notable as containing the first known example of a complete mortality table. This table was constructed from the deaths in Breslau during the five years from 1687 to 1691. The table was based on the assumption that the population was stationary and that the deaths above a certain age would equal the number living at that age. It was the first table that considered from actual experience a large number of persons and showed how many would be alive at each age until all had died.

Referring to the work of Graunt and Petty on the Bills of Mortality, Halley remarked that these Bills failed to specify the total number of the population and the ages of the people who died. Halley's table seems to have been the first to show both causes of and ages at death—facts essential to the development of true mortality tables. Halley's table, along with the development of the laws of probability by Pascal, de Fermat, Huygens, and others, combined with the attempts to record mortality by Graunt, De Witt, and others, provided the basis for insurance on a scientific level.

Halley's *Degrees of Mortality* was accurate enough to survive to comparatively modern times and to give responsible English businessmen the urge to set up permanent life insurance companies. In 1699, there appeared in London an assessment association named the "Mercers Company of London," organized to give insurance protection to widows and orphans. This appears to have been the first life insurance association founded separately from other businesses or financial organizations. The first life insurance companies established in London in the eighteenth century made use of Halley's table.

Two contributions of Halley were major advances in actuarial science. He provided the first complete enumeration of a population, which enabled him to indicate the proportion of the population dying at a given age. He also obtained a complete tabulation of the ages at death of the people in his sample. He was relatively fortunate in his sample because there was relatively little migration to and from the city of Breslau in the period. Citizens were born, raised, and died in the city. The result was a complete enumeration of christenings and deaths with little error.

TABLE 19.1   Table of Mortality Prepared by Edmund Halley in 1693 Drawn from the Bills of Mortality of the City of Breslau During the Period 1687-1691

Age	Number Living	Total Population	Age	Number Living	Total Population	Age	Number Living	Total Population
1	1,000		31	523		61	232	
2	855		32	515		62	222	
3	798		33	507		63	212	1694
4	760		34	499		64	202	
5	732		35	490	3604	65	192	
6	710		36	481		66	182	
7	692	5547	37	472		67	172	
8	680		38	463		68	162	
9	670		39	454		69	152	
10	661		40	445		70	142	1204
11	653		41	436		71	131	
12	646		42	427	3178	72	120	
13	640		43	417		73	109	
14	634	4585	44	407		74	98	
15	628		45	397		75	88	
16	622		46	387		76	78	
17	616		47	377		77	68	
18	610		48	367		78	58	
19	604		49	357	2709	79	49	
20	598		50	346		80	41	
21	592	4270	51	335		81	34	
22	586		52	324		82	28	
23	579		53	313		83	23	
24	573		54	302		84	20	253
25	567		55	292				
						100		107
26	560		56	282				
27	553		57	272		Sum Total		34,000
28	546	3964	58	262				
29	539		59	252				
30	531		60	242				

Newton and the Binomial Theorem

The role of Sir Isaac Newton in the history of actuarial science has seldom been given proper recognition. In 1665, as a twenty-three year old undergraduate student at Cambridge, he discovered the Binomial Theorem and the Differential Calculus. In 1666, he discovered the Integral Calculus. These contributions provided the major mathematical structure of actuarial calculations.

Bernoulli
and the Law of Large Numbers

In 1713, Jacob Bernoulli published the principle of large numbers which underlies all of sampling theory.[5] Briefly, his principle states that "as the number of trials increases the proportion of favorable results approaches the underlying probability." First used in gambling problems, this theory implies randomness and the stability of mass phenomena.

The law of large numbers states the predictive basis of insurance. It asserts that the observed probability of an event in a random sample will tend to approach the underlying probability as the sample size increases. By approximating the requirements of this law, insurers are able to provide their services at an average cost that is predictable within acceptable limits.

Implicit are the requirements of:

1. Mass,
2. Identifiability of the unit of observation or exposure,
3. Independence,
4. Homogeneity, and
5. Fortuitous or accidental selection.

Operational Implications
of the Law of Large Numbers

The operational significance of the law of large numbers arises from the attempt on the part of insurance companies to duplicate the prerequisites for the law in everyday terms. Hence the principal areas affected are: rate making, underwriting, claims adjustment, and marketing.

Mass, or numbers of observations, is achieved by intensive marketing through a variety of techniques that are oriented toward gaining as large a volume of business as possible. Through differential commission formulae companies stimulate the sale of insurance on a broad scale. Additional mass is achieved by accepting reinsurance cessions from other companies. This serves to increase the number of exposure units or risks in the portfolio of an individual insurer.

Identifiability of the unit of observation is achieved through underwriting of the risks at the time of policy issue, or at the time of presentation of claims. Unless there is a clear definition of the hazard under the terms of the contract, the rate structure will be materially in error.

Independence of exposure is the attempt to gain territorial diversification

[5] Jacob Bernoulli, *The Law of Large Numbers* (1713). Reprinted in part in James R. Newman, *op. cit.*, pp. 1452-55.

of risks. This is done by operating in as many different areas as possible, by underwriting with a view to avoiding disasters, and by reinsurance.[6]

Homogeneity, the equiprobability of loss of the different exposures in a class, is more difficult to achieve. The risk classification systems in use by insurance companies attempt to achieve this.

Fortuitous events are assured in large part through underwriting inspections and careful surveillance of claims. Despite these precautionary measures, however, a certain amount of moral hazard loss occurs as evidenced in suicides and arson. The rational approach to insurance company management strives to maximize predictability of experience on the basis of duplicating the preconditions of the mathematical models of large numbers. Operationally, nothing should be done that will change the deviation of experience from that which is predicted mathematically.

De Moivre and
The Doctrine of Chances

In 1718, *The Doctrine of Chances* was published by Abraham de Moivre. His most important contribution to the field of actuarial science was a formula that enabled a complete table of annuity values to be computed with little more labor than was formerly necessary for the calculation of a single value. He also gave the value of a reversion in terms of the annuity value and the rate of interest, but in a form that seems to have contemplated a complete annuity.

James Dodson
and Permanent Life Insurance

James Dodson is credited by many scholars with founding modern life insurance by virtue of his determination of rates and reserves for the first long term life insurance contracts. He was associated with the old Equitable, the first English life insurance company to be chartered. A well regarded mathematician, his rate schedules and plan of operation were the first to succeed and endure on a modern basis.

His published writings on the subject are contained in volumes two and three of the *Mathematical Repository*, a three-volume work published in 1747, 1753, and 1755. He worked out the progress of an insurance company on various assumptions and by striking a balance at the end of twenty years calculated the reinsurance reserve. His work was of significant importance to the development of scientific life insurance. The concept of a "Model Office," a

---

[6]A. L. McCrindell, "The Insurability of Natural Catastrophes," *Journal of the Chartered Insurance Institute*, Vol. 69 (1972), pp. 87-107 reviews the literature on this subject.

technique for calculating the profitability of a class of life insurance policies is attributed to Dodson.

Richard Price and the
Northampton Table

A *Treatise on Reversionary Payments* was published in 1769 by Dr. Richard Price of Wales. The following year he wrote a paper for the Royal Society "on the proper mode of calculating the values of contingent reversions." In 1783, the fourth edition of his treatise, which contained the famous Northampton Table, was published. This table, which was used extensively for many years, was crudely constructed because Dr. Price ignored several important factors affecting mortality. The statistics on which he based his results consisted of a record of the deaths in two parishes in the town of Northampton. No census of the population was taken, but the tables were formed from ages at death. Dr. Price also had a record of the baptisms that had taken place in the community, and he found that the number of deaths exceeded the births in the period 1735-1780. He therefore assumed that the additional deaths were largely the result of baptisms being less numerous than births. This assumption was inaccurate, and it was later determined that the mortality of the two parishes from which the figures were taken was higher than the average of other towns. The table was extensively used for many years because it showed excessive mortality, and large profits were earned by life insurance companies that adopted its figures. Alternatively, annuity companies suffered severely because their annuitants lived longer than the table indicated.

Between 1773 and 1776, Richard Price, Benjamin Franklin, and Adam Smith lived in London, where Smith was completing his *The Wealth of Nations.* Franklin was a friend of Price's and shared with him some of the ideas that later gave birth to the first American life insurance companies.[7]

Commutation Columns

John Nicholas Tetens, George Barrett, and Francis Baily were associated with the invention of commutation columns and the application of them on a practical, simplified basis.

A commutation column is simply a shortcut in which all the values of a given function are provided in tabular form so that calculations can be made

---

[7]An excellent reference on the early history of actuarial science is Barry Supple, *The Royal Exchange Assurance: A History of British Insurance, 1720-1970* (Cambridge: Cambridge University Press, 1970). See also, Edwin W. Kopf, "The Early History of the Annuity," *Proceedings of the Casualty Actuarial Society,* XIII, Part 11 (May, 1927); Robert Henderson, "Prominent Names in Actuarial History," *Actuarial Society of America, Transactions,* XXXII, Part 1 (1923).

very quickly. One example of a commutation column is a compound interest table. There are commutation columns for almost all of the functions with which the actuary deals. Today, commutation columns are generated by computers, and the number of possibilities is so large that only the more commonly used functions are published with the rest available as programs on call by actuaries. Some actuarial societies publish inventories of programs that are available.

The Carlisle Table

The Carlisle Table, published in 1815 by Joshua Milne, was prepared on scientific principles and from satisfactory statistics. It was constructed from a census of two parishes in Carlisle, England, in 1780 and the deaths in the same parishes from 1779 to 1787. Allowance was made for an increase in population so that the ratio of deaths to the number of living could be satisfactorily obtained. There happened to be a larger number of female than male lives included in the statistics, and the result was to show light mortality at the older ages. The table was used extensively.

ACTUARIAL DEVELOPMENT
IN THE UNITED STATES

In the first half of the nineteenth century no American life insurance company had a special actuarial officer. The American tables and rules were fairly accurately calculated by following the experience and practice of the older English companies. Most American companies based their premiums on the Carlisle Table of Mortality. Around 1850, the growing size and complexity of company operations brought about a need for skilled mathematical help. Where American companies had been carefully following the pattern of the older British companies, it was now felt that mortality and investment opportunities in the United States might be better than in England.

Actuarial science was at an embryonic state in America, and operational errors were not uncommon. For example, when a company insured a number of people for life, charging the same premium for each year of life, the company might not have recognized the need to save part of the first year's premium in order to pay heavier losses that occurred as the group became older. It was generally understood that the risk of death increases somewhat with increased age, but how much it increased and what provisions should be made for the greater hazard was known only by a very few. False assumptions were made in conducting the business, and tragic results often followed. It was during this time that directors of insurance companies began to recognize the importance of the actuary.

Sheppard Homans
and the American Experience Table

In 1868, a new mortality table was introduced in the United States. Developed by Sheppard Homans this table became the standard for American life insurance companies. Interesting comments about the table's development were made by Mr. Homans at the organizational meeting of the Actuarial Society of America:

> When I first entered life insurance, American companies were dependent on foreign tables entirely. We had no statistics on American mortality.

He reported that when he first investigated the experience of American life insurance companies there was a manifest and marked difference in the rates of mortality among the holders of different kinds of policies.

> I reasoned with myself as to the causes, and I came to the conclusion that if men were left to their own judgment and inclinations they would by instinct, not necessarily by any process of reasoning, select that form of policy which was best suited to their own individual interests: that those who had some reason to believe that they would die sooner than the law of nature would indicate would naturally select the short term policy; that those who had no reason to believe they would die sooner or later than nature allowed would naturally select a whole life; while those who had reason to believe they would live to enjoy the benefit, selected the endowment.

> I also found, very much to my gratification, in comparing the rates of mortality in this country with the rates of mortality in Great Britain, as shown by the Actuaries' Table, and still more by the Carlisle Table, that the rates at younger ages and older ages were greater; I accounted for those peculiarities on these grounds: we live faster; we burn the candle at both ends; young people are apt to die more rapidly here than in a more settled and conservative community, and the same would hold good with men in advanced years. Our energetic way of living would carry men in the middle period of life over periods when, in a more staid community, they would succumb to influences prejudicial to health. I believe these peculiarities have been found to exist in all later experiences.

> I also collated the experience with regard to geographical districts. I followed the plan of dividing the United States into six territorial districts. The first was the New England and Middle States; the second, the Western States; the third, the Southern States on the Atlantic seaboard; the fourth, the Southern States on the Gulf; the fifth was California; and the sixth were those which could not properly be included in either one of the other divisions. I found a marked difference in respect to mortality in that those

differences are fading away. In the West, in early days, through the want of proper sewerage, and want of water supply, the rate of mortality was greater. In the South, I think, there is a marked improvement. In California, of course, the differences are very marked.

The result was that after I had collated the experience of the Mutual Life, I drew a curve representing the approximate rates of mortality at different ages; and then found, by a simple method of adjustment, the rates of mortality now called "The American Experience Table"—a name, however, that was not given by me. The table has for its basis the experience of the Mutual Life; but it is not an accurate representation of the experience of that individual company. In other words, it is not intended to be, and never was claimed to be an accurate interpretation of the experience of the Mutual Life. I take it that no mortality table, however correct it may be as an exponent of the mortality of the past, will necessarily be a correct exponent of the mortality in the future, it may be a close approximation, and that is all we want. We want, in the first place, a table which will be safe. The American table is safe because it is based on the mortality of lives where the experience in the first five years is eliminated; and, the effect of recent medical selection is eliminated. It was more of a happy accident, or a happy thought, than anything else, that I made the termination of that table the age of ninety-six. In all the records of experience in different countries—Great Britain, France, Germany, and this country—there is no record of any individual attaining the age of one hundred years being insured.[8]

The Actuarial Societies of America

The Actuarial Society of America was organized in 1889 by a number of actuaries who responded to the invitation of five leaders in the actuarial field to meet in New York for the purpose of forming a professional organization. The meeting combined fellowship, organization, business, and discussion of professional papers. Another group of actuaries, the Casualty Actuarial Society of America, was organized later in 1914.

In 1909, the Actuarial Society of America and the Association of Life Insurance Medical Directors undertook a broad study analyzing the effect of certain conditions, such as occupation, and certain impairments, such as overweight, on the length of life. The first report of this study, known as the Medico-Actuarial Investigation, was made in 1912, but supplementary research continued for many years. The conclusions of this investigation were of immeasurable value to life underwriting and also useful for life conservation efforts of various kinds.

[8] Cited in J. B. Maclean, *Life Insurance* (New York: McGraw-Hill Book Company, Inc., 1957).

The American Men Mortality Table

In 1915, the larger life insurance companies of the United States cooperated in gathering experience for the *American Men Mortality Table*. This experience was taken from the records of insured lives from 1900 to 1915 inclusive and shows not only the "ultimate" rate of mortality for the period after the effect of medical selection has disappeared (assumed to be five years) but also shows the adjusted rates of the five-year period during which the medical examination and other selection methods are effective.

The Guertin Committee and the
CSO Table

In 1937, the National Association of Insurance Commissioners appointed a committee to study the need for a new mortality table and related matters. The seven-man committee consisted of five State Department actuaries and one representative of the Actuarial Society of America and the American Institute of Actuaries. (Those professional societies did not combine as the Society of Actuaries until 1949). The committee worked for about two years and submitted detailed recommendations. Continuation of the work was authorized. The committee was informally called the Guertin Committee for its chairman, Mr. Alfred N. Guertin. A second report was made in 1941 and was designated the *Commissioners 1941 Standard Ordinary Mortality Table*. This was abbreviated to the *CSO Table*.

It was recognized that if all companies in the country constructed their own tables of monetary values on the new mortality standard the duplication in work would be enormous. World War II was in progress, and the shortage in manpower was acute. Accordingly, the Actuarial Society of America and the American Institute of Actuaries arranged to collaborate through a joint committee of five actuaries to produce the vast number of monetary value calculations required by the entire insurance business. To meet the broad and varied requirements of the business seven rates of interest were used, and the results were published in twenty-four volumes, giving 1,850,000 values. A survey made not long after the last volumes were distributed indicated that nineteen of the twenty-four volumes appeared to be entirely free of mathematical error. Mr. Guertin commented that it was the first time in actuarial history that monetary tables were constructed on such a broad base.

The table in most widespread use is the *CSO 1958 Table*, which replaced the *CSO 1941 Table*. The 1958 table is based on death rates recorded by insurance companies during the years 1950 to 1954.

Prior to the time of the Guertin Committee, it was common practice for a company to measure the reserves for life insurance purposes, add a surrender charge, and the difference became the cash value under an insurance policy. After the committee did its work, cash surrender values were calculated independently of the reserves. The simple surrender charge disappeared. There were two completely separate techniques for calculating cash values and reserves. The impact of the Guertin Committee's work was not so much on the price of life insurance as it was on the public image of life insurance. The public realized that the companies were using modern up-to-date tables. The rates themselves did not change in any significant way.

The Variety of Mortality Tables

Different mortality tables are used for various purposes. Some of the more important ones used by American insurance companies during the twentieth century include: the *American Experience Table,* which was replaced by the *CSO 1941 Table;* the *National Fraternal Congress Table,* based upon the lives of persons insured in fraternal organizations; the *Standard Industrial Mortality Table,* based on the experience of companies writing industrial policies; the *1937 Standard Annuitants Mortality Tables,* for the valuation of annuities; and the *Commissioner's Standard Ordinary Table, 1941 and 1958.* The *United States Life Table* reflects the mortality experience of the general population, as distinguished from insured lives. The mortality assumption is crucial in rate making and in setting reserves for life insurance. Most insurers follow a conservative practice in selecting such tables for their calculations.

PROBABILITY CONCEPTS IN INSURANCE

The Concept of Probability

The concept of probability lends itself to a wide variety of possible interpretations. There are many schools of thought with distinctive approaches to the nature and meaning of probability.[9] The a priori mathematical, the empirical relative frequency, and the Bayesian approaches are of greatest interest for the field of insurance for practical applications.

A Priori Mathematical Probability

The mathematical theory of probability is founded upon a set of definitions and theorems that is essentially definitional.

Definition 1. The minimum probability value is zero.

Definition 2. The maximum value is one.

Definition 3. If an event can occur in W ways and fail to occur in L

[9] Irving Pfeffer, *op. cit.,* pp. 153-85, discusses the foundations of probability.

ways, all of which are equally likely and mutually exclusive, the probability P of the occurrence of the event is

$$P = \frac{W}{W + L}$$

and the probability of the nonoccurrence of the event is

$$Q = \frac{L}{W + L}$$

Theorem 1.   If

$$P = \frac{W}{W + L} \quad \text{and} \quad Q = \frac{L}{W + L} ,$$

then

$$P + Q = \frac{W}{W + L} + \frac{L}{W + L} = \frac{W + L}{W + L} = 1$$

and therefore, $P = 1 - Q$ and $Q = 1 - P$. Also, $P + Q = 1$ and $1 - (P + Q) = 0$. It follows that $P = (1 - Q)$ and $Q = (1 - P)$. This is usually referred to as the Negation Theorem.

The Negation Theorem and its definitions are used most commonly in the field of life contingencies. For example, the probability of survival beyond the terminal age on a mortality table is assumed to be zero. The probability of death during the year prior to the terminal age on a mortality table is assumed to be one. The probability that a man will die within a given year is equal to one minus the probability that he will survive, and, conversely, the survival probability is one minus the mortality probability.

Theorem 2.   If two or more events are mutually exclusive, the probability that at least one of the events will occur is the sum of the respective probabilities of the individual events. This is called the Addition Theorem.

An endowment policy promises to pay the proceeds in the event of death during the term (Q) or in the event of survival (P). The Addition Theorem is applicable for this pair of contingent events.

Theorem 3.   If two events are not mutually exclusive, the probability that at least one of the events will occur is the sum of the respective probabilities of the individual events less the product of their separate probabilities. Conceptually, we may think of an overlapping sample space for the possible events, and it is the overlap area that must be excluded to distinguish this Disjunction Theorem from the Addition Theorem.

Theorem 4.   The Multiplication Theorem states that the probability of the occurrence of all of a set of mutually exclusive independent events is the product of the respective probabilities of the individual events. Another statement of this joint probability is the following: the probability of a first event is P_1, and the probability of a second event is

P_2. The probability that both events will happen in the specified order is $P_1 P_2$. This is sometimes referred to as the Conjunction Theorem. The probability that both A and B will die within one year is the product of the separate probabilities of these two events.

From this limited set of theorems the mathematician may generate a formidable variety of models to meet theoretical contingencies.

Empirical Relative Frequencies

The statistician recognizes that there are few situations that meet the assumptions of a priori probability theorems. Sample populations do not typically consist of mutually exclusive events; it is impossible to enumerate all of the ways in which an event may occur; and the size of the universe is usually not precisely known.

If we assume that there is an underlying probability of an event, that the future will be identical with the past, that we can approximate the underlying probability by increasing the sample size, and that we can identify or define our sampled events, then we may assert that the probability of an event is the limit of the ratio m/n where m is the observed event and n is the total number of possible occurrences: $P = \lim_{n \to \infty} m/n$.

In effect, we assert that the "best" theory of the probability of occurrences of an event in the real world is the best approximation to the underlying probability, and this is achieved by increasing the sample size.

Another view of this relationship would be $P = m/n + e$, where e is the variance about the mean values of m/n and e decreases as n increases. The size of e measures the credibility of the ratio m/n.

Even where the conditions of the model cannot be fully met, the actuary finds it instructive in providing criteria or norms for his statistical work. Empirical relative frequencies have countless applications in insurance. In practice they are the basis of the laws of large numbers and form the actuarial or scientific foundation of insurance.

Mortality rates are the relative frequency of deaths to the total population of given characteristics and constitute an essential tool of modern life insurance. Morbidity rates are used in health insurance. Property insurance companies are concerned with loss ratios, and liability insurance companies with average losses per unit of exposure. The actuary could make little contribution to the business of insurance without empirically derived ratios.

Bayesian Approaches

The marriage of the a priori and empirical approaches is not a very satisfactory one because the problem of application is difficult to resolve.

Observed events are not mutually exclusive. Catastrophe, war, epidemic, environment, and other phenomena create interdependence of events. Traffic volume affects accident frequency; sanitation affects health; hurricanes affect multiple properties; and the judicial process affects liability awards. Events or exposures are not identical. People, homes, and lawsuits can only be grouped into broad classifications. The future does not duplicate the past. Trends of all kinds alter the underlying probabilities of events in the real world, and individual judgments must be used at all stages in the analysis of empirical data.

The Bayesian Approach suggests a more rational estimation of the probability of a future event by combining the a priori and empirical approaches and adding as an additional factor the best estimates we have of the impact of unobserved data of all kinds on the probability of the event under consideration. It is an eclectic approach that couples judgment with observations. Used intuitively for more than two hundred years, it is being given more formal application at present.[10]

SUMMARY

Originally, the actuary was a clerk. Then he became a mathematician, and then a statistician. Today, he has also become a businessman. Where the actuary in the eighteenth century was proficient in mortality and simple probabilities, by the turn of the twentieth century he was conversant with most phases of the insurance business as we know it today.

Graduation of irregular data, commutation of expansions, development of various contingencies, and compliance with the regulatory requirements of reserves and nonforfeiture values became the heart of the work of the actuary.[11]

The life actuary passes on all unusual cases in the capacity of an underwriter, prepares rates and proposals, and participates in the decisions relating to most phases of the insurance business. He is concerned with investment policy nearly as much as he is with rate making.

The actuarial societies have served to enlarge the field through examination programs of different kinds, most of which include a blend of mathematical work with the practice of insurance company operation.

The casualty actuary emerged in the twentieth century to meet the needs of the workmen's compensation statutes. The fire actuary remains relatively scarce.

[10] Jack Hirschleifer, "The Bayesian Approach to Statistical Decision: An Exposition," *The Journal of Business,* XXXIV (1961), pp. 471-89 offers an excellent introduction to Bayesian methods.

[11] Charles A. Spoerl, "Actuarial Science–A Survey of Theoretical Developments," *Journal of the American Statistical Association* (1951).

The ideas of actuarial science are straightforward. One idea is the theory of probability; another, the theory of statistics. A third idea is the law of large numbers. A fourth is the commutation column. And, finally, the use of modern data based on insurance experience is a basic idea for actuarial science. The whole development of actuarial theory consists of the elaboration and refinement of these basic ideas. There is a need for refinement in terms of the law of large numbers, using different distributions. Not only do actuaries use the normal distribution, or the Bernoulli distribution, but also the Poisson, which is applicable where two probabilities have very significant differences in their size. The Poisson distribution is used for accident tables. The notion of probability and the compounding of probabilities is elaborated far beyond the original few theorems into a full-fledged branch of mathematics. The theory of risk is an important branch of mathematics. The actuary today is at work in all these areas with more sophisticated tools such as computers.

REVIEW QUESTIONS

1. The task of the underwriter is to approximate the requirements of the law of large numbers. Discuss this proposition.

2. There are several requirements which must exist before the law of large numbers is operative. Explain how each of the prerequisites is achieved.

3. According to the *Commissioners 1958 Standard Ordinary (CSO) Mortality Table* for male lives, the yearly probability of dying (q_x) at age 21 is .00183. What is the yearly probability of surviving (p_x) at age 21? Explain.

4. Has the computer displaced the actuary in the insurance business? Discuss.

5. "The actuary is the insurance technician. He is the designer and the engineer of insurance coverages. Yet, his role is commonly misunderstood. His colleagues tend to regard him as a mathematical wizard who is a bit peculiar and quite impractical. Nonetheless, his work ranks among the most important in any insurance company organization." Explain why the actuary is misunderstood.

STUDY QUESTIONS

6. Five 21 year olds enter into a pact. If one of them should die during the year, the four survivors will each contribute an equal amount to provide a memorial scholarship of $1,000 to be awarded to a needy student. Assuming the mortality rate at .00183, how much should each survivor expect to pay? Explain.

7. Some authors distinguish dynamic risks from static risks. Dynamic risks arise out of political, economic, or catastrophic events such as wars, depressions, price level changes, or floods, and are uninsurable. Static risks are free of the catastrophic hazard and therefore are insurable. Why can't the law of large numbers be used to make predictions concerning dynamic risks?

8. Prepare a job description for a life insurance actuary. In what respects does your description differ from that which you might prepare for a statistician? Discuss.

9. Why does a commutation column simplify the work of an actuary? What contemporary discovery has led to the less extensive use of commutation columns?

10. What were the functions of the Guertin Committee? To what extent did the work of this committee affect the operations of life insurers?

20

Life Insurance
Premiums

INTRODUCTION

The actuary, as the expert who calculates degrees of risk and premiums, is concerned with the technical aspects of his discipline and the practical business of operating a profitable insurance company. Actuarial science provides the mathematical and statistical tools for the measurement of probable benefit costs. Business judgment determines the extent to which modifications of the data are desirable for reasons of safety, profitability, or competitive pressure.

Insurance statutes are concerned with the safety of the funds accumulated for the benefit of policyholders. These statutes usually provide limitations on the assumptions that may be employed in calculating life insurance premiums and policy reserves. Insurance companies are expected to grow and operate on a profitable basis, so that margins for contingencies and profits are important considerations. There is more price competition in life insurance than is commonly believed. The pricing problem is not only one of determining the lowest reasonable price, but also what price will be most compatible with a particular company's marketing strategy in the long run.

The actuary views the life insurance policy as a contractual obligation for future performance of a set of promises, each of which has a fixed monetary value. The set of promises may cover: varying time periods, ranging from one day to more than a century; varying contingencies, ranging from early death of one insured to retirement benefits for a beneficiary as yet unborn; varying settlement patterns, ranging from lump sums to combinations of annuities; varying premium payment modes, ranging from single premiums to installments of all kinds.

The actuary's first task is to specify each of the benefits provided in the life insurance policy in order that its cost may be estimated. Ultimately, the premium that the policyholder must pay will be calculated as the sum of the costs associated with each promise contained in the contract. Ordinarily, one might expect that the fewer or less valuable the benefits of the policy the lower the cost.

RATE MAKING FACTORS

There are six basic factors that are considered in pricing life insurance.[1] For purposes of gross premium calculation, these may be identified as:

1. a mortality rate,
2. a rate of interest,
3. a rate of withdrawal or persistency,
4. unit expense factors,
5. a factor for contingencies and fluctuations in experience, and
6. a profit factor.

Each of these elements is subject to considerable discretion on the part of the actuary, but he must strive for a formula that provides an adequate, equitable, and competitive premium level. Statutory constraints and adverse experience set the lower limits of any premium. Alternatively, competition in the marketplace provides a ceiling on prices.

Mortality

The mortality table used for premium calculation of a given policy should reflect the probable experience of the appropriate population group. This suggests the need to use different tables for policies on the lives of people with different ages, occupations, and so forth.

Mortality tables are based upon the past experience of various populations. They indicate the number of deaths expected during a given year of age related to the number of individuals of a particular age who are exposed to the risk of

---

[1] Alfred N. Guertin, "Life Insurance Premiums," *The Journal of Risk and Insurance,* XXXII (1965), pp. 23-49, offers an excellent non-technical discussion of the subject.

death in that year. The death rate is the ratio of persons dying in a period to survivors of the preceding period. Death rates may be calculated as age specific death rates, death rates by cause, race, nationality, or by any other attribute.

The Development of a Mortality Table. A mortality investigation begins with the measurement of the number of deaths within a predetermined group by age and other characteristics. The population of lives exposed to the risk of death at each age is also determined. From these data the rate of mortality at a given age is calculated (see Table 20.1).

TABLE 20.1 Calculation of Mortality Rates

(1)	*(2)*	*(3)*	*(4)*
		Population Relevant	*Age Specific*
Age	*Number of Deaths*	*to Each Age*	*Death Rate*
			(2) ÷ (3)
20	895	500,000	.00179
21	732	400,000	.00183
22	1302	700,000	.00186
23	1890	1,000,000	.00189
24	668	350,000	.00191
25	1158	600,000	.00193

With age specific death rates derived from empirical investigations, a modified mortality table (see Table 20.2) can be constructed. An initial age is chosen, and a convenient number of lives, called the radix, is assumed to exist at that age. This number is rounded to 100,000 or 1,000,000 or 10,000,000. For example, the *CSO 1958 Table* begins with a radix of 10,000,000 at age 0. The mortality rate of 0.00708 applied to an exposure base of 10,000,000 lives

TABLE 20.2 Portion of 1958 CSO Mortality Table - Males

Age	*Number Living*	*Number Dying*	*Death Rate*
x	l_x	d_x	U_x
0	10,000,000	70,800	.00708
1	9,929,200	17,475	.00176
2	9,911,725	15,066	.00152
3	0.896,659	14,449	.00146
98	19,331	12,916	.66815
99	6,415	6,415	1.00000
100	0	00	0

produces 70,800 expected deaths between the ages of zero and one. At age one there are assumed to be 9,929,200 survivors. A mortality rate of 0.00176 at age one applied to the number presumed to have survived to their first birthday, 9,929,200, implies 17,475 deaths. Subtracting the presumed deaths from the number presumed living leaves 9,911,725 survivors at age two. The process continues up to the table's limiting age, which is defined as the first age at which no survivors exist. In the case of the *CSO 1958 Table* for males, the limiting age is 100; that is, all persons are assumed to have died by age 100.

Adjustment of Mortality Tables.   Given the difference in sample sizes used to calculate each age specific death rate and the potential for random fluctuations, death rates may not proceed smoothly from age to age. A process of graduation is applied to the raw data to obtain a smooth curve that lends itself more readily to mathematical manipulation. Numerous techniques for graduation of data are available to the actuary.

Graduation should be distinguished from modification, which is a change in either the shape or location of the curve, for the purpose of establishing safety margins on a basis of judgment. For example, assume that (1) future mortality rates will be higher than in the period under investigation, and (2) infant mortality rates will drop sharply. Given this assumption the actuary's modification would shift the curve upward within the quadrant and alter its shape in the early years. In Figure 20.1 this modification would be a shift of the curve from aa_1 to bb_1. Graduation might be a curve such as dd_1, instead of the series of irregular points.

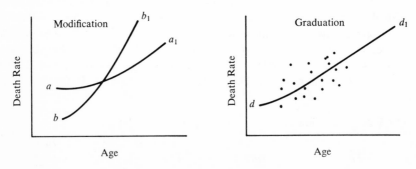

FIGURE 20.1   Modification and Graduation

Other Tables Used by the Life Insurer.   The life insurance contract may contain benefits in addition to those that relate to the peril of premature death. For example, a provision for waiver of premium in the event of disability is quite common. Thus, the life actuary has an interest in other, nonmortality, tables of contingencies or mathematical expectations.

The same techniques used in the construction of mortality tables are applied to the construction of tables that depict the risk of becoming disabled. The morbidity rate is the ratio of persons becoming disabled at a given age to the total number exposed to this contingency. For example, the *1952 Report of the Society of Actuaries* with data for the period 1935-1939 and a benefit based on a ninety-day waiting period, provided the rates shown in Table 20.3.

TABLE 20.3   Illustrative Rates of Disability per 1000

Age	Disability Rate
20	2.44
30	3.26
40	5.43
50	11.69

SOURCE: Charles A. Ormsby, "Life Insurance Riders - Disability and Accidental Death Insurance," in Davis W. Gregg, ed., *Life and Health Insurance Handbook*, 2nd ed. (Homewood, Illinois: Richard D. Irwin, Inc., 1965), p. 264.

Less widely used tables that can be constructed from census or other data include natality tables, tables available for marriage, divorce, and remarriage. Because these latter "risks" may be planned by individuals, the events lack the contingent quality that insurance companies seek, and hence, are not regarded as proper bases for conventional insurance coverages.

Interest

The interest assumption must recognize the long term nature of most life insurance contracts. The insurer is concerned with probable average interest rates for the next twenty to fifty years. Current rates are almost irrelevant as failure to earn these rates in the future is a distinct possibility. If an insurer used an interest assumption of 5 percent (noting that in 1971 the average rate earned on investment portfolios by U.S. insurers was 5.44 percent) and was unable to achieve this investment yield throughout the long term life of the policies, the resulting deficit would lead to losses on the balance sheet. If the drain in surplus was significant or persistent, the company might be forced into insolvency. As Table 20.4 indicates, prudence in the past would have dictated an interest assumption of not more than 3.11 percent. In fact, most companies have used assumptions such as 2.5, 3, and in some special cases, 3.5 percent.

Participating Insurers vs. Nonparticipating Insurers.   Insurers that issue participating policies are more conservative in estimating interest earnings because policyholder dividends can be used as a means of adjusting the cost of

TABLE 20.4   Net Rate of Interest Earned on Investment Funds
U.S. Life Insurance Companies

Year	Rate
1915	4.77%
1920	4.83
1925	5.11
1930	5.05
1935	3.70
1940	3.45
1945	3.11
1950	3.13
1955	3.51
1960	4.11
1965	4.61
1970	5.30

SOURCE: *1971 Life Insurance Fact Book* (New York: Institute of Life Insurance, 1971), p. 63.

the policy to reflect actual investment results. Participating insurers frequently use a low interest assumption such as 2.5 percent.

Nonparticipating insurers cannot avail themselves of the *ex post* adjustment opportunity provided by "dividends" to policyholders. While nonparticipating insurers assume a rate of interest that should be safely earned over the long run, the need to maintain a competitive price generally requires selection of interest rates higher than those assumed by participating insurers. Interest assumptions in the range of 3 to 3.5 percent are typical for nonparticipating life insurers.

Effects of Varying the Interest Assumption.   The force of interest, which is the rate at which a given sum increases at different rates of interest and over different time intervals, is crucial in understanding the rate making process in life insurance. For example, the value of $1 deposited each year and left at compound interest grows exponentially at a surprising rate depending upon the interest and time assumptions. Even without periodic deposits, $1 left at compound interest expands rapidly. At 2 percent, $1 doubles itself in thirty-six years; at 3 percent it requires twenty-four years; and at 4 percent only eighteen years. The long term nature of most life insurance contracts allows the force of interest to reduce premiums by substantial discounts.

Changes in interest assumptions have a significant impact on premiums. This is particularly true for policies issued at lower ages and which might be in force for several decades. For example, a company that assumes a 3 percent interest rate will calculate a net level annual premium, for a twenty-five year old insured, 9 percent less than it would have calculated using a 2.5 percent interest assumption. At higher ages the effect of varying the interest assumption is diminished because the potential interest earning period is reduced.

Persistency Rates

A persistency rate measures the probability that a policyholder will discontinue or lapse his life insurance policy before maturity by failing to maintain his premium payments or by forfeiting the policy in exchange for the cash surrender value. When combined with mortality, lapses provide a termination rate that can be used to indicate the probable volume of premiums that will not be collectable in each period.

While persistency rates vary significantly by company and are more difficult to project than mortality, it has been determined that lapses tend to occur more frequently in the early years of a policy. Termination of a life insurance contract in the first few years usually results in the insurer failing to recover the costs associated with issuing the policy (e.g., sales expenses, underwriting, and administration costs, etc.). In order to recover the insurance company's marketing and underwriting outlays, the costs of early lapses are distributed among all policyholders.

Persistency is a function of the age and type of contract, the way in which the policy was sold, and the experience of the agent. New companies tend to have less favorable persistency than older ones. Persistency also varies with economic conditions.

Expenses

Expense factors are estimated on the basis of cost accounting. They may be related to: (1) size of premium, and include commissions, expense allowances and state premium taxes; (2) amount of insurance, and include medical examinations, inspection reports, underwriting costs, and policyholder service costs; (3) number of policies, and include administrative expenses and general overhead; and (4) investment income, and include costs of buying, selling, and managing the portfolio of securities. The expense factor differs for alternative methods or scales of operation and for individual company experience.

Contingency and Profit Margins

Contingency margins are implicit in the assumptions used for the mortality, lapse, and expense elements, but, as an alternative approach they may be identified and dealt with specifically. In the first instance, specific contingency and profit margins are not established because they have been incorporated in the mortality and other tables. The explicit approach to these margins requires the use of more precise actuarial assumptions.

Profit margins in gross premium calculations are characteristically small and are usually grouped with contingency factors. Profits, or gains, arise when actual experience is better than expected. Various ratios based upon these gains are used as both management tools and as determinants of possible policyholder dividend distributions. Of particular interest to the insurer are (1) the ratio of actual to expected mortality, and (2) the margin of overall net investment income over contractual interest required to maintain policy reserves.

NET SINGLE PREMIUMS VS.
GROSS SINGLE PREMIUMS

The net single premium is the result of combining only the factors of mortality and interest. This is the pure insurance cost of the contract. The gross single premium combines the net single premium and a loading, or markup, that covers such factors as persistency, operating expenses, contingencies, and profit.[2] When the insured pays for a life insurance policy with a single premium, he pays the gross single premium. Most commonly, he will pay a gross annual premium on an installment plan.

ASSUMPTIONS FOR PREMIUM CALCULATIONS

In order to simplify illustrative computations, it is assumed that premiums are paid at the beginning of each year, although they may be payable at any time. Death benefits are assumed to be paid at the end of the year of death. Calendar years and birthdays are presumed to be coincident.

MODES OF PREMIUM PAYMENT

All of the installment methods of paying premiums are referred to as modes. Monthly, quarterly, semiannual, and annual modes are the most common. The monthly mode has been increasing in popularity with the use of automatic bank drafts for periodic payments.

Regardless of the mode of premium payment, most computations of rates in life insurance begin with the net single premium and the net annual level premium.

[2] Richard M. Sellers, "The Calculation of Gross Premium Rates," *The Journal of the American Society of Chartered Life Underwriters*, VII (September, 1953).

NET SINGLE PREMIUMS FOR
ONE-YEAR TERM INSURANCE

A one-year term policy makes a single promise: if death occurs within the policy term, the proceeds of the policy will be paid to the beneficiary. Assuming that premiums are collected at the beginning of the year and claims paid only at the end of the year, premiums will be invested for the entire year and thus earn interest. This procedure reduces the insurance cost.

To calculate the net single premium three factors must be known: the face amount of the policy, a discount rate that reflects the interest assumption, and a mortality rate. Assume that the actuary must calculate the net single premium for a $1,000 one-year term insurance policy for a 35-year-old standard male risk. Using a 2.5 percent interest assumption and the *CSO 1958 Table*, he might proceed as follows. At age 35, according to the *CSO 1958 Table*, there are 9,373,807 persons living, of whom 23,528 are expected to die before reaching age 36. The mortality rate at age 35 is therefore:

$$\frac{\text{Number of Deaths During Period}}{\text{Number Living at Beginning of Period}} = \text{Mortality Rate}$$

$$\frac{23,528}{9,373,807} = 0.00251$$

At 2.5 percent, the present value of $1 payable at the end of one year, the discount factor, is 0.975610. The present value of $1,000 payable a year hence is therefore:

$$.975610 \times \$1,000 = \$975.61$$

The formula for the net single premium is the product of the mortality rate, the discount factor, and the face amount of the policy:

	Face Value of Policy	x	Mortality Rate	x	Discount Factor	=	Net Single Premium
	$1,000	x	$\dfrac{23,528}{9,373,807}$	x	0.975610		
or	$1,000	x	0.00251	x	0.975610		
or	$975.56	x	0.00251			=	$2.45

NET SINGLE PREMIUMS
FOR FIVE-YEAR TERM INSURANCE

A five-year term policy makes five separate promises: to pay the proceeds to the beneficiary if death occurs during any one of five distinct annual periods of time.

The calculations for a 35-year-old male, using the same tables and assumptions as were employed for the one-year term policy, would be as follows:

	Face Value of Policy		Mortality Rate		Discount Factor		Net Single Premium
(1)	$1,000	x	23,258 / 9,373,807	x	0.975610	=	$ 2.449
(2)	$1,000	x	24,685 / 9,373,807	x	0.951814	=	$ 2.507
(3)	$1,000	x	26,112 / 9,373,807	x	0.928599	=	$ 2.587
(4)	$1,000	x	27,991 / 9,373,807	x	0.905951	=	$ 2.705
(5)	$1,000	x	30,132 / 9,373,807	x	0.883854	=	$ 2.841
					Net Single Premium	=	$13.090

The net single premium is less than the sum of five net single premiums for one-year renewable term policies for two reasons. First, interest is being earned for periods from two to five years in the former, while interest would only be earned for one-year periods in the latter. The net single premium for the fifth one-year term policy when purchased four years hence would have a discount factor of 0.975610, as opposed to 0.883854, as in the example above. Second, regardless of when death occurs in the five-year term case, the full five year premium has been collected. However, if a series of five one-year renewable term policies was used, those who died in the early years would not pay premiums during the remainder of the five year period.

WHOLE LIFE INSURANCE

A whole life insurance policy promises to pay the proceeds whenever death occurs up to the last year (limit age) of the mortality table, at which time death is treated as a certainty. The computation is the same as that for the five-year term policy, except that the procedure continues until the end of the mortality table. In brief, the whole life insurance policy is the same as a term to age 100 life insurance policy.[3]

ENDOWMENT POLICIES

An endowment policy makes two sets of promises: (1) to pay the proceeds in the event of death during any year of the endowment period, and (2) to pay the proceeds in the event of survival to the end of the endowment period.

The first set of promises is valued as a set of term insurance promises. The second is a pure endowment—a promise to pay a sum of money only to those members of an original group who survive to the end of the endowment period.

Using the *CSO 1958 Table* and a 2.5 percent interest assumption, a 35-year-old male would pay a net single premium for a five-year pure endowment of $1,000 as follows:

$$
\begin{array}{ccccccc}
\text{Face of} & & \text{Survival} & & \text{Discount} & & \text{Net Single Premium} \\
\text{Policy} & \text{x} & \text{Rate} & \text{x} & \text{Factor} & = & \text{for Pure Endowment} \\
\\
\$1,000 & \text{x} & \dfrac{9,241,359}{9,373,807} & \text{x } 0.883854 & & = & \$871.37
\end{array}
$$

This equation states that of an original group of 9,373,807 males at 35 years of age, 9,241,359 will survive five years to age 40. The survivors will receive $1,000, which will have been prepaid and therefore discounted at 2.5 percent for five years by a factor of 0.883854.

It was determined that the net single premium for a five-year term policy issued at age 35 was $13.09. Thus, by addition, the five-year endowment net single premium will be:

$$
\begin{array}{ccccc}
\text{Net Single Premium} & + & \text{Net Single Premium} & = & \text{Net Single Premium} \\
\text{for Term Policy} & & \text{for Pure Endowment} & & \text{for Endowment} \\
\$13.09 & + & \$871.37 & = & \$884.46
\end{array}
$$

ANNUITIES

An annuity is a series of periodic payments. It is a device that makes possible the systematic liquidation of an estate over the remaining lifetime of an older

---

[3] Assuming that death must inevitably occur by age 100, according to the tabular mortality assumption. A whole life policy is similar to a term to age 100 policy and the endowment at age 100 on this set of assumptions.

person, or for a certain period. Life insurance companies offer a variety of annuity contracts with varying provisions. There are many different ways in which a stream of payments can be made to an annuitant. The premium or cost varies with the promises made in the annuity contract. Some common types of annuity include:

1.   Annuities due, where the first payment occurs at the inception of the contract;

2.   Annuities immediate, where entry into annuitant status occurs at once, but the first periodic payment occurs at the end of the first period;

3.   Deferred annuities, where annuitant status begins at some future time;

4.   Ordinary annuities, where payments stop at the time of death of the annuitant;

5.   Guaranteed annuities, where payments are made for a stipulated period, even if death precedes the end of the period;

6.   Cash refund annuities, where the guaranteed period is as long as necessary to assure recovery of the original premium or principal sum;

7.   Joint annuities, which cover two or more lives, with annuity benefits terminating at the time of the first death;

8.   Joint and last survivor annuities with payments continuing until the last annuitant under the policy dies; and

9.   Variable annuities, where benefit payments fluctuate in amount corresponding with fluctuations in a diversified portfolio of securities, which act as a proxy for price level changes.

Because the concept is also essential to the computation of net annual level life insurance premiums, consider the five-year annual annuity due of $1. Under a five-year annual annuity due, the insurer promises to make a payment at the inception of the contract and four additional payments in the event of the insured's survival to the end of each of the first four years. This is also the premium payment pattern of insureds who pay for a five-year life insurance policy in annual installments, rather than with a gross single premium for the entire contract.

The net single premium for any annuity is calculated as a series of pure endowments, each based upon the probability of survival, the amount of the payment, the discount or present value factor, and the manner in which annuity payments are to be made.

Assuming the *CSO 1958 Table*, 2.5 percent interest and a male age 35, the net single premium for a five-year annuity due of $1 is:

Survival Rate			Discount Factor		
(1) 9,373,807 / 9,373,807	x	$1	x 1.000000	=	$1.0000
(2) 9,350,279 / 9,373,807	x	$1	x 0.975610	=	$0.9732
(3) 9,325,594 / 9,373,807	x	$1	x 0.951814	=	$0.9469
(4) 9,299,482 / 9,373,807	x	$1	x 0.928599	=	$0.9212
(5) 9,271,491 / 9,373,807	x	$1	x 0.905951	=	$0.8961
					$4.7374

NET LEVEL PREMIUMS

Most people are unable or unwilling to pay their life insurance premiums in a single lump sum. They need an installment program whereby premiums may be paid annually or at more frequent intervals.

The temporary life annuity due is the same as the stream of annual premium payments made by an insured—one in advance and one at the beginning of each year thereafter. Premiums are paid during the term of the policy only while the insured survives.

The net level premium is calculated as follows:

$$\frac{\text{Net Single Premium}}{\text{Present Value of a Temporary Life Annuity due of \$1}} = \begin{array}{c}\text{Net Level Annual} \\ \text{Premium}\end{array}$$

For a 35-year-old male, the illustrative net single premium for a five-year $1,000 endowment was $884.46. The present value of a five-year annuity due of $1 was $4.7374. Combining these factors, the net annual level premium for a five-year $1,000 endowment issued at age 35 is:

$$\frac{\$884.46}{\$4.7374} = \$186.70$$

Net level premiums may be computed for any period of years and at any age by the same method.

GROSS PREMIUMS

Loading is the amount added to the net premium to produce the gross premium. The loading covers all operating expenses of the company, except investment expenses. The latter are deducted from investment income to derive net investment income, which is reflected in the interest assumption. The loading also includes margins for contingencies and profits. Under participating policies margins for future dividend payments may also be included in the loading.

The cost analysis of a life insurance company results in a complex loading formula, which is calculated to be an adequate estimate of outlays. It is designed to be equitable for different classes of insureds and to be competitive. The loading factors used by U.S. life insurance companies vary widely as shown in the sampling of Table 20.5.

TABLE 20.5   Five-Year Term Policies, Gross and Net Level Premiums per $1,000

Company[1]	Gross	Hypothetical Net	Estimated Loading	Loading Percent
A	8.77	2.79	5.98	214
B	12.70	2.79	9.61	344
C	12.97	2.79	10.18	365
D	15.15	2.79	12.36	442
E	16.82	2.79	14.03	502

[1] All sample companies are nonparticipating.

Loading factors tend to be largest for small short term individual policies, smaller for larger face amount longer term contracts, and smallest for group insurance contracts, where handling of individual files is minimized.

Loading excesses on participating policies may be refunded to policyholders by means of dividends. On nonparticipating policies the loadings tend to be smaller and more closely related to actual experience because the net cost to the policyholder is permanently fixed.

SUMMARY

The calculation of life insurance premiums is based on assumptions about the mortality rate which the insurance company anticipates, investment earnings on prepaid premiums, persistency of policyholders in maintaining their policies in force, overhead costs, a margin for contingencies, and a profit factor. Each of these variables is subject to business judgment as well as to technical requirements.

The construction of a life insurance or annuity premium begins with a net single premium which is based on mortality and interest assumptions alone. The promises of the contract are individually priced and combined in the net single premium. When the loading factors are added to the net single premium, the gross single premium is determined. The use of the temporary life annuity due makes possible the calculation of premiums payable under any mode of payment from annual to more frequent such as monthly or quarterly.

Participating policies, by virtue of their obligation to refund a portion of the excess premium charged in the form of dividends, generally are based on more conservative assumptions than are nonparticipating policies. This results in par premiums being higher than non-par premiums in a given company, contract for contract.

Competition compels insurance company executives to consider the assumptions underlying their rates very carefully. If they are not sufficiently careful, they may lose money without the possibility of changing prices on existing contracts.

REVIEW QUESTIONS

1. To what extent are life insurance premiums which are charged to the public scientifically determined? What are the unscientific elements? Discuss.

2. Why is the net level premium on a ten year policy greater than the net single premium divided by ten? Explain.

3. Life insurance premiums are based on predictions of probable mortality, probable interest yields, and probable future expenses. The actuary nonetheless employs high-powered mathematical techniques in his premium computations. Is there an inconsistency in building a highly refined premium structure on a crude set of underlying assumptions? Explain.

4. How might a life actuary estimate an appropriate lapse rate? Explain.

5. Distinguish between a net single premium, a gross single premium, and a net level premium.

STUDY QUESTIONS

6. A statistical service recently published the following comparisons:

Company	Ratio of Actural to Expected Morality
A	88.33%
B	64.06%
C	55.95%

Critics argue that this kind of table lends itself to material misrepresentation. Discuss. If you were a policyholder in Company C, would the ratio given above prove that you were being overcharged for your life insurance? Explain.

7. Assume that the net level premium for a five year term policy is

$2.79 per $1,000 at age 35. The company used the *1958 CSO Mortality Table* and a 2.5 percent interest assumption. Obtain the rate of an insurance company for five year term insurance at age 35 and calculate the percentage of loading involved. Does it pay an insurance company to issue such contracts for very small face amounts? Discuss.

8. In order to accurately calculate life insurance premiums, the actuary must obtain cooperation from accountants, underwriters, top management, etc. Describe the information which the actuary must obtain from other areas within the company.

9. "A more modern mortality table for life insurance is the equivalent of a reduction in the interest assumption in life insurance premium calculations." Discuss.

10. The life insurance rate making process is not regulated as extensively as rate making in property and liability insurance. Minimum assumptions are set, but that is the only apparent concern of the statutes. Why? Explain.

21

Rate Making

in Property and

Liability Insurance

INTRODUCTION

The actuary in life insurance has an advantage over his counterpart in the property and liability insurance field because the risks of primary concern to the life actuary are few and relatively homogeneous. While the mathematical aspects of life rate making are perhaps more complex, the assimilation of empirical data and the statistical analysis required by the casualty actuary is more sophisticated. In property and liability insurance, groups of insured units exposed to the same collection of perils may have significantly different characteristics and underlying probabilities of loss. These inherent differences tend to limit the extent to which statistical averaging of all risks can provide prop rty and liability insurance rates that will be regarded as equitable either at law or in the marketplace. The actuarial techniques employed in property and liability insurance are more varied and more empirically based than in life insurance.

The casualty actuary's responsibility[1] is to select the most appropriate techniques from his growing collection and apply them to meet the criteria for

[1] The classic article on this subject is C. A. Kulp, "The Rate-Making Process in Property and Casualty Insurance—Goals, Technics, and Limits," *Law and Contemporary Problems*, XV (Autumn, 1950), pp. 493-533. See also Thomas O. Carlson, "Rate Regulation and the Casualty Actuary," *Proceedings of the Casualty Actuarial Society*, XXXVIII, and Ralph M. Marshall, "Workmen's Compensation Ratemaking," *Proceedings of the Casualty Actuarial Society*, XLI.

rate making set by law and required by sound business practice. The most common techniques include Judgment, Manual, Merit, and Retrospective rating.

JUDGMENT RATING

The earliest method used for rating property and liability risks was called judgment rating and consisted of a subjective appraisal of the chance of loss for a particular risk. The insurer would establish a rate on a case by case basis using intuitive judgment to determine the degree of risk involved. If the rate was set too low, the insurance company would lose money; if the rate was set too high, the prospective insured would buy insurance elsewhere. By basing his judgment on past experience and with a knowledge of current developments and future prospects, a competent insurer will estimate the probabilities well enough to assure a long run profit.

Judgment rating is necessary when a risk cannot reasonably be included in a homogeneous group of risks. While judgment rating is not scientific, it is a pragmatic approach that does not readily yield to statistical methods. The insurer reviews the information that is relevant to the risk and assigns crude but carefully thought out estimates for the maximum loss potential and the probability of partial or total loss. In arriving at these estimates the rate maker compares any relevant data or experience of this specific risk with data on any other risk that appears to have similar characteristics. For example, while the Boeing 747 aircraft was a unique risk with high catastrophe loss potential, loss data on other large jet aircraft played an important role in establishing a rate for the risks associated with the 747.

MANUAL RATING

With the growth in variety of risks and kinds of insurance a systematic approach to rating was required, and this led to the development of manual rating and its modifications. Manual, or class, rating requires the grouping of all homogeneous exposures into predetermined classes, and all members of a class are charged the same premium. Exposures are grouped according to general criteria, which are presumed by the insurer to affect the underlying loss potential of the class of exposure units. For example, automobiles are grouped according to territory, the location where the car is principally garaged (urban vs. rural); type of car (make and model); age and sex of the driver; average mileage per year; and so on.

Class criteria result from (1) an analysis of loss experience data, (2) the need to establish statistically significant class sizes, and (3) the business judgment of actuaries and other insurance company executives. Rate classes are subject to review by the regulatory authorities and must be reasonable and fair in light of available loss statistics. Thus, rate groupings are not static. They undergo periodic change to reflect new experience or changing circumstances. Furthermore, competitive pressures frequently lead to changes in rate classifications.

Construction of Manual Rates

The rate charged each class of exposures is constructed of two parts: (1) a pure premium, which is composed of expected losses and loss adjustment expenses, and (2) a loading to reflect all other expenses and a reasonable underwriting profit.

The pure premium is derived for a specific experience period as follows:

$$\text{Pure Premium Rate} = \frac{\text{Losses and Loss Adjustment Expenses Incurred}}{\text{Number of Exposure Units}}$$

This rate represents the loss cost per unit of exposure. A unit of exposure is a simple homogeneous statistical category, such as a car-year (an automobile exposed to the risk of loss for a full year), a man-year, $100 of payroll, and so forth. The rate times the number of units of exposure yields a net pure premium.

Calculation of manual premiums is a complex procedure varying from one type of insurance to another, but the process generally begins with the development of the indicated net pure premium. To these results there is applied a credibility formula (levels of significance in general statistics) that yields the established pure premium. In addition, various adjustments are made to correct for trends, regional differences or other special factors, and the result is a set of selected net premiums. To these are added expense loadings to produce the gross premiums that are charged to the insurance buyer.

Manual Rating and the Loss Ratio

The loss ratio is the ratio of losses and loss adjustment expenses incurred as related to premiums earned. The loss ratio, or the relationship of losses to premiums, is used without further refinement when exposure unit information is either unavailable or when, because it is heterogeneous, as in the case of industrial or commercial buildings, exposure unit information cannot be assimilated efficiently. The expenses paid, when related to premiums written, result in the expense ratio. As illustrated in the equation below, if the sum of these two ratios is less than 100 percent, the company is presumed to have earned an underwriting profit; if it is more than 100 percent, they have probably sustained an underwriting loss.

$$\text{Loss Ratio} \quad + \quad \text{Expense Ratio} \quad = \quad \begin{array}{c}\text{Underwriting}\\ \text{or Trade Profit}\\ \text{(Loss)}\end{array}$$

$$\frac{\text{Losses \& Loss Adjustment Expense}}{\text{Premiums Earned}} + \frac{\text{Expenses Paid}}{\text{Premiums Written}} = \begin{array}{c}\text{Underwriting}\\ \text{or Trade Profit}\\ \text{(Loss)}\end{array}$$

These ratios are widely used in the United States as a measure of insurer performance.

MERIT RATING

Merit rating provides the actuary with several techniques for assigning different rates to insureds who fall within the same broad class of risk exposures. Merit rating is appropriate for those insureds who have either a sufficient number of exposure units to achieve a measure of statistical credibility or sufficient control over loss frequency and severity to justify a deviation from the class rate. Merit rating may lead to either an increase or a decrease from manual rates. There are three basic types of merit rating: schedule rating, experience rating, and retrospective rating.

Schedule Rating

Any two property insurance surveyors who inspect the same building using judgment methods may frequently evaluate the property with materially different results. They might assign different weights to the positive or negative aspects of the risk based upon different personal judgments. Awareness of this potential inconsistency in underwriting judgment led to the development of schedule rating.

Construction of Schedule Rates. To arrive at a systematic evaluation of the factors affecting the risk, a schedule of uniform rate debits and credits is applied to each insured property. Thus, schedule rating is a systematic procedure for recognizing variation in the traits of relatively similar exposures. It isolates the variation of individual features of a risk from the standard or average of the class.

Schedule rating requires that appropriate characteristics for evaluating an exposure be identified and measured, and an average for each characteristic be determined. Furthermore, the underwriters must understand these criteria and be able to apply them consistently to individual risks. Unless these requirements are met, the underwriter will be unable to establish uniform net schedule rates. He will not have the means for applying standard debits and credits to individual risks. Too often, under schedule rating plans, the risk characteristics are given as broad generalities, and their application is at the discretion of the underwriters.

The Case for Schedule Rating.   The principal arguments for schedule rating are based upon the incentives that the technique provides for improved loss prevention or loss control efforts. Schedule rating rewards, and thus encourages, loss prevention and loss control activities. Failure to provide safety equipment, to remove hazards, or to use fire-resistent construction, may result in the loss of credits or the application of debits to the basic rate of the insured. The potentially higher cost of insurance provides a monetary stimulus to minimize losses. Schedule rating also makes possible more equitable discrimination among risks of the same class but with different safety characteristics.

The disadvantages of schedule rating include the high cost of administering the schedule rating process and the potential abuse arising from the attempt to meet competitive pressures for lower rates on a specific risk by improper application of credits.

Use of Schedule Rating.   Schedule rating was extensively used in workmen's compensation, but its use in this field of insurance has decreased significantly. The decline is attributed to the recognition by insurance technicians that physical hazards currently play a minor role in the prevention of on-the-job accidents. With overall improvement in plant safety, nonphysical hazards such as employee morale and attitudes toward safety are more important. Thus, a system that relies upon debits and credits based upon an engineering inspection is less efficient than one that deals with the totality of factors affecting problem loss. However, schedule rating systems that place less emphasis on physical hazards are still in use. For example, a business with five or more vehicles (and a premium base of at least $500) may qualify for schedule rating under some circumstances. Table 21.1 outlines an example of the debits and credits that are sometimes used in commercial automobile liability insurance. The criteria for applying rate modifications are very general and leave the underwriter with much latitude in their application. Insurers that use schedule rating as a competitive tool consider this discretion particularly important. Corporate risks, who might otherwise consider selfinsurance, will frequently be satisfied with appropriately modified schedule rates.

Experience Rating

Experience rating is a merit rate modification system based on the loss ratio experienced by the insured rather than on a system of predetermined credits and debits. Thus, experience rating is based on actual results rather than

TABLE 21.1   Automobile Schedule Rating Illustration

		Range of Modification		
		Credit		*Debit*
A.	Management: cooperation with insurance company	5%	to	5%
B.	Employees: selection, training, supervision	5%	to	5%
C.	Safety organization: periodic meetings to review accidents with drivers, accident reports, and records	10%	to	5%
D.	Equipment: type, condition, servicing	5%	to	10%

anticipated losses. A credibility factor is applied to the loss ratio of the insured, and this yields the rate modification to be used for that risk. In addition, the expense factor is adjusted to reflect actual costs.

Experience rating is prospective in nature. The rate is calculated at the beginning of a rating period and is not changed to reflect experience during the period. Furthermore, experience rating in contrast with schedule rating is based on actuarial formulae that assign weights to the experience of the insured and the credibility of the risk. Thus, experience rating lacks some of the discretion or subjectivism found in schedule rating procedures.

Construction of Experience Rates.   The actuary's first step in using an experience rating system is to determine the experience rating modification factor (M). As a percentage of manual rates this factor is calculated for automobile liability insurance as follows:

$$M = \frac{A - E}{E}$$

A = loss ratio actually incurred in the previous period

E = expected loss ratio used in determining the manual premium for the given class

For example, assume an actual loss ratio of 70 percent and an expected loss ratio of 65 percent. The modification factor would be:

$$\frac{.70 - .65}{.65} = .0769$$

which would suggest the need for a 7.69 percent rate increase if the level of rates for the next period is to be high enough to meet the experience of the last period. After initially calculating M, the actuary applies an appropriate credibility factor. Credibility is the extent to which the actuary believes that a set of sampled data can be relied upon to reflect the underlying statistical population from which the sample has been drawn. Actuaries have developed mathematical formulae that provide measures of credibility on a scale from zero to one.

An additional modification would be necessary if there is an upward or downward trend T of loss experience that is expected to continue through the next period. The rating modification factor M is adjusted for credibility and trend as follows:

$$M = \frac{A - E}{E} \times Z \times T$$

$$Z = \text{credibility factor}$$

$$T = \text{trend factor}$$

If the adjusted modification factor is negative, the rate is reduced (rate credit); if it is positive, the rate is increased (rate debit).

The loss ratio experience adjustment method has the inherent deficiency of increasing the entire premium on the basis of changes exclusively in the loss ratio. Included in the premium is an expense factor, which may or may not change proportionately with the trend in losses. However, if a rate is divided into a pure premium and a loading factor, the individual components can be adjusted to reflect the appropriate changes in both losses and operating expenses.

The Case for Experience Rating. The most important advantages of experience rating are its objectivity and economy of application. If the actuary is furnished with the required experience data, the manual rate can be adjusted at the insurer's office. Physical examinations of the risk are not required. Furthermore, the rate charged is based on actual experience rather than merely on anticipated risk factors.

Experience rating is criticized for providing an illusion of simplicity and equity. It is contended that, given the complexities of rate making and credibility and the inherent problem of projecting statistics from past data, some of the relatively simple experience rating systems are subject to wide margins of error.

Retrospective Rating

Retrospective rating is similar to experience rating except that credits are awarded by the insurance company for favorable experience during the insurance policy year. An anticipatory dividend, or rate credit, is applied at the inception of the policy period with an adjustment made after the close of the period. This is sometimes referred to as the anticipatory dividend method.

Under a retrospective rating system, the insured does not know the exact cost of its insurance coverage until after the close of the policy period. However, the rate is usually bounded. A minimum and a maximum rate may be established before the policy is issued, and the eventual charge will fall somewhere within these limits. Without the use of minimums and maximums, there would be a violation of a basic principle of insurance—transfer of risk by pooling of exposures—so that those who incur loss are reimbursed by those who do not.

Participating insurance, where the insurer pays policyholder dividends at the end of the policy period, may also be classified in the retrospective rating category because the dividends are a reflection of actual incurred costs, which may fall below the expected costs used to calculate the initial premium.

Those insureds who qualify and elect retrospective rating are initially charged a basic premium, which is a percentage of the full experience modified premium. After the insured period a charge (up to any agreed upon maximum) is added to cover losses and loss expenses incurred in the policy period and premium taxes.

Those insureds who adopt a retrospective rating plan assume the risk of potential variation in their insurance costs. Such variation can add to the inherent risk of a business. However, if losses are expected to be low because of extensive loss prevention activities, the insured may be willing to accept some cost variability in exchange for the possibility of lower overall insurance costs. Thus, retrospective rating can provide a reward for successful loss prevention.

RATE MAKING CRITERIA

Statutory Criteria

Insurance statutes generally require that property and liability insurance rates meet three fundamental criteria: adequacy, reasonableness, and no unfair discrimination.

Adequacy. The rates charged by an insurance company must be high enough to allow the insurer to recover the costs of losses, loss adjustment expenses and overhead, plus a modest profit. If the company consistently loses money in a given classification, rates are inadequate. Inadequate insurance rates are regarded as contrary to good public policy because they may lead either to company insolvency or to destructive competition.

Reasonableness. Reasonableness means that rates should not be too high in view of the cost factors involved. If a company sustained high profits in a given line year after year, this would imply that its rates were unreasonable.

Generally, competitive pressure is sufficiently strong to keep rates from becoming or remaining unreasonably high.

No Unfair Discrimination.   No unfair discrimination means that like risks will pay like rates. Where rates differ, there must be some reasonable difference inherent in the risk if the company is to treat its policyholders fairly and comply with the rating laws of the state.

Other Criteria

From a practical standpoint, insurers apply three additional rate making criteria:

1. The rate structure must be consistent. The underlying basis of the rate structure must apply a uniform system of classification to all risks.
2. The rate structure must be flexible so that demonstrated variations among insured risks can be accommodated.
3. The rate structure must be comparatively stable in order to permit statistical experience to be developed at a given level of rates.

These criteria require a considerable degree of business as well as actuarial judgment in the rating process.

Regulatory Enforcement

While insurance regulators have the task of assuring the public that property and liability insurance rates meet the criteria of adequacy, reasonableness, and no unfair discrimination, most statutes fail to provide a clear set of standards for each criterion. Furthermore, those standards whose effects are apparent do not address these questions: What are the insurer's net earnings as a result of a specific rate? Is this rate of earnings "fair" in relation to the inherent risks of the business?

In attempting to judge the propriety of any rate and the resulting profit potential, the regulator is faced with three problems. First, underwriting results must be adjusted to reflect possible inaccuracies in the calculation of insurance reserves. For example, an overestimate of loss reserves results in an understatement of underwriting earnings. An insurer might overestimate loss reserves in order to present the appearance of low earnings and thus provide a basis for seeking a rate increase.

Second, underwriting gains are only one source of possible earnings for a property and liability insurer. In addition, any gain or loss from investments must be considered. While most insurance regulators and practitioners recognize a need to consider investment results in the rate making process, there is considerable debate as to an appropriate composite measure of property and liability insurer profits.[2]

Third, there is the unanswered question: What is a fair return to an insurer? How great a return is necessary for a property and liability insurer to attract and keep sufficient capital to provide a socially desired insurance market? Until these questions are resolved, it will continue to be a difficult task to judge accurately whether a specific rate is adequate or excessive.

Economic Enforcement

Several states have adopted rating statutes that place a greater burden on the marketplace as a judge of rate propriety. For example, competitive rating laws generally state:

> No rate shall be held to be excessive unless (1) such rate is unreasonably high for the insurance provided, and (2) a reasonable degree of competition does not exist in the area with respect to the classification to which such rate is applicable, or such rate will have the effect of destroying competition or creating a monopoly.
>
> No rate shall be held inadequate unless (1) it is unreasonably low for the insurance provided, and (2) continued use of it would endanger solvency of the company, or (3) such rate is unreasonably low for the insurance provided and the use of such rate by the company using same has, or if continued, will have the effect of destroying competition or creating a monopoly.[3]

Interpretation of a competitive rating statute indicates how criteria for the vague concept of "unfair discrimination" are established by regulators:

> . . . the existence or application of any difference in rate with respect to risks apparently alike that is not based on a corresponding and demonstrable difference in cost, constitutes unfair discrimination. The very expression "unfair discrimination" infers that there is such a thing as "fair" discrimination. Discrimination is fair if it accurately reflects anticipated cost differences. Consequently, no less obviously than inappropriate differences in rates, failure to establish appropriate differences in

---

[2] For a discussion of alternative composite measures of property and liability insurer profit, see: *Prices and Profits in the Property and Liability Insurance Industry: Report to the American Insurance Association* (Boston: Arthur D. Little, Inc., 1967). J. D. Hammond and Ned Shilling, "The Little Report on Prices and Profits in the Property and Liability Insurance Industry," *The Journal of Risk and Insurance*, XXXVI (March, 1969), pp. 129-44; Richard Norgaard and George Schick, "Profitability in the Property and Liability Insurance Industry," *The Journal of Risk and Insurance*, XXXVIII (December, 1970), pp. 579-88; Stephen W. Forbes, "Rates of Return in the Nonlife Insurance Industry," *The Journal of Risk and Insurance*, XXXVIII (September, 1971), pp. 409-22; James S. Trieschmann, "Property-Liability Profits: A Comparative Study," *The Journal of Risk and Insurance*, XXXVIII (September, 1971), pp. 437-53.

[3] State of Illinois, *Insurance Code*, 1970, Article XXX 1/2.

rates for risks that are demonstrably different in cost is an unfair discrimination. Justice requires that like cases be treated alike; it also requires that cases that are unlike be treated differently. The test is the burden each risk puts on the insurance system, so far as that can be measured.[4]

CALENDAR YEAR VS. POLICY YEAR

Insurance policies are written at any time during a year, and they typically run for periods of one year or more. On December 31, few policies written during the year will have been on the books for a full twelve months. Therefore, the calendar year is an impractical period for rate making purposes. For example, a growing insurance company will issue more policies at the end of the year than at the beginning, and its loss experience may not become apparent until a subsequent period. Furthermore, seasonal factors may affect the results drawn from calendar year data. To overcome these problems the policy year is usually employed. This is a twelve month period beginning with the date of inception of the policy. Relating all experience to policy years makes it possible to determine a more equitable allocation of premiums and claims to the relevant period. The distortions that might otherwise arise are exemplified in Table 21.2.

TABLE 21.2   Calendar and Policy Years

Calendar Year				Policy Year			
Year	Premiums	Losses	Loss Ratio	Year	Premiums	Losses	Loss Ratio
1	100	10	10%	1	100	600	600%
2	200	10	5%	2	200	10	5%
3	300	600	200%	3	300	15	5%

Suppose that the insurer incurred a loss in year 1 that was not reported until year 3. The calendar year data for year 1 would appear highly favorable but would be misleading. The policy year data would reflect the actual results for the year and would provide a better basis for decision-making. Insurance companies favor the policy year approach.

RATING BUREAUS

Rating bureaus are organizations formed for the purpose of gathering loss and

[4] State of Illinois, Department of Insurance, *Commentary on Article XXX 1/2 Illinois Insurance Code*, 1970, p. 10.

expense data from numerous member insurance companies and calculating property and liability insurance rates based on these data. Manuals of rates and underwriting guides are provided for the use of bureau members and subscribers. Rating bureaus evolved for four reasons.

First, few insurers have sufficient experience in individual lines of property and liability insurance to form a credible base for rate calculations. By combining data contributed by all of its members the bureau can assimilate sufficient experience to calculate credible rates in each line of insurance.

Second, bureaus generally can collect data and calculate rates more efficiently, and economically, than many of their individual member companies. Individual insurers are not required to incur the full cost of maintaining actuarial staffs. They share this cost with other bureau members.

Third, most states require that property and liability insurance rates, and the statistics upon which they are based, be filed with the state insurance department. Rate manuals are frequently very extensive technical documents, and an insurer's compliance costs may be reduced significantly if the filing requirement is handled by a rating bureau. Bureau members are not only required to notify the regulator of compliance with all bureau rates, or notify the regulator of any specific deviations from bureau rates.

Fourth, insurers generally do not have the resources, or the legal authority, to engage in effective lobbying before state legislatures or the Congress. On many occasions rating bureaus have used the power and funds of their membership to lobby for legislation favorable to their member companies. Furthermore, it is common practice for a bureau to establish and maintain close ties and channels of communication with regulatory officials. While these activities are not essential to the bureau concept, they may provide potential benefits for members of effective rating bureaus.

RATING, PRICE COMPETITION, AND PRODUCT AVAILABILITY

Property and liability insurers generally engage in nonprice competition to a greater extent than price competition. However, a trend toward more price competition and increased price flexibility has evolved. Three factors have contributed to this trend: (1) a reduction in the pricing restrictions imposed by insurance statutes, (2) the increased pressure on property and liability insurers to make their products more readily available to all consumers, and (3) the relative success in gaining larger market shares by insurers who have emphasized price as a competitive tool.

Insurance regulators and state legislatures are under increasing public pressure to improve the market availability of certain "necessary" insurance products (e.g., automobile insurance and residential and commercial property insurance in congested urban areas). In response to these pressures, regulators have attempted to reduce insurer inability to implement flexible price structures.

Legislative actions to remove price restrictions range from the deletion of mandatory bureau laws (e.g., laws that require all insurers in a state to use bureau rates) to the implementation of open competition rating laws.[5]

Increased insurer rate flexibility should lead to less emphasis on strict underwriting criteria and greater stress on rate structures that allow acceptance of nearly all risks. However, if increased rate flexibility is accomplished by means of an extensive expansion of rating factors or rate classifications, premiums for many risks will be prohibitive. The actuary's task is to provide a workable compromise between the pooling concept and fair discrimination.

An alternative solution to the property and liability insurance availability problem would be to reduce or remove rate classes. It has been suggested that any significant expansion of the numbers of rate classes would violate the pooling concept of insurance. A drastic but appropriate solution to the availability problem would be the implementation of one rate for all exposures to the same peril.[6] Under this proposal all automobile owners would pay identical automobile insurance premiums for similar policy limits. The contended benefits of such a system include: (1) reduced operating cost to the insurer, and thus, a reduction in the "average rate"; (2) a more socially efficient distribution of insurance costs; that is, a "complete" automobile insurance policy would be affordable to a greater number of consumers; and (3) more automobile owners would be insured. While "low risk" automobile owners might justly claim that such a plan would require them to subsidize "high risk" automobile owners, others suggest that the net social gain offsets any potential discrimination. Furthermore, if recognition is given to the potential benefits provided one individual because others are fully insured, the claim of unfair discrimination may be discounted.

The one class rating system would be workable only under a system of compulsion. Any insurer that voluntarily implemented a single rate system would probably incur financial ruin because it would tend to lose insureds who previously had rates below the average rate. These clients could obtain insurance from a competitor at their previous lower rates. Insureds who were liable for above average rates would remain on the books of the insurance company and be joined by large numbers of other "high" risks seeking a bargain. This phenomenon is referred to as adverse selection.

SUMMARY

The rate making process in property and liability insurance is both more

---

[5] David R. Klock, "Competitive Rating Laws and Insurer Conduct: A Case Study," *The Journal of Risk and Insurance*, December 1972, pp. 589-603.

[6] Comments by Senator Philip A. Hart, *Hearings Before the Subcommittee on Antitrust and Monopoly of the Committee on the Judiciary of the United States Senate*, 92nd Congress, First Session, Chicago, May 17 and 18, 1971, pp. 14113-14115, pp. 14634-14635.

complex and more simple than it is in life insurance. A greater range of techniques, including judgment rating, manual, merit, schedule, experience, and retrospective rating, is employed by the casualty actuary, but the life actuary uses more high powered mathematics in manipulating his tabular data.

Property and liability insurance rates must meet the statutory criteria of reasonableness, adequacy, and fairness in addition to practical business and technical requirements. Rating bureaus have offered statistical services that are indispensable for insurance companies whose experience is not sufficiently large for credible rate making.

Competitive rate making and greater availability of insurance coverage are among the important current trends in the field of nonlife insurance rate making.

REVIEW QUESTIONS

1.   Do the pricing problems encountered in the property and liability insurance industry differ from those encountered in the life insurance industry? What are the differences and the similarities?

2.   Explain the concept of "credibility." How is this concept used in property and liability insurance rate making?

3.   The expected loss ratio for fine arts exhibitions insurance is 60 percent; the actual loss ratio is 30 percent. Based solely on this information, what percentage adjustment would be indicated in the rate level for this class of insurance? Explain.

4.   Why are there significant differences in rates charged by different insurers for the same risks? Explain.

5.   What would be the social costs and benefits of implementing a rating system for automobile insurance in which all risks would pay the same flat rate? Discuss.

STUDY QUESTIONS

6.   How does the actuary determine the risk classes in manual rating? What are the criteria for a properly defined class? Discuss.

7.   How does this rate making process in property and liability insurance deal with the inflation problem? Discuss.

8.   Rate making bureaus are essentially price-fixing organizations. Why do state legislatures permit such bureaus to operate in the insurance industry? Doesn't this violate the anti-monopoly laws? Discuss.

9.   Explain and evaluate the loss ratio method of rate making in fire insurance. Cite some of the objections which have been raised against this system.

10.   Some authors contend that the pure premium or statistical method of making insurance rates removes the arbitrariness of personal judgment and makes the rate "scientific." To what extent is the judgment of the actuary really eliminated in the process of making pure premiums? Explain.

22

Insurance
Reserves

THE NATURE AND PURPOSE
OF INSURANCE RESERVES

Most individuals are aware that insurance companies have substantial invested assets. However, few laymen are aware of the nature of the liabilities that offset these invested assets. The largest share of insurance company assets is held to meet obligations that have either matured or are anticipated. These obligations are represented among the liabilities on an insurance company financial statement and are referred to as reserves. Because reserves are so large a proportion of the liabilities of an insurer, they generally determine the type of assets required to maintain solvency in a technical or statutory sense.

State statutes generally specify both the type of reserve liabilities that must be maintained and the methodology that must be employed to calculate minimum reserves. The need to supervise insurance company reserves is tied to the primary goal of regulation: the safeguarding of insurer solvency. Regulatory authorities contend that the supervision of insurance company reserves provides a useful test of the ability of insurers to meet their contract obligations. The reserve represents a potential debt to either policyholders or claimants, and by the surveillance of reserves the regulator guarantees that these potential debts are recognized in the accounts of the insurer and that sufficient assets will be available to match the maturing obligations.

The extent to which actual reserves exceed the minimum requirements varies as a result of the skill, prudence, and goals of insurance company management. The minimum requirements also vary with the nature of specific reserve obligations and the use of conservative margins to offset unpredictable variations between expectations and actual results.

CLASSIFICATION OF RESERVES

Reserves are classified in several ways. One classification scheme distinguishes between involuntary and voluntary reserves. Voluntary reserves are appropriations of surplus to meet special contingencies that are not specified in any statute. These may include special reserves for security price fluctuations, catastrophes, undeclared policyholder dividends, and the like. Involuntary or statutory reserves are liabilities and are specified in the insurance codes of the various states. Involuntary reserves include claim reserves, unearned premium reserves, tax reserves, legal reserves for life insurance, and so on.

A second classification of reserves differentiates between retrospective reserves for items that have already accrued, and prospective reserves for contingencies that have not yet occurred but are expected. Retrospective reserves include claim reserves, claim expense reserves, reserves for taxes, reserves for dividends voted, and miscellaneous reserves. Prospective reserves include legal reserves for life insurance, the reserves for noncancellable disability income insurance and unearned premium reserves for fire, marine, and liability insurance.

Finally, reserves may be classified by type of insurer—life insurance as contrasted with property and liability insurance reserves.

RESERVES OF A
PROPERTY AND LIABILITY INSURER

There are two principal reserves maintained by a property and liability insurer: the loss reserve and the unearned premium reserve.

Loss Reserves

The casualty actuary operates under two distinct handicaps with regard to obtaining estimates of the frequency and severity of insured losses. First, the casualty actuary is concerned with a large number of different risks. Many of these risks have (1) only a few exposure units, (2) dynamic or unknown probabilities of loss, or (3) indefinite loss potentials. In contrast the life actuary deals with a few well defined, large groups of homogeneous exposures. Furthermore, he uses mortality tables that provide fairly accurate estimates of the underlying probabilities of loss.

Second, in property and liability insurance the time between the occurrence of the insured event and final settlement can range from a few hours to several decades.[1] However, there is generally little delay between the occurrence of a death and the payment of life insurance proceeds. The claims process in life insurance consists primarily of the beneficiary providing and the insurer verifying the appropriate information about the time and nature of the insured's death. In addition to verifying the occurrence of a loss, the property and liability insurer will investigate the loss to determine the extent of any obligations to either the insured or a third party claimant, negotiate an equitable settlement, and defend the insured against claims that appear to be unjustified. While the life insurance contract is a valued policy and loss values are agreed upon at the outset, the property and liability contract is usually one of indemnity and loss adjustments are frequently subject to differences of opinion and negotiation.

Nature of the Loss Reserve.   The potential liability of a property and liability insurer for unpaid losses incurred during the reporting period must be estimated and included in a loss reserve. The loss reserve is composed of three factors: (1) losses incurred and reported, (2) losses incurred but unreported, and (3) expenses associated with adjusting and settling the losses.

The size of the loss reserve is a function of the incidence of claims and the time required before disbursements are completed. In fire insurance it is possible to determine the amount of loss precisely and quickly. Accordingly, the unpaid reserves of a fire insurance company (generally) are relatively small. However, in liability insurance, many years may elapse before losses are fully paid. For example, in workmen's compensation insurance the claimant may be entitled to medical payments and monthly disability income payments for the remainder of his life. Such active claims remain on the books and must be reserved for almost indefinitely.

The loss reserve must also account for losses incurred during the year but not yet reported. For instance, the victim of surgical malpractice may not become aware for many years of a condition that might justify a claim against a negligent surgeon. Such claims may be reported long after the incident causing the loss occurred, and prudence dictates that the insurer be prepared for these contingent liabilities.

---

[1] In the case of medical malpractice insurance, the statute of limitations on a negligence action does not begin to run until the victim discovers the apparent negligent act. A boy undergoing surgery may not know for many years that a malpractice has been committed. Long after, a lawsuit may be filed on his behalf. Periods in excess of twenty years are not uncommon.

Because claims may be paid, or disputed, over an extended period of time, and adjustment expenses are incurred on a continuing basis, a reserve for loss adjustment expenses is required. In a workman's compensation claim the insurer incurs continuing expenses to verify that medical treatment is progressing. In a complex automobile liability suit legal expenses may be extensive and continue for several years.

Reported Losses. There are three methods of estimating the eventual cost of reported losses: (1) individual case method, (2) average value or statistical method, and (3) formula or loss ratio method.

The individual case method requires an analysis of each claim and a projection of its eventual settlement cost. The initial estimates are usually made by the claims adjuster assigned to the case. The adjuster's estimates are revised by claims supervisors and also reviewed periodically by the insurer's legal department. However, it is often difficult for even the experienced claims supervisor to estimate accurately the potential cost of individual losses. This is particularly true of recently reported losses where the adjuster has not had sufficient time to obtain information on which to base a reasonable projection of costs. For freshly reported claims, the reserve estimate is based on any available data, experience with similar cases, or intuition. When judgment plays a key role, there is a potential for excessive or inadequate reserving. If an insurer has a large number of claims occurring each year, individual loss reserving is both costly and time consuming. However, if the insurer writes only those lines of insurance where claims are investigated and settled rapidly (e.g., property damage insurance, collision insurance, etc.) or where the insurer has a relatively small volume of claims, the individual method may be a viable technique for estimating the potential costs of reported losses.

The average value method is used by insurers who experience patterns of consistency in the type and distribution of reported losses. As each loss is reported the claims adjuster reviews the file and assigns it to one of several predetermined loss categories. For each category an average loss value has been calculated based on the insurer's experience with similar losses. The loss reserve for each category is the sum of the number of losses in the category multiplied by the appropriate average loss value. The total reserve (for reported losses) equals the sum of all individual weighted loss categories. Because judgment plays only a limited role in the determination of loss categories and average loss values, the subjective factor in the average loss method is less significant than in the individual case method. For the large insurer the average loss method is more economical because it avoids the expense of a thorough review of each case. If the insurer receives only a small number of claims each year, and if each loss varies significantly in size, the average value method would not be appropriate. If such were the case, average loss values would not be credible indicators of actual losses incurred.

The formula, or loss ratio, method estimates losses as a set percentage of earned premiums and the appropriate percentage that varies by type of insurance. The loss ratio method evolved primarily as a regulatory tool for setting minimum reserve requirements. Regulators were concerned that insurers using the individual case method might underestimate losses and thus set too low a reserve. To avoid this potential problem, regulators set minimum reserve requirements based on a loss ratio method. For example, a requirement that reserves for automobile bodily injury liability claims be at least 60 percent of earned premiums is not uncommon. However, loss ratio requirements are generally not accurate projections of losses that will be incurred by individual insurers. Thus, most insurance companies use an alternative method and rely on the loss ratio method solely as an indicator of minimum reserves.

Unreported Losses. In addition to reported losses the insurer must establish reserves for those losses that occurred in the accounting period but have not been reported. While the loss ratio method accounts for both reported and unreported losses, the individual and average loss methods do not. Thus, insurers who use one of these two methods must also make a projection on the potential cost of unreported losses. These projections vary by company and type of insurance. Using alternative statistical methods, the past experience of each insurer serves as a guideline for the projection of unreported loss costs. For example, an insurer might analyze the relationship between reported and unreported losses in the past five years. If a significant correlation exists, unreported losses can be estimated as some percentage of the projected reserve for reported losses.

Loss Expenses. Loss reserves must include the projected expenses associated with adjusting all losses that occur in the accounting period. An insurer relies on a financial interpretation of its cost structure and policy mix to estimate these expenses. If the insurer is small and must hire independent adjusters, the cost per loss may be higher than for an insurer that is large enough to efficiently employ its own full-time staff of loss adjusters. The insurer that writes liability policies and provides legal defense for insureds incurs greater expenses per loss than an insurer that writes only first party property damage insurance.

Loss Reserving Criteria. Regardless of the method selected for the determination of loss reserves, uncertainties affect their accuracy. Judgment is required at all steps in the reserving process. Furthermore, there are industry considerations that may not be directly related to a goal of setting accurate reserves.

The following criteria are commonly considered by insurers when setting loss reserves:

1. high enough to more than adequately meet loss payments,

2. high enough to soften the effect of any adverse conditions,
3. not so high as to present a distorted picture of loss experience,
4. not so high as to significantly reduce current earnings, and
5. not so low as to lead to a higher than necessary short run taxable income.

Loss Reserves and Underwriting Profit. The estimates used to calculate the loss reserve liability are also used in the determination of statutory underwriting profits. Underwriting profit is the income that arises solely from insurance operations and does not include investment gains or losses. Underwriting profit is calculated as follows:

$$
\begin{matrix} \text{Statutory Underwriting} \\ \text{Profit} \end{matrix} = \begin{matrix} \text{Earned} \\ \text{Premiums} \end{matrix} - \begin{bmatrix} \text{Losses} \\ \text{Incurred} + \begin{matrix} \text{Loss} \\ \text{Adjustment} \\ \text{Expenses} \end{matrix} + \begin{matrix} \text{Other} \\ \text{Expenses} \\ \text{Incurred} \end{matrix} \end{bmatrix}
$$

The deduction for loss and loss adjustment expenses is generally the same figure used in the establishment of loss reserves; that is, an estimate of claims payments and expenses required for losses that occurred in the accounting period. Thus, to the extent that loss reserves are inaccurate, underwriting profit will be an inaccurate measure of real gain or loss resulting from insurance operations.

Unearned Premium Reserves

The unearned premium reserve represents the portion of the premium that corresponds to the unexpired term of the policy. In property and liability insurance the insured has the right to cancel the policy and receive a return of premium. The amount returned is referred to as a short rate cancellation refund and is less than the pro rata share of the premium. Because the insured was responsible for cancelling the policy, the insurer is allowed to retain an amount to cover the costs associated with issuing the policy. However, should the company cancel the policy, the premium refund must be proportional to the unexpired term of the policy. This gives rise to the need to maintain a pro rata unearned premium reserve. The unearned premium reserve represents the potential liability the insurer would incur if it were to cancel all existing policies.

In theory, the insurer should examine all policies and determine the unearned portion of each premium (i.e., the portion of time left before the contract expires multiplied by the total premium). However, in normal business practice insurers use either an annual or a monthly formula method.

The Annual Method. This method is appropriate for insurers that issue insurance policies at an even rate throughout the year. For the purpose of calculating the unearned premium reserve it is assumed that all policies are written at the exact midpoint of the accounting period (e.g., June 30 when using a calendar year). The reserve is calculated as a given percentage (depending on the length of the contracts) multiplied by all written premiums for policies of equal length. If a calendar year is used, it is assumed that all one-year policies were issued on June 30, and the unearned premium reserve as of December 31 is one-half of all premiums written in the year. For three-year policies the amount of premium earned in the first year would be one-half of a year, or one-sixth of the policy period. The reserve would be five-sixths of the written premium. For a five-year period the reserve for unearned premiums during the first year would be nine-tenths of the written premiums for the year.

The Monthly Method. The monthly method also assumes an even distribution of policy issue dates. However, it differs from the annual method in that all policies are assumed to be written evenly throughout the month in which they are issued. All policies are assumed to be written on the fifteenth day of the issue month. For example, assume a one year policy issued in April with a premium of $120. The unearned premium reserve as of December 31 would be calculated using the following format:

$$\frac{A - B}{A} \quad \text{x} \quad W.P. \quad = \quad \text{Reserve}$$

A	=	period of policy (12 months)
B	=	length of time since assumed issue date (April 15th)
$W.P.$	=	written premium ($120)

Thus:

$$\frac{12 - 8.5}{12} \quad \text{x} \quad 120 \quad = \quad \text{Reserve}$$

$$\frac{3.5}{12} \quad \text{x} \quad \$120 \quad = \quad \$35$$

In this example the company has legally earned that amount of premium represented by the passage of time from April 15 to December 31 but has not as yet earned the premium for the period from December 31 to the following April 15. The period from December 31 to April 15 is equal to $\frac{3.5}{12}$ of a year, and reflects the unearned premium reserve factor.

The monthly method is appropriate for insurance companies whose policies are not written evenly throughout the year. For example, some automobile insurers write a majority of their policies in the fall when automobile model changes are introduced. For these companies the monthly method provides a compromise between the distortions of the annual method and the unnecessary refinement of an individual policy reserving method.

THE POLICY RESERVES OF A LIFE INSURER

The life insurance policy reserve is designed to be an amount sufficient to meet the maturing obligations contained in the life insurance contract. Under the level annual premium plan of life insurance, the premiums paid in the early years are more than sufficient to cover the costs of providing policy benefits. In the later years the premiums are not adequate to cover the promises of the insurer. This gives rise to the need for a life insurance policy reserve, which is the amount required to make up the difference at any time between prospective benefits and prospective premiums. Thus, as illustrated in Figure 22.1, the reserve in an endowment or whole life insurance policy increases as the contract remains in force and approaches maturity.

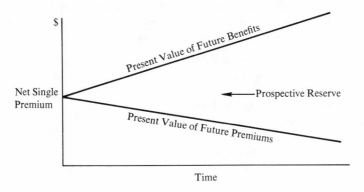

FIGURE 22.1 The Prospective Reserve

The policy reserve may be calculated on a retrospective basis, measuring actual deficiencies according to the experience of the company; or on a prospective basis, measuring the projected deficit indicated by the actuarial tables in use at the time. If the actual experience and the tabular assumptions are identical, both methods will result in the same reserve factor.

Calculating the Policy Reserve

The policy reserve is calculated as an aggregate for all policies in force. The retrospective terminal reserve is equal to the value of accumulated net level premiums less the accumulated value of losses incurred (death claims plus maturities) for life insurance. In contrast, the prospective terminal reserve is equal to the present value of future claims ess the present value of future net level valuation premiums. The prospective method is generally required by regulatory authorities.

The Valuation Premium.   The net level valuation premium is used by the actuary in the calculation of the policy reserve to represent the stream of future payments to the company by the insured. It is not the same as the premium charged the consumer. It contains inputs only for mortality and interest assumptions. The net valuation premium does not contain a loading factor for expenses or profits. Furthermore, in calculating the net valuation premium the actuary may use different (usually more conservative) interest and mortality assumptions than those used in calculating the actual premium charged the consumer. Use of the net level valuation premium is required by regulators in order to add another element of conservatism to reserve calculations.

Calculating the Prospective Reserve.   The prospective reserve is the equalizing factor between the present value of future claims or benefits and the present value of future net valuation premiums. Assuming an insured, age 45, and a whole life insurance policy paid-up at age 65, issued when the insured was age 30, the reserve could be calculated as follows:

(1)   Reserve   = $\begin{array}{c}\text{Present Value}\\\text{of Future Claims}\end{array}$ $-$ $\begin{array}{c}\text{Present Value of}\\\text{Future Valuation Premiums}\end{array}$

(2) Recall that the New Single Premium is the same as the Present Value of Future Claims. Thus,

Reserve   = $\begin{array}{c}\text{Net Single}\\\text{Premium}\end{array}$ $-$ $\begin{array}{c}\text{Present Value of}\\\text{Future Valuation Premiums}\end{array}$

(3) Furthermore, the Present Value of Future Valuation Premiums is the same as the Net Level Valuation Premiums times the Present Value of a Life Annuity Due of \$1 for the remaining premium paying period. Thus, the terminal reserve is calculated as:

$\begin{array}{c}\text{Reserve at}\\\text{age 45}\end{array}$ = $\begin{array}{c}\text{Net Single}\\\text{Premium at}\\\text{age 45}\end{array}$ $-$ $\begin{array}{c}\text{Net Level}\\\text{Valuation Premium}\\\text{at age 30}\end{array}$ x $\begin{array}{c}\text{Present Value}\\\text{of Life Annuity}\\\text{Due of \$1}\\\text{for 20 years}\end{array}$

Varying Actuarial Assumptions

Variations in the calculated life insurance policy reserves result from different actuarial assumptions. The steepness of the mortality curve is an important determinant of reserves and premium calculations. Those insurers who assume a higher mortality rate will set aside greater reserves. Higher mortality implies a smaller flow of future premiums with an earlier stream of policy benefits falling due.

Varying the interest assumption has a significant effect on reserve development because the interest assumption affects both reserve earnings and the calculation of net valuation premiums. For example, assume a $1,000 whole life insurance policy in force for 20 years. If the interest assumption is 2.5 percent, then the terminal reserve would be $352 under one set of conditions. If the interest factor is 3 percent, a reserve of $334 would be calculated. Finally, if the actuary used a 3.5 percent assumption he would establish a reserve of $316.

MISCELLANEOUS RESERVES

State premium taxes, federal income and payroll taxes, and real estate taxes accrue monthly, although their payment dates may be quarterly or annually. Accruals for taxes must be set up as reserves if the balance sheet at the close of any month is to reflect properly the financial condition of an insurance company.

Declared but not yet disbursed stockholder and policyholder "dividends" are reserved because they are true liabilities as of the time of declaration.

If a life insurer charges the policyholder a gross premium less than the valuation net premium, a deficiency reserve must be created and maintained. The use of a larger valuation net premium may overestimate the flow of future premiums and lead to a potentially inadequate reserve (Reserves = Present Value of Future Claims − Present Value of Future Valuation Premiums). While the valuation net premium is usually less than the gross premium charged insureds (i.e., providing more conservative assumptions for reserve purposes), competition and mortality have, on occasion, led to reduced net premiums and the need for deficiency reserves.

Life insurers who provide either accidental death (double indemnity) or waiver-of-premium disability benefits must maintain a reserve to offset these potential liabilities. Accidental death benefit reserves are calculated in the same manner as policy reserves, except that the actuary uses an accident mortality table instead of a standard one. Morbidity, or disability, tables are used to calculate the reserves necessary for disability waiver-of-premium benefits.

ACCURACY OF RESERVES

Because an insurer strives to estimate its reserve liabilities with care, the judgment factor is very important. If the assumptions underlying the actuary's work are biased, this will have a material impact on the adequacy of the reserves. This potential problem is made all the more acute because surplus is small as compared with statutory reserves in most insurance company balance sheets. For example, in 1971 policy reserves for all life insurance companies exceeded $179 billion, while total surpluses were approximately $16 billion. A small insurer might find itself technically insolvent if there was a 10 percent variance in its reserves as a result of an insurance department audit examination and revaluation.

Redundancy in the Unearned Premium Reserve

The unearned premium reserve is based on the gross premium and is reduced proportionally with the passage of time. Thus, premiums are earned only with the flow of time. But the property and liability insurer must pay expenses as they occur, and most expenses occur in the early part of the policy period. Sales commissions, expenses, and overhead are usually paid immediately. An extreme example of the balance sheet accounting format might be as follows:

1.   January . 1, Apex Insurance Company begins operations with $1,000,000 of capital and $500,000 of paid-in surplus.

Assets		Liabilities	
Cash and	$1,500,000	Capital	$1,000,000
Securities		Surplus	500,000
Total	$1,500,000	Total	$1,500,000

2.   During the year, Apex writes $2,000,000 of net premiums on five-year fire insurance policies, on which it has an excellent 40 percent loss ratio, pays agents' commissions at a low rate of 20 percent, and has an overhead factor of only 10 percent.

3.   Having had an excellent first year in business, Apex is insolvent on a statutory basis and will be obliged to take drastic remedial action to remain in business. Its year-end balance sheet shows the following:

Assets		Liabilities	
Cash and	$1,500,000	Unearned	$1,800,000
Securities		Premium	
(+ Premiums)	2,000,000	Reserve	
(- Losses)	160,000	(9/10ths of	
(- Commissions)	400,000	written	
(- Overhead)	200,000	premium)	
Total	$2,740,000	Capital	$1,000,000
		Surplus	(60,000)
		Total	$2,740,000

The balance sheet does not reflect the substantial value in the portfolio of insurance-in-force that will only emerge as the policies mature. The premium is reflected as being earned on an accrual basis, but the costs of acquisition and underwriting are not permitted to be amortized. They are treated on a cash basis. If Apex had been an established insurer with new insurance policies written at an even rate over a period of years and with a flow of investment and underwriting profits, surplus would tend to grow.

In general, a growing insurance company will sustain a drain on surplus as it builds up its unearned premium reserve; a static company is not subject to this strain; a shrinking company will have gains to surplus as business runs off the books. Any equity in the unearned premium reserve will flow into the surplus account with the passage of the policy term.

If the unearned premium reserve was based on incurred loss costs (or expected benefits), it would not include company underwriting expenses and overhead, and the reduction in surplus would be abated. However, regulators demand a gross premium reserve because of the requirement that when an insurer cancels a policy the pro rata share of the gross premium must be refunded to the policyholder. Prudent management dictates the maintenance of funds sufficient to cover the full potential pro rata liability of the insurance company.

The unearned premium reserve is sometimes referred to as a reinsurance reserve because withdrawal from a line of insurance can often be achieved by purchase of reinsurance covering the unearned portion of the exposure. Thus, it is suggested than an amount equal to the unearned premium reserve should be maintained to cover potential reinsurance costs. However, the cost of reinsurance would probably be less than the unearned premium reserve because many of the expenses associated with the policies have already been absorbed by the initial insurer. Ceding of all unearned premiums to a reinsurer would restore any redundancy in the reserve to the insurer's surplus.

Accuracy of Loss Reserves

While there is no inherent reason for loss reserves to be either excessive or inadequate, there are incentives for an insurer to set loss reserves at levels above or below projected losses.

The overstatement of loss reserves not only provides a safety margin in the event actual payments exceed loss estimates, but also leads to an understatement of underwriting profits and to a reduction in the flow of funds to surplus. Accordingly, an insurer can create an equity in its loss reserves. A reduction in current underwriting profits offers the additional benefit of deferring tax obligations. The understatement of earnings may also be used as a means of obtaining rate increases from regulatory agencies.

The understatement of loss reserves results in an increase in earnings and surplus. An apparent improvement in earnings might provide the stimulus for an increase in the market price of the insurer's common stock. Such a misleading sign of solidity may temporarily mask an insurer with financial problems and possibly delay regulatory detection or intervention. Furthermore, company officers may be tempted to overstate earnings in order to achieve recognition for their accomplishments.

Any discrepancy in loss reserves will become apparent when claims must be paid. The time necessary for errors to be revealed varies by line of insurance. Property damage losses are paid relatively quickly. Liability losses take longer. It is difficult to test for discrepancies in loss reserves, and this kind of information is not generally available to the public.

Insurance commissioners are aware of potential inaccuracies in loss reserves and have tried to detect inconsistencies between loss reserving practices and eventual loss payments. However, there is a lack of reliable techniques for evaluating loss reserve practices in the short run.

Redundancy in Policy Reserves

Life insurers may also have a potential equity in their policy reserves. While the property and liability insurance company unearned premium reserve is potentially redundant because of the use of a gross premium, the policy reserve of a life insurer may be redundant because of the use of a net premium. This apparent paradox is caused by differences in reserving methods. The unearned premium reserve is calculated directly from the gross premiums, whereas the policy reserve of a life insurer is calculated by subtracting the net valuation premium from the present value of future claims. If a gross premium were subtracted, the reserve would be smaller.

The use of a policy reserve based on the net valuation premium causes a drain on the surplus of an insurer. The life insurer incurs and pays most of the expenses associated with a new policy in the initial period. First year expenses for a new life insurance policy usually exceed 100 percent of the annual premium, in addition to the costs associated with insurer overhead and death benefits paid in the first year.[2] If reserves are calculated using a net valuation premium, nearly all of the first year expenses are offset against surplus. Unless a new or rapidly growing insurer is able to adjust the required policy reserves to offset the surplus drain created by high initial expenses, technical insolvency is a distinct possibility.

Recognizing the validity and importance of this need, insurance laws permit the use of a "modified reserve" system in life insurance. The Commissioners Reserve Valuation Method provides a technique for significantly reducing first year reserve requirements by permitting the amortization of nonrecurring policy start up costs.

---

[2] For a discussion of distortions in costs, see Irving Pfeffer, "Measuring the Profit Potential of a New Life Insurance Company," *The Journal of Risk and Insurance*, XXXII (September, 1966).

SUMMARY

The reserves of an insurance company represent potential claims of policyholders. Regulatory authorities specify both the type of reserves that must be maintained and their minimum requirements in order to ensure that contract obligations are fulfilled. The two primary reserves required of a property and liability insurer are the unearned premium reserve and the loss reserve. For a life insurer the major liability is the policy reserve.

The life insurer may rely upon mathematical procedures for the determination of the policy reserve. The life actuary employs many of the same inputs and calculations for policy reserves as he uses to determine life insurance premiums. Judgment plays a role only in the selection of actuarial assumptions in arriving at the policy reserve.

The property and liability insurer has little discretion in setting the unearned premium reserve. Statutes specify that initially the unearned premium reserve must equal the total premium charged the consumer and may be reduced only with the passage of time. However, since the insurer cannot practically set up an unearned premium reserve for each individual policy, some latitude is given in arriving at estimates of premium flows and the required reserves. Loss reserves are estimates of future claims payments. While it is possible for some insurers to examine individual claims and set a reserve for each loss, most insurers attempt to reduce the need for judgment in the setting of loss reserves by using statistical averages to project the cost of losses.

Conservatism permeates the reserve procedure. Both the regulator and the insurer strive to avoid conditions that might endanger the solvency of the insurer. Since reserves represent such a large portion of the insurer's balance sheet, underestimates can result in financial jeopardy for the insurance company, its policyholders, and its claimants.

REVIEW QUESTIONS

1. Explain the purpose for each of the principal reserves maintained by either a property and liability insurer or a life insurer.

2. What is the relationship between the regulation of insurance company reserves and the maintenance of insurance company solvency? Explain.

3. Contrast the retrospective and prospective methods of determining reserves in life insurance. Are these reserves equal if the assumptions are the same in both cases? Discuss.

4. What is the "equity" in the unearned premium reserve? Discuss.

5. "The faster a company grows, despite the profitability of the book of business, the faster it is likely to become insolvent." Discuss.

STUDY QUESTIONS

6. How can one determine whether the loss reserves of an insurance company are adequate? Discuss.

7. Why do many life insurance companies use preliminary term or modified reserve methods? Explain.

8. The expression "Buy term and keep the reserves in your pocket," was very popular in the fraternal insurance movement at the turn of the century. Why do life insurance companies believe that reserves are necessary? Discuss.

9. In evaluating the financial status of an insurer, what adjustments in the balance sheet are appropriate? How would you go about making these adjustments?

10. The "L" Mutual Life Insurance Company announced a substantial increase in dividends to be distributed among all policyholders "on an equitable basis." Assume you are an actuary for the "L". Explain briefly an "equitable" method for dividing this surplus among policyholders. No answer is complete without supporting *reasons*.

23

Contemporary
Actuarial
Developments

INTRODUCTION

The frontier areas of modern actuarial work are not unlike those of a century ago. They relate to the theoretical limitations of the actuary's projections, the status of the actuary in the insurance industry, and the recognition by the public and by the law of actuarial science as a closed field worthy of special licensure.

The work of the actuary is so diverse that virtually every important insurance problem is his problem.[1] Every phase of insurance is the subject of some research exploration. Some of the more important problem areas have included: identification of insurable hazards; the financial consequences of exporting to other countries that are subject to fewer problems of regulation, taxation, and so on; the no-fault problem in private passenger automobile insurance; adaptation of reporting requirements to the capabilities of modern electronic data processing equipment; and rate making statistical uniformity. Other business problems include: improved rate making classifications for fire insurance; subrogation; net cost rate making; small premiums; and simplified rate manuals.

[1] Laurence H. Longley-Cook, "Actuarial Aspects of Industry Problems," *Proceedings of the Casualty Actuarial Society*, XLIX, Part II (1962), pp. 104-08.

LIMITATIONS IN ACTUARIAL SCIENCE

At least six major areas of weakness in modern actuarial work can be identified. They include: (1) data refinement needs, (2) the inadequacy of industry aggregates, (3) adverse selection, (4) credibility criteria, (5) retention limit theory, and (6) capacity resolution.

Data Refinement Needs

The collection of statistical data on a company by company basis or even on a bureau basis is unsatisfactory. The data that flow into the computers are inadequate for refined statistical analysis because of countless policy deviations and rate variations. This means that crude data are being used for projections, the validity of which is crucial for insurance companies. Some effort has been made to gather more refined data, but the job is not adequately done because of a lack of obligatory reporting.

Inadequacy of Statistical Aggregates

There is a serious deficiency in aggregate statistics in the United States. Private organizations, such as rating bureaus, public relations institutions, financial reporting services, and trade publications, offer a wealth of data. State insurance departments publish very little for budget reasons. The federal government does not collect many of the kinds of statistics required for important actuarial analysis for lack of regulatory interest.

At present there is no source from which to obtain a comprehensive tabulation of insurance. This scarcity makes it difficult to discuss in a precise manner the growth and structure of the business and lines of insurance.

Adverse Selection

There is a need for the development of more adequate means for dealing with the problem of nonrandom variations, which adversely affect the selection process in insurance underwriting. The classification of exposures is somewhat less than reasonable where misclassification is easy or where arbitrary decisions to cut rates are concealed behind misclassification.

The rigidity of rate regulatory practice provokes the imagination of insureds and their brokers to find ways of achieving better rates within the existing structure. This can occur by shifting the risk to a more favorable classification than it warrants. In life insurance this may result from concealment of medical history or occupation, faulty medical examinations, or careless underwriting. In automobile insurance it may arise from concealment of facts relating to accident history, use of the car, identification of drivers, or mechanical alterations that may affect safety. In workmen's compensation faulty descriptions of occupations or operations are not uncommon.

Avoidance of adverse selection is essential to the validity of rate structures. The actuary has the task of ascertaining that his inputs are conformable to his assumptions.

Credibility Criteria

The concept of credibility is substantially the same as that of statistical levels of significance.[2] There are general statistical functions that provide measures of the level of significance of the variance of the probable loss. There is no 100 percent level of significance in a sample that embraces less than the total universe of observations. There are only approximations of ever higher degrees of probability. Pragmatically, the insurance industry has adopted arbitrary cutoff points, which are negotiated and to which they assign a value of 100 percent credibility.

The insured with a considerable number of exposure units, such as car-years, intuitively believes that his experience is superior to that of the rate classification to which he has been assigned by the underwriter. He may have 100,000 units, 10,000, or even fewer than 100 units. If his loss experience has been good, he expects to be treated favorably with rate reductions. Questions that must be considered although unanswered are: to what extent is the experience of a risk a result of underlying factors as opposed to mere luck, and how much weight should the actuary assign to the experience of a particular risk?

By fitting a Poisson curve to represent the underlying distribution of the number of claims in a specified time interval, it is possible to answer the question: what is the number of observed claims that will permit the actuary to assert with a probability of a given percent that the results observed are not due to chance fluctuations?

One credibility table used in private passenger automobile liability rate making provides the following partial credibilities.[3]

[2] Laurence H. Longley-Cook, *An Introduction to Credibility Theory*, Casualty Actuarial Society, (1962) is a standard reference work on this subject. See also Jerome D. Braverman, "Credibility Theory: A Probabilistic Development," *The Journal of Risk and Insurance*, Vol. XXXV (September, 1968), pp. 411-23.

[3] See C. A. Kulp and John W. Hall, *Casualty Insurance*, 4th ed. (New York: The Ronald Press Company, 1968), pp. 823ff.

Actual Number of Claims	*Credibility (%)*
0 - 10	0
43 - 97	20
173 - 270	40
390 - 530	60
694 - 877	80
1,084 and over	100

The credibility concept is used primarily in casualty insurance and when carried to its extreme it permits a single automobile car-year to have a credibility factor as large as 10 or 20 percent. The accident free driver is given discounts as if there were some underlying justification other than random results. To resolve the problem requires a much more careful look at the implications of the concept of credibility and the rationale for deviations from the norms suggested by general statistical theory.

Retention Limit Theory

There is at present no adequate theory that can predict the appropriate amount of any risk that an insurance company should retain for its own account. The ratio of the largest individual exposure to the capital and surplus of an insurance company is generally inadequate. Most insurance companies forego undertaking risks that they can and should accept and thereby forfeit not merely the possibility of rendering an important business service but also profits. The lack of an accepted theory of retention limits not only takes its toll of profits but also contributes to the capacity problem.

In recent years, particularly under the leadership of the Scandinavian actuaries, there has been a rapid growth and expansion of what has come to be known as collective risk theory.[4] This branch of actuarial mathematics deals with deviations that are produced by random fluctuations rather than with average probabilities. Instead of considering only the number of claims in a fixed time period as a random variable, using an average size of claim as a constant, risk theory treats the number and size of claims and the time interval as random variables.

Collective risk theorists have been exploring nonnormal distributions and are concerned with laws of small numbers. The "ruin problem," where a chance fluctuation of abnormal frequency of severity of loss in a particular time interval might cause insurer insolvency, is a central issue.

---

[4] An excellent introduction to collective risk theory is R. E. Beard, T. Pentikainen, and E. Pesonen, *Risk Theory* (London: Methuen and Co., 1969). See also Hans Ammeter, "Practical Applications of the Collective Risk Theory," *Scandinavian Actuarial Journal*, Supplement (1969), pp. 99-117; Hans Bühlmann, *Mathematical Methods in Risk Theory*, (Springer-Verlag, 1970); Hilary L. Seal, *Stochastic Theory of a Risk Business* (John H. Wiley and Sons, Inc., New York, 1969).

Risk theory is being applied to business planning in limited ways. Safety measures against the random or chance risk are taken by insurers. Further applications include: premium rating of excess-of-loss and stop-loss reinsurances, profit planning, stability of loss experience, solvency, and credibility. However, whereas risk theory methods offer a certain rationality to the estimation process, the risk attitudes of responsible insurance executives and the constraints of the institutional framework have not been incorporated in the models in such a way as to inspire confidence in their safety and dependability.

Capacity

Capacity is the ability of an insurance company or of the insurance industry to absorb risk exposures of large size. The lack of a theory of retention limits has resulted in companies absorbing far less than they should of the risks presented to them.[5] The actuary has a responsibility for answering the questions: what is the capacity of the insurance industry to absorb risk, and what are the limiting factors that mark the capacity level? This need is accentuated by the resistance to government intervention and the refusal to write certain categories of risk.

STATUS OF THE ACTUARY

The actuary has become a rare breed in our society because the growth of the insurance industry has far surpassed the growth rate in the number of accredited members of actuarial societies. Those actuaries employed in company ranks tend to be concentrated among the largest life insurance companies. Indeed, there are fewer actuaries than there are licensed insurance companies. This scarcity has propelled the professional actuary into the top ranks of company management and has served to give the profession substantial status within the industry. Many of the chief executives of the fifty largest life insurance companies are Fellows of the Society of Actuaries. More vigorous recruiting and training are urgently needed if the requirements of the business are to be met.

The shortage of actuaries in the insurance industry may be explained by the rigorous examination process and the movement from company ranks into private consulting. In 1949, forty Fellows of the Society of Actuaries reported that they were engaged in consulting work. By 1960, this had increased by 715 percent to a total of 326. During the period, the overall number of Fellows in

---

[5] Ingolf H. E. Otto, "Capacity," *Journal of Insurance*, XXVIII (March, 1961), pp. 53-70, provides an excellent review of the economic and institutional aspects of the problem.

the Society increased 177 percent for a total of 1193 new members in the decade.

The job description of the life insurance actuary defines his role as that of an insurance mathematician whose primary responsibility is to keep insurance and pension plans financially sound. He estimates premium and investment income, reserves for payment of future benefits and future operating costs. He is a statistician concerned with revenue and cost implications of new forms of coverage, new developments in marketing or underwriting, in investments, and in general management. At a minimum, he must have an adequate training in mathematics, electronic data processing, and the technology and law pertaining to insurance and statistical techniques. At an optimum, he will possess the management skills that lead to the executive suite of an insurance company, government post, or an actuarial consulting firm.

LICENSING OF ACTUARIES

Despite the limited supply of qualified actuaries the actuarial profession has gradually been moving toward monopolistic closure of the field through state or federal licensing. The objective is to raise the standards of professional conduct and requirements for entry into the field. A number of professional societies have emerged and, with the formation of the American Academy of Actuaries, most practitioners are registered with a central body.[6]

Licensing is economically important to actuaries because it leads to granting them exclusive rights: to certify financial statements of insurance reserves, to value insurance portfolios, to propose financial projections for regulatory review, to represent insurers or pension fund trustees before governmental bodies, and so on. Very little formal licensing of actuaries has occurred in the United States.

SUMMARY

The actuary's role as an applied insurance business mathematician is changing as he comes to grips with some of the most difficult techniques on the frontiers of

---

[6]The primary goals of the American Academy of Actuaries as discussed in the early meetings of the Society of Actuaries (*Transactions of the Society of Actuaries*, XVI: D3, 1964) were to achieve accreditation and certification of professional status. It was expected that following attainment of a federal charter, the Academy would proceed to promote legislation in each of the states which would provide for certification of actuaries of the Academy.

his science. If it can be harnessed properly, collective risk theory may make possible capacity expansion and profit realization for insurance companies on a new scale. Professionally, the status of the actuary is rising. License requirements will restrict entry to the profession and make the field even more exclusive than at present.

REVIEW QUESTIONS

1. Discuss the role of the actuary today in the insurance company executive suite.

2. The credibility concept is primarily applied in property and liability insurance. Why?

3. Explain the relationship between retention limit theory and the underwriting capacity of either individual insurers or the insurance industry as a whole.

4. Adverse selection can generate non-random variations in loss data. How might an actuary deal with this problem?

5. What are the merits of tight restrictions on entry into the actuarial profession? Is this in the public interest? Discuss.

STUDY QUESTIONS

6. The medical and legal professions are integrated. These professions regulate their own activities as a matter of law. Should the actuarial profession be accorded the same status? Discuss.

7. The United Nations has proposed collecting world-wide insurance data on a uniform basis. What problems are likely to arise in the early stages of such an undertaking? Discuss.

8. What is the optimum size of deductible as a retention for an insurance company? For an individual insured? Discuss.

9. The United States insurance industry has resources aggregating in the tens of billions of dollars. How then do you explain the capacity problem? Discuss.

10. How does an actuary contribute to the development of new insurance products? Explain.

VI

MANAGERIAL
PERSPECTIVES

The management of companies and the measurement of their performance are two of the most important aspects of any study of the insurance industry. In this part, the structure of insurers and the various types of carrier are discussed. Each of the important functional areas of insurance company operations is surveyed. The performance of insurers is studied in terms of objective measurements, such as widely used analytical ratios, and more general external and operational criteria.

24

The Management
of Insurance Companies

INTRODUCTION

The managerial problems of insurance companies are similar to those found in
any other type of business enterprise. The insurer attempts to use available
financial and human resources in order to optimize the flow of benefits to
company owners. In order to achieve its goals the management of an insurance
company must: (1) devise and implement a viable corporate strategy, (2)
establish an efficient corporate structure, and (3) hire, train, and motivate
employees to perform the functions incorporated in the organization plan. The
uniqueness of an insurer relates to the available forms of legal organization, the
comprehensive regulatory framework within which insurance companies operate,
and a technology characterized by costs that typically are not known until long
after the product has been sold and paid for.

CORPORATE DECISION-MAKING AND STRATEGY

In an efficient insurance organization there are well defined levels of managerial
authority understood by all employees. There should be a specific strategy for
achieving the goals of the company. Departmental plans, budgets, and review

procedures should be formulated to evaluate and correct the corporate strategy. The "invisible organization chart," which represents the actual power structure that emerges over time, should be reconciled periodically with the "official organization chart." Channels of communication among the various parts of the organization should be open. There should be a minimum of conflict between personal and organization goals, or between departmental and organizational goals.

Levels of Authority

Five levels of authority or management can be identified in any insurance company. These five levels are: ownership, directorial, executive, managerial, and supervisory.

Ownership. The ultimate power within the corporate structure comes from the owners of the enterprise, regardless if these owners be stockholders, policyholders, or the state. This group determines the size and legal form of the carrier. The initial capitalization of the firm can assume any level within the capacity of the ownership group, although subject to minimum limits set by law. The legal forms 'that an insurance company can take include capital stock companies, mutuals, reciprocals, Lloyds, fraternals, nonprofit associations, and state corporations. The most important decisions to be made by the prime mover of the ownership group relates to the size and form of the enterprise and the election of a board of directors to translate intentions into more specific long range plans.

Board of Directors. The board of directors performs a trusteeship function and is concerned with such matters as long range planning, finances, and evaluation of results. The role of the board is more important than its composition.[1]

There is much confusion about the role of the board of directors. It is uncertain whether the board should be active or inactive, large or small, a legislative body or a review group for a prime mover. In practice the insurance codes of the various states assign certain specific responsibilities to the board. These responsibilities include approval of all investments, appointment of officers, and endorsement of any significant changes in the direction or thrust of

---

[1] An early study of a random sample of 100 medium and large sized life insurance companies and their boards of directors found: "There is no relationship between the size of a Board of Directors, in and of itself, and the efficiency of a life insurance company." Irving Pfeffer, "The Nature and Significance of Insurance Principles," *The Annals of the American Society of Chartered Property and Casualty Underwriters* (1958).

the company. The most influential of the board's tasks is usually the appointment of a president, or chief executive officer, and ratification of executive compensation.

Because of the fiduciary aspects of the insurance business, membership on the board carries with it the potential of personal liability for improper actions taken by the company.

Executive Officers. The president is responsible for the successful achievement of the goals of the company. He is the ultimate manager, and if the enterprise is to be profitable he must be effective in his planning, organizing, staffing, coordinating, and controlling functions. Perhaps his most important task is the determination of the precise goals and levels of achievement to be sought for the company. Once these have been quantified, it is possible to engage in systematic organization, financial, and market planning designed to achieve the corporate goals.

Managers. The officers of the company provide the managerial structure for the direction of the various departments or divisions of the enterprise. Achievement of departmental objectives, cooperation with other departments, and participation in the decision-making processes of the company are characteristics of the managerial level.

Supervisors. The supervisory level is the bottom rank of managerial authority. This level is concerned with the implementation of plans on a day to day basis through clerical, technical, and sales personnel.

Organization Planning

The tasks of the organization may be classified by:

1. function, including sales, underwriting, administration, claims, etc.,
2. product, including life, property and liability, marine insurance, etc.,
3. territory, including local, regional, national, and international,
4. customer type, including individual consumers, commercial enterprises, private institutions or government, and
5. executive interest.

A current trend is in the direction of very broad functional groupings based on primary management functions, followed by subgroupings based on territory, and other subgroupings by functions. However, the availability of talent and the predilections of management will determine the feasibility of any organizational structure. One pattern of organization for an all lines group of insurance companies is shown in Figure 24.1.

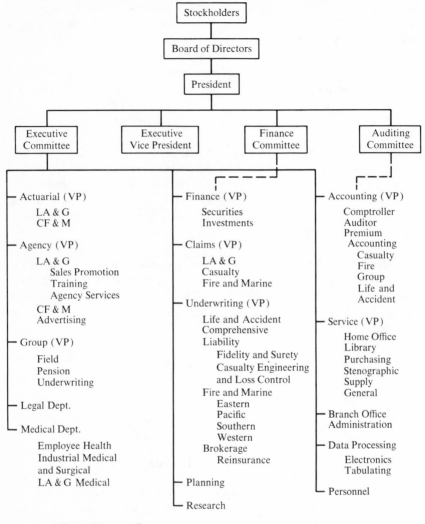

LA & G   Life, Accident and Group
CF & M   Casualty, Fire and Marine
LA & H   Life, Accident and Health

FIGURE 24.1   Organization Chart of an "All Lines" Insurance Company

Financial Planning

As large financial institutions with fiduciary responsibilities, insurance companies are concerned with prudent management of their asset portfolios, optimum use of their underwriting capacity in order to increase profits, and equitable distribution of earnings to policyholders and company owners. In contrast to a manufacturing concern, physical plant and equipment is a small part of an insurer's balance sheet. Most of the assets of an insurer are in the form of securities. Within the restrictions imposed by statute, regulatory promulgation, and prudent financial practice, the investment manager seeks a strategy that will optimize investment returns and provide sufficient liquidity to meet company expenses and claims.

Policyholder surplus is the primary determinant of an insurer's capacity to supply insurance. If an insurer is to grow, it must plan for the efficient use of its limited surplus. Sources of capacity generating surplus include: underwriting gains, investment earnings, increases in market value of the investment portfolio, new funds contributed by owners, and adjustment of reserve accounts. Surplus must be sufficient to meet expanding market needs for the insurer's products. If demand for insurance increases, and insurers are unable to attract or generate new surplus, the demand may not be met even at higher and more profitable prices. However, surplus should not be so excessive as to result in an inefficient use of financial resources. The purchase of an insurer by a conglomerate, and the concomitant transfer of surplus funds from the insurer to the parent, has often been stimulated by the insurer's use of surplus. The parent company believes that the "surplus surplus" can be more profitably employed in alternative business ventures.

Market Planning

An insurance company must adopt a market strategy that is appropriate for its needs.[2] While marketing strategies are numerous, and the insurer may elect to combine a number of different methods, factors within the business make it customary to adopt a single market plan and adhere to it. This may involve the use of: (1) a brokerage system, whereby independent insurance agents or brokers place business with the company on a nonexclusive basis; (2) an agency system, using indirect agencies to solicit business; (3) a direct writing system, whereby the insurer hires salaried sales employees; or (4) a branch office system, in which a branch manager develops business from a territory using a variety of sales tactics. In the United States the independent agency system is in conflict with alternative methods of distribution, and many companies find it difficult to produce business by multiple channels of distribution.

---

[2] Joseph W. Newman, *Marketing Management and Information* (Homewood, Ill.: Richard D. Irwin, Inc., 1967). The Hawthorne Insurance Company case deals with adjusting corporate strategy to a changing environment.

CORPORATE STRUCTURES: AN OVERVIEW

Several distinct types of insurance carrier have evolved for historical, financial, and social reasons. Each has a number of peculiar features that may be advantageous to consumers or to insurance company management.

Stock Companies

A stock insurance company is owned and controlled by its common stockholders. The stock insurer's ability to attract additional capital from stockholders gives this form of organization possible financial advantages over the mutual insurer. While stock insurance companies predominate in the property and liability insurance industry, the volume of business in life insurance attributable to stock companies is small, but growing.

Historically, the independent agency system has been the traditional sales outlet of the stock companies. However, since the Supreme Court handed down its famous South-Eastern Underwriters Association (S.E.U.A.) decision, there has been a movement toward greater diversification of sales outlets. The independent agency system still predominates, but direct mail, captive agencies, and over-the-counter selling techniques have been adopted by stock insurers. The lines of insurance written by stock insurers are limited only by company policy and statutory limitations.

The long run trend of the industry is in the direction of more stock companies as the advantages of other forms are eroded by legislation.

For example, at one time the cost of entry, in the form of minimum capital and surplus requirements, was significantly higher for stock insurers. Contemporary legislation has provided for uniform entry requirements regardless of the legal form of the carrier.

Stockholders exercise their control primarily through the election of the board of directors. Realistically, the control tends to be concentrated among a small number of shareholders, who own a minority interest in the company but control sufficient proxies to elect the board. The majority of stockholders, who are usually scattered all over the country and world, seldom attend annual meetings. The small stockholders are more concerned with dividends and possible capital gains than with the power of their votes. Dissatisfaction with management is more often expressed by the sale of the company's stock than with attempts to alter corporate plans.

Mutual Companies

Mutual insurance companies are owned and controlled by policyholders. The initial surplus for a mutual insurance company is contributed by either the policyholders or a financial intermediary who must be repaid with interest as surplus accumulates.[3] The initial capital requirements for a mutual insurer were traditionally very low; thus providing ease of entry into the insurance business. However, in recent years capital requirements for mutual insurers have been raised to the level required for the licensing of stock companies. This has deprived the mutuals of one of their principal attractions.

Outside the field of life insurance, small mutuals are sometimes assessable (i.e., the policyholders may be assessed for additional financial contributions beyond the premium charged), but such assessability is usually limited to an additional year's premium. The assessability feature is usually eliminated when the insurance company achieves a minimum size specified by statute. Many small mutuals initially operate within a limited geographical territory, such as a single town, county, or state on the theory that policyholders would know one another and have better control over underwriting. However, there is a trend toward greater geographic dispersion of marketing efforts by the mutual insurance companies for competitive reasons.

Historically, the primary sales outlet of the mutual insurer was a staff of salaried sales employees. This form of direct writing remains the principal sales channel among smaller mutual insurance companies. But, as the mutual insurers have grown, they have adopted alternative sales outlets, such as the independent agency system, captive agents, and direct mail. The underwriting policy of mutuals has traditionally been selective with only preferred risks being written. But competition has led the mutuals into all lines of insurance including the substandard or high risk markets.

The control of a mutual company is technically under the direction of policyholders. The policyholders have voting control in the election of the board of directors, who in turn select and evaluate the management team. This is the legal arrangement. However, not unlike the shareowners of stock companies, few policyholders attend the annual meetings. Control shifts to the hands of a small group, usually the managers of the business. They obtain control of the firm by virtue of owning policies and by holding proxies obtained from other policyholders.

Both in mutual and stock insurance companies, effective control usually rests with company management. However, the fact that control has been surrendered by stockholders or policyholders should not suggest that management operates without restraints. Insurance is a tightly regulated industry. Any individual policyholder or stockholder has the right to file a protest at the state insurance department with regard to any alleged misconduct of management. The state insurance department is responsible for the determination and correction of any abuses. If an investigation of management activities warrants,

---

[3] The contribution certificate, a debt instrument repayable at the discretion of the insurance company with the consent of the insurance commissioner, is frequently used to provide capital funds to stock and non-stock insurance companies. It is subordinated debt in the nature of equity but not part of the permanent capital of the company.

the regulator has the power to force the resignation of company officers who have failed to properly conduct the insurance company's business.

While stockholders or policyholders may frequently allow the usurpation of their power, consistently poor performance by top management will probably lead to forceful change. Proxy fights to gain effective control of an ailing insurer, while uncommon, have occurred. Thus, the potential for owner disenchantment and eventual participation in management is an important constraint on the activities of the existing management team.

Reciprocals or Interinsurance Exchanges

In a reciprocal or interinsurance exchange each policyholder assumes or insures a proportion of all risks presented by other policyholders. In effect, the members exchange insurance contracts with one another. The reciprocal is managed by an Attorney-in-Fact under an exclusive long term contract. The Attorney-in-Fact receives an overwrite commission on all premiums for performing management functions. Initial capital is obtained from either: (1) prepayment of excessive premiums by members, which are contributions to surplus, or (2) contributions in the form of subordinated loans made by the Attorney-in-Fact. Surplus is also accumulated by retention of earnings. Like some small mutuals, the reciprocal usually has an assessment feature while its capitalization is below a statutory minimum. The assessability usually does not extend beyond an additional one year's premium.

Many states prohibit the reciprocal type of carrier. While most reciprocals operate within only a given state, some very large ones extend their operations to a number of states (most commonly in the western United States). Sales outlets are provided by the Attorney-in-Fact who generally uses "captive" commissioned salesmen. Traditionally, only preferred classes of risk were written by reciprocals, but contemporary reciprocals have moved toward more venturesome underwriting in all lines except life insurance.

Lloyd's of London

Lloyd's of London is an association of individual underwriters, each of whom is organized as a sole proprietor who underwrites insurance for his own account. The more than 6,000 individual underwriters control the operations of Lloyd's through an elaborate committee structure that is headed by a board of governors. Required capitalization is very high because all members are obliged to maintain deposits of at least $50,000 in a trust fund. The trust is to meet extraordinary contingencies and to provide investment income for the operation of Lloyd's. Premium trust funds are maintained in addition to this trust. Ultimately, the insured is protected by the unlimited personal liability of the·

underwriters, each of whom is a wealthy individual in his own right. There is no assessability of policyholders.

The operations at Lloyd's of London are worldwide and extend into all lines of insurance. Sales outlets consist of brokers and surplus lines offices throughout the world. The underwriting policy is liberal and somewhat innovative. It has been said that Lloyd's will place insurance on any risk, of any kind, anywhere, if there be an insurable interest, regardless of the lack of previous statistics or experience. In this sense, Lloyd's is the market of last resort for the hard to place risks of the worldwide insurance industry. In addition to conventional and unusual risks, reinsurance is particularly important as a source of premium volume for the underwriters at Lloyd's of London.

American Lloyds

The American Lloyds carrier was a phenomenon of the southern United States. Originally patterned after the Lloyd's of London operation, the financial strength of these underwriters was inadequate, and many were dissolved. Most states now prohibit this form of operation. Currently such carriers are a small factor in the American insurance market. They are incorporated; and, while owned and controlled by their underwriting members, they are more in the nature of closed corporations than of groups of individual underwriters. The stockholders own and control the American Lloyds company. Capital and surplus is generally small, and there is no assessability of policyholders. Territorial limits are very narrow, and business is placed by brokers or by members representing insurance agencies. Underwriting policy tends to be somewhat liberal, but because of the small capitalization, retention limits are small.

Nonprofit Service Associations

The Kaiser Foundation Health Plan and the Blue Cross and Blue Shield are relatively new groups of "insurers," who are owned by their member doctor and hospital associations. While these organizations are generally controlled by the associations, management is contracted to an independent firm. Capitalization is typically small and is derived by retention of earnings after guaranty capital is returned to the original investor members. Typically, there is no assessability, although services may be discontinued or curtailed under the terms of contracts between the members and the insureds. There is technically no reserve liability, and many of these organizations fall outside the province of state insurance codes. The benefits provided by these organizations are medical services as opposed to cash indemnification for losses. Often such plans are limited to operations in a single state, and they frequently will operate only within a given community. Sales are by salaried personnel, although brokers are sometimes paid commissions for obtaining clients. At the outset, underwriting policy is usually selective and preferential but tends to be relaxed after a time.

The advent of pressures for improved medical care at the national level has led to the expansion of "Health Maintenance Organizations" (HMO), who offer a given population a wide range of health services in exchange for flat prepayments on a monthly or quarterly basis. The Kaiser Foundation Health Plan, with more than 2,000,000 members in five states, 2,000 participating doctors and a string of privately owned and operated hospitals, pioneered the HMO concept. The Health Insurance Plan of greater New York was another early entrant in this field with about 750,000 members. Because they offer benefits in the form of service units, whose quality and volume are determined by the doctors who operate these programs, such plans may grow to very substantial size with relatively little concern for 'loss reserves." Statutory controls on their fiscal responsibility and the quality of their services have been increasing.

Self-insurance

Self-insurance is not strictly an insurance plan. When organized rationally, it is a form of budgeting for the retention of a risk by the would-be insured. The policyholder does not generally capitalize a separate insurance entity. The self-insurer rarely maintains a cash reserve, but generally makes accounting transfers into a contingency reserve of an amount equal to the premiums that would normally be paid to a commercial insurer. When specific assets are set aside, all losses are borne by the self-insurer out of normal cash flows or borrowed funds. Self-insurance tends to be limited to risks that recur frequently. To protect the self-insurer from catastrophic occurrences, excess limits insurance is generally purchased in the commercial insurance market.

State Corporations

Government bodies have entered the insurance business and have employed the device of a state corporation as an insurance carrier. Owned and controlled by the federal or state government, such corporations are initially capitalized by the government unit. This initial capital is later returned, and subsequent equity is developed by retained earnings. There is no assessability of policyholders, and the territory is usually limited to the jurisdiction of the government body.

Sales are usually by salaried employees, although direct mail is often used. The underwriting programs of government insurers are usually limited to the insurance lines specified in the statute. Examples include the State Compensation Insurance Fund in California for the writing of workmen's compensation insurance and the Federal Deposit Insurance Corporation for insuring bank deposits.

Some foreign governments have insurance entities operating in other countries in direct competition with private enterprises, but this is not an American phenomenon. The Soviet Union and The People's Republic of China are prime examples of governments maintaining insurance companies that are not involved in the insuring of domestic risks but are active insurers in foreign countries.

Insurance Groups

By forming groups of companies, which include members of various insurance carriers, the advantages of these various types of insurance carrier may be achieved. Historically, the group mechanism provided greater flexibility in marketing a variety of insurance coverages than did the sole carrier operation. Group formation was also aimed at obtaining sufficient size to incur economies of scale in marketing, underwriting, claims adjustment, financing, and computer operation.

The need to form groups resulted from statutory restrictions on the number and type of insurance lines that could be written by any one company. These laws were based on the premise that an insurer might spread its technical competency too thin when it operated in several lines of insurance. However, support of this contention has declined, as have legal restrictions on the types of insurance that may be sold by any one insurer. The states have granted multiple line writing powers to many insurers. Group formations have slowed, and existing groups are consolidating their membership. Mergers and acquisitions of insurance companies continue, but the purchased companies are usually consolidated in the parent company rather than left as separate entities in a group.

FUNCTIONAL STRUCTURE OF AN INSURER

The uniqueness of the insurance industry arises in large part from the level of required technology. Insurance is an industry of specialists. The basic task is the achievement of the model of large numbers, but the means of accomplishing this goal involve numerous functions of an insurer into three groups:[4] (1) those necessary to perpetuate the identity and health of the corporate entity,

---

[4]T. E. Walton, "Company Organization and Management," in John D. Long and Davis W. Gregg, eds., *Property and Liability Insurance Handbook* (Homewood, Ill.: Richard D. Irwin, Inc., 1968), pp. 877-92.

including the president, secretary-treasurer, controller, and investments; (2) those necessary for the offering of insurance protection, including sales, underwriting, and claims adjustment; and (3) those that complement and allow the other functions to operate, including general counsel, actuarial, statistics, engineering, personnel administration, and so on. Any analysis of these functions is complicated by the fact that each varies in some degree among different lines of insurance. The underwriting of fidelity bonds is unlike the underwriting of life insurance; malpractice liability is unlike fire insurance; and marine insurance hardly resembles annuities.

Accounting

Insurance accounting is different from that for other businesses because of the blend of accrual and cash bases and the use of regulatory valuation methods. Much of the accounting relates to reserves for contingencies, which are difficult to predict.

Insurance accounting practices have been determined on a statutory basis. The insurance codes set forth the form and content of accounting statements that must be filed with the state. These reporting requirements are designed to assist the insurance commissioner in evaluating the financial strength, performance, and solvency of an insurer. Thus, the individual accounting requirements focus on insurer solvency, rather than the status of the insurer as a going concern. For example, an insurer may only include in its annual statement to the state those assets that can readily be converted to cash. These are referred to as admitted assets, as opposed to nonadmitted assets, such as the depreciated value of office furniture or equipment.

The principal financial report for an insurance company is the annual statement or convention blank that must be filed with the state each year. In order to achieve uniformity of reporting, all states with minor exceptions have adopted the annual statement as prescribed by the National Association of Insurance Commissioners. The required annual statement consists of: a balance sheet, income statement, statement of sources and uses of surplus, and a group of additional schedules supporting the income statement and balance sheet.

To supplement the statements required by law, the insurance accountant may also prepare more conventional accounting statements. Balance sheets and income statements that reduce potential distortions resulting from the emphasis on liquidity and solvency are made available for management decision-making. For example, the balance sheet may be adjusted to include nonadmitted assets, or it may be adjusted to transfer to surplus any redundancy in reserves resulting from required overestimates of unearned premiums.[5]

[5] The American Institute of Certified Public Accountants has published a set of accounting rules known as Generally Agreed Accounting Principles (GAAP) which introduces uniformity between insurance and general accounting. These principles were adopted by insurance departments and the insurance industry in 1973 for use in published financial reports.

Since 1973, insurance companies have been required to report their results on the basis of Generally Agreed Accounting Principles (GAAP) as well as on a statutory basis. GAAP provides a set of formulas for adjusting statutory results to conform more nearly with those of other types of business corporation.

Investment

Insurance companies have been referred to as "closed end investment trusts engaged in the underwriting of risks as a means of obtaining funds for investment." Investment activity is crucial although not the dominant function. Funds are held for long periods of time, interest rates are guaranteed to the policyholder, and the insurer is obliged to seek the best possible rates of return. The investment problem is complicated by the large size of insurance company investment portfolios. When a portfolio manager is concerned with billions of dollars, the investment outlets tend to be limited in scope, and there is a great need for organized programs to keep the cash flow in balance.

The investment department is responsible for managing the insurer's portfolio of investments, which may include: government securities, corporate bonds, direct placement loans, mortgages, preferred stock, common stock, real estate, and other business interests. Within the constraints of regulation and prudent financial management, the investment department attempts to optimize income and capital gains. If the investment department is successful, there will be an increase in surplus which will raise the insuring capacity of the company.

Communication between the investment and underwriting departments is imperative. Both functions place the assets of the insurer at risk. Both deal with risk portfolios. When combined, the two portfolios represent the total risk to which the insurer's assets are exposed. The two departments must be aware of each other's activities and goals in order that the potential variation in earnings created by the total portfolio of risks does not exceed some predetermined level.

Sales and Marketing

The sales department of an insurance company, like that for any other firm, plays a vital role in the achievement of corporate goals. However, the marketing function is particularly important to the insurer. The law of large numbers requires the insurer to attract a sufficient number of exposures to allow credible loss ratio prediction. An insurer dares not operate on the premise of limited marketing to a few high quality customers. The sales department must generate a sufficient volume of risks to allow the actuaries to predict that actual losses will not vary considerably from expected losses.

Insurance is a service business, and the marketing department plays a key role in the delivery of such service. Few consumers of insurance have the skill to select the combination of insurance products that will best meet their needs. The statement "insurance is sold, not bought" has validity.

To stimulate serious consideration of the need for life insurance, in the face of resistance by the prospect toward the product, is an extremely difficult task. There is steady pressure brought to bear on the salesman's cycle of prospecting, interviewing, processing, servicing, and reprospecting in order to build his volume of life insurance sales. In property and liability insurance, there is more of a sellers' market because the consumer is generally more aware of his needs. Thus, the sales effort is less stressful. The problem is one of obtaining a proper distribution of risks by territory, line, or class.

Underwriting

The underwriting department is responsible for selecting, classifying, and rating risks. The underwriters' goals are: to select a set of risks that will make an optimum contribution to the profits and surplus of the insurer, to achieve equity among the policyholders, to avoid adverse selection against the insurance company, and to protect the company from the danger of catastrophic losses. This department is concerned with policy forms, policy writing, determination of prohibited risks, reinsurance, and experience review. The criteria of underwriting vary by line and are in large part based on the experience and judgment of an underwriting specialist. For example, in life insurance the underwriter must be able to interpret medical findings. He must also be aware of causes of death and disability in a medical context and be able to evaluate reports on moral hazards, financial condition of insureds, and the like.

The underwriter has primary responsibility for the success of the insurer. He must determine the extent to which the assets of the firm will be subjected to risk by setting limits of retention on each line of insurance. The underwriter formulates and enforces rules that specify the characteristics, rates, and reinsurance requirements of risks that he is willing to accept.

It is essential to have substantial information on the nature of individual risks for the effective performance of the underwriting function. The underwriter has access to many possible sources of underwriting information. In life insurance, these include the application, the medical history form, the results of any required physical examination, the report of the agent who solicited the business, and credit bureau reports. In property and liability insurance the underwriter may obtain information from the application, a physical inspection of the property and a credit bureau report. If the property and liability risk is a commercial enterprise, the underwriter may also review the financial status of the risk and the extent to which it engages in loss control or loss prevention activities.

A number of insurance industry organizations have been formed for the purpose of providing central clearing houses for information about medical records of insura ce applicants, loss experience of automobile drivers, claims experience of liability insurance claimants, their doctors and their lawyers, and arson investigations. Credit agencies, appraisal services, and investigation bureaus are extensively used in insurance.

Claims

Ultimately, the social purpose of an insurance company is to pay claims. The key function of the claims department is to verify and settle all claims presented. This requires an awareness of coverages, an ability to quantify losses, and a capacity to settle claims on a fair basis. Litigation and subrogation decisions are made by this department. Finally, the claims department is often responsible for the establishment and revision of loss reserves.

In life insurance losses are settled relatively quickly with little need for extensive claims investigation. The only exceptions are deaths that may have been caused by excluded perils, such as suicides, or death claims arising from mysterious disappearance. In most other lines of insurance the investigation required by the adjuster can be extensive. A claim for disability income insurance benefits requires the determination of the extent and nature of the alleged disability. A claim for property damage insurance benefits requires an examination of the damaged property to determine if the damage was caused by a covered peril and, if so, the value of the loss. Liability insurance claims probably require the most extensive investigations by the claims department. Liability claims have a higher loss potential, and they also involve many human and subjective factors that are not easily communicated on a claim form.

The adjustment process for an automobile liability insurance claim is as follows. First, the adjuster reviews the report filed by the claimant, or his attorney, to determine if the loss is one covered by the insured's policy. Assuming it is a covered loss, the adjuster must interview and take signed statements from the insured, the claimant, and any known witnesses to the accident. If the claimant is represented by an attorney, the adjuster generally is unable to obtain a statement directly from the claimant, but discusses the facts of the case with the attorney. If the adjuster and the attorney do not initially agree on the facts of the accident, both parties will usually proceed to collect additional data relevant to the event. After analyzing these data, the adjuster makes a determination of the possible negligence of the insured and discusses the case with his supervisor. Then, the adjuster will usually recontact the attorney and attempt to obtain a settlement. If settlement attempts are unsuccessful, the attorney will probably file a lawsuit against the insured. At this point, the adjuster will transfer his claim file to either the legal department or to outside counsel representing the insurance company. Periodically, the adjuster is asked by the legal department to furnish additional information needed for defense of the case.

Legal

All contracts and much of the routine activity of the insurance company have a legal aspect, and the legal department is necessary to maintain order in the multitude of conflicting statutes and court rulings. In addition to the design and interpretation of insurance contracts, the legal department has responsibility for: counseling the claims department, determining the validity of security covenants, foreclosing on unpaid mortgage debts, reviewing agency contracts for the sales department, and providing advice on insurance statutes and regulatory promulgations. Legal departments seldom try cases; outside counsel is retained as needed.

Actuarial

The actuarial department is concerned with all of the monetary functions (e.g., the calculation of premiums, policy reserves, nonforfeiture values, and dividends) of a life or health insurance company and with rate making in property and liability insurance. The actuary prepares the convention statements of companies, determines rates and reserves, and conducts mathematical studies for management on various aspects of the business. Actuaries also play a key role in the development of new insurance products.

Statistical

The statistician is an important technician within the company, particularly in property and liability insurance where the accumulation of intercompany experience is required to provide an adequate statistical base for rate making. Rarely is this a large department, but the coding and statistical output are very important to both the actuary and the underwriter.

Reinsurance

Reinsurance is regarded as a function of the underwriting department. However, it usually warrants special attention by top management because it is an indispensible feature of safe operation particularly for the small insurance company. On an automatic treaty basis reinsurance permits underwriting to flow smoothly; on a facultative basis, reinsurance gives additional scope and flexibility to the management of risks larger than or different from those that the company would normally assume.

Engineering

The insurance engineer deals primarily with loss control or loss prevention and is used most frequently in property and liability insurance. The evaluation of the effectiveness of safety guards around machinery, of boiler and other pressure vessel capacities, and of elevator conditions is the responsibility of the engineer. Furthermore, he contributes data for the underwriter whereby the latter may determine the rate structure appropriate for a given technical risk.

Administrative

The administrative department performs a wide range of services ranging from personnel to purchasing, mailrooms to storage, stenographic to inventory maintenance. All of the housekeeping arrangements including the maintenance of properties usually fall within the purview of this department.

A SYSTEMS APPROACH
TO AN INSURANCE ORGANIZATION

Contemporary management research emphasizes the systems approach toward the activities of an organization. The systems approach recognizes the importance of integrating functions in an effective organization. When a systems approach is utilized, the focus is not a specific goal or set of goals, but rather a model of a business unit that is capable of efficiently achieving many alternative goals. Thus, in addition to requiring an assessment of all functional relationships, the systems approach requires an analysis of the relationship between the organization and its environment. The environment consists of any suprasystem: market, political, social, economic, and so on.

Figure 24.2 provides an illustrative model of an insurance company. The model depicts the important relationships between the technical requirements and other aspects of the organization and the need for a corporate strategy and policy that is responsive to the needs and demands of the external environment.

Resource Subsystem

The existence of the technical subsystem presupposes that the insurer will be able to obtain technical resources to perform specialized functions, input resources required by the technicians, and administrative resources to coordinate the technicians. Figure 24.2 presents a listing of technical resources generally required by an effective insurance organization. The list is not intended to be complete because alternative types of insurers will require specialized resources. For example, a boiler and machinery insurer must obtain expert loss engineers. Alternatively, a workmens' compensation insurer may require medical technicians trained in physical rehabilitation.

The insurer is not required to employ all technical resources full-time, but it may obtain the services of technical specialists. For example, a small insurer may not hire an actuary but may indirectly obtain such services by membership in a rating bureau or by the use of actuarial consultants.

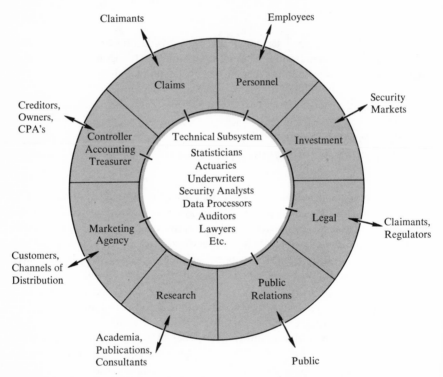

FIGURE 24.2   Systems Model of an Insurance Company

Administrative Control

In addition to identifying several alternative subsystems of an insurer, Figure 24.2 demonstrates the importance of interaction between the functional subsystems. Functional areas will usually adopt a set of subgoals that functional supervisors conclude are prerequisites to attainment of perceived corporate goals. Conflict arises when the attainment of one subgoal may reduce the possibility of obtaining another functional subgoal. Any such conflict must be resolved at the administrative level. The administrator is required to blend the two sets of demands in order to optimize the overall status of the organization. An example of potential conflict in an insurance organization exists between the underwriting and agency functions. The agent perceives his goal as increasing sales, whereas the underwriter seeks a grouping of risks that will generate a favorable loss ratio. The agent has been referred to as the yes man, and the underwriter is often called the no man.

The management of conflicts and the achievement of balances between subsystem goals is referred to as a problem of organizational rationality. If the administrators in their tasks of control and integration are able to achieve organization rationality, then organizational effectiveness is increased.

Environmental Support

In addition to the problem of organizational rationality, administrators are also concerned with environmental acceptance. For example, in order to retain the support of governmental bodies, insurers must contribute to generally accepted social goals. However, social goals and criteria are dynamic and subject to change.

> Many corporate presidents and their boards are adequately sensitized by now to the importance of pollution control, consumer protection and other like matters that are currently having significant impact on business. But what will be the issues of the future? One can be sure only that new issues will arise, and if they are as unanticipated as the events of the recent past, management and directors will deservedly continue to be embarrassed and put on the defensive.[6]

Thus, the need to complement social goals can create uncertainty for an insurance company administrator who is unable to perceive the relationship between his organization and society.

An insurer's ability to contribute to the solution of social problems is a function of its financial solidity. An insurer is under conflicting pressures. One pressure is to survive in a competitive environment. Spurred by the profit motive, a company tends to take only those risks and actions that a competent management feels will not endanger the profitable survival of the firm. But a second pressure also weighs on an insurer. Through its governmental agencies society believes that insurers should participate in the solution of social ills. For example, public policy regards many forms of property insurance as necessities

---

[6]Frazer Wilde and Richard Vancil, "Performance Audits by Outside Directors," *Harvard Business Review*, L (July-August, 1972), p. 115.

that should be made available to all.[7] Thus, insurers face the dilemma of avoiding financial ruin for themselves and avoiding economic ruin for society. Economic ruin, or failure, may be defined as "nonfulfillment of a social purpose in particular light of public interest." The avoidance of the two concepts of failure require organizational and social actions that may be in conflict. Thus an effective insurance organization will plan to avoid being hurt by the conflicting goals of owners and society.

SUMMARY

The management of an insurance company requires organizing, planning, staffing, controlling, and coordinating. The insurer must first establish a set of goals and a practical strategy for achieving these goals. The strategy consists of a plan for an optimum form of capitalization, marketing, underwriting, claims handling, and administration. To carry out the tactics of the predetermined strategy, the insurer needs a cohesive corporate structure in which delegation of authority and acceptance and performance of responsibility are clear. Effective lines of communication among all levels of the corporate structure must be established and maintained in order to control, evaluate, and redirect the efforts of the firm and its employees.

The management of an insurer is unique because of the numerous technical requirements of the business. The costs of insurance cannot be completely predetermined because they are the result of contingencies that only occur after the sale of the product. The skill of an actuary is needed to provide mathematical estimates of costs. The insurer does not sell his product to everyone, but rather uses underwriting skills to select that group of risks or customers that will allow the insurer to make a profit.

REVIEW QUESTIONS

1. Explain the functions and responsibilities of a typical casualty insurance company underwriting department.

2. What differences are there between the goals of insurance accounting for regulatory purposes and for management use in decision making? Explain.

3. Insurance companies lend themselves readily to operations research techniques because of their intensive use of statistical data. Discuss.

---

[7]President's National Advisory Panel on Insurance in Riot-Affected Areas, *Meeting the Insurance Crisis of Our Cities*. Washington, D.C., U.S. Govt. Printing Office, 1968.

4. The increase of regulation in the insurance field has led to an increase in the proportion of stock companies to the total number of insurance companies. How do you account for this change? Discuss.

5. Describe the advantages and disadvantages of each of the following insurance company structures: (a) stock, (b) mutual, (c) reciprocal, and (d) Lloyd's.

STUDY QUESTIONS

6. What is the relationship between the underwriting function and investment decision making?

7. In addition to the independent agency system, what channels of distribution are available to insurers? Discuss.

8. Draw a typical organization chart for a casualty insurance company showing the lines of authority down to the executive levels. How would the chart for a large life insurance company differ? Discuss.

9. Why might an insurer delegate its rate making function to a rating bureau? Explain.

10. Compare commission arrangements in life insurance with those in property and liability insurance. Explain.

25

Reinsurance

INTRODUCTION

Reinsurance is the transfer by one insurance company to another of a part or all of a given risk. This process is referred to as a cession of reinsurance. The company that transferred or ceded the risk is called the primary or ceding company, while the company that accepted the reinsurance risk is known as the reinsurer. Reinsurance contracts are referred to as treaties. The reinsurance process may proceed beyond the initial reinsurer. The reinsurance company may transfer a portion of the risk to a third company. This process is referred to as retrocession.

The insured is generally not aware of the reinsurance process because the insurer remains fully liable to the insured in the event of loss. Furthermore, the insured has no legal basis for proceeding against either a reinsurer or a retrocessionaire.

PURPOSES OF REINSURANCE

Reinsurance is an indispensable mechanism in insurance underwriting because it enables an insurance company to: (1) achieve greater distribution of risk, (2) strengthen policyholder protection, (3) build or reduce its premium volume in a given line of business, (4) avoid loss of volume by use of reciprocity, (5) stabilize profits and losses by limiting the amount of risk retained, and (6) reduce required reserves, which will be maintained by the reinsurance carrier.

Risk Distribution

No insurer has the financial capacity to provide unbounded amounts of insurance for any one risk. The capacity of any one insurer is restricted by surplus requirements. Insurers are generally restricted, by regulatory authorities, as to the amount of insurance they can write with a given surplus. This relationship is summarized in the ratio of written premiums to policyholder surplus. A maximum ratio of three to one is not uncommon, but if reinsurance can be obtained, the insurer may be allowed to exceed this limit.

Sound underwriting practice dictates that an insurer spread its exposures to avoid a catastrophic loss. In order to obtain a wide distribution of its underwriting capacity, an insurer will usually set a dollar limit on the maximum amount of risk it will assume on any one exposure. However, exposures that are beyond this predetermined retention limit may be insured by a company if reinsurance can be obtained. Reinsurance allows a company to seek out all potentially acceptable risks regardless of size, to provide full insurance coverage under one policy, and to cede a portion of the risk to the reinsurer.

The use of reinsurance is more efficient than having several insurers underwrite and issue separate insurance policies for portions of the exposure. As long as the initial insurer is known to use sound underwriting practices, uneconomical duplication in sales and underwriting effort are not required. In addition, the insured is obliged to deal with only one insurance company and need buy only one policy. For example, assume a large corporation requires a $5 million key man life insurance policy on the life of its president. Few insurers would assume $5 million on one life. The alternatives available are to require the corporation to purchase several policies from different companies, or to write one policy and distribute the risk by means of reinsurance. The latter is less costly and more efficient. Frequently, the insurer must obtain reinsurance facilities or it risks the loss of the sales prospect to a competitor.

In practice, life insurance companies are more likely to issue a single policy for the total exposure to protect the competitive position of the agent than are property and liability companies. The life insurance agent prefers having his policyholder client deal with a single insurance company because that is the only company represented by the agent. This competitive factor is less urgent in nonlife insurance because the insured tends to look to the agent or broker for his coverage rather than to the insurance company. It requires less effort for a nonlife insurer to accept only that which fits its line limits than to accept larger risks and seek out reinsurance on a facultative basis.

Policyholder Protection

In addition to efficient distribution of the risk, the use of reinsurance serves to strengthen the protection provided by an insurance policy. While the insured does not have a contractual relationship with the reinsurers, the ability of the ceding carrier to proceed against the reinsurer for partial reimbursement of a loss strengthens the contractual promise given by the insurer. The reinsurer acts as a guarantor of the promises of the insurance company that issued the original policy.

Adjustment of Premium Volume

Through reinsurance an insurer may add blocks of business in a particular line or withdraw from a line of insurance or a geographic area without disrupting the market. For example, assume an insurance company no longer wishes to write automobile insurance in a particular state. The reason for withdrawal may range from a deteriorating regulatory climate to the inability of the insurer to generate a desirable level of premium volume. Whatever the reason, the insurer has three alternatives: (1) cancel all policies in the area and return the pro rata share of the premium to policyholders, (2) refuse to renew policies, or (3) obtain reinsurance for all risks in the area. The first two methods might disrupt the automobile insurance market in the state and create public disfavor for other lines of insurance that the insurer might still wish to sell in that state. Furthermore, the first approach may produce a strain on the insurer's cash flow. The reinsurance alternative will not cause immediate disruption and will allow the insurer time to retreat gradually from this market. The cost of reinsurance should be less than the pro rata premium because the insurer has already borne most of the nonclaims expenses associated with the policies.

Reciprocity

Reinsurance is often employed to obtain business reciprocity. Reciprocity is a mutual exchange of business, usually to the advantage of both parties. Reciprocal reinsurance is very common between U.S. insurers and the international reinsurance market. For example, a U.S. insurer operating in Europe may agree to reinsure all or a portion of its European exposure with its European partners, and the European insurer may agree to cede all or part of its U.S. risks to the U.S. partner.

Stabilization of Experience

Reinsurance can add to the stability of an insurer's earnings and cash flow. Extreme fluctuations in earnings and cash flow increase business risk and are a matter of profound concern to insurance companies. Action taken to reduce the variability of earnings is beneficial to the insurer. By obtaining reinsurance the ceding company can place limits upon the potential losses it is likely to incur and thus reduce the element of uncertainty in underwriting. Just as individuals benefit from reduced uncertainty, so do insurers. This is particularly important for smaller companies in planning the efficient use of limited cash flows. Reinsurance may reduce the need for liquidity in the investment portfolio of a ceding company.

Surplus Relief

Reinsurance enables insurers to obtain unearned premium reserve relief by transferring the reserving requirement to a reinsurer. In assuming new business the reinsurer will set up the reserves on its own balance sheet rather than upon that of the reinsured company. This can be of particular importance for the new, or rapidly expanding, insurer. By the purchase of reinsurance the ceding insurer may obtain relief from the effect on its surplus caused by the statutory requirement for increasing premium reserves. The ceding company is usually allowed a balance sheet credit only on premiums ceded to a company authorized to write reinsurance in the state. Nonadmitted reinsurance is not credited because, in case of default by the reinsurer, the state lacks the means of securing policyholder benefits. Since the reinsurance cost (or the transfer of cash to the reinsurer) is the reinsurer's portion of the premium less any incurred expenses, part of the burden of financing the redundancy in the reserves (i.e., prepaid expenses) is transferred to the reinsurer.

METHODS OF OBTAINING REINSURANCE

The most common approaches to reinsurance include: (1) facultative treaties, (2) automatic treaties, (3) pools, and (4) coinsurance agreements.

Facultative Treaties

Facultative treaties are intercompany agreements providing for optional or voluntary reinsurance transactions. There is no advance agreement between the ceding company and the reinsurer with respect to acceptance of any particular exposure, rates, or specific terms of any reinsurance assumption. However, the ceding company and the reinsurer may enter into an advance agreement on reinsurance commissions and settlement terms for convenience. The reinsurer retains the right to accept or reject any business offered by the insurer.

Furthermore, the insurer retains the right to decide whether and how much to submit for reinsurance.[1]

Automatic Treaties

An automatic reinsurance treaty is a contractual relationship between two insurance companies that provides for automatic cession and acceptance of some specific amount or percentage of all insurance of a given type written by the primary insurer. Such an agreement reduces the uncertainty for both parties. The ceding company knows in advance that it will be able to obtain reinsurance for all exposures that meet the conditions specified in the treaty. Furthermore, the reinsurer is guaranteed against the risk of adverse selection.

Pools

Reinsurance pools or syndicates have been formed to provide a better spread of risk for their members. Each member of the pool agrees to accept from and cede to the pool a specific amount of reinsurance. Usually, the constitution of the pool specifies the reinsurance formula adhered to by the membership. Examples of pools include the Workmen's Compensation Reinsurance Bureau and the Factory Insurance Association. Syndicates include the Jewelers Block Syndicate and the Furriers' Customers Syndicate.

Coinsurance Treaties

Coinsurance, as a method of reinsurance, is similar to the pooling method except that the lead company in nonlife insurance issues combination policies that contain the names of all members. This does not fall under a strict definition of reinsurance and may too easily be confused with the coinsurance concept of loss sharing between the insured and the insurer (or the sharing of loss between the insurer and its reinsurer). Coinsurance is a popular form of life reinsurance.

REINSURANCE ARRANGEMENTS

The most important types of property and liability reinsurance include: (1) quota share reinsurance, (2) pro rata reinsurance, (3) excess of loss reinsurance,

---

[1] Under the terms of a facultative obligatory treaty, the ceding company may cede risks of a defined class in its discretion and the reinsurer agrees to accept all such ceded insurance.

and (4) loss ratio reinsurance. Life reinsurance is usually referred to as either yearly renewable term or coinsurance.

Quota Share Reinsurance

The insurer agrees to cede a set percentage of all business in approved lines to the reinsurer under a quota share agreement. The reinsurer receives a quota share of both the exposures and the premiums, less agreed costs incurred by the ceding company in writing the business. The cost allowance is referred to as a reinsurance commission. Quota share reinsurance agreements are useful for the new and rapidly growing company that may wish to write risks larger than it is willing to retain for its own account. Reinsurance agreements between members of the same insurance company fleet are usually of the quota share type.

Pro Rata Reinsurance

Pro rata reinsurance agreements state that the insurer will assume all risk up to some specific policy limit, and will cede a portion of the risk above the retention limit. For example, a fire insurer might agree to cede four-fifths of the liability above $20,000 per policy.

Excess of Loss Reinsurance

Excess of loss reinsurance specifies the extent of reinsurance in terms of losses rather than in terms of liability.[2] Under such a treaty, the ceding company would pay all claims up to a specified amount per event or per period. Any losses over the agreed amount would be paid in full (or in part), as agreed, by the reinsurer. In contrast to the quota share and *pro rata* arrangements, the premiums are not shared proportionally in excess of loss reinsurance because the agreement does not refer to any specific policy but covers all of the insurer's business. The primary advantages of this agreement are the reduction in detailed record-keeping and reporting on specific policies, and the automatic nature of the plan. However, the excess of loss agreement usually does not provide credit for surplus relief.

Excess of loss reinsurance is catastrophe reinsurance. It can only be arranged to provide protection against the large loss. It may be considered similar to a large deductible clause, with the amount retained a function of the

---

[2] Excess of loss reinsurance is a generic term for reinsurance plans which indemnify the ceding company against the amount of loss in excess of a specified retention. It may include various types of reinsurance, such as catastrophe, per risk, per occurrence, and aggregate excess of loss.

ceding company's capacity and financial stability. The plan is sufficiently flexible to allow the insurer to cede losses due to specified perils only, or losses which occur exclusively during a specified time or in a specified geographical territory.

Loss Ratio Reinsurance

Loss ratio contracts provide for reimbursement by the reinsurer when a specified loss ratio is exceeded. The loss ratio is the ratio of losses incurred to premiums earned. Usually, the loss ratio when used as a basis for payment is set well above that normally incurred by the company and at a level that the insurer could not bear without sustaining severe damage to its financial condition. Thus, the loss ratio method is also used to provide catastrophe coverage.

Aggregate excess of loss reinsurance may be written to indemnify the ceding company against the amount by which the ceding company's losses incurred during a specific period, usually twelve months, exceed either (1) a predetermined dollar amount, or (2) a percentage of the company's subject premiums, or loss ratio, for the specific period. This is often referred to as stop loss reinsurance or excess of loss ratio reinsurance. Nonproportional reinsurance is a form of aggregate excess of loss, frequently employed in life insurance.[3]

YRT Reinsurance

Yearly renewable term (YRT) life reinsurance may be thought of as risk premium reinsurance because the reinsurer is liable only for the net amount at risk above a set retention limit.[4] The net amount at risk is defined as the difference between the face amount of a policy and the terminal reserve. Thus, given that the terminal reserve will grow each year that the policy is in force, the reinsurance liability decreases each year. In effect, the ceding company buys yearly renewable term insurance from the reinsurer to cover a portion of the mortality risk above the retention limit. The ceding company retains for its own account the premium reflecting its retained mortality risk plus the difference between the gross premium and the cost of the yearly renewable term portion transferred to the reinsurer.

Coinsurance

The coinsurance plan of life reinsurance is similar to pro rata reinsurance. The ceding life insurer retains a specified amount of each risk and cedes all or

---

[3] Herbert L. Feay, "Introduction to Non-Proportional Reinsurance," *Transactions of the Society of Actuaries*, XII (1960).

[4] See Dan M. McGill, "Reinsurance of Life Risks," *Journal of the American Society of Chartered Life Underwriters*, XII (1958); John T. Rohm, "Life Reinsurance," *Proceedings: Conference of Actuaries in Public Practice*, V (1955).

part of the remaining liability. In addition to being liable for a pro rata share of claims, the reinsurer also shares in payment of nonforfeiture values and dividends.

Frequently, the reinsurer will buy a block of business under a coinsurance arrangement and pay a flat commission, such as 180 percent of the first year's premium, for it. In the largest insurance fraud in history, the Equity Funding Life Insurance Company was found in 1973 to have sold more than $1 billion of non-existent policies in force to a group of reinsurers. The insurance company executives in this instance falsified computer records and created more than 80,000 policies on insureds who did not exist and false death claims for dummy individuals. Failure to detect the fraud sooner led to massive losses by reinsurers and the insolvency of the insurance company. Those insureds who had bona fide policies issued by the insurance company were able to recover their benefits after only a slight delay.

RETENTION LIMITS

The maximum amount of potential loss on any one risk, or any class of exposures, is referred to as the retention limit of the insurance company. Its determination is among the most crucial decisions of insurance company management. This limit may be expressed in terms of a maximum dollar limit per occurrence, a max mum proportion of the aggregate loss arising out of an occurrence, or as a maximum permissible loss ratio. The retention limit is designed to be small enough so that any one loss, or series of losses, will not have a disproportionate impact on the financial condition of the insurance company. The larger the insurance company, the higher are its retention limits, but there is no universally adopted formula for determining what those limits should be.

REINSURANCE MARKETS

Reinsurance is provided by both specialists who are exclusively in the reinsuring business, and by insurers who also provide broad insurance covers directly to the public. In addition, many insurers have reciprocal agreements for the mutual exchange of reinsurance.

Professional reinsurance specialists provide worldwide markets for reinsurance, and the majority of the business is ceded to these reinsurance companies. In addition to providing reinsurance under a wide array of agreements, professional reinsurers also serve as efficient distributors of worldwide exposures through the mechanism of retrocession. Many of the major professional reinsurers are based outside the United States, primarily in London, Switzerland, and Germany.

The London carriers, especially the underwriters at Lloyd's of London, offer the most important world market for reinsurance. A portion of all large exposures will usually find its way into the London market. Since members of Lloyd's are rarely licensed in the United States, the use of Lloyd's will not normally assist an insurer with unearned premium reserve problems. Much of the reinsurance business placed at Lloyd's is handled through brokers. Furthermore, United States brokers wishing to cede reinsurance at Lloyd's use a London broker as an intermediary. Reinsurance brokers have developed a level of expertise that is an important element in successful insurance and reinsurance operations.

Table 25.1 summarizes the reinsurance transactions between United States and foreign insurers. The net outflow of reinsurance premiums is significant. In 1964, the effect of reinsurance transactions on the U.S. Balance of Payments was a net loss of $49.4 million. By 1971, the net loss had increased to $105.4 million. The international portion of the U.S. reinsurance business in 1971 was relatively small. Of a total of $2,579,000,000 in net premiums, only $309,100,000 was received from abroad.

THE REINSURANCE TREATY

A reinsurance treaty is an insurance contract entered into between two or more insurance companies and is based on the principle of utmost good faith between the parties and the agreement by the reinsurer to "follow the fortunes" of the ceding company. A typical First Surplus Fire Treaty might include the following provisions:[5]

1.   Agreement by the ceding company to cede, and by the reinsurer to accept, a fixed share of the first surplus (a line, or retention, equal to that which the ceding company will retain for its own account) on all insurances, whether accepted direct or by way of reinsurance, against the risk of fire or other insured property perils.

2.   A list of the perils, risks, and kinds of insurance that are excluded under the agreement. This list might include ocean marine business, automobile, growing crops, flood, water damage, and Target Risks, such as bridges, tunnels, and valuable art collections.

3.   The time and manner of attachment of the reinsurance.

4.   Agreement to "follow the fortunes of the ceding company in all respects as if being a party to the underlying insurances or reinsurances."

[5] An excellent discussion of reinsurance treaty negotiation is to be found in Robert C. Reinarz, *Property and Liability Reinsurance Management* (Fullerton, California: Mission Publishing Company, 1969).

5.   Provision for reporting losses and paying premiums.

6.   Provision for accounting between the parties and establishing commissions.

7.   The ceding company reserves to itself the sole right to settle losses as it sees fit. All settlements are unconditionally binding on the reinsurer.

8.   The ceding company provides the reinsurer with specified statistical reports, usually on a quarterly basis.

9.   Cancellation and amendment provisions are spelled out.

10.   In case of insolvency of the reinsurer, or the ceding company, the obligations of the parties are stated in the contract. As a general rule the reinsurer remains liable in spite of the insolvency of the ceding company.

11.   Arbitration of differences is a common requirement of the reinsurance treaty.

There is little standardization of terms of reinsurance treaties, except for the understanding that these engagements are entered into by men of honor. Despite the lack of uniformity, litigation in the reinsurance field is relatively uncommon. The customs and usages of the business, coupled with the professional skill of the reinsurers and their brokers, appear to satisfy the needs of this branch of insurance.

THE REINSURANCE PREMIUM

There is active price competition for reinsurance business. Thus, reinsurance premiums usually provide for a relatively small expense loading. In addition to the influence of competition, the size of any required expense loading is reduced by the fact that the ceding insurer absorbs most of the selling and underwriting costs.

Rates charged for reinsurance are based on judgment. Agreements that are maintained over a period of time generate sufficient experience to allow for proper establishment of rates. Because rates are adjusted frequently to reflect individual insurer experience, it has been argued that reinsurance is merely a convenient method of financing large losses other than for those catastrophic losses that affect the entire industry.

If the reinsurance agreement is pro rata the premium is also usually a pro rata share of the total premium charged by the ceding insurer, net of commission. However, if the reinsurance is on an excess basis, the premium may be either a part of the total premium charged the policyholder for that portion of the policy reinsured or a specified portion of the total premiums obtained by the insurer from all policyholders regardless of policy limits.

TABLE 25.1 Reinsurance Transactions—U.S. And Foreign Insurers

Reinsurance transactions of United States insurance companies with insurers resident abroad, 1964-1971, by specified countries
(In millions of dollars)

	1971p	1970p	1969p	1968	1967	1966	1965	1964
A.—Net premiums paid on reinsurance ceded abroad								
All areas	470.9	447.7	416.7	408.1	381.9	353.9	305.8	299.5
Western Europe, total	399.0	392.5	375.8	373.7	354.5	324.9	285.8	280.6
Switzerland	24.3	21.3	16.5	15.9	17.6	17.9	16.3	16.6
United Kingdom	321.7	321.1	328.7	326.6	311.3	284.9	250.5	242.5
Other	53.0	50.1	30.6	31.2	25.6	22.1	19.0	21.5
Canada	14.8	12.3	10.3	8.3	6.6	6.0	3.7	4.5
Latin American Republics	10.8	12.8	9.6	8.8	7.6	8.9	7.1	6.7
Other Countries	46.3	30.1	21.0	17.3	13.2	14.1	9.2	7.7
B.—Losses recovered from abroad on ceded reinsurance								
All areas	263.1	287.8	269.3	291.2	302.6	310.2	288.8	226.8
Western Europe, total	220.4	253.8	243.1	266.4	280.8	288.8	273.1	212.9
Switzerland	13.2	13.7	14.1	11.2	15.1	15.3	13.2	9.7
United Kingdom	172.4	203.7	205.9	232.1	244.0	253.7	237.6	184.5
Other	34.8	36.4	23.1	23.1	21.7	19.8	22.3	18.7
Canada	13.1	12.5	8.5	9.2	7.5	7.5	5.8	6.2
Latin American Republics	2.5	3.4	4.2	3.9	2.7	4.4	3.2	2.4
Other Countries	27.1	18.1	13.5	11.7	11.6	9.5	6.7	5.3

C.—Net premiums received on reinsurance assumed from abroad

All areas	309.1	251.4	205.7	170.7	143.2	125.3	107.0	103.5
Western Europe, total	198.5	165.2	133.3	112.4	96.5	76.4	67.9	62.3
Switzerland	12.5	9.7	4.4	4.7	3.1	2.4	1.4	2.2
United Kingdom	111.3	101.3	89.5	70.0	54.5	43.4	39.8	36.1
Other	74.7	54.2	39.4	37.7	38.9	30.6	26.7	24.0
Canada	41.5	33.2	29.0	23.1	19.4	20.3	16.9	15.5
Latin American Republics	31.9	26.0	23.9	17.7	15.3	18.1	15.4	17.5
Other Countries	37.2	27.0	19.5	17.5	12.0	10.5	6.8	8.2

D.—Losses paid abroad on assumed reinsurance

All areas	206.7	174.2	163.2	151.7	126.9	118.7	98.0	80.2
Western Europe, total	143.1	121.4	107.7	109.8	90.1	86.8	70.2	54.1
Switzerland	7.4	6.3	2.6	4.5	1.7	1.7	1.5	1.6
United Kingdom	79.8	72.5	70.6	67.5	54.2	59.8	43.4	33.1
Other	55.9	42.6	34.5	37.4	34.2	25.3	25.3	19.4
Canada	19.8	20.0	20.2	15.5	13.8	13.4	10.8	10.4
Latin American Republics	19.9	19.9	20.8	10.3	15.3	11.2	9.9	9.6
Other Countries	23.9	12.9	14.5	16.1	7.7	7.3	7.1	6.1

Reinsurance transactions in the U.S. balance of payments

Net U.S. receipts (C-D)	102.4	77.2	42.5	19.0	16.3	6.6	9.0	23.3
Net U.S. payments (A-B)	207.8	159.9	147.4	116.9	79.3	43.7	17.0	72.7
Net balance on U.S. reinsurance transactions with foreigners	-105.4	-82.7	-104.9	-97.9	-63.0	-37.1	-8.0	-49.4

SOURCE: U.S. Department of Commerce, Bureau of Economic Analysis.

405

SUMMARY

Reinsurance is a device whereby an insurance company may decrease its risk by transferring a portion to one or more other insurance companies. Many different arrangements are employed depending on the needs of the ceding company. Reinsurance is a specialized, highly technical, competitive industry whose existence makes possible a more effective distribution of risk.

REVIEW QUESTIONS

1.   What are the basic purposes of reinsurance? How do these functions differ from those of insurance? Discuss.

2.   How does reinsurance assist in the entry to or exit from a specific market? Explain.

3.   What is the contractual relationship between a reinsurance company and the ultimate consumer of the insurance product? Discuss.

4.   Why do giant insurance companies buy reinsurance? Explain.

5.   Explain the comparative advantages and disadvantages of *treaty* and *facultative* reinsurance. Under what circumstances might each be more desirable? Discuss.

STUDY QUESTIONS

6.   Under what circumstances might an insurer find each of the following reinsurance agreements most appropriate: (a) quota share, (b) *pro rata*, (c) excess of loss, and (d) loss ratio? Explain.

7.   As a general rule, a life insurance company which cedes insurance to a reinsurer has no control over the retrocession policy of the reinsurer. This suggests the need for careful selection of reinsurers. Why should a ceding company be concerned about retrocessions? Discuss.

8.   In order to conserve foreign currency, some countries require all domestic insurers to cede a portion of their reinsurance to a national company before they are permitted to cede reinsurance abroad. This practice reduces the volume of insurance exports and in the short run has favorable balance of payments effects. Is this a sound public policy? Discuss.

9.   Explain the potential effects of reinsurance on reserves and earnings.

10.   Explain the relationship between reinsurance and underwriting.

26

Measuring
the Performance
of an Insurance Company

INTRODUCTION

Effective performance by an insu er may be measured by the degree to which its goals are realized. Consequently, the identification of goals is a first step in evaluating the organizational effectiveness of an insurer. However, defining the actual goals pursued by an insurer is at best difficult. The goals suggested either by the company charter or by economic theory may not be the real goals of the corporate officers. While not in direct conflict with the goals of the owners, the informal goals of the management team may be oriented toward servicing the most immediate needs of employees or the corporate structure. An analysis of corporate performance, based on formal goals, might reveal a relatively ineffective organization; the same analysis performed from the perspective of informal goals could reveal a highly effective one.

The problem of goal determination is compounded by recognition of the sociopolitical obligations prescribed for the private insurance industry. Insurers are conscious of the public interest in that the private insurance mechanism provides a "necessary" supply of insurance at a "reasonable" price. A conflict between corporate and social goals is usually resolved by modifying the strategy of the insurance company. To do otherwise might endanger the freedom of operation that society permits the insurer. Such conflicts are relatively infrequent because most insurance executives are aware of their obligations to society.

Resolution of the goal specification problem is achieved by making assumptions about the aims of all insurers and recognizing that any review of the performance of an individual insurer requires both the determination of the objectives that are operative and their feasibility. In the effective organization, assumed and actual goals are seldom incompatible, nor are there significant variations.

CRITERIA FOR EVALUATION OF PERFORMANCE

Measuring the performance of an insurance carrier is unlike that for companies in other industries because the most important factors of performance are rough estimates. One approach to the analysis of performance recognizes three types of criteria and attempts to evaluate the elements of each of these. The criteria are: external, operational, and ratio analysis. Another approach uses the tools of scientific management to analyze the effectiveness of each activity within an insurance company and to predict or simulate the effect of alternative management decisions.

EXTERNAL CRITERIA

The public is concerned with bases for comparing the external performance of companies. External criteria include: (1) service, (2) cost, (3) equity among policyholders, and (4) financial strength of the carrier. Each of these bases for comparison has a nonquantifiable element that makes evaluation difficult.

Service

Service to policyholders is essentially a function of the speed and fairness of claims settlement, the extent of contract coverages, and the reasonableness of underwriting practices. Service entails a ready response to policyholder inquiries, the recognition and implementation of all rights under a contract, and flexibility in amending contracts to meet the needs of insureds. Liberality with respect to cancellation features and stability of practices are other criteria.

While the typical consumer might recognize a need for information on the quality of services offered by an insurer, reliable and unbiased sources of information on this aspect of the insurance product are neither numerous nor precise. The negative aspect of services offered by an insurer may be measured by the number and type of complaints submitted to state insurance departments by policyholders. While state insurance departments may sometimes be informed sources of information, few consumers can afford to travel to the state capital for the purpose of reviewing such available public regulatory files on complaints. Most insurance regulators are willing to answer requests for general information about an insurer. However, they generally do not provide (for public distribution) summaries of complaints against insurers doing business in the state. The consumer must rely on local sources of information, such as bankers, lawyers, corporate insurance managers, friends, and insurance agents.

Cost

Traditionally, actuaries and insurance regulatory officials have been more concerned with alternative mortality tables, credibility of experience, and other mechanisms of rate making than with price studies which might assist consumers in their purchasing decisions. However, a recent trend toward the provision of comparative pricing data has emerged and the consumer can have access to several sources of comparative pricing data.[1]

The problem of price comparison is particularly relevant to the life insurance product. Given the technical nature of both the living and testamentary benefits of life insurance, an accurate price comparison of similar products is a difficult task for the typical consumer. Contemporary insurance analysts have concluded that a fair comparison of alternative life insurance prices requires more than an examination of premium charges. A fair comparison of life insurance costs requires inputs for the timing and quantity of both dividends and cash values. Furthermore, the more sophisticated analysts also include assumptions for alternative lapse and mortality rates. However, few insurance consumers have the time, desire, or capability to make the necessary technical reviews. In recognition of this potential problem several states, most notably Pennsylvania, have provided consumers with simple cost comparisons of numerous life insurance products. While there is extensive debate as to the merits of these "shopping list" comparisons, a trend toward more extensive price disclosures has started. The growth of consumerism has been influential. The National Association of Insurance Commissioners has considered a model price disclosure law, and this is being considered in many states.[2]

---

[1] *Cost, Facts in Life Insurance* (Cincinnati, Ohio: National Underwriter Company) provides detailed comparisons of life insurance prices with periodic revisions. Joseph M. Belth, *The Retail Price Structure in American Life Insurance,* (Bloomington, Indiana: Indiana University, 1966) is the standard reference on life insurance policy cost comparisons.

[2] See "Knauer, N.A.I.C. Differ on Way to Compare Life Policy Costs," *National Underwriter: Life and Health Insurance Edition* (July 18, 1972), pp. 1, 17.

Late in 1973, the Insurance Commissioner of California proposed a set of regulations requiring life insurance companies to disclose interest factors so that potential customers could make valid cost comparisons. The proposed "index" would outline for the prospective insured how much interest he could expect to earn if his premium payments, plus any dividends he might receive, were invested. The example would be required to use an interest rate of not less than 4 percent compounded annually and dividends based on the current dividend scale used by the insurance company.

Equity

Individual equity in insurance means that the insured pays a premium that reflects the hazards presented by him. However, where there is perfect equity, there is no way for the law of averages to work and there is zero credibility. To generate credible rates, the insurer must combine a large number of homogeneous risks in a group. If risks are divided into subgroups according to minute differences, the experience (or sample size) of each subgroup will be inadequate for the calculation of credible rates. Companies must compromise credibility with equity. Rate structures reflect an attempt to charge like rates for like risks. Insurance department examiners are concerned that equity prevails because this is required by the statutory definition of "not unfairly discriminatory" rates.

Financial Strength

Although there are no rigid guidelines, the financial strength of an insurance carrier is perhaps easier to quantify than the other external criteria. Generally, a company should have sufficient adjusted net worth, or policyholder surplus, to permit the offsetting of any unusual variance or experience. Reinsurance programs can help reduce the variance, but there is always a net retention that can prove troublesome, especially in lines where reserves are significant and difficult to estimate.

There are several sources of general information on the financial strength of insurers,[3] but the consumer must rely upon the regulatory authorities to ensure that all licensed insurance companies are able to meet policy obligations. Recognizing that some insurers become insolvent each year despite regulatory supervision, the professional insurance company analyst depends upon his informed judgment to adjust and evaluate reported financial data. Furthermore, the analyst may seek additional information from the insurer, regulator, or any other informed source. The first step usually taken by an analyst is to adjust the reserves (e.g., the unearned premium reserve and claims reserve of a property and liability insurer) to provide a more accurate reflection of an insurer's conventional earnings and surplus. The process of estimating claims reserves can easily lead to over or underreserving, and thus, a concurrent over or underestimate of profits.[4] The statutory requirement that property and liability

---

[3] Alfred M. Best and Company (Morristown, New Jersey) and The Spectator Company (Philadelphia, Pennsylvania) are perhaps the best known sources. For an evaluation of the rating system used by Best's, see Herbert S. Denenberg, "Is 'A-Plus' Really a Passing Grade?" *The Journal of Risk and Insurance,* XXXIV (September, 1967).

[4] John J. Anderson and Howard E. Thompson, "Financial Implications of Over-Reserving in Nonlife Insurance Companies," *The Journal of Risk and Insurance,* XXXVIII (September, 1971), p. 333. See also, Stephen Forbes, "Loss Reserving Performance Within the Regulatory Framework," *The Journal of Risk and Insurance,* XXXVII (December, 1970), pp. 521-38; and Dan Robert Anderson, "Effects of Under and Over-Evaluation of Loss Reserves," *The Journal of Risk and Insurance,* XXXVIII (December, 1971), pp. 585-600.

unearned premium reserves be based on the gross premium (including underwriting expenses and commissions) results in a distortion of surplus. While conservatism and prudence dictate the regulatory requirements, financial analysis requires adjustment of the data to determine relative strengths and weaknesses.

OPERATIONAL CRITERIA

In order to gain a realistic appraisal of an insurance company's effectiveness, the organization should be evaluated in functional terms. The elements include: organization and management, product research and development, underwriting and reinsurance, pricing flexibility, claims control, marketing, investments, financial planning, personnel training, and environmental adaptation. An analysis of these factors can provid a profile of the caliber of management.

Organization and Management

The successful company is normally characterized by a carefully designed organization structure with competent management. There should be a strong first echelon of executives, with at least one strong supplemental second echelon. The one man company is too vulnerable to autocratic leadership along with the hazard of sudden death or disability. The perpetuation of a business is largely dependent upon effective staffing and planning. The managerial functions must be performed well and not on an erratic basis.

Adam Smith stressed the importance of specialization and the economies derived from the division of labor. Organizations that have a higher degree of specialized departmentalization are more likely to be effective than organizations that have a low degree of specialization. Departmentalization is the manner in which the organization allocates the work among various divisions. Specialization is the degree to which the work of the division is interdependent.

Within an insurance organization there are several distinct functions that require specialization of labor. The actuary, the underwriter, the agent, and the claims adjuster all perform distinct functions requiring specialized training. Furthermore, if several of these functions are combined in one individual or decision center, there may be severe conflicts of interest. For example, the underwriting function generally should not be included in the sales department.

Product Research and Development

Of the myriad of products to be found in the insurance field, each company must develop its area of expertise or specialization. To attempt all things, or merely to follow the leader, is likely to leave a company behind in the race for better than average performance. The extent to which a company is able to respond to dynamic market conditions by designing new products, attempting new market approaches, and exhibiting a fresh enthusiasm about the product line will affect its performance.

Underwriting and Reinsurance

The underwriting procedures of a successful company are clearly defined and supervised. All of the rating criteria that can be codified are in manuals, and the underwriter is left to make decisions based upon processes that are carefully developed.

Reinsurance programs should be reviewed at regular intervals to determine whether the company is maximizing its opportunities under the various contracts in force.

Pricing Flexibility

Bureau rates and regulations govern a large part of the insurance field, but companies must be flexible in order to meet unusual situations. Where a company abdicates its rate making powers completely, it is unable to compete as effectively as it should.

Claims Control

A relatively tight claims control function with speedy follow-up on claims and procedures and the systematic and frequent review of files is an essential factor in good company management. The delays between occurrence and reporting of claims, between reporting of claims and investigation, and between investigation and settlement must be kept to a minimum. There are no norms here for guidance other than the criterion that wherever possible, the claims process should be shortened without allowing the quality of service to deteriorate.

Marketing

The loss ratio is an external measure of marketing effectiveness. However, an analysis of the selling cost per unit coupled with the loss experience may be more appropriate. Effective marketing requires: an agency force that is vital, a minimum policy size that is maintained at an adequate or economical level, and an average size of written premiums that is profitable.

Investments

The effectiveness of the investment program can be measured in terms of rates of return and the quality of the portfolio. Industry averages are readily available. A company should strive for the best combination of risk and return on investments available for companies of its size.

Financial Planning

Aside from the very large insurance companies, the amount of long range financial planning by insurers is minimal. Companies seem to plan for the current quarter or year with little thought for the long run. This results in many of the managerial functions being neglected because long range investments in staff and systems are not given adequate consideration. An efficient company will have a five-year plan with at least three years plotted on a quarter by quarter basis.

Personnel Training

Another important area of management that contributes to the performance of an insurer is effective training of company personnel. The insurance analyst might examine the extent to which employees are provided both formal and informal training. Even if an insurer hires only experienced personnel, new employees need a review of the specific work processes and employee standards under which they must operate. While some insurers implement extensive training programs, other insurance companies use on-the-job training. Either approach may achieve the goal of trained personnel. The point is not to favor any particular form of training but to emphasize the effectiveness of controlled guidance or supervision.

Personnel training may also take the form of providing a stimulus for self-education. This includes the provision of reading material, payment of education costs or salary increases for the attainment of degrees, diplomas, certificates, or professional designations. For example, insurance companies frequently pay the costs associated with an employee becoming a Chartered Life Underwriter (CLU) or a Chartered Property and Casualty Underwriter (CPCU). Both of these are professional designations obtained after passing a series of examinations on numerous topics (e.g., economics, finance, accounting, insurance principles, insurance law, etc.) and after working in the insurance industry or related institutions for a specified number of years.

Environmental Adaptation

Regulatory patterns and insurance customs differ so that each state has a somewhat unique environment. The successful company is able to adapt to local needs with an awareness of the special characteristics of different markets.

RATIO ANALYSIS

Ratio analysis is designed to transform the data in the insurer's balance sheet and income statement into a form that is more useful for decision-making. The balance sheet depicts the financial status of a business entity at a specific point in time. The income statement discloses the revenues, expenses, and net income (or net loss) resulting from the operation of a business over a period of time. While the financial statements of an insurer may appear complete, they have distinct limitations. First, they are essentially interim reports; the actual status of an insurance company cannot be known with certainty unless the business is sold or liquidated. Second, the exact dollar amounts shown in the statements give a misleading impression of accuracy. This is particularly true of insurance company loss reserves, which are at best educated estimates of potential losses. Third, transactions summarized in the statements occur at different times and present varying dollar values. Inflation automatically tends to increase dollar values and distorts the meaning of increases. A rising sales volume may reflect inflated prices rather than an increased number of units sold. Thus, comparisons between transactions at varying time periods can be misleading unless adjustments are made. Fourth, the financial statements fail to include "goingness" factors, such as the insurer's reputation or the number and quality of personnel. To the extent that these limitations affect an insurer's statements, the published figures require adjustment before meaningful ratios are constructed, or before comparisons of alternative ratios in various time periods are made.

Even if the financial statements were subject to none of these limitations, the insurance analyst would have difficulty in arriving at dependable decisions based on the raw data. He needs performance criteria, which are susceptible to easy comparison, and benchmarks of performance that reveal important relationships between the elements of insurance company financial statements. Ratios are commonly used to express, measure, analyze, and interpret these financial relationships.

While each financial ratio serves a useful purpose in the evaluation of an insurer, safe conclusions cannot be drawn from a review of a single ratio. No one ratio provides a comprehensive index of performance or solvency. The analyst examines groups of ratios and draws inferences from many observable trends. Expert judgment based on familiarity with a particular insurer is one of the most important complements to ratio analysis.

Insurance Ratios

Numerous ratios for the measurement of performance are employed in the insurance industry. Widely used are: the loss, expense, combined, Kenney, and cover ratios, among others.

The Loss Ratio. The most popular measure of underwriting performance is the loss ratio: the ratio of losses incurred to premiums earned. This is sometimes called the pure loss ratio because it does not include loss adjustment expenses. The ratio of losses plus loss adjustment expense incurred to premiums earned is the loss ratio used by financial analysts. Because there is a considerable time lag between calendar and policy years, the ratio of losses and loss adjustment expense incurred plus the reserve for losses incurred but not reported is sometimes related to net premiums written. For uniformity and intercompany comparisons it would appear that the ratio of losses and expense incurred to premiums earned is the most meaningful. Where different premiums are charged for the same class of risks (as in mutuals vs. stocks), the denominators will differ. Hence, it becomes necessary to verify rate structures in making intercompany comparisons.

The Expense Ratio. Expenses incurred to premiums written is widely used because much of the expense is related to the acquisition factor. Furthermore, the cost of sales must measure the full costs rather than just that which is reflected in earned premiums. However, a proper measure of underwriting profit would relate expenses incurred to premiums earned. These ratios may be distorted by special marketing practices or by the particular commission structures in use by a company.

The Combined Ratio. The combined or trade ratio is the sum of the loss and expense ratios. The measure is crude because it requires the addition of two fractions with unlike denominators. Nonetheless, its widespread use makes it a useful analytical tool.

The Kenney Rule. Roger Kenney published a number of popular ratios for measuring the capacity of an insurance company.[5] The Kenney ratios are widely employed, particularly by the regulatory authorities. One such rule of thumb is that a company in the property or liability insurance business should limit its net premiums written to no more than three times its policyholders' surplus. Another is that policyholder surplus should be no less than one-half of the reserves of the company. There are no counterpart ratios in life insurance.

---

[5] Roger Kenney, *Fundamentals of Fire and Casualty Insurance Strength,* 4th ed. (Dedham, Mass.: The Kenney Insurance Series, 1967).

While the Kenney ratios are commonly used as performance criteria, there is no scientific basis for their adoption.

The Cover Ratio.   In Great Britain and other countries the cover ratio is used as a measure of financial strength. This is the ratio of net premiums written to loss reserves plus policyholders' surplus. It is generally prescribed that there should be at least 250 percent of cover for the net premiums written. In workmen's compensation it is suggested that the net premiums written in a given year should not exceed 100 percent of the loss reserves for this line of insurance.

Actual to Expected Mortality.   In life insurance the ratio of actual to tabular mortality is sometimes used as a test of the adequacy of rates and reserves. This measure is useful internally but is ambiguous for intercompany comparisons because of differences in underwriting classifications, rates, and tables.

Interest Earned to Assumed.   Because of the importance of interest rates in life insurance contracts, a useful ratio is: interest actually earned to interest assumed for reserve calculations. This ratio should exceed 100 percent.

The Lapse Ratio.   In life insurance the potential return on sales is deferred for some years from the date the sale is made. Lapse or termination for any cause results in a loss of the potential income inherent in the insurance-in-force. Lapse ratios are therefore significant. The measure may be by policies or by insurance-in-force, but it is essentially the ratio of lapses during the year to total in force at the beginning of the year.

The Attrition Ratio.   In some respects the attrition ratio is more meaningful than the lapse ratio. This is measured as follows: the insurance-in-force at the beginning of the year, plus the insurance written during the year, less the insurance-in-force at the end of the year, divided by the insurance written during the year. This measures the ratio of lapse to insurance written. It indicates how much new production is required to overcome the force of attrition of business already on the books.

Ratio Analysis: An Example
of Regulatory Use

Many regulators review sets of financial ratios for the purpose of examining the financial stability of an insurer. However, the specific ratios examined and the extent of analysis vary from state to state. The variations result from the lack of conclusive evidence that any one set of ratios is optimum. Thus, the ratios used by specific states are not necessarily authoritative, but they provide useful guidelines for analysis. The following extract presents (1) an analysis of the ratios examined by one state insurance department, and (2) the standards established by that state for evaluating each ratio.

SOLIDITY CLASSIFICATION CRITERIA AND STANDARDS

These tests are intended to provide a means of identifying those companies that could have problems. No single test is generally sufficient to determine that a company is in hazardous condition, unless the degree of failure is extraordinarily excessive. Therefore, the percentages used are not absolute criteria, and conclusions will generally be based on the failure of several tests. When more than three tests are failed, additional analysis is done to assist in reaching a final conclusion.

1.   Bonds, Cash, and Preferred Stock % of Total Liabilities

Liabilities reflect the obligations of the insurance company and as such must be available at all times at specific values. This is necessary for continuous protection especially under the conditions of impairment or insolvency. In the case of impending insolvency the company must maintain the ability to retire all liabilities for their full value. To do so requires that liabilities be supported by such assets as bonds, cash and preferred stock. We utilize a standard of 90 percent rather than 100 percent, recognizing the equity in the unearned premium reserve.

2.   Common Stock % of Policyholders' Surplus

If over 100 percent of policyholders' surplus is placed in common stocks, then a portion of the liabilities payable by the company are in assets, the redemption value of which is uncertain. Any decline in the stock market would be reflected by a similar decline in surplus.

3.   Agents' Balances % of Policyholders' Surplus

It is apparent from a study of liquidated companies that substantial agents' balances have been used to inflate company assets. In every case studied to date, where a company has been liquidated, the agents' balances have been excessive or they have been reduced by extraordinarily heavy reinsurance transactions. Agents' balances equal to 1/3 of policyholder surplus would amount to 6.66 percent of that surplus if 20 percent of the balances were uncollectable. Double this amount of agents' balances or 2/3 would amount to almost 14 percent of surplus if 20 percent of the balances were uncollectable. It is this thinking that has produced a 1/3 rule-of-thumb.

4.   Policyholders Surplus % of Total Liabilities

Minimum of 35 percent.

5.   Risk Ratio (Net Written Premium/Policyholders Surplus)

Maximum of 400 percent.

6. Combined Loss and Expense Ratio

Maximum of 100 percent.

7. Policyholders Surplus % Change over Previous Year

A decrease of 20 percent would mean that a company would be out of business in five years; any amounts in excess of 20 percent would shorten this period of time.

8. Dividends Stockholders or Policyholders % of Net Income before Federal and Foreign Taxes

Maximum of 100 percent.

9. Paid Loss and Loss Expense Ratio to Outstanding Loss and Loss Expense Ratio

This test compares expenses actually paid on paid losses to the expenses reserved for unpaid losses. It is reasonable to assume that loss expenses on the unpaid will be comparable to expenses on the paid losses except for the fact that some expenses have been paid on claims still outstanding, so we allow for this fact by using a criterion of 70 percent.

10. % of Policyholder Surplus Invested in Owned or Controlled Subsidiaries

This test combined with the test immediately below would account for 58 percent of policyholder surplus leaving only 48 percent for deficiencies in the other tests. The existence of this permissible ratio on this item and the one below would more than double the exposure represented by the risk ratio. Maximum of 33 percent.

11. % of Policyholders' Surplus in Special Deposits Not Held for Protection of All Policyholders

When placed in light of the results of other critical tests, a 25 percent commitment of surplus to other than the company's policyholders is an item of critical concern. As in other tests, this item must be considered in light of the other weaknesses affecting the policyholders surplus.

12. Reinsurance Unearned Premium and Loss Recovery % of Policyholders' Surplus

Heavy reinsurance transactions have often been the vehicle for hiding nefarious activities of company officers. Perhaps more important, reinsurance does not solve basic underwriting problems that have a tendency to get worse when heavily reinsured because management does not take necessary underwriting steps when they are protected by reinsurance. The peril is that sooner or later the reinsurer gets tired of paying losses; the company has a very poor book of business and there is no place to go except down. Maximum of 100 percent.

13.   Schedule O Reserve Deficiency

This test compares the company's losses estimated last year with actual developments this year and in effect says that their estimates should have been at least 90 percent of the actual losses paid or not in excess of a 10 percent deficit. The 10 percent margin is allowed recognizing that some losses occurring at the end of last year may not be adequately reserved for.

14.   Schedule P Reserve Deficiency

Schedule P represents long term liability as opposed to the first party claims in Schedule O, but the comparison is identical. The 10 percent margin is allowed for those cases occurring at year end, which may not have been adequately reflected in either case base reserves or the IBNR.

15.   Losses that Should Have Been Reflected

Maximum of −10 percent.

SCIENTIFIC APPROACHES
TO INSURANCE COMPANY MANAGEMENT

The technology of insurance consists of a vast number of major functions, each of which can be analyzed in terms of specific tasks. Given the complexity of insurance operations, which are interrelated, the improvement of an insurer's performance lends itself to the application of a scientific approach in some areas.[6]

Extensive use of scientific methods as aids to decision-making in management evolved from World War II. During the war, the armed services developed applied mathematical approaches to complicated and detailed decision problems (e.g., submarine deployment, supply distribution, etc.). Concomitant with the development of applied mathematical approaches to decision-making was the development of sophisticated computer hardware and software (e.g., programming procedures). The availability of advanced electronic data processing equipment allowed the practical application of decision techniques that previously had only theoretical or experimental use.

The increasing emphasis on quantitative concepts and methodology did not neglect the behavioral sciences. Contemporary developments in management have emphasized the exploitation of advances in sociology, psychology,

[6] Alfred E. Hofflander and Milton Drandell, "A Linear Programming Model of Profitability, Capacity and Regulation in Insurance Management," *The Journal of Risk and Insurance,* XXXVI (March, 1969), p. 41. Linear programming approaches are being superceded by the technique of goal programming which permits a shifting of priorities among numerous goals in the solution of decision problems.

anthropology, and other social sciences. Managers have used the social sciences as a basis to reveal and solve problems that are relevant to the attitudes and actions of both workers and consumers.

Operations Research

Operations research uses scientific methods in order to represent complex functional relationships as mathematical models. This provides a quantitative basis for decision-making and uncovers new problems for quantitative analysis. Thus, the goal of operations research is to provide the primary decision-maker with information on individual factors, or the relationship between factors, that determine the end results of the business; how the business may respond to changes in these factors; and plan modifications that might tend to optimize the goals of the firm. The output of an operations research project is useful to the extent that it assists the decision-maker in either recognizing or solving important problems.

Proponents of operations research make the following distinctions between their work and that of allied groups.

Operations Research vs. Statistics.   The operations research analyst uses statistical methods when applicable, but he is not limited to these methods. His viewpoint differs from the statistician. Statistics is concerned primarily with reaching an understanding of the operation—of the underlying physical system which the numbers represent, rather than the decision process, *per se.*

Operations Research vs. Accounting.   The goals of the accountant are to implement controls and report financial data in accordance with conventional or standardized procedures. The operations research analyst is concerned with the analysis of problems and, therefore, needs data that are assimilated in terms of relevance to the problem in hand. Operations research, using the same raw accounting data, may use its own definitions, which serve the special needs of the particular study. One of the hurdles in the organization and implementation of an operations research study is the sorting of relevant cost data for analysis from accounting records.

Operations Research vs. Marketing Research.   Operations research differs from marketing research in that where the latter seeks an understanding of the market, the former is concerned with the marketing operation itself. The objective of operations research is to obtain a fundamental characterization of consumers for use in the model. Much of operations research in marketing problems is directed toward clarifying the interdependencies between marketing and other company operations. It draws on techniques well beyond the scope of conventional marketing research.

Operations Research as a Science. The essential distinction between operations research and allied disciplines is the fact that the operations analyst is not an "expert" but rather a "scientist." His value is not in his knowledge or business experience but rather in his attitude and methodology.

Operations Research in Insurance. For operations research to be an effective management tool there must be: (1) opportunities for decision between alternative courses of action, (2) feasibility of quantitative study or measurement, (3) availability of relevant and accurate data, (4) a means of rapid data manipulation (e.g., computer facilities), and (5) the capacity to comprehend and have faith in decisions suggested by the methodology. Unless these conditions are met, operations research may become an irrelevant and expensive exercise in the generation of useless data "output." Many problems in insurance company management are subject to solution by operations research. For example, developing an optimum organizational structure, product and marketing plans, pricing, underwriting and claims policies, reinsurance and retention programs, agents' compensation and investment plans.

The "Model Office" in Life Insurance. A model office has been defined as a mathematical formula that represents a particular cause and effect relationship so that assumed data, representing a particular course of action, can be inserted and an estimation of the results to be attained observed. It is used constantly in actuarial studies of the impact of different decisions on the book of business or on existing practices. The life insurance actuary uses the operations research approach extensively in his rate making and reserving activities. Some applications include: using numerical methods in underwriting, testing for different retention policies in reinsurance, testing different combinations of fixed and variable costs in acquisition costs and testing direct mail runs and other lead advertising media in marketing. As a forecasting device, the model office can be used to develop norms for decision-making about growth rates, policy lines, surplus strain and numerous other factors. The life insurance company is compelled to maintain substantial unit information and, perhaps, lends itself, more than other types of carrier, to the operations research approach. The earliest applications of computers were in this area.

SIMULATION MODELS IN PROPERTY AND LIABILITY INSURANCE

Because the underlying distributions of the frequency and severity of losses by exposure are reasonably well known to the casualty actuary, it would appear that model offices could be developed using simulation techniques in the multiple lines fields. In fact, this approach is still relatively uncommon. Precisely the same kinds of analysis that are used in life insurance would be applicable to the determination of underwriting and claims policy, reinsurance, and marketing strategies. The unit statistical data is presently collected through bureaus for conventional rating purposes, and there is the belief (but inadequate explanation) in many companies that classifications are too thin to permit valid experimentation. Reinsurance models have been used extensively as training devices. These simulation devices can be applied to concrete problems, and their inferences used meaningfully in the decision-making process.

The Behavioral Sciences and Insurance Company Management

The behavioral scientist is concerned with the study of human responses to various stimuli. He relies primarily on the body of theory and postulates provided by psychology, sociology, social psychology, and anthropology. His method is to assimilate data in a systematic and valid manner, analyze data based on generally accepted criteria, and apply the results of his experimentation to the solution of problems relevant to a business environment. Whereas a physical scientist generally functions in the controlled environment of a laboratory, his behavioral counterpart deals with human emotions, perceptions, and responses which cannot be fully observed or controlled in an experiment. The lack of scientific precision in observation and results does not negate the contribution of the behavioral scientist to informed decision-making. Insurance companies have used behavioral science in such areas as: (1) recruiting, testing, training and motivating individual employees; (2) evaluating and changing group and organizational behavior, and (3) consumer research and product development.

Individual Behavior.   Management must be able to evaluate and influence employee attitudes and actions in order to achieve its objectives. Individuals respond to their need for self actualization, esteem, love, and safety more than they do to the needs of their employers. Failure by management to recognize, evaluate, and respond to these needs may lead to goal conflicts that are detrimental to the organization. Insurance companies have been active supporters of research in the problems of individual behavior.

Group Behavior.   In addition to individual responses, the behavioral scientist is concerned with how individuals, groups, and organizations will interact under varying conditions; what lines of communication are generally required in order to facilitate required interaction, and what motivation or leadership style is most effective. The question is: are the needs of the formal and informal groups compatible with the goals of the firm? If not, the behavioral scientist attempts to determine the reasons for incongruity and ways to resolve it. Like individuals, groups wish to contribute to the establishment of organizational goals, to be judged by them, and to receive feedback as to their contribution. The understanding of group dynamics is a research objective pursued in some insurance companies.

Market Behavior.   The behavioral scientist is also concerned with consumer responses to the insurer's product. Insurance is generally purchased for the dual purpose of achieving financial security and reducing anxiety. The behavioral scientist evaluates the extent to which insurance contracts (and their associated services) reduce or remove consumer anxiety. Thus, he must deal with consumer perceptions of the benefits of specific insurance products. If the insurer fails to effectively communicate a specific anxiety reducing product benefit, the behavioral scientist may be able to determine the cause and advise the insurer. Furthermore, he may be able to assist the insurer in developing a marketing strategy that will communicate the benefits of the insurance product.

SUMMARY

The performance of an insurer may be measured in many ways. One approach defines criteria that are expressed objectively and measured by various ratios. These may be derived from external data, operational information, or by a combination of factors. Another approach studies performance with the aid of operations research methods. Yet another analysis examines the company in terms of behavioral science norms.

The most important consideration is the set of goals of the firm and the manner of their realization. There are many paths to the common objective of optimization of performance. Regulatory authorities are more concerned with marginal performance and have developed solidity classification tests as guidelines.

The principal determinant of an acceptable measure of insurer performance is the objective of the analyst. The consumer is concerned with service, cost, and equity; the stockbroker with profitability, management, product research, and marketing; the regulator with solvency, product availability, and market practices.

REVIEW QUESTIONS

1. Ratio analysis is widely used in the evaluation of the financial strength of fire and casualty insurance carriers. What are the principal ratios employed for this purpose? Explain each carefully.

2. What general factors should a consumer evaluate in selecting an

insurance carrier? Where can he obtain information about these factors? Discuss.

3. The "non-admitted assets" and "unearned premium reserves" provide margins of safety in fire and casualty insurance company balance sheets. Explain.

4. What criteria do you believe to be important in evaluating the effectiveness of a liability insurer's claims department? Discuss.

5. "The only market research I need is the name and address of a life insurance prospect for my salesman to talk to tomorrow morning." Discuss this assertion made by a senior executive of a medium size life insurance company.

STUDY QUESTIONS

6. What would you expect the effect of the movement toward Generally Accepted Accounting Principles (GAAP) to be on inter-company performance comparisons? Discuss.

7. The potential for computer fraud presents significant limitations on ratio analysis for insurance company financial strength and performance. How can such fraud be detected by auditors? Explain.

8. Insurance companies typically do not have major research and development departments. How do you account for this? Explain.

9. Reduction of the expense ratio may reflect (1) better cost controls, (2) a prevailing rate level which is too high, or (3) a shift in the product mix. Discuss.

10. The Large Insurance Company is interested in the possibility of acquiring one of two available insurance companies with a view to merger. The only criteria they are interested in relate to the size of policyholders' surplus and the underwriting experience of the two candidates for merger. Both candidates write the same lines of insurance in approximately the same proportions. The available data for 1972 and 1973 are as follows:

	Carrier A	Carrier B
Policyholders' Surplus (1972)	$5,000,000	$4,000,000
Unearned premium reserve (1972)	4,500,000	5,500,000
Loss reserve (1972)	4,000,000	4,500,000
Assets (1972)	15,000,000	14,750,000
Unearned premium reserve (1973)	3,500,000	3,500,000
Loss reserve (1973)	3,000,000	3,000,000
Losses paid (1973)	2,000,000	2,000,000
Premiums written (1973)	4,000,000	4,500,000
Expenses paid (1973)	1,000,000	1,500,000

(a) Calculate the policyholders' surplus for each company and indicate which has the more favorable position.

(b) Calculate the loss ratio of each company and indicate its significance.

(c)   Calculate the expense ratio of each company and evaluate.
(d)   Which of the two carriers should the Large Company buy? Explain.

VII

CONSUMERIST
PERSPECTIVES

The consumer is interested in the availability of the kinds of insurance he needs, at fair prices, with adequate information about the product, and with proper treatment by those who are licensed to supply the service.

Part VII describes social insurance and some of the techniques of risk management and estate planning that provide guidelines for the intelligent buyer of insurance. The consumerist movement in the insurance field is explored in terms of health, automobile, life, and workmen's compensation insurance.

The insurance industry supplies the products that appear to be in greatest demand. The consumer who understands his needs can be a force for change.

27

Social

Insurance

INTRODUCTION

Unlike many other nations, the problem of economic security in the United States is attacked with a great variety of approaches whose extremes are private insurance and social insurance.[1] There is some overlap in coverage, but the philosophy and basis of the two approaches are fundamentally different. To the extent that private enterprise is able to meet the problem of economic security at a level of performance that is socially acceptable, it is free to function on a profit seeking basis. However, when private insurers are unable or unwilling to achieve social goals, the government enters, and social insurance mechanisms evolve. The balance of power between private and social sectors varies in different countries. The trend has been toward a greater role on the part of government.

[1] See J. Douglas Brown, *An American Philosophy of Social Security* (Princeton, N.J.: Princeton University Press, 1972); *Social Security Programs throughout the World* (Washington, D.C.: Dept. of Health, Education and Welfare Publication No. (SSA) 72-11802, 1971); George E. Rejda, "Social Security and the Paradox of the Welfare State," *The Journal of Risk and Insurance*, XXXVII (March, 1970), p. 17.

EVOLUTION OF U.S. SOCIAL INSURANCE

Despite the adoption of social insurance legislation in Europe during the nineteenth century, the United States waited until the Great Depression of the 1930s before taking affirmative action. Prior to 1935, private charity and public welfare or relief were the only economic provisions made for the destitute. The Social Security Act of 1935 provided public assistance, unemployment insurance, and old age insurance. This act has been amended at every session of the Congress since 1935, and all aspects of the program have frequently been liberalized. However, the continuing philosophy underlying Social Security is that the government should provide only a floor of subsistence income.

PURPOSE AND SCOPE OF SOCIAL INSURANCE

Social insurance is designed for problems in which a social need is best met by a combination of the insurance mechanism and government participation. This is the case where the solution to a social problem is beyond the capacity of individuals or the private enterprise system. For example, mass unemployment or old age dependency for low income families are catastrophic events that are not insurable hazards.

Security may be defined as "freedom from economic uncertainty." Economic security requires confidence that lost income will be replaced. Social insurance mechanisms are designed to help provide this security.

Social Insurance vs. Public Assistance

There is an important distinction between social insurance and public assistance. Social insurance is provided as a matter of statutory right, whereas public assistance is usually based on a means test with benefit amounts within the discretion of an administering agency. Of the two, only social insurance provides guaranteed benefit rights.

· The contrasts between Social Security and public assistance can be seen in the many differences in the principles of operation of the systems.

1. In social insurance, benefits are based on presumptive need. For example, it is presumed that all persons reaching retirement age will need a stream of income to replace what was generated by gainful employment. The presumption exists regardless of actual need. In public assistance, benefits are granted only to those who can demonstrate hardship or need; and social workers determine the amounts of what are, in effect, public charity benefits.

2. Social insurance contemplates a floor of protection for everyone at a

level related in some manner to the cost of living. The vast majority of individuals will be kept at a level above destitution, and those still in need can be cared for by supplementary public assistance. In contrast, the public assistance program contemplates interim assistance according to individual needs with no firm formula for what constitutes adequacy.

3. In social insurance, benefits are related to earnings by a statutory formula. However, the formula is weighted so that there is only moderate individual equity. Lower income workers receive benefits in a higher proportion to their contributions than do higher income contributors. In public assistance there may be no statutory formulas and no actuarial linkage between benefits and earnings.

4. Individual equity, balanced by social adequacy, is a principle of social insurance not found in public assistance. The latter program is not concerned with individual equity in a contractual sense. The welfare agency has no contractual obligations to provide an equitable flow of benefits.

5. Actuarial balance, whereby the program is expected to be selfsupporting, is a principle of social insurance.[2] Public assistance, however, is regarded as a form of relief or charity and is based on needs as they arise. While the Social Security System withdraws a specified amount from each individual's earnings, there are no similar taxes earmarked for public assistance programs.

6. Fixed duration of benefits is characteristic of social insurance but not of public assistance.

7. Federal administration is a feature of social insurance that is not characteristic of public assistance, even though the federal government provides a large share of the financing.

Social Insurance vs. Private Insurance

Social insurance may also be compared with private insurance:

"1. Private insurance must be based on individual equity; social insurance, although possibly having certain individual equity features, must generally contain a considerable degree of emphasis on social adequacy principles.

2. Private insurance is on a voluntary basis as to participation (under some employee benefits plans, the employee must participate, but the employer's action in establishing the plan is voluntary—even under collective bargaining); social insurance almost invariably is based on compulsory participation.

3. Private insurance involves complete contractual rights between the

[2] Robert J. Myers, "Various Proposals to Change the Financing of Social Security," *The Journal of Risk and Insurance*, XXXVI (September, 1969), p. 355.

two parties (the insurer always has the right to terminate the contract on nonpayment of premiums; but usually, it must continue the contract in force for the period specified; social insurance does not involve a strictly contractual relationship, although the benefits involve a statutory right (but the statutory provisions can be changed from time to time by the legislature).

4. Private individual insurance must be fully funded so that the rights of the insureds are protected, and this is a desired goal of private pension plans (but note that under the latter, full funding is often not present, especially with regard to prior-service benefits); social insurance, because of its compulsory and statutory nature, need not be fully funded—in fact, it is generally thought that from an economic standpoint, full funding is undesirable."[3]

There are conflicts between private insurance companies and the advocates of an enlarged federal government role in social insurance. However, the individual consumer as taxpayer and premium payer does well to consider his personal economic security plan as a combination of all programs available to him. The Economic Security Pyramid (see Figure 27.1) suggests that government, the employer, and the employee each has a contribution to make to a program of personal income maintenance.

FIGURE 27.1 The Pyramid of Economic Security

In brief, the main characteristics of social insurance appear to be: (1) compulsory contributions, (2) set formulae or benefit levels, (3) a floor of protection, (4) subsidy, (5) flexibility to allow payment to those elements of the

[3] Robert J. Myers, *Social Insurance and Allied Government Programs* (Homewood, Ill.: Richard D. Irwin, Inc., 1965), p. 9.

population in greatest need, and (6) unpredictable or catastrophic nature of losses covered by the system.

RECOGNITION OF NEEDS FOR SOCIAL INSURANCE

The changing attitudes of the general public, governmental bodies, and private business led to a wider recognition of the problems that may be solved with social insurance.

Due to increased education and communication, the public has become aware of its ability to influence the economic environment. This public awareness has been promoted by all of the communications media.

The low income and depressed groups increasingly recognize and use their economic and political bargaining power. Economic and political institutions are geared for well-organized complaints by such groups.

The government is aware of unmet social needs. There is recognition that no democratic society can long endure the existence of a substantial number of citizens who feel deeply aggravated as a group.

Businessmen have also learned that disregard of social needs can be fatal to an economy or an industry. Unless problems of income insecurity are solved, the potential acceptable market for various industries may fail to grow.

THE SCOPE OF SOCIAL INSURANCE

The scope of social insurance has been defined along the following lines:

> Generally . . . social security is defined as including only a . . . restricted scope of programs, namely, (1) those providing cash payments to persons and families whose income from earnings has ceased or diminished, either temporarily or permanently; (2) those furnishing medical care to persons and families receiving benefits under item (1), or, under certain circumstances, to all persons of a given category; and (3) those providing cash payments to all children of a given category, regardless of the presence or absence of parents who could support such children, and regardless of whether such support is being given or in what quantity.[4]

The International Labor Organization (Convention No. 102) provides a good summary of the potential branches or types of social security: (1) old age benefits, (2) survivor benefits, (3) disability benefits, (4) unemployment benefits, (5) sickness benefits, (6) medical care, (7) maternity benefits, (8)

[4]*Ibid.*, p. 3.

industrial injury benefits, and (9) family allowances. Private insurance is directly involved in all of these, with the possible exception of unemployment insurance.

OLD-AGE, SURVIVORS, DISABILITY, AND HEALTH INSURANCE (OASDHI)

The OASDHI Program contains the various elements of the Social Security Act. OASDHI is the only major social insurance program in the United States that is both federally administered and financed. While the original 1935 Social Security Act provided only for retirement income, the act has been amended frequently to expand the set of potential benefits. The actual dollar benefits paid to a beneficiary vary significantly from case to case, depending on such factors as period of coverage in the system and average wages. Benefits include: retirement income, survivor benefits to dependent widows (or widowers) and children, disability income, and medicare.

Eligibility

Employees who are eligible for retirement, disability, or survivorship benefits are classified as either fully insured or currently insured. Current status is obtained when an individual has been in covered employment for at least six quarters during a thirteen quarter period. A quarter of employment is a calendar quarter, or three months, in which the employee earned at least $50 in a job that is not exempt from Social Security. To qualify for fully insured status, a worker must have worked at least one quarter per calendar year since either 1950 or the attainment of age twenty-one. However, once an individual has worked forty quarters he is fully insured. Table 27.1 shows the requirements for fully insured status.

TABLE 27.1   Social Security Insured Status[a]

If you reach 65 (62 for women) or die, or become disabled	You will be fully insured if you have credit for this much work
In 1971	5 years
*1975	6
*1979	7
*1983	8
*1987	9
*1991 or later	10

[a]The data provided in this text are for illustrative purposes only. Current information is available from the Social Security Administration and its many publications.

*For 1975 and after, consider the year in which men reach age 62.

Attainment of fully insured status qualifies the worker for certain benefits that are not available to workers with only current status. For example, for a widow with no dependent children to receive survivors' benefits, the deceased spouse must have been fully insured. Fully insured status is also a requirement for disability income benefits.

Nearly all individuals over age sixty-five qualify for Medicare[5] (health insurance for the elderly), including many individuals who are not eligible for cash income Social Security benefits. All individuals reaching sixty-five prior to 1968 were automatically qualified. Those reaching sixty-five after 1967 needed only three-quarters of coverage for each year after 1965 to qualify. After 1974, those reaching sixty-five required fully insured status to qualify.

Retirement Income

Retirement income is available at age sixty-two to all qualified workers. However, the worker can obtain a larger retirement income by waiting to age sixty-five. The income received is a direct function of the worker's average wages during the period from age twenty-two to retirement (excluding the five years when wages were lowest).

While retirement income increases with average wages, the formula adopted by the government favors lower income workers. Average wages above a maximum amount are not included in the calculation of retirement income. Furthermore, a 1972 amendment to the Social Security Act provided a special minimum benefit for low income workers. The minimum benefit is equal to $8.50 multiplied by the number of years of covered work in excess of ten (up to a maximum of thirty years). Thus, a low income worker who has been in covered employment for thirty years or more would receive a minimum individual retirement benefit of $170 per month (or $255 minimum for a couple). The special minimum benefits are paid as an alternative to regular benefits when the regular benefits would be lower.

In addition to the primary insurance amount provided the retired worker, there are benefits for dependents. These benefits are expressed as a percentage of the primary insurance amount. However, the total monthly income provided any one family is subject to a specified maximum.

Table 27.2 shows the average benefits[6] received by retired workers between 1940 and 1971. The benefits paid have obviously increased substantially, but the current level of payments remains low in relation to the cost of living.

---

[5] Robert J. Myers, *Medicare* (Homewood, Ill.: Richard D. Irwin, Inc., 1970).

[6] Theoretically, a retired worker with full coverage could collect $354.50 in 1972, but most work records are not at maximum levels for benefits and most workers receive considerably less than the benefit rates advertised. The disparity between the maximum and actual benefit levels are greater for the dependent spouse and dependent children.

TABLE 27.2   Average Retirement Benefits Paid, 1940-1971

Year	Retired Worker	Dependent Spouse	Dependent Children
1940	$22.60	$12.13	$9.70
1945	24.19	12.82	11.74
1950	43.86	23.60	17.05
1955	61.90	33.07	20.01
1960	74.04	38.72	28.25
1965	83.92	43.63	31.98
1970	118.10	61.19	44.85
1971	132.16	68.35	49.64

SOURCE: *Social Security Bulletin,* U.S. Department of Health, Education and Welfare (Washington, D.C.: U.S. Government Printing Office, April, 1972), p. 40.

Table 27.3 shows the benefits available to a retired worker (and his dependents) at varying rates of average monthly income. Note that the insured worker also receives benefits for his wife, the amount of which is dependent upon whether she is sixty-five or under when her husband retires. If she is sixty-five or older, her benefit is one-half as much as her husband's, but only one-third if she is between sixty-two and sixty-five. Should the insured worker elect to retire at age sixty-two, his primary benefits would be 80 percent of those received if retirement starts at age sixty-five. However, the benefits for the wife remain as if the worker retired at age sixty-five.

TABLE 27.3   Retirement Benefit Levels, 1972

	Average Monthly Wage			
	$450	$550	$650	$750
Worker at 65	$250.60	$288.40	$331.00	$354.50
Wife at 65	125.30	144.20	165.50	177.30
Worker at 62	200.50	230.80	264.80	283.60
Wife at 62	94.00	108.20	124.20	133.00

SOURCE: U.S. Social Security Administration.

If the insured worker predeceases his wife, total payments to the wife at age 65 are 100 percent of the benefits that the husband would have received at age 65. However, if the widow starts receiving benefits at age 62, her benefits will be 82.5 percent of her husband's benefits. While this is a relative increase to the wife, total benefits for the family unit are reduced upon the husband's death.

The retired worker's ability to collect his full retirement benefits is subject to an earnings test. A retired worker can earn up to $2,100 in annual wages (or $75 in any one month) without affecting his Social Security benefits. However, benefits are reduced by $1 for each $2 of wages above $2,100. Prior to a 1972 amendment, benefits were reduced by $1 for each $1 of earnings above $2,880. But Congress believed this placed an unfair burden on those who desired to earn additional wages. The 1972 Amendment assures a retired worker that the more he works and earns, the more discretionary income he will have.

Survivors' Benefits

Survivors' benefits under Social Security include: a small lump sum payment to the surviving spouse, monthly income to a spouse over age sixty-two, monthly income for dependent children or parents, and monthly income for a mother until the youngest child reaches age eighteen. The amount of these benefits is a specified percentage of the worker's primary insurance amount.

Table 27.4 outlines the benefits that have been available to the survivors of a fully insured worker.

TABLE 27.4 Survivors' Benefits

Type of Benefit	Amount of Benefit (as % of insured worker's amount
A. Monthly income	
1. Widow 65 or older	100%
2. Widow over 62 or, if disabled, over 50	82.5%
3. Widow under 62 with children under 18	75.0%
4. Children up to 18, or to 22 if continue in school	75.0% each
5. Dependent parents over 62	150.0% so long as both alive 82.5% for only one
B. Lump Sum Paid to either spouse or bearer of burial expense	300.0% or $255, whichever is less

Disability Insurance Benefits

Should the worker become permanently and totally disabled before age sixty-five, he would be eligible to receive a monthly income after a waiting period. The Social Security Administration defines disability as "unable to engage in substantial gainful activity by reason of a medically determinable physical or mental impairment that is expected to last or has lasted for twelve months or can be expected to result in death."

The amount of the disability benefit is calculated as if the worker were retired. Disability payments continue to age sixty-five, at which time benefits are changed to retirement payments at the same rate. In addition to income payments, the disabled worker may be provided with vocational rehabilitation by a state rehabilitation agency.

Health Insurance

In 1965, the Social Security Act was amended to include hospital insurance (i.e., Medicare). The supplement to Social Security provides persons at least sixty-five years of age with hospital, extended care facility, and home health service benefits. In addition to these benefits, which are automatic, there is voluntary supplementary medical insurance. This program provides doctor's services and medical supplies for a modest annual charge.

Funding

The Old-Age, Survivors, Disability, and Health Insurance (OASDHI) program is financed through compulsory payroll-tax deductions. Workers and employers each pay 5.85 percent of the first $10,800 earned each year. This wage base is automatically adjusted upward as wage levels rise. Table 27.5 shows the contribution rate schedule for employers, employees, and self-employed workers. The schedule applies to the first $10,500 of earnings for 1973, the first $12,000 for 1974, with automatic increases thereafter.

Critics of Social Security funding contend that Social Security is a tax rather than a premium. Originally, OASDHI payments were to be made from an accumulated reserve fund on an actuarially sound basis. In 1939, the act was amended to permit "pay-as-you-go" financing. At present, payroll taxes are transferred from the Internal Revenue Service to OASDHI trust funds from which disbursements are made. If taxes and interest on trust-fund investments exceed benefits paid, the size of the trust fund increases. Reserves are calculated on the basis of covering only nine months in benefits. The regressive nature of the Social Security tax as a method of financing income maintenance programs has led to proposals for a negative income tax as a more equitable method of spreading the costs over a broader tax base.[7]

---

[7]Donald J. Mullineaux, "Paying for Social Security: Is it Time to 'Retire' The Payroll Tax?" *Business Review*, April, 1973, Federal Reserve Bank of Philadelphia, pp. 3-10. See also, John A. Brittain, *The Payroll Tax for Social Security* (Washington, D.C.: The Brookings Institution, 1972); Martin Feldstein, "The Incidence of the Social Security Payroll Tax: A Comment," *American Economic Review*, 72 (1972), pp. 735-38.

TABLE 27.5 Social Security Funding Schedule

Year	OASDHI	HI	Total
	Employer and Employee (Each)		
1973-77	4.85%	1.00%	5.85%
1978-80	4.80	1.25	6.05
1981-85	4.80	1.35	6.15
1986-92	4.80	1.45	6.25
1993-97	4.80	1.45	6.25
1998-2010	4.80	1.45	6.25
2011 and thereafter	5.85	1.45	7.30
	Self-Employed		
1973-77	7.00%	1.00%	8.00%
1978-80	7.00	1.25	8.25
1981-85	7.00	1.35	8.35
1986-92	7.00	1.45	8.45
1993-97	7.00	1.45	8.45
1998-2010	7.00	1.45	8.45

SOURCE: Social Security Administration.

Automatic Adjustment of Benefits and Costs

Starting in 1974, Social Security cash benefits were subject to automatic "cost-of-living" increases. The law specified a formula that ties benefits with a change in the arithmetical mean of the Consumer Price Index (CPI) prepared by the Department of Labor for April, May, and June. The mean CPI for any one year is divided by a like mean for a base year (i.e., 1972 or the year in which the last "cost-of-living" increase occurred). If the quotient is greater than or equal to 3 percent, a benefit increase of the same percentage becomes effective on January 1 of the following year.

When an automatic increase in benefits occurs, a determination is also made of the need to automatically increase the maximum taxable earnings. In general, contribution adjustments are made in light of changes in the average taxable wages of all employees included in the Social Security program.

UNEMPLOYMENT INSURANCE

Unemployment insurance is designed primarily for short term involuntary unemployment.[8] This type of insurance is not intended to deal with all forms or

[8]William Haber and Merrill G. Murray, *Unemployment Insurance in the American Economy* (Homewood, Ill.: Richard D. Irwin, Inc., 1966). William Papier, "What's Wrong with Unemployment Insurance?" *The Journal of Risk and Insurance*, XXXVII (March, 1970), p. 63.

causes of unemployment. The most obvious exclusions are: the disabled worker who is unable to accept a job (i.e., usually a requirement for benefits), and victims of long term unemployment. Furthermore, state laws do not require all workers to be covered. Uncovered employments frequently include: farm workers, part-time workers, domestic servants, employees of nonprofit organizations, and self-employed workers. In addition, the states usually exclude employees working for firms with a minimum number of workers or working for a covered employer less than a minimum period. It has been estimated that a little over one-half of all unemployed workers are actually covered by unemployment insurance.

Benefits

Since the states administer their own programs, there are variations in benefit levels and requirements for coverage. In most states the benefits received are a specified percentage of wages earned during the year prior to presenting a claim. Furthermore, benefits will usually not be paid beyond twenty-six weeks. Benefit receipt is usually conditioned upon willingness to accept suitable work, availability for work, and nonreceipt of other specified benefits (e.g., workmen's compensation). To solve the problems of the disabled worker who does not qualify for unemployment benefits, a few states have adopted temporary disability laws. These laws provide benefits to temporarily disabled workers. The benefits are usually comparable to unemployment compensation.

Funding

Unemployment insurance is partially financed by the federal government, but is administered at the state level. The Federal Unemployment Tax Act provides the financing of the insurance. Employers are taxed at a flat rate on a maximum earnings limit per employee. However, the employer is allowed to credit against the federal tax a significant portion of any contributions made under a state unemployment compensation plan.

WORKMEN'S COMPENSATION

Workmen's compensation was the first form of social insurance implemented in the United States. It is referred to as social insurance only because: (1) the states require its use by most employers, (2) the states administer the benefits and costs of workmen's compensation insurance, and (3) several states actually provide the required insurance. However, most workmen's compensation insurance is provided by private insurers. Many large industrial firms self-insure their exposures.

TABLE 27.6 Workmen's Compensation Payments: 1950 to 1970

[Workers in millions; benefits in millions of dollars. Prior to 1960, excludes Alaska and Hawaii. See also Historical Statistics, Colonial Times to 1957, series H 175-185]

Item	1950	1955	1960	1965	1967	1968	1969	1970
Workers covered per month, estimate	37	41	45	51	55	57	59	59
Benefits paid during year	615	916	1,295	1,814	2,189	2,369	2,624	2,927
Type of insurance:								
Private carriers[1]	381	563	810	1,124	1,363	1,482	1,641	1,844
State funds[2]	149	238	325	445	524	557	607	669
Employers' self-insurance[3]	85	115	160	244	303	331	376	414
Type of benefit:								
Medical and hospitalization	200	325	435	600	750	830	920	1,050
Compensation payments	415	591	860	1,214	1,439	1,539	1,704	1,877
Disability	360	521	755	1,074	1,284	1,374	1,519	1,672
Survivor	55	70	105	140	155	165	185	205
Percent of payroll covered:								
Workmen's compensation costs[4]	0.89	0.91	0.93	1.00	1.07	1.07	1.07	1.13
Benefits	0.54	0.55	0.59	0.62	0.64	0.63	0.63	0.68

[1] Net cash and medical benefits paid under standard workmen's compensation policies.

[2] Net cash and medical benefits paid by competitive and exclusive State funds and by Federal workmen's compensation programs.

[3] Cash and medical benefits paid by self-insurers, plus value of medical benefits paid by employers carrying workmen's compensation policies that exclude standard medical coverage.

[4] Premiums written by private carriers and State funds and benefits paid by self-insurers increased by 5-10 percent to allow for administrative costs. Also includes benefits paid and administrative costs of Federal workmen's compensation programs.

SOURCE: U.S. Social Security Administration, *Annual Statistical Supplement* to the *Social Security Bulletin.*

Workmen's compensation is based on state statutes that hold the employers liable for industrial accidents. Prior to workmen's compensation laws, an employee seeking compensation for his injuries had to demonstrate that: (1) the employer was negligent, (2) the employee himself or a fellow worker was not contributorily negligent, and (3) the employee had not assumed the risk that led to his injury. Furthermore, there was a natural reluctance to sue one's employer if continued employment was desired. The need for a more equitable and efficient system for compensating industrial accident victims led to the adoption of workmen's compensation laws.

The Occupational Safety and Health Act of 1970 was designed to create action programs for reducing injuries, illnesses, and deaths connected with working conditions, increase the numbers of people trained in health and safety techniques, develop greater knowledge of occupational accidents and illness, announce and enforce effective standards for compliance. The Act also established the National Commission on State Workmen's Compensation Laws whose task was to study and evaluate the existing system of workmen's compensation. The 1972 report of the National Commission concluded that the current state laws were neither adequate nor equitable and numerous recommendations were made for legislative and administrative reform. The impact of OSHA on safety engineering and legislative change in the states was impressive.

AN INTERNATIONAL VIEW OF SOCIAL SECURITY

The term *social security* is in wide international use. Article 25 of the Universal Declaration of Human Rights as proclaimed by the United Nations (in 1948) provides for "freedom from want and social security." The concept of social security has spread universally, and institutions designed to provide income security are found in most nations. However, the degree to which these institutions provide income protection for covered workers varies from country to country. It has been estimated that only one-tenth of all people in the world are covered by social security institutions. But in some countries expenditures for social security account for a very significant portion of national income.

A study conducted by the European Common Market in 1972[9] indicated the proportions of national income devoted to social security by various western countries as follows: France, 20.9 percent; West Germany, 21.4 percent; Italy, 20.3 percent; Belgium, 21 percent; Netherlands, 21.5 percent; U.S.S.R., 11 percent; Japan, 6 percent; and the United States, 7 percent. In most European countries contributions are made by employers, employees, and by the government.

The most generally accepted meaning of the term social security is found in the Declaration of Human Rights of the United Nations, which refers to "the

---

[9]"Social Security Costs Represent More Than 20% of the Revenues of the Six Countries of the Common Market," *Le Soir*, Paris (July 8, 1972), p. 11.

right to security in the event of unemployment, sickness, disability, widowhood, old age, or other lack of livelihood in circumstances beyond his (the individual's) control" and "a standard of living adequate for the health and well-being of himself and his family, including food, clothing, housing, medical care, and necessary social services." However, what is considered as "adequate" varies significantly by region.

Social Security has been provided in numerous ways, but two major methods of social security have evolved: public assistance and social insurance. Public assistance evolved much earlier than social insurance and still holds a position of great importance. Social insurance is a relatively new concept.

The greatest growth in social insurance occurred after World War II. During this period, many countries expanded their industrialization and adopted relatively comprehensive social insurance laws. However, the expansion of social security and social insurance has brought with it an awareness that such programs are no guarantee of automatic and immediate economic security. Increased productivity of goods and services and an equitable distribution of the resulting national income must complement social security.

SUMMARY

Social insurance is a technique for providing economic security by means of income maintenance benefits to victims of uninsurable hazards, such as mass unemployment, old age dependency, permanent disability, and old age medical care. First launched by Bismarck in Germany in the 1800s, the social security idea rapidly spread throughout the world.

The Social Security Act of 1935 launched the United States into ever expanding programs of social insurance. The current program, Old-Age, Survivors, Disability, and Health Insurance (OASDHI), embraces a wide range of benefits from pensions to life insurance and from disability to medical care for the aged.

The Unemployment Insurance Program is jointly operated by the federal and state governments under a financial offset plan. The proportion of the labor force covered under the program is only slightly over one-half, which is regarded as too low by many critics. Workmen's compensation is regarded as an important form of social insurance despite the fact that insurance benefits may be provided by private carriers and self-insurers as well as state funds and other government carriers.

REVIEW QUESTIONS

1.   Which of the hazards covered by Social Security do private insurance carriers presently insure? Why is Social Security coverage of these hazards required? Explain.

2. What factors determine the amount of Social Security retirement benefits an individual worker may receive? Discuss.

3. Compare and contrast social insurance and public assistance from the standpoint of the operation of the two systems.

4. In *Fleming v. Nestor*, 363 U.S. 603 (1960), the Supreme Court upheld the constitutionality of a provision which prohibits Social Security payments to persons deported for subversive activities. The majority opinion declared: "The noncontractual interest of an employee covered by the Act cannot be soundly analogized to that of the holder of an annuity, whose right to benefits is based on his contractual premium payment." Is social insurance insurance? Discuss.

5. "Creeping socialism with its steadily mounting proportion of federal expenditures going toward charity to the improvident will slowly but surely strangle the economy." (Total Social Security taxes as a percent of national income in the U.S. was 0.8 percent in 1947, 2.1 percent in 1957, 4.4 percent in 1967, 5.8 percent in 1973). Discuss.

STUDY QUESTIONS

6. What is the negative income tax? What are its merits? Discuss.

7. How do you account for the fact that medical care costs have risen so sharply in the United States during the past decade? Explain.

8. What are the advantages or disadvantages of state administration of unemployment and workmen's compensation as compared with federal administration? Discuss.

9. Are Federal Deposit Insurance Corporation activities a branch of social insurance? Discuss.

10. Explain briefly each of the benefits currently available under the Social Security Act to a man age 23 who is married with a wife age 20 and a son age 2. (Assume that the man is both fully and currently insured).

28

Corporate
Risk Management

INTRODUCTION

Corporations spend billions of dollars in the aggregate on group life insurance, accident and health insurance, pension programs, fire and casualty insurance, workmen's compensation, and in the form of taxes for the financing of social insurance programs. Yet, because corporations characteristically do not report their insurance costs, it is difficult to estimate the magnitude of corporate insurance programs. However, there is little doubt that the efficiency of corporate risk management in recent years has improved considerably by virtue of the professionalization of this management function. [1]

THE RISK MANAGEMENT FUNCTION

The process of risk management is an emerging discipline designed to identify

[1] The American Society for Insurance Management is a professional organization of corporate insurance managers with chapters throughout the United States. ASIM is dedicated to raising standards of professional competence among insurance buyers and risk managers.

and evaluate those static risks to which a business is exposed.[2] Businesses are subject to numerous forms of risk: when the entrepreneur forms the business, his capital is exposed to the risk of business failure; when a new product is introduced, the business is exposed to a risk of market failure; when the business issues debt instruments to raise additional funds for expansion, the corporation is exposed to financial risk. However, these risks not only create a possibility of loss, but also generate an opportunity for greater profit. They are referred to as dynamic risks. While the risk manager is concerned with the total exposure to risk incurred by the business, his major concern is with static risk. Static risk refers to perils that are normally insurable: including physical damage to assets, fraud, criminal violence, liability, death or disability of employees, and so forth.

The fundamental goal of the risk manager is to preserve the assets and earning power of the company from damage or destruction. Through the achievement of his goal, he contributes to the profitable survival of the firm.[3] The risk manager evaluates exposures to risk and selects those methods for handling static risk that optimize the efficiency of the firm. Problems incurred by the risk manager include the identification of risk, determination and measurement of relevant costs and benefits, and formulation of a risk management program that is compatible with the activities of other departments and company policy.

The term risk manager may be a misnomer. While a firm is faced with numerous types of risk, the risk manager is concerned primarily with static risk. However, the title of risk manager is more appropriate than insurance manager or insurance buyer. The efficient management of static risk requires more than effective purchasing of insurance. Insurance is only one of many available tools for risk management. In schematic form, Figure 28.1 presents the typical functions performed by risk managers.

RISK IDENTIFICATION

Risk identification requires a thorough and systematic assimilation of relevant data from reliable sources. Information on existing and potential exposures to static risk can be obtained from: (1) a physical inspection of plant, equipment, and products, (2) communication with other company personnel, and (3) a review of company accounting and other records.

---

[2] See H. Wayne Snider, ed., *Risk Management* (Homewood, Ill.: Richard D. Irwin, Inc., 1964). Also, Robert I. Mehr and Bob A. Hedges, *Risk Management in the Business Enterprise* (Homewood, Ill.: Richard D. Irwin, Inc., 1963); C. Arthur Williams, Jr. and Richard M. Heins, *Risk Management and Insurance*, 2nd ed. (New York: McGraw-Hill Book Company, Inc., 1971).

[3] Marshall W. Reavis, "The Corporate Risk Manager's Contribution to Profit," *The Journal of Risk and Insurance*, XXXVI (September, 1969), p. 473.

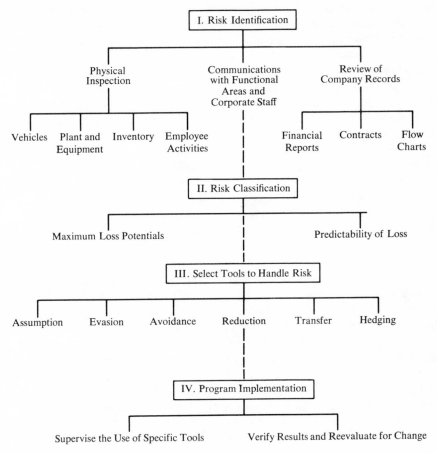

FIGURE 28.1   The Risk Management Functions

Physical Inspection of Premises

The physical inspection of all company assets and operations is an impossible job unless the risk manager devises a systematic procedure for periodic review. Most risk managers use checklists or surveys that list possible exposures to assist in the task. A typical checklist for a manufacturing firm might require information about the following items: (1) building and premises locations and values, (2) boilers and power machinery, (3) contents, (4) accounts receivable, (5) goods in transit, (6) numbers and classifications of employees, (7) money and securities, (8) public liabilities, (9) business interruption, and (10) automobiles, aircraft, or boats.

The risk manager determines the type of construction of buildings in which the firm is located (walls, floors, roof, number of stories, etc.). He is also concerned with: the location of the building with respect to water supplies, fire stations, and hospitals; cost to replace the building if totally destroyed; the nature of any mortgages; status of any sprinkler system; and the portion of the property occupied by other tenants. Furthermore, if the building is rented, the risk manager should be aware of the nature and term of any leases.

Boilers and power machinery should be examined and at least the following information recorded: number and type, fuel used, and other equipment that is dependent on each power system. Cold storage and other temperature control facilities are inspected, and their location, use, and nature of contents are recorded.

The contents of buildings are inventoried as to age, use, and value. Items examined include: raw goods, goods in process, finished products, furniture, fixtures, betterments, dies, patterns, tools, salesmen's samples and exhibits, scientific instruments, and property in the custody of others.

Other important assets requiring evaluation are accounts receivable (e.g., total, average per account; average payment time, place of storage, etc.) and goods in transit, including those in trucks, ships, trains, air, and mail.

Automobile exposures are evaluated to determine year, make, serial number, cost, and garaging of each vehicle. Other requisite information includes: average distance travelled in year; area of travel; employee use of vehicles for personal travel; and nature, number, and cost of each property damage and bodily injury loss occurring during the past three years.

By the systematic review of the items on the list, the risk manager (or his staff) can identify the relevant values. In the process of the examination, the risk manager studies each section of the survey to determine if his checklist is complete. The list will undergo change as items are deleted and new exposures are identified. The checklist is only used as a reference tool and is not a complete listing of all possible exposures.

Communication

Because many of the questions raised by a checklist of exposures require expert interpretation, a detailed discussion with other company personnel is necessary for effective decision-making. Thus, the risk manager and his staff must develop a skill for asking probing questions and eliciting useful responses. Effective communication requires mutual respect, awareness of mutual problems, and compatible language. The risk manager must explain clearly the nature of his work and the need for cooperation. While company policy may require department heads to forward certain types of information to the risk management department, an awareness of how cooperation can benefit individual departments may stimulate more extensive and detailed communication. A frequent problem in establishing lines of communication is the variation in terminology used in specialized branches of a firm. The risk manager must understand the technical language used in the firm. For example, to identify the perils associated with industrial pollution, he must be able to communicate with chemists and industrial engineers.

Company Records

The financial reports of a firm play an important role in the task of exposure identification. The flows of income and cash associated with various operations and equipment are outlined in the balance sheet and income statements. This information is particularly important in the identification and evaluation of potential consequential losses. For example, the income statement helps determine the "business interruption" exposure.

Company records also include sales contracts, leases, mortgages, patent licenses, warranties on products, and the like. While the corporate attorney can furnish and comment on these documents, he generally is not an expert in static risk identification. Thus, the risk manager cannot rely solely on the attorney for this area of potential exposure to loss. The risk manager must meet with the corporate attorney to obtain supplementary information on the specific obligations associated with individual contracts and to advise him of potential loss exposures that may arise from contract provisions.

Corporate flow charts are useful in risk management. These charts outline the specific flow of raw inputs through the production process and the movement of goods within the plant. Careful analysis of the flow charts should reveal where any bottlenecks might occur in the event of damaged equipment. Vulnerable sections of the production process should receive special attention.

RISK CLASSIFICATION

After identifying exposures to risk, they should be classified as to type or potential influence on the firm. While alternative classification schemes may be used, the risk manager usually divides the exposures into property, liability, and life and health. This classification scheme has evolved as a parallel to that used in insurance. However, the risk manager is most concerned with risks that could have a catastrophic effect on the firm. Thus, in addition to the foregoing classification, exposures to risk may be categorized as to (1) the probability or predictability of loss, and (2) the maximum loss potential and its effect on the financial status of the firm. By grouping exposures according to these two variables, the risk manager can emphasize or "red flag" those risks that might be most detrimental to the firm.

SELECTION OF TOOLS FOR HANDLING RISK

After identifying and measuring the risk exposures, the manager must determine which combination of techniques will be most effective for dealing with the various perils. Risk management tools include: assumption, evasion, avoidance, reduction, transfer, combination, and neutralization, or hedging.

Risk assumption takes the form of retention programs and includes self-insurance and the use of large deductibles.[4] Evasion is achieved by loss adjustment programs that favor the corporation by virtue of its financial position in forcing compromise settlements. Prevention and loss control or protection programs are avoidance measures in addition to being reduction strategies. Pure avoidance would arise from nonexposure of the firm to possible risks. Transfer programs include insurance, guarantees, and hold-harmless agreements. Pooling and insurance are examples of combination approaches. Neutralization, or hedging, is the offsetting of risks, particularly of price level changes, and is used primarily in cases where commodities play a large role in corporate activity.

The risk manager first determines the resources needed to prevent the occurrence of loss. He then decides in consultation with top management whether the firm's resources are sufficient to absorb potential losses. The firm may decide to use assumption if the maximum potential loss is not too great. However, when there are gaps between resources needed and those available, the risk manager may have to decide either to reduce or eliminate the exposures to static risk or to increase the flow of resources that would be available in the event of loss. The costs and benefits associated with each alternative must be considered. However, many of the benefits and costs are not easily quantified, and the extent to which each tool is used will depend upon the company's objectives, ability to absorb losses, and risk aversion attitudes or policies.[5] For example, a firm may have sufficient resources to assume several property damage exposures. However, because the risk taking propensity of corporate management may be very low, insurance may be purchased. The subjective probabilities adopted by management, although difficult to quantify, are implicit in company policy and play an important role in risk management decisions.

PROGRAM IMPLEMENTATION

Following a decision on an appropriate set of risk management tools, the program must be implemented and administered. For example, assuming that loss control and prevention is considered appropriate, the following questions must be answered. What safety devices will most effectively do the required job

---

[4] See Robert C. Goshay, *Corporate Self-Insurance and Risk Retention Plans* (Homewood, Ill.: Richard D. Irwin, Inc., 1964).

[5] An example of corporate risk retention policy is found in the 1965 *Annual Report* of E. I. Dupont de Nemours & Company, p. 19.

"While it has been the company's policy, with some exceptions, to assume the risks of losses from property and plant damage, substantial increases in property values led to the decision, in 1953, to purchase "excess loss" insurance. This insurance provides coverage against direct losses from fire, lightning, explosions, windstorms, etc. Under the policy, the company assumes the first $2.5 million of each loss and the insurers assume the remainder of the loss up to $25 million above the $2.5 million. The insurers' liability is limited to $75 million in any policy year."

at the least cost? Are employees being instructed in the use of the devices? Are employees using the devices as instructed? Are the devices still doing the desired job? It is apparent that the risk management function is dynamic by nature. As the technological and physical environment change, the risk manager must constantly reevaluate the exposures to loss and methods for their management.

Given the numerous duties required of a risk manager, it is difficult to outline his specific job description. The risk management function requires a combination of engineering, industrial hygiene, law, accounting, statistics, finance, government, medicine, and insurance. To perform the tasks of the risk management function well, an individual must possess a conservative and analytical outlook.

THE RELATIONSHIP OF RISK MANAGEMENT TO OTHER BUSINESS FUNCTIONS

The effective manager does not operate in a vacuum. He initiates and maintains contact with all key company personnel and departments. This is particularly important for the risk manager because his primary function is to protect the assets and cash flows that are vital for the operation of all areas of the business. In addition, the risk manager must complement the other activities of the firm to implement its policies. In particular, there must be coordination with: (1) accounting, (2) production, (3) marketing, (4) research and development, and (5) finance.

Accounting

The accounting department is a primary source of information on exposures to consequential losses. A consequential, or indirect, loss is one that results from the destruction or damage of property. Consequential losses include loss of income, extra expense, loss of a leasehold interest, and loss of advantageous tax factors (e.g., depreciation). The income and the cash flow statements reveal the timing and amount of income and cash flows that might be discontinued in the event of a direct property loss. The risk manager must be aware of these data. The accounting statements also give the risk manager necessary information for determining the company's ability to absorb losses. If the company is maintaining a tight cash flow, its ability to assume risk safely will be reduced. Furthermore, the balance sheet provides information on financial strength and the extent of any safety margins in the net worth of the firm.

The accounting department also plays a key role in the implementation and execution of risk management strategies. The corporate accountant is an internal auditor and can identify and confirm information related to assets, income, and cash flows. This is obviously related to the risk manager's task. For example, the risk manager is concerned with the risks associated with employee dishonesty and fraudulent manipulation of funds. In cooperation with the accounting department the risk manager can implement loss prevention and control techniques that will deter employees from stealing corporate assets and help identify those responsible.

Production

The production department furnishes the risk manager with information on work flows and the contribution to production provided by each piece of equipment. This information is essential to the risk manager's task of identifying the key exposures to loss. In addition, the production manager assists the risk manager in loss prevention and control. The design and timing of production flows is an important factor in plant safety. The placement or accessability of safety equipment (e.g., fire extinguishers) also contributes to the elimination or reduction of loss potentials. The risk manager cooperates with production personnel in developing and implementing safety training programs. Quality control is another area of mutual concern. Steps must be taken to reduce the potential hazards in the product due to incorrect or negligent assembly.

Marketing

Since the marketing department is in contact with customers it is an important source of information on usage of company products. Products may be sold for a single use but be adopted for an unforeseen purpose. While the product may be safe for its intended purpose, it may be unsafe as actually used. The potential for a products' liability lawsuit is apparent. The marketing department is also responsible for communication of any warranties or guarantees to the customer. The risk manager must determine any implied or oral warranties communicated to customers. If such warranties have created a new exposure to loss, the risk manager must cooperate with the marketing department either to eliminate the risk or clarify the exact effect of the risk and provide for it. For example, a salesman may warrant that a product will perform a specific function safely in response to competitive pressure. However, the product may not have been tested to verify the claim. If the product is used and causes damage to the purchaser, the seller may be liable. The risk manager instructs salesmen on the problems of possibly misleading sales statements and attempts to reduce the impact of product warranties.

Research and Development

The risk manager should maintain contact with research and development personnel to advise them of risks inherent in a new product and to obtain advance notice of products that may evolve from current research. The expertise of research personnel will be used by the risk manager to devise methods for dealing with problems caused by existing products. The risk manager is not only concerned with the problems of product liability but also with the hazards involved in the production processes required for new products.

Finance

The risk manager is probably more concerned with the functions of capital budgeting and financing than any other corporate area of responsibility. Capital budgeting is involved with decisions that affect the future asset structure of the firm. The financing decisions directly affect the use of alternative risk management tools.

Capital Budgeting. Capital budgeting deals with the efficient allocation of scarce resources with the goal of optimizing long run benefits to the firm. Specifically, capital budgeting decisions determine the asset and liability structure of the firm. Because different sets of assets and liabilities will produce alternative sets of static risks, the risk manager must observe and participate in the capital budgeting process.

Assume a firm is deciding whether to build a new plant. If the plant is deemed necessary, additional questions include where to put the plant and how to finance it. The risk manager is concerned with all of these decisions. He is often asked to assess the hazards created by a new plant and whether the risks can be handled effectively. The risk manager may conclude that the risks inherent in the new building are too large to be assumed by the firm. Unless insurance can be obtained, the investment should not be undertaken. To do otherwise would add significantly to the potential variation in the firm's net cash and income flows. The increased variation might increase the firm's risk as evaluated by stockholders and lead to an increase in the required rate of return to satisfy investors. The decision to build the plant would be influenced strongly by the availability and cost of appropriate insurance. The risk manager might examine alternative plant sites and layouts to determine the combination that would be acceptable to an insurer or which would significantly lower the cost of available insurance. For example, the location of an adequate supply of water would be an important consideration for fire insurance.

The Financing Decision.   The financing decision is also important to the risk manager. Static risk is only one type of risk incurred by a firm. Financial risk as measured by the degree of financial leverage[6] is also important. Both types of risk may affect the financial market's evaluation of a company's income flow and worth. Thus, decisions related to financial risk and static risk cannot be made independently. For example, the use of debt to finance a new plant would increase the potential variation in earnings due to financial leverage. If it was independently decided to assume all or a large part of the static risks associated with the plant, the potential variation in corporate earnings would be increased even more. There must be joint action between the finance and risk management personnel to achieve an optimum balance between financial and static risk.

RISK MANAGEMENT AND
THE PURCHASE OF INSURANCE

One approach to an understanding of an effective insurance buying program is to determine the extent to which sound principles of risk management are used. There is wide variation in the extent to which formal programs exist. Many companies have piecemeal programs in which they purchase various insurances without regard to overlap or long range planning.

While the literature of corporate risk management provides no universally agreed upon set of principles, one can identify the basic ingredients of an efficient program of insurance buying.[7]

Centralized Responsibility

The first principle of management is the coordination of the lines of authority within the firm. All too often this is not done in insurance matters. To avoid duplication of services, to gain the economies arising from a unified purchasing program, and to eliminate a diversity of insurance buying practices, the authority to purchase and administer the insurance program should be centralized in a single division. In the absence of a centralized responsibility, confusion may create special problems. It is not uncommon for the legal department of a firm to have responsibility for the purchase of court bonds, for the construction department to have authority for certain types of bid bonds, for the corporate secretary to be responsible for fire insurance, and for the

[6]Paul M. Van Arsdell, *Corporation Finance: Policy, Planning and Administration* (New York: The Ronald Press Company, 1968), pp. 303-15 offers a detailed discussion of the concepts of financial risk and leverage.

[7]Irving Pfeffer, *The Placement of Insurance by The State.* Assembly Interim Committee Reports, Vol. XV, No. 14 (Sacramento, Cal.: State of California, March 1957). This report outlines a program and applies it to an analysis of the insurance buying practices of the State of California.

personnel department to manage the group insurance. Under a regime in which there are many executives responsible for insurance buying, it is probable that the corporation will forego some of its mass purchasing power.

Adequate Staffing

The complexity of a large organization's insurance problem demands a collection of legal, actuarial, and administrative skills beyond the capacity of any single individual. An adequate staff is essential if the division is to meet all of the problems inherent in, its complex job. Unless the corporation has personnel who are skilled in the purchase of insurance contracts, it is inevitable that it will become dependent on an insurance broker. When this happens, the broker's needs rather than those of the client may be overemphasized. At a minimum, the risk management department should have one person who is a qualified insurance buyer. Optimally, the risk management department should have a staff of experts (e.g., experts in loss prevention, persons who are competent in the administration of group insurance programs, etc.). Without a full-time staff it should be possible for the risk manager to have access to independent counsel, either from the ranks of consulting actuaries or independent insurance consultants.

Manual of Procedures

In order that established policies may readily be communicated, and to insure consistent and uniform practice, a manual of procedures should be developed and maintained. The Manual of Procedures may be a formal document of the kind recommended by the American Management Association,[8] or it may merely be a file of correspondence classified by subject matter. It should assist the administrator in determining past practices and in setting policies for future use. Unless there is a manual of procedures, confusion is likely to occur when there are personnel changes. The mistakes of prior periods may be avoided by the availability of explicit statements of systems and procedures.

Insurance Surveys

Periodic comprehensive surveys of exposures and insurable values must be undertaken to determine the continuing need for existing coverages and the necessity or desirability of new coverages. The field of insurance surveys has developed substantially in recent years. The main purpose of the survey is to identify the exposures afresh and provide a basis for reevaluation of retention limits. Except for the most complex risks, surveys can be conducted in a

[8] James C. Cristy, *Corporate Insurance Manuals, Reports and Records*, Research Report No. 25 (New York: American Management Association, 1955).

relatively short time and be kept current by periodic review. It is virtually impossible for the manager to perform his function properly without a survey.

Contract Analysis

A continuing analysis of existing insurance policies should be conducted in order to determine the appropriateness of such contracts in terms of current conditions. Policy language and insurance company practices change. The broadening of such terms as "accident" to cover "occurrence," the expansion of coverage into new and more comprehensive multiperil packages, and related developments suggest the need for a continuous review of contract terminology. Insurance contracts should be reviewed from the standpoint of current needs. Sometimes, a policy may include language that is standard but unintentionally exclude perils to which the insured is exposed. For example, a labor union should be interested in "riot attending a strike," which is a common policy exclusion. Firms with seasonal operations should carefully consider the "vacancy or unoccupancy clauses" in fire insurance policies.

Rate Analysis

Actuarial studies should be conducted in order to determine whether the rates in effect on existing insurance policies are the best in terms of changing conditions. In an economy with shifting values and changing price levels, a time lag of substantial proportions may develop between existing rates, which are based on past experience, and those that are now appropriate. In some lines, such as fire insurance, it is not uncommon for rates to be set on a three or five-year basis. Yet the corporation is undergoing change much more rapidly than would be indicated by such long term rate projections. By pursuing actuarial analyses of rates on a continuing basis, it should be possible to take advantage of improvements in the market. The firm may forego substantial savings if it waits for an insurance broker to recommend an improvement in the insurance program.

Market Studies

A continuing study of insurance markets and current developments within the state and elsewhere should be pursued. The technique of public bidding on insurance is one method of periodically ascertaining the nature of the market for particular kinds of insurance. Too often, the risk manager, for want of time or staff or because of biases engendered by friendship or background, may ignore important segments of the market for the various insurances that are needed. Failure to utilize the services of mutuals, reciprocals, or other types of carrier is sometimes the result of an unreasonable prejudice in favor exclusively of stock insurance companies. New companies are constantly moving into given markets, and old companies are constantly moving out. Unless continuing studies are made, it will be impossible for the corporate risk manager to know whether his insurances are placed with the best companies on the best terms.

Open Bid Purchasing

A procedure should be established and maintained for purchasing new insurance and renewing existing contracts. Such a system should permit the free forces of market competition to operate for the benefit of the insurance program. Where access to the set of bid specifications and experience statistics of the risk is available, there is a strong likelihood that effective competitive pricing will prevail. It is not sufficient that a better rate be received; rather the company should receive the very best rate possible in the current insurance market. While open bid purchasing procedures may be favorable as a technique for insurance buying, there are some inherent limitations in it.

The open bid purchasing procedure has fallen from favor in personal service contracts. The auditor who supplies his services as a C.P.A. on the basis of open bid purchasing may have to compromise the quality of his services because of the temptation to overeconomize on time. The brain surgeon who receives his assignment on the basis of open bid purchasing would hardly be recommended to most patients. The attorney defending an important action who is engaged on an open bid basis might not be expected to do the best job. By the same token, the insurance broker whose services are obtained on this basis may give less service than he should if he is to perform his professional responsibility well. It would appear that the open bid purchasing procedure is effective on a periodic basis to check the cost of services rendered. In the long run insurance companies will tend to add a margin for special contingencies to the rates that they quote. A company using open bid purchasing may find the low bid to be somewhat higher in the long run than the cost of insurance purchased through a single broker or group of brokers. On balance, the insurance carrier bearing the risk must have an opportunity to recoup his losses over a period of time, and the open bid purchasing procedure deprives him of that opportunity. Frequently, state agencies and governments require as a matter of law that open bid purchasing procedures be used.

Annual Reports

The preparation of annual reports is useful for the appraisal of overall insurance results. Such reports should present the basic statistical actuarial data pertaining to the experience of the program and its component parts. Annual reports help insure a sound and practical appraisal of the overall risk management program. While the annual report concept is indispensible for a public agency, it would seem to have considerable merit for corporations as well. If properly prepared, the annual report offers a historical account that can prove of enormous value as a record of the experience of the company and as a guideline for evaluating the extent to which the corporation should self-insure certain risks. In the absence of some form of systematic reporting it becomes impossible to determine whether the insurance buying policy has merit.

Independent Audits

To determine that the best insurance practice is being followed, the overall program should be subjected to a periodic independent audit.[9] While it is not necessary that a firm use an independent insurance consultant, nonparticipating brokers should be given an opportunity to review the existing coverage. In the absence of an independent audit, it becomes possible for uneconomic practices to be maintained over a period of years on a basis of social friendships rather than on business need. Inasmuch as substantial sums of money are expended for insurance purposes and much more is at risk, an independent audit is prudent.

SELECTION OF INSURERS

Given both the number and varying quality of insurers doing business in various insurance markets, it is imperative that the risk manager establish a set of criteria for evaluating alternative sources of insurance. The potential criteria may be divided into the following classes: (1) financial strength, (2) contract provisions, (3) services, and (4) price.

Financial Strength

Financial strength, or the security of the insurer's promises, should take precedence as a primary criterion in carrier selection. Unless an insurer survives to complete its contract, its promises will not reduce anxiety but will merely aggravate it. This is the type of situation the risk manager wants to avoid.

The first step in evaluating an insurer is to ascertain its existing and potential financial strength and to examine those factors (e.g., underwriting, reinsurance, etc.) that can directly affect its future security.

The insurer's financial statements, as presented in the annual report, provide one source of information on insurer solvency. In addition to a review of

---

[9] See Robert I. Mehr and Stephen Forbes, "The Risk Management Decision in the Total Business Setting," *The Journal of Risk and Insurance*, 1973; also, Fred Molineaux, "How to Effectively Use Consultant and Broker Service," *Risk Management*, Vol. 20 (March, 1973), p. 26.

the insurer's annual statements, the risk manager may consult various insurance company rating services, insurance agents, brokers, or consultants. Furthermore, other risk managers, bankers, and security analysts may be good sources of information on the financial strength of an insurer.

Contract Provisions

After determining that an insurer meets a set of solvency standards, the contracts available from an insurer should be examined. Does the insurer provide the specific contracts and contract covenants that are needed by the risk manager? If not, is the insurer prepared to provide custom-designed policies? Answers to the foregoing questions will require a detailed examination of policy forms and an inquiry of insurers for more detailed information on the specific meaning of any unclear phrases. It is dangerous to enter into a contractual relationship unless the meaning of all terms and conditions is clear. While the courts may tend to interpret any ambiguities in favor of the insured, the risk manager should not have to rely on the courts for payment of losses.

Of particular importance to the risk manager, who has very large or unusual exposures, is the insurer's ability or willingness to provide nonstandard covers. While many insurers provide typical policies, the needs of some risk managers may require the construction of a unique policy form. If such is the case, the risk manager must ascertain the insurer's willingness to provide the desired covers.

Service

Services that should be reviewed include: (1) evaluation of exposures, (2) loss prevention and control assistance, (3) fair and prompt claims settlement, and (4) extension of credit. In addition, the risk manager needs to ascertain the extent to which any of the services are provided on a national or international basis.

The need for these services will vary among individual companies. Thus, the risk manager should establish individual service standards. For example, the corporation that has an extensive risk management department with experts in exposure analysis will not require risk evaluation services. However, all risk managers will be concerned with the costs of these services. Some insurers may be willing to negotiate the price of insurance based on the services required.

Price

Insurers do not charge uniform prices. There exist significant price differences, and the effective risk manager shops for the best terms. Costs must be balanced against services and policy covenants in order to determine the best price. Furthermore, the best price does not necessarily mean the lowest initial premium. One insurer may base its premium on a level commission to the agent, whereas another insurer may use a declining commission scale. The former will show a lower initial premium, but the net cost over several years may be the same. Finally, net cost may not be measurable in advance. The cost of insurance with a mutual insurer may depend on unpredictable dividend flows. Interest and expense assumptions of insurers may be inaccurate, and net costs will vary. In such cases the risk manager must review the past experience of alternative insurers and make a projection as to cost.

TRENDS IN RISK MANAGEMENT

The most important trend in risk management is the expanded recognition of the role played by the risk manager. This recognition has taken two forms: increasing use of risk managers, and placement of the risk management function higher in the corporate structure. The basis for this expanded use lies with the risk manager's increasing contribution to the goals of the corporation.[10] Assuming the corporate goal is to optimize the flow of benefits to the owners, the risk manager makes two contributions. First, he can help reduce the net risk of the firm. Realizing that the value of capital is a function of the risk-return composite, a reduction in corporate risk (assuming return remains stable) should increase the value of common stock and reduce the firm's cost of capital (both equity and nonequity). Second, the efficient management of a firm's portfolio of insurance policies should reduce the costs associated with insured risks and thus increase a firm's profits. This factor has been of increasing importance as the supply of many corporate insurance products has tightened and as the cost of insurance has significantly increased.

Within the risk management framework the most significant trend is the increasing use of risk retention. Firms have expanded the use of risk assumption, self-insurance, captive insurers, and large deductibles.[11] Corporate managers are awakening to the value of risk management programs that are comprehensive and do not rely solely on insurance. Furthermore, the rising cost and unavailability of many types of insurance has forced risk managers to reevaluate the relative benefits and costs of risk retention alternatives.[12]

[10] Marshall W. Reavis, *op. cit.*, pp. 473-79.

[11] For a detailed review of alternative deductibles and an application of decision making under uncertainty techniques see D. Hugh Rosenbaum, "Deductible and Risk Management," *Risk Management*, Vol. 20 (March, 1973), p. 20. Also, Michael Murray, "A Deductible Selection Model-Development and Application," *The Journal of Risk and Insurance*, September, 1971, p. 423.

[12] David B. Houston, "Risk, Insurance and Sampling," *The Journal of Risk and Insurance*, December, 1964, p. 530 uses quantitative methods for analyzing the benefits of insurance in alternative risk situations.

INDIVIDUAL RISK MANAGEMENT

The problem of risk management is no less important for the individual consumer than it is for the corporation. He must make decisions about which risks to avoid or reduce; which ones to assume or evade; which ones to transfer or hedge. He must identify and evaluate the risks to which he is exposed, develop a strategy for dealing with them, and follow through with a program to manage risk and reduce his anxiety about potential bad luck.

In simpler form, the same criteria apply to the individual's risk management efforts as apply to the corporation's. The same elements are applicable. Some guiding principles are:

1. Assume risks that are bearable and budgetable. Use the largest deductibles that you can afford in buying insurance in order to keep the costs down.

2. Identify your priorities and buy insurance to cover the most urgent and potentially catastrophic risks first.

3. Carry high limits on liability insurance.

4. Insure to value, less a *planned* retention, in property insurances.

5. Shop for a good agent or broker. The best costs no more than the average.

6. Keep your insurance records in one place.

7. Have an insurance agent review your liability, property, and income exposures at regular intervals.

8. Read your insurance policies. Have your agent explain provisions that are unclear.

9. Check prices. Get insurance rate quotes from companies other than the ones who have your present policies.

10. Shop for insurance. Let a number of companies or agents make presentations before you decide to renew your policies or buy additional insurance. About four months before an insurance premium is due, or before expiration date, check prices and coverages that are available in the market.

11. Keep records of your insurance accounts, premiums, and losses.

12. Use independent audits. Invite another agent or broker to review and make recommendations about the work of your insurance adviser.

13. Do not be intimidated by insurance procedures. Claims should be reported promptly, and losses should be indemnified by the insurance carrier within the limits of the policy.

SUMMARY

Risk management is an essential business function which is gaining recognition as risks become more complex and potentially disastrous for the firm or individual. The risk manager is concerned with static rather than with dynamic risks. His method is essentially scientific: identification of the problem, classification, analysis and prescription, restatement and review.

The risk manager interacts with many different departments in the typical firm and brings to bear a wide range of possible solutions to risk situations. For the rational buyer of insurance the basic ingredients of a program include: centralized responsibility, adequate staffing, manuals of procedures, insurance surveys, contract analysis, rate analysis, market studies, open bid purchasing, annual reports, and independent audits.

The individual consumer has an equally large stake in proper risk management. He can apply some simple precepts to improve the effectiveness of his insurance buying decisions.

REVIEW QUESTIONS

1.   What are the objectives of the risk management function? What problems are encountered in attempting to reach these objectives? Discuss.

2.   Outline the principles of a program of effective insurance buying for an individual.

3.   Differentiate between the "best" price and the "lowest" price in the use of open-bid procedures in insurance buying.

4.   "There are in general six possible responses to risk and uncertainty situations:

(a) assumption	(b) evasion
(c) reduction	(d) transfer
(e) combination	(f) neutralization

These techniques may be employed either singly or in a wide variety of possible combinations."
Explain the nature of the "responses" mentioned in the above quotation and provide illustrations of each.

5.   The Acme Bolt Company has 150 employees ranging in age from 16 to 59. Management has been considering the provision of a life insurance benefit for each employee in an amount equal to 20 percent of his average annual wage. Since the life expectancy of Americans is about 68 years and the average age of all employees on the Acme payroll is only 40, an officer of the company suggests that Acme should self-insure the risk and thereby save the expense factor in the life insurance company's gross premium. Do you think that Acme should self-insure this risk? Explain why or why not.

STUDY QUESTIONS

6. A grain elevator operator buys wheat from farmers at $2.75 a bushel and sells it to millers for $2.95. During the period between purchase and sale the market price may change. Accordingly, the operator sells a contract for future delivery at the same time he buys the wheat. The selling price for the future contract is $2.85 a bushel. He regards this as an imperfect but adequate hedge. Is this an illustration of *hedging* or of *arbitrage*? Explain. Why is the future price higher than the spot or current price? Explain.

7. A private zoo printed the following statement on the reverse side of all of its tickets of admission:

"The person using this ticket assumes all risk of personal injury and loss of property. Management reserves the right to revoke the license granted by this ticket."

What is the legal effect of this type of hold-harmless-agreement? Does it effectively release the zoo of its legal liability? Discuss.

8. Is risk management a "profession"? Discuss.

9. Discuss the relative merits of placing all of one's personal insurance with a single agent as contrasted with distributing it among several different agents.

10. Corporate insurance administration is an emerging field of specialization in management. The field is complex, guidelines are not numerous, and principles are not well established. Prepare a memorandum for the newly appointed corporate insurance buyer outlining a set of "principles" which he might follow in managing the risk problems of the company. Explain each of your "principles" carefully.

29

Estate

Planning

INTRODUCTION

Estate planning is the process whereby the individual attempts to achieve an ideal balance between the attainment of his personal goals and his economic potential.[1]

Personal goals may not necessarily be expressed or clearly understood, but they underlie most of the actions taken in everyday affairs. These goals may conflict with one another; they may shift in uncertain ways; and, for the individual, they may be incapable of expression. Power, recognition, creative success, happiness, security, a sense of accomplishment, a full life, and freedom are merely labels for a set of implicit personal goals.

The economic potential of the individual may be expressed as the maximum net worth, earning power, or net worth ultimately transmitted to one's heirs. Each of these ideas is rooted in the same concept—the enlargement of the economic power of the individual with conservation and orderly liquidation during the years after death and for the longer period during the lifetimes of the heirs or other natural "objects of one's bounty."

Achievement of personal goals and economic potential are not necessarily incompatible. There are many paths to economic success that do not conflict

[1] See Irving Pfeffer, "The Nature and Scope of Estate Planning," *California Management Review,* Fall, 1966, from which this section is adapted.

with personal goals. Aided by certain tools and strategies, the individual can make his personal and economic goals complementary.

PERSONAL GOALS

The first step in estate planning is identifying the goals of the individual as he perceives them. Such a statement may take any one of a great variety of forms. Its utility arises from the discipline of clarifying these ideas and making them explicit. Four such goals might be considered nearly universal.

1. The most important single goal is realizing the maximum potential of the individual in terms of cultivating and applying his skills. These may be technical, human, or conceptual; they may be theoretical or applied; they may be esthetic or merely practical. But they are intensely personal, regardless of their nature or degree.
2. The achievement of a well adjusted and mature family relationship.
3. Economic security in terms of adequate resources to meet daily needs with cushions of liquidity to meet nonrecurring major expenses, such as illness, education, and holidays.
4. The creation and preservation of the largest possible estate compatible with the striving for the first three objectives.

The statement of goals serves to identify the considerations that the estate planner must employ in doing his work. It establishes a frame of reference and a set of benchmarks for evaluating the quality of the planning that is conducted. It also limits the degree to which tax planning and risks may be undertaken. Unless the individual is concerned solely with the accumulation of wealth for its own sake, he must sacrifice some of his immediate economic objectives for basic psychological and social considerations. Effective estate planning helps to achieve a balance among the complete set of goals.

THE PERSONAL ANNUAL REPORT

Once the goals have been determined, the next step is the analysis of the existing estate. This should begin with the preparation of an annotated statement showing the financial status of the individual. This may be called the Personal Annual Report. It resembles the report of a corporation and reveals the history, achievements, current progress, implicit goals, and plans for the future of the individual.

The Income Statement

The first part of the report is an income statement that may be reconstructed from personal income tax returns and checkbook stubs. This financial data sheet includes information for three years ago, last year, and for the third year hence. Footnotes explaining some of the items and assumptions should be included. An exhibit of this kind will assist- the planner to evaluate recent progress and to specify some of the planning objectives.

The Balance Sheet

The second part of the report is a balance sheet drawn up to reveal progress and prospects. This should array assets and liabilities for the third year previous, the most recent year end, and the third year hence.

Annotations for this balance sheet will reveal the titles in which all property is held and the tax liabilities that will be incurred in the event of liquidation, sale of property, or in the event of death. Location of legal documents such as wills, trusts, and insurance policies should be footnoted.

Consanguinity Chart

The third part of the statement is a chart showing all of the natural objects of one's bounty in the absence of a valid will and listing potential beneficiaries and heirs who can be protected only by a will. The footnotes to such a chart reveal the individual's intentions with regard to each of the persons on the chart. For example, the question of who should serve as guardian for the children in the event of the death of the parents in a common disaster would be noted on the chart.

At this point, it becomes meaningful to perform a "trial balance" to estimate the extent to which the estate as presently structured conforms to the goals of the individual. A number of obvious weaknesses in the program (or lack of program) will ordinarily be evident. The next step is to develop a plan that will result in achieving the intermediate and long range goals of the individual.

ESTATE BUILDING

The management of estate building is essentially the same as that for any other business activity. Problems arise from a poverty of skills, and their solution is found in more effective management. Numerous books and articles have been written on the subject of "how to get rich," but insufficient attention has been given to situations where luck is not a major element. While less spectacular, these cases are our immediate concern.

Attitude is an important element in estate building. It has been suggested that "money-mindedness" is essential. The millionaire has been characterized as one who is "money-oriented"—he thinks about money making, consciously or subconsciously, all the time. He has a high regard for money and tends to be somewhat parsimonious. He tends to be disciplined and austere about his money and has a powerful accumulation motive. Such generalizations may be gross oversimplifications, but an attitude that is strongly disposed toward effective estate building is vital. If the desire is present and the goals are known, the building process can begin.

ESTATE CONSERVATION

Estate conservation problems relate to the proper evaluation and control of four classes of risk: business, investment, legal, and tax.

The successful management of business interests requires an understanding of and provision for the wide spectrum of risks that confront a firm. These include insurable hazards, such as legal liability for negligence, property damage, fidelity and surety bonds, and life, accident, and health risks. Beyond these types of business risk, there is the set of fundamental hazards arising from economic conditions and the political environment. Overcoming the economic risks that are a part of the environment of business is one of the major tasks confronting every businessman, and success in this activity is at the heart of massive estate building.

The investment risk is dealt with through the techniques of the portfolio analyst. These techniques include diversification of various kinds and the selection of securities on the basis of their relative invulnerability to surprise.

The legal risk arises from the failure to execute the documents that are essential to the carrying out of the plans of the individual. A will that is technically invalid or out of date, a trust instrument improperly executed, titles to property that are inappropriate, forms of business organization that are not suitable, assumption of obligations that are not intended, contracts that are poorly drawn are all parts of the legal risk that is embraced in the concept of "preventive law."

The tax risk is the most complex of all because it includes the problems of minimization of income tax erosion and the planning of tactics for eliminating or reducing the confiscation of estates through transfer taxes, such as gift, inheritance, estate, and capital gains levies. Frequently, the tax risk is regarded as the exclusive problem in estate planning, but such a viewpoint is distorted because tax avoidance may occur at a higher price than the thoughtful individual really wants to pay.

ESTATE DISPOSITION

Proper management of the estate should make it possible to achieve a high degree of goal satisfaction along with risk minimization and control.

Estate disposition problems are similar in many respects to those of conservation, except for the differing importance of the various types of risk and the accuracy of the individual's judgment of the motivations, character, and financial ability of his family beneficiaries.

Traditionally, the greatest stress has been upon the tax risks. The probability of estate shrinkage through poor tax planning is so high that special care is required. The differential treatment of property in terms of ordinary vs. capital gains income, of gifts in contemplation of death vs. valid gifts, of attribution rules in property ownership, and most devastating of all—successive taxation of estates when surviving heirs pass on shortly after the death of the individual—demand a high degree of skill in the estate planning process.

The activities of the probate courts indicate the legal hazards that should be dealt with. Ill-defined objectives, procrastination, poorly drawn legal documents, and uncoordinated planning result in designs that are unstable and vulnerable to attack. The attorney who is versed in preventive law can eliminate most of the sources of frustration in the legal aspects of estate planning.

As a rule the investment risk is secondary because of the conservative bent of executors. The same may be said of the business risks. The dangers inherent in continued operation of a business by executors are so well known that the exposure tends to be relatively small.

Properly gauging the needs, aptitudes, capacities, and temperament of the potential successors is a major area of weakness in estate disposition planning. Will a minor son be able to.run the business? Will he be able to manage his financial affairs in a mature manner? Will the children be able to exploit their opportunities adequately? These are but a few of the issues that must be resolved in the light of present information and intuition.

ESTATE LIQUIDITY

Surprise factors coupled with short term planning provide the major sources of severe liquidity problems in estate planning.[2] The sudden death of a key individual in the economic sense—disability, mortality, unemployability, voluntary retirement—brings shock losses with cash drain implications for the estate. Sudden tightening of terms with a shortening line of credit; market adjustments; tax audits; major new commitments; falling out of family members through divorce or litigation are sources of the surprises that can create sudden liquidity needs.

[2] See Irving Pfeffer, "The Liquidity Problem in Estate Planning," *Journal of The American Society of Chartered Life Underwriters*, XIX (Spring, 1965), from which this section is adapted.

Needs for Liquidity

Chronologically, the incidence of a material need for liquidity may be classified into three time periods: (1) during the continued activity of the individual; (2) at the time of economic death; and (3) during the remote period, years after the passing of the decedent.

During the active lifetime period, liquidity may be needed for budget planning, acquisition of fixed assets, exploitation of opportunities that arise suddenly—or the sustaining of shock losses that arise equally suddenly, payment of income taxes that are not adequately anticipated or met, or payment of gift taxes.

At the time of death of the client, the principal cash needs would seem to relate to probate and administration costs, estate and inheritance taxes, potential income tax liability, and costs of purchase or sale of business interests by the estate.

Finally, in the remote period after death of the decedent there may be gift tax problems associated with trusts or foundations where once more the liquidity problem arises, although probably in less acute form than in other time periods.

Inadequate time is the culprit behind the liquidity problem. Given enough time, orderly liquidation of estates could be properly planned and credit stringency would be of minor consequence.

Life Insurance. Life insurance is an increasingly important medium for the funding of business continuation buy and sell agreements because of all the methods in widespread use, this is uniquely suited to the purpose. The cost is very low, particularly when favorable tax treatment is considered. Settlement of life insurance claims is very speedy because of the nature of the contract. Safety is possibly higher than that for any other financial instrument. Control is secure. Asset retention is unaffected, and simplicity is assured. The mechanics of life insurance as a funding medium are familiar, and there is no practical limit to the aggregate insurance available for a single insurable life. The chief limitation of the life insurance approach arises from the fact that some people are uninsurable.

TOOLS OF ESTATE PLANNING

The most commonly used tools of the estate planner are: wills, trusts, estates, gifts, investment analysis, tax avoidance, and insurance. Each of these basic devices is highly complex and generally requires its own specialists.

Wills

Each state has probate laws, relating to intestacy, that outline the way in which property passes in the event that there is no will left by the decedent. Such laws provide for the orderly distribution of the net estate to the immediate family, and if the executor is unable to locate the heirs, the property passes under the escheat laws to the state. Intestacy is avoided by executing a valid will. The laws of the various states differ somewhat in the requirements for a will. Obviously, estate planning, if it is to effect proper disposition of assets, requires a current will. Attorneys recognize the adage that, "If a man dies without leaving a will, his property goes to the nearest villain."

Trusts

A trust is a legal device whereby a new entity or "legal person" is created with some of the attributes that most individuals would like to possess. These include a duration, which can be virtually as long or as short as desired, a separate tax basis, and a great deal of flexibility in management. Creation of a trust is simple in most instances. There is a need for a creator or grantor; a document expressing the intent of the grantor; a corpus or portfolio of some kind—one dollar is not uncommon; beneficiaries; and a trustee or trustees, the individuals who will operate the trust and manage the funds. While no recording or filing is necessary, in most states a trust agreement must be in writing and preferably should be witnessed and notarized.

Trusts are of many varieties. They fundamentally serve two purposes: (1) to remove certain property from the estate of the individual for tax or other reasons, and (2) to provide property management for one who lacks the time, inclination, or skill to manage his own property. Where there are minor children or adults who are legally incompetent, trusts are indispensable in properly designed plans.

Estates

Technically, estates are the ways in which title to property is held. Each state has a different set of laws relating to property ownership. The question regarding the ownership of property is far more complex in the case of larger estates than appears on the surface. In California the attorney must know the value of the estate owned by both spouses, the sources of the property, the testamentary objectives of both spouses, the state of their marriage and its vitality, the dates on which the various elements of the property estate were acquired, and the manner of their acquisition. All of these factors are important in determining the way in which title to a particular asset is recorded.

A mere listing of some of the estate choices is instructive: joint tenancy,

tenancy in common, separate property, community property, quasicommunity property, and conversions of title from one to another of the forms. The tax consequences of improper choices are significant; the legal results of ignorance can be frustrating; and the practical results may be disastrous. Proper counsel is obviously indispensable.

Gifts

Gifts offer an excellent means of realizing family goals while providing favorable tax treatment. There is very little rationale for the transfer of property to one's family or to charitable outlets at only one point in time—the death of the giver. Lifetime giving is more advantageous from many viewpoints. It permits the giver to observe the use of the gift so that modifications can be made with regard to future gifts, and it enables the giver to enjoy participation in the activities of the grantee, even if only vicariously. It is taxed on a more favorable basis under the gift tax laws than the estate tax or the combined estate and state inheritance tax program. The pitfalls are primarily the potential loss of control of the property and the red tape that may be associated with outright gifts to minors, but these hazards can be overcome with proper planning.

Gifts have tax implications that require certain formalities as to nature, timing, amount, tax basis, and probabilities of reversion. These formalities demand technical competence and care.

Investment Analysis

The importance of a sound approach to the expansion of an investment portfolio in the estate cannot be overestimated. The application of proper principles of investment is particularly essential during the creation phase of estate planning. What might be appropriate for a person of substantial means may be inappropriate for a salaried individual, and what is correct for an entrepreneur of modest means is probably not suitable for his widow.

While there is no universal agreement on a set of investment principles, it is evident that the goal of a mixture of optimum rate of return with minimal risk can only be achieved on the basis of a careful search for appropriate investments, careful selection of individual securities, careful supervision of the developing portfolio, and a striving for diversification in terms of the cyclical qualities of different industries.

Tax Planning

Tax avoidance has a poor connotation. It smacks of illegality or immorality. In fact, it possesses none of these elements. Tax evasion is another matter, and the ethical estate planner stays clear of such fraudulent practice. The

Supreme Court of the United States has enunciated the doctrine that the taxpayer has no duty to pay more taxes than the statute requires,[3] and the tax adviser relies upon this doctrine as the foundation of his work. He would have his client pay no more than the minimum amount due.

Insurance

Life insurance is unique among the property interests of the individual because it provides the best means available for capitalizing the prospective income stream and providing estate liquidity. The payment of an initial premium, which may be relatively small, creates an instant estate. Life insurance is an effective medium for indemnifying the estate for the loss of income arising from premature death; for funding stock redemption or buy and sell agreements in business; and as an investment outlet. Life insurance plays such a large role in estate planning that it is a major technique. Favorable tax treatment, great liquidity, stability of principal, flexible settlement options, cash value loan features, instant capitalization, and other ramifications account for the importance of this element in the overall design.

Disability income insurance and health insurance play the important estate role of protecting the insured's stream of income. Disability or illness may create a greater financial problem than death because the estate must continue to support and care for the victim. These costs can erode even large estates. Liability insurance is an important estate tool for the same reasons. The catastrophic potential inherent in the liability exposure is a problem faced by all estate planners. Life insurance programming is a method of integrating insurance into the estate plan.

LIFE INSURANCE PROGRAMMING

Insurance programming is a systematic procedure for determining the specific insurance needs of an individual and for filling these needs with the most appropriate set of policies and policy options. Insurance programming answers the questions: How much insurance do I need? What type of insurance should I buy? Furthermore, insurance programming is a method for efficiently integrating noninsurance estate resources into an appropriate program of insurance purchasing. The basic concepts are applicable to all forms of insurance.

[3] In *Commissioner v. Newman*, 159, F. 2d 848, 850, 851 (2d Circ. 1947), Justice Learned Hand stated: "Over and over again the courts have said that there is nothing sinister in so arranging one's affairs as to keep taxes as low as possible. Everybody does so, rich or poor; and all do right, for nobody owes any public duty to pay more than the law demands; taxes are an enforced exaction, not voluntary contributions. To demand more in the name of morals is mere cant."

Programming and the Insurance Agent

The professional life insurance salesman has a variety of approaches toward the sale of his services and products. The simplest is the one product approach, whereby a single need is met by the sale of a single product. As he gains in experience, the agent finds that he can sell package plans that are designed to meet more than just one need. As the agent becomes more skilled and sophisticated, he is ready to provide tailor-made protection for his clients.

Skillful programming appeals to the life underwriter because it is "needs" selling in its highest form, it provides a basis for the purchase of more appropriate amounts of insurance, and it provides the foundation from which further sales to the client may be made. The agent who is a master of programming techniques typically has higher average sales and higher persistency than the man who is able to sell only a single product or a single mix of products.

Programming may be regarded as simple, where the formula applied is exclusively a life insurance program; advanced, where complex tax considerations are introduced into the plan; and estate planning proper, when all of the elements of a man's estate are taken into account.

The Programming Technique

The programming procedure has four steps. First, the postloss needs of the individual are identified and, based on the goals and resources of the individual, a dollar amount is assigned to each need. Second, the available or existing resources that may be used after a loss are subtracted from the total needs in order to obtain the net required resources. Third, the voids in the program (the net required resources) are filled with an appropriate package of insurance products. Fourth, any required estate safeguards are determined and implemented.

Needs.   The primary resources required after the death of an estate owner include: executor fund, family period income, and lifetime income to spouse. In addition, there may be a need for mortgage retirement, education of dependents, and an emergency fund.

The executor fund, sometimes referred to as a clean up or last expense fund, should be sufficient to complete the administration and distribution of assets in the estate, pay all final expenses (funeral, medical bills, etc.), and clear the estate of any debts. The amount required will be a function of the size and nature of the estate and the type of distribution desired. For example, it will cost more to administer an estate that contains a close corporation than an estate containing only marketable bonds and stocks.

The family income period is usually divided into an adjustment period and a dependency period during which minor children must be supported. Most estate owners cannot afford to program an amount of family period income equal to the present income. However, the programmer realizes that the family would have difficulty in adjusting to a lower standard of living immediately. Thus, the program usually includes an initial adjustment income period when the income is gradually reduced to the affordable level.

After the youngest child has reached age eighteen (or completed the college dependency period), the program may provide a life income to the widow. While it is feasible to assume that dependent children will care for the surviving parent, this concept goes against contemporary social policy. Neither the children nor the parent appreciate this kind of dependency. However, if the spouse has a skill, trade, or work experience, it may not be unreasonable to assume that he or she will be self-sufficient after the family rearing period.

Resources.   Accumulated resources that may become available in the event of death include: (1) financial assets (stocks, bonds, demand deposits, savings accounts, etc.), (2) tangible assets (house, car, boat, etc.), (3) existing life insurance, (4) employee benefits (group life insurance, health insurance, pension plan, profit sharing, etc.), and (5) Social Security.

The programmer will identify the extent to which each of these resources is available and will apply them to the individual needs. Assets and life insurance will vary significantly with each individual as a result of previous spending and investment patterns. However, the individual has less control over the extent of any applicable employee and Social Security benefits. These will vary by type and extent of previous work experience. Social Security death benefits are frequently overlooked by individuals. While most people recognize Social Security retirement benefits, many consumers are unaware of the Social Security widow's allowance, dependents' allowance, and lump sum death benefits. The widow may receive a monthly income until the youngest child reaches eighteen years and again when she reaches age sixty-five (or age sixty-two at a reduced amount). The widow may also receive monthly allowances for each child under age eighteen (up to a maximum amount for all children). Furthermore, under some circumstances a child attending college may be eligible for a monthly stipend.

Requirements.   To illustrate a typical insurance program and show how voids in the program are highlighted, consider the following set of individual goals and circumstances:

1. Family—father, age 30; wife, age 30, two children, ages 2 and 4.
2. Executor fund required—$2,250.
3. Desired level for family—adjustment income (two years following death) of $900 a month; family period (until youngest child reaches 18) of $800 a month; lifetime income of wife of $600 a month; and income to children while in college of $100 a month.

4. Mortgage—lump sum to pay off net outstanding debt of $23,000.
5. Emergency fund—$2,500.

Total needs are programmed in Figure 29.1. In addition, this figure demonstrates the use of the following resources that will be available to the family:

1. Bank account—$1,500.
2. Existing life insurance—$15,000.
3. Social Security—widow's and dependency allowance of $350 a month in family period; lifetime income to wife at age 65 of $150 a month; income to child while in college of $100 a month; lump sum at death of $250.
4. Employee benefits—group life insurance of $10,000; pension benefits of $100 a month to the wife.

The data in Figure 29.1 indicate that the emergency fund, mortgage, executor fund, and education income needs are met with existing resources. However, there are the following voids in the income program:

1. Dependency period—$450 a month in adjustment period, $350 a month for remainder of family period.
2. Lifetime income for wife—$500 a month between ages 46 and 62; $350 a month after age 62.

The insurance programmer would devise a set of policies and policy options to fill the gaps in the program. Figure 29.2 shows how this might be done. The programmer often works from right to left in filling the voids (from the period when the wife is oldest to the date when the husband dies). For example, the agent might determine that $50,000 would be needed to fill the $350 monthly income need in the period beyond age 62. The programmer assumes this fund will be provided by a $50,000 life insurance policy (Policy #1) with the benefits paid under a life income option. However, the husband is assumed to die when the wife is age thirty, and she will not use the life income option until age sixty-two. The funds may be left with the insurer under the interest only option until the wife reaches age sixty-two. The interest paid by the insurer is paid to the widow in the years between ages thirty and sixty-two. If we assume interest on the $50,000 proceeds as $200 per month, all monthly voids in the program between the ages of thirty and sixty-two will be reduced by $200.

The agent would next determine the amount necessary to remove the remaining $300 per month deficiency during the years between ages 46 and 62. Assume a $50,000 policy paid under the fixed amount option would provide the necessary income. Again the option would not be implemented until the wife

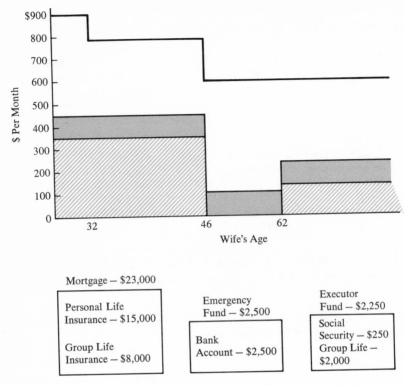

Mortgage — $23,000

| Personal Life Insurance — $15,000 | Emergency Fund — $2,500 | Executor Fund — $2,250 |
| Group Life Insurance — $8,000 | Bank Account — $2,500 | Social Security — $250 Group Life — $2,000 |

FIGURE 29.1   A Hypothetical Program for Life Insurance: Before

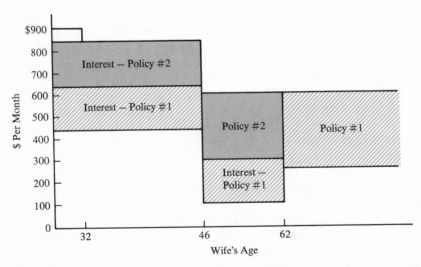

FIGURE 29.2   A Hypothetical Program for Life Insurance: After

reached age forty-six. Prior to age 46, the $50,000 proceeds would be left with the company, and the $200 monthly interest distributed to the wife. The interest would be more than sufficient to fill all remaining program voids except for $50 per month during the readjustment period. This remaining gap could be filled by an additional, small, life insurance policy (which could provide $50 per month for two years). However, the estate planner may decide that $850 per month adjustment income is sufficient.

It is a difficult programming task to provide insurance benefit flows that coincide exactly with individual needs. However, the agent or estate planner might be able to demonstrate that the purchase of $100,000 in additional life insurance and the use of three settlement options (life income, interest only, and fixed amount) can solve the problem reasonably well in our hypothetical case. The types of policy suggested for purchase will depend on the resources and supplementary needs of the individual.[4] If he desires to use life insurance for retirement and death protection, then it would be appropriate to use whole life insurance or endowment insurance with their cash values. However, if the individual's only need is temporary death protection, term insurance would be best. Furthermore, the ability to pay will be a key determinant. Unless the individual has sufficient discretionary income to pay premiums on $100,000 of whole life insurance, he must either purchase some or all term insurance or reduce the level of desired benefits for his family.[5]

Safeguards. To assure the completion of the program and its goals, the individual should consider the following safeguards: (1) removal of uncertainty in case of common disaster, (2) proper designation of beneficiaries, (3) protection from the dynamic perils of inflation and rising standards of living, and (4) frequent reevaluation of the program.

A common disaster occurs if both the insured (e.g., the estate owner) and the beneficiary (eg., the wife) die simultaneously in the same occurrence. In such a case, the estate administrator or the court may have difficulty in determining which party died first and, thus, how the assets should be distributed. If it is assumed that the wife died first, the estate would pass to the husband's estate. However, if it is assumed that the wife survived the husband, the assets would have temporarily passed to the wife and would eventually be distributed to her beneficiaries. Obviously, if the timing of the two deaths is unknown there can be confusion as to who should receive the estate assets.

---

[4] The advanced estate planner devotes more attention to a balance of life insurance and non-life insurance solutions than a life insurance programmer might be inclined to do. Property assets, potential inheritances, business interests are elements in more sophisticated planning.

[5] The cost of alternative plans of insurance in the face amount of $100,000 for nonparticipating ordinary life would be about $1,583 at age 30. For five year convertible and renewable term insurance at age 30 the cost of $100,000 of protection would be about $750.

While various state laws create presumptions as to which party died first, these may be contrary to an individual's intent. Thus, it is usually advisable for the estate planner to insert common disaster clauses into insurance policies.

A common disaster clause provides that it should be presumed the beneficiary died before the insured, if both die as a result of a single accident. This does not completely solve the distribution problem when it is known which party died first. Another approach uses settlement options. For example, the life insurance proceeds can be held at interest for a specified period of time, and, if the beneficiary survives the insured beyond this point, the proceeds may be distributed to her. However, should the beneficiary die during the specified period, the proceeds can be distributed to a secondary beneficiary.

Beneficiary designation should not be taken as a simple and obvious task. For example, to name "my wife and children" as the beneficiary could lead to confusion. What if the insured remarried and had additional children? What if the insured has children out of wedlock? It is important to name the beneficiaries with full names or by a clearly identifiable class. In addition to the primary beneficiary, it is important to name secondary, or contingent, beneficiaries to receive funds not distributed to the primary beneficiary. Unless the policyowner specifically names beneficiaries and indicates how the proceeds are to be distributed, the decision will be made by the state. There is no guarantee that the state will satisfy the goals of the estate owner.

While the insurance program has provided the beneficiaries with specified income flows, there is no certainty that the income provided will satisfy the projected needs. The purchasing power of the dollars provided may decline or there may be a rise in the requirements for a reasonable standard of living. Inflation and a rising standard of living reduce the real value of fixed income. Thus, the programmer must take steps to offset the effects of potential inflation. One method is to diversify asset holdings. In addition to the guaranteed fixed income flow of settlement options, variable income flows from investments and variable annuities may be included in the estate plan.

Changing estate goals, family circumstances, and financial capabilities of the estate owner give rise to a need for periodic review of the program and the goals it is attempting to achieve. The program is static by nature, but individual needs and desires are dynamic. Reevaluation of the plan at least annually is appropriate for insurance programming and other aspects of estate planning.

MINIMIZING TAXES

There are six broad strategies employed in tax minimization programs as an aspect of estate planning. All of the various tactics, schemes, and "gimmicks" employed in the field may be subsumed under one of these approaches. The following classifications suggest the variety of possibilities.

1. Substitution of fringe benefits for ordinary income—accident and health insurance; company-owned transportation facilities; company-paid physicians, attorneys, accountants, and the like; company dining room facilities for meals; group life insurance; company credit cards.

2. Substitution of cash flow for income—depreciation; depletion and amortization; tax-exempt securities.

3. Substitution of capital gains for income—stock options; plowback stocks (stock dividend paying); leveraged real estate; profit-sharing trusts.

4. Exploitation of tax free exchanges—realty for realty; stock for stocks; miscellaneous property for noncommercial annuities.

5. Vertical distribution of income and tax exposure over time—deferred compensation contracts; pensions; profit-sharing trusts; long term employment contracts with income-spread provisions.

6. Horizontal distribution of income and tax exposure over entities—gifts; trusts; family corporations; family and other foundations.

All of these tools, and many more, are part of the kit of the estate planning team.

JUDGING EFFICIENCY

An efficient estate plan is characterized by at least the following four attributes: comprehensiveness, flexibility, economy, and liquidity.

The "one-shot" approach of preparing a will or buying a life insurance policy defeats the objectives of the individual because these pieces of a plan are not correlated with other goals or elements. There is no best kind of life insurance policy, other than that which is most suitable considering all of the circumstances. There is no best type of investment without regard to the total portfolio. There is no best kind of trust without regard to the tax consequences. Unless the plan is comprehensive, working from sets of goals to integrated solutions, it is unlikely to be efficient, to withstand change, or to endure.

A good plan is flexible so that it can be modified appropriately as time passes. Overattention to tax consequences can "lock-up" an estate should divorce, inheritance, premature death, or adverse tax changes occur. There is a price to be paid for tax opportunities. For example, the assignment of a life insurance policy on an irrevocable basis may remove the property from the estate of the insured for estate tax purposes, but does the insured want to surrender control over his major assets to his spouse or some other party? Flexibility is important.

Economy is the raison d'être of estate planning work, and sloppiness can run the ultimate costs of poor planning very high.

Liquidity in the estate is an important element, particularly after a death occurs, because the liabilities of the decedent fall due promptly, whereas realization of the assets may suffer erosion and delay. The historic role of life insurance has been to help provide this essential liquidity.

THE ESTATE PLANNING TEAM

Estate planning advisors include: life insurance agents, nonlife insurance agents and brokers, attorneys, accountants, trust officers, realtors, investment advisors, and other personal and financial counsel. Competent advice may be one of the best investments made by an estate owner.

It is not possible to provide a single set of criteria for choosing estate advisors which would be suitable for everyone. The nature, desires, and needs of each estate owner vary. While some individuals only need indirect guidance, others need direct management of assets. Furthermore, whereas some individuals only need suggestions, others need to be motivated to take action. The estate owner should find compatible advisors. Common sources of information used for the selection of professional estate advisors include friends who have used the services of professional advisors, local businessmen or bankers, and the estate planners themselves.

People are too often reluctant to interview and select their professional advisors. Just as a consumer might gather information about alternative products, he also needs to investigate the services of his potential professional counsel. A preliminary interview may help avoid future problems.

SUMMARY

Estate planning is an art which, if well performed, can make an important contribution to the realization of the goals of the individual and his family. The tools employed in this field, of which life insurance is among the most important, are not difficult to understand, but they possess legal and economic characteristics that require specialized skills. The government's fiscal structure has been so constructed that one who is knowledgeable and imaginative can devise a program with propriety, which will effectively minimize or postpone the erosion of wealth by death and taxes.

REVIEW QUESTIONS

1.   Should an unmarried college student buy and pay for any kind of personal insurance? Discuss.

2. Tom and Mary have been married for ten years. He is 31, and she is 29. They have three children: Helen (age 7), Margaret (age 5), and Bill (age 2). They recently bought a new home with a down payment of $2,000, a first mortgage of $25,000, and a second mortgage of $15,000. Tom is an engineer and earns $16,000 per year. Mary earns $4,000 per year in a part-time job. The Smiths are getting started in a swimming pool contracting business in their spare time. What insurance program would you recommend for this family? Explain.

3. Life insurance is among the best investments because it has the highest leverage. A monthly premium of $10 can produce an estate worth $100,000. Discuss.

4. The text suggests six broad tax minimization strategies: fringe benefits for ordinary income, cash flow for income, capital gains for income, tax-free exchanges, vertical distribution of income, horizontal distribution of income. Show how life insurance can be used to take advantage of each of these legal strategies.

5. What is a life insurance trust? Explain.

STUDY QUESTIONS

6. Frank did not have a will because he had only two living relatives: Aunt Jane, who took care of his house, and Cousin Bill, who had not been heard from since leaving for Canada thirty years ago. In the event of Frank's death, who will inherit his estate? Explain.

7. Beneficiary designations in life insurance policies are important because of the probate and tax implications. Explain.

8. Compare the settlement made under a "property will" with that made under a "life will" (life insurance settlement agreement) as to economy of administration and creditor protection.

9. What barriers are there to the estate planning team working under the direction of a life insurance agent? Discuss.

10. Design an insurance program for your family, setting out the basic data about needs and resources. What is the best life insurance program for your family situation? Discuss.

30

Consumerist Developments
in Insurance

INTRODUCTION

Among the more important social and economic developments of the past decade has been the rise of consumerism as a potent force. At first a muckraking development, and then a boisterous minority viewpoint, consumerism in due course became respectable and a force to be contended with. Consumer councils were created in every state, and representation was sought at the highest political and economic levels. Inevitably, the insurance industry became the object of consumerist attacks. Criticism came at a number of different levels and in large measure was predicated upon the assumption that the insurance industry has a social responsibility beyond providing a service at a profit—it is a mechanism that should be used to solve social problems. Much of the vulnerability of the private insurance industry arose from its inability or unwillingness to solve some of America's recognized ills. The pressure for change has been strongest in the areas of product availability at reasonable prices, product development, and delivery of services.

The major themes of modern consumerism relate to full disclosure, implied warranties of service, cost, fairness and equity, and discrimination.[1] Statutory protections and legal approaches are increasingly common with the class action lawsuit as the ultimate threat. Among the fields of insurance most affected by the consumerist movement are health, automobile liability, life, and workmen's compensation insurance.

THE HEALTH INSURANCE CONTROVERSY

The delivery and financing of adequate medical care for Americans has been an active political issue for several decades. There is some prospect that one of the numerous plans being advocated by partisan groups, including the executive branch of the government, will soon be enacted into law at the federal level. The issue is one of inefficient technology, inefficient delivery systems, and inefficient financial programs. Critics contend that "health care is the fastest-growing failing business in the nation—a $70 billion industry that fails to meet the urgent needs of our people. Today, more than ever before, we are spending more on health care and enjoying it less."[2] The more telling argument, as reported in the *Congressional Record*, runs as follows:[3]

> The United States today is the only major industrial nation in the world without a system of national health insurance or a national health service. Instead, we have placed our prime reliance on private enterprise and private health insurance to meet the need.
>   . . . the private health insurance industry has failed us. It fails to control costs. It fails to control quality. It provides partial benefits, not

[1] Betty Furness stated the objectives as follows:
"From the insurance industry the consumer wants to know that he can put in a claim without having his policy arbitrarily cancelled—and that that same policy will be renewed next time around.
He wants the insurance industry to work toward controlling the rising costs of health insurance . . .
He wants to be sure that his automobile insurance pays him fully for his losses without penalty of cancellation. And he wants his money now, not after five years of expensive litigation.
He wants to be able to buy personal property insurance no matter what his neighborhood or the color of his skin is. And he wants to be able to protect his business against fire and theft—without having the high cost of that insurance drive him out of business.
But what the consumer wants from the insurance business above all else is information." *1971 Proceedings of the National Association of Insurance Commissioners,* Vol. II, p. 6.
[2] Edward M. Kennedy, "Health Security for America," *Congressional Record,* 92nd Congress, First Session (January 25, 1971), p. 2.
[3] *Ibid.*

comprehensive benefits; acute care, not preventive care. It ignores the poor and the medically indigent.

Despite the fact that private health insurance is a giant $12 billion industry, despite more than three decades of enormous growth, despite massive sales of health insurance by thousands of private companies competing with each other for the health dollar of millions of citizens, health insurance benefits today pay only one-third of the total cost of private health care, leaving two-thirds to be paid out of pocket by the patient at the time of illness when he can least afford it.

Consumer advocates contend that nearly all private health insurance programs provide only partial and limited protection. Health insurance coverage is either nonexistent or more loophole than protection for most citizens. In 1968, of the 180 million Americans under age 65:

1. 20 percent, or 36 million, had no hospital insurance;
2. 22 percent, or 39 million, had no surgical insurance;
3. 34 percent or 61 million, had no in-patient medical insurance;
4. 50 percent, or 89 million, had no out-patient X-ray and laboratory insurance;
5. 57 percent, or 102 million, had no insurance for doctors' office visits or home visits;
6. 61 percent, or 108 million, had no insurance for prescription drugs;
7. 97 percent, or 173 million, had no dental insurance.

The American Dental Association estimates that there are about one billion untreated cavities, or five per capita. Some 25 million adults have lost all their teeth, and another 25 million have lost half.[4]

... private health insurance today is a major part of our current crisis in health care. Commercial carriers siphon off the young and healthy, leaving the old and ill to Blue Cross, vulnerable to escalating rates they cannot possibly afford.

Too often, private carriers pay only the cost of hospital care. They force doctors and patients alike to resort to wasteful and inefficient use of hospital facilities, thereby giving further impetus to the already soaring cost of hospital care and unnecessary strains on health manpower.

Valuable hospital beds are used for routine tests and examinations which, under any rational health care system, would be conducted on an out-patient basis.

Unnecessary surgery is encouraged. We know that far more surgery takes place in the United States than in other nations with far better health records. We know that under the Federal Employees Health Benefits program, more than twice as much surgery takes place on federal

[4]*The Wall Street Journal* (July 28, 1972), p. 30.

employees enrolled in the indemnity reimbursement plan as on those enrolled in prepaid group practice plans in the federal program. The figures are especially striking for female surgery and for surgical procedures like appendectomy and tonsillectomy.[5]

The insurance industry is quick to respond to this bill of particulars by arguing that its role is to provide a service the public is willing to buy at prices the public is willing to pay. It is not the responsibility of private industry to provide services below cost for those who lack the means to purchase adequate insurance programs. When the private health insurance industry reaches beyond this argument to contend that the government should leave the field exclusively to private industry, it invites the residual market argument—that government must step in to fill the gaps where a need exists.

The problem of health care costs is crucial, and the consumer is aware of the need for better programs. Countless examples of hardship cases have been cited in the newspapers and elsewhere.

MEDICAID AND MEDICARE

The federal government's first large scale attempts to cope with the medical care dilemma were the Medicare and Medicaid programs. Medicare and Medicaid were aimed respectively at the old, whose medical demands are large, and at low income members of society. Since 1966, these two programs have injected billions of dollars each year into the medical care delivery system. Yet, there is still considerable concern about inadequate care, in part because these programs do not deal with alleged problems in the organization and operation of the medical system. Both Medicare and Medicaid were simply grafted on to existing medical facilities. These programs were not intended to reorganize or improve the efficiency of the system. However, they have increased the demand for medical services dramatically. As a result, many observers suggest that the inflation of medical costs is partially the result of the Medicare-Medicaid programs.[6] There is evidence that both the quality and quantity of hospital care has increased because of these programs. In addition, the hospital admission rate per 1,000 people covered under Medicare alone rose 8.5 percent in the first four years of the program.

[5] Edward M. Kennedy, *op. cit.,* p. 2.

[6] See J. P. Newhouse and V. Taylor, "The Insurance Subsidy in Hospital Insurance," *Journal of Business* (October, 1970) p. 453; Mark V. Pauley, *National Health Insurance: An Analysis* (Washington, D.C.: American Enterprise Institute for Public Policy Research, 1971), p. 1. "Simultaneously with the implementation of Medicare and Medicaid in 1966, the rate of inflation in medical care prices, which had consistently been higher than that of the general price index, began to increase at an even greater rate."

MAJOR NATIONAL HEALTH INSURANCE PROPOSALS

The concept of national health insurance is not new to the United States. As early as World War I, the American Medical Association proposed a tax financed health insurance program. Similar proposals came up during the Roosevelt and Truman administrations, but the opposition was able to defeat the legislation. It was not until 1950 that Congress passed a form of health care assistance when it instituted a program to assist the states in providing medical care for welfare and public assistance recipients. This was expanded and liberalized in 1960 to include medical assistance grants for the aged. In 1965, the federal government adopted the Medicare and Medicaid programs. These programs gave an indication of the federal government's concern for the provision of medical services. Thus, it should not be surprising that the extensive contemporary criticism of the American health insurance and medical system led to numerous national health insurance proposals. Table 30.1 outlines the provisions of several leading proposals.

TABLE 30.1 National Health Insurance Highlights of Some of the Major Proposals

---

Proposal A: National Health Insurance Partnership Act

Financing: Mandatory coverage premiums paid for by employer (75%)-employee (25%). Group rate pools established for state and local government employees, self-employed, small employers and persons outside labor force. Pay plans for costs of coverages for low income persons on a sliding scale based on income. Pays all costs of extremely poor.

Principal Provisions: 1. National program requiring health insurance protection through employer-employee mechanism.

2. Civil lawsuits and fines used to gain employer compliance.

3. For persons not covered by other means establish "pools."

4. Both employees and "pool" plays underwritten by private insurance carriers.

5. Employees must be offered opportunity to enroll in more than one plan.

6. Encourage development of health maintenance centers, medical-dental training centers by grants and loans.

Proposal B: Health Security Act

Financing: Equal contribution from general revenues and payroll taxes. Employee rate 1.0%, self-employment rate 2.5%, employer's tax rate 3.5% on entire payroll.

Principal Provisions: 1. Completely eliminate private health insurance plans.

2. Provide "cradle to grave" health insurance through new and existing federal taxes.

3. Unlimited physician and hospital services.

4. Absorb Medicare and Medicaid into the new system.

5. No phasing in period.

6. Complete federal administration (under Secretary of HEW) of all health care financing.

Proposal C: Health Care Insurance Act (Medicredit)

Financing: Costs of qualified private plan shared by employers and employees. Other individuals pay by sliding scale of tax credits based on income. Low income persons through premium payment vouchers.

Principal Provisions: 1. Tax credits for all U.S. residents under 65 to offset cost of voluntarily purchasing a qualified health insurance plan.

2. Employers subject to tax penalty for failure to comply.

3. Poor and near poor purchase private health insurance with payment vouchers.

4. Set minimum federal standards for health insurance plans.

Proposal D: National Health Care Act

Financing: Employer and employee share premiums for qualified private plans. Other individuals pay own policy premiums. States and federal government, from general revenues, subsidize premium costs up to 100% for low income persons.

Principal Provisions: 1. Health insurance protection provided by private carriers.

2. Imposes minimum federal standards for qualified plans.

3. Employers eligible for 100% tax deduction for qualified employee plan premiums (only 50% nonqualified plans).

4. Medicare would remain; Medicaid absorbed into state "risk" pools.

5. Phase in benefits to prevent overloading present health care delivery system but poor and near poor phased into system at faster rate.

6. Copayment system to hold down premium costs and prevent over utilization.

7. Private and group plans to offer equal yearly protection by 1976.

8. Ambulatory care center construction emphasized to reduce costs.

Proposal E: Catastrophic Illness Insurance Act

Financing: Similar to Medicare, financed by special tax on wages and special tax on self-employment income subject to Social Security taxes. Tax rate 0.3% on first $9,000 to increase to 0.4% in 1980.

Principal Provisions: 1. Provide catastrophic health insurance protection for almost all persons under age 65.

2. Superimpose national program on existing private health insurance.

3. Extend Medicare program to almost all persons under 65 only after large medical expenses incurred.

4. Federally financed by payroll taxes.

5. No provision for private insurance industry participation.

6. After deductibles and coinsurance, provides unlimited hospital, home health and extended facility care.

The National Health Insurance Partnership Act, described in Table 30.1, was proposed by President Nixon in 1971 but was modified in 1973 to overcome the objections that there were many gaps in coverage which differed for the rich and the poor. Alternatives under consideration were proposals to give every person a credit card for medical and hospital expenses, and a catastrophic coverage program coupled with a federal requirement of health insurance for all workers. The Health Security Act, supported by organized labor, was criticized on grounds of cost. It was estimated to cost between $40 billion and $60 billion each year. Senator Edward M. Kennedy, its chief advocate, argued that passage of this legislation would save Americans the $83.4 billion that went for health care costs in 1972.

THE PREPAID GROUP PRACTICE APPROACH

Prepaid group health plans, such as the Kaiser Foundation Health Plan in California and the Health Insurance Plan of Greater New York, offer an alternative method of delivering health care to the public. These plans provide the hospitals, doctors, and laboratory services for a fixed yearly fee, which is paid monthly, rather than simply paying the bills when certain types of sickness or injury occur. More importantly, they have a vested interest in preventive medicine because the healthier a member is the less he will use the facilities, hence the smaller the cost to the organization. The organization takes on the responsibility of insuring the medical care for members and suffers the financial consequences of failing to keep members healthy. Doctors are paid salaries and are provided with monetary incentives to use the facilities and treatment techniques efficiently. If revenues are more than costs at year's end, doctors receive a bonus. Moreover, they spend all their time practicing medicine rather than engaging in billing, worrying about patients' financial status, gearing treatment to fit the type of insurance coverage he has, and hiring and supervising office personnel. Many advocates of change in health insurance argue for the expansion of group medical practice.

Prepaid group practice plans were resisted by the medical profession with varying degrees of success. There were twenty-two states that prohibited or greatly limited the role of prepayment group practice organizations in 1972. At least one state legislature considered a proposal to outlaw proprietary or "for profit" hospitals. The medical profession contends that such programs tend to lower the quality of medicine practiced by invading the private patient-doctor relationship.

AUTOMOBILE INSURANCE

The automobile and its accident victims have been matters of public concern since the beginning of the century when the major hazard arose from horses panicking and charging away from the noisy machines. As the auto became indispensable and universal in its use with accident frequencies and severities rising rapidly, the insurance industry found itself with a fast growing set of opportunities and problems. The legal profession and the court system came under pressure, and the public found the system of dealing with the hazard of automobile accidents a source of dissatisfaction.

Major reform proposals were advocated in the 1930s and again in the 1950s and 1960s. Legislation pertaining to this field was remolded and updated at every session of most state legislatures. Furthermore, during the late 1960s the federal government and Congress instituted numerous investigations into various aspects of auto insurance.

Initial Federal Action

The first Congressional action taken considered the problem of auto insurance company insolvencies. On January 26, 1967, Senator Thomas Dodd introduced a bill calling for the establishment of a Federal Motor Vehicle Insurance Guaranty Corporation. Dodd proposed to pattern the organization after the Federal Deposit Insurance Corporation. All auto insurers would be required to pay a percentage of premiums received into the corporation so that policyholders and claimants of insurers that become insolvent would be protected in a manner similar to the way FDIC protects bank depositors. Although the bill never gained support and no action was taken upon it, Dodd's proposal served as a catalyst. Congressional reaction to the problems facing the insurance system increased.

House Antitrust Subcommittee Study.   In July 1967, Emanuel Celler, Chairman of the House of Representatives Antitrust Subcommittee, instructed the staff of the Subcommittee to conduct a preliminary study of the following subjects:

1.   An analysis of federal-state legal and regulatory relationships;
2.   An evaluation of current practices in the automobile insurance industry that generate problems and complaints;
3.   An analysis of the adequacy of state regulation of the automobile insurance industry;
4.   Delineation of the areas that warrant further investigation, including a definition of needed statistical and financial data, and industry and regulatory conduct relevant to the inquiry; and
5.   Procedures recommended for the conduct of any necessary further investigation.

After less than three months, the staff issued a report that indicted the auto insurance industry and the tort-fault system. The staff concluded that a further investigation of the automobile accident reparations system was in order. It recommended that further investigation should be concerned with two basic considerations:

1.   Shall the federal-state relationship that is established in the McCarran-Ferguson Act for regulation of the automobile insurance business be continued?
2.   Does the function of the automobile under modern economic and social conditions require changes in U.S. compensation systems applicable to individuals that suffer economic losses and personal injury as a result of automobile accidents?

Thus, Congress was to consider both insurance company practices and the real value of continuing the auto-tort system.

Department of Transportation Study.   On December 14, 1967, House Joint Resolution 958 and Senate Joint Resolution 129 were introduced. They called for a $2 million study of the entire automobile accident reparations system by the Department of Transportation. Both insurance company practices and the adequacy and effectiveness of the tort system were to be examined.

Impetus was added to the Congressional resolutions on February 6, 1968, when President Johnson delivered his Consumer Message. He stated:

> One area of major concern to the consumer is automobile insurance. Every motorist, every passenger and every pedestrian is affected by it—yet the system is overburdened and unsatisfactory.
> Premiums are rising—in some parts of the country they have increased by as much as 30 percent over the past 6 years.

Arbitrary coverage and policy cancellations are the cause of frequent complaint—particularly from the elderly, the young, the serviceman, and the Negro and Mexican American.

A number of "high risk" insurance companies have gone into bankruptcy—leaving policyholders and accident victims unprotected and helpless.

Accident compensation is often unfair; some victims get too much, some get too little, some get nothing at all.

Lawsuits have clogged our courts. The average claim takes about 2.5 years to get to trial.

This is a national problem . . .

The Department of Transportation's "Auto Insurance and Compensation Study" was comprehensive and covered virtually all aspects of the auto insurance industry. The goal of the study was to provide Congress and the general public with useful information on the status of the industry and the potential need for reform. While the Department of Transportation concluded that a form of "no-fault" auto insurance would be appropriate, the Department also concluded that any required program should be instituted at the state level.

Senate Judiciary Antitrust Subcommittee Study. While the Department of Transportation study was underway, an investigation was also being conducted by the Senate Judiciary Antitrust Subcommittee under the direction of its Chairman, Senator Philip A. Hart. The Subcommittee was concerned with the business aspects of auto insurance. It considered matters such as company underwriting practices, the trend toward mergers and the formation of holding companies, the growing interest in mass merchandizing, and the industry's profit structure. Hart's committee and others were waiting for the results of the Department of Transportation study.

Renewed interest has arisen regarding insurance insolvencies. On May 23, 1969, Senator Hart and others introduced a bill that was similar to the measure Senator Dodd introduced two years before, calling for a FDIC type corporation for auto insurance. The significant difference in the new proposal was that it sought a Federal Insurance Guaranty Corporation for the entire property, casualty, and surety insurance field. No action was taken on this bill.

State Action

In addition to studies in Washington, the states' legislatures were also active. Many state investigations of the auto insurance industry and the auto accident reparations system were undertaken between 1967 and 1973.

The first U.S. no-fault plan was enacted in Puerto Rico. During the years 1970 to 1973, no-fault plans were introduced in most state legislatures. By mid-1973, most states had enacted variations of "No-Fault Automobile

Insurance," and Congressional committees were moving forward with proposals to make no-fault mandatory according to federal guidelines in the event that all of the states failed to enact adequate bills.[7]

THE PROBLEM OF AUTO ACCIDENT REPARATIONS

The auto reparations problem centers around four distinct but related issues: (1) auto damageability and safety, (2) tort liability vs. "no-fault" as the most desirable, equitable, and efficient reparations system, (3) the specific language of the "best law," and (4) federal vs. state promulgation and supervision of an automobile reparations system.

The central issue in any analysis of alternative systems for reimbursing the auto accident victim has been the degree to which any remedy reduces or eliminates certain individual legal "rights." This issue is of such importance that it must be resolved on a basis of social justice rather than of absolute cash savings or additional expense. However, the way in which individuals evaluate the relative social benefits and costs is a political question. The values attached to certain individual freedoms and the costs of relinquishing these freedoms varies with one's political philosophy. While the conservative presents an appeal for "traditional methods" and "individual rights," the liberal presents an equally strong appeal for "social equity."

The controversy surrounding the problems of indemnifying the victim of automobile accidents generates strong emotional reactions. Thus, it is not surprising that the controversy extends into a whole set of social, political, legal, and economic problems and debates. Both sides of the "no-fault" debate have important points.

No-Fault vs. Tort Liability

Much of the public confusion on this issue arises from simplistic approaches that merely point the finger at the driver, the highway, the insurance company, the lawyer, or the automobile manufacturer, as if any one group were responsible for the problem of the auto victim. The problem is much more complex and affects the whole structure of the economy and legal system. The issue is one of finding ways and means of improving existing solutions to the auto reparations problem while preserving the legal rights of those who are the victims of accidents.

---

[7]Despite rapid movement toward enactment of no-fault laws, the standards adopted in many of the states were regarded as inadequate. Many insurance executives argued that "the only meaningful way no-fault-insurance can be made available to the public within a reasonable length of time is through passage of a federal minimum standards bill incorporating the key components of true no-fault." B. P. Russell, Chairman of Crum & Forster, May 22, 1973.

The most popular label is "no-fault", which seems to suggest more than it really means. Those who advocate no-fault insurance plans usually mean reform of the elements of the system rather than destruction of the rights of victims to use the judicial processes. There is little consistency in the enacted or proposed no-fault programs.

The Case for No-Fault Auto Insurance. The proponents of no-fault auto insurance claim that the tort system was heaping abuse and disaster on the general public. Statistics indicate that less than 50 percent of automobile insurance premiums were ever returned in the form of claims payments.[8] The other 50 percent went to the insurer and the costs associated with determining fault. Furthermore, it was argued that the tort liability system led to the overpayment of small nuisance claims and underpayment of the more serious losses. Benefits were not only small but often late in arriving. Automobile lawsuits involving serious injury would require several years to reach termination. The system was also attacked for its failure to adequately compensate the victim of a "true accident," in which the accident was unavoidable or not the result of any neglect.

The most frequent criticism of the tort system related to an alleged bias against the poor and the uneducated. The potential for inequity resulted from the fact that only a very small percentage of auto claims reached the courts; the majority were settled by individual laymen and insurance adjusters. Thus, it was suggested that reform was needed in the required adjustment process rather than the judicial system.

The Case Against No-Fault. The opponents of a no-fault auto accident reparations system argued that such a system would lead to the abandonment of individual rights and responsibility. One opponent stated that any reform that deletes fault would "inevitably put an end to the moral and legal responsibility of individuals who inflict injuries upon their fellows. The regimentation of all injured persons in 'basic protection' without regard to guilt or innocence would certainly lead to the simultaneous destruction of the dignity of the individual and the evenhanded justice of the common law."[9]

It was further argued that "there is no proven certainty that costs to the premium paying public will be lower. There are many claims, but the actuaries are in fundamental disagreement." Subsequent experience demonstrated that no-fault caused a reduction of frequency of insured losses.

Because the benefits available under many no-fault proposals are tied to direct losses (e.g., income lost) and delete pain and suffering, the opponents

---

[8] Robert Keeton and Jeffrey O'Connell, "Basic Protection Automobile Insurance," *Law Forum,* Fall, 1967, p. 402.

[9] William E. Knepper, "Alimony for the Accident Victim," *Defense Law Journal,* XV (1966), p. 533.

argue that no-fault discriminates against the housewife, minor, elderly, disabled, unemployed, and the low income worker.

Accident Prevention and Other Related Issues

The problem of the auto accident victim is that the entire system whereby accidents and their consequences are controlled is less efficient than it might be. Auto accidents occur more frequently than they should because of deficiencies in: (1) the way cars, highways, and roads are built, (2) traffic congestion, (3) lack of restriction on careless and drunken drivers, (4) court discrimination, and (5) the legal system.

Auto Damageability. The automobile industry has come under attack for manufacturing cars that cannot withstand collisions even at very low speeds. The Department of Transportation requires that automobiles manufactured after 1973 must meet the standard of withstanding impact at five mph. without damage to vital car systems. The standard is two and one-half mph. for rear bumpers. At five mph., the average front end damage has been about $300. The fact that bumpers are of different heights, so that instead of bumper to bumper accidents we have bumper to sheet metal, serves to increase the costs of collisions. Present technology permits bumpers with water or air cushions to withstand collisions at speeds up to forty mph.

Many insurance companies are now offering substantial premium discounts for cars with reasonably crash proof bumpers. Ultimately, the consumer must decide whether he is willing to buy a safe car and pay a lower insurance premium or buy a fancy car and pay the cost of insurance appropriate to the risks he insists on taking. The federal government's intervention in reducing this freedom of choice is slow but certain.

Highway Safety, Traffic Congestion, and the Drunk Driver. Highway safety standards have been rising rapidly in recent years, and many states are conducting important research on even more effective ways of dealing with the problems of highway traffic and accidents. Numerous commissions have explored the highway construction and safety problem and have advocated improvements in the use of emergency facilities, such as helicopter rescue operations, medical communication networks, special offramps, special guard devices, and techniques for dealing with motorist confusion at onramps of freeways.

Of the 60,000 deaths on the highways each year caused by the automobile, more than 30,000 involve persons who are legally classified as drunk drivers. Chronic alcoholism is the major factor in auto deaths, and yet society refuses to regard the problem drinker as an ill person who should be kept off the road. Better ways of testing for drunkenness have been proposed, and there are bills being considered by the various legislatures to curtail the right to drive of persons who are chronic alcoholics. With drunk drivers discouraged from getting behind the wheel, better training of new drivers, refresher courses for traffic offenders, and greater safety consciousness, the driver's contribution in solving the auto problem can be materially increased.

Court Congestion. The court congestion problem is real and serious. The average time from filing a case to ultimate conclusion takes much longer than court administrators or the public desire. Numerous approaches are being attempted to speed up justice. Several substantial reforms have been urged.

For small cases involving amounts under $3,000—and these comprise the vast majority of all auto bodily injury claims—a simple arbitration procedure has been recommended to relieve court congestion without depriving the parties of their legal rights. For cases involving less than $10,000, a regular court action would be available using a short form procedure whereby the parties agree in advance on the judge and most of the issues not in dispute. A jury could be dispensed with and the matter resolved very quickly for these cases.

For large cases, involving $10,000 or more in dispute, the parties would use the present legal procedure with the important difference that the victim would have had his medical and hospital bills, if any, paid by his own insurance company, so that the only matter to be litigated would relate to the other economic losses sustained by the victim.

One change that has proved effective in Arizona is to require a sufficient number of judges by basing them on population density rather than on broad categories of need. Thus, Arizona provides 1 judge for every 35,000 population. For most states this would mean a material increase in judicial manpower.

The Legal System. Perhaps the most significant change advocated for the legal system is to provide for comparative negligence instead of contributory negligence, so that a greater number of injured people are compensated when the accident is chiefly the fault of another. The current practice of most insurance companies is to operate as if the comparative negligence doctrine was the law. Attempts to avoid claims where the victim is partially at fault have been reduced or eliminated in most auto company claims practices. Changing the law in this regard would give the parties greater certainty with respect to the treatment they would have a right to demand.

GROUP AUTOMOBILE INSURANCE

Mass merchandizing of insurance has been slow to emerge outside of the fields of life insurance, pensions, and health insurance. The group concept of selling, which tends to achieve economies of scale by simplifying marketing, underwriting, administration, and claims, was feasible in life and health insurance because of the nature of the rating laws in those fields. Minimum standards are set for policyholder protection. However, in property and casualty insurance the rating laws seek adequacy, equity, and reasonableness, and most states have resisted the contention that group rates in auto insurance would not be unfairly discriminatory. Agents' associations have led the fight to block this kind of marketing.

A survey of labor unions conducted in 1969 showed that most workers feel that group automobile insurance is a worthy goal for fringe benefit negotiation. Most said it would be a sound union benefit for members. No-fault plans, which would convert automobile insurance into life and health insurance and bring with them compulsory insurance, may tend to accelerate the movement toward group auto insurance.

LIFE INSURANCE PRICING

Critics of life insurance have long argued that there is widespread existence of unreasonable overcharges regularly made by insurance companies, that there is avid overselling; that lapses are excessive because of improper selling; that savings through life insurance is a poor investment.[10] The public is unaware of the price, product, and service variations because they do not tend to shop for insurance. The comparison of prices in life insurance is not a simple process. The difficulty is one of estimating future dividends and assuming that past dividend history can be projected for a mutual life insurance company. Recently, more stress and publicity have been given to the matter of life insurance price differentials.

The State of Pennsylvania Insurance Department developed a shoppers' guide for life insurance in 1972, which showed that some major companies charge more than twice as much as others for similar policies and that some of the best known companies charge the most for coverage.[11] The national guide shows the actual cost of insurance after the insured person has paid premiums and deducted the ultimate cash value of the policy and the money paid back by the company as dividends. The chief conclusion of the national guide is that the firms charging the lowest premium are not necessarily the best buys. The guide comparisons were done on the $10,000 straight life policy because it is the most popular and representative of life insurance offerings. About seven in every ten people have life insurance. The average family has $20,900 in coverage. Total life insurance-in-force was more than $1.4 trillion in 1972.

The National Association of Insurance Commissioners appointed a task

---

[10] See, for example, James Gollin, *Pay Now, Die Later* (New York: Random House, 1966); Ralph Hendershot, *The Grim Truth About Life Insurance* (New York: G. F. Putnam's Sons, 1957).

[11] "Shopper's Guide to Policies," *Time* (July 10, 1972), p. 42. For an incisive attack on the methodology of the Shopper's Guide, see Frank W. Podrebarac, "Consumerism," *Transactions of the Society of Actuaries*, XXIV, Number 4, p. D471-72.

force on life insurance cost/price illustrations to develop a method that is both comprehensible to the typical consumer and accurate in portraying actual costs.

While there is extensive contemporary debate about the most appropriate method for comparing the costs of alternative life insurance products, there is a consensus that the traditional net cost comparison is insufficient and potentially misleading. The traditional twenty-year cost comparison uses the following approach:

1. Annual premium   x   20 Years   =   Total cost
   (e.g.) $100   x   20   = $2,000
2. Less:
   a.   Cash value at end of 20 years   = $1,700
   b.   Accumulated dividends   =   400
                                                  $2,100
3. (1) − (2)   = Total cost   − $100
4. (1) ÷ 20 years   = Net cost per year   − $2.50

This methodology is considered deficient for three reasons. First, it fails to consider the interest that an insured would earn on the cash values and dividends if placed in an alternative program. Second, it provides a cost basis for only one point in time (i.e., twenty years after policy issuance). Third, it can mislead the consumer by implying that the insurance product is free.

Several alternative cost comparison methods have been suggested. Belth has devised a "level price" method that considers time preference. Rather than computing cost for a single point in time, the level price method requires determination of prices for each policy year. Furthermore, the level price method adopts a basic premise that the savings element of a life insurance policy is an asset from the policyholder's point of view. Life insurance is thus viewed as a combination of savings and protection. The level price relates only to the protection element. Belth provides the following method for calculating the price for the sixth year of a life policy:[12]

Cash Value at End of Fifth Year	$613.00
Add Premium for Sixth Year	250.00
Total Investment Beginning Sixth Year	863.00
Add 3 percent Interest	25.89
Total Investment End of Sixth Year	888.89
Subtract Cash Value End of Sixth Year	773.30
Price of Protection in Sixth Year Before Dividend	115.59
Subtract Sixth Year Dividend	50.00
Price of Protection Sixth Year	$ 65.59

[12] Joseph M. Belth, *The Retail Price Structure in American Life Insurance* (Bloomington, Ind.: Indiana University, 1966), p. 37. See also, Joseph M. Belth, *Life Insurance: A Consumer's Handbook,* Indiana University Press, 1973.

The final figure, along with those for each year in the specified comparison period, is used to determine a level price.

Under the authority of the American Life Convention, the Institute of Life Insurance, and the Life Insurance Association of America, the Joint Special Committee on Life Insurance Costs evaluated more than twelve price comparison methods. In 1970 the Committee favored the "Equalizing Cost Method" utilized by the National Underwriter Company. This method is called the "interest-adjusted" method for clarity of understanding. The interest-adjusted method resembles the traditional net cost method except that it: (1) uses premiums (and dividends) accumulated at a risk free rate of interest instead of using "total" premiums and dividends paid, and (2) divides the total cost by the present value of $1 received each year in the comparison period (e.g., the present value of $1 received each year for twenty years using a 4 percent discount rate) rather than by the number of years in the comparison. The interest-adjusted cost of a $10,000 policy issued at age 35 with a premium of $240 per year is calculated in Table 30.2. The National Underwriter Company uses the interest-adjusted method to prepare *Cost Facts on Life Insurance,* a comparison of policy costs for 231 life insurance companies.

The interest adjusted method of price comparisons came into widespread use in 1973 as a result of strong endorsement by the National Association of Insurance Commissioners and adoption by the marketing departments of many large insurers.

TABLE 30.2   Interest-Adjusted Cost, $10,000 Whole Life, Age 35

	Ten Years	Twetny Years
Accumulated Premuims	$2,997	$7,433
Less Accumulated Dividends	517	2,003
	2,480	5,430
Less Cash Value	1,710	3,610
	770	1,820
Accumulation of $1 per year at 4 percent	12.486	30.969
Cost Index, Per Year	61.67	58.77
Cost Index, Per Year Per $1,000 Insurance	6.17	5.88

SOURCE: *Cost Facts on Life Insurance,* (Cincinnati, Ohio: National Underwriter Company, 1971)

WORKMEN'S COMPENSATION ISSUES

In 1972, the National Commission on State Workmen's Compensation reported adversely on the status of United States workmen's compensation laws. It found that in 31 states less than $4,137 in benefits were provided to injured workers.

The government defined this amount as the poverty level for a nonfarm family of four. Created under the Occupational Safety and Health Act of 1970, the commission began its work in June 1971 and recommended eighty changes in the workmen's compensation programs to the Congress. The commission recommended that the states be given until 1975 to raise their standards to acceptable levels or face federal intervention in this field.

The seven "top priority" items whose adoption by the states were regarded as imperative were:

1. Weekly cash benefits for temporary or permanent total disability cases or death cases should be no less than two-thirds of the worker's gross weekly wage, subject to a maximum benefit of at least two-thirds of the state's average weekly wage by July 1, 1973, and 100 percent of the state's average weekly wage by July 1, 1975. In 32 states, weekly benefits were found to be less than 60 percent of the state's average wage.

2. Weekly cash benefits should be paid without arbitrary limits on duration or sum of benefits. One-third of the states were found to limit the period of permanent disability benefits, and two-thirds had death benefit limits.

3. Coverage under state laws should be compulsory rather than elective; neither employers nor employees should have the right to reject coverage. Seventeen states currently have elective laws.

4. State laws should not exempt any occupational groups and should cover all employers with one or more employees, including most farm workers and household workers.

5. State laws should provide full coverage of work related diseases. Ten states still cover only a list of enumerated diseases.

6. Full medical care and physical rehabilitation services should be provided for any work related impairment without statutory limits on dollar amounts or length of time.

7. Employees should be allowed to file claims in the state where injured, hired, or where employment is principally based.

The program for workmen's compensation reform is estimated to cost between 10 percent and more than 50 percent in rate increases. Public pressure for improvements in the system will probably take effect over a period of time.

CONSUMER ADVOCACY IN GOVERNMENT

The consumerist movement has found an attentive ear in the halls of the legislatures and in the insurance oriented areas of the executive branch as well.

At the federal level, the Consumers' Counsel to the President has taken vigorous public stands on insurance matters. The Federal Insurance Administration and the Department of Transportation have not shown a reluctance to speak out on consumer issues. Increasingly, state insurance commissioners are taking a more aggressive consumer oriented approach to their problems. Change comes slowly, but the social control of the insurance industry is growing.

REVIEW QUESTIONS

1. Outline some of the variables which must be considered in comparing the prices of two life insurance policies from a net cost point of view.

2. The State of Maryland enacted a no-fault law which offers no restrictions on the right to sue in tort. The law covered only bodily injury liability and provided $2,500 aggregate for various benefits. Was this a "pure" no-fault law? Explain.

3. What are the principal advantages and disadvantages of prepaid group medical practice? Discuss.

4. "State insurance departments are among the oldest, if not in fact the oldest, consumer protection agency in the country." Discuss.

5. Is a national health insurance plan feasible without socialized medicine? Discuss.

STUDY QUESTIONS

6. "I feel that the agent will sell me whatever he happens to carry or whatever he gets the best commission on." How valid is this criticism? How can it be overcome? Discuss.

7. What is the role of the Federal Insurance Administration in the field of consumer protection? Discuss.

8. What are the arguments against the manufacture of "safer" automobiles? Discuss.

9. A recent report showed that the five year *net cost* figures for a *non-participating* $10,000 whole life insurance policy for a male age 41 were as follows:

Company	Net Cost per $1000
A	$ 5.46
B	$12.50
C	$17.66
D	$20.14

(a)   Explain *net-cost* and *non-participating*.

(b)   How can the extreme price differentials be explained? Discuss.

(c)   Would you expect the 20 year net cost figures to be materially different? Explain why or why not.

10. Discuss the case for a "Truth in Insurance" law. What should such a law include?

Appendix A Mortality Tables

Age	American Experience (1843-1858) Deaths Per 1,000	American Experience (1843-1858) Expectation of Life (Years)	Commissioners 1941 Standard Ordinary (1930-1940) Deaths Per 1,000	Commissioners 1941 Standard Ordinary (1930-1940) Expectation of Life (Years)	Commissioners 1958 Standard Ordinary (1950-1954) Deaths Per 1,000	Commissioners 1958 Standard Ordinary (1950-1954) Expectation of Life (Years)	Annuity Table for 1949—Male (1939-1949) Deaths Per 1,000	Annuity Table for 1949—Male (1939-1949) Expectation of Life (Years)	United States Total Population (1959-1961) Deaths Per 1,000	United States Total Population (1959-1961) Expectation of Life (Years)
0	154.70	41.45	22.58	62.33	7.08	68.30	4.04	73.18	25.93	69.89
1	63.49	47.94	5.77	62.76	1.76	67.78	1.58	72.48	1.70	70.75
2	35.50	50.16	4.14	62.12	1.52	66.90	.89	71.59	1.04	69.87
3	23.91	50.98	3.38	61.37	1.46	66.00	.72	70.65	.80	68.94
4	17.70	51.22	2.99	60.58	1.40	65.10	.63	69.70	.67	67.99
5	13.60	51.13	2.76	59.76	1.35	64.19	.57	68.75	.59	67.04
6	11.37	50.83	2.61	58.92	1.30	63.27	.53	67.78	.52	66.08
7	9.75	50.41	2.47	58.08	1.26	62.35	.50	66.82	.47	65.11
8	8.63	49.90	2.31	57.22	1.23	61.43	.49	65.85	.43	64.14
9	7.90	49.33	2.12	56.35	1.21	60.51	.48	64.89	.39	63.17
10	7.49	48.72	1.97	55.47	1.21	59.58	.48	63.92	.37	62.19
11	7.52	48.08	1.91	54.58	1.23	58.65	.49	62.95	.37	61.22
12	7.54	47.45	1.92	53.68	1.26	57.72	.50	61.98	.40	60.24
13	7.57	46.80	1.98	52.78	1.32	56.80	.51	61.01	.48	59.26
14	7.60	46.16	2.07	51.89	1.39	55.87	.52	60.04	.59	58.29
15	7.63	45.50	2.15	50.99	1.46	54.95	.54	59.07	.71	57.33
16	7.66	44.85	2.19	50.10	1.54	54.03	.55	58.10	.82	56.37
17	7.69	44.19	2.25	49.21	1.62	53.11	.57	57.13	.93	55.41
18	7.73	43.53	2.30	48.32	1.69	52.19	.58	56.17	1.02	54.46
19	7.77	42.87	2.37	47.43	1.74	51.28	.60	55.20	1.08	53.52
20	7.80	42.20	2.43	46.54	1.79	50.37	.62	54.23	1.15	52.58
21	7.86	41.53	2.51	45.66	1.83	49.46	.65	53.27	1.22	51.64
22	7.91	40.85	2.59	44.77	1.86	48.55	.67	52.30	1.27	50.70
23	7.96	40.17	2.68	43.88	1.89	47.64	.70	51.33	1.28	49.76
24	8.01	39.49	2.77	43.00	1.91	46.73	.73	50.37	1.27	48.83
25	8.06	38.81	2.88	42.12	1.93	45.82	.77	49.41	1.26	47.89
26	8.13	38.12	2.99	41.24	1.96	44.90	.81	48.44	1.25	46.95
27	8.20	37.43	3.11	40.36	1.99	43.99	.85	47.48	1.26	46.00
28	8.26	36.73	3.25	39.49	2.03	43.08	.90	46.52	1.30	45.06
29	8.34	36.03	3.40	38.61	2.08	42.16	.95	45.56	1.36	44.12
30	8.43	35.33	3.56	37.74	2.13	41.25	1.00	44.61	1.43	43.18
31	8.51	34.63	3.73	36.88	2.19	40.34	1.07	43.65	1.51	42.24
32	8.61	33.92	3.92	36.01	2.25	39.43	1.14	42.70	1.60	41.30
33	8.72	33.21	4.12	35.15	2.32	38.51	1.21	41.75	1.70	40.37
34	8.83	32.50	4.35	34.29	2.40	37.60	1.30	40.80	1.81	39.44
35	8.95	31.78	4.59	33.44	2.51	36.69	1.39	39.85	1.94	38.51
36	9.09	31.07	4.86	32.59	2.64	35.78	1.49	38.90	2.09	37.58
37	9.23	30.35	5.15	31.75	2.80	34.88	1.61	37.96	2.28	36.66
38	9.41	29.62	5.46	30.91	3.01	33.97	1.73	37.02	2.49	35.74
39	9.59	28.90	5.81	30.08	3.25	33.07	1.87	36.08	2.73	34.83
40	9.79	28.18	6.18	29.25	3.53	32.18	2.03	35.15	3.00	33.92
41	10.01	27.45	6.59	28.43	3.84	31.29	2.22	34.22	3.30	33.02
42	10.25	26.72	7.03	27.62	4.17	30.41	2.48	33.30	3.62	32.13
43	10.52	26.00	7.51	26.81	4.53	29.54	2.80	32.38	3.97	31.25
44	10.83	25.27	8.04	26.01	4.92	28.67	3.19	31.47	4.35	30.37
45	11.16	24.54	8.61	25.21	5.35	27.81	3.63	30.57	4.76	29.50
46	11.56	23.81	9.23	24.43	5.83	26.95	4.12	29.68	5.21	28.64
47	12.00	23.08	9.91	23.65	6.36	26.11	4.66	28.80	5.73	27.79
48	12.51	22.36	10.64	22.88	6.95	25.27	5.25	27.93	6.33	26.94
49	13.11	21.63	11.45	22.12	7.60	24.45	5.88	27.07	7.00	26.11
50	13.78	20.91	12.32	21.37	8.32	23.63	6.56	26.23	7.74	25.29

Age	American Experience (1843-1858) Deaths Per 1,000	American Experience (1843-1858) Expectation of Life (Years)	Commissioners 1941 Standard Ordinary (1930-1940) Deaths Per 1,000	Commissioners 1941 Standard Ordinary (1930-1940) Expectation of Life (Years)	Commissioners 1958 Standard Ordinary (1950-1954) Deaths Per 1,000	Commissioners 1958 Standard Ordinary (1950-1954) Expectation of Life (Years)	Annuity Table for 1949—Male (1939-1949) Deaths Per 1,000	Annuity Table for 1949—Male (1939-1949) Expectation of Life (Years)	United States Total Population (1959-1961) Deaths Per 1,000	United States Total Population (1959-1961) Expectation of Life (Years)
51	14.54	20.20	13.27	20.64	9.11	22.82	7.28	25.40	8.52	24.49
52	15.39	19.49	14.30	19.91	9.96	22.03	8.04	24.58	9.29	23.69
53	16.33	18.79	15.43	19.19	10.89	21.25	8.84	23.78	10.05	22.91
54	17.40	18.09	16.65	18.48	11.90	20.47	9.68	22.99	10.82	22.14
55	18.57	17.40	17.98	17.78	13.00	19.71	10.56	22.20	11.61	21.37
56	19.89	16.72	19.43	17.10	14.21	18.97	11.49	21.44	12.49	20.62
57	21.34	16.05	21.00	16.43	15.54	18.23	12.46	20.68	13.52	19.87
58	22.94	15.39	22.71	15.77	17.00	17.51	13.48	19.93	14.73	19.14
59	24.72	14.74	24.57	15.13	18.59	16.81	14.54	19.20	16.11	18.42
60	26.69	14.10	26.59	14.50	20.34	16.12	15.66	18.48	17.61	17.71
61	28.88	13.47	28.78	13.88	22.24	15.44	16.87	17.76	19.17	17.02
62	31.29	12.86	31.18	13.27	24.31	14.78	18.20	17.06	20.82	16.34
63	33.94	12.26	33.76	12.69	26.57	14.14	19.67	16.37	22.52	15.68
64	36.87	11.67	36.58	12.11	29.04	13.51	21.28	15.68	24.31	15.03
65	40.13	11.10	39.64	11.55	31.75	12.90	23.07	15.01	26.22	14.39
66	43.71	10.54	42.96	11.01	34.74	12.31	25.03	14.36	28.28	13.76
67	47.65	10.00	46.56	10.48	38.04	11.73	27.19	13.71	30.53	13.15
68	52.00	9.47	50.46	9.97	41.68	11.17	29.58	13.08	33.01	12.55
69	56.76	8.97	54.70	9.47	45.61	10.64	32.20	12.46	35.73	11.96
70	61.99	8.48	59.30	8.99	49.79	10.12	35.09	11.86	38.66	11.38
71	67.67	8.00	64.27	8.52	54.15	9.63	38.27	11.28	41.82	10.82
72	73.73	7.55	69.66	8.08	58.65	9.15	41.77	10.71	45.30	10.27
73	80.18	7.11	75.50	7.64	63.26	8.69	45.62	10.15	49.15	9.74
74	87.03	6.68	81.81	7.23	68.12	8.24	49.85	9.61	53.42	9.21
75	94.37	6.27	88.64	6.82	73.37	7.81	54.50	9.09	57.99	8.71
76	102.31	5.88	96.02	6.44	79.18	7.39	59.61	8.58	62.96	8.21
77	111.06	5.49	103.99	6.07	85.70	6.98	65.22	8.10	68.67	7.73
78	120.83	5.11	112.59	5.72	93.06	6.59	71.37	7.63	75.35	7.26
79	131.73	4.74	121.86	5.38	101.19	6.21	78.11	7.17	83.02	6.81
80	144.47	4.39	131.85	5.06	109.98	5.85	85.50	6.74	92.08	6.39
81	158.60	4.05	142.60	4.75	119.35	5.51	93.59	6.32	102.19	5.98
82	174.30	3.71	154.16	4.46	129.17	5.19	102.44	5.92	112.44	5.61
83	191.56	3.39	166.57	4.18	139.38	4.89	112.11	5.54	121.95	5.25
84	211.36	3.08	179.88	3.91	150.01	4.60	122.67	5.18	130.67	4.91
85	235.55	2.77	194.13	3.66	161.14	4.32	134.18	4.84	143.80	4.58
86	265.68	2.47	209.37	3.42	172.82	4.06	146.71	4.51	158.16	4.26
87	303.02	2.18	225.63	3.19	185.13	3.80	160.33	4.20	173.55	3.97
88	346.69	1.91	243.00	2.98	198.25	3.55	175.12	3.90	190.32	3.70
89	395.86	1.66	261.44	2.77	212.46	3.31	191.15	3.62	208.35	3.45
90	454.55	1.42	280.99	2.58	228.14	3.06	208.49	3.36	227.09	3.22
91	532.47	1.19	301.73	2.39	245.77	2.82	227.19	3.12	245.98	3.02
92	634.26	.98	323.64	2.21	265.93	2.58	247.33	2.88	264.77	2.85
93	734.18	.80	346.66	2.03	289.30	2.33	268.96	2.67	282.84	2.69
94	857.14	.64	371.00	1.84	316.66	2.07	292.12	2.47	299.52	2.55
95	1,000.00	.50	396.21	1.63	351.24	1.80	316.83	2.28	314.16	2.43
96			447.19	1.37	400.56	1.51	343.12	2.10	329.15	2.32
97			548.26	1.08	488.42	1.18	370.97	1.94	344.50	2.21
98			724.67	.78	668.15	.83	400.35	1.79	360.18	2.10
99			1,000.00	.50	1,000.00	.50	431.20	1.65	376.16	2.01
100							463.41	1.52	392.42	1.91
101							496.87	1.40	408.91	1.83
102							531.39	1.29	425.62	1.75
103							566.76	1.20	442.50	1.67
104							602.71	1.10	459.51	1.60
105							638.96	1.02	476.62	1.53
106							675.14	.94	493.78	1.46
107							710.90	.86	510.95	1.40
108							745.82	.75	528.10	1.35
109							1,000.00	.50	545.19	1.29

Index

INDEX OF NAMES

INDEX OF SUBJECTS